The Persistence of Whiteness

The Persistence of Whiteness investigates the representation and narration of race in contemporary Hollywood cinema. Ideologies of class, ethnicity, gender, nation and sexuality are central concerns as are the growth of the business of filmmaking. Focusing on representations of Black, Asian, Jewish, Latina/o and Native American identities, this collection also shows how whiteness is a fact everywhere in contemporary Hollywood cinema, crossing audiences, authors, genres, studios and styles.

Bringing together essays from respected film scholars, the collection covers a wide range of important films, including *Guess Who's Coming to Dinner*, *The Color Purple*, *Star Wars* and *The Lord of the Rings*. Essays also consider genres from the western to blaxploitation and New Black Cinema; provocative film-makers such as Melvin Van Peebles and Steven Spielberg and stars including Whoopi Goldberg and Jennifer Lopez.

Daniel Bernardi provides an in-depth introduction, comprehensive bibliography and a helpful glossary of terms, thus providing students with an accessible and topical collection on race and ethnicity in contemporary cinema.

Contributors include: Susan Courtney, Thomas Cripps, Tani Dianca Sanchez, Gabriel S. Estrada (Nahuatl), Lester D. Friedman, Bambi L. Haggins, Keith M. Harris, Dale Hudson, Susan Hunt, Peter Lehman, Gina Marchetti, Celine Parreñas Shimizu, Priscilla Peña Ovalle, Charles Ramírez Berg, Sean Redmond, Josh Stenger, Beretta E. Smith-Shomade, Deborah Elizabeth Whaley, Young Eun Chae.

Daniel Bernardi is Director of Film and Media Studies and Associate Professor at Arizona State University. He is the author of *Star Trek and History: Race-ing Toward a White Future* (1998) and the editor of *The Birth of Whiteness: Race and the Emergence of US Cinema* (1996) and *Classic Hollywood, Classic Whiteness* (2002).

I dedicate this book to my fellow "junior" colleagues in the Department of Media Arts at the University of Arizona (1999 to 2004):

Beretta Smith-Shomade, my media arts wife, for her breathtaking courage and devout honesty.

Barbara Selznick, for her radical sincerity and playful willingness to mix it up.

Michael Mulchay, for his tenacious fairness and tireless dedication.

Kevin Sandler, for his incurable enthusiasm and unwavering integrity.

Yuri Makino, for her quiet determination and beaming originality.

We made it!

So what be next?

The Persistence of Whiteness

Race and contemporary
Hollywood cinema

Edited by Daniel Bernardi

Routledge
Taylor & Francis Group

LONDON AND NEW YORK

First published 2008
by Routledge
2 Park Square, Milton Park, Abingdon, Oxon OX14 4RN

Simultaneously published in the USA and Canada
by Routledge
270 Madison Ave, New York, NY 10016

Routledge is an imprint of the Taylor & Francis Group, an informa business

© 2008 Editorial selection and material, Daniel Bernardi; individual chapters, the contributors

Typeset in Bembo and Gill Sans by
Book Now Ltd, London
Printed and bound in Great Britain by
Antony Rowe Ltd, Chippenham, Wiltshire

British Library Cataloguing in Publication Data
A catalogue record for this book is available from the British Library

Library of Congress Cataloging in Publication Data
The persistence of whiteness: race and contemporary Hollywood cinema / edited by Daniel Bernardi.
    p. cm.
Includes bibliographical references.
1. Minorities in motion pictures. 2. Race in motion pictures.
3. Motion pictures–United States. I. Bernardi, Daniel, 1964–

PN1995.9.M56P47 2007
791.43′6552–dc22   2007008736

ISBN10: 0–415–77412–8 (hbk)
ISBN10: 0–415–77413–6 (pbk)
ISBN10: 0–203–93974–3 (ebk)

ISBN13: 978–0–415–77412–3 (hbk)
ISBN13: 978–0–415–77413–0 (pbk)
ISBN13: 978–0–203–93974–1 (ebk)

Contents

Notes on contributors   ix
Acknowledgments   xiv
Introduction: race and contemporary Hollywood cinema   xv
DANIEL BERNARDI

PART I
Generic history   1

1 Manifest myth-making: Texas history in the movies   3
CHARLES RAMÍREZ BERG

2 Mapping the beach: beach movies, exploitation film and geographies of whiteness   28
JOSH STENGER

3 Boyz, boyz, boyz: New Black Cinema and black masculinity   51
KEITH M. HARRIS

PART II
Anthropomorphism   67

4 *Star Wars* episodes I–VI: Coyote and the force of white narrative   69
GABRIEL S. ESTRADA (NAHUATL)

5 The whiteness of the *Rings*   91
SEAN REDMOND

6 Neo-abolitionists, colorblind epistemologies and black
   politics: the *Matrix* trilogy   102
   TANI DIANCA SANCHEZ

PART III
Blood and bodies   125

7 Vampires of color and the performance of multicultural
   whiteness   127
   DALE HUDSON

8 The naked and the dead: the Jewish male body and
   masculinity in *Sunshine* and *Enemy at the Gates*   157
   PETER LEHMAN AND SUSAN HUNT

9 Framing Jennifer Lopez: mobilizing race from the wide
   shot to the close-up   165
   PRISCILLA PEÑA OVALLE

PART IV
Desire to desire   185

10 *Guess Who's Coming to Dinner* with Eldridge Cleaver and
    the Supreme Court, or reforming popular racial memory
    with Hepburn and Tracy   187
    SUSAN COURTNEY

11 Master–slave sex acts: *Mandingo* and the race/sex paradox   218
    CELINE PARREÑAS SHIMIZU

12 The tragedy of whiteness and neoliberalism in Brad Kaaya's
    O/Othello   233
    DEBORAH ELIZABETH WHALEY

13 *Romeo Must Die*: interracial romance in action   253
    GINA MARCHETTI

PART V
Provocateurs   267

14   **The dark side of whiteness: *Sweetback* and John Dollard's**
     idea of "the gains of the lower-class negroes"   269
     THOMAS CRIPPS

15   **Black like him: Steven Spielberg's *The Color Purple***   292
     LESTER D. FRIEDMAN

16   **Crossover diva: Whoopi Goldberg and persona politics**   315
     BAMBI L. HAGGINS

17   **Surviving *In Living Color* with some *White Chicks*:**
     whiteness in the Wayans' (black) minds   344
     BERETTA E. SMITH-SHOMADE

     Glossary of terms   360
     Select bibliography   373
     COMPILED BY YOUNG EUN CHAE

     Index   384

Contributors

Charles Ramírez Berg is University Distinguished Teaching Professor in the Department of Radio-Television-Film at the University of Texas at Austin. He is the author of *Latino Images in Film: Stereotypes, Subversion, and Resistance* (University of Texas Press, 2002), *Cinema of Solitude: A Critical Study of Mexican Film, 1967–1983* (University of Texas Press, 1992), and *Posters from the Golden Age of Mexican Cinema* (Chronicle Books, 2001). In addition, he has written many journal articles, book chapters and encyclopedia entries on Latinos in US film and on Mexican and world cinema.

Daniel Bernardi is Director of Film and Media Studies and Associate Professor at Arizona State University. He is the author of *Star Trek and History: Race-ing Toward a White Future* (Rutgers University Press, 1998) and the editor of *The Birth of Whiteness: Race and the Emergence of US Cinema* (Rutgers University Press, 1996) and *Classic Hollywood, Classic Whiteness* (University of Minnesota Press, 2002).

Susan Courtney directs the Film Studies Program at the University of South Carolina, where she is also an associate professor in the Department of English, and is the author of *Hollywood Fantasies of Miscegenation: Spectacular Narratives of Gender and Race, 1903–1906* (Princeton, 2005). She is currently at work on a book, tentatively titled *Regional Projections: Imagining the South, the West, and the USA at the Movies*, that juxtaposes two exceptionally mythic locations in film culture to consider how cinema has helped shape our conceptions not only of regional identity, but also of a larger, imagined "America" comprised of such filmic parts.

Thomas Cripps is University Distinguished Professor, Emeritus, at Morgan State University. He has written five books, first among them *Slow Fade to Black: The Negro in American Film, 1900–1942* (Oxford, 1977), in addition to many articles and television scripts. *Black Shadows on a Silver Screen* (Post-Newsweek TV, 1976), for which he wrote the script, won several gold medals in international festival competitions. He has held numerous fellowships, among them from the Guggenheim, Rockefeller, and Dedalus

Foundations, as well as resident fellowships at the Woodrow Wilson International Center for Scholars; the National Humanities Center in the Research Triangle, NC; and the Rockefeller Center in the Villa Serbelloni, Bellagio, Italy. He has been visiting professor at Stanford, Harvard, and other universities. He and his wife reside in Baltimore where he continues to write and occasionally teach, most recently in the Communication in Modern Society program at the Johns Hopkins University.

Gabriel S. Estrada (Nahuatl) is a Mexican Indian of Nahuatl, Raramuri, Mestizo, and Basque heritages. He is a proud child of the Chicana and Chicano Movements and an activist grandchild of the indigenous revolutions of Mexico. He holds a joint Assistant Professor position in Chicano/Latino Studies and American Indian Studies at California State University, Long Beach. His interests range from Aztec codices to California Indian media to queer Latino literature.

Lester D. Friedman is Senior Scholar in Residence at Hobart and William Smith Colleges. The author or editor of numerous publications – including *American-Jewish Filmmakers* (University of Illinois Press, 1993), *Unspeakable Images: Ethnicity and American Cinema* (University of Illinois Press, 1991), and *Bonnie and Clyde* (British Film Institute, 2000) – he is co-editor of *Screen Decades: American Culture/American Film*, and will edit a volume on the 1970s in this series for Rutgers University Press. This spring Wallflower Press will publish the second edition of his anthology, *Fires Were Started: British Cinema and Thatcherism*, and the University of Illinois Press will publish *Citizen Spielberg*, the first comprehensive analysis of the films of America's most commercially successful director.

Bambi L. Haggins is an Associate Professor of Screen Arts and Cultures at the University of Michigan. She teaches about television history, representations of class, ethnicity, gender and sexuality across media as well as fan and popular culture. Her first book is an examination of the place of black comedy as comedic social discourse in American popular consciousness, *Laughing Mad: The Black Comic Persona in Post Soul America* (Rutgers University Press, 2006). She has begun work on a second volume focusing on "for us, by us" black comedy and the nature and significance of insider laughter.

Keith M. Harris is a graduate in Cinema Studies at New York University. He is an assistant professor in the Departments of English and Program in Film and Visual Culture at the University of California at Riverside. His areas of specialization include film, African American and Africana Cinema, gender studies and queer theory. However, his recent research and writing interests primarily concern masculinity, performance and gender(s) as ethical constructs within performance and cultural production. His recent publications include "'Stand up, boy': Sidney Poitier, 'Boy,' and Filmic Black masculinity" in *Gender and Sexuality in African Literatures and Films* (Africa World Press, 2007), *Boys, Boyz, Bois: An Ethics of Masculinity in Popular Film, Television and Video* (Routledge, 2006), and "'Untitled': D'Angelo and the visualization of the black male body" in *Wide Angle*.

Dale Hudson received his doctorate from the University of Massachusetts Amherst and presently teaches in cinema studies at Ithaca College. His research and teaching focus on global and national cinemas, particularly constructions of race, ethnicity, and nation implicit in film production, distribution, and audience reception. He has written articles on French and Israeli cinemas, as well as online media fan subcultures, and has presented work at various conferences including Screen Studies, the Society of Cinema and Media Studies (CMS), and the Modern Language Association (MLA).

Susan Hunt is a faculty associate at Santa Monica and Pasadena City Colleges. Her essays on the representation of sexuality and the mind/body split in films – co-authored with Peter Lehman – have appeared in *Titanic: Anatomy of a Blockbuster* (Rutgers University Press, 1999), *Enfant Terrible! Jerry Lewis in American Film* (New York University Press, 2002), *Framework*, and *Jump Cut*. She and Lehman are currently writing a book on the same subject for Rutgers University Press.

Peter Lehman is Director of the Center for Film, Media, and Popular Culture at Arizona State University, Tempe. He is author of *Roy Orbison: The Invention of an Alternative Rock Masculinity* (Temple University Press, 2003), the revised, expanded second edition of *Running Scared: Masculinity and the Representation of the Male Body* (Temple University Press, 1995), and *Unmaking Love: Essays on the Male Body, Pornography, and Sexuality* (forthcoming). He is editor of *Pornography: Film and Culture* and *Masculinity: Bodies, Movies, Culture* (Rutgers University Press, 2006).

Gina Marchetti teaches in the Department of Comparative Literature, School of Humanities, at the University of Hong Kong. In 1995, her book, *Romance and the "Yellow Peril": Race, Sex and Discursive Strategies in Hollywood Fiction* (University of California Press, 1993), won the award for best book in the area of cultural studies from the Association for Asian American Studies. Her recent books are *From Tian'anmen to Times Square: Transnational China and the Chinese Diaspora on Global Screens* (Temple University Press, 2006) and *Hong Kong Film, Hollywood and the New Global Cinema*, co-edited with Tan See-Kam (Routledge, 2007).

Priscilla Peña Ovalle is Ford Dissertation Fellow and Assistant Professor of Film Studies in the English Department at the University of Oregon. Her work on Latinos/as and new media appears in *Television After TV: Essays on a Medium in Transition* (Duke University Press, 2004). Ovalle also works in media production and has most recently collaborated with the Labyrinth

Project at the University of Southern California's Annenberg Center for Communication. Her primary research focuses on dance, race and sexuality in Hollywood film.

Sean Redmond is a senior lecturer in Film Studies at Victoria University of Wellington. He has research interests in black and Asian cinema, science fiction, stardom and celebrity, film authorship, and whiteness and identity. He is the co-editor of *Framing Celebrity: New Directions in Celebrity Culture* (Routledge, 2006), *Stardom and Celebrity: The Reader* (Sage, 2007), and *Hollywood Transgressor: The Cinema of Kathryn Bigelow* (Wallflower Press, 2003), and editor of *Liquid Metal: The Science Fiction Film Reader* (Wallflower Press, 2004). He is currently working on *The War Body on Screen* (with Karen Randell, forthcoming, 2007), and *The Cinema of Takeshi Kitano* (forthcoming, Wallflower Press, 2009).

Tani Dianca Sanchez is a faculty member in Africana Studies at the University of Arizona. Her work focuses on black feminism, visual culture, cultural studies and art appreciation. She serves as a state president of the National Association of Colored Women's Clubs and worked for a number of years as an editor, news journalist, and as a media relations specialist.

Celine Parreñas Shimizu is an associate professor of Film and Video in the Asian American Studies Department at University College Santa Barbara. Her publications include articles in *Yale Journal of Law and Feminism*, *Theatre Journal*, *Signs* and *Wide Angles*.

Beretta E. Smith-Shomade is an associate professor of Media Arts at the University of Arizona. She is the author of *Shaded Lives: African-American Women and Television* (Rutgers University Press, 2002) and *Pimpin' Ain't Easy: Selling Black Entertainment Television* (Routledge, 2007). Her work centers on the intersections of race, gender, sexuality, class and generation in visual culture.

Josh Stenger is an assistant professor of Film Studies and Literature at Wheaton College, where he teaches courses on film history, genre, cultural studies, gender and race in film, and critical theory. His research focuses on the relationship between cinematic representation and urban space (with specific attention on how Hollywood film and Los Angeles's cultural landscape interact with one another) and constructions of masculinity in contemporary film.

Deborah Elizabeth Whaley is a visiting assistant professor at Saint Louis University in the Department of American Studies. Her research and teaching fields include comparative American studies, black cultural studies, popular culture and the visual arts, and feminist theory. She has been a resident visiting scholar at the Center for Cultural Studies at the University of California, Santa Cruz, and was a recipient of a grant from the William

Monroe Trotter Institute for Black Culture for research on responses to 9/11 in black art and popular culture. Whaley has published original art, poetry, as well as articles on popular culture, fine art, photography, and film. Her first book manuscript, "By Merit, By Culture," is an interdisciplinary investigation of the cultural and public sphere work of a historically black sorority.

Young Eun Chae is a PhD student in the Department of Communication Studies at the University of North Carolina at Chapel Hill. She studied philosophy, film history and theory, and cultural studies at Kyunghee University, University of Chicago, and University of Arizona. Her master's thesis dealt with rearticulation of white superiority in the James Bond film, *Die Another Day* (2002). Her dissertation focuses on transnational media traffic in the East Asian region, including China, Japan, Taiwan, Hong Kong, and South Korea.

Acknowledgments

I would like to thank all of the contributors to this volume for sticking with the project as it went through three years of revision. Their commitment to challenging racism in Hollywood cinema deserves our collective praise and my everlasting gratitude. All faults with this book belong to me. I also would like to thank three research assistants who helped put this project together: Jacob Pantoja, Michael Green and Alexis Cabrera. I really appreciate the help and extra effort! Finally, I would like to thank my wife, Helen Na, for giving me plenty of room to finish this and other projects during our move to Arizona State University, pregnancy, and the birth of our ItKoRican (Italian/ Korean/Puerto Rican) son on October 5, 2006, Sojin Rock Soto Bernardi (a.k.a. Mr Cool).

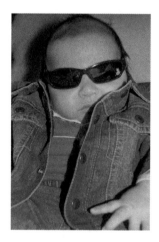

Introduction

Race and contemporary Hollywood cinema

Daniel Bernardi

This is the third collection of essays on race in US cinema that I have edited. The first, *The Birth of Whiteness: Race and the Emergence of US Cinema*, published in 1996, focuses on the aesthetic, ideological and institutional meaning of race in early cinema from 1896 to the introduction of sound. The second, *Classic Hollywood, Classic Whiteness*, published five years later, focuses on the meaning of race from the birth of sound in 1927 up until 1960, the start of what many scholars consider the contemporary period.[1] In both collections scholars from a range of disciplines bring distinct methodologies and unique insights to the enduring problem of the American color line in Hollywood cinema. And while both books are mindful of history – in fact, directed by historical concerns – they work to undermine the power of whiteness shared by both periods of filmmaking. This is to say that, although the meaning of race shifts in the sixty-five years covered by these two collections, they share an overarching point: "US cinema has consistently constructed whiteness, the representation and narrative form of Eurocentrism, as the norm by which all 'Others' fail by comparison."[2]

Building on these two books and concluding a long-term project that intends to promote sustained research on race in US cinema, *The Persistence of Whiteness* is as diverse in scope as its predecessors. Contributors to this collection investigate the representation and narration of blackness, brownness, redness and yellowness. Whiteness is addressed explicitly as a racial code and indirectly as an implicit discourse that fractures the representations and stories of other colors. Ideologies of class, ethnicity, gender, nation and sexuality are central concerns to several of the contributors to this book, as is the growth of the business of filmmaking. Whether focusing on color or its apparent invisibility, this collection also shows how whiteness is a fact everywhere in contemporary Hollywood cinema, crossing audiences, authors, genres, studios and styles.

Hollywood functions as a sort of prism, refracting the colors we see on cinematic screens by separating them from whiteness. Misrepresenting whatever is seen through it, Hollywood attempts to segregate whiteness from color in ways that make the former invisible and the latter isolated and stereotypical. Yet white light and the structure of the Hollywood prism itself are not that difficult to see if one focuses in areas where it is either overwhelming or where its absence nonetheless structures the meaning of color. Scholars, students and audiences merely need to turn their critical attention to the intermittent beams of light that result in the escapist ideology of Hollywood realism.

The discourses of race and whiteness are anything but mutually exclusive. A film need not represent Europeans and European Americans as "white" to be about whiteness; it need not be about, for example, "white trash" or "white money" to be about whiteness. Films about people of color are also about whiteness in so far as they are directed and contextualized by the ubiquity, however unquestioned or under-analyzed, of the US racial formation. For that matter, films by people of color, though they often bring unique shades to the refraction of race in film, are also often about whiteness, either directly as Beretta Smith-Shomade reveals in her essay on *White Chicks* (2004) or indirectly as Keith Harris's essay on New Black Cinema suggests. I will go as far as arguing that all studies of racism in Hollywood film are in some ways also studies of whiteness, since to talk or write about racism in this country is to at least implicitly acknowledge white supremacy. *The Persistence of Whiteness*, like the two collections it follows, pursues this line of criticism without compelling each contributor to address the particularity of whiteness.

Borrowing from sociologists Michael Omi and Howard Winant, "race" names a historical process – racism/white supremacy/resistance – that is socially meaningful and politically consequential.[3] Race is conceived as both a social structure and a cultural discourse, susceptible to change, that informs how we see ourselves, how we see others, how others see us, and how we represent each other. In this way, race is an identity that is simultaneously imposed on us and that we elect to assume. Anything but an illusion, race as identity is meaningful, even if not biological or divinely determined, because it has a real impact on everyday life, on social practice, and on the stuff of representation. Hence, while race and identity are often erroneously perceived as natural or divine, they are in fact historical and cultural processes fraught by oppression yet marked by resistance.

In terms of cinema, a dominant cultural institution, the meaning of race and the representation of identity impact our historical lives and future because, like race, cinematic representations, styles and stories are ubiquitous. Cinema is everywhere a fact in our lives, saturating our leisure time, our conversations, and our perceptions of each other and of self. Because of this, race in cinema is neither fictional nor illusion. It is real because it is meaningful and consequential; because it impacts real people's real lives. It is anything but trivial or inconsequential. We learn about other people, other cultures, ourselves by watching Hollywood films over and over again – all too often without questioning what we see. Hence, we do not escape reality when watching cinema uncritically; we perpetuate real ideologies when we think of cinema as "only the movies." To question cinema – the central goal of this book and its contributors – is to resist ideology.

What we see and experience in Hollywood race relations is a performance about who passes as white and who does not. As is the case off-screen and outside the theater, there are no "true" white people. As I have argued elsewhere, there are only people who pass as white.[4] And as Noel Ignatiev suggests in his important book, *How the Irish Became White*, who counts as white and who does not depends on place as much as it does time.[5] Given the demands of assimilation, for example, Italian and Jewish Americans often self-identify and are seen as white in significant areas of the USA, having successfully passed through the so-called melting pot by adopting its racial myths and privileges. However, both groups, along with Irish Americans as Ignatiev shows, were once considered anything but worthy of the privilege of whiteness.[6] They might not have been black or red, but they weren't pure white either. Now too many people and institutions position them as white; now too many people think of themselves as white. Interestingly, Latinos seem to now be at the point where the Irish, Italians and Jews were decades ago: struggling with the power of an assimilationist discourse that wants them to either play white, and thus conform to the racial formation standard (to speak only English, for example), or to return to their origins across a geographical border that continues to move under their feet.

Due to changing social and cultural practices across American history, the articulation of race in contemporary film is not only distinct from the articulation of race in early and classical film, but also in the contemporary period itself. From the Civil Rights Movement of the 1960s to the neoconservative movement of the Bush administrations, from the Cold War to the neverending war on terrorism, from Vietnam to Iraq, the last fifty plus years have seen dramatic and traumatic change. In fact, we see a different color of race in certain genre films, as contributors such as Charles Ramírez Berg and Josh Stenger point out in their contributions to this book, as well as in the star discourses associated with the colorful characters who make up Hollywood, as Priscilla Peña Ovalle and Bambi Haggins reveal in their essays. Every contemporary film is different in complex ways from the other films that comprise contemporary cinema; so too is the representation of race from film to film. As Gabriel Estrada, Sean Redmond and Dale Hudson point out in their contributions, race can look like an extraterrestrial humanoid in *Star Wars* (1977), an animated hominid in *The Lord of the Rings* (2001), and vampires in *Vampire's Kiss* (1989). Ironically, given the function of stereotypes, no two forms of race are identical.

This collection attempts to embrace historical specificity, the diversity of race in cinema, while recognizing the persistence of whiteness. It may seem counter-intuitive to say that the meaning of race shifts and changes with time and space while whiteness remains supreme, especially since race and whiteness are inherently intertwined quanta, but this historical fact characterizes the US racial formation and accounts, I think, for its determinacy across time. The racial formation is directional, adjusting to sociopolitical movements, but its benefactors, those who pass as white, focus like a laser beam on maintaining the status of their power and privilege. Like a light-bending cloak, whiteness bends and contorts in order to achieve a kind of consent from historical period to historical period. And its primary tactic, as cultural theorist Antonio Gramsci might argue if he was applying his neo-Marxist method to the locality of the US, is cultural articulation as opposed to bullets and bombs (at least, generally speaking, not domestically).[7] This is to say that, along with politics and law, culture is one of the primary terrains in the struggle over the power of whiteness.

Using various analytical methods and addressing a variety of genres, films and stars, the contributors to this collection intercede in the trajectory of Hollywood's white lights in an attempt to eclipse the blinding power of whiteness in contemporary cinema. Their work contributes to a growing scholarly interest in both the color of race and its privileged benefactor. Collectively and in relation to both *The Birth of Whiteness* and *Classic Hollywood, Classic Whiteness*, contributors engage in a kind of critical intervention that exposes both racism and resistance. Their goal, and thus the goal of this book, is to move the field of film studies – and in, I hope a small, way, cinema itself – toward a more concerted and rigorous approach to the complexity, tenacity and blinding transparency of race in Hollywood cinema.

Generic history

In the first section of the book, Generic History, contributors address the manifestation of race in genres that speak consistently to the history of American racism, including the Western in the 1950s and today, beach films from the 1960s, and New Black Cinema. Genres are perhaps the most obvious places to look for the reflection of ideologies and myths over cinematic time, mainly because they rely on recurring themes and motifs in order to play to viewer expectations. We go to genre films looking for these recurring elements, hoping that our expectations are satisfied with modest surprise from film to film. Contributors to this section of the book look at genre films in order to reveal how some forms of race and whiteness change over time while others remain the same.

In the first essay, "Manifest Myth-Making: Texas History in the Movies," Charles Ramírez Berg corrals Hollywood Westerns that recount the birth of Texas, from Howard Hawks' *Red River* (1948) to John Lee Hancock's *The Alamo* (2004). In doing so he reveals the ways that Hollywood's familiar three-act quest narrative and the concomitant stereotyping of Latinos and Others are overdetermined by the nineteenth-century American experience of westward expansion.

> The purpose of Hollywood's 'Manifest myth-making' was to rationalize – and sanitize – the history of US's North American imperialism and transform it into an entertaining, guilt-free narrative that conformed to core American beliefs (liberty, democracy, freedom, equality) and values (truth, honesty, fair play).

(p. 3)

We see, in Westerns about Texas history, the persistence of whiteness manifesting in recurring myths about America's westward expansion.

In the next essay, "Mapping the Beach: Beach Movies, Exploitation Film and Geographies of Whiteness," Josh Stenger looks at the segregated spaces of beach films produced by American International Pictures, including *Beach Party* (1963), *Muscle Beach Party* (1964), *Bikini Beach* (1964), *Beach Blanket Bingo* (1965), and *How to Stuff a Wild Bikini* (1965). By reinscribing natural landscapes and public spaces as private sites defined by an exclusive and excluding commonality, Stenger shows us how these "films evoked, and to a degree reproduced, the same racial and spatial anxieties that motivated the *lebensraum* of suburban enclavism" (p. 30). In making his case, he reveals the cultural power and ideological ramifications of beach films in the 1960s, specifically the way they exploited and replicated the racialized geography in the early days of "white flight" (or the move of European Americans from the inner city to the suburbs in response to African Americans' migration, bussing, and affirmative action). We learn a great deal about the ideology of whiteness and transient power of segregation from Stenger's analysis of the geography of race in beach films.

In the final essay in the Generic History section, "Boyz, Boyz, Boyz: New Black Cinema and Black Masculinity," Keith Harris investigates the ways in which New Black Cinema takes on the project of cultural intervention and the recoding of blackness as a political and subversive act. In *She's Gotta Have It* (1986) and *Boyz N the Hood* (1991), we see the intentional articulation of "the problematics and paradoxes of black masculinity" (p. 51). New Black Cinema is complicated by its progressive politics, its willingness to confront racism directed at black masculinity, but also by its regressive contradictions. These contradictions point to the discourse of whiteness that justifies in many ways the need for a genre (and label) called New Black Cinema. Harris' work sheds light on our understanding of race as a discourse that operates behind the scenes, in production, as well as on the screen, in genres.

Anthropomorphism

Race in Hollywood cinema is often played out, encoded and articulated, in the representation of humanoids of all kinds, from aliens to hobbits to post-humans of color. In these colorful characters, phenotypes such as skin color and hair provide clues to racial identity. In some cases these clues are either literal, as in the case of the software program that is embodied as the African American Oracle (Gloria Foster) in *The Matrix* (1999), or metaphoric, as in the case of many of the creatures that make up *Star Wars* and *The Lord of the Rings*. I first wrote about representations of phenotypes in *Star Trek and History: Race-ing Toward a White Future*, where I argued, among other things, that Trek's vision of the alien is warped by the gravity of the US racial formation, producing a whitewashed space-time defined by the liberal humanism of the 1960s and neoconservative idealism of the 1980s and 1990s.[8] In similar ways, contributors to this section of this book identify the way humanoids of various kinds form the site of both racial fantasy and critical resistance.

In the first essay, "*Star Wars* episodes I–VI: Coyote and the force of white narrative," Gabriel Estrada engages the distant space-time of alien diversity in the *Star Wars* epic (1977; 1980; 1983; 1999; 2002; 2005). For Estrada, the series mystifies "pure" white masculinity as the "new" hope for a peaceful universe. Yet Lucas's representation of race makes little sense when grounded in historical Native American and Latino "Coyote" narratives. Uncovering the ideology in filmmakers' vision of a white space-time, Estrada offers us an indigenous methodology to deal with cinematic articulations of whiteness. Coyote narratives, he suggests, comprise a method that "can teach Lucas that an intersection of class, multiracial, and pansexual hierarchies mar a greater vision of social equality and evolution" (p. 88). Indeed, one of the many strengths of Estrada's analysis is that he brings to it a methodology grounded in Native American, Mestizo, and Nahuatl cultural sensibilities.

In the second essay in this section, "The Whiteness of the *Rings*," Sean Redmond offers an analysis of racial cartographies in Peter Jackson's *The Lord of the Rings: The Fellowship of the Ring*. For Redmond, race is played out in the film's spatial arrangements of high/low and rural/city oppositions. Yet unlike Estrada, Redmond sees a critique of whiteness in the film. He argues, among other things, that *The Lord of the Rings* posits that too much whiteness, or "hyper-whiteness," is "a dangerous, ultimately destructive subjectivity" (p. 91). For Redmond, the first film in Jackson's Tolkein trilogy more forcefully connects the metaphors of hobbits and other anthropomorphic beings to the space-time of today's multicultural racial formation. His analysis of space in *The Lord of the Rings* stands in interesting contrast to Stenger's aforementioned work on space in beach films.

In the third and final essay in this section, "Neo-Abolitionists, Colorblind Epistemologies and Black Politics: The *Matrix* Trilogy," Tani Dianca Sanchez reads the popular science-fiction films (1999; 2003; 2003) against the framework of African American ideology and critical race theory. Her work compliments Estrada's use of Native American, Mestizo, and Nahuatl ideas to critique the *Star Wars* saga. Yet, unlike Estrada and similar to Redmond, Sanchez sees a critique of whiteness operating in The *Matrix* trilogy. She argues that the directors, Andy and Larry Wachowski, were inspired by the work of critical race theorist and Princeton University Professor Cornell West and his critique of American racism and patriarchy.[9] In fact, Professor West was actually given a small part in the story, playing a wise but critical Zion elder and councilman in *The Matrix Reloaded* (2003). Informed by West's work, the trilogy, Sanchez argues, "is shown to use black ideology to challenge whiteness and to suggest possible routes into social change, human coalitions, and understandings of what it means to be human" (p. 103). Instead of perpetuating stereotypes and racism, *The Matrix* promotes resistance by revealing whiteness as a Matrix-like ideology rather than a norm we should believe is real.

Blood and bodies

The third section of this book focuses on the ways in which race is materialized through bodily fluids, phenotypes, and visual style. Blood is a powerful signifier of whiteness and its many discourses, having been used by courts and the government to classify people as races. Vampire films, for example, draw out our fears of contamination and mixing; the often pasty white skin of the blood-sucker providing metaphoric clues to contemporaneous racial anxieties. Indeed, we see whiteness in the bodies of actors and actresses as they perform race on screen. Our eyes are led to their racialized features, from skin color to different body parts, by the work of the camera, which in many cases functions as a sort of eugenics tool designed to exaggerate – ostracize, demean, and sexualize – colored bodies. As the contributors to this section discuss, the sign of race that takes shape in the blood and bodies we see on screen forms a kind of racial language limited by the anxieties of white supremacy.

In the first essay, "Vampires of Color and the Performance of Multicultural Whiteness," Dale Hudson looks at three vampire films produced during the late 1980s: *Vamp* (1986), *Vampire's Kiss* (1989), and *Carmilla* (1990). Hudson shows how the living-dead in these films reflect great deals of racial diversity while at the same time remaining "largely neoconservative" (p. 127). Vampires in the 1980s provide interesting metaphors for race relations in the 1980s, touching on difference centered on blood and a supernatural evil that, like the stereotypes of welfare queens common to the period, end up being parasitic and living off the labor and flesh of (white) humans. The rhetoric of "reverse discrimination" operates in these Reagan-era films about "bloodsuckers" and "creatures of the night."

In the next essay, "The Naked and the Dead: The Jewish Male Body and Masculinity in *Sunshine* and *Enemy at the Gates*," Susan Hunt and Peter Lehman look at contemporary representations of Jewish masculinity that form a history linked to the mounds of naked corpses in footage of Nazi concentration camps. They argue "that images of Jewish masculinity in international cinema since WWII have been profoundly affected by documentary images of seemingly passive, weak, starving, naked men on the verge of death or in fact dead: their naked bodies a testimony to a very public, failed masculinity" (p. 157). Addressing an important element of whiteness, specifically the role ethnicity and difference plays in the hierarchy of who can and cannot pass as white, Hunt and Lehman focus on two contemporary films, *Sunshine* (2000) and *Enemy at the Gates* (2001). Although these films are very different works of filmmaking, each represents the Jewish male body as both naked and dead, not unlike concentration footage, and the mind, typically the "positive" stereotype of Jewish identity, as metaphorically lifeless.

Moving from bloodsuckers and dead penises to an altogether different kind of embodiment, the final essay in this section tackles the representation of a Latina from the territory of Puerto Rico. In "Framing Jennifer Lopez:

Mobilizing Race from the Wide Shot to the Close-Up," Priscilla Peña Ovalle investigates the ways in which the Puerto Rican American's body is framed by the camera as a way to mobilize racial signs. She argues that "the close-up encapsulates the cosmetic changes Lopez has made to access mainstream Hollywood film while the wide shot reiterates her difference by reinstating the popularity of her butt and the nonwhiteness it represents" (p. 166). We see, in other words, the alienation of Lopez as a racial sign through the work of the camera as much as the narrative and star discourses surrounding the performer's "plump" parts. Like Hunt and Lehman, Ovalle shows us why it is as important to study visual style – the work of the camera – as it is to study representation and narration.

Desire to desire

The next section of the book, Desire to Desire, is a play on Mary Ann Doane's important feminist work, *Desire to Desire: The Woman's Film of the 1940s*.[10] Doane, who has also written an insightful essay on race,[11] provides in *Desire to Desire* a psychoanalytic reading of the repression of women in melodramas during the 1940s. Women in this "woman's film" desire to desire, to express sexual intimacy, and are often punished brutally for it even though that desire is caught in an economy of repression. "The woman's exercise of an active investigating gaze," she writes, "can only be simultaneous with her own victimization."[12] This is not unlike the way interracial relationships are represented in contemporary film: repressed, desiring to desire, punished painfully when, in rare instances, that desire even hints at rising to the surface. We see, in short, the pleasure and subsequent violence of race relations in Hollywood's representation of miscegenation.

In the first essay, "*Guess Who's Coming to Dinner* with Eldridge Cleaver and the Supreme Court or Reforming Popular Racial Memory with Hepburn and Tracy," Susan Courtney addresses the quintessential "desire to desire" film of the 1960s, *Guess Who's Coming to Dinner* (1967).[13] Reading the film against a number of other texts and social events, Courtney reveals the ways it "masked the most critical histories of the phobia it allegedly renounced" (p. 188). It accomplishes this form of desire through cinematic forms of vision, space, and spectatorship. "[I]nterracial desire is only speakable, and visible in 1967," she writes, "when those who have the most to lose are still positioned as if telling and seeing the story, surveying and projecting the field in which it appears as if they have no part to play but that of liberal judge or benevolent father" (p. 213). Ironically, the 1933 version of *King Kong*, with its political metaphor and social allegory, seems more honest to history than does the classic 1967 *Guess Who's Coming to Dinner*.

In the next essay, "Master–Slave Sex Acts: *Mandingo* and the Race/Sex Paradox," Celine Parreñas Shimizu reveals how much and how little interracial relationships changed in the eight years since *Guess Who's Coming to Dinner*.[14] Shimizu's "work emphasizes the way in which spectators of color must practice, as they have since the beginning of race films in the turn of the century, a particular self-displacement in consuming the telling of their history and their sexuality within and against limited terms of whiteness." Focusing on the sex act itself, where a female master seduces a black slave, Shimizu sees both a formation of domination and a site of subject formation. There is opportunity for spectators of color to see in the repressive elements of the sex act more than just the repression and violence it represents and brings about. In this way it is similar to the ending of *King Kong*, in that our sympathies lie with the recipient of violence and hate rather than the perpetuators of violence and hate.

In the next essay, "The Tragedy of Whiteness and Neoliberalism in Brad Kaaya's *O/Othello*," Deborah Whaley looks at the contemporary remake of Shakespeare's *Othello*, *O* (2001), drawing connections between these texts and the larger contexts of a sort of self-absorbed neoliberalism. In the process, she shows how, despite liberal calls for plurality and respect for difference, we have regressed in many ways from *Mandingo* back to *Guess Who's Coming to Dinner* (1967). "*O* works as a multivalent metaphor for disparate race and social relations in contemporary US society," she writes, "and brings to focus the ways that the neoliberal ruling force responds to and within those social relations" (p. 234). Complicating her analysis, Whaley recognizes that, in the end, the cultural work of the film lies, not in its problematic articulation of whiteness, but in its latent possibility in helping young audiences "work at rejecting" neoliberal articulations of race.

In the last essay in this section, "*Romeo Must Die*: Interracial Romance in Action," Gina Marchetti, the only scholar to contribute essays to all three collections, continues her important work on the representation of interracial relationships in *Romeo Must Die* (2000).[15] Marchetti argues that:

> Although action and romance occasionally mix in action plots (particularly in the action-adventure genre) and "Romeo and Juliet" stories are a staple of Hollywood fiction, the pairing of a Chinese man and an African American woman in a mainstream commercial film challenges many deeply held prejudices about Asian masculinity, African American femininity, and the racial politics of romance in Hollywood.
>
> (p. 254)

We learn from Marchetti's work that an interracial relationship that does not include a white partner is capable of sustaining many of the elements desired in *Guess Who's Coming to Dinner*, *Mandingo*, and *O*. And this realization tells us a great deal about blackness and yellowness in the white imagination.

Provocateurs

In the last section of the book, contributors walk the line between the intentional fallacy, which places the meaning of films problematically at the direction of filmmakers instead of audiences, and the need to recognize that
filmmakers and stars nonetheless function discursively to facilitate meaning
and social discourse. Although audiences are ultimately responsible for the
persistence of whiteness in Hollywood cinema – we can, after all, walk out
of the theater when we come across a racist film; or, better yet, recognize it for
the ideology that it is – filmmakers should nonetheless be held responsible
for the choices they make in moving texts from pre-production to exhibition.
This is especially the case in the contemporary period, as many of the filmmakers discussed in this book continue to produce films for diverse audiences.
After the audience they are our best hope for effecting cinematic change.

In the first essay, "The Dark Side of Whiteness: *Sweetback* and John Dollard's
Idea of 'the Gains of the Lower-Class Negroes,'" Thomas Cripps, a scholar
who pioneered the study of race in cinema, continues the work on whiteness
he started in *The Birth of Whiteness* with an analysis of Melvin Van Peebles's
Blaxploitation classic, *Sweet Sweetback's Baadasssss Song* (1971). For Cripps, the
filmmaker left the ending and the moviegoer in an ambiguous position with a
frame that promises a vengeful sequel that has yet to come out. After *Sweet
Sweetback's Baadasssss Song*, he argues:

> in the age of the so-called *blaxploitation* movie and commercially driven
> hip-hop and rap music, there emerged a one-dimensional portrayal of
> African American culture that insisted on a sort of retreat to the ghetto, a
> surrender to the status quo, indeed a conservatism on the part of men –
> *Sweetback* is mainly about men – who had little to conserve.
>
> (p. 269)

For Cripps, the film's progressive promise doesn't lead to progressive results.

In the next essay, "Black Like Him: Steven Spielberg's *The Color Purple*,"
Lester Friedman studies a much different filmmaker, Steven Spielberg, who is
more popular than Van Peebles but, from a critical race perspective, no less
consequential or controversial. As Friedman points out: "Given the intensifying debates swirling about commercial filmmaking, the most successful
Jewish director in Hollywood, the man who adapted Alice Walker's book for
the screen, unwittingly became part of the ongoing controversies between
blacks and Jews" (p. 293). Part of a book-length study of the filmmaker, *Citizen
Spielberg*, this essay is focused on *The Color Purple* (1985) in order to show how
the director added a Jewish American accent to the voice of Alice Walker's
blackness in the novel.[16]

In the next essay, "Crossover Diva: Whoopi Goldberg and Persona Politics,"
Bambi Haggins details the ways Goldberg "navigated crossover waters by
mobilizing multiple personae, dependent upon both intended audience and the

limitations of the given medium" (p. 315). Haggins places Goldberg in the context of black female comics who came before her, showing "how the construction of their personae are inextricably tied to tropes of black femininity – for better *and* for worse" (p. 315). Goldberg becomes a crossover star, spanning multiple media markets and racial categories. In many ways, she is like Jennifer Lopez, another crossover star; in ways that reveal the difference between representations of Latinas and black women, she is not. Lopez's body is shot in ways that we do not see in the shooting of Goldberg, revealing the way sexuality and representation inform racialized performers as they cross over to stardom.

In the last essay in the book, "Surviving *In Living Color* with Some *White Chicks*: Whiteness in the Wayans' (Black) Minds," Beretta Smith-Shomade investigates gender/race passing in *White Chicks* and other Wayans productions. Smith-Shomade sees in the Wayans' project an attempt to imagine whiteness from the eyes of black folks, as well as several problematic contradictions and missed opportunities. For Smith-Shomade, the Wayans' view of whiteness was more cutting edge when they were producing the hip *In Living Color* (1990–4) television series on the neoconservative Fox television network than it has been in their neoliberal feature films such as *White Chicks* and *Scary Movie* (2000). Revealing both contradiction and subversion in the work of the Wayans brothers, Smith-Shomade provides a fair and balanced critique of their work in general and of whiteness in particular.

All of the contributors to this collection offer readers an array of insights from a variety of critical methodologies. Some of the scholars are established and pioneering academics. Others are recent additions to the professorial ranks. Some use social history as their primary methodology; others use critical theory, textual analysis and cultural studies. Collectively, they shine the full spectrum of light on the colors of whiteness in Hollywood, making *The Persistence of Whiteness* a work that challenges racism in cinema while acknowledging Hollywood's progressive moments and resistant elements. More importantly, these authors reveal the shared experience of color – in all its diversity – in relation to the persistent domination of whiteness.

The story of race in cinema does not end with *The Persistence of Whiteness*. As with any collection, this one has its gaps. Important films and genres are not addressed; Mel Brooks' *Blazing Saddles* (1974) and animation immediately come to mind, but there are others. Key issues such as globalization are touched upon but not as developed as warranted by contemporary industry norms. Some of these gaps are addressed by work referenced in the bibliography at the end of this book. Others are left for future scholars. As I suggested at the start of this introduction, it is my hope that this book and its predecessors, *The Birth of Whiteness* and *Classic Hollywood, Classic Whiteness*, will promote additional critical work on race and whiteness in cinema. We need to keep up the intensity of attention paid to the power of cinema to divide white from color.

Notes

1 See Daniel Bernardi, ed., *The Birth of Whiteness: Race and the Emergence of US Cinema* (New Brunswick, NJ: Rutgers University Press, 1996) and *Classic Hollywood, Classic Whiteness* (Minneapolis, MN: University of Minnesota Press, 2001).

2 Daniel Bernardi, "Race and the Emergence of US Cinema," in *The Birth of Whiteness*, p. 5.

3 Michael Omi and Howard Winant, *Racial Formation in the United States: From the 1960s to the 1990s*, 2nd edn (New York: Routledge, 1994).

4 Daniel Bernardi, *Star Trek and History: Race-ing Toward a White Future* (New Brunswick: Rutgers University Press, 1998).

5 Noel Ignatiev, *How the Irish Became White* (New York and London: Routledge, 1996).

6 See, also, Karen Brodkin, *How Jews Became White Folks and What That Says About Race in America* (New Brunswick: Rutgers University Press, 1999); Jennifer Guglielmo and Salvatore Salerno, eds, *Are Italians White? How Race is Made in America* (New York: Routledge, 2003); and David R. Roediger, *Working Toward Whiteness: How America's Immigrants Became White: The Strange Journey from Ellis Island to the Suburbs* (New York: Basic Books, 2005).

7 See Stuart Hall, "Gramsci's Relevance to the Study of Race and Ethnicity," *Journal of Communication Inquiry* 10, 2 (1986): 5–27.

8 See especially Chapters II and III of *Star Trek and History*.

9 For West's seminal work on race, see *Race Matters* (New York: Vintage, 1994).

10 Mary Ann Doane, *Desire to Desire: The Woman's Film of the 1940s* (Bloomington, IN: Indiana University Press, 1987).

11 See Mary Ann Doane, "Bark Continents: Epistemologies of Racial and Sexual Difference in Psychoanalysis and the Cinema," in *Femmes Fetales: Feminism, Film Theory, and Psychoanalysis* (New York: Routledge, 1991).

12 Mary Ann Doane, *Desire to Desire*, p. 136.

13 This essay is part of a larger project. See Susan Courtney, *Hollywood Fantasies of Miscegenation: Spectacular Narratives of Gender and Race, 1903–1967* (Princeton, NJ: Princeton University Press, 2005).

14 The essay in this volume is a revision of a previously published essay. See Celine Parreñas, "Master–Slave Sex Acts: Mandingo and the Race/Sex Paradox," *Wide Angle* 21, 4 (October 1999): 42–61.

15 See, for example, her wonderful and important book, *Romance and the "Yellow Peril": Race, Sex, and Discursive Strategies in Hollywood Fiction* (Los Angeles, CA: University of California Press, 1994).

16 Lester Friedman, *Citizen Spielberg* (Chicago, IL: University of Illinois Press, 2006).

Part 1

Generic history

Chapter 1

Manifest myth-making
Texas history in the movies

Charles Ramírez Berg

Over more than a decade and a half I have researched and written on Latino images in US cinema, resulting in several articles and book chapters, and culminating in a book, *Latino Images in Film*, published in 2002.[1] Since then, I have expanded my critical focus to analyze not only the images themselves, but also the matrix from which they sprang. The first piece along these lines looked at the discourse about Mexicans and Mexican Americans in Southern California during the first third of the last century, the time when the film industry relocated there and established itself as a leading world cinema.[2] I continue the investigation of context and imagery here by sketching out the ways that the basic Hollywood adventure narrative – and the concomitant stereotyping of Latinos and Others – was overdetermined by the nineteenth-century American experience of westward expansion.

My claim is that although Hollywood's familiar three-act quest plot, the basis for many of its action films, had many classic antecedents, the American experience gave it a distinctive, local inflection. Specifically, the three-act structure found in Hollywood adventures and Westerns had two major shaping influences. The first is the dogma of America's civil religion, positing the USA as a nation of God's chosen people who were delivered to a Promised Land. The second is the nineteenth-century enactment of this doctrine, Manifest Destiny, which can be considered the civil religion's "continental crusade," the impetus for the settling and annexation of the West by the USA. Viewed from this perspective, Hollywood films, particularly those about the "winning of the west," proselytized Manifest Destiny, simplifying and organizing the experience into a coherent conquest myth that recounted the "crusade's" exploits in epic, God's-on-our-side, happy-ending fashion. The purpose of Hollywood's "Manifest myth-making" was to rationalize – and sanitize – the history of the USA's North American imperialism and transform it into an entertaining, guilt-free narrative that conformed to core American beliefs (liberty, democracy, freedom, equality) and values (truth, honesty, fair play).

A tall order, to be sure, but the result can be clearly seen in Westerns, which deal directly with westward expansion. Therefore, in order to examine how Manifest Destiny informed Hollywood movies and how both were derived from civil religious dogma, in this essay I will discuss Hollywood Westerns that recount the birth of Texas by analyzing six films: Howard Hawks' *Red River* (1948) and five Alamo movies: the D.W. Griffith-produced *Martyrs of the Alamo, or The Birth of Texas* (1915), Walt Disney's *Davy Crockett, King of the Wild Frontier* (1954), Frank Lloyd's *The Last Command* (1955), John Wayne's *The Alamo* (1960), and the most recent version, John Lee Hancock's *The Alamo* (2004).

This is primarily a work of narratology. I'm not interested in comparing history and movies in order to grouse about Hollywood's changes and distortions – movies always alter history. Rather, I want to begin to understand how America's civil religion and Manifest Destiny combined with Hollywood's adventure narrative paradigm to form a colonizing master movie narrative: a stirring quest story of a God-fearing, Anglo male protagonist who enters, claims, tames, and civilizes the wilderness. Of course, it is impossible to make America's foundational values (equality, life, liberty, and the pursuit of happiness) jibe with the thievery and violence that characterized much of what was perpetrated under the banner of Manifest Destiny. So it should not be surprising that the history of Manifest Destiny, the crusade as well as Hollywood's recounting of it, is deeply conflicted ideologically. The acceptance of the assumptions driving Manifest Destiny policy and the ensuing crusade was widespread, but not universal. There were always pockets of disagreement and resistance, stemming from differing interpretations of the nation's civil religious doctrine, just as there was an ongoing debate about its enactment as the Manifest Destiny campaign. Similarly, regarding Hollywood's mythologizing of that history, there were reluctant and resistant filmmakers whose films questioned or sometimes subverted the prevailing doctrine.

Looking at the Alamo films treated here in rough chronological order, we see an interesting progression from simplistic legend formation to richer and more complex treatments of the battle. Griffith's *Martyrs of the Alamo* is the earliest existing movie version (none of the previous ones have survived), and it is the Ur-text, establishing the Alamo movie formula in the simplest partisan and racist terms. Though less blatant, Disney's *Davy Crockett, King of the Wild Frontier* carefully follows the *Martyrs of the Alamo*'s narrative template; it is the best structured, most straightforward and economical telling of the Alamo legend, taking just 30 minutes of screen time. Like these two films, Wayne's rendition is uncritical of Manifest Destiny, but its presentation of the Texas–Mexican conflict is far from one-sided, displaying sensitivity to Mexican history and culture. And Frank Lloyd's *The Last Command* is more complex still, presenting a nuanced account of Tejano and Texas colonial culture as well as the events leading up to the battle.

Finally, Hancock's *The Alamo* tries to debunk received history and revise the Alamo sub-genre. But, judging by its lackluster box office performance and so-so critical reception, it paid a heavy price for doing so.[3] The film's failed revisionism is illuminating, however, in revealing how Hollywood's quest-story template not only affirms the national civil religion and supports Manifest Destiny, but also fulfills key movie narrative functions, such as providing a coherent dramatic structure, clarifying heroic character motivation, and delivering a happy ending. Hancock's tampering with history undermined all that.

One non-Alamo film, Hawks' *Red River*, is included here because it too covers the birth of Texas, the state as cattle empire. As Robert Sklar notes in one of the earliest essays to chart the film's ideological undercurrents, *Red River* is "a film about the notions of empire. . . . about the territorial expansion of one society by the usurpation of land from others, and the consequences arising therefrom."[4] The fascinating thing about it – what, in fact, may account for its classic status – is just how ideologically conflicted it is. Its intent at the start, however, seems simple and single-minded. An introductory note scrolling on the screen before the action begins, accompanied by Dimitri Tiomkin's grandiose theme music, states the film's straightforward goal: to depict the founding of cattle ranching in Texas and recount the heroic saga of the first cattle drive along the Chisolm Trail. Then the film proper begins. Act I takes place 15 years after the Battle of the Alamo, then the rest of the film jumps ahead nearly 15 years after that, and, as the story unfolds, the jubilant jingoism is gradually undercut by a critical examination of the ruthlessness beneath imperialism. For all its exultant trappings, *Red River* is an exploration into the toxic effects of enacting Manifest Destiny. It is thus a good place to begin our discussion because its cowboy-turned-rancher protagonist demonstrates the poisonous workings of Manifest Destiny on a human scale.

The human toll of Manifest Destiny

Red River's first act is a fictionalized account of the origins of Texas's famed King Ranch. Tom Dunson (John Wayne) and his cantankerous side-kick, Groot (Walter Brennan), break away from a California-bound wagon train. The time is 1851, and Tom wants to go south in search of land to raise a herd of cattle. After a nighttime skirmish with a band of Native Americans, they cross the Red River and ride south through Texas. Along the way they pick up a young boy, Matt (who will grow up to be Montgomery Clift), who has been orphaned by a Native American attack. Nearing the Rio Grande, Tom finally finds the land he wants. "This is it," he announces, "this is where we start growing good beef."

Groot agrees. "Sure looks good, Tom. Worth coming 2,000 miles fer." "Everything a man could want," says Tom. "Good water and grass – and plenty of it." It is the boy who raises the legal sticking point. "Who this belong to?" he asks. "To me," Tom snaps back. "Some day that'll all be covered with good beef and I'll put a mark, a brand on 'em, to show they're mine too." He proceeds to describe his Red River D brand by drawing it on the ground with a stick, tells Matt he'll add his "M" to it when he's earned it, and, being a man of action, sets to work branding his lone bull. No sooner is that done than two

Mexican *vaqueros* ride up. They patrol the range for the owner, Don Diego. When it turns out that he lives some 400 miles south, Groot articulates the legal basis for the squatter's rights Tom has enacted. "That's too much land for one man. Why, it ain't decent. Here's all this land achin' to be used and never has been. I tell you it ain't decent."

To show he is a reasonable man (and to make sure the audience has the geography straight), Tom offers to split the difference with Don Diego's emissaries. "What's that river you were talking about?" he asks.

"El Rio Grande," the *vaquero* replies. "But I told you that—"

"Well," says Tom, interrupting the Mexican, "tell Don Diego that all the land north of the river is mine. Tell him to stay off of it."

Once again the Mexican explains that Don Diego is the rightful owner of the land, having acquired it many years before by grant and patent from the king of Spain.

"You mean," says Tom, reducing the Mexican's legal explanation to its basest bottom line, "he took it away from whoever was here before. Indians maybe? . . . Well I'm taking it away from him."

This leads, of course, to a shoot-out: the Mexican draws first but Tom is quicker and kills him with a single shot. When the surviving *vaquero* decides not to fight, Tom sends him back to tell Don Diego what happened. They bury the dead Mexican and Tom dutifully reads over his grave from his Bible. It's a brief, cursory ceremony because Tom still needs to brand Matt's cow. Afterwards, as the bull and the cow drift off to roam his newly acquired land and begin propagating the Dunson herd, Tom predicts that in a decade his brand will be on the gates of "the greatest ranch in Texas."

Over a series of dissolves that show Tom's dream materializing he continues his voiceover, providing the justification for stealing the land: it's in the national interest. "Ten years and I'll have that brand on enough beef to feed the whole country," he says. "Good beef for hungry people. Beef to make 'em strong, make 'em grow. But it takes work, and it takes sweat, and it takes time, lots of time. It takes years."

Creating an empire by boldly taking what he wants and ruthlessly eliminating the competitors in the name of feeding the nation, Tom is the personification of Manifest Destiny. But underneath the film's majestic surface lie disturbing verities at the heart of Manifest Destiny, which the remainder of Hawks' film explores. To appreciate the links between America's civil creed, Manifest Destiny and the film's opening, let's delve into the history of how Texas and the Southwest became part of the United States.

From history to narrative in *Red River*

Act I of *Red River* gives a highly abbreviated but essentially accurate recap of the origins of the state of Texas. North American settlers did indeed come to Texas, in droves, and liked what they saw. Though it was resolved by 1851 when *Red River* begins, there was a contested strip of land between the established settlements in central Texas and the Rio Grande, claimed by both Mexico and the USA. Despite losing the battle of the Alamo in 1836, Texas won its independence in the same year and was briefly a republic, then became the 28th state of the Union in 1845. In 1846, the US Army (like Tom Dunson) provoked an attack by Mexicans over the disputed land, getting them to "draw first," which prompted a swift and deadly response from the USA. That incident led to the Mexican–American War which Mexico lost, forcing it not only to forfeit its claim on the disputed land but also to cede a vast expanse of its northern territories to the USA on top of that ("All the land north of the river is mine.").

Even the dramatic motivations of *Red River*'s Anglo-Mexican confrontation scene have their basis in history. The notion of "that's too much land" for a Mexican – though not too much for an Anglo – is consistent with the sweeping racist and ethnocentric assumptions supporting Manifest Destiny. The land-grabbing and empire building that typified much of the expansion to the Pacific was masked under the guise of national interests, namely strategic military and profitable business interests that summarily negated the interests – and the ownership rights – of any other Latino or Native American peoples or nations. And, as in Tom's voiceover in *Red River*, the USA's entrepreneurial ambitions and fortune-hunting were transformed by contemporary politicians, then later by history books and Hollywood, into a beneficent crusade. North Americans were rightfully and divinely entitled to the land from sea to shining sea – the future well-being of the nation depended upon it.

But, as I've said, the rest of *Red River* complicates such simplistic imperialism. Director Howard Hawks' development of the character of Tom Dunson and John Wayne's portrayal of him as a stubborn, unrepentant hard case reveals his tyrannical nature in the course of the cattle drive. In the process, the film exposes the shadow side of the pioneering personality and the dualistic nature of Manifest Destiny: brave but brutal, daring but obsessed, bold but ruthless. Tom Dunson, like Ethan (again John Wayne) in *The Searchers* (1956), provides a candid display of the two seemingly inseparable sides of Manifest Destiny: the courageous risk-taker and the cold-blooded killer.

Finding whether Tom can proceed beyond violence is the subject of the second half of the film. *Red River*'s key conflict is animated when Matt takes the cattle drive away from the despotic Tom, after Tom nearly kills a drover who accidentally caused a stampede, then later orders the hanging of two deserters. Matt's mutiny pits his more temperate approach (which Tom repeatedly calls "soft") against Tom's severe pioneer pragmatism. Will Tom actually kill Matt, as he has sworn to do, just as he killed all the others the film has told us have tried to take Tom's ranch from him over the years? Resorting to familiar Western film binaries (the law of the gun vs. the rule of law, greed vs. selflessness), *Red River* probes the barbarity of colonizing the West, and raises these questions about Manifest Destiny:

- When exactly does the use of force condoned by Manifest Destiny end? When does the rule of law supersede the rule of violence?
- Who can stop the regime of violence? Who dares to confront a violent architect of Manifest Destiny like Tom and propose a more moderate program?
- Once law and order have replaced guns and killing, making way for railroads, paved streets, businesses, courts, and schools, how does society deal with the perpetrators of that violence? How does a "civilized society" handle the unbridled violence at the core of its creation?

As has been widely noted, violence lies at the heart of the Western's mythic structure – and of Manifest Destiny – both as policy and myth. As Richard Slotkin says:

> . . . the ethics of Western violence coincide with the imperatives of entrepreneurial ideology which are the core of the political-economic mythology of the United States. However, the Western deflects, masks or denies the validity of economic self-interest – 'greed' – which is the motivating principle of that ideology. In this Westerns perform the classic function of cultural myth, offering a vehicle in which the culture can both affirm its values and express its doubts and ambivalence.[5]

Simultaneously asserting and questioning national values, the Western genre looks back at the deeds rationalized by Manifest Destiny with a mixture of celebration and guilt. Accordingly, *Red River* tries to maintain the mythic tone that characterized its opening as it goes on to recount the first successful Chisolm Trail cattle drive, but ends up scrutinizing this ambivalence, seeking a way to honor Tom's bravery yet critique – and distance itself from – his cruelty. Across the genre, if not in every film, the same tension occurs. Usually the celebratory narrative predominates, but it does not completely obscure the guilt-ridden one. *Red River*'s dark, introspective narrative shadows its brighter, uncritical myth-making one, producing a fascinating ideological tug-of-war, which the film resolves by having it both ways.

The climax of the Tom–Matt confrontation is really an anti-climax. Matt refuses to use his gun, so they fist fight, and nobody gets hurt. They acknowledge that they love each other, and Tom adds an "M" for Matt on the cattle brand. Tom the ruthless empire-builder is rehabilitated and ideologically quarantined from the more moderate characters (and from viewers) in two interesting ways. The first is generational: after the 1851 prologue, most of the film takes place in 1865, when Tom has reached late middle-age and has become the gray-templed patriarch. Matt, the orphan he raised as his own, is the heir apparent, with the narrative making clear just how different they are from one another. Society's transformation to Matt's more reasonable ways, then, is evolutionary, automatic. Ruthlessness naturally gives way to decency.

The second distancing of Tom, by biology, is more definitive. Tom never married so his kind dies out when he dies. And since no blood ties between Tom and Matt exist, Matt can inherit the family's ranching business without being genetically tainted by Tom's brutality and avarice. *Red River* is the perfect Manifest Destiny balancing act, tempering Tom's audacity and hard-hearted cruelty with Matt's moderation, reason, and restraint. It celebrates courage and condemns ruthlessness. It revels in the spectacle of violence, then establishes its limits. It acknowledges guilt, then expiates it. Able to deliver pleasures to viewers of every political stripe, no wonder it's a revered classic.

By exploring *Red River*, I have tried to show the links between civic creed, Manifest Destiny and narrative. In order to proceed to a deeper reading of several Alamo films, and to trace the interrelationships among the USA's civil religion, Manifest Destiny, and the essential Hollywood narrative in that often-repeated story, it will be necessary to know more about America's civil religion and how it provided the impetus for Manifest Destiny.

The USA's civil religion

America's civil religion derives from a broader Eurocentric discourse. As outlined by Ella Shohat and Robert Stam, Eurocentrism may be characterized as a justification of First World actions by claiming a direct democratic lineage flowing from Greece directly to the metropolitan capitals of Europe and the USA. By thinking of the West as the "'motor' for progressive historical change," Eurocentrism posits Western civilization as progressing unswervingly toward democratic institutions (conveniently writing off figures such as Torquemada, Mussolini, and Hitler as aberrations). Non-European democratic institutions are elided, and the West's part in subverting democracies abroad is obscured. The West's oppressive practices – slavery, colonialism, imperialism, fascism – are minimized as is the historical link between the highly profitable imperialistic institutions and the present cultural, economic, technological, and political dominance of the First World. In short, Eurocentrism cleanses history so that the West is framed "in terms of its noblest achievements – science, progress, humanism" – and "the non-West in terms of its deficiencies, real or imagined."[6]

In the USA, the discourse of Eurocentrism formed the basis for its imperialism, Manifest Destiny, on this continent and the Monroe Doctrine in the southern hemisphere, and structured its operative assumptions. Commonplace though seldom explicitly acknowledged, they are implicitly understood, becoming a quasi-religious set of tenets. The USA's implicit dominant ideology becomes, in the words of Robert N. Bellah, its "civil religion," a credo that "was able to build up . . . powerful symbols of national solidarity and to mobilize deep levels of personal motivation for the attainment of national goals." Founded on "biblical archetypes: Exodus, Chosen People, Promised Land, New Jerusalem, and Sacrificial Death and Rebirth," America's civil religion posits America as "the promised land," where "God has led his people to establish a new sort of social order that shall be a light unto all the nations."[7] Though harkening back to biblical antecedents, Bellah argues that:

> . . . it is also genuinely American and genuinely new. It has its own prophets and its own martyrs, its own sacred events and sacred places, its own solemn rituals and symbols. It is concerned that America be a society as perfectly in accord with the will of God as men can make it, and a light to all nations.[8]

For Noam Chomsky, such presupposed doctrines set "the bounds of discourse, . . . the bounds of thinkable thought,"[9] informing everything from state policy decisions to the writing of history books, and, I'm arguing, to Hollywood filmmaking. The core formative assumptions, what Chomsky calls the USA's "necessary illusions," are these:

- Americans are a chosen people, selected by God to bask in the glory of democracy.
- As God's elect, Americans are called on to propagate democratic freedom around the world. A "yearning for democracy," Chomsky says, guides the USA's foreign policy.[10]
- Unlike other countries, which habitually act out of base self-interest, the USA acts out of benevolent and moral motives, never ignoble or selfish ones.
- The USA always acts defensively, responding to aggression, never offensively as the aggressor. "The use of force can only be an exercise in self-defense and . . . those who try to resist must be aggressors, even in their own lands."[11]
- "No country has the right of self-defense against US attack, and the United States has the natural right to impose its will, by force if necessary and feasible."[12]

Hollywood movies internalized the assumptions of America's civil religion and its necessary illusions within their narratives. Consciously, of course, what most filmmakers were doing was shaping the raw material of history to conform to American cinema's classically well-plotted narrative. In a nutshell, Hollywood's standard three-act story features a goal-oriented Anglo (usually male) protagonist, the causal arrangement of gradually escalating story events building to a near-the-end-of-the-movie dramatic climax, an intertwined romantic subplot, all tied together with a suitably upbeat and, preferably, triumphant resolution. Obviously the three-act (beginning–middle–end) quest narrative predates film by centuries. The tale of the young hero leaving on a journey, encountering and overcoming a series of tests and challenges, then returning home is the basis for myriad stories ranging from *The Odyssey* to *Sir*

Gawain and the Green Knight. What was distinctive about the Hollywood version was its incorporation of national history and civil religion to present a pageant of American colonialism, what Arthur G. Pettit called "conquest fiction."[13] In Hollywood's Manifest Destiny-inflected quest variant, a white man leaves home, journeys to some remote location, plants a flag, and claims the land in the name of order, civilization and democracy.

Several of Chomsky's necessary illusions, for example, are evident in *Red River*'s first act. Tom steals the land, but it's not really greed because his motivation is pure: he's feeding the nation. And his killing of Don Diego's *vaquero* is not really murder: it's self-defense. Another good example of Hollywood's narrative construction meshing with these ideological assumptions is a story also set in Texas and the subject of numerous screen treatments – the Battle of the Alamo. It is Manifest Destiny's creation myth, the story of sacrifice and martyrdom for democracy that marks the opening of the West. In order to appreciate the role it played in the shaping of Hollywood adventure narrative, a short summary history of Manifest Destiny, particularly as it played out in the Southwest, seems in order.

Texas and Manifest Destiny: the continental crusades in the southwest

As the coiner of the phrase, John L. O'Sullivan, put it in 1845, Manifest Destiny was the notion that the USA was fated to "overspread the continent allotted by Providence for the free development of our yearly multiplying millions."[14] In his estimation, David Montejano has written that what Manifest Destiny decreed was that "The Anglo-Saxon nation was bound to glory; the inferior, decadent Indian race and the half-breed Mexicans were to succumb before the inexorable march of the superior Anglo-Saxon people."[15] Settling and claiming western lands, then, was considered civilizing the heathens and was approached with missionary zeal. "Our whole history," wrote Ralph Waldo Emerson, "appears to be a last effort of Divine Providence on behalf of the human race."[16]

The Louisiana Purchase of 1803 began the United States' growth westward, and initiated the country's dispute over the ownership of Texas, which some felt had been included in the Purchase. Later, several unauthorized military expeditions into Florida secured control of Spanish posts there and gave the USA leverage to bargain for the Transcontinental Treaty in 1819, which ceded Florida to the USA in exchange for abandoning its claim to Texas.

This only postponed the United States' designs on Texas. But for that to come to pass two wars would have to be fought. The first, the Texas war, was a revolt of Anglo settlers against the Mexican state. In 1821, after Mexico had won its independence from Spain, it opened Texas to Euroamerican colonizers, led by Stephen F. Austin. The growth of their settlement in Texas was dramatic: from the fewer than 2,500 Euroamericans in 1820,[17] to 20,000 settlers and 2,000 slaves by 1830; by 1835, when Austin called for an armed revolt, the number of settlers was somewhere between 30,000 and 35,000,[18] roughly ten times the Mexican population in the region.[19] With the numbers on his side, Austin argued that the best interests of the USA required that "Texas should be effectually, and fully, Americanized – that is, settled by a population that will harmonize with their neighbors on the *East*."[20] The best way for Americanization to proceed in Texas would be for it to separate itself from Mexico.

The causes of the war were many and complicated. Certainly Mexican President Antonio López de Santa Anna's annulling of the nation's Constitution was an important one, since it caused some Tejanos (Mexicans born in Texas) and Texians (North American immigrants to Texas) to seek to return to a federalist state, if not within Mexico, then outside it. Other Tejanos and Texians, nevertheless, continued to support the Mexican government.[21] And there were numerous other reasons as well: the desire of the Texians to maintain their slaves after Mexico abolished slavery in 1829; the USA's longstanding desire to acquire Texas (it made repeated offers to purchase Texas from Mexico, and Mexico always declined); Mexico's prohibition of further North American immigration to Texas in 1830, which enraged Anglo settlers (and made all North Americans who entered Texas after 1830 – including many of those who fought in the Alamo – technically illegal immigrants); the settlers' failure to adhere to Mexican laws and the Mexican government's flexing its muscle by moving troops into nearby Coahuila; the Anglos' refusal to pay customs duties and engaging in widespread smuggling; and the sale of parcels of Texas land by US land companies to unsuspecting buyers who did not know that the scrip they purchased was worthless so long as Texas was part of Mexico.[22]

Then there were the hostile attitudes of Anglos toward Mexicans. As Arnoldo De León argues, if racism was not *the* cause of the Texas war, it was certainly a very prominent one. The roots of the racism "were planted in the unique psychohistorical experience of the white Texas pioneers and settlers."[23] Some migrants who came to Texas brought with them certain racist attitudes which adversely affected their estimation of the Mexican. For example, many may have shared English antipathy towards Spain, Spaniards (Texas was a Spanish colony until 1821) and Catholics. Furthermore, many may have harbored prejudices against Native Americans and blacks. For such settlers, Mexicanos, who were mostly *mestizos* (a mixture of Spanish, *indio* and black ancestry), "were doubly suspect, as heirs to Catholicism and as descendants of Spaniards, Indians, and Africans."[24]

These anti-Mexicano sentiments were naturally exacerbated by the violent events of the war, particularly the Mexican victories over Anglos at the Alamo and the garrison at Goliad in which they killed all Anglo combatants. The Mexicans were eventually defeated in the Battle of San Jacinto by Sam Houston, who captured Gen. Santa Anna. The Mexican general signed a treaty that ceded Texas to the insurgents, and the Republic of Texas was born.

But it was not long before the USA began looking for ways to annex Texas into the Union. When Congress voted to make Texas a state in 1845, Mexico broke off diplomatic relations in protest. The USA sent troops to Texas under the command of General Zachary Taylor, and here is where the beginning of *Red River* symbolically recreates history. General Taylor promptly crossed what the Mexicans regarded as their northern border with Texas at the Nueces River and led his men 150 miles south to the Rio Grande, the boundary line the USA was claiming. After Mexicans attacked a small search party of Taylor's soldiers ("drawing first"), President Polk asked Congress to declare war, because Mexico had "invaded our territory and shed American blood upon the American soil."[25]

The Americans attacked Mexico and waged a bloody war, killing thousands of Mexicans as they drove southwards to Mexico City. US forces captured the capital city in 1847, and soon thereafter, in February, 1848, the two countries signed the Treaty of Guadalupe Hidalgo which ended the war and declared that the Rio Grande was the USA–Mexico border. It also gave Manifest Destiny a tremendous boost at bargain prices: Mexico ceded more than one million square miles of its northern territories – all or part of the present-day states of California, Arizona, New Mexico, Nevada, Utah, Wyoming, Colorado, Kansas, and Oklahoma – to the USA for $15 million.[26]

Although provisions of the treaty called for equal citizenship for the Mexicans who chose to stay in place, in effect they were regarded – and widely treated – as a defeated people. "Within a year of the treaty's ratification," Martha Menchaca writes, "the United States government . . . began a process of racialization that categorized most Mexicans as inferior in all domains of life." The legal system was used "to confer privilege upon Whites and to discriminate against people of color."[27]

Anglo discrimination toward Mexicanos that had been present since the two groups came into contact in the 1821–36 period was the foundation for the intense denigration that followed. At heart, the prejudice was racist. It might arise in a discussion of the significance of color, as in the Austin *Southern Intelligencer's* note in 1865 that "white was the emblem of light, religious purity, innocence, faith, joy and life," while black was its opposite, indicating "the earth, darkness, mourning, wickedness, negation, death, and was appropriate to the Prince of Darkness."[28] Such "color coded" world views might be extended to the kind of pseudo-ethnology found in the *San Antonio Herald's* claim that blond, fair-skinned, blue-eyed races were given to investigation, invention and improvement, while the dark-skinned, black-eyed, black-haired ones held fast to their customs and religions, thus their lack of progress.[29]

But, however it was expressed, the main message was that the *mestizo* Mexicans were an inferior "mongrel race." The racial prejudice of the North American settlers expressed itself most directly in the fear of miscegenation. The *Southern Review* published an editorial condemning "mongrelism," holding that the mixing of these "two unequal races is . . . a cancer, an unpardonable sin against mankind and against nature."[30] When racial discrimination and the fears of racial pollution were added to the obvious religious and cultural differences, these formed the basis for Anglos' longstanding stereotypical beliefs about Mexicans, marking them as dirty, lazy, uncivilized, immoral, and irresponsible.[31]

Texas is where the events leading to the Treaty of Guadalupe Hidalgo played out and where many of the stereotypical attitudes towards Mexicans, Tejanos, and Latinos in general were established. But similar prejudices were exhibited by many Anglos towards Mexicans as they carried out the US expansion across the southwest. Throughout the area in the nineteenth century, this stereotypical defamation of Mexicans provided the justification for their social and economic control by Anglos. In region after region, the pattern of Anglo colonization was the same: Mexicans went from being the land-holding majority to an impoverished minority; as such, they were deemed second-class citizens, especially after the Texas and Mexican wars; they were given few rights; they had little recourse to legal remedies for their plight (for example, legal proceedings were held in English, and Mexicans could neither serve on juries nor testify in court); and they gradually lost most of their land, personal wealth and, in the eyes of Anglos, their worth as human beings. By the time Arizona and New Mexico were admitted as states in 1912 – around the same time that the film industry was moving from the east coast to Hollywood – Mexican Americans in the US southwest were at the bottom of the social scale, alongside African, Asian and Native Americans.[32]

It is important to remember, however, that not all Anglos discriminated against Mexicans. There were those who saw that the nation's expansionist ambitions too often contradicted the founding ideals of liberty, equality and freedom, and who treated Mexicans fairly and decently. Some members of Congress, including Abraham Lincoln, opposed the Mexican War. One congressman from Ohio went on the record to call it "a war against an unoffending people without adequate or just cause, for the purpose of conquest," and stated that he would "lend it no aid, no support whatsoever."[33] There were those, such as Abiel Abbott Livermore, who saw the Mexican War as an expansionist hoax that could not be squared with the USA's supposedly egalitarian principles or its purported Christian beliefs. "The Anglo-Saxons," Livermore wrote in *The War with Mexico Reviewed*, a winner of an American Peace Society prize in 1850, "have been apparently persuaded to think themselves the chosen people, anointed race of the Lord, commissioned to drive out the heathen, and plant their religion and institutions in every Canaan they could subjugate."[34] But if there was opposition to the general run of oppression and vilification of Mexicans, it was a minority sentiment that was overwhelmed by the Anglos' prevailing lust for land and accumulation of wealth.

Narrative structure and ideology

"What the American public wants in the theater is a tragedy with a happy ending."

William Dean Howells to Edith Wharton, explaining the failure of her tragic play, *The House of Mirth*

Wharton's play, based on her best-selling novel, was a archetypal tragedy about a woman who, near the mid-point of the story, makes a bad decision and pays for it with her social standing, her reputation, and ultimately her life. That is, it was a tragedy with an ending that tragedies have – an *unhappy* one. Leaving aside for the moment whether such a thing as a tragedy with a happy ending could even exist, it's worth noting that Wharton's tale failed as a film as well. A recent British–US co-production, written and directed by Terence Davies and starring Gillian Anderson as the ill-fated Lily Bart, was a modest critical success but a box office failure.[35]

Since its inception, Hollywood has thoroughly subscribed to the Happy Ending and so, aside from adaptations of Shakespeare, tragedies in mainstream studio-produced cinema are rare indeed.[36] Yes, there are movies with sad or bittersweet endings, but that's not the same thing. A tragedy depicts the downfall and demise of an individual as the result of a fateful decision. It may be due to a sense of honor (Brutus partaking in the killing of Caesar in *Julius Caesar* to prevent him from becoming king), or honor leading to revenge (Hamlet avenging his father's murder), or simply a moral weakness (Macbeth's ambition). In Hollywood cinema, the best-known tragedy is probably Orson Welles' *Citizen Kane* (1941), whose title character, Charles Foster Kane, abandons his ideals, loses his moral bearings, and becomes a monster of Shakespearian proportions. The structure of a tragedy that would apply to *Hamlet*, Wharton's *The House of Mirth*, and *Citizen Kane* would look like this:

CLIMAX

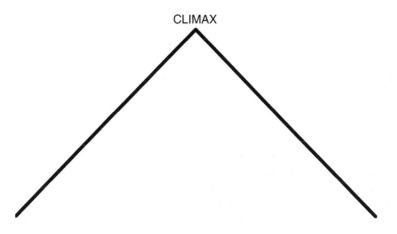

The roughly mid-point climax marks the main character's major decision, one that seals his or her downfall (Hamlet deciding to kill his uncle the king but mistakenly killing Polonius instead; Kane's compromising his values by buying the rival newspaper's editorial staff; Macbeth's murder of the king, which occurs somewhat earlier than the play's exact mid-point).

Aiming for uplifting endings, American studio films have typically – and doggedly – avoided tragedy. Protagonists might make bad decisions but they are corrected in a last-minute flurry of recognition, repentance, and redemption. Often that redemptive turnaround is the film's climax, the character's near-the-end-of-the-film decision to do the right/courageous/noble thing. Luke Skywalker decides to "trust the Force," fly his spaceship manually, and destroys the Death Star; Rick decides that fighting the Nazis is more important than his love for Ilsa and sends her off with her husband at the end of *Casablanca* (1942). The plot line of the classical Hollywood protagonist would look like this:

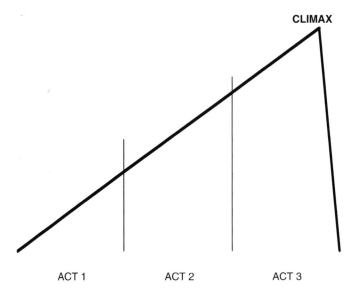

The main decision resolves all the narrative's loose ends and, coming before the ending, allows most Hollywood films to conclude on a stirring high note. The plane carrying Ilsa and her husband departs Casablanca and Rick and Captain Renaut walk off to begin a life fighting Nazism.

Each narrative structure has a specific dramatic function. The tragic structure is good for moral analysis and well-suited for cautionary tales. *Macbeth* critiques overreaching ambition; *Citizen Kane* examines the American Dream and concludes that money brings not happiness but corruption, misery, and a sad and lonely death. The climax placement near the plot's center forces audiences to consider the ethical consequences of characters' actions for some time and in some depth. The happy ending structure, on the other hand, is good for uplift, and perfect for fables and morality plays: the moral of the typical Hollywood story is that doing the right thing is redemptive, yielding both individual and social benefits. The placement of the climax just before the end ensures a positive, triumphant conclusion. Luke Skywalker destroys the Death Star, there's a celebration, and, accompanied by John Williams' soaring fanfare, *Star Wars IV* ends. Roll credits.

Since tragedy and the happy ending stem from separate structures, combining the two as Howells suggested appears impossible. But *Red River*, I'd argue, does just that. It critiques dominant policy (i.e. Manifest Destiny) and on the whole hews to the tragic structure, yet it delivers a Hollywood happy ending.

For 131 of *Red River*'s 133-minute running time, Tom Dunson's plot line is completely tragic. When Matt puts an end to Tom's killing and takes over the cattle drive, Tom swears revenge. "I'm going to kill you, Matt," Tom says, just 15 minutes past the film's exact mid-point (minute 82), signaling the tragic climax. The rest of the story leads to Tom and Matt's inevitable showdown, and if this were Shakespeare, Matt would kill Tom. Tom's demise would be the heart-rending fall of a good man gone wrong. A valiant warrior morally deformed by the violent demands of Manifest Destiny, he is killed by his stepson, the man who – ironically, tragically – loved him most. But this is Hollywood, and the film is rescued from being Shakespeare by a last-minute turn of events. Tom pulls a gun on him, but Matt refuses to draw his pistol. So they get into a fist fight. Matt's love interest (Joanne Dru) draws a gun on them, demands that they stop and admit they love each other. Which they promptly do. Tom sketches out the new ranch brand, which now includes an "M" for Matt. The stepson smiles his approval and the film ends. By redesigning the brand, Tom redesigns his plot line, transforming *Red River* from tragedy to Hollywood happy ending. That is, by shifting the dramatic structure from

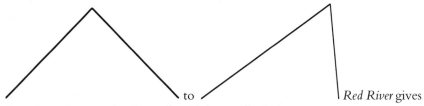

to   *Red River* gives American viewers what Howells said they really desire.

It's a stunning, cunning sleight of hand, ushering viewers out the door before they can question Tom's last-minute conversion, much less reflect on the corrosive effects of Manifest Destiny. But Tom's implausible transformation becomes plausible only with the aid of audience participation. In order for that ending to make sense, many American viewers will comprehend Tom's sudden change of heart by activating civil religious doctrine. Seen through that dogmatic lens, the reversal is rationalized in this way:

Tom's brand of fierce determination was what it took to settle the frontier, and let's not forget that in doing so he fed an entire nation. Sure, he might have some rough edges, but when pressed, Tom Dunson showed his true colors, avoided the unforgivable wrong killing your adopted child would be, and did the right thing.

It's a dazzling recuperation of Manifest Destiny. Of course, the more you think about it, the less neatly it holds together, but *Red River* doesn't give you time – screen time at least – to think about it.

However, during most of the film before the happy ending resolution the tragic narrative prevailed, containing a built-in critique of Manifest Destiny and the sort of untrammeled violence that enforced it, and viewers have to deal with that. Tom's actions on the cattle drive are clearly framed as crazed, demented, and just plain wrong. Initially the heroic protagonist, he mutates into the film's antagonist, alienating Matt, the most decent character in the film, and his life-long sidekick, Groot, who sides with Matt. Viewers who could rationalize Tom's violence in the film's first act will have a more difficult time denying that as his program of brutality persists he becomes the film's core problem, becomes in fact the villain. Though its critique is suddenly reversed, *Red River* is mainly a meditation on the use of force needed to execute Manifest Destiny.

Structuring the Alamo: from history to legend to film

I. Familiar movie tropes

As source material for a Hollywood movie, the history of the Alamo immediately presents problems. Of all the events out of Texas history, or of the settling of the West for that matter, one wonders why a defeat so total has been so popular, so often repeated in novels, poems, paintings, songs, and films. Why the near-obsessive need to "Remember the Alamo"? How can the death of all its defenders provide the requisite happy ending? In its favor, it does have several viable American movie selling points, beginning with its two well-known heroes, Jim Bowie and David Crockett. They present an opportunity to create a historical buddy film whose partner protagonists gallantly join forces to lead their besieged, greatly outnumbered men against a despotic villain, Santa Anna, the "Napoleon of the West." As such, the story is an action spectacle featuring ample doses of derring-do.

In addition, it contains one of the most reliable American movie tropes, the siege narrative, a Hollywood staple since D.W. Griffith. Ideologically, the siege/circle the wagons/hold out at the fort trope is handy in a Manifest Destiny story because, as Tom Englehardt has pointed out, it "flips history on its head," turning the terms of the native–outsider confrontation upside down.[37]

With the Texians outnumbered and surrounded, they become the defenders of their land against the attacking Mexican interlopers who want to take it away. The perfect Manifest Destiny movie siege occurs in *Drums Along the Mohawk* (1939), where the Anglo settlers are encircled, and the hero (Henry Fonda) runs for help through enemy Native American lines, bringing aid just in the nick of time.

Since the time when Griffith perfected it in 1908–09, the standard conclusion to the siege formula is the last-minute rescue. But history presents a problem in the case of the Alamo because the rescuers never arrived.[38] The ensuing calamitous defeat seemingly makes it unsuitable either as Manifest Destiny myth or Hollywood happy ending. Legend solved the problem by restructuring the narrative, in much the same way that we saw in *Red River:* by giving the tragedy an uplifting turnaround. History became Manifest mythology became Hollywood happy ending with the insertion of "the line in the sand," a decisive moment in which the defenders could profess their belief in core civil religious values and thereby transform defeat into sacrifice.

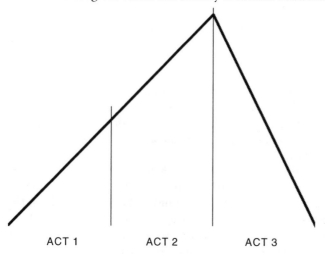

ACT 1   ACT 2   ACT 3

The historical Alamo's tragic structure – on the face of it, the Alamo's historical narrative is classically tragic: Act 1 introduces the situation, from worsening Texas–Mexico relations to all-out war; Act 2 assembles the defenders at the Alamo mission, where they fight skirmishes and wait for reinforcements; Act 3 begins with the realization that help will not arrive and depicts the defenders' deaths in the final catastrophic battle.

II. The line in the sand

Genre theory posits that some stories are formulaically repeated because the recurring narration serves important ideological functions. As a structured myth, the oft-told Alamo narrative is like a genre, or more precisely a Western sub-genre. Its ideological function is to depict sacrifice and rebirth, casting the defenders as martyrs who died so that freedom, liberty and democracy could spread to Texas and throughout the West. Their deaths vindicate Manifest Destiny.

First in legend then in film, the Alamo story's historic elements were rewritten into a potent myth that reiterated Manifest Destiny's formative assumptions better than any other westward expansion narrative. Partly this is achieved by narrative condensation that occurs when the Texan's colonial experience is abridged from 15 years to 13 days. This reduces the aforementioned complex relationship between Anglo immigrants and their host, the fledgling Mexican nation, into a simplified armed conflict between reasonable, freedom-loving Anglos and tyrannical, proto-fascist *mexicanos* (buckskin shirts and coonskin hats versus carefully appointed uniforms). Jettisoned in the interests of Hollywood's narrative streamlining is the shared culpability found in questionable political and military decisions on both sides, as well as the messy economic, legal, social and cultural issues that, over the span of a decade and a half, contributed to the friction between Anglo settlers and the government of Mexico. Of all the Alamo films, it is one of the least known, *The Last Command*, that best acknowledges this complexity. "It is strange how it [the impending battle] has come," muses a thoughtful General Santa Anna (J. Carrol Naish) to his old friend Jim Bowie (Sterling Hayden). "Little pieces fitting together, one at a time. No one wanting it. How did it come to be?"

The condensed historical time frame is driven by another time compression, the roughly two-hour length of a Hollywood movie, necessitating many adjustments, additions and subtractions to fashion history into three neatly escalating acts.[39] To work within this time frame and this narrative structure, Hollywood films follow long-established dramatic and melodramatic conventions. Character motivations need to be straightforward, obvious, and unambiguous; protagonists are guided by noble altruism, villains by baser instincts. In the case of the Alamo myth, civil religion furnishes the reason the defenders sacrifice their lives: the survival and propagation of democratic ideals. "Republic," says Davy Crockett (John Wayne) in Wayne's *The Alamo*, "I like the sound of that word. Means people can live free, talk free, go or come, buy or sell, be drunk or sober, however they choose. . . . Some words give you a feeling that make your heart warm. Republic is one of those words." Delivering democracy, then, becomes the rationale for the Battle of the Alamo, the Texas rebellion, and, for that matter, Manifest Destiny.

This motivation is reiterated in one of the most famous tropes of the Alamo sub-genre, Colonel Travis' drawing a line in the sand and asking the defenders to step over it and join him in defending freedom. "Those who wish to die like heroes and patriots," Travis says in *Martyrs of the Alamo*, "cross this line to me." It's the stuff of legend that's unsubstantiated by historical fact, but it is as crucial ideologically to Manifest Destiny as it is dramatically to Hollywood storytelling. It restructures the Alamo narrative, moving the story's climax to the end and giving it an inspirational spin. Structurally, rather than being the tragic climax, the line in the sand becomes instead a transcendental moment of nationalistic courage that leads to Act 3 and the decisive, fatal battle. Dramatically, the defenders' crossing the line restates the stakes (sacrificing one's life), makes plain each man's decision to stay, fight, and die, states their reasons for doing so (the defense of liberty), and ennobles them.

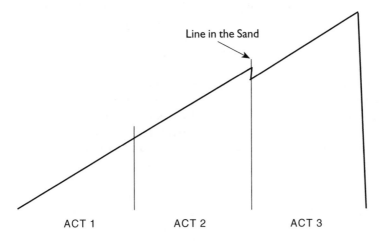

Legend and Hollywood's Alamo structure – with the addition of the line in the sand, the Alamo tragedy is transformed into a conventionally heartening Hollywood ending, especially when interpreted with the aid of civil religious doctrine. The line in the sand becomes the momentous turning point from Act 2 to Act 3. The final climax is now the men's sacrificial death, a soaring conclusion that can be understood as the heavy price required to protect liberty.

Civil religious discourse helps ensure that viewers understand the defeat-into-sacrifice narrative in clear, unequivocal terms. Historical associations facilitate comprehension. For instance, once liberty is identified as The Cause, the Alamo story produces a neat historical echo linking the Texas rebels with the American revolutionaries who fought for identical principles 60 years earlier. The Alamo is westward expansion's Valley Forge – a desperate low point in the saga of American freedom where the civil religion's creed is severely tested. The Texans are the American colonists, the Mexicans are the British, Santa Anna is Cornwallis, Houston is Washington and the Texas rebellion becomes a nineteenth-century, western-frontier version of the American Revolution.

In fact, for the purposes of spreading the civil religious "faith," the Battle of the Alamo is symbolically superior to Valley Forge, at once providing martyrs for the cause of American freedom and the justification for continental expansion. Beyond simply supplying a rallying cry for the Texas Revolution, the Alamo endures in American mythology – and in the movies – as Manifest Destiny's creation myth by reassigning Revolutionary ideals to the "winning of the west." As mythologized in legend and film, the Alamo narrative is a near-perfect civil religious text. Conveniently continuing the American Revolution on the western front, it rationalizes the appropriation of lands belonging to Mexico, Mexicans, Mexican Americans, and Native Americans not as stealing property but rather as the birth of freedom in the face of tyranny. As the titles that introduce Wayne's *The Alamo* put it, in 1836 Texans "faced the decision that all men must face . . . the eternal choice of man . . . to endure oppression or to resist." According to the Alamo myth, then, the American colonists to Texas are not *taking* anything away from Mexico, they are *bringing* liberty to the western frontier.

Just as with *Red River*, a narrative adjustment combines with civil religion to rescue the tragic ideological implications of the Alamo story. The revised, uplifting Alamo narrative is extremely useful ideologically, able to extend its mythic reach across time and space. Seen through the lens of the dominant discourse, 185 deaths is not a demoralizing ending because *that's not the ending*. Not only will civil religion's "faithful" grasp the upbeat resolution of martyrdom, they can use it to make sense of American history from 1836 to the present: the Alamo led to Texas independence, which led to statehood as territory by territory, state by state, liberty blossomed throughout the west. "They fought to give us freedom," the song that concludes Wayne's *The Alamo* says, linking past to present, "that is all we need to know."

The Alamo (2004): history, legend, and narrative structure

If *Red River* begins by rhapsodizing Texas history, John Lee Hancock's *The Alamo* begins by challenging it. Sam Houston (Dennis Quaid) is an alcoholic and William Barret Travis (Patrick Wilson) abandons and divorces his pregnant wife and admits to gambling and going with whores. Davy Crockett (Billy Bob Thornton) stumbles into the fracas by mistake, coming to Texas thinking that the war with Mexico is over.

Both *Red River* and *The Alamo* equivocate, but in different ways. *Red River* is torn between celebration and guilt but is so elegantly sly about it that – against the odds – it succeeds in proselytizing and discrediting Manifest Destiny at the same time. The newest *Alamo* is clumsy and unsure of what it wants to do. It purports to tell the truth, but it doesn't have the strength of its convictions. At times it mounts a critique, at others it is mawkishly jingoistic. Despite wanting to be historically and politically correct, it falls into old stereotyping traps. According to the film's publicity, Hancock and the Mexican actor portraying Santa Anna, Emilio Echevarría, were both "determined to create a more complex portrayal of the often-reviled general than had been seen in previous films." Echevarría states that he resisted playing the army commander as a stock villain, noting that Mexicans often viewed him with admiration.[40] Nevertheless, his Santa Anna is another stereotypically despotic Latin American dictator:

vain, cruel, impulsive, demonic, a womanizer and a tyrannical leader who terrifies his more moderate subordinates.

This might have been offset by the part of Juan Seguin (Jordi Molla), the Tejano who fought with the Texians, but the small role hardly conveys a Tejano point of view. This is unfortunate, because elaborating the position of Tejanos would have brought into relief much of what Texas independence – the return of constitutional law in Mexico's northern states – was about. Character-by-character, then, the film's fidelity to history is a representational draw. The Anglo leaders are flawed, the Mexican one is far worse, and the Tejanos are minor players.

Finally, the film's historical honesty plays havoc with traditional Hollywood dramatic structure. In the interests of historical accuracy, the traditional line-in-the-sand climax scene is omitted. Inaction and silence take its place. In the pivotal scene were Travis gathers the men and grimly announces that the likelihood of help arriving is slim, he goes on to define Texas. "There have been many ideas brought forth in the last few months of what Texas is, of what it could become," he begins. "We are not all in agreement. I'd like each of you to think of what it is you value so highly that you are willing to fight and possibly die for. We will call that Texas." He then gives them the same three choices that all the Travises in this sub-genre give: escape, probably resulting in capture and execution; surrender; or fight to the death. But with no line to cross there's no way for the men to indicate their decision or why they make it. They do nothing and say nothing – just stand around in motionless silence, each presumably thinking about what he considers worth dying for and passively accepting his fate.

This might be more true to history, but because cinema is a visual medium it's impossible for viewers to know precisely what characters think unless their thoughts are indicated by words or action. And more than any other, Hollywood is the cinema of certainty, not ambiguity. Key points are stated not once, but multiple times. "Optimally, a significant motif or informational bit should be shown or mentioned at three or four distinct moments," writes David Bordwell of the classical Hollywood cinema. "An event becomes important if it is mentioned three times. The Hollywood slogan is to state every fact three times, once for the smart viewer, once for the average viewer, and once for the slow Joe in the back row."[41] In contrast are Hancock's hushed, pensive men. Ultimately they fight, but we don't know why. Fidelity to history and poor dramaturgy join forces here to frustrate viewers naturally expecting unambiguous motives in a high-profile studio-produced film. As Carla Meyer, film critic for the *San Francisco Chronicle*, wrote, "Questions about the rebels' motivation nag throughout."[42] Ambiguity also thwarts the interpretive power of civil religion. The men at the Alamo may be driven by ideals like liberty and freedom, but it's all conjecture unless they say so; they might just as well have been moved by greed, ignorance, or stupidity.

Of course, Hancock might have stuck to his revisionist guns to pursue either a critique of Manifest Destiny or a more nuanced account of it. There are notable precedents in the Western genre. John Ford's retelling of the Battle of Little Big Horn, *Fort Apache* (1948), for example, indicted imperialistic arrogance and showed its disastrous effects on rank and file soldiers. If *Red River* presented megalomania as a dark side of Western heroics, Ford's *The Searchers* (1956) posited racism as another shadowy factor. Ford's *The Man Who Shot Liberty Valance* (1962) as well as Clint Eastwood's *Unforgiven* (1992) showed the media's role in glorifying history. ("This is the West, sir," says the newspaper editor at the end of *The Man Who Shot Liberty Valance*, as he destroys the true story of who killed the notorious bad man. "When the legend becomes fact, print the legend.") *Unforgiven* and Sam Peckinpah's *The Wild Bunch* (1969) portray the heroic exploits of the Old West as a volatile mix of violence, alcohol, and suicidal fatalism, with traces of nobility. All these mainstream films adhered to the Hollywood dictum demanding explicit thematic clarity; Hancock's *Alamo* removed myth but replaced it with vagueness. Using the Hollywood paradigm to critique the status quo requires more than simply erasing dominant doctrine. Something else must be put in its place.

The film's hesitant, conflicted revisionism is further complicated by its depiction of the concluding Battle of San Jacinto. To start with, Sam Houston's morphing from a drunken real-estate salesman into a master military tactician strains credulity. Of course last-minute character mutations are nothing new in Hollywood cinema, as the case of *Red River* readily demonstrates. But Hawks' film also illustrates that the most successful uses of deus-ex-machina devices are best executed extremely rapidly, not, as happens here, in a protracted coda.

Then there is Hancock's contradictory view of the battle. Is it a morally justified response to the defeat at the Alamo? Or a vicious, vengeful settling of scores? It begins as the first, with a righteous Sam Houston – astride a rearing white stallion no less – leading his troops into battle shouting "Remember the Alamo!" But when the battle concludes with Texians shooting the fleeing Mexican soldiers in the back and killing them as they flail about helplessly in a river, it looks like murder. Having lost the moral high ground, the Texians exhibit the savagery they are supposedly fighting against. But then the film switches back to high heroic mode for the next scene, where Houston rejects his bloodthirsty troops' call for the execution of Santa Anna and mercifully grants the general his life – in exchange for ceding Texas to the rebels. (Maybe Houston was just a real-estate broker after all.)

What is this *Alamo* saying, then? It's a fair guess that many viewers, like many critics, were confused. "This is the Texas battle's most confused treatment yet," wrote David Edelstein in *Slate*, "a definitive Hollywood muddle." What it boiled down to in the end, he concluded, was that "nothing motivates us like revenge."[43] For David Ansen of *Newsweek*, "not just the storytelling but the original intention has gotten muddled. . . . You leave 'The Alamo' uncertain of what you're meant to feel: is this a celebration of patriotic sacrifice or an illustration of war's futility?"[44] And according to the *Boston Globe*'s movie critic, the film's vaunted revisionism backfired and produced just the opposite: a "chest-beating paean to Manifest Destiny."[45]

In revising history, Hancock tampered with three interlocking sacred elements: America's civil religion, Manifest Destiny, and Hollywood's three-act structure. Civil religion is the most important of these three. Not only is it the engine that drives the other two, it is also the "master code" used to decipher much of American life, everything from State of the Union addresses to foreign policy to Westerns. Hancock attempted a postmodern, post-colonial, anti-imperialistic revision of the Alamo story, but it was doomed because his ambivalent, confused, and mightily conflicted revisionism collided with Hollywood's literal-minded form. As a result, he produced a film the Hollywood paradigm couldn't accommodate and the "master code" couldn't decipher.

I have tried to describe the genesis, operation, and effects of a dominant discourse, one comprised of a belief system (civil religion), a national policy (Manifest Destiny), and a media propagation platform (Hollywood cinema). This discourse is so pervasive and so powerful that it created the conditions for both producing particular kinds of films and understanding them. Viewers who internalize and agree with the beliefs and values of the civil religion are best equipped to read and comprehend these films. However, just as some Americans had differing interpretations of the civil religion and just as some objected to Manifest Destiny, there is always the possibility of films questioning the creed and critiquing the policy. Similarly, some spectators will read the films against the grain. But resisting this discourse is not easy. It entails interrogating its three longstanding sub-components – national creed, state policy, and a mode of filmic narration – that have been naturalized nearly to the point of invisibility. It is difficult to question what society trains its members to accept on faith, sight unseen. This essay has sought to begin tracing these unseen or dimly seen features in order to better understand this quasi-religious faith, its resultant policies, and its movie narratives.

Notes

1 *Latino Images in Film: Stereotypes, Subversion, and Resistance*. Austin, TX: University of Texas Press, 2002.
2 "Colonialism and Movies in Southern California, 1910–34," *Aztlan: A Journal of Chicano Studies*, 28: 1 (Spring 2003), pp. 75–96.
3 According to the Internet Movie Database (IMDb), its domestic gross at the end of its first run was approximately $22 million, a very poor return on a film whose cost was an estimated $95 million. See IMDb, *The Alamo* box office information, at www.imdb.com/title/tt0318974/business and www.imdb.com/BusinessThisDay?day=18&month=July.
4 Robert Sklar, "Empire to the West: *Red River* (1948)," in John E. O'Connor and Martin A. Jackson, eds, *American History/American Film: Interpreting the Hollywood Image* (New York: Frederick Ungar Pub. Co. Inc., 1979), p. 169.

5 Richard Slotkin, "Violence," in Ed Buscombe, ed., *The BFI Companion to the Western* (London: British Film Institute, 1988), p. 235.
6 Ella Shohat and Robert Stam, *Unthinking Eurocentrism: Multiculturalism and the Media* (New York: Routledge, 1994), pp. 2–3.
7 Robert N. Bellah, "Biblical Religion and Civil Religion in America," *Daedalus, Journal of the American Academy of Arts and Sciences*, 96: 1 (Winter, 1967), pp. 1–21. Republished at the author's website, www.robertbellah.com/articles_5.htm.
8 Bellah, "Biblical Religion."
9 Noam Chomsky, *Necessary Illusions* (© 1989; accessed at www.zmag.org/Chomsky/ni/ni-c03-s01.html), Chapter 3, "The Bounds of the Expressible," Segment 5/8.
10 Chomsky, *Necessary Illusions*.
11 Chomsky, *Necessary Illusions*.
12 Chomsky, *Necessary Illusions*.
13 Arthur G. Pettit, *Images of the Mexican American in Fiction and Film* (College Station, TX: Texas A&M University Press, 1980), pp. 17–79.
14 Quoted in Buscombe, p. 181. Himilce Novas, in *Everything You Need to Know about Latino History* (New York: Penguin Books, 1994), gives the same quote (without the word "yearly") and says the author of the term is unknown, p. 75.
15 David Montejano, *Anglos and Mexicans in the Making of Texas, 1836–1986* (Austin, TX: University of Texas Press, 1987), p. 24.
16 Quoted in Eldon Kenworthy, *America/Américas: Myth in the Making of US Policy Toward Latin America* (University Park, PA: The Pennsylvania State University Press, 1995), p. 24.
17 Pettit, *Images of the Mexican American*, p. 5.
18 Arnoldo De León, *Mexican Americans in Texas* (Wheeling, IL: Harlan Davidson, Inc., 1993), p. 28, cites the higher number; Rodolfo Acuña, *Occupied America: A History of Chicanos* (New York: Harper & Row, 1988), p. 10, the lower figure.
19 David G. Gutiérrez, *Walls and Mirrors: Mexican Americans, Mexican Immigrants, and the Politics of Ethnicity* (Berkeley, CA: University of California Press, 1995), p. 19.
20 Quoted in Arnoldo De León, *They Called Them Greasers: Anglo Attitudes Toward Mexicans in Texas, 1821–1900* (Austin, TX: University of Texas Press, 1983), p. 3.
21 See Richard Flores, *Remembering the Alamo: Memory, Modernity, and the Master Symbol* (Austin, TX: University of Texas Press, 2002), p. 24; also Stephen L. Hardin, *Texian Iliad: A Military History of the Texas Revolution* (Austin, TX: University of Texas Press, 1994), pp. 57, 156.
22 Acuña, *Occupied America*, pp. 7–10.
23 De León, *Greasers*, p. 12.
24 De León, *Greasers*, p. 4.
25 "Polk's Message on the War with Mexico, May 11, 1846," *Documents of American History*, Vol. I, p. 311.
26 Gutiérrez, *Walls and Mirrors*, p. 13.
27 Martha Menchaca, *Recovering History, Constructing Race: The Indian, Black, and White Roots of Mexican Americans* (Austin, TX: University of Texas Press, 2001), p. 215.
28 Quoted in De León, *Greasers*, p. 20.
29 De León, *Greasers*, p. 20.
30 Quoted in De León, *Greasers*, p. 22.
31 De León, *Greasers*, pp. 20–4.
32 See my essay, "Colonialism and Movies in Southern California, 1910–34," for a discussion of how the Californios (Mexican Americans in California) in Los Angeles went from being the dominant majority to a dispossessed minority, all in the space of about fifty years.
33 Quoted in Alonso Aguilar, *Pan-Americanism from Monroe to the Present: A View from the Other Side* (New York: Monthly Review Press, 1968), p. 33.

34 Quoted in Acuña, *Occupied America*, p. 15.

35 The Internet Movie Database (IMDb) estimated the film's cost at $10 million; the *Guardian* reported a cost of $8 million. In its two prime markets, the film was a box office disappointment. IMDb reported US box office revenue at just over $3 million and the British Film Institute reported the film earned about $1 million in Britain. For IMDb information, see: www.imdb.com/title/tt0200720/business. For the *Guardian*, see "First Steps in Show Business," by Simon Hattenstone: http://film.guardian.co.uk/interview/interviewpages/0,,377979,00.html. For the BFI see: www.bfi.org.uk/filmtvinfo/stats/boxoffice/ukfeatures-00.html.

36 Other examples of Hollywood studio tragedies are several of Martin Scorsese's films (*Raging Bull* [1980], *GoodFellas* [1990], *Casino* [1994]). Another from Hollywood's Golden Age is William Wyler's *Jezebel* (1938), depicting the fall of a proud, head-strong woman, Julie (Bette Davis), in antebellum New Orleans. A classic Golden Age Western tragedy is John Ford's *The Searchers* (1956). And, though it is not strictly speaking a Hollywood film, David Lean's *Lawrence of Arabia* (1962) is another example of a classic two-part tragedy: T.E. Lawrence's idealistic imperialism ends and his moral decline begins midway through the film when he executes an Arab friend in order to placate bickering tribal factions and maintain unity. In one reading of what happens afterwards, the film recounts the toll imperialism takes on him.

37 "Ambush at Kamikaze Pass," in Donald Lazere, ed., *American Media and Mass Culture* (Berkeley, CA: University of California Press, 1987), p. 481.

38 Texian delegates were attending a convention to decide Texas's fate. By the time independence was declared, the Republic of Texas had been formed, and Sam Houston had been reappointed commander of the army and left, the Alamo had fallen. Hollywood, therefore, scripted a series of simplifications. Rescuing Texians tried to reach the fortress but did not get there in time (*Martyrs of the Alamo*), were ambushed along the way (Wayne's *The Alamo*), couldn't spare the men (*Davy Crockett, King of the Wild Frontier*), or they had equipment problems and couldn't move (*The Last Command*).

39 The existing copy of *Martyrs of the Alamo* runs approximately 70 minutes. *Davy Crocket, King of the Wild Frontier*, a compilation of three television shows, runs 93 minutes; however, the Alamo section which ends the film lasts only 30 minutes. Originally running at 3 hours and 12 minutes, Wayne's *The Alamo* was trimmed to 140 minutes for its general release, though the DVD runs 162 minutes, and the special edition wide-screen VHS version ran 193 minutes. *The Last Command* runs 110 minutes. Like the Wayne version, the recent *The Alamo* was said to have been cut from around 3 hours to its release length of 137 minutes.

40 Frank Thompson, *The Alamo: The Illustrated Story of the Epic Film* (New York: Newmarket Press, 2004), p. 45.

41 Bordwell, Chapter 3, "Classical Narration," in Bordwell, Janet Staiger, and Kristen Thompson, *The Classical Hollywood Cinema* (New York: Columbia University Press, 1985), p. 31.

42 Carla Meyer, "Only Thornton Emerges Unscathed in 'The Alamo,'" *San Francisco Chronicle*, April 9, 2004 (n.p., e-edition).

43 *Slate*, April 8, 2004; www.slate.com/id/2098492.

44 David Ansen, "Mexicans? Bring 'em On!" *Newsweek*, April 19, 2004 (n.p., e-edition).

45 Ty Burr, "A Problematic Epic seems Torn between the Legend and the Facts of Texas," *Boston Globe*, April 9, 2004 (n.p., e-edition).

Chapter 2

Mapping the beach

Beach movies, exploitation film and geographies of whiteness

Josh Stenger

Near the end of *Muscle Beach Party* (1964), the highly successful follow-up to *Beach Party* (1963), perennial teenager Frankie (Frankie Avalon) explains to an Italian contessa named Julie (Luciana Paluzzi) why he can't requite her love or accept her offer to support him while he surfs around the world: "There's people for people, but also people for places. This is my place, and these are my people. This is where I belong." Frankie's speech couches the film's (dis)articulation of a growing class tension between the ostensibly classless surfers and the cartoonishly wealthy contessa in his continued commitment to Dee Dee (Annette Funicello) and to the beach itself. However, his "people for people, people for places" proclamation cannot be read so ahistorically; nor can it be read outside contemporary dynamics of race and space. Located within the contexts of the Civil Rights movement, white flight, and anxieties about integration, Frankie's dictum also suggests that the beach – "America's dream backyard – predictable, serene, and white"[1] – resonated with white suburban audiences as an historically specific, utopian geography of whiteness.

From 1963 to 1965, American International Pictures (AIP) released *Beach Party*, *Muscle Beach Party*, *Bikini Beach* (1964), *Beach Blanket Bingo* (1965), and *How to Stuff a Wild Bikini* (1965).[2] Though often dismissed as mass-cultural detritus, the hugely popular cycle capitalized on the studio's canny ability to anticipate emerging trends and to package them in productions that were highly responsive to incipient aspects of the cultural *Zeitgeist*. Drawing on its history of exploitation, AIP used the purchase of the beach to enshrine Frankie Avalon and Annette Funicello in the pantheon of teen idols, garner new industry credentials, tap the merchandising power of popular music and the teen subculture, and generate huge profits.[3]

Despite their sizeable impact on the popular culture, scant serious attention has been paid to AIP's beach films. This may owe in part to the fact that the films never took themselves seriously. AIP co-founder Jim Nicholson suggested the films were nonsensical, inconsequential fun: "These are busy, bustling films. They don't even have to make sense if they move fast enough. They do not hold up any mirrors to Nature. There are no messages."[4] Indeed, the entire production company seemed eager to distance the pictures from any kind of social commentary. Franchise director William Asher regarded the films as a "comic strip" working to document "the longest summer on record."[5] If there was a message in the films, Asher proffered, it was simply this: "there was such a thing as kids *not* in trouble."[6]

At first glance, the films bear this out. AIP's beach is quaintly carnivalesque, a space where hints of transgression are always recuperated for the dominant order. Sanitized, privatized, and earnestly apolitical, the cinematic beach became a fantasy *topos* in which toothless teen rebellion, chaste flirtation, and good-natured inter-generational conflict found comical, hermetic expression. Yet to dismiss the films as mere fodder for an increasingly hungry teen audience would be to overlook several key areas in which the beach cycle impacted 1960s attitudes about race, sex and space. First, AIP's successful packaging of conservative mainstream values about these issues for a youth market often reluctant to embrace such values signaled important ideological and political-economic shifts in exploitation filmmaking practices. Second, the films' construction of the beach as a "raceless" utopian landscape worked to naturalize whiteness and to regulate racial, sexual and geographic mobilities at a time when such mobilities constituted a crisis for many whites and a precondition of citizenship for people of color. Finally, the material and symbolic links the films constructed between the southern California beach and the American suburb promoted the privatization and commodification of white community, leisure and consumption; drawing ties to popular music and other forms of consumerism in the process, they established a new industrial model for the production, distribution and exhibition of film as a multimedia commodity.

At the center of all these processes is the cinematic landscape of the beach. The landscape is crucial. Oft-overlooked yet omnipresent, it is the site where cultural myth, political economy and social relations converge. When read through the lens of cultural geography AIP's beach films must be understood as participating in a more ambitious and ideologically consequential project than many who see the films as insignificant ephemera are usually inclined to acknowledge. Fastening specific constructions of white community to the over-determined site of the beach, the films not only racialized space, they spatialized race. As Matthew Frye Jacobson has argued in his study of ethnic whiteness, this is a key strategy through which racial hierarchies are reified: "The awesome power of race as an ideology resides precisely in its ability to pass as a feature of the natural landscape."[7] Thus, we must understand the beach as an important site of the disavowal and containment of racial difference during a period in the country's history when racial formations underwent a series of radical realignments.

Exploited by the films as an idyllic white landscape, the beach was offered to 1960s audiences as an escape from contemporary racial and political turmoil, "present[ing] a detailed but vastly different tableau of the culture than what one could see in the dark, deteriorating major cities of 1950s [and 1960s] America."[8] The cinematic beach envisioned by AIP was a distinctly segregated oasis. By reinscribing a presumptively natural landscape and public space as a private site defined by community, commonality and containment, moreover, AIP's beach films evoked, and to a degree reproduced, the same racial and spatial anxieties that motivated the *lebensraum* of suburban enclavism. In what follows, I argue for a new consideration of the cultural significance and ideological consequences of AIP's beach films and the geographies of whiteness exploited both in their narratives and through their exhibition and promotion in suburban communities.

AIP and the mainstreaming of exploitation film

Founded as the American Releasing Corporation in 1954 by James Nicholson and Samuel Arkoff, American International Pictures (so named in 1956) spent most of its twenty-five years perfecting low-budget exploitation films targeted more often than not at the youth markets of the 1950s and 1960s before eventually taking aim at urban black audiences in the early 1970s. After a series of moves in the mid-1970s that fatally over-extended the studio's resources under Arkoff, it was absorbed into Filmways in 1979, which in turn was quickly acquired by Orion.[9]

In the early years, AIP subsisted on horror films, monster movies and biker flicks.[10] Such films kept the company afloat financially, but the threadbare fare hardly gained Nicholson and Arkoff much in the way of industry credibility. Eager to ensure their continued solvency while improving their cachet among critics, rivals and audiences alike, Arkoff and Nicholson employed their most valuable asset, director Roger Corman, to direct a series of very successful and well-received Edgar Allen Poe adaptations throughout the early 1960s.[11] AIP's early teen kitsch and middlebrow-aspiring Poe films demonstrated how well AIP parlayed liabilities like limited resources and often dreadfully low production values into merchandising assets.

Above all else, the studio's first decade of film production and distribution revealed Arkoff's aptitude for discerning, then exploiting nascent currents in popular culture. Such a skill was invaluable in the 1960s and early 1970s, one of Hollywood's most financially inglorious and creatively inchoate periods. Struggling to adapt to a rapidly changing entertainment landscape and to find more solid economic and creative footing, virtually every major studio absorbed sharp financial losses at some point during this time.[12] As "market conditions rendered the studios ripe for takeover," many of the studio-era majors such as Paramount, Warner Bros, MGM, Universal, and United Artists were acquired throughout the 1960s by more solvent corporate entities during a period of conglomeration.[13] The tumult confronting the majors – who stood to lose the most and whose recent acquisition proved a harbinger of new, sometimes unfamiliar managerial practices – allowed room for more mobile, less entrenched independents to exploit niche markets with greater success than their more mature counterparts.

As the industry turned its attention to the "cultivation of the youth market,"[14] upstart companies like AIP were already well positioned to bring product to teen audiences. Despite being an early target of industry ridicule, AIP ranked among the most financially profitable and culturally influential of the industry's smaller players during this period. Indeed, AIP survived the turbulent industrial climate spanning the late 1950s through the mid-1970s without posting a loss in any fiscal year. This remarkable-for-its-time statistic was not lost on *Variety*, which in 1972 cited AIP's exceptional success to suggest that the company had become a bellwether of Hollywood's health: "For 18 years, American International Pictures has been . . . sustaining a chaotic and undirected industry with an otherwise long absent brand of confident showmanship, innovative production, distribution and sales. When AIP falters, the metastasis of current film industry ills is complete."[15]

It would be difficult to overstate the degree to which the studio's success followed from Arkoff's savvy pop-culture prognostications and his ability to package emerging trends:

> Arkoff was a finger-in-the-wind filmmaker who never let a trend go by without having his cut at it . . . and he didn't hesitate to move on when the *Zeitgeist* shifted. His willingness to cut bait was both ruthless and inventive. Take his best-remembered pictures, the lovably dimwitted beach-party movies. These films have made such a dent in pop culture that it's surprising to note the six-picture series lasted a mere two years, from 1963 to 1965. And when the wheel started to turn, Arkoff was ready, keeping one foot on the beach while he reached ahead in search of the next big thing.[16]

Never an initiator of trends, Arkoff was actually an accomplished imitator who "always waited for someone else to test the water first."[17] This is perhaps most evident with the studio's beach films and blaxploitation movies. For instance, *Beach Party* (1963), the first of AIP's beach franchise, only arrived after three other studios "tested the water" – *Gidget* (Columbia, 1959), *Where the Boys Are* (MGM, 1960), and *Blue Hawaii* (Paramount, 1961). A decade later, Arkoff watched the staggering returns of Melvin Van Peebles's *Sweet Sweetback's Baadasssss Song* (Cinemation, 1971) and Gordon Parks's *Shaft* (MGM, 1971) before relocating the studio's resources to the inner-city with *Slaughter, Blacula,* and *Black Caesar* (all 1972).

AIP's utilitarian approach to exploiting new fads did more than return consistent profits; it also packaged in innovative and eclectic ways American International's subtly trenchant conservativism. Nowhere was the studio's ability to wrap its mainstream values in an edgy subcultural appeal more fully realized than with the *Beach Party* cycle. The films' absurdly quirky narratives, miniscule production budgets, location shooting, and multimedia promotional strategies each played a part in this. Together, they conjured the beach as an insulated, raceless geography in which middle-class white youth could engage in self-segregating, consequence-free leisure without ever having to acknowledge their own mobility, privileged subject positions or social power. In so doing, the films marked a watershed moment in the studio's conservative appropriation of exploitation cinema's one-time marginal industrial status and cultural politics.

In his work on the subject, Eric Schaefer celebrates exploitation cinema as "the most sustained domestic challenge to Hollywood's hegemony over aesthetics and content in the commercial cinema."[18] Given that he sees exploitation film "shaking the entrenched industry's definitions of acceptable form and subject matter," Schaefer is quick to take issue with what he sees as the common (mis)application of the term to AIP products: "It is probably already clear that I'm not writing about the films that have most often come to be identified with the term exploitation movie: those cheap genre pictures directed at the teen market by outfits like American International Pictures in the 1950s and 1960s."[19] For Schaefer, AIP falls outside the historical purview of exploitation film proper, which he identifies as having "roughly paralleled the rise and fall of the classical Hollywood cinema."[20] Yet the economic and cultural barriers separating Hollywood studios and exploitation films grew considerably more porous during the era of industrial reorganization that held sway from the 1950s through the mid-1970s. Absent a highly centralized motion picture industry to ensure its marginal position, the exploitation movie no longer derived its appellation through its contradistinction to a weakening mainstream center.

Representative of this shift, AIP's beach films augured an era of more conservative exploitation cinema, one defined less through oppositional values than through the narrative and ideological conciliation it sought with its competitors and audiences. The turn to more ideologically affirmative values signaled by the beach movies requires that we recover dimensions of "exploitation" not specifically addressed by Schaefer's model, namely, the political-economic and racial. Certainly these must become central areas of concern when films are made on the cheap for, aggressively marketed to, and designed to profit from audiences that are commonly excluded from the major circuits of economic and cultural production and symbolic exchange (e.g. teenagers in the 1960s or African Americans in the early 1970s).

And it is here that we may begin to understand how American International worked contrapuntally to the oppositional exploitation films discussed by Schaefer. Their notoriety for promoting teen rebellion and transgression notwithstanding, AIP films, especially those in the *Beach Party* cycle, commonly reinforced, rather than interrupted or subverted, dominant cultural values and industry standards. From the 1960s forward, AIP used its most successful franchises to shed its outlier status and to gain entry into the industry mainstream. Gary Morris notes that "the inevitable effect of this move was . . . to increase its role as participant in – that is, endorser of – mainstream, conformist cultural values."[21] This had been going on to some degree for years. For instance, in 1958 Arkoff famously disowned the studio's reputation for licentiousness, chiding that even though his horror films pandered to teens, unlike many characters in more respectable fare, AIP's "monsters do not smoke, drink, or lust."[22]

As it often does, the assimilation from a marginal position to a central one required embracing and participating in the dominant group's values and practices. In the case of American International, this was not achieved by matching the majors' production values, star power or box-office; rather, it was accomplished by embracing hegemonic attitudes about sex roles, whiteness and racial difference and mapping them onto one of the era's most symbolically valent and racially overdetermined cultural geographies: the southern California beach.

The political ramifications of the films and their use of the beach landscape are disputed by R.L. Rutsky. In "Surfing the Other," Rutsky notes dismissively that "the idea that these films are conventional, white, and middle class, that their 'normality' serves to deny social problems and to support ideological conformity, is hardly an astonishing revelation."[23] Here, he suggests that criticism of the beach films' conservatism is at best obvious and at worst blind to alternative reading positions from which teen audiences might experience the films; yet he gives the films too much credit when he alleges that they represent "the allure of non-Western cultures" and that "the attraction of the surfing films, and of surf subculture, is . . . the thrill of nonconformity, the attraction of a certain difference, both sexual and otherwise."[24] Rutsky is, of course, nominally correct about surfing's non-Western origins and American surf subculture's non-conformist characteristics. Emphasizing individuality and closely connected with bohemianism and the beat counter-culture, surfers often rejected 1960s bourgeois values. However, the assertion that AIP's beach films and American surf subculture appealed to the same groups or gave rise to the same "attraction" is hardly axiomatic.

Though they glorified surfing, the *Beach Party* films actively distanced themselves from its non-Western origins and rejected its non-conformist ethos. Depoliticizing the subculture, the films transformed surfing and the beach into palatable commodities for mainstream suburban movie-goers. So remote from authentic surfing communities was AIP's "antiseptic, virtually sexless, wink-and-leer society"[25] that real surfers who attended *Beach Party*'s southern California premiere "turned away in disgust" at the film's "desecration of everything they held sacred" and its "criminal misrepresentation" of their subculture.[26] Far from engendering an anti-bourgeois, non-conformist reception in which teens would find pleasure in "a certain kind of difference, both sexual and otherwise," the films worked in virtually the opposite capacity, interpellating audiences into hegemonic ideas about sex roles and racial identities.

Policing race, space and sex on the beach

The inclination to see the films' attraction residing in an appeal to otherness relies on reading the films as being more about "surfing" than about the "beach"; yet even the titles of the films (*Beach Party*, *Muscle Beach Party*, *Beach Blanket Bingo*) suggest they were always more about the "turf" than the "surf." More importantly, such a reading fails to address the distinct racialized histories of surfing and the beach, especially in southern California. As the *locus classicus* of both mainland surfing and beach culture, the area has a long-established if paradoxical history of both exoticizing and Anglicizing surfing and its Hawaiian origins. At the same time, the region has long looked to built environments such as the beach as sites within which racial formations and mobilities could be policed.

In the late nineteenth century, for instance, Los Angeles boosters characterized the region as a semi-tropical paradise. When this motif fell out of favor amidst shifts in racial discourse – conjuring unwelcome images, as it eventually did, of an opprobrious cultural "primitivism" – boosters modified their promotional rhetoric and touted the city as a Mediterranean resort. Designed to mobilize associations with European culture and the promise of "impending civilization," the Mediterranean was expected to retain the earlier emphasis on the region's scenic beauty but to balance it with connotations of cultural prestige and racial exclusivity.[27] Thus, the new touristic imagery rhetorically repositioned southern California as a white utopia.

By the 1920s, when one of surfing's founders – dark-skinned, Hawaiian-born Duke Kahanamoku – popularized surfing in southern California, the beach had stronger local associations with the Mediterranean than with the South Pacific. Kahanamoku's arrival, then, did not signify the "primitive" debasement of or encroachment on the Anglo landscape. Rather, he embodied the civilizing effects of whiteness on the racial Other. Transforming the surfer into both a man of leisure and "the preferred local form of the noble savage,"[28] Kahanamoku proved a fitting ambassador for southern California's tourism industry, which managed to market the region's landscape as both an exotic paradise and an Anglo arcadia.

While surfing could accommodate a degree of ethnic and racial otherness insofar as its non-white origins were easily appropriated by white beach-goers and city boosters, the beaches themselves were far less open to racial difference and hybridity. Kahanamoku's fetishized body functioned as both male spectacle and exotic other; at the same time, his athletic body served as a site where competing discourses of race, space, leisure and mobility could be mapped onto one another. Local African Americans finding themselves at the beach, however, embodied no such cultural polysemy or spatial mobility; on the contrary, for blacks in Los Angeles, the beach was simply another site wherein the city enacted its strategy of racial containment through spatial regulation. In this context, we can understand the AIP beach films as participating in southern

California's decades-old project of mapping the beach as a specifically white landscape. The films commodified the beach, along with the nexus of racial and socioeconomic connotations the beach spatialized, for white suburban teen consumption. One *Beach Party* Production Fact Sheet touted location shooting and the film's setting, promising exhibitors lush views of "Southern California's famous ocean fun resorts at the height of the annual vacation season. Surfing, swimming, boating, dancing and other fun sports are highlighted."[29] Both press kits and the films themselves emphasized the "fun" enabled by the beach, a defining aspect of which proved to be the ostensible racelessness of both the beach landscape and the films' own narratives. In each of these capacities, then, AIP's exploitation of the beach as an idyllic, naturally occurring geography located the beach and whiteness outside the social, and therefore outside the troublesome domains of history, politics, race relations, and urban space.

Beach Party initiated the cycle and established the formula for the ensuing films. Frankie and Dolores/Dee Dee[30] are in love; tensions arise (for him over their sexless present, for her over their uncertain future); they resort to flirtation to provoke jealousy, only to reaffirm their love for one another in the end. At the same time, the idyllic community of surfers is threatened by and defends itself against some outside force, be it a parodic middle-aged biker named Eric Von Zipper (Harvey Lembeck) or muscle-bound body-builders. Both plots constructed the beach as a setting organized around the tropes of community, togetherness, and containment. In what may seem initially ironic, the *Beach Party* films' emphasis on community and cohesion is most manifest in the (sometimes absurd) steps the narratives take to keep the teenagers apart and to contain their sexual desires. Though the studio merrily promoted the films as teen sex romps, the films themselves are positively prudish. In the strange world of AIP's beachfront, casual sex is simultaneously the *sine qua non* and anathema, while a strong identification with one's peer group and a lasting romantic union based on true love are the privileged forms of social relations. Promoting *Beach Party* with the titillating tagline, "The perfect summer when the urge meets the surge" and *Muscle Beach Party* with salacious promises like, "When 10,000 biceps go around 5,000 bikinis, you know what's gonna happen," AIP embraced its tried and true method of misleading ballyhoo, promising teen audiences one thing and delivering another.[31] Once in the theater, movie-goers were invited to listen to pop-infused surf music, ogle scantily clad bodies, watch B-roll of real surfers, and, most importantly, laugh at and sympathize with Frankie and Dolores/Dee Dee's ongoing romantic entanglements.[32]

The constant *coitus interruptus* endured by Frankie and Dolores/Dee Dee is often cited as proof of the films' blandness and sexual conservatism. Thomas Doherty typifies critics' takes on the films' engagement with adolescent sexuality: "[although] parents were banished altogether . . . there was little in this portrait of teenage life that would disturb a worried father. Adults were usually absent, but their values were always present."[33] Among the most ubiquitous of these was that sexual propriety invariably triumphed over teen lust. Typically this is established from the outset. Both *Beach Party* and *Muscle Beach Party* begin with the arrival of the young couple to the beach for the summer, each film using the set-up to establish not only the potential for, but also the limits on, sexual behavior. In *Beach Party*, for instance, when Frankie and Dolores pull up to their summer rental, they see the vacation as a rehearsal of adult married life. Frankie points out, "There it is honey; it's all ours." Dolores responds, "Just you and me, all alone. . . . just like we're married." As they approach the front door, Frankie insists that they "do this right," then scoops Dolores up to carry her across the threshold.

"Doing this right" is an organizing, albeit overdetermined, narrative concern. Thus, as soon as the two enter the house, Frankie realizes that Dolores has invited the whole gang to the house for the summer. Dolores attempts to palliate Frankie, reminding him, "You know it's more fun with the whole gang." Knowing there is now no chance to consummate their "marriage," a nonplussed Frankie retorts, "Not with what I had in mind." Lest she be mistaken too early as a prude, Dolores quickly outflanks Frankie's effort to cast her as such: "That's just it. I don't trust myself when I'm alone with you." However, later that same day, Dolores makes it clear she is a girl who wants to "do this right." Chatting on the beach with her friend, Rhonda (Valora Noland) – who is so hyper-sexualized that she is renamed "Animal" in *Muscle Beach Party* – Dolores sees Frankie's sexual frustration as an opportunity to reform Rhonda and to reassert her own virginity:

DOLORES: Did it ever occur to you that there's more to life than getting a boy?
RHONDA: Like what?
DOLORES: Love.
RHONDA: What's the problem? Frankie giving you the cold treatment or something?
DOLORES: Deep freeze would be more like it.
RHONDA: You can't really blame him. He invites you down here alone and you turn the place into a teenage flophouse.
DOLORES: Well, at the last minute I got cold feet.
RHONDA: If somebody had wild plans for me, why stop him?
DOLORES: Rhonda, I want Frankie to think of me as more than just a girl.
RHONDA: There's something else?
DOLORES: Yes. A wife!
RHONDA: Wife? But you're not even a woman.
DOLORES: But I'm close. And I'm not getting any closer until I'm a wife!

Exchanges such as these are common throughout the beach films, and their emphasis on sex and romance has understandably guided critics in their assessment of the cycle's cultural impact in those areas. However, such a focus ignores the ineluctable fact that, particularly with respect to 1960s racial dynamics, the films' effort to curb adolescent sexuality cannot be considered outside contemporary anxieties about integration and miscegenation. Matthew Frye Jacobson reminds us that "[t]he policing of sexual boundaries – the defense against hybridity – is precisely what keeps a racial group a racial group."[34] To a similar degree, the policing of spatial boundaries circumscribed the mobilities that enabled racial hybridization. Thus, when the "adult values" of containment and purity enter AIP's cinematic beach, they apply not only to sex, but to race and space as well; indeed, (the fear of) sexuality is so securely yoked to (the fear of) otherness and hybridity that the films' abrogation of teen sex also serves as a defense of the sexual and geographic territory of whiteness.

Beach Party goes so far as to have a fictitious evolutionary anthropologist narrate the links between sex, race and space. Unbeknownst to the teens, who have come to the beach for summer vacation, they are being "studied". Dr R.O. Sutwell (Bob Cummings) has taken up residence on the beach to observe the rituals of the inscrutable American teen. When Sutwell explains to his assistant, Mary Anne (Dorothy Malone), that he is researching his latest book, *The Behavior Pattern of the Young Adult and Its Relation to Primitive Tribes*, she fires back: "I've got a shorter title. *Teenage Sex.*" But her title does not work either for Sutwell's research or the film's racial politics because it no longer imbues teen sex with racial alterity.

Indeed, so foreign to Sutwell are the teens and their sexual habits that he can only compare them to "primitive" subaltern groups from exotic lands, such that the two become equated through their shared otherness and, importantly, their ties to the beach as a site where potential transgressions can be contained, or at least rendered intelligible through an ethnographic discourse. Early on, Sutwell insists to a skeptical Mary Anne that "[t]hey live in a society as primitive as the aborigine of New Guinea." Later, as he watches the teens dance around in a circle, Sutwell likens their behavior to a "Haitian voodoo ceremony" before exclaiming that their gyrations suggest the "Samoan puberty dance all over again." Later, after befriending Dolores and gaining an invitation to join the teens on the beach, Sutwell's swimwear further develops the juxtaposition between surfing, teen sexuality, and racial otherness. Dressed in a kimono and an unusual pair of sandals, Sutwell leaves Dolores aghast. After she demands to know where he got those "banana boats," Sutwell explains that he acquired them in Africa, to which Dolores quips, "How'd you get them away from the witch doctor?" Failing to sense the joke, Sutwell once again serves as the mouthpiece for the film's conflation of otherness with tribal primitivism: "[T]hey weren't his. They belonged to the chief." Dolores insists he take them off but allows him to leave the kimono on when she sees that underneath it Sutwell is wearing a most unmanly, turn-of-the-century style bathing suit. Though we are invited to laugh off (and at) Sutwell's desexualization, the scene is interesting because by stripping him of his shoes, Dolores essentially denies Sutwell any claim to the sort of "primitivism" that both he and the film equate with the sexual economy of the beach.

Sutwell's repeated assignation of racial alterity to teen sexuality, along with his ill-fated attempt to clothe himself in the signifiers of the former to gain access to the latter, at once identifies and effaces whiteness as a construct. And, as is true of all racial constructs, the contours, complexions, costumes and desires associated with whiteness require constant regulation. Each of these aspects becomes visible through *Beach Party*'s relationship to both literal and figurative forms of darkness. Richard Dyer offers a useful model for understanding how the beach allows the film to reconcile conflicting desires – such as the desire for sexual experience and transgression the film associates with adolescence and the desire for homogeneity and insularity it associates with the white middle class: "The projection of sexuality on to dark races was a means for whites to represent yet dissociate themselves from their own desire. . . . Dark desires are part of the story of whiteness, but as what the whiteness of whiteness has to struggle against."[35] That it must struggle at all, of course, suggests that "the whiteness of whiteness" is always, to some degree, contingent.

Beach Party complicates Dyer's model. It does "project sexuality on to dark races," but it also, through Sutwell's observations, projects dark races on to (white) sexuality. The beach landscape allows the narratives to treat these as reciprocal processes in part because it provides so many diegetic opportunities to literalize the conflation of sexuality and darkness. The most prominent of these is the ritual of tanning, a leisure pursuit that occupies much of the teens' time within the films. As Dyer notes, tanning consolidates economic privilege and racial mobility:

> [Tanning] is associated with leisure, with time not devoted to work and the necessities of life . . . and therefore . . . with money. . . . [Nevertheless,] a tanned white person is just that – a white person who has acquired a darker skin. There is no loss of prestige in this. On the contrary . . . not only does tanning bespeak a wealth and life style largely at white people's disposition, but it also displays white people's right to be various, literally to incorporate into themselves features of other people.[36]

The teenagers in AIP's beach films are never troubled by the "necessities of life." On the contrary, they are at the beach to socialize and to test the boundaries of acceptable sexual interaction. Tanning enables both activities. Requiring a state of partial undress and affording ample opportunities for the homosocial discussion and heterosocial pursuit of romance and sex, moreover, it also provides a device through which both the diegesis and *mise-en-scène* can elaborate the equation between the darkening of white skin and the enactment of sexual desire.

If tanning destabilized sexual and racial boundaries, the films' star-couple worked to resecure the territory of whiteness and the sanctity of adolescent virtue. Frankie and Dolores/Dee Dee are indeed strident advocates for keeping the community safe from disruptive outside forces and for allowing chaste adolescent romance to blossom into marriage before having socially sanctioned, presumably procreative sex. As was the case in *Beach Party*, this is established immediately in *Muscle Beach Party*, which inaugurates the film's preoccupation with policing boundaries by clarifying the summer's sleeping quarters in the first scene. Both films ensure that the boys sleep in one room and the girls in another, but whereas this produced a crisis for Frankie just one summer earlier, he no longer finds this surprising or inconvenient. The set-up is narrativized as a voluntary form of self-segregation, but few of the teens other than Frankie and Dee Dee seem content with what quickly becomes characterized as a contested border. The boys encourage the girls to "sneak across the border," promising that they "will gladly take in refugees." When Johnny tells Animal "if you want to defect, we believe in peaceful coexistence," Frankie stops the badinage and calls instead for peaceful detumescence: "Okay guys, knock it off. Let's bag some z's. Somebody shoot out the lights."

Throughout *Muscle Beach Party*, Dee Dee and Frankie confront and occasionally even test boundaries; by the end of the film, however, these boundaries are always reaffirmed and, like the teen couple around whom the films revolve, stronger than ever. As was true in *Beach Party*, none require more vigilant affirmation or are more constantly embattled than those boundaries understood to be sacrosanct to the middle-class couple, the nuclear family, even to the American suburb itself – be they sexual, generational, socioeconomic, racial or geographic. Though *Muscle Beach Party* makes no explicit references to non-white cultures until the penultimate scene, the film mobilizes an opposition between unmarked whiteness and accented ethnicity to clarify the range of outside threats facing Frankie and Dee Dee, and by extension, the sexual, gender, racial and economic hierarchies that structure and define white middle-class life.

This first becomes an explicit danger to the social and sexual geography within which the teen community exists when Frankie refuses to accept the responsibilities of manhood. Midway through the film, impatient with Frankie's refusal to embrace a more mature, adult lifestyle that will lead to marriage, parenthood and home ownership, Dee Dee confronts her boyfriend, who in turn launches into an overly earnest celebration of the carefree surfer's forever-young lifestyle: "This is how I want it. I want it easy and I want it free. I want it without the ropes, squares, bills or bombs. This is my world because I don't ask anything of it . . . you swing with me on that or you don't swing at all." While the reference to "bills and bombs" is one of the few moments when the reality of the world intrude on the film, it would likely have been difficult even for teens in the theater to take this paean to bohemian wanderlust too seriously, delivered as it was by Frankie Avalon, a cherub-faced 25-year-old who was already married and a father.

Still, within the diegesis, Frankie's tantrum precipitates his temporary estrangement from Dee Dee and a brief courtship with the Italian contessa, Julie. Julie's interest in Frankie incites Dee Dee's ire and provokes a curiously unselfconscious spate of anti-Italian slurs. When the gang runs into each other at a local hangout, Dee Dee tells Julie she should "start peddling [her] pasta somewhere else," and later refers to her as "the Mafia" before sarcastically asking Frankie if he's "had enough pizza." Without a character like Sutwell to codify adolescent sexuality as "primitive" racial otherness, *Muscle Beach Party* instead invokes ethnic difference – embodied by the contessa, who immodestly uses her money to procure men to sate her sexual appetite – as an equally disruptive force that will jeopardize the social dynamic of the group.

Julie is an unsuitable partner for Frankie not only because she is rich and he is not, but because she is marked as a foreigner who does not fit in with the "native" surfers. This provides the film with a strange but functional ideological sleight of hand. On one level, Julie's status as an outsider naturalizes the white characters' "native" claim to the beach; on another, her Italianness secures the whiteness of the film's romantic couple, played, ironically, by two of popular culture's most well-known Italian-Americans. As in *Beach Party*, in which Frankie is pursued by the oversexed and heavily accented Ava (Eva Six), women who openly desire men are exotic and a threat to the middle-class white couple; their sexuality and foreignness confirm not just Frankie's and Dee Dee's whiteness and moral superiority, but the moral superiority of whiteness itself.

Bringing the beach to the 'burbs

At once a *sui generis* natural landscape and a utopian built environment, a site of free public leisure and restrictive private consumption, the southern California beach became an increasingly liminal space in the years leading up to AIP's *Beach Party* films. When considering the films' appeal to the audiences who set AIP rental records attending them, therefore, it is important to understand that, despite representing the allure of a landscape to which most Americans did not have quick or easy access, the cinematic beach nevertheless evoked values that reflected, and were embraced by, an increasingly suburban nation. To be sure, AIP's beach mirrored suburban life in important ways; most notably, each site implied that spatial and sexual regulation, conspicuous but classless consumption, and racial homogeneity were at once the preconditions and rewards of a white community.

Despite going to great lengths to distance themselves from the social problems of the world outside the beach, the *Beach Party* films' aforementioned containment of sexual promiscuity and defense of the beach community must be understood in historical context as being at least partially motivated by contemporary anxieties about Civil Rights, miscegenation and integration. Of course these anxieties were visible throughout the country, even close to Paradise Cove in Malibu, where much of the location shooting for the beach films took place. One month prior to *Beach Party*'s July 1963 premiere, for instance, the United Civil Rights Committee organized "the largest march for black civil rights in the history of Los Angeles"; in that same month, 300 residents in the primarily white South Bay suburb of Torrance attended a City Council meeting to insist "that the council close all roads leading into the city on weekends to prevent people who 'have no business being there' from entering."[37]

Like the Torrance residents, the teenagers in AIP's beach films are silent on the matter of their own whiteness and proactive about defending their territory from those who "have no business being there." In *Beach Party* and *Beach Blanket Bingo*, this takes the form of Eric Von Zipper and his motorcycle gang. A spoof of the angst-ridden teen rebel immortalized by Marlon Brando, Von Zipper and his gang register as a disruption not only because they are clearly too old to be antagonizing a group of kids on summer vacation, but also because they cannot be assimilated into the film's (or the suburb's) geography of whiteness. In a *mise-en-scène* dominated by the "natural" beauty of the sand and surf and by brightly if barely clothed bodies, the black leather-clad motorcycle gang are pronouncedly out of place – generationally, intellectually, sexually, culturally, and visually. This last point is significant. The *Beach Party* films envision their landscape in highly saturated colors; ocean and sky often seem unnaturally blue, the beach gleams white, and the cast's bathing suits splash color across the screen. Both narratively and visually, the beach films occupy a primarily diurnal world, all the better to showcase healthy white bodies undulating in the California sun. It is not insignificant, therefore, that Von Zipper and his gang appear almost exclusively at nighttime; thus they are marked as always already intrusive, dangerous and dark. Von Zipper is, to be fair, an absurd, incompetent character who poses no real threat; still, as the closest thing the beach films offer to a "black" character, he transcends mere parody and personifies a kind of return of the repressed.

Although *Beach Party* freely grafts "tribal" behaviors from Africa, Haiti, Samoa and New Guinea onto white teen sexuality, the film never directly engages race relations within the USA. Thus, it is significant that when Von Zipper first appears in the narrative, he is immediately racialized. Walking into Big Daddy's – the bar where the teens hang out at night – Von Zipper and his entourage are greeted by the manager, Cappy, who complains, "Great, just what we needed, the Black Plague." The metaphor links Von Zipper to blackness, and invokes the overdetermined rhetoric of disease, a rhetoric that has historically been used to call for the containment of those whose mobility (or "spread") is perceived as a threat to national security and an inviolate body politic: communists, Jews, blacks, immigrants, homosexuals, etc. Furthermore, his gang is called The Rats, a none-too-subtle device that relegates Von Zipper to social vermin, someone who warrants extermination when containment fails.

At Big Daddy's, we see why Von Zipper constitutes such a threat as he forces himself on to a reluctant Dolores. Confronted with a situation that falls well outside the consensual flirtation he witnessed on the beach earlier that day, Sutwell moves in to stop Von Zipper from "molesting this girl." In the process, he abandons his earlier references to tribal practices in favor of the language of sexual assault, foreshadowing the biker's next appearance in the film and ensuring that he be read outside the framework of the teenagers' social dynamic. The following night, The Rats descend on the beach seeking revenge. The gang arrives shortly after a campfire, which ends when couples retreat to private nooks, wedge surfboards in the sand for privacy and commence making out. *This* sexual behavior is acceptable. What follows after Von Zipper arrives, however, is not.

Dolores heads back to the house, alone. Thinking her window is Sutwell's, the forever clueless Von Zipper climbs into her bedroom and falls onto the sleeping Dolores, whose screams raise the alarm for Sutwell to come to her rescue yet again. The scene is played mostly for laughs, and Dolores is never in any express danger. Still, the film has just used the campfire scene to underscore the link between darkness and sexuality; so when a group of black-clad gang members show up where "they have no business being" in the middle of the night only to hoist their leader into a young white girl's bedroom, it is impossible not to read the scene as a perverse fantasy about rape and home invasion. Indeed, as Dolores – who, remember, is "not even a woman" – cries out in the night, we are seeing a thinly veiled nightmare of the threat predatory, if bumbling, "black" masculinity poses to virginal white femininity. Von Zipper's leather outfit has replaced the burnt cork films once used to "blacken" white actors, but he nevertheless descends from the same painful history of racial caricature and animalization.

Von Zipper's gang implies the need to protect the community from unwanted intrusions, especially from groups who suggest blackness. Still, the *Beach Party* films remain astonishingly quiet on the matter of African American culture, community and subjectivity. In that film, blackness is either reduced to Africanness or displaced onto delinquent white masculinity. One of the cycle's only explicit gestures to black identity comes at the close of *Muscle Beach Party*, in which Little Stevie Wonder sings "Happy Street" at Big Daddy's. Through Wonder, the film acknowledges blackness as part of American popular culture, yet marks it as distinctly performative in a manner that departs from the musical numbers performed by Dick Dale and the Del-Tones, Frankie Avalon or Annette Funicello. For instance, he is introduced by name to the diegetic (and theatrical) audience, an ambiguous move that certifies the young artist's credentials as an entertainer (he was fourteen years old when the film was released) but which also signals that he may well be unknown to the spectators. The films offer no such introductions, by way of comparison, for Dick Dale, whose fame as the "king of the surf guitar" could be safely assumed.

The beach films feature a number of guitar-heavy "surf rock" numbers that foreground the frolicsome lifestyle of beach culture; in these, both musicians and audience occupy the same social space and share in the production of each other's entertainment, if only through dancing around in bathing suits for one another's visual pleasure. Wonder's "Happy Street," on the other hand, operates in a noticeably different idiom, one marked by the film's inability to include him in the carnivalesque atmosphere of the other musical numbers. Wonder cannot be absorbed into the social, the sexual or the spatial field of the film's teenagers. On the contrary, he is kept in his "place" – on stage – like so many black performers before him, singing for an all-white audience at a club in which he would not be welcome were he not the "entertainment". Moreover, Wonder, of course, cannot participate in the sexual economy of white adolescence. His age assures us that he is just a "boy", too young to be a romantic rival, and because he is unsighted, he cannot see the white women's bodies writhing in front of him. He poses no threat to white femininity the way Von Zipper does in *Beach Party*, though, like Von Zipper, he does not really "belong" in this space. Even the song lyrics underscore this, locating Wonder, along with the whole of black culture he is asked to represent, in "the happy street." As the film's only reference to urban space, "the happy street" is indeed a fantasy site, a non-place that allows the film simultaneously to gesture to such spaces while eliding the contemporary racial and political foment that defined them.

Both Wonder and his performance challenge us to question the veracity and limits of the film's earlier claim to "believe in peaceful co-existence." Clearly, Frankie was right: there *are* "people for people, and people for places." Like Wonder's appearance, certain promotional materials for *Muscle Beach Party* underscored the degree to which, even in their absence, blackness, integration and miscegenation structured the all-white space of the beach. In a publicity still photographed at an airport outside the Eastern Airlines terminal, contract player Darlene Lucht poses with local body-builders. Flanked by shirtless weight-lifters all posing for, and looking at, the camera, Lucht smiles at the attention. The only non-white person in the photograph is an African American body-builder who faces, on bended knee, not the camera, but Lucht. Rather than allowing his body to be the object of the gaze he has taken hers as one, something Wonder could never do. Interpreting this as a threat to white femininity (and thus an affront to white masculinity), the man to Lucht's immediate right has pivoted his body to accept the perceived challenge, arms outspread just enough to imply the invitation of a physical conflict. The photograph crystallizes much of the beach films' vision of whiteness – attractive, strong, healthy, happy, and united against potential threats to their homogeneous communities. To the very limited degree racial otherness is acknowledged, it exists on the periphery and, even there, is construed as a crisis for whiteness and to normative sexuality.

Evacuating people of color from the cinematic beach in order to authenticate the racelessness of that space, the films exploited a long-shifting dynamic between racial formations and sites of leisure and consumption in the USA. An important consequence of this was to erode the beach's connotations as a public space and to promote it as a site for semi-private consumption, leisure and insularity. As Eric Avila has noted, the emerging mass culture of the late nineteenth and early twentieth centuries "reinforced a mutually constitutive relationship between *public* and *white*."[38] Thus, as southern California's population swelled in the early twentieth century, beach communities such as Venice, Ocean Park and Santa Monica served as privileged sites of public amusement and leisure; the huge crowds were themselves part of the spectacle and attraction of such spaces. However, Avila explains that the rapid diversification of urban centers and public spaces in the postwar era led to a pronounced "reconfiguration of race and space . . . [and an] accompanying transition from public to private modes of entertainment."[39] Thus, even though the beach continued to attract large crowds, its status as a public space became more conditional as it came to signify in the popular imagination specific forms of leisure, spatial regulation and racial containment that were wholly commensurate with the suburban enclave. The concurrent processes of suburbanization and the privatization of the beach in the 1950s and 1960s expressed in spatial terms a felt need to consolidate geographies of whiteness. Such geographies were commonly represented as besieged by a diverse range of social and cultural forces that included everything from poverty and racial difference to political radicalism and rock'n'roll. Catherine Jurca usefully highlights the degree to which suburbanites – whom she describes as a "white diaspora" – ironically guarded themselves against such threats by viewing their enclosed built environment as material proof of their own suffering. For Jurca, suburbia is a loosely connected geography of distinct communities united by "a fantasy of victimization that reinvents white flight as the persecution of those who flee, turns material advantages into artifacts of spiritual and cultural oppression, and sympathetically treats affluent house owners as the emotionally dispossessed."[40]

The flight to and fortification of white spaces, combined with the increasing popularity of the beach landscape and lifestyle, produced drastic limits on access to coastal communities. As Reyner Banham pointed out in the early 1970s:

> from Malibu Pier to Santa Monica pier . . . [the southern California coast is] covered by sizeable middle-class houses in such close contiguity that for miles there is no way to squeeze between them and get to the beach, which thus becomes a secluded communal backyard for the inhabitants.[41]

With property ownership and class privilege combining to restrict access to and mobility on the beach, popular culture provided one of the only ways for many, even in southern California, to actually experience the beach: "The seven million people within an hour's drive of Malibu got Beach Boys music and surfer movies, but the twenty thousand residents kept the beach."[42] The growing popular-cultural appeal and accelerating residential exclusivity of the coastline proved mutually reinforcing. This allowed AIP and other Hollywood studios to market the southern California beach to a national audience as a space that was accessible and enjoyable, but only to the "right" kind of people. Well beyond its titular significance in *Beach Party*, *Muscle Beach Party*, *Bikini*

Beach and *Beach Blanket Bingo*, the cultural landscape and social values of AIP's beach enjoyed vigorous cross-promotion in printed materials, suburban shopping malls and movie theaters, and through the concurrent surf music craze.

The most successful effort to reify connections between the beach and the suburb was through AIP's plan to have exhibitors who booked *Beach Party* host their own "beach parties" right at the theater. Working to ballyhoo the film, press materials cited the success of four theaters in Toledo, Ohio that "imported a truck load of white sand and created their own beach setting." The press book urged other theater owners to follow suit, promising that the simulated beach atmosphere would be met with the same kind of increased attendance and profits experienced in Toledo, where "free admission to the first fifty couples who showed up in bathing suits spelled B-E-A-C-H P-A-R-T-Y and any way you cut it [sic] also spelled D-O-L-L-A-R-S at the box office."[43] These virtual beaches helped generate single-day and opening week records for the Toledo theaters, and were met with similar results in a number of other markets in suburbs and mid-sized cities like Providence, RI, Flint, MI, York, PA, Wilmington, DE and Appleton, WI.

The films also exploited the popularity of surf music to bolster box-office appeal:

> By 1963, the year that *Beach Party* was released, surf music had become a craze. The Beach Boys had six songs go into the Top 40, including "Surfin' USA" (no. 3) and "Surfer Girl" (no. 7). Jan and Dean had a number one hit with "Surf City," while The Surfaris' "Wipeout" reached number two. . . .[44]

Despite performances by respected surf music icons like Dick Dale and His Del-Tones and some collaboration with the Beach Boys' Brian Wilson, many of the musical numbers in the films are performed by Frankie Avalon and Annette Funicello. Andrew Caine notes that the two were often so affected and insubstantial that, among both critics and fans of surf music, they "remain[ed] derided, forever associated with the dilution of classic 1950s rock'n'roll rebellion into bland pop."[45] This "dilution," however, served an important diegetic function, for it purged the music of, and distanced the films from, any associations with rock's origins in black culture or surf music's emphasis on non-conformity.

A year after AIP's successful effort to stage beach parties at movie houses and drive-ins, the release of *Bikini Beach* occasioned promotional beach-themed parties at local shopping malls. As McGee recalls of one such party, "Five thousand kids swarmed a Canoga Park shopping center where Sam Riddle, emcee of KHJ-TV's *9th Street West*, hosted a Zody's Department Store 'Bikini Beach' Dance Party."[46] Moving into the mall and enlisting the help of local TV and radio personalities, the studio developed an even more transparent parallel between the beach and the suburban consumer landscape. More importantly, the practice revealed the increasing imbrication of the movies, music and shopping, and thus began to articulate a marketing philosophy from which Hollywood as a whole would reap immeasurable rewards in the decades to come.

Certainly, these promotional gimmicks strove to recreate for white audiences across the country the utopian beach geography imagined in the films themselves, further cementing the links between the cinematic beach, suburban racial insularity, and private sites of consumption. However, the legacy of their promotion and marketing exceeds even this, for in many respects, American International Pictures transformed the beach franchise into the kind of multimedia commodity that would eventually come to define the New Hollywood's blockbuster ethos.[47] The success of this business model, which ultimately informed production, distribution and exhibition practices industry-wide, would, perhaps ironically, guide the studio to even greater heights when it relocated its exploitation apparatus from the southern California coastline to the American city center in the early 1970s.

From the beach to blaxploitation

Throughout this essay I have argued that in the early 1960s AIP exploited the cultural, material and symbolic value of the beach in order to promote dominant attitudes about racial containment and perceived needs to protect white communities. Mapping whiteness onto the cultural and cinematic landscape of the beach, the *Beach Party* franchise revealed the tremendous signifying power of such a space. The ability to envision and exploit geographies of race would further guide American International Pictures into its most financially successful and politically controversial period when it reoriented its release schedule away from the youth market and toward the burgeoning black audience of the early 1970s.[48] Consequently, I would like to close by briefly mentioning how AIP borrowed strategies it perfected with its beach films in order to play a central role in the blaxploitation movement.

Obviously, there is no room in this essay to untangle the Gordian knot of political, economic, cultural and social forces that catalyzed the industry's exploitation of black culture and communities during this period.[49] Initially, it may seem hard to imagine two groups of films more disparate in tone, style, content and audience than AIP's beach films and blaxploitation movies; yet the studio's prioritization of the urban black audience from 1972 to 1975 serves as a compelling lesson on how the same formula employed in its exploitation of the beach a decade earlier could be updated and relocated to a new racial geography so as to produce similar results with a sharply different demographic. In its spate of films aimed at black audiences, AIP combined the same fundamental strategies discussed above with respect to the beach films, mapping historically specific attitudes and anxieties about race onto an overdetermined racial landscape – in this case, the inner-city "ghetto" – in order to wield cultural influence and to realize the studio's greatest box-office returns.[50]

As with the *Beach Party* franchise, AIP's blaxploitation films employed production and marketing techniques often associated with exploitation cinema in order to embed conservative racial values in an outwardly oppositional package. Having seen with the beach cycle the potential for film to reify dominant values by attaching those values to a racialized geography, Hollywood followed AIP's lesson when the entire industry turned its attention to the "ghetto" in order to authorize representations of black space, and by extension, black subjectivity. In this, the films often worked to interpellate audiences into a racial hierarchy that, despite appearing within the narratives to be weakened by physically and politically empowered black characters, nevertheless often remained intransigent for people of color in the world outside the theater. Further, like the beach films, which taught audiences how *not* to see the institutional and material aspects of their own social power and white privilege, the majority of Hollywood's blaxploitation films either elided the institutional and political-economic dimensions of American racism, or worse, invoked "the Man" as the apocryphal, nameless and faceless personification of black subjugation.

Also like the beach films, blaxploitation movies benefited from their occupation and articulation of a symbolically potent racial geography. However, whereas the beach films positioned the coastal geography as being outside of, and untouched by, the political, social and racial problems of the 1960s, blaxploitation movies envisioned the "ghetto" as a site where most of those problems converged or, worse, originated. The unfortunate and all-too-common result was to represent rampant drug use, violence and prostitution as the inevitable *causes* – rather than the avoidable *effects* – of economic neglect, urban blight and institutionalized racism in the "ghetto". Reducing the geography of blackness to a site of crisis, blaxploitation films used the black "ghetto" to spatialize through the *mise-en-scène* a politics of racial containment and immobility, even when their narratives ostensibly challenged such a politics. In *Black City Cinema*, Paula Massood points out that discourses about the "ghetto" coming out of the social sciences, urban planning and popular culture effaced the complexities and heterogeneity of black life and urban space; effectively superimposing the city and the geography of blackness onto one another such that "the trope of the black ghetto defined the American urbanscape as a whole."[51] It is important to understand, therefore, that among blaxploitation's most far-reaching, albeit under-examined consequences is how it mapped blackness onto a falsely consolidated urban geography much like the beach films from a decade earlier inscribed whiteness onto an expansive yet equally confabulatory suburban geography.

As it did with its *Beach Party* franchise, then, AIP continued to turn to the built environment and cultural landscape in order to map its racial politics. Indeed, despite their many differences, the beach films and blaxploitation movies released by American International Pictures – which brought the studio its greatest cultural influence and box-office successes – were actually guided by very similar organizing principles: first, the exploitation of audiences with limited options for cultural consumption and reception; second, the reinforcement of dominant white values and anti-black racism in films packaged to conceal their own mainstream interests; third and perhaps most importantly, the mapping of racial formations, containment and mobilities onto specific geographies. As perfected in the cycle of beach films and repeated in the turn to blaxploitation, the racialization of space and the spatialization of race have played key roles in perpetuating Americans' ideas about emplacement, community, and belonging. It is no coincidence, therefore, that these symbolically resonant racial geographies emerged in the popular culture during historically specific moments when these very issues were being simultaneously challenged, defended and redefined.

Notes

1   Gary Morris, "Beyond the Beach: AIP's Beach Party Movies," *Bright Lights Film Journal*, 21 (May 1998), www.brightlightsfilm.com/21/21_beach.html.
2   AIP produced several other films that were less expressly about the relationship between a community of white youth and the beach landscape, but which worked to capitalize on the beach films' success. These included *Pajama Party* (1964), *Ski Party* (1965) and *Dr Goldfoot and the Bikini Machine* (1965).
3   *Beach Party*, shot on a budget of $350,000 over a three-week period, returned approximately $4 million in rentals (Internet Movie Database, http://us.imdb.com/title/tt0056860/business). *Muscle Beach Party*, originally released around Easter in 1964, was brought back into theaters during Christmas of that same year. In between these two runs, *Bikini Beach* was released in July, bringing record returns for American International at that time. Mark Thomas McGee, *Faster and Furiouser: The Revised and Fattened Fable of American International Pictures* (Jefferson, NC: McFarland & Company, Inc., Publishers, 1996), pp. 229, 230.
4   Robin Bean and David Austen, "USA: Confidential," *Films and Filming*, November 1968, pp. 22–3.
5   Quoted in McGee, *Faster and Furiouser*, p. 229.
6   Quoted in McGee, *Faster and Furiouser*, p. 222.
7   Matthew Frye Jacobson, *Whiteness of a Different Color: European Immigrants and the Alchemy of Race* (Cambridge, MA: Harvard University Press, 1998), p. 10.
8   Morris, "Beyond the Beach."
9   For more on the history of AIP, see McGee's *Faster and Furiouser* and Thomas Doherty's *Teenagers and Teenpics: The Juvenilization of American Movies in the 1950s* (Boston, MA: Unwin Hyman, 1988), especially pp. 153–60.
10 For a full list of AIP productions, see McGee's *Faster and Furiouser*, which provides an AIP filmography that is as comprehensive as it is compendious.
11 The cycle of Poe adaptations included *House of Usher* (1960), *The Pit and the Pendulum* (1961), *The Raven* (1962), *Tales of Terror* (1962), *The Masque of the Red Death* (1964), *The Tomb of Ligeia* (1965).
12 In "The New Hollywood" (*Film Theory Goes to the Movies*, ed. by Jim Collins, Hilary Radner and Ava Preacher Collins. New York: Routledge, 1993, p. 15), Thomas Schatz notes that from 1969–71, the industry lost a total of $600 million.
13 Schatz, "The New Hollywood," p. 15. During the period of conglomeration in Hollywood, a number of key takeovers occurred. In 1962, the Music Corporation of America (MCA) acquired Universal-International Studios; Gulf & Western

bought Paramount in 1966. In 1967, United Artists was absorbed by TransAmerica Corp, a division of the Bank of America, while Jack Warner sold off his controlling interest in Warner Bros to Seven Arts. Two years later, Warner Bros-Seven Arts, saddled with its own debts, was acquired by Kinney National Services. That same year, Las Vegas hotelier Kirk Kerkorian acquired MGM.

14 Schatz, "The New Hollywood," p. 15.
15 *Variety* (n.d., n.p.), quoted in McGee, *Faster and Furiouser*, p. 292.
16 Bill Barol, "The Overstuffed World of AIP: Remembering the World's Greatest Producer of Bikini-spy-blaxploitation Flicks," *Slate* (29 October 2001), www.slate. com/id/117299.
17 McGee, *Faster and Furiouser*, p. 219.
18 Eric Schaefer, *"Bold! Daring! Shocking! True!": A History of Exploitation Films, 1919– 1959* (Durham, NC: Duke University Press, 1999), p. 14.
19 Schaefer, *"Bold! Daring! Shocking! True!"*, pp. 14, 2.
20 Schaefer, *"Bold! Daring! Shocking! True!"*, p. 8.
21 Morris, "Beyond the Beach."
22 Quoted in Doherty, *Teenagers and Teenpics*, p. 159. The commitment to selling to young audiences however bland or brash a worldview the youth market seemed to require continued until that market gave over to the blaxploitation juggernaut. As late as 1971, Arkoff continued to assert the studio's devotion to "clean" pictures, which he saw as a necessary adjunct to courting the teen market, especially with the advent of the new MPAA ratings system. As *Variety* reported, "In their continuing effort to milk the last drops of the flagging youth market, the studio says they'll avoid 'consciously producing' any R or X rated films and instead will commit to exhibitors only distributing G or GP pics" ("American Int'l Will Make on G or GP-Rated Films," 1 March 1971, p. 1).
23 R.L. Rutsky, "Surfing the Other: Surf Films from the 1950s, 1960s and how Teenagers Responded," *Film Quarterly* (Summer 1999), p. 13.
24 Rutsky, "Surfing the Other," pp. 13, 14.
25 Morris, "Beyond the Beach."
26 Domenic Priore, quoted in Andrew Caine, "The A.I.P. Beach Movies – Cult Films Depicting Subcultural Activities," *Scope: An Online Journal of Film Studies* (20 November 2001), www.nottingham.ac.uk/film/journal/articles/aip-beach-movies.htm.
27 Kevin Starr, *Inventing the Dream: California Through the Progressive Era* (Oxford: Oxford University Press, 1985), p. 46.
28 Reyner Banham, *Los Angeles: The Architecture of Four Ecologies* (New York: Penguin Books, 1971 (1990)), p. 49.
29 American International Pictures, *Beach Party* Production Fact Sheet (Courtesy of Margaret Herrick Library).
30 Funicello's character is named Dolores in *Beach Party* and Dee Dee in subsequent beach films.
31 Arkoff understood that sexualized imagery would pique teens' desire and addle adults. The promotions had the intended effect. As quoted in McGee's *Faster and Furiouser*, Arkoff recalled that "at least 200 newspapers throughout the country brushed out the belly buttons of the ads for the *Beach Party* movies. As though some evil lurked in the belly button" (p. 233).
32 It is worth noting that when AIP re-released the beach films in 1973, social attitudes about sex had changed and the original audiences of the films were no longer teenagers. Consequently, the studio was far more tongue in cheek about the distance separating the promise of sex in the original 1960s ads and the withholding of it in the films themselves; press materials for the re-release winked knowingly to the earlier subterfuge: "See! Actual simulated hand holding!" (American

International Pictures, "Beach Party Combo Shows are SOLID GOLD from A. I.P.," press materials, 1973).

33   Doherty, *Teenagers and Teenpics*, p. 195.

34   Jacobson, *Whiteness of a Different Color*, p. 3.

35   Richard Dyer, *White* (London: Routledge, 1997), p. 28.

36   Dyer, *White*, p. 49.

37   Josh Sides, *L.A. City Limits: African American Los Angeles from the Great Depression to the Present* (Berkeley, CA: University of California Press, 2003), pp. 164, 166.

38   Eric Avila, *Popular Culture in the Age of White Flight: Fear and Fantasy in Suburban Los Angeles* (Berkeley, CA: University of California Press, 2004), p. 4.

39   Avila, *Popular Culture in the Age of White Flight*, p. 6.

40   Catherine Jurca, *White Diaspora: The Suburb and the Twentieth-Century American Novel* (Princeton, NJ: Princeton University Press, 2001), pp. 8–9.

41   Banham, *Los Angeles: The Architecture of Four Ecologies*, pp. 40–1.

42   Thomas Mikkelson and Donald Neuwrith. Quoted in Mike Davis, *Ecology of Fear: Los Angeles and the Imagination of Disaster* (New York: Metropolitan Books, 1998), p. 109.

43   American International Pictures, "'Beach Party' Gets Promotional Blast in Toledo!" (Courtesy of Margaret Herrick Library).

44   Rutsky, "Surfing the Other," pp. 13, 14.

45   Caine, "The A.I.P. Beach Movies."

46   McGee, *Faster and Furiouser*, p. 230.

47   For more on the New Hollywood, see Thomas Schatz's essay of the same name in *Film Theory Goes to the Movies*, edited by Jim Collins, Hilary Radner and Ava Preacher Collins (New York: Routledge, 1993), pp. 1–35.

48   From 1972 to 1975, AIP released roughly 18 films aimed primarily at the burgeoning black audience: *Slaughter* (1972), *Black Mama, White Mama* (1972), *Black Caesar* (1972), *Blacula* (1972), *Slaughter's Big Rip-Off* (1973), *Scream Blacula Scream* (1973), *Hell Up in Harlem* (1973), *Coffy* (1973), *Heavy Traffic* (1974), *Abby* (1974), *Sugar Hill* (1974), *Foxy Brown* (1974), *Truck Turner* (1974), *Sheba Baby* (1975), *Cooley High* (1975), *Cornbread, Earl and Me* (1975), *Bucktown* (1975).

49   For more on the historical, cultural and political-economic dimensions of black exploitation film see: Chapter 3 of Ed Guerrero, *Framing Blackness: The African American Image in Film* (Philadelphia, PA: Temple University Press, 1993); Chapter 4 of Mark Reid, *Redefining Black Film* (Berkeley: University of California Press, 1993); Chapter 2 of William R. Grant, *Post-Soul Black Cinema: Discontinuities, Innovations and Breakpoints, 1970–1995* (London: Routledge, 2004); and Gladstone L. Yearwood, "Towards a Theory of a Black Cinema Aesthetic," in *Black Cinema Aesthetics: Issues in Independent Black Filmmaking*, ed. by Yearwood (Athens, OH: Ohio University Papers on Afro-American, African and Caribbean Studies, 1982), pp. 67–81.

50   In 1973, following on the heels of successful runs with *Blacula, Black Caesar, Slaughter* and *Black Mama, White Mama* in 1972, and *Coffy, Heavy Traffic, Slaughter's Big Rip-Off, Hell Up in Harlem* and *Scream Blacula Scream* in 1973, the studio realized a 175 percent increase in profits from 1971–2 ("AIP Scores Big Gains With Income Up 175% for Year," *Hollywood Reporter*, 21 May 1973, n.p.). In 1975, the studio posted single-week, single-quarter and annual records, owing in part to the well-received *Cooley High* and *Cornbread, Earl and Me* (both 1975) ("AIP's 20th Year Is Best Yet; 9-Mo. Earnings $2,891,000 As Gross Up 59% to $37 Mil," *Variety*, 15 January 1975, p. 1; "Record One-Week Billings of $1.8 Million for AIP," *Box Office*, 8 September 1975, n.p.).

51   Paula J. Massood, *Black City Cinema: African American Urban Experience in Film* (Philadelphia, PA: Temple University Press, 2003), p. 84.

Chapter 3

Boyz, boyz, boyz

New Black Cinema and black masculinity

Keith M. Harris

In the Hollywood tradition of "mainstream film," the visual codes surrounding blacks and blackness on the screen have been stereotypical images, more contemporarily drug dealers, prostitutes, single mothers and complacent drag queens. These are the traditional encodings informed by popular discourse of race and gender, reflecting and sustaining popular convictions about blackness and black sexuality. Implicit in these encodings of blackness as deviancy is the encoding, the way of seeing whiteness as the social and sexual norm, as reason and rationality, as civility and tradition. In the realm of popular culture, these discursive images, as film transcodes them, dispense the "framework[s] of symbols, concepts and images through which we understand, interpret, and represent aspects of our 'racial' existence."[1] However, since the mid-1980s, Hollywood and independent American cinema have seen a rise in films by African American filmmakers. Often touted as being "by, for, and about African Americans," these films are social commentaries, indictments of racism and depictions of "everyday" African American lives. Afrocentrism and nationalistic pride often inform the aesthetic frameworks of these films, and they are replete with black cultural signifiers.

Juxtaposed against the traditional representations of blacks and blackness, New Black Cinema[2] takes on the project of cultural intervention and the recoding of blackness, "revising the visual codes surrounding black skin on the screen and in the public realm."[3] This is ultimately a political project within its relationship to the Hollywood tradition and the traditional racialist and, at times, racist codings of blackness and a project which is dialectical within the real/representation relationship of New Black Cinema. My interest is in the representational dialogic of racial difference within film and the real/representation dialectic of cultural, gender and sexual identity.

The number of films that I have viewed in preparation for discussion raises various complicated issues of race, class and gender and the representation of race, class and gender, ranging from sexual liberation in Spike Lee's successful independent film, *She's Gotta Have It*, to the coming of age story in John Singleton's *Boyz N the Hood*.[4] At the core of these films' complexities are the problematics and paradoxes of black masculinity and images of black men and black masculinity. The operation of recoding masculinity from established, now historic, Hollywood codings of black men and black masculinity visualizes a more ambiguous, more discursive image, producing the meanings of an intricately constructed masculinity, more complexly dimensional than the submissive, docile Tom or the morally corrupt, conniving, sexually threatening drug dealer.[5]

However, these more aggressive, politically charged black masculinities, now turned difficult, involved, ideological metaphors, construct themselves, in the arena of meanings, from the existing, pop cultural and filmic representations of masculinity. By operating referentially to the popular cultural images of black men which are visibly recurring, or simply fixed, instructing homogeneous, monolithic, and culturally familiar (and therefore, quite culturally consumable) constructs, the critical attention that New Black Cinema markets as black men and masculinity then seemingly becomes reinforcement of singular, monologic meanings, only within different popular images. What is culturally familiar – hip-hop, rap music, commodified neo-nationalism and the cool, posed, "endangered black man" – becomes representationally and culturally totalized as the Black Experience of the young, heterosexual urban black man, the only experience possible.

I have chosen to examine three of the earliest New Black Cinema films: Spike Lee's musical, *School Daze*; Reginald and Warrington Hudlin's teenpic, *House Party*; and John Singleton's coming of age tale, *Boyz N the Hood*. I have chosen these three films for the purposes of critiquing the discursive visual recodings of black masculinity. I have selected these three particular films because the codings and recodings of masculinity and black masculinity are different across the genres of musical, teen comedy, and the more literary coming of age story. By examining these three films in a sequential order, I propose to interrogate patterns of formation of black masculinity as these patterns position (and reposition) women and female sexuality, male homosexuality, and the patriarchal construction of the family. These films, if unmediated, serve to construct a master narrative of black men and masculinity and sexuality that attempts to be seamless, unitary and phallic.

School Daze

> This film is . . . about our existence as a people in white America.[6]

School Daze is a musical, but not quite what one might expect. As Toni Cade Bambara notes: "Lee . . . chooses an enshrined genre of the dominant cinema . . . whose conventions were not designed to address an embattled community's concerns."[7] In the big MGM Hollywood tradition of elaborate sets, choreography, pageantry and spectacle, *School Daze* is a musical fused with the black cultural signifiers of jazz, Motown sound, and DC go-go. Using an all black, ensemble cast, the musical takes place during the homecoming events on the fictional campus of the historically black Mission College.

The focus of the film revolves around four gendered social groups: the Gammites, men; the Wannabees, women; Dap and da fellas, men; and the Jigaboos, women. The tension of the film lies in the shade/caste/class racial identity and community conflict that subdivides, and heterosexually aligns, the gendered groups into two binaries: the Jigaboos, the dark-skinned group, led by Dap and Rachel, made up of predominately working-class black folk, *versus* the Wannabees, led by Julien and Jane, made up of light-skinned, upwardly mobile, middle-class black folk. The women confront the shade complex and racial identity issue. What is at stake is who, culturally, is the "blackest," has internalized white aesthetics of beauty more, and is more naturally black. The men confront the class and community division as being one of who is going to lead black people and what political ideology will inform a people's cultural and economic mobility. The campus is divided along these lines, representing the political and cultural dilemma of black communities at large.

Thus in keeping with the popular, yet oppositional, cultural positionality of New Black Cinema, the musical takes place during the homecoming events on the Mission College campus, examining the politics of race in an embattled community. It is in this setting that Lee subverts the use of the musical. Richard Dyer analyzes entertainment, and particularly the Hollywood musical, as utopian fantasies inverting the signifiers of scarcity, exhaustion, dreariness, manipulation and fragmentation with the utopian sensibilities of abundance, energy, intensity, transparency, and community.[8] The entertaining inversions finally serve as temporal and spatial escapes from the "inadequacies of the society." With the musical, the result is a "utopian world" in which tension and conflict resolve in a burst into dance and song.

Dyer further notes that the "utopian world" of entertainment responds to real needs in society, but entertainment is also defining and delimiting what is a legitimate, real need in society. What are defined out of the category of "real need" within the utopian vision of entertainment are the social-cultural problems of race and gender, among other things. Spike Lee disrupts the musical form by placing the problem of race and racial identity into the field of vision, and by orienting this disruption in the utopian sensibility of community, the problem of race and racial disunity is then seen as an impediment and hindrance to community formation and function within an oppressive environment. Though Lee disrupts the utopianism inherent in the musical form, *School Daze* is not simply an alternative dystopian vision of the world in that it does not represent the imaginary as a wretched, fearful place. The disruption of the form allows for the representation of a black community as a thinking, self-critical body of people.

As the film is not a dystopian one, it is a masculinist one. The political question and possibility of unification seems to be the debate of the film, and by positioning the unification of black people and black communities within a

narrative history of slavery, emancipation, reconstruction, migrations, segregation, civil rights, and economic plight (all of which are set in the photo
montage as the film's credits appear on screen), *School Daze* and the question of
unification then flow into a cultural current of self-determination and survival.
With the Afrocentric vision, nationalist iconography, and urban, hip-hop
cultural infusions, the fluent visuals, rhythms, and language of the film become
messengers for the unification of a retrograde nation, a nation informed by the
patriarchal demarcations of power and gender inherent in the nationalistic
agenda.[9] As informed by the ideological and sexual paradigms of cultural
nationalism, sexual difference becomes the discourse mediating intraracial relations, separating racial identity and community into heterosexual, gendered
domains. Racial identity, the light/dark conflict, is feminine and signified by
the female body; community and leadership are masculine. Unification then
falls into the traditional construction of racial oppression and the recovery from
racial oppression as a "man's problem," as racial emasculation, as the recovery
of the phallus.

The women's color/shade problem is introduced in the first musical number, "Straight and Nappy." In the narrative, the two groups of women, the
Jigaboos, the dark-skinned women, and the Wannabees, the light-skinned
women, confront each other in the dormitory corridor. What ensues through
the musical number is an argument over shade, weaves, naps, contact lenses,
and men. In "Madame Ree Ree's Hair Salon," the Jigaboos and Wannabees
are in a gang fight set to the sound of big band. The territory of dispute is the
female body, the black female body. Rachel, Dap's girlfriend and head Jigaboo,
and Jane, Julian's girlfriend and head Wannabee, face off to the chorus:
"Talkin' 'bout good and bad hair / whether you are dark or fair / go on and
swear / see if I care / good and bad hair." At one point in the number, the
Jigaboos and the Wannabees don fans bearing images of Hattie McDaniel/
Mammy and Vivian Leigh/Scarlet O'Hara, the perennial Hollywood images of
the black woman *versus* the white woman. The fans of McDaniel and Leigh as
they circulate within the spectacle serve as the choice for the women, neither
one of which is a real choice for black women. The racialized masquerade, as
indicated by the donning of fans, directs the spectator to the constructedness of
women and racialized femininity and to the female body as the demarcation of
the color difference and intraracial community problem. The female body is
spectacle, objectified, scandalous, and contemptible. The spectacle of "Straight
and Nappy" is cathartic in that it removes the skin color conflict of racial identity from the men and embodies it in the female body. Racial identity is then
separated from the community of men, becoming an object for recovery.

Not surprisingly, in the narrative of the film, Rachel and Dap argue, in the
course of which Rachel suggests that Dap only dates her because of the shade,
the darkness, of her skin. Rachel argues that Dap's association with her, "the
darkest thing on campus," is "good for [his] all-the-way-down pro-black
image." The female body and the skin color/shade of the female body become

commodities in exchange for power and control. As commodities, certain values are assigned. In this case there is the historic value of white over black, light over dark. The skin color/shade of the objectified woman, now the black body, determines the politic of the man in possession of the body.

A more explicit example than the demonstrated use of Rachel's body is the use of Jane's body in the Gammites' rite of passage. After the pledges go over, joining the fraternity and becoming Gamma men, Half-Pint (Spike Lee's character) is still a virgin. What follows is Julian's (the head Gamma) trickery and coercion of both Jane and Half-Pint: Jane is raped/what she bodily possesses – Half-Pint's manhood and racial identity – is exchanged for Half-Pint's virginity. Half-Pint, now a Gamma man, enters into the ranks of the future leaders of the race. The sexual act, his initiation into manhood, recuperates his authenticity, his blackness, and his political alignment with the Wannabees, as a class and as a community.

Even though Lee's disruption of the musical form allows for an interrogation and re-presentation of the representation of black masculinity, Lee does not subvert the male gaze (however, he does racialize it).[10] Operating in a classic narrative form, the images of the women remain static, eroticized and fragmented; the men are active agents, representing movement and resolution. Race and sexual difference are collapsed; the black woman then simultaneously represents the lack of blackness and the phallus. Consequently, race and sexual difference are fetishized. Sexual difference becomes containment in a conventional construction of masculinity.

House Party

> I wanted to make a movie that had social messages, but was also entertaining, nonstop fun. . . . [11]

In Warrington and Reginald Hudlin's *House Party*, coding of male homosexuality and the representation of the male homosexual both situate the recoding of black masculinity as racial and class responsibility. *House Party* is a teenpic as characterized by the simple plot, the narrative of the rebellious youth, submerged in the urban, counter-cultural lifestyle of the day, the rhythms of hiphop and rap. This is a very deliberate film, very much in dialogue with Hollywood, mainstream film and popular cultural images of black people, especially black men, and very conscious of its youthful black audience. Therefore, what is very formulaic and exploitative (of teenagers, music and adolescent angst) in a Hollywood convention is rendered critical and interventionist, foregrounding race and oppression.

What is so deliberate and intentional about this film is the inversion of the common, stereotypical representations of black men and black communities with opposing cultural codings that, in turn, bring into question the fabrication and falsity of the stereotype itself. These critical inversions lead Lisa Kennedy to comment: "[*House Party*] touches on many of the signs of the black familiar – the projects, police brutality, teen sex, teen drinking, . . . black on black crime. . . ."[12] By "touching" on these signs of the "black familiar," and inverting them, the Hudlins construct a cinematic portrait of a utopian, "imagined community," inventing the visual meaning of a nation of black people, in which the stereotypes are supplanted, in the case of this film, with revised, "positive" images: there is the single-parent family with a black man, Pop, who is the head of the household in contrast to the much-media-dogged single black mother; there is the absence of a drug-plagued, inner-city black ghetto, replaced by the sanitary, drug-free suburban community; class strife is submerged; the black middle class is attendant and responsible for the entire representational community; and there is the representation of sexually responsible black youth.

Kid, the protagonist, is introduced to the audience as the only child in a male-headed household, trustworthy, and obedient, a clean-cut young man. This introduction is determining of two things: first, it establishes the narrative of the teen film as one of disobedience; the acting out of disobedience and punishment becomes the narrative motivation and plot closure for the film. Second, the family setting with Pop, as the widower father, is in opposition to the abandoned, single black mother image that is so pervasive in the media and Hollywood representation of the black family (which leaves the image of the single black mother intact and unexamined, simply suggesting that a man is better). Placing Kid next to Pop and suspending them in idiomatic language and the hip-hop culture codings of the *mise-en-scène*, Kid and Pop become authentic community role models for black youth. The role model itself offers a unitary symbol of man, black man, and manhood, informing class, sexual, and aesthetic standards to which the nation is to aspire and maintain. Respectability, as in Kid's responsibility in sexual abstinence and respect to and for his father, defines the parameters of moral codes, what is acceptable and not acceptable, what is good or bad. The role model, then, becomes a form of social control delimiting the parameters and the permanence of the construct of the black man.

As a role model, Kid's disobedience must be a punishable and redeemable learning experience. In the cafeteria scene immediately following his introduction, Kid wrangles with thugs – Stab, Zilla, and Pee Wee. The premise: Kid accidentally spills milk, a sexual slur is directed at his mother, and finally the pheromonal battle cry, issued simultaneously from Stab, Zilla and Pee Wee: "I smell pussy!" Thus, Kid is effeminized. The "smell of pussy" leads to a fight, in which Kid is beaten and reprimanded and Stab is expelled. As the film continues, it becomes clear that the premise of the film, Kid's going to the party without his father's consent, is ultimately a test of his manhood.

Now I want to turn the discussion to a close reading of two of the film's discursive maneuvers: the manipulation of the presence of homosexuality and the absence of the homosexual in this film. Homosexuality is present and detached from the black man and the black community. This presence and detachment serves two purposes. First, there is the establishment of homosexuality as a deviation from and threat to heterosexual black masculinity. When Kid is arrested, the responsible heterosexual sex scene in which the use of the condom, the trope of safe sex, is solely contraceptive precedes the jail scene, which is ostensibly about safe sex and anti-rape. The fixed use of the condom as contraception without a hint of its prophylactic use reconfigures any configured safe sex message, as it re-inscribes heterosexuality. What is articulated in the homosocial jailhouse setting of leering, caged men is that homosexuality is solely a homosexual act of violence and rape – with AIDS as the signifier of a wrongful act of violence. (Not surprisingly, the discourse of AIDS is conducted in the confines of a jail cell as something arrested and criminal in the black community.[13]) The second use of homosexuality lies in the submerged text of class difference. If homosexuality is a metaphor for the conflict between black men and criminality, the metaphor of disavowal, then metaphor intersects with metonym at the point of class. Class is submerged in a discourse of heterosexual, masculine difference, and is defined, and subsequently undefined, by the removal of homosexuality and the differentiation of a good, straight black man from a bad, straight black man, a positive image from a negative image. The presence of homosexuality demonstrates a black masculinity that is fluid between the heterosexual poles of good and bad. The concealment of class difference behind the veil of a good/bad dualism and pervasive morality refigures class on a moral plane transcoding the accoutrement and the materiality of class into moral signs. In this refiguration "Jheri" curls, bulging muscles, tank tops, and dark skin, the working-class signifiers of black masculinity, become the signifiers of the morally corrupt. The narrative identification of Kid as the protagonist positions spectators to identify with middle-class righteousness, privileging the middle-class aesthetic of the film.

Curiously missing in the presence of homosexuality is its embodiment in the homosexual. The absence of the homosexual, the lack of the physical display or some textual disclosure of a character, is deceptive in that the physical absence itself gives presence to the homosexual. I mean that homosexuals, specifically gay men, are not in the film, but figuratively still there. The first three gay men appear on the body of Bilial, the dj for the evening's infamous party. Bilial is bedecked with Keith Haring "Free South Africa" buttons, the oversized Willi Smith clothing, and Patrick Kelly designer buttons and combs.[14] These three men, a pop artist and two designers, respectively, were all dying or had already died of AIDS by the release of *House Party*. All three of these men were gay; two of them, Willi Smith and Patrick Kelly, were black. During the jail scene, the last two gay men, Rock Hudson and Liberace, appear in reference to their deaths from AIDS.

The presence of the absent homosexual totalizes the coding of black men and masculinity as unitary and heterosexual. Gay black men, for example Willi

Smith and Patrick Kelly, are commodified and erased, in the appropriated commodity form, from the representational black community, and gay white men, Rock Hudson and Liberace, signify the homosexual body. The cathexis of the homosexuality onto the absent, white, male homosexual body negates the possibility of a black gay man. Of course in view of the jail cell finale, the absent homosexual body, indeed the performative body, is doubly negated from the black community as it is contained within the film's insidious AIDS discourse, a discourse of criminality, confinement and race.

Again, as with *School Daze*, there is an oppositional aesthetic which foregrounds race and the construction of race, only to re-inscribe race in a discourse of patriarchy and heterosexuality. The reversal of denigrating stereotypes into the positive role model character of Kid is problematic in that the role model and role modeling are generative of another stereotype, perhaps more moral and corrective, but nonetheless a stereotype – a fixed and fixing conventional conception of black masculinity. The positive/negative image abstraction, as conceived, only serves to transpose one stereotype with another. The positive stereotype of black is exchanged with the negative stereotype of white. This limits the film's visual analysis of social messages to an us/them binary opposition, replacing "them" (white folk) with "us" (black folk), without interrogating the construct of us/them. The blind-sighted contradiction of this binary opposition is the re-inscription of the oppressor and the oppressed, or as in the film, heterosexual, masculine subject formation as determined by the negation of the homosexual.

Boyz N the Hood

> My film has a lot of messages in it . . . but my main message is that African American men have to take responsibility for raising their children, especially their boys. Fathers have to teach their boys to be men. The audience will be able to see the direction that the characters take when there is an absence or a presence of fathers in their lives.[15]

In *Boyz N the Hood*, John Singleton employs some of the narrative conventions of the melodrama, as Jackie Bayars has outlined them, which provide a mode for constructing moral identity. As Bayars explains, the melodramatic form functions as a site of conflict over social values, is often situated in family struggle, and often serves to define and redefine gender and its relationship to the structure of the family.[16] Bayars also discusses the male-oriented melodramas in which men are coming of age and establishing identity and relationships with their fathers.[17] In a traditional reading, a masculine coming of age story follows a young man as he finds himself, establishes his masculinity, and masters his sexual awakening and sexual urges.[18] *Boyz N the Hood* does not break with this tradition; however, in an expansion of the notion of family to an inclusion of community, the film places the story in South Central Los Angeles, an urban black community. Again as with *School Daze* and *House Party* race is centered, central to the melodrama.

Unlike *School Daze* and *House Party*, *Boyz* does not use sexual difference and sexuality, women and homosexuality, to define and negotiate black masculinity and black men. In turn, in the absence of homosexuality and with the oppositional symbolism of father and mother, black men are defined against heterosexual, masculine differences, and, once defined, black men are presented in an Oedipal opposition to black women as mothers in a family structure. This distinction of the definition by differences in masculinity is crucial because it then is the cause for the filmic opposition of black men and women.

First I want to examine the men, Furious, Tre, Ricky, and Doughboy. There is a parental figure, Furious, from whom the codings of masculinity and the fraternal order of Tre, Ricky, and Doughboy are derived. The representation of black men and masculinity is in dialog with the representation of male heterosexuality. In this dialog the film gives an age and maturation continuum of black men. This allows the audience to see the men through childhood, adolescence and manhood. This also allows for the visualization of difference in black men, how this difference, supposedly, develops and how, finally, the singular image of black man is created. The difference in masculinity pivots on the representation of Doughboy. As a visual image, Doughboy is both narratively and aesthetically abject, the low point, the lost, the dispossessed, the visually banished, yet not disavowed, forcing, but not bursting, the seams of masculinity: Doughboy is very much a black man, not removed from the film's range of black masculinity, but nonetheless, not what a black man should be. Within the narrative Doughboy is the bad seed, the disfavored son of Ms Baker; he is unemployed and criminal. Aesthetically, and in contrast to the well-built, toned and well-groomed images of Tre and Ricky (Doughboy's brother), Doughboy is fat and physically sloppy, malt liquor totting and "Jheri" curled, all the trappings that have come to code the masculinity of the black underclass.

As the abject, Doughboy defines the possibility of black masculinity, indeed the nadir, which is descendent from Furious, the peak of black masculinity. This construction of masculinity, with its highs and lows, allows for the totalizing monolith of Furious as the father and re-claimer. For, once abject-ed, Doughboy challenges and narratively motivates the reconstruction of masculinity. Consequently, Furious must meet the challenge by raising his son, Tre, as only a man can, and since Furious is the only father, absent or present in the film, as only he can.

To Singleton's credit, the audience is not bombarded with heavy, and naively simplistic, good/bad moralism. Doughboy's abjection is not represented as bad in that he is not good, but Doughboy is an anti-hero, conscious of his abjection, knowing his environment and mastering it. As the rejected son and the ex-con, Doughboy creates his own community of men in which he is the leader and protector. On the fringes of black masculinity, beyond recovery, Doughboy defines black masculinity and, while avenging his brother's murder, redeems black masculinity.

At the core of the representation of masculine difference and the reconstruction and reclamation of black masculinity is the representation of women and the family, and family values. The singular father image of Furious is projected against that of three images of the mother: Ms Baker, the crack mother and Reva, Furious' ex-wife. While Furious is the instructive, politically aware, community-based entrepreneur, Ms Baker, Ricky and Doughboy's mother, is a single mother with no narrative means of income. Doughboy as the abject is the product of a female-headed, single-parent household. In contrast to Furious, who provides parental guidance and Afrocentric encouragements of self-determination, Ms Baker favors Ricky over Doughboy, giving some guidance and encouragement to Ricky and nothing but verbal abuse to Doughboy. The only other neighborhood mother whom we see is the crack mother across the street. This is the mother who allows her young child to wander, unattended, into traffic. This is the mother who offers fellatio to buy crack.

Reva, Tre's mother, who gives her son up to Furious because she feels she is unable to raise her man child, is depicted later in the film, surrounded by the professional, single-woman opulence of her plush apartment, as upwardly mobile and meddling, opportunistic in her request for Tre to return to her parental custody. In the café scene between Furious and Reva, what would otherwise be a pro-feminist stance is rendered feminist backlash as Reva asserts that by raising his son, Furious has done nothing special, has done nothing that black mothers have not been doing for years. This comes only after Reva has shown that she cannot raise Tre herself, nor can any other woman in the film rear a son.

These images of black mothers would not be so damning if they were not so pervasive. These three images are very calculated and positioned in a masculine coming of age narrative, in a community of men, in opposition to the only father in the film. This community of men is in struggle for salvation and survival. Consequently, Furious, as the father, is a messianic figure, bearing salvation, bringing control and order back to the community. With Tre as the son and protagonist growing up in the mire of South Central Los Angeles, the salvation of the community is through the resurrection and preservation of this masculinity. Again, as in *House Party*, there is the instructional representation of the role model. In the case of *Boyz*, Tre is posited as the role model because he has a role model: his father, Furious Styles. As a consequence, Tre is invested with the future of the filmic community.

In 1991 there were some nineteen films by black directors scheduled for release. By the end of 1991, at least twelve of these films were released with the backing of big Hollywood studios.[19] Clearly these films were popular and profitable, but the content and subject matter of these films – black people, black people's lives and cultural space and identity – were seemingly in contrast to

Hollywood's racial traditions. In terms of popular trends, New Black Cinema was preceded by rap and hip-hop music, the popular image of the "endangered black man" and the sociological interest in drugs, crime and the inner city, all of which are portrayed by the media as a black dilemma.[20] The strategy of New Black Cinema was to recode the existing codings of blackness, informing the symbolic with the social and cultural sensibilities of black culture, Afrocentrism, and the everyday experiences of black people.

On the one hand, the issues of blackness, nationalism, and masculinity present in these early New Black Cinema films, in my reading, raise critical questions about the representations themselves; on the other hand, as Guerrero notes, these filmmakers in their mainstream, independent, and insurgent forms and tendencies expose and negotiate discriminatory practices in Hollywood (around marketing, promotion, and development of "black-themed" films) and, in doing so, engage and often explicitly provide a reading, a hermeneutic investigation, of American culture: as problematic as *School Daze*, *House Party*, and *Boyz N the Hood* are, they do present blackness and black masculinity as a site of interpretation, critique, and ethical engagement, as ongoing projects and cultural formations.[21]

In the New Black Cinema films examined above, race as a discourse, especially as popular American discourse, functions in models of exceptionalism, talent and virtuosity, as these models are deployed for racial, social, and political uplift (not surprisingly, most of these films are often described as masculine narratives). Furthermore, the use of blackness is critical of the invisibility of whiteness as an organizing trope and discourse. In other words, the emphasis on blackness as a constructed visual representation, as generic and hermeneutic devices, directs viewers to the use of race, notions of black and white as organizing narrative and visual elements. This New Black Cinema moment is an example of the early self-positions in Cornel West's new cultural politics of difference, and exclusive "talented tenth" grouping, a grouping which opened market and audience doors. Yet, there has been a marked shift; the issues and questions of racial representation have markedly changed. One can, on the one hand, argue that New Black Cinema has integrated and been assimilated into the American film machine (older filmmakers who have benefited include Michael Schultz and Bill Duke, and, more recently, Forrest Whittiker); on the other hand, black filmmakers are now the interpreters of whiteness. By this I mean that black cinema has, through the efforts of New Black Cinema, developed a market and audience, which reflect not only its success as a popular form, but also its critical interrogations and interpretations of blackness and race. This latter aspect of black cinema as critical interrogation and interpretation is where New Black Cinema has shifted in emphasis.

Let me clarify: two high-profile national and media incidents reframed the discursivity of black masculinity in the 1990s: the Rodney King beating, the Simi Valley jury's acquittal of the police officers responsible and the subsequent protests and riots (1992); and the O.J. Simpson verdict (1995). With the

Rodney King beating, verdict and riot, black masculinity is reiterated in notions of aggression, submission, and criminality, and simultaneously repositioned within notions of collective and historical victimhood and denied and delayed state justice. The black masculine is violently removed from a liberal discourse of race pathology and re-inscribed in a Foucaultian notion of the state. The simultaneity of iteration and inscription, on the one hand, serves to universalize the black man as victim (in that the Rodney King beating is an incident of state control, of which everyone is a victim); on the other hand, the simultaneity of iteration and inscription serves to particularize the state's relationship to the black body (in that the black male body is the demonstrative body).

In the O.J. Simpson case, there is a greater sense of cultural betrayal. As an actor and entrepreneur, Simpson was an exemplar of the democratic ethos of celebrity; a model of the athletic masculine ideal; and an exemplar of integration and racial harmony. However, the trial for the murder of Nicole Brown Simpson and Ronald Goldman re-blackened, so to speak, his celebrity and masculinity: the black man is re-criminalized as the brute, the rapist, and the threat to white femininity and civility. With his acquittal, O.J. Simpson became a figure of "black" justice (especially in light of the initial Rodney King verdict); at the same time, he became a figure of liberal white injustice. By this I mean that Simpson valorized the American justice system of fair trial, while he vilified the American dream and the American ideal of integration.

The question becomes, what is the impact of these ambiguous, discursive black masculinities in the realm of representation, mass media and entertainment? These two figures, Rodney King and O.J. Simpson – the quotidian and the celebrity, the everyday and the iconic – become a split image fused in the cultural imaginary as the limit and horizon of the representation of black masculinity.[22] It is the horizon of the representation of black masculinity because it is ambiguous, rendering the representation of black masculinity as inassimilable to stereotype and stereotypic representation; the split image is the limit of the representation of black masculinity because in its ambiguity the split image reveals the disavowed contradictions of American class and racial ideals, a productive and profitable disavowal, indeed the disavowal of entertainment itself.

The mediations of this split image have been subtle, partially through the co-optation and absorption of black-themed narratives and characters into popular culture as economically viable entertainment (films and especially hip-hop inflected films which use rap artists as actors) and partially through the movement of black filmmakers into more mainstream projects.[23] In the post-Rodney King/Simpson verdict era, the standardized hood film, unable to engage the conflicts and contradictions of the 1990s black masculine, fell into redundancy similar to Blaxploitation. At the same time, there were "applications" similar to those of Blaxploitation (the application of blackness to standard, tried and true narratives) in films like *Tales from the Hood* (1995) and *Vampire in Brooklyn* (1995), exploring race and horror. However, films that confronted race more historically, critically and confrontationally in the established masculine narrative mode of New Black Cinema failed at the box office.[24]

In partial recognition of the shifting significations of race and masculinity, Guerrero notes that the racial climate and popular audience mood immediately following the O.J. Simpson verdict contributed to the box office failure of two films; specifically, *Devil in a Blue Dress* (1995) and *Strange Days* (1995).[25] It is my contention that, yes, on that October weekend in 1995, the majority American audience was unwilling to confront a film like *Devil* or *Strange Days* because of their emphasis on race, but also I contend that black cinema, in its New Black Cinema permutation, can no longer support the masculine narratives of a film like *Devil* because of the conflicting split imagery of media black masculinity. In other words, the prototypical, recuperative images of black men in the early films of New Black Cinema are no longer viable representations because of their uncomplicated, simplistically redemptive discursivity.

Two things have happened. First, New Black Cinema has succeeded in changing the face of American cinema in that black-themed films, black male characters, and black male stars have multiplied and done so with economic and industrial success.[26] The aesthetic emphasis of these films has been on the representation and interpretation of filmic and pop cultural images of blackness as these images have been deployed to the service of representing whiteness as the norm, as normativity. Second, in the expansion of market and audience, there are greater demands on the black film. With the ambiguity of the black male and the black male narrative, there is necessarily a change in subject matter, different themes of racialized subject formations, different thematic contexts for the black male. This has entailed a move away from the masculine, urban-centered narrative of the initial outpouring of New Black Cinema[27] to the decidedly post-New Black Cinema focus on family (both urban and rural), the black middle class, and female-centered narrative, and to the post-New Black Cinema shift in the signifying practices of race and black cinema. With the second significatory component, I mean to suggest that blackness is inscribed in recent films in a more aesthetic manner as a way of looking, as a way of being, as opposed to the black character or *mise-en-scène* of blackness determining and defining the films of New Black Cinema. In the first instance and the broadening of narratives, I refer to films like *Soul Food*, *Down in the Delta*, *Eve's Bayou*, *Friday*, *The Brothers*, *Kingdom Come*, *Set It Off*, and *Waiting to Exhale*, to name a few. In the second instance, I refer to films like *Summer of Sam* and the more recent *From Hell* in which blackness is rendered as a transgeneric hermeneutic device which provides an interpretation of whiteness in narratives about white men.

Notes

1 Michael Omi, "In Living Color: Race and American Culture," *Cultural Politics in Contemporary America*, eds Ian Angus and Sut Jhally (New York: Routledge, 1989), p. 114.
2 New Black Cinema refers to a period of black cinema, roughly between 1985 and 1995. This periodization follows Tommy Lott's demarcation of black cinema. See Tommy Lott, "A No-Theory Theory of Contemporary Black Cinema," *Black Literature Forum* (currently *African American Review*) 25.2 (Summer 1991): pp. 221–36.
3 James Snead, "Recoding Blackness: The Visual Rhetoric of Black Independent Film," *Whitney Museum of American Art: The New American Filmmakers Series*, Program 23, pp. 1–2.
4 These films include *Do the Right Thing, House Party, Def by Temptation, Juice, A Rage in Harlem, New Jack City, Five Heartbeats, Boyz N the Hood, Jungle Fever, Mo' Better Blues, Chameleon Street, School Daze, Straight Outta Brooklyn,* and *Harlem Nights.*
5 For example, see the three images, and their differences, among Nola Darling's suitors in Spike Lee's *She's Gotta Have It.*
6 Spike Lee, *Uplift the Race: The Construction of School Daze* (New York: Simon & Schuster, 1988), p. 179.
7 Toni Cade Bambara, "Programming with *School Daze*," *Five by Five: The Films of Spike Lee*, ed. Shirley L. Poole (New York: Stewart, Tabori & Chang, Inc., 1991), p. 49.
8 Dyer defines the utopian sensibilities as follows: energy, the capacity to act vigorously; human power, activity, potential (e.g. dance); abundance, the conquest of scarcity; having enough to spare without sense of poverty of other; enjoyment of sensuous material reality (e.g. spectacle); intensity, experiencing of emotion directly, fully, unambiguously, "authentically" without holding back (e.g. "incandescent" star performers); transparence, a quality of relationships – between represented characters, between performer and audience (e.g. sincere stars; love and romance); and community, togetherness, sense of belonging, network of phatic relationships (e.g. singalong chorus numbers). See Richard Dyer, "Entertainment and Utopia," in *Genre: The Musical*, ed. Rick Altman (London: Routledge and Kegan Paul, 1981), pp. 175–89.
9 George Mosse, *Nationalism and Sexuality: Middle-Class Morality and Sexual Norms in Modern Europe* (Madison, WI: Wisconsin University Press, 1985).
10 Here I am referring to Mulvey's "Visual Pleasure and Narrative Cinema." However, I will not attempt to engage in questions of spectatorship. At this point, I am interested in Lee's structuring of the male gaze. See Laura Mulvey, *Visual and Other Pleasures* (Bloomington, IN: Indiana University Press, 1989).
11 Reginald Hudlin interviewed in Marlaine Glicksman, "They Gotta Have It," *Film Comment* (May–June 1990), pp. 65–9.
12 Lisa Kennedy, "Wack House," *Village Voice* (March 13, 1990), p. 65.
13 Warrington Hudlin argues that this scene is anti-rape (*versus* anti-gay): "The point is the guy is in danger of being raped. We're not taking a position on homosexuality, we're taking a position on sex against someone's will." However, the confinement of the anti-rape discourse to a homosocial space of the prison cell directs the viewer not only to the potential of rape but also to rape as forced homosexuality; see Glicksman, "They Gotta Have It."
14 See Kennedy's reading of Bilial.
15 John Singleton interviewed in Thomas Doherty and Jaquie Jones, "Two Takes on *Boyz N the Hood*," *Cineaste* 18.4 (1991), pp. 16–19.

16 Jackie Bayars, *All That Heaven Allows: Re-Reading Gender in the 1950s Melodrama* (Chapel Hill, NC: The University of North Carolina Press, 1990), p. 8.

17 Bayars, pp. 217–26.

18 Jonathan Rutherford, "Who's That Man?" *Male Order: Unwrapping Masculinity*, eds Rowena Chapman and Jonathan Rutherford (London: Lawrence & Wishart, 1988), pp. 21–67.

19 Patrick Cole, "Cinema Revolution," *Emerge* (January 1992), pp. 36–40.

20 Jacqui Jones, "The New Ghetto Aesthetic," *Wide Angle* 13.3–4 (1991), pp. 32–43.

21 Ed Guerrero, "A Circus of Dreams and Lies: The Black Film Wave at Middle Age," *The New American Cinema*, ed. Jon Lewis (Durham, NC: Duke University Press, 1998), pp. 328–52.

22 Here I am using Judith Mayne's notion of the limit and horizon. See Judith Mayne, "A Parallax View of Lesbian Authorship," *Inside/Out*, ed. Daina Fuss (New York: Routledge, 1991), pp. 173–84.

23 For more discussion of this see Guerrero, "Circus of Dreams and Lies."

24 Films like *Panther* (Mario Van Peebles 1995); *Dead Presidents* (The Hughes Brothers 1995); *Clockers* (Spike Lee 1995); and *Devil in a Blue Dress* (Carl Franklin 1995), for example.

25 Guerrero, "Circus of Dreams and Lies," p. 349.

26 This is most apparent in the increased and increasing number of black male stars and celebrities: Denzel Washington, Will Smith, Eddie Murphy, Ice-T, Ice Cube, Samuel Jackson, Laurence Fishbourne, Roger Guenevere Smith, Savion Glover, Cedric the Entertainer, Bernie Mac, Steve Harvey, Chris Rock, Chris Tucker, Jamie Foxx, to name a few. And also the expansion of the role of the thug or the gangsta to that of the anti-hero in American film, for example Ice Cube's character in *Escape from Mars* (John Carpenter 2001) or *XXX: State of the Union* (Lee Tamohori 2005) and Snoop Doggy Dogg's character in *Bones* (Ernest Dickerson 2001).

27 Indeed, one can examine John Singleton's return to the hood film, a genre and black male narrative which he, arguably, formalized, and the closure of that genre and narrative in *Baby Boy* (2001). In this film Singleton rewrites the ambiguous and abject figure of the gangsta, Doughboy (Ice Cube) from *Boyz N the Hood* (1991), as threat, menace and impossibility in the imagined black community, through the annihilation of the gangsta character Rodney (Snoop Dogg) in the protection of family and class and economic mobility. The archetypal gangsta character, which functioned as the consciousness of the black community in so many hood films, is no longer viable and, instead, replaced by the conscientious, jobless, yet upwardly mobile, "baby boy" (Jody as portrayed by Tyrese Gibson), a figure of mockery and revision.

Part 11

Anthropomorphism

Chapter 4

Star Wars episodes I–VI

Coyote and the force of white narrative

Gabriel S. Estrada (Nahuatl)

Previous scholarship confirms that *Star Wars* creator George Lucas avoids overt white racism. For Richard Dyer, whiteness covertly slips in and out of racist sexualities throughout Lucas' first *Star Wars* trilogy. For example, Dyer notes Princess Leia's stereotypical "pure white Victorian womanhood" pitted against Darth Vader's evil "black" presence, as well as the heroic prominence of black character Lando Calrissian.[1] Kenny's post-*Star Wars Episode I* anthology (2002) offers a more biting multicultural, sexual, and class commentary on Lucas' series. Its contents also focus heavily on the well-established black–white racial tension that Dyer begins to describe. However, its publication prior to the last two episodes and limited cultural perspectives create space for this further analysis into the tricky nature of *Star Wars* whiteness.[2]

George Lucas' anti-classist, anti-sexist, and anti-racist representations predictably fade throughout the *Star Wars* series. As he gains production power and money, he abandons the working-class male heroes of *Episodes IV–VI* and creates a prequel trilogy *I–III* starring elite heroes. In both trilogies, however, the main white woman protagonist is always a member of an elite who must fight off male desire. *Star Wars* cyclically chronicles the decline of white women's power as white men rise to defend them from dark male sexual threats, especially those of tribal origins. Of course, tribal cultures have more to offer science fiction film than stereotypes. This essay reflects the indigenous traditions of Coyote in order to explain *Star Wars* whiteness. As fool, mixed-breed, and exploiter, Coyote wreaks havoc with any consistent visions of cultural equality throughout the *Star Wars* series.

The Force and Coyote philosophies

Indigenous Coyote stories mostly argue against seeing a cosmos of good and bad forces as Lucas often does. Ironically, traditional Coyote and Warrior stories first inspired Lucas guru Joseph Campbell to write about universal/archetypal characters such as "the trickster" or "the hero." Campbell lauded Lucas' work as a modern myth of heroism.[3] In an historical context of Christian colonization, anti-Chinese immigration laws, and religious wars, Lucas does expand a popular audience's sense of humanistic spirituality as he mixes Chinese Taoist monks, Japanese samurai, and Judeo-Christian saviors in order to create the Jedi. He explicitly depicts spiritual Jedi warriors of various species, races and genders in order to show the nonracist nature of virtue. However, while Campbell was clear that no culture lacked archetypes, heroes are sometimes scarce among the non-white, working-class, and female characters that Lucas creates. In seeking to nail down the absolute truths of democracy and humanism, Lucas inserts his own white male identity as the deliverer of absolute truth. Elite white males end up protecting truth when a diversity of others fails one by one. Pure truth is a problematic idea in many primal traditions that emphasize balance over purity. For Lucas, as for many Western philosophers, one truth must be superior to the opposite truth as in the case of light/dark, male/female, good/bad etc.[4] The Force misses out on Yin–Yang balance as it pursues moral hierarchy. Both good and bad sides dress in their respective light or dark colors as a reminder that the *Star Wars* ethical galaxy is mostly "a black and white" one with "very few shades of gray, much less of brighter, more interesting moral colors."[5] While traditional coyote stories do not follow racial or moral absolutes, Lucas does because of colonially rooted patterns of whiteness. According to bell hooks and Edward Said, Western colonization mandates a cinematic portrayal of pure whiteness as a sign of absolute morality, intelligence, and power. This is meant to justify the historical and continued oppression of "inferior" non-whites.[6] White is the good that must oppose darkness as a racial sign in neocolonial films. Instead of teaching social equality, Western states use the cinematic apparatus to seal racial borders.

The good/light opposition with evil/dark is symbolically clear in the finale of *Star Wars Episode III: Revenge of the Sith* (2005) in which Obi-Wan confronts Darth Vader over Padme's suffocated body. From the view of Darth Vader's offensive position, Obi-Wan stares back dressed in a light tunic. Below his waistline rage orange volcanic eruptions from the open veins of the planet Mustafar. The flames represent the hells of pelvic passion that animate Anakin's new life of treachery, fatherhood, and mass murder. Padme lies near death, out of sight at Obi-Wan's feet where Anakin has strangled and released her. The digitally produced amber rays stain his garments and light beard with hellish highlights and cast shadows about his blue eyes. Digitally animated flames threaten to devour both Jedis. Above Obi-Wan's shoulder, and symbolic masculine side, a bright white star shines through the darkness of sooty clouds, the light of Western Truth. The weakness of the white starlight indicates that Obi-Wan is but one of two remaining Jedi who constitute a greatly weakened force for the Light Side while the placement of a gleaming heaven above a smoldering hell cements the moral "high ground" that Obi-Wan will defend with his light saber. The light gleams from heaven with promises of redemption just as light shines from heaven into the hellish realms of sinners in the Catholic *ex-votos* and *retablos* of colonial Latin America and medieval Europe. The Jedi stands like a saint whose message of white light will ultimately redeem

Anakin who only rejoins the Light Side after killing the Emperor in *Return of the Jedi*. However, the young Sith must first burn in the fires of hell that await him in the image. Even when Obi-Wan amputates Darth Vader's legs and arm and leaves him to burn by a lava flow, he has compassion for the good he tried to nurture within Anakin. "I hate you!" screams a burning Anakin. "I loved you" softly returns his regretful teacher. Obi-Wan's intention to defend the pure Light Side burns like the star behind him, even through the sooty layers of the Mustafar sky that represents Anakin's dark hate and confusion. Obi-Wan's image marks the pinnacle of the six-part series plot and clearly dramatizes both the internal and external fight of pure elements, the good Light Side and evil Dark Side of the Force.

The haloed Obi-Wan is supposed to represent the exoneration of white male oppressors through a protection of compassion and democracy rather than the pursuit of women and greedy elitism. However, the notion that women and oppressed peoples could speak and empower themselves is a message that Lucas ultimately undermines. In the image, Padme's white female body lies limp as the light-bearded blue-eyed Jedi stands alone against Vader. In fact, her body rests just below the right knee level of the Jedi showing that she is literally out of the picture in terms of resistance. It is fitting that Padme's body should grace the earth, for it is the organic human that Padme embodies as her husband makes the opposite thrust towards unnatural cyborg power. Anakin seizes dark power in order to protect Padme from a death in childbirth he foresees in dreams. His desire to control her fate is his downfall. Dyer's pronouncement "empire; the white female soul is associated with its demise" helps to explain Padme's role.[7] In a sense, this last frame captures her place in the demise of two empires. First, she unwittingly motivates the downfall of the Republic she loves through a series of political maneuvers and a marriage with Darth Vader. Second, her pregnancy with the twins Luke and Leia foretells the downfall of the evil Empire she despises. Padme is the female body that elicits the passion to move plots. Her body moves Anakin to the Dark Side in a way that no man can. Like Eve before her, Padme is an unwitting love temptress who plays into the downfall of Man. Her final *Sith* scenes attempt to exonerate her from any desire as she regains her virginal glow and gives birth in a pure white hospital gown. At the same time, Darth Vader becomes encased in his famous black armor and respiration suit that keeps him artificially alive. His dark desire for her pure love resonates with early and classic Hollywood images in which the empowered dark male desires the passive white female, especially those of middle and upper classes.[8] Unfortunately, Padme is the good white woman who must die rather than succumb to Anakin's "dark" sexual libido with its racist overtones.

As hooks and Said would predict, Obi-Wan's defense of Padme resonates with the overtly racist *Birth of a Nation* to which American audiences also flocked to see in record numbers, from 1915 to 1937. Both films hinge on images of good white morality versus dark sadistic sexuality.[9] D.W. Griffith's plot unabashedly supported the Ku Klux Klan's lynchings by purporting that they prevented black men from raping white women and destroying white civil freedoms. *Star Wars* also links goodness, godliness, superiority, and purity as natural descriptors of whiteness while sexually demonizing "dark" men. As a dark Sith, Anakin strangles his pregnant wife Padme when she rejects Darth's murderous ways and appears to harbor Obi-Wan who had secretly stowed away on her ship to the fiery planet of Mustafar. Obi-Wan prevents Vader from killing Padme on the spot, but he is too late to save her from a broken heart that drains the life from her. Padme lies passed out as the two prepare to battle with light sabers. As protector of the Light Side, Obi-Wan cuts off the "dark" Sith Anakin's arm and legs in the ensuing fight thereby castrating the young Darth Vader's sexual power. Anakin is then literally transplanted into a black cyborg body making his transformation into a "dark" man complete. Lucas even casts black actor James Earl Jones as the voice of Darth Vader, a subliminal message that behind Vader's black outfit is a black virile man. The black actor's resonant voice is used only so long as Darth Vader is evil.[10] Unfortunately, racial stereotypes widely impact science fiction and fantasy plots as white male heroes are pitted against a "Dark Lord" in the box office hits *Harry Potter*, *Lord of the Rings*, and *Star Wars*.[11]

Not only does *Sith* exclude women and non-whites from key heroic roles, it excludes the majority of whites who are not elites, further limiting those who can represent glowing white goodness in the *Star Wars* universe. While *Sith* does return with the strongest anti-Empire whiteness since the original trilogy, it does so in a classist way. With his elite English Lord accent, Obi-Wan resonates with a class elitism that was not so evident in the original trilogy. The first *Star Wars* trilogy sides with young working-class and anti-Imperial characters while demonizing the older elite who run the Empire. For example, Han Solo's working-class vernacular "ain't" defines his leading man character. As a smuggler who successfully fights the Empire, Han invites sympathy for working-class whites whose "illegal dealings" hurt far less peoples than Empire wars do. As a white space cowboy complete with a low-hanging leather holster and gun, Han Solo evokes the images of John Ford's Westerns that sympathized with the ethnic white cowboy on the marginal frontlines of war, "refugees from constricting societies."[12] The original *Star Wars* trilogy invites youthful rebellion against an older, richer, and repressive US empire. It echoes anti-Vietnam sentiment fermenting in the late sixties and early seventies. Sixteen years later, multimedia empire mogul Lucas created prequel galaxies featuring a white elitism he once resisted in the first three films. As Lucas' prequels teach the futility of resisting Empire, sympathy for the common white person disappears. Instead, well-established royalty and elite Jedi hold central prequel roles. The Jedi knight's lone white figure prevents working-class whites from symbolizing pure virtue as well.

Coyote stories don't segregate characters in color-coded shades of good and evil as Obi-Wan's image seems to do. Like color symbolism, Coyote stories derive from their local origins in wildly varying varieties, even within California. For example, one Maidu story of Old Man Coyote explains how Coyote carries off beautiful women from a dance and has sex with them, only to find that each one turns into his wife, Frog Old Woman. "He threw her down in a dark place / and stuck it into her" the story goes as Coyote experiences much sexual frustration in badly executed attempts at unfaithful copulations.[13] L. Frank Manriquez (Tongva/Ajachmem) muses that Coyote reminds her that "it doesn't do to take ourselves too seriously"[14] as many choices of the heart can end up in chaos. Without judgement, she recounts Coyote who stole the heart of his own dead father at a funeral. Coyote was beaten by others with fire sticks which left his fur messy and charred. Manriquez does not label Coyote as evil for he was simply fulfilling his heart's desire without regard for the larger group. Making foolish mistakes is part of the learning process humans share with coyotes. Coyotes, like people, also tend to get burned for their foolishness. In many ways, Anakin and Manriquez's Coyote are similar. Both get literally and symbolically burned as a result of community punishments after they seek to fulfill selfish desires at the community's expense. While Coyote retains his charred fur, a burnt Darth Vader retains his iron lung suit: a reminder of past infractions. Were it not for Anakin's professed devotion to evil, Anakin's chaotic desires could be read as a kind of Coyote story. His story deviates by pursuing a need for redemption. Manriquez's Coyote simply lives on to commit more foolishness as many kids do, quite apart from Christian ideals of self-righteousness. Thanks to indigenous coyotes' passionate antics, there are no absolute laws of static good and evil such as those that rule the Jedi and Sith.[15] Unlike the *Star Wars* plot of good versus evil, indigenous narratives often relate a cosmos which honors both chaos and order with truths that are seasonal, locational, or merely evolving through changing stories.

Because a Coyote-like abandon for desire and sexual libido is not within the controlled *Star Wars* universe of white masculine sexuality, the homoerotic tension that surrounds the evil Emperor can only represent the ultimate betrayal of homoerotic molestation. Obi-Wan's glowing father-like mentorship of Anakin captured in the image is meant to be a direct contrast to the evil Emperor's homoerotic seduction which is shrouded in shadow. Throughout the series, the Emperor "seduces" young white males as he lures them into the Dark Side. When he confronts Luke in *Episode VI*, he arches back his head with eyes closed as he hisses "Goooooooood! I can feel your anger!" in a clear attempt to arouse Luke's dormant passions. The Emperor basks in Luke's passionate feeling in an odd moment of sensual empathy that is completely wrapped in narratives of dark betrayal and subliminal homosexual predation. He delights in the prospect that another man will attempt to penetrate his body with a phallic light saber as he dares Luke to "Strike me down . . . !" This Sith prefers to operate behind the vaginal folds of his hood, behind the light sabers of other men who defend him as if he was damsel in distress. He is the antithesis of Obi-Wan who always honorably announces his intentions to fight, as pictured in the image. Beneath all of the Emperor's rage for power is a deep need to feel emotional connection with other men that he ultimately expresses through male domination and castration. The homoerotic S/M implications of Darth Vader's unquestioning service to his "Master" should not be underestimated. The Emperor's penchant for corrupting young boys is reminiscent of the black-robed Catholic priests who molested young boys while also pretending to serve society's best interests. For hinted homosexual infractions, the Emperor dies most horribly – as did more than 80 percent of gays and lesbians in Hollywood films between 1934 and 1970, due to homophobic censorship[16] backed by Catholic censorship.[17] Homosexuality is a force too chaotic to survive within Lucas' world of dual oppositions, so it, too, must be relegated into the deep folds of darkness that symbolize anal, oral, and vaginal sites of pleasure. These are exactly the sites that Coyote stories openly engage quite humorously and often for an audience of adults and children alike. As a heterosexist white male, Lucas is not so open. It is into the central deep hole of the Death Star that the Emperor must fall to his death, consumed by his own dark feminine space. For Lucas, sex is much more frightening than violence. The only depicted sexual union is marred by Padme's strangled body at Obi-Wan's feet. The thought of males pleasuring males is one that Lucas can only attack through the hinted sexual predation of the Sith Lord. The more repressed pansexual Coyote desires become, the more violently men war.

Lucas plays the Coyote fool by advancing the very cyborg digital technology that creates Obi-Wan's warrior figure meshed with a fantasy fiery background. Ironically, both Donna Haraway and Lucas share an ecological condemnation of human greed fed by cyborg empires and defense systems. Haraway rejected the Cold War technologies of Reagan's "Star Wars" missiles as Lucas protested Reagan's use of the "Star Wars" name for anti-nuclear technology in the eighties. However, Haraway argues that Lucas' reliance on visual technology, marketing, and individual male heroes is out of line with the more resistant "Coyote" nature she envisions.[18] She writes:

> The specific historical markings of a Star Wars-maintained individuality are enabled by high-technology visualization technologies, which are also basic to conducting war and commerce, such as computer-aided graphics, artificial intelligence software, and specialized scanning systems . . . military culture . . . draw[s] directly from and contribute[s] to video game practices and science fiction.[19]

For her, all sciences and media are fictions that feed off each other. Too often, these fictions draw upon capitalist patriarchal racism to achieve elite goals. In mass marketing light saber confrontations and war games to kids, Lucas envisioned the supremacy of capitalist white male aggression that convinced President Reagan to market the Strategic Defense Initiative missiles as "Star Wars" to the masses. Millions of kids have replicated in play the confrontation between Darth Vader and Obi-Wan and, in doing so, accepted that war and weapons are the only real political options in an ethically "black and white" world. Haraway is but one of many critics who believe that Lucas ushered in a more conservative age in the early eighties with his emphasis on laser warfare.[20] In this instance, Lucas became Coyote, a bumbling victim of his own selfish drive for success as his series came to name the very military greed that he sought to condemn.[21]

Through Obi-Wan's condemnation of Darth Vader, Lucas attacks white male aggression as being foolishly Coyote prone. His confrontation dialog sent waves through media. At *Sith*'s debut in an anti-US/Iraq War France, Cannes critics were quick to draw parallels between Darth Vader and President George W. Bush as elite leaders of oppressive empires. Anakin's "If you're not with me, then you're my enemy!" paralleled Bush's post-9/11 war ultimatum to international audiences, "Either you are with us, or you are with the terrorists."[22] In the frame taken immediately after this ultimatum, Obi-Wan's face mirrors Lucas' shock at American empire wars in Iraq and Vietnam. Lucas' rejection of Bush's war was a warning that has already proved prescient since Iraq has plummeted into political chaos and US voters have expressed their dissatisfaction with costly Republican war. Obi-Wan soberly replies "Only a Sith deals in terms of absolutes," a condemnation of greedy white male leadership. While Lucas does not consistently allow for non-white, female, and working-class agency, he begins to see white male elites as the coyotes they often are. Only the fire and brimstone judgment that the Mustafar hell conjures overshoots a more simple admission that elite white males can be less abusive by sharing power with the diverse groups they formally oppressed. No more lone white male saviors like Obi-Wan are needed in that scenario.

Filmmakers such as George Lucas always risk playing the Coyote when their desire for public acceptance gets mixed critical reviews. Robert Warrior (Osage), like L. Frank, does not support the good versus evil universe George Lucas provides and offers a complicated reading of the film. When Warrior compares the excitement of seeing *Star Wars* with that of viewing the Coeur d'Alene Indian coming of age story, *Smoke Signals*, he does so without pitting Indians against whites as envisioned so often in American Westerns. Instead, he relates an Indian audience viewing Indians on screen.

> In the summer of 1998, I sat in a Tempe, Arizona, movie theater packed with several hundred people from the Native American Journalists Association's annual meeting for a sneak preview of Chris Eyre's breakthrough film *Smoke Signals* . . . The young people I saw at the film with were enthralled, seeing reasonable facsimiles of themselves and their lives on the big screen – most of them, for the first time . . . I remember thinking that it was like they were watching *Star Wars* . . . But rather than special effects and a galaxy far far away, what those young people in Tempe and thousands of filmgoers that summer saw was pretty much new to

them: American Indian actors playing American Indian characters, saying words written by American Indian screenwriters, and following direction from an American Indian director.[23]

Warrior reports that a new combination of Native American writing, acting, directing, and movie watching is a thrill related to the thrill of seeing *Star Wars* special effects. Without obvious moral condemnation of *Star Wars* racial exclusion, he shows a clear support of greater Native American representation in film production. In fact, given larger budgets, Native American filmmakers of the future may adopt some of Lucas' visual effects to heal their respective nations and remake their own images.

Coyote miscegenations and white masculinity as Oedipal complex

Given popular culture's equation of white with good, the mixing of white and nonwhite sends a mixed moral message that Lucas avoids. Fueled by miscegenation fears, *Star Wars* focuses on the protection of white lives and loves through white male agency. In fact, segregation still secures a film's potential box office draw from racist and colonized audiences. Lucas did not cast blaxploitation star Glynn Turman as Han Solo for fear of creating an interracial couple with white actress Carrie Fisher. "I didn't want to make *Guess Who's Coming to Dinner?* at this point, so I sort of backed off," Lucas admitted about that particular casting choice.[24] Because only whites can love and win key confrontations, their deaths mean more. Only white protagonist lovers elicit John Williams' swelling digitized scores that explode with the aid of Lucasworks THX systems. The *Sith* orchestral score crescendos as Padme dies and Anakin is melded to his black cyber-body. While supportive black characters Mace Windu and Lando Calrissian lead anti-Sith military to make key gains, they fall short when actually facing the Sith in face-to-face combat. Black characters certainly never date. In a related way, Lucas also shuns the mixed-race realities of Hispanic colonial life that found new uses for the Spanish term *coyote*. During Spanish colonization, *el coyote* represented the "thieving" offspring of a "pure" Indian and "mixed" Mestizo who fell below the ranks of "purely" white Spaniards yet above "full-blooded" Indians and Africans in a racial scale of *castas* or castes. Carmen Tafolla notes that *Star Wars'* lack of Latina/o characters demonstrates how being racially mixed can still lead to cinematic exclusion.[25] Lucas' horror of Mestizo miscegenation guides much of his casting and plot development. Even in the southwestern setting of *Tatooine* Mestizos are absent, a shock since, previous to 1848, the Southwest was recognized as Mexican. The lack of Spanish named characters in *Star Wars* points to a rejection of *coyote*-type mixing common in Latin America. *Arturito*, *Cipitrio*, and *Chuy Baca* are Latino names absent from the series. Instead, R2D2, C3PO and Chewbacca are Anglicized names that indicate a system of racial purity in contrast to the mixed race realities that openly typify Latinos. Through Anglo names and characters, Lucas avoids the reality of *el coyote*-type *castas* that still impact American race relations across borders.[26] He also fails to dramatize how whiteness attains purity by segregating mixed-blooded offspring from the "pure" whites who father them. Spanish Catholic priests often fathered children with African and Indian converts even though they, like the Jedi spiritual warriors, were supposed to be celibate. Afro-Asian-Indian-European racial permutations were supposed to serve "pure" whites in US and Latin American histories, although most subverted the racist plan through interracial class alliances. What *Star Wars* representations belie is that those once termed *coyotes*, *mestizos* or *mulattos* have occupied political and demographic leadership across the Americas despite ongoing racism.[27]

The borders that separate *coyote* and other Indian-black-white-mixed bodies from "purely" white or dark ones amplify the desire to maximize political borders between the USA and Latin America. Perhaps Latino actor Jimmy Smit's role is Lucas' belated recognition of the large political roles that "*coyote*" and "mixed-blooded" peoples play in Latin America and the USA. Even so, limited Latino casting typifies *Star Wars*. Only Puerto Rican/Surinamese Smits momentarily speaks in prequel scenes as Senator Bail Organa. While he is a leading moral critic of the evil Emperor, he is also the only supporting character to never physically defend himself, even when shot at. His weak, effeminate Latino presence symbolizes the rare *Star Wars* fusion of African, European, and Indian bloodlines. When he adopts Leia in the last minutes of *Episode III*, he is pictured with a non-speaking Latina or Asian-looking wife rather than a white one who might raise questions of white–nonwhite racial miscegenation. His planet is the only planet that is completely destroyed by the Death Star, and this complete obliteration resonates with the sense that mixed peoples should not really exist within the realm of *Star Wars*. Even the Sith alien menace may subtly replicate other sci-fi movies that capitalize on the US rhetoric of "anti-alien," "anti-Hispanic" laws by subliminally creating "alien" or "anti-immigrant" phobias in film.[28] The lack of Latinos in *Star Wars* resounds with an absence of English media coverage that exposes the exploitative relations that the USA has secured over many Latin American countries. These are the multinational politics that motivate largely Mestizo migrations across current US borders, often with the help of racially mixed guides who are also called *coyotes*. Through the absence of *coyote*, *mulatto*, and *mestizo* mixed "races," Lucas is slow to overcome a fear of borderlands Latino cultures that permeate the Americas.

The absence of *coyotes* and mixed-bloods is meant to show that true difference really does separate whites and tribal peoples. Underlying the white fear of mixed-blooded peoples is the fear of dark tribal peoples who must be shown as technologically and morally inferior in a hierarchy that is topped by white elite males. In *Return of the Jedi*, Lucas idealizes that difference when the Miwok-based Ewoks overpower Empire clones with only primitive wooden weapons in the historically Miwok Sequoia forests of Northern California, once home to Lucas' cutting-edge Skywalker Ranch, Lucas Films Ltd., THX, Skywalker Sound, and Industrial Light and Magic. Lucas' white male dominance in film technology is meant to contrast with the primitive Ewoks. The Ewok lack of technology, superstitious worship of C3PO, and attempt to roast Han and Luke, play out classic stereotypes of tribal peoples as primitive low-tech inferiors. Lucas' Ewoks play into historical racism against California Indians and Miwoks in particular. Historical California Indian technological differences were unethically used to justify Indian genocide as State and Federal policy, especially after the 1849 Gold Rush. Popular resistance to modern California Indian sovereignty derives in part from K–12 education that depicts Native Californians as restricted to anachronistic basket weaving and acorn pounding, rather than also existing within contemporary technologies. In anthropological lore, California Indian "hunting and gathering" tribes were long seen as culturally inferior to farming tribes of the southwest because the latter more closely resembled European civilizations. Even though the teddy bear Ewoks fight off Empire soldiers and side with the good guys, they are more like the "lovable" loyal sports mascots that so many Native Americans ridicule.[29]

Star Wars Episode II: The Attack of the Clones also pivots on the savage image of tribal peoples who most resemble Apache tribes of the desert southwest, an image that contrasts to that of the Skywalkers who are "civilized" like farming Pueblo Indians. The Sand People "raid" for a living, wear masks, use rifles, and live in tipi-like wikiups; like the Apaches, they popularly represent a "loss of frontier" to "savages."[30] The original *Star Wars* Sand Peoples easily link to Ford's savage Indians who massacre innocent white settlers in *The Searchers* (1956).[31] With undertones of sexual violation and miscegenation, the Sand People stereotypically return to torture and murder Shmi Skywalker. An anti-feminist version of white womanhood appears in the image of a dead Shmi in the arms of her avenging son. The primitive wood and leather torture and/or rape rack stands behind the kneeling Anakin who now drapes his mother in his arms in a reversed *Pieta* pose. The product of immaculate conception holds the crucified mother inside a wikiup-like Sand People shelter made of dark rough hides and bathed in a hellish orange fire. Shmi has been freed from slavery only to die by "savage" torture. It is a pathetic end to a life showing no agency from this lowest-class woman, once a slave. Even her giving birth to Anakin did not really come of her own will as she was impregnated by a Sith through manipulations of Force-producing chloromidians. Shmi's impregnation by a "dark" Sith man without her consent is the root of the evil that Anakin comes to embody as a quasi-mixed-breed child. This racial taint is symbolized by the darkness of the image and the hellish orange light that defines the pair. Shmi's limp body and the bloody scar on her cheek mark her as used and abused territory of the Sand People. Her dried blood denies the power of white women's blood in menstruation and birth as it freezes her in victim mode. White patriarchy ideally envisions white frontier women such as Shmi as tortured, dead, and bloody because it proves the need for white male protection from indigenous savagery. While white men survive and excel when faced with castration, white women die rather than regenerate from sexual assault because Lucas views them as a weaker sex unable to adapt to "savage" violence. It also sends the false message that women will experience more sexism and rape within tribal cultures, a "fact" that is supposed to make the sexism and rape conditions of white culture relatively palatable or even pleasing. Here, Lucas denies white women's abilities to fight back as Leia does so adequately in the original *Star Wars*. Shmi's tortured end on the frontier ties in with the absence of Mexicans in the southwestern setting of Tatooine. Her death prevents the horror of white–Indian and hence eventual *coyote*-type miscegenation as a result of either rape or adoption as a wife and mother by tribal members.

Lucas' fear of mixed-blooded and nonwhite Others is complicated by attempts to bridge racial divides. After Anakin massacres the women, children, and men of the Sand Peoples who captured his mother, he vengefully recounts that he "slaughtered them like animals!" Given a belief in white superiority, white men will naturally be able to best indigenous peoples in battle as Anakin demonstrates in his easy win.[32] However, Anakin reverts to a more "civilized" tone when he later laments, "I'm a Jedi. I know I'm better than this." In this statement, Lucas replicates the stereotype that Apache-like Sand People really are savages, but implies that to resort to the same "savage" tactics of revenge makes the civilized no better. While *Episode II* shows that both technologically advanced Republic and "primitive" tribal cultures can descend to "savagery," the film naturalizes the assumption that semi-nomadic indigenous people are more prone to do savage acts. To equate a white Anakin with the Sand People's murderous Apache-like ways is to erase key historical relations. In white and Indian wars, Native Americans hold a different moral ground from white frontiersmen because they are defending their indigenous homelands, most often with peace treaties already signed that guarantee rights to their aboriginal land. Because Lucas cannot come to terms with white attempts to eradicate and enslave indigenous peoples across the globe, he falls into stereotypes of civilized whites versus savage indigenous peoples.[33] Lucas cannot fully acknowledge whiteness as a form of exploitation, what some indigenous peoples call *coyotl*.

Rather than embrace the *coyote* realities of mixed-race peoples, Lucas fantasizes a morally white-dominated universe in which races are separated by fetishized Oedipal differences. Consider the sequence from *Episode V* that begins after Darth Vader cuts off Luke's hand in a catwalk duel above the metal abyss of the Sky City ship. Darth Vader attempts to convert Luke to the Dark Side by revealing that Luke is his son. Vader affirms, "No, *I* am your father!" as the camera cuts to frame his dark phallic hood and lingers dramatically upon his shadowy head against the checkered metal backdrop of the Sky City. The metallic backdrop emphasizes Vader's inhuman cyborg nature that brings death to the masses. Composer John Williams' powerful score, amplified by Lucas' innovations in sound, create Darth Vader's slow mortuary theme that is reminiscent of a requiem mass.

"No, no. That's not true; that's impossible!" grates Luke with a cut to his contorted face close up. "Search your feelings. You know it to be true," commands Darth Vader. "NOOOOOO! Nooooooo!" Luke screams in agony, hugging a metal cylinder with his only remaining hand. Luke is overwhelmed that the father he trained to avenge is the evil leader who now stands victorious before him. In battling Darth Vader, Luke is also evolving in the Oedipal complex in which a son desires to kill his father in order to sexually possess his mother, the original object of desire. The glowing light sabers represent the phallic power to penetrate, possess, and protect objects of desire. As Luke's light saber and right hand are severed from his body, Luke symbolically loses phallic power at the hands of his father's more powerful red light saber. Lucas himself explains that "impotency is cutting off hands and legs and arms" further linking losing sexual power with losing limbs.[34] Darth Vader castrates his own son, rather than letting Luke's Oedipal impulse to kill his own father to run its course. A son normally grows into desiring sex outside the family incest boundaries. However, after Luke kisses and lusts after his twin sister, Leia, he remains a virgin. Luke cannot find his way out of the Oedipal complex and remains a castrated, sexually confused adolescent forever. Luke's image emphasizes his adolescent response as he desperately clings to the Death Star like a child clings to his mother. His scabby face and messy hair are less reminiscent of a warrior man than of a snotty-nosed injured child who defiantly denies the sexual knowledge that adults "know . . . to be true."

Darth Vader's shiny black leather outfit, mouth grill, and large phallic hood embody Lucas' obsession with the fetishization of the black phallus. The smooth black eye globes relate the inhuman prison of racial terror that surrounds Darth, a terrible Imperial legacy that Luke inherits as his son. Again, James Earl Jones' virile black voice over of Darth Vader adds to the subliminal message that Darth Vader is racially black.[35] Carson comments:

> the fact that Darth Vader turns out to be Luke's father is less important than the way Luke experiences it as a taint . . . part of what makes the whole Dark Father business powerful is the way we register it, subliminally, as a projection of what used to be Western culture's idea of the ultimate sexual horror: miscegenation.[36]

Luke's horror that electrified audiences isn't simply the realization that his father is evil. The horror is a subliminal message that Luke's father is black and wields black phallic power over Luke's white mother and Luke. Lucas explains that Darth Vader derives from "dark father," further cementing this association of blackness in the audience.[37] Vader's evil tendencies spring from a genetic mixing of his dark Sith father with his white slave mother, Shmi. The shock of miscegenation that Luke's blond-haired and blue-eyed face registers and rejects is also a white rejection of Afro–white mixing common among African American and Afro-Latino populations. Vader's phallic appearance as a giant black dildo is compensation for his inability to sexually possess his dead white mother and wife. His black phallic presence sends movie lines around the block for the same reason that "monstrous" black dildos sell so successfully in sex stores, a racist fetishization imbedded in US culture. White lesbian Heather Findlay explains, "the black dildo fetish can 'make acceptable' a specific racial lack – the lack, that is, under white hegemony of a relation between races." She continues:

> If sex *itself* is the location of racial terror and desire, we might say that the more general (and apparently lucrative) sexual fantasy of Black superpotency . . . is another powerful cultural fetish that allows us to circumvent the Real of racial disintegration.[38]

Central to racial disintegration is the reality of mixed peoples who result from the sexual colonization of Indian and African slaves in the Americas. This is the Force of white sex that Lucas denies as he reverses American history to blame dark peoples for sexual violations of white women.

Oedipal issues of miscegenation and castration are clearly multicultural in *Star Wars* as Lucas struggles to make pan–ethnic archetypal themes. While African American males are fetishized as being hypermasculine, Asian males are fetishized as being effeminate and impotent. As Luke takes on the phallic sword symbol of the Asian male warrior, he also loses his virility and sexual desire. A stereotype of Asian masculinity in US media is that Asian men have "small dicks" and "no desire" while gay pornography often links Asian men to anally receptive "boy" roles for white male pleasure.[39] Luke's castration by Darth Vader is, on one level, a castration of Asian masculinity. Although neither blacks nor Asian males are more masculine than the other, Lucas creates a fight scene in which a powerful black phallus easily castrates an Asian boy phallus in a "who's your daddy?" revelation. In *Episode VI*, Luke can only passively plead to his father for help when the Emperor attacks him. Darth Vader finally uses his black male prowess to defeat his Sith master while the Asian-boy Luke can only watch on. Lucas uses Asian male stereotypes of asexuality to create tension with black hypermasculine stereotypes. In this reading, father and son do not duel to establish good and evil. Instead, they duel to polarize fetishized masculinities and to heighten the sexual tension between the white father–son characters.

Star Wars provides a number of examples of fetishized Asian male "lack." The cowardly Asian-accented Trade Federation leaders who attack Naboo contrast with the brave white Jedi who lead a successful revolt against their tyranny. Trade Federation leaders wear Fu Man Chu-type effeminate dresses on their frog-like digitally reproduced bodies that spout stereotypical Chinese accents that do not match the lip movements. Another example of Orientalism is Watto, a dirty Arab or Jewish-accented alien who owns Shmi and Anakin. His digital anti-Semitic depiction unnerved Muslims whose mosques were burning in the USA and the Middle East during the Iraq War. Although Yoda is both valiant and wise, his fortune-cookie linguistics mark him as an Asian Other. Even when he is digitally animated to fight the Sith, his green pee-wee sized saber is comical as are his tiny physique and advanced age. While Yoda's knowledge of the Force is as large as his frame is "small," his asexuality is in keeping with doubts about Asian male virility and sexual desire. Asian asexuality also resonates with anti-immigration laws that kept Asians from US shores, especially "breeding" females. Yoda transfers this Asian lack of sexuality to Luke to begin a new cycle of Asian passivity. Eerily, none of these depictions use Asian actors to play the parts. Lucas mistakenly believes that digitally animated stereotypes are kosher. Only a human East Indian plays the new Queen of Naboo, but her leadership is quickly undermined as focus shifts to Padme's more heroic white actions in the *Episode II* Clone Wars.

Coyotl exploitation of tribal men and white women

Lucas is not just foolish or wily as a coyote, he is *coyotl*, a term synonymous with exploitative whiteness within modern Nahuatl communities of Mexico, formally known as Aztec. This critical definition contrasts with the popular Coyote as Trickster who usually gets it in the end as Wile E. Coyote did in *The Road Runner* cartoons modeled after many Native American stories. *Coyomeh* or *koyomej* is the modern plural Nahuatl form of *coyotl*. Consider the poem stanzas by Natalio Hernandez Hernandez:

> Na ni indio
> Pampa ijkinoj nech tokatijekej koyomej
> (I am Indian
> because the white man named me thus)[40]

These lines show that naming is mutual across cultures. An indication that "Indians" are named pejoratively by whites is not only in the succeeding stanzas that recount historical white "discrimination" against "*Indios*," but also in the fact that Nahuatl are also naming whites "*coyomej*" in the process. Alan Sandstrom explains that to be called a "*coyotl*" is no great compliment within Nahuatl ethnography.

> Although James Taggart translates the term as "gentleman," he does point out that the Nahuatl word *coyotl* . . . is an animal the Nahuas view as a mischiefmaker and backbiter as well as being clever and self-serving. The coyomej are seen as aggressive and arrogant, people who exploit others when allowed.[41]

Coyomeh aren't just the Spanish or Old World ethnics, they are also the mixed-blooded Mexicans and Indians who greedily assimilate into Eurocentric culture. For the purposes of this essay, *coyotl* emphasizes the white exploitation of working-class, multiethnic and pansexual groups. At times, Lucas is *coyotl* – white, accomplished, exploitative, and tricky all rolled into one indigenous word. Lucas succeeds, but through a noted measure of exploitation of other classes, races, and sexes. However, although Lucas does have great productive power, he does not have the last word in what his movies mean. As Hernandez Hernandez concludes his poem with cultural affirmation:

> Na ni indio
> uan namaj sampa nech neluayotia tlatipaktli
> tonana tlatipactli
> (I am Indian:
> and now the earth returns to give me roots,
> our mother earth)[42]

so this essay continues to affirm the many voices that speak out against Lucas' *coyotl* tendencies, even when that voice is Lucas' own.

In *coyotl* fashion, concern for the lives of digitally created nonwhite soldiers is either absent or patronizing as race and class exploitations collide in *Star Wars*. While Lord Sidious mandates a complete eradication of the lowly Afro-Caribbean Gun-guns in the critically panned *Episode I*, Jedi liberally propose to reform the nonwhite racial inferiors. White Jedi must convince the Gun-guns to fight Sith forces because the Gun-guns are too stupid to understand that they are about to be destroyed by a droid army. Popular outcries of racism targeted the Stepin Fetchit-reminiscent Jar Jar Binks who faithfully served his "white master" Jedi. "Me sah your humble servant!" Jar Jar tells the white Jedi in a thinly digitally disguised version of the black man as slave-buffoon. The dread-lock-like long ears reference the black actor whose rhythmic gait was the model for the dinosaur-human creature. Gun-guns die on the front lines of the army and are never adequately mourned, in contrast to the suffering of white supporting and leading characters such as Han Solo, Luke Skywalker, and Shmi Skywalker. Gun-guns are simply too stupid and too black to be missed in one of Lucas' more racist *coyotl* moments.[43]

Jango Fett is the ultimate *coyotl* who sells out his own clones in immoral wars, even as he is respected for his virile fighting abilities. The fighter clones digitally replicated from Maori actor Temuera Morrison's dark body are also meant to contrast with Obi-Wan's superior white ethics. The clones "have been genetically altered to take any order" a cloner explains in *Episode II*. The dark hordes of dead indigenous cloned men are not mourned because they suffer through no ethical struggles as they battle for whatever side controls them. Lucas fails to show that pain is felt by people of all races in war, especially poor dark masses who are pressed into service on opposing sides. In *Episode III*, the clones mindlessly fight for the Republic until killing off the Jedi at one treacherous "Order 66" from Darth Sidious. The white sheen of the clone protective clone armor is a Trojan horse metaphor for the dark treachery that looms behind the veneer of whiteness. The dark clone bodies are completely encapsulated in a whiteness of assimilation that forces them to die and kill for their white Sith master. These clones represent nonwhite peoples as lacking moral conviction and agency, falling into complete servitude to corrupt whites. At a time when Maori are taking back land and language in New Zealand, Lucas chooses to depict them as mindless servants. Fiona Cram (Maori) specifically objects to cloning stating:

> Of the species that exist humankind is the youngest and therefore does not have the right to dominate other species who are our *tuakana* or elders. Our relationship with the land, the waters, and the animals and plants of Aotearoa is therefore one of respect and *kaitiakitanga* (guardianship). Genetic manipulation of the human genome places *whakapapa* [genealogies] at risk.[44]

As clones attack their masters, Lucas generally condemns cloning as do the Maori. However, Lucas could have let the Maori–identified actors make that realization. Instead, through Morrison's Jango Fett character, Lucas exposes the powerlessness of colonized indigenous peoples in war, yet excludes their voices of protest, sovereignty, and resistance. The clones' lack of ethics upholds the colonial myth that white male protagonists and antagonists should ultimately decide universal fates.

Lucas materially succeeds, but through a noted measure of *coyotl* exploitation of women who are less than heroic, less than the white male elite Jedi. Daughter–mother duo Leia and Padme begin with strong political positions in the first episode of their respective trilogies, *Star Wars Episode IV: A New Hope* (1977) and *Star Wars Episode I: The Phantom Menace* (1999), but their political effectiveness wanes as they become more sexualized objects in *Star Wars Episode V: The Empire Strikes Back* (1980), *Star Wars Episode VI: The Return of the Jedi* (1983), *Star Wars Episode II: The Attack of the Clones* (2002), and *Star Wars Episode III: The Revenge of the Sith* (2005). Because *Star Wars* white women master neither technology nor the Force, they resort to passive resistance against dark masculinity as their white male counterparts claim heroic victory or failure for them. Unfortunately, the feminist visions of the first episodes of both trilogies are also the most white supremacist as Lucas upholds virginal white womanhood in greatest opposition to nonwhite immorality. Good white and nonwhite male characters only gain more power once the squeaky white purity of protagonist women is sullied by their female desires for men. Rather than pursue a logic that both men and women can grow in power and sexual maturity together, Lucas reinvests in the old colonial and segregation narrative that dark male sexualities must force weak white women to rely upon elite white male saviors.

In an epic attempt to prevent Coyote-type miscegenation, Lucas ultimately seeks to control the reproductive parts of the strong white women he originally idealizes. White women protagonists slowly lose their sexual powers to white men as each trilogy unfolds. Yet, each series has its glowing moments of white feminist resistance. In the original *Star Wars* (1977), Princess Leia breaks barriers for white women by acting as a spy, a tactical leader, and a gun-wielding Rebel as she consistently defies Han Solo's misogynistic comments. Part of Leia's appeal is that she is not the typical princess of Grimm Brothers lore who passively waits for her prince to save and marry her. When Luke Skywalker and Han Solo do free her from Darth Vader's death row cell on the Death Star, she immediately turns the tables by leading the escape through a sewer line. Once clear, Han attacks her, barking "If we can just avoid any more *female* advice, we oughtta be able to get outta here." "Female" is meant as an epithet of inferiority, as though female were another species or ignorant animal. In his mind, female "booty" isn't supposed to take charge of his rescue. He is unaware that she is a primary tactical leader in the rebellion against the Empire. A subsequent shot of Leia played by Carrie Fisher is telling. Swathed in her white Hopi-like garb, a close up of her face and shoulders fills the screen as she slightly tilts her face up to the camera in what is meant to be a direct eye contact gaze with the taller Han Solo. In fact, through tilting her head up, her gaze is meant to simulate actually looking down on the taller hunk played by Harrison Ford. Her lips are glistening and appealing painted in that 1970s cherry red lipgloss with dark eye-liner and rosy cheeks that mark a context of free love and sexual experimentation. However, her dark brown hair is pulled into Hopi squash blossoms and her skin is white, marking her as exotically intelligent rather than blonde, stupid, and easy. Subliminally, audiences may register the strong Hopi women's presence as a potential Clan Mother of political and religious weight symbolized through hair and costume. Unflinching eyes actually widen to show her anger and power with a direct unblinking gaze. Her intense stare also draws attention away from her clingy wet attire that testifies that she wears no bra. Leia's bralessness brings in a context of 1970s bra-burning feminists like Gloria Steinem who flaunted their bodies as expressions of their own sexual power rather than as repressed objects of male desire. The stare, high neckline, and shoulder cropping of the image indicate that Leia is commanding Han to focus on her intelligence, not her cleavage. Her voice is crisp and slow, as if speaking to an immature boy. "Listen," she slowly lays it out for him, syllable by punctuated syllable. "I don't know who you are or where you came from," she commands, "but from now on, you do as I tell you – OK?" The question is completely rhetorical and dismissive. She charges past him and Luke by pushing Chewbacca out of the way, and reassumes the lead position she feels she should occupy. The image focuses on Leia's mouth exaggerating the emphasized word, "NOW," which is also the acronym for the National Organization for Women that was aggressively fighting for women's rights in 1977. "NOW" emphasizes that privileged white women like Leia are fed up and want immediate reactions to their voices, which rise up in anger against sexism. Leia's "now" frame also exposes her teeth and incisors that indicate that her "biting" voice will have retribution if not obeyed. Her teeth are reminders that women's mouths will not just kiss or suck for male pleasure. When angered, they will bite, and Han clearly feels that bite in the scene. Although Leia has her back to the gray Death Star wall that symbolizes male destructive power, she is backlit and glowing with lights of virtue, giving her a moral standing that sees her through in this scene. Later, when Solo leaves the Rebels with his rescue reward, Leia is completely willing to let him go. "Luke, he's got to follow his own path," she tells young Skywalker. In *Episode IV*, Han and Luke do fight to claim Leia as their sexual territory, but she never gives in to their boyish competition as she reigns on high and battles in the feminist trenches with an almost lesbian flair. But such a thing was not meant to last.

Coyotl sexist oppression mandates that women cannot be too smart, commanding, and sexually confident without retribution. That would mean gender power equality with the likes of Harrison Ford. The slight downward camera angle that disempowers Leia's gaze, the pin-up girl makeup, and wet chest from the "now" frame predict the future relinquishment of her sexual sovereignty. In subsequent episodes, Leia allows herself to take misogynistic orders from Han as she sexually blossoms. Her initial resistance to patriarchy becomes framed as mere sexual frigidity. "You could *use* a good kiss!" Han Solo admonishes her in *The Empire Strikes Back*, scenes before they actually do kiss. As the trilogy progresses, Leia appears to "need" more male commands in order to overcome her sexual inhibitions which she "hides" as strength and leadership. As dark men enter into her presence she loses sexual power and becomes an object of white male desire and protection. In *The Empire Strikes Back*, Han fends off a treacherous Lando Calrissian's advances on Leia. Lando, played by black actor Billie Dee Williams, puts the "smoothie"/pimp moves on Leia who finds him mildly interesting, to Han's discomfort. Han never worries about Luke's competitive efforts to woo Leia, especially as Luke is transformed by an Asian-stereotyped Jedi philosophy of celibacy. As the first trilogy evolves, Leia loses her wardrobe and leadership capabilities as her twin Luke develops Jedi powers that seem mostly passed from father to son. However, Leia's white feminist leanings never completely leave her character. For example, she strangles Jabba the Hut to death with the same chain that he had used to claim her as his scantily clad sex slave in *Star Wars Episode VI: The Return of the Jedi*. Men never portray that level of sexual degradation unless carefully masked by phallic symbol and homoerotic innuendo.

The prequel series seems hopeful as Lucas gives Padme combined sensual and political strengths that Leia never realizes. Padme's wartime leadership resonates with the role of her daughter as military strategist and leader, but she is able to more openly discuss her romantic desires. In *Episode I*, a teenage Padme is a leading voice for a non-violent democracy in the Senate and the elected queen of her planet. Unlike Leia, Padme more easily expresses and receives affection from other cast members without fearing that emotion and sensuality are inherently weak qualities. Padme's last words, "there is good in him . . . I know . . . I know there is still," are a statement of hope that ultimately predicts the series resolution in which Darth Vader destroys the Emperor out of compassion for Luke. Padme's beliefs show that cycles of violence cannot end by violent means. Passively, she rejects Anakin's patriarchal control over their relationship and galactic politics. Even more passively, she teaches Anakin how to relinquish personal power and die for love.

Like Leia, Padme loses much of her feminist leanings as her prequel trilogy evolves. Padme, who once led a galactic movement for legislative reform, can barely fight being "relegated to a romantic trophy for the white male central character" in *Sith*.[45] As soon as she pursues sexual interests with Anakin, she becomes domestically trapped. She hides her pregnancy for fear that the elite Jedi or Queen of Naboo would admonish the pair for their illicit marriage. Being an upper-class white woman is a key limitation for her romance as it is for Princess Leia. Both don themselves in ethnically exotic outfits that place them above sexual reach. Along with classic screen wipes, Lucas incorporates a rather 1950s sense of the dangers that white women face from bad men, especially bad dark men. Rather than hint at interracial relationships and female sexual desire, Lucas has Padme finish her *Madame Butterfly* performance by taking her life once her Imperial man rejects her. Like Butterfly's suicide in the 1915 film, Padme's "suicide is for love lost"[46] as Padme relinquishes her life of her own will. The presumption is that women are a class of peoples who will always die for their man's honor or dishonor. In a similar way, Shmi's death predicts Anakin's fall into the Dark Side.

One path out of *coyotl* oppression of women that white suffragettes and feminists have taken is to seek out non-sexist indigenous teachings. Oral traditions retold by Laguna Pueblo author Leslie Marmon Silko provide insight into *Star Wars* white women's sex. White women's oppressed sexuality contrasts with Pueblo celebrations of female fertility and the sacredness of the earth. For Silko, the themes of escape from earth into space are laden with a hatred of mother earth and earth-linked female sexuality. Cherokee feminist Henrietta Moore comments that "Silko's plot and characters illustrate the imbalance that occurs when humans become alienated from their earthly origins . . . characters alienated from the land are also alienated from their bodies and exhibit the most perverse and destructive sexual behavior." This is contrary to the earth-rooted Indigenous characters who pursue what could be termed "mutually satisfying, non-exploitative sex . . . twice a day."[47] Padme and Anakin's violent relationship is emblematic of their alienation from their respective Earths and sexualized bodies. The further they go from their home worlds, the more fetishized and destructive their relationship becomes. Had Padme really exhibited the kind of Yellow Woman sexual allure that her Pueblo trappings promised, she would have seduced a man who had more to offer herself and her planet. After all, it was Yellow Woman's fling with Buffalo Man that allowed the Pueblo people to hunt the buffalo with the buffalo's permission.[48] Leia's romance with Han Solo was much more productive in accomplishing her political goals to destroy the Empire and to save remaining earths from Death Star annihilation. In a sense, she does vindicate her mother who tragically and stubbornly parlayed for a more peaceful and romantic universe. Like Yellow Woman, Leia shows that seduction is not the evil Lucas imagines it to be. Seduction can help the group realistically fulfill its political and sexual needs. Desire, which is at the unpredictable core of Coyote narratives, flourishes in indigenous traditions that relate a complicated range of feminine and masculine powers.

Conclusion

Lucas often exhibits *coyotl* patterns of stereotyping race, class, and gender, despite his sporadic desire to foster human compassion and to raise consciousness. Indigenous peoples are among a large host who can teach Lucas that intersections of class, multiracial, and pansexual hierarchies mar a greater vision of social equality and evolution. To reflect on more traditional Coyote stories is to understand how foolishness needs not meet eternal condemnation as all peoples, including Lucas, have evolved through making and paying for mistakes. If Coyote is blinded by individual desire, then to become a better relative who can dialog across transnational, class, and sexual communities is a remedy. To refuse to dialog with working class, queer and multiracial movements may be to fall into multiple *coyotl* oppressions. By grounding this analysis in coyote, *coyote*, and *coyotl* concepts from respective Native American, mestizo, and Nahuatl cultures, one can further decolonize their understanding of popular culture in general and *Star Wars* in particular. While current Cultural Studies critiques document the poor representation of Indians, few are able to tap into the languages and complexities of indigenous philosophies to do so. In contrast, this essay maintains that indigenous cultures are not simply objects of white stereotypes; they are also generators of ideas, movements, and media that can help heal the oppressive forms of whiteness that films such as *Star Wars* attempt to maintain.

Notes

1 Dyer, Richard, *White* (London: Routledge, 1997), p. 65.
2 Kenny, Glenn, ed., *A Galaxy Not So Far Away: Writers and 25 Years of* Star Wars (New York: Henry Holt and Company, 2002).
3 Moyers, Bill, *Joseph Campbell and The Power of Myth*. Joseph Campbell, Bill Moyers, George Lucas (Mystic Fire Video, 1988).

4 Waters, Anne, "Language Matters: Nondiscrete Nonbinary Dualism," *American Indian Thought*, ed. Anne Waters (Malden: Blackwell, 2004), p. 102.

5 Dees, Richard H., "Moral Ambiguity in a Black and White Universe," *Star Wars and Philosophy: More Powerful Than You Can Possibly Imagine*, ed. Kevin S. Decker and Jason T. Eberl (Open Court: Chicago, 2005), p. 39.

6 Dyer, *White*, p. 13.

7 Dyer, *White*, p. 184.

8 Dyer, *White*, p. 127.

9 Wiegman, Robyn, "Race, Ethnicity and Film," *Film Studies: Critical Approaches*, eds John Hill and Pamela Church Gibson (Oxford: Oxford University Press, 2000), p. 181.

10 Dyer, *White*, p. 66.

11 Mitchell, Elvis, "Works Every Time," in Kenny, ed., *A Galaxy Not So Far Away*, p. 84.

12 Joseph McBride quoted in Berg, Charles Ramírez, *Latino Images in Film* (Austin, TX: University of Texas Press, 2002), p. 133.

13 Shipley, William, ed., *The Maidu Indians Myths and Stories of Hanc'ibyjim*, trans. William Shipley (Santa Clara, CA: Heydey Books, 1991), p. 95.

14 Manriquez, L. Frank, *Acorn Soup* (Berkeley: Heyday Books, 1999), p. 17.

15 Waters, "Language Matters," p. 97.

16 Russo, Vito, *The Celluloid Closet: Homosexuality in the Movies* (New York: Harper and Row Publishers, 1989), p. 52.

17 Estrada, Gabriel, "The Macho Body as Social Malinche," *Velvet Barrio: Popular Culture and Chicana/o Sexualities*, ed. Alicia Gaspar de Alba (New York: Palgrave, 2002), p. 54.

18 Haraway, Donna, "The Promises of Monsters: A Regenerative Politics for Inappropriate/d Others," *Cultural Studies*, eds Lawrence Grossberg, Cary Nelson and Paula A. Treichler (New York: Routledge, 1992), p. 332.

19 Haraway, "The Promises of Monsters," p. 320.

20 Carson, Tom, "Jedi Uber Alles," in Kenny, ed., *A Galaxy Not So Far Away*, p. 161.

21 Yazzie Burkhart, Brian, "What Coyote and Thales Can Teach Us: An Outline of American Indian Philosophy," *American Indian Thought*, ed. Anne Waters (Malden: Blackwell Publishing, 2004), p. 15.

22 Associated Press (May 16, 2005).

23 Warrior, Robert, "Foreword," *Wiping the War Paint Off the Lens: Native American Film and Video* (Minneapolis: University of Minnesota, 2002), p. vii.

24 Mitchell, "Works Every Time," p. 79.

25 Tafolla, Carmen, *To Split a Human: Mitos, Machos, and La Mujer Chicana* (San Antonio, TX: Mexican American Cultural Center, 1985).

26 Noriega, Chon, "Ramona," *The Birth of Whiteness: Race and the Emergence of US Cinema*, ed. Daniel Bernardi (New Brunswick, NJ: Rutgers University Press, 1996), p. 203.

27 Gonzalez, Juan, *Harvest of Empire: A History of Latinos in America* (New York: Penguin Books, 2000), p. 228.

28 Berg, Charles Ramírez, "Immigrants, Aliens, and Extraterrestrials: Science Fiction's Alien 'Other' as (Among Other Things) New Hispanic Image," *The Howard Journal of Communication*, 2, 3 (1990), pp. 286–300.

29 King, Richard C. and Springwood, Charles Freuhling, eds, *Team Spirits: The Native American Mascots Controversy* (Lincoln, NE: University of Nebraska Press, 2001).

30 Dilworth, Leah, *Imagining Indians in the Southwest: Persistent Visions of a Primitive Past* (Washington, DC: Smithsonian Books, 1996).

31 Kenny, Glenn, "Introduction: Jedi Mind Tricks," in Kenny, ed., *A Galaxy Not So Far Away*, p. xxvii.

32 Prats, Armando Jose, *Invisible Native: Myth and Identity in the American Western* (Ithaca, NY: Cornell University Press, 2002), p. 174.

33 Aldama, Arturo J., *Disrupting Savagism: Chicana/o, Mexican Immigrant, and Native American Struggles for Self-Representation* (New York: Duke University Press, 2002).

34 Lucas, George, quoted in *Rolling Stone*, 975 (June 2, 2005), p. 46.

35 Taylor, Clyde, "The Master Text and the Jedi Doctrine," *Screen*, 29, 4 (1988), pp. 96–104.

36 Carson, "Jedi Uber Alles," p. 169.

37 Lucas, *Rolling Stone*, p. 44.

38 Findlay, Heather, "Lesbian Dildo Debates," *Feminist Theory and the Body: A Reader*, eds Janet Price and Margrit Shildrick (New York: Routledge, 1999), p. 472.

39 Hamamoto, Darrell Y., "The Joy Fuck Club: Prolegomenon to an Asian American Porno Practice," *Countervisions: Asian American Film Criticism*, eds Darrell Hamamoto and Sandra Liu (Philadelphia, PA: Temple University Press, 2000), p. 75.

40 Sandstrom, Alan R., *Corn Is Our Blood: Culture and Ethnic Identity in a Contemporary Aztec Indian Village* (London: University of Oklahoma Press, 1991), pp. xiii–ix.

41 Sandstrom, *Corn Is Our Blood*, p. 69.

42 Sandstrom, *Corn Is Our Blood*, p. 69.

43 Carson, "Jedi Uber Alles," p. 168.

44 Cram, Fiona, "Backgrounding Maori Views on Genetic Engineering," *Sovereignty Matters: Locations of Contestation and Possibility in Indigenous Struggles for Self-Determination*, ed. Joanne Barker (Lincoln, NE: University of Nebraska Press, 2005), p. 55.

45 Ho, Jeffrey, "The Matrix: Using American Popular Film to Teach Concepts of Eastern Mysticism in the College Classroom," *Reversing the Lens*, eds Lane Ryo Hirabyashi and Jun Xing (Boulder, CO: University Press of Colorado, 2003), p. 209.

46 Browne, Nick, "The Undoing of the Other Woman: Madame Butterfly in the Discourse of American Orientalism," in Bernardi, ed., *The Birth of Whiteness*, p. 238.

47 Moore, Henrietta, "Native American Literary Analysis, Poetry, and Prose," *An Introduction to American Indian Studies: Sovereignty, Culture, and Representation*, ed. Gabriel S. Estrada (Boston, MA: Pearson Custom Publishing, 2004), pp. 154–5.

48 Silko, Leslie Marmon, *Storyteller* (New York: Arcade Publishers, 1981), p. 69.

Chapter 5

The whiteness of the *Rings*

Sean Redmond

In this essay on *The Lord of the Rings: The Fellowship of the Ring* I want to explore the way whiteness is metaphorically represented as a contradictory subjectivity that is as much about absence and negation as it is about racial power and idealization. On one level, *The Lord of the Rings: The Fellowship of the Ring* is saturated in racial metaphors and imagery that work to position whiteness as a universal ideal and Otherness as a horrifying and destructive force that comes into being through a monstrous form of reproduction. Idealized images of whiteness are found right across the film: in certain key forms of embodiment and costume; in the stylistic streams of bright light that bathe the good, the innocent, and the pure; in the Edenic, utopian natural settings; and in and through a number of the central characters, particularly Arwen and Galadriel, whose purity and innocence light up the screen in a well-choreographed form of heavenly white female beauty.

Evil, by contrast, is not only symbolically Other in the film, but racially encoded in the corporeality and actions of the Orcs and the Uruks. Created below ground in the smelting fires and liquid metal of an unnatural and polluted industrial hell, they are white stereotypes of the savage and dangerous Negro – all-body bucks who will fuck and fight their way through white communities if given the chance. The racial politics of the film, then, is also often played out in its spatial arrangements, with a high/low and rural/city binary opposition in place. Above ground, man, beast, water, earth and air are, or can be, in perfect, idyllic unison: below ground, chaos reigns, as hordes of barbaric "negroes" threaten to take flight. Frodo and Sam leave the shires – or their white rural Eden – and head off to the "city", where they are in constant danger from ghetto dwellers dead-set on ruining their quest.

However, *The Lord of the Rings: The Fellowship of the Ring* is also more contradictory in its representation of whiteness, and more critical of particular forms of whiteness as they are given representational definition. The film posits that too much whiteness – what Bonnett would call "hyper-whiteness" – is a dangerous, ultimately destructive subjectivity.[1] The two key figures in this respect are Saruman and Arwen. Saruman is excessively white (with white robes and long, flowing white hair) who has let the power that whiteness brings him *go to his head*. He is a death-like figure, a living corpse, so close is he to the absence effect at the centre of this type of cerebral-inflected whiteness. Saruman is a sorcerer whose alchemy and science has allowed him to reproduce, colonise, and reincarnate those slave negroes who will actually threaten the very survival of the white species. As such, he is doubly dangerous: he is incapable of his own reproduction (since he lives in/through his head) and he begets a species that threatens the annihilation of the white race.

Arwen is the personification of white female beauty: she is made up and out of light and is pure and innocent. However, such radiance is also imagined to be a type of death for her: a type of ephemeral spirituality that has little (sexed) flesh to it – something she so clearly yearns for. This will not do for Arwen: she desires Aragorn and will willingly sacrifice her immortality (here read idealized whiteness) for love, sex, and intimacy with him.

In more general terms, when whiteness is made symbolically visible it is essentially connected to the highest ideals of human civilization: to purity, innocence, rationalism, naturalism, and to the "higher" motifs of Christianity, such as ascending angels and the concept of "spirit." However, this purity in spirit and thought is also considered to be death-like because it necessarily brings white people closer to, or in touch with, the lack of life, corporeality, or sex drive that such higher ideals brings to bear on them as white subjects. When one reaches the highest ideals of whiteness, one literally disappears into the ether: in fact, one is already dead, since "the very things that makes us white endangers the reproduction of whiteness."[2] In *The Lord of the Rings: The Fellowship of the Ring* it is through the figures of Saruman and Arwen that this life-and-death struggle is principally played out and arguably to devastating consequences.

Nonetheless, it is the "one true ring" that seems to best represent the contradictory nature of whiteness in the film. On the one hand, the power of the ring to make those who wear it invisible and the vision it gives those who possess it to control past, present and future, speak of the racial power of whiteness itself; the power to be not seen as a racial category at all; the power to create a vision of the world in one's own image of whiteness.[3] The ring, in effect, comes to stand for, is a symbol of, the racial privilege that whiteness secures for (its) people. It reproduces the I/eye of whiteness or that master vision and meta-subjectivity which holds the centre ground of identity formation. At the same time, the ring itself confirms how whiteness is itself a potentially terrifying and species-destructive subjectivity. Those who possess the ring, those who are enamoured by its power, become pathological: they suffer a form of white schizophrenia – desperate for the power that whiteness brings, and yet terrified by the death that will come with its possession.

In *Lord of the Rings: The Fellowship of the Ring* there is an absent/present paradox at the core of much of the representation of idealized whiteness, constantly threatening to tear it apart as a possible or ultimately desirable form of subjectivity. The more *present* or visible white people become in the film, the more culturally ideal they appear, the more *absent* or death-like/death producing they are.

Idealized whiteness: terrifying negrophobia

A great many of what are supposedly the most prized of human qualities are symbolized through a visual aesthetic and a signification chain that encodes idealized white people with the highest attributes available to humankind. For example, one can find the extraordinary nature of whiteness in the stories of ephemeral, ascending angels; the hi-tech laboratories of scientific invention; in the embodiment of white-haired, white-coated inventors and scientists; and in the "make-up" of heavenly film stars who "light up" the silver screen – situating this iconic version of whiteness as the highest, brightest racial ideal available to humankind and one, therefore, it is culturally enunciated, that should be reached for.

In the main, whiteness is brought into the racially concrete through highly positive connotations, manifest in semiotically rich images that fill the cultural world with extraordinary visions of the power and the beauty of whiteness. Whiteness is located as a source of light: reflective, bright, shiny, and positive. This idea of light, of purity and "goodness" seems to be repeated, in a series of inter-textual relays, across a number of representations. For example, in terms of Western culture, especially in Western myth and fairy-tale, it is white skin, white body, blond hair, blue eyes which signifies radiant beauty, and in particular, it is idealized white femininity which resonates at the core of the beauty myth.[4] Idealized white women are bathed in and permeated by light: it streams through them and falls on to them from above. It is light that makes them glow, appear angelic, heavenly, and, ultimately, to be not-of-this-world, heavenly absences rather than fleshed beings.

In *Lord of the Rings: The Fellowship of the Ring* one can argue that both Arwen and Galadriel appear as heavenly creatures: as idealized white women who radiate light. They are narrativized in symbolically loaded white settings, with carefully selected iconography, that uses both the colour white to connote ideas of purity, innocence and radiance, and high key light to bathe them in an imaginary halo that marks them out as translucent, ephemeral, spiritual beings.

Arwen enters the film in a stream of bright, white light at the moment that Frodo is being taken over: he is soon to pass "into the shadowland" where he will become a spectre, a living corpse. Frodo's face is itself chalk-like: in fact the closer he gets to death the whiter he becomes, confirming the close proximity that exists between whiteness and the figure of the corpse. Arwen's entrance pours light onto Frodo's face and in his feverish state she appears as an apparition. Her "ideal" light momentarily brings him back into a state of near well-being. Initially there is no grounded corporeality to her: she is just an expanse of white light that floats towards Frodo. Chamber/choral music accompanies Arwen's arrival and in the Edenic setting of a hushed, lush green forest, she is enchanted and enchanting. As she moves further into view she is given greater physical definition: she has blue eyes, long, flowing black hair, wears a white satin dress and a white (gold) pendent that hangs from her neck. Nonetheless, a striking back light continues to illuminate her so that the very edges of her body, face and hair continue to glow, and this glow fills the scene with a not-of-this-world ethereality. Light is also central to this scene in the way it is used as a metaphor to keep Frodo away from the Shadowlands, and to differentiate between good and evil. Arwen softly calls to Frodo, "hear my voice: come back to the light", and in her "race against time" horse ride back to her kingdom, she is chased by the Black Riders/ringwraiths – diabolical henchmen for Lord Sauron. Arwen defeats the Riders at the river crossing, the boundary to Rivendell, her Elf home, by creating a tidal wave of white horses who take them down stream. *Lord of the Rings: The Fellowship of the Ring* is full of such light/dark, day/night, white/black binary oppositions, with light/day/ white the generally favoured ideological position – something I will briefly return to later in the essay. Galadriel enters *Lord of the Rings: The Fellowship of the Ring* in a strikingly similar way to Arwen: in an expanse of flooding white light and radiant white clothes before she is given corporeal characteristics. However, her physical introduction has been preceded by Gimli's description of her as an "elf witch of terrible power . . . all who look at her fall under her spell." When Galadriel emerges from the aura of her own being, she has long, blonde hair and blue eyes, and she is given a penetrating stare that sees through people – concretized through her telepathy which grants her direct access to people's subconscious. Galadriel, then, is also a white witch, in contrast to the black art of Lord Sauron.

Nonetheless, Galadriel's entrance occurs in a setting itself imbued with real spiritual meaning. She enters the film at the apex of a network of ornate, inter-connecting bridges and passageways – all of them flooded with light – so that she stands at the head of what is a glowing cathedral. Frodo and the other Fellows of the Ring have had to move from the low to the high to meet her: rising up in what can be read as a mini-ascension scene. Galadriel's heavenly, spiritual appearance, then, is also confirmed because of the film's spatial posi-tioning of her.

In summary, Arwen and Galadriel are idealized white women: an ideal-ization that, by corporeal and symbolic definition, only thin white females can achieve. The film suggests that the glow that passes between them and through them is a natural essence that belongs to them, and to their made-of-nothing, or very little, white bodies. Suffused in this glow, caught up in all this inno-cence and tranquility, they appear to be able to float right off the screen. In fact, Galadriel seems to walk on air and travel through time because of the way she is enigmatically captured. In cultural terms, thin bodies do this *passing through* best because there is not "much to them" in the first place, their lines and shapes economical. But with glow, with haze and shimmer alongside, above, beyond, and flowing over the skin, the thinness makes it easier for the body borders to be seen to disappear, or float upwards.

But not only this: Arwen and Galadriel's thinness produces the sense that their bodies have been kept natural, unpolluted, and pure. The implied absti- nence suggests containment and self-control. In this oscillating mix of fluidity and yet self-control, of translucence and yet fixity, the cultural significance/ importance of the idealized, thin white woman is realized. She is body that is self-contained and controlled, and through such self-regulation marked by abstinence (nothing, or very little, enters her body) she is pure; by being pure she naturally glows, and in glowing the very minimal borders of her body are allowed to float away into a heavenly state of grace. Arwen is virginal, pure (although as I will go onto argue this is a death for her, since she loves and wants Aragorn), and Galadriel refuses Frodo's offer of possession of the ring – something that would have turned her inside out, white-to-black, innocent to sinful, according to the fantasy scene in which she plays out the scenario of having accepted the ring.

The star biographies of both Liv Tyler (Arwen) and Cate Blanchett (Galadriel) are important here. Liv Tyler is often found in films that foreground and problematize her purity and innocence. In *Stealing Beauty* (Bertolucci, 1996), for example, she plays the part of Lucy Harmon who visits Italy to lose her virginity. Liv Tyler, then, brings to the part of Arwen a character history of absent/present paradoxes that she is found resisting or transgressing. Similarly, Cate Blanchett often appears in films in which she is identified with the figure of the white corpse: alabaster white, cold and calculating, haunted, and engi- neered by her own death instinct. In *Elizabeth* (Kapur, 1998) this is brilliantly played out in the way that she paints herself white to appear as the Virginal Queen, only confirming her closeness to death in the process.

Versions of whiteness and idealized whiteness find their way into many of the core representations in the film. The Shires are rural, middle "England" and Frodo and Sam innocent white children who have no knowledge of the multiracial ghettos that exist outside their rolling hills and valleys, but who, nonetheless, have to travel there if the sanctity of "home" is to be protected and preserved. Frodo, in effect, is charged with securing for white people their continued privileged position at the centre of things – if (when) he throws the ring into the fires of Mount Doom, light will flood back into the world and the racial purity of the Shires will be ensured. Rivendell, the Enchanted Wood, the Aryan (blond, blue-eyed) Elves, Legolas, Gandalf, are places and people of (racial) purity and innocence, largely free of the shadows and darkness that stretches into the other lands and cities, and out of people/monsters who are less securely white and Other in the film.

Lord of the Rings: The Fellowship of the Ring produces its own racial hierarchy of whiteness. The whitest of white people are those who are the purest or who hold positions of power in the film – Gandalf, Saruman, Galadriel, Arwen –

while those who are darker, more ruddy in complexion, more explicitly corporeal, are charged with undertaking the quest and/or threatening it. These white identities are also class-inflected. Spirit, purity and power become the markers of the refined upper class or nobility, while nature, earth/dirt, and primitive urges become the ideological indicator of the working class.

Bonnett writes about the "symbolic production of whiteness in nineteenth-century Britain," suggesting that white hue was pivotal in indicating the status and power differences between the gentlemanly bourgeoisie, who were located as hyper white and "almost superhuman," and the urban working class, who were located as "marginal" to this idealized paradigm.[5] The urban working class were in fact made to appear "dark", to have some of the colour of the primitive negro. The conflation between race and social class added symbolic weight to the idea that the working classes were themselves primitive, animalistic, and mindless.

There is a degree of this class and racial conflation in *The Lord of the Rings: The Fellowship of the Ring*. Gollum appears as a stereotype of the gentile Eastern European Jew: bony, sickly and sinewy, driven by a desire to possess or own the ring (here read the economic power that such jewellery, or gold, would bring him). Gimli, the "celtic" dwarf miner, is working-class embodied: mesamorphic, brutish, physically "dirty", crude, with traces of the simian in his movements. However, it is the unnatural and cannibalistic Orcs (fallen Elves) and Uruks who best demonstrate the film's racial hierarchy and suggested negrophobia. In particular, it is through the figure of Lurtz that *Lord of the Rings: The Fellowship of the Ring* reproduces the racist figure of the "bad buck" or the all-body negro brute, who is "over-sexed and savage, violent and frenzied as [he] lust[s] for white flesh".[6]

Lurtz, an Uruk-hai, is begot in a monstrous birthing scene. Industrial sounding music scores the *mise-en-scène* as a delicate white butterfly floats perilously over a large, burning gash in the earth. Under Gandalf's influence, the butterfly makes its way down into the semi-darkness: into the bowels of this flaming abyss, again confirming the contrast between light and dark, good and evil in the film. Tunnels, walkways, bridges, scaffolding, black holes and flame towers fill the underground landscape with the look and sound of large-scale industrial production. Steel is being forged: helmets and swords are being produced, and rivers of glowing, red hot metal pour forth. Orcs rush about, dirty, bruised, snarling, and unable to speak: revelling in the pain of their own tortuous subjugation, as far from the idealized perfection of the Aryan Elves as one could get. Nonetheless, at the same time, ancient trees are being cut up and thrown into the "engines" that fuel this inferno, and there is an organic, if oozing texture, to the landscape. A violent, ugly form of "nature" is found underground: one that when it is conjoined with the industrial seems to seed the violent births that are about to take place there.

At the very bottom of this underground pit, one finds a bubbling birthing pool of thick mud. At the exact moment Saruman appears to marvel at and direct proceedings, an Orc reaches into the mud to reveal a twisted face pressed beneath a soiled sac. In a terrifying reconstruction of the human birthing scenario, a brutish figure roars into existence, ripping open the sac it was contained within, killing the Orc who had moments earlier acted as his midwife. The sheer size, strength and ethnic identity of this man-beast are quickly established. Shot in close-up, his blazing nostrils, dreadlock hair and animalistic posturing directly recalls the stereotype of the all-body/no-brain black buck of racist imagination. This is confirmed later in the film when such "beasts" adorn themselves with tribal paint and leave the pit to scour the earth in search of white man-flesh.

At the core of *Lord of the Rings: The Fellowship of the Ring*, then, is a story of the fear of racial mixing and miscegenation: the black and bestial Uruk-hai uncontrollably reproduce themselves and leave their underground ghetto on a mission to destroy middle England and the white communities that live there. Frodo foresees such a destruction of the Shires in the mirror that Galadriel asks him to stare into. Frodo's journey into the heart of darkness is to protect white people from such species destruction. If he fails, whiteness fails.

Nonetheless, white people are under threat in the film in another sense, and the racial hierarchy constructed in the film is itself faulty and subject to internal contradictions. In *Lord of the Rings: The Fellowship of the Ring* whiteness is haunted by its own definition of perfection, by its own death instinct, and by those who are less securely white but have a vitality or corporeality that idealized white people crave.

The death of whiteness

In terms of representation, the white body exists in a paradoxical state of being. On the one hand, the white body is represented as not-flesh and natural absence, or, as Dyer puts it, "what is absent from white is any *thing*; in other words, material reality".[7] On the other hand, the white body is subjected to and the object of a virulent construction process which attempts to make the white body ideal through identifying the absence quality of white flesh with the most prized attributes in dominant culture, such as purity, spirituality, and "light." In essence, this rather perverse form of white embodiment ensures that white bodies are seen and yet not seen as white bodies, and that this transparency *and* simultaneous corporeality has to be "manufactured" or put into representation to ensure its ideological meanings are rendered comprehensible, cohesive, and culturally dominant. However, this putting into representation of the contradictory nature of whiteness has the potential to not only draw attention to its inherently unstable and potentially unsatisfactory nature, but to reveal it to be as much a living tyranny of absence and negation for those who come to embody it, as an empowering and empowered subjectivity.

In *Lord of the Rings: The Fellowship of the Ring* Arwen seems to be suffering such a living tyranny: identified as an angelic, immortal creature, she yearns only for real and lasting intimacy with Aragorn. The spirit and purity that defines Arwen is one she wants to reject: her immortality – her idealized white-ness – is death-like since it forbids sexual relations and reproduction. As she laments to Aragorn, "I choose a mortal life," a life that is grounded, rooted, embodied, and therefore, in subtextual terms, not ideally white.

This desire is actually represented in corporeal terms: Arwen is the one who takes Frodo to his safety because she is the faster rider; and her sexualized body constantly threatens to sully or taint the very innocence that she is connected to – her body, her desire, is always there as a troubling presence in the film. In the courtship scene with Aragorn (set at night, under moonlight, on a bridge between two worlds) she is at her most physical and sexually charged: her body breathes, heaves, is full of curves, and it is as if her body (the heart-beat, the racing temperature, the first kiss) has more to offer her than the ultimately rather sterile spirit, absence, and grace of idealized white womanhood.

Asexual reproduction is central here, because it draws into the narrative one of the key signifiers, one of the key contradictions of what it means to be ideally white. To be ideally white is to be above and beyond those primitive, and impure, sexual and reproductive drives that "emerge" in and between hetero-sexual, sexed individuals. To be an ideally white male is to have resisted, denied, or negated the "dark drives" of sexuality.[8] To be a hyper-white female is not " . . . to have such drives in the first place . . . The model for white women is the Virgin Mary, a pure vessel for reproduction who is unsullied by the dark drives that reproduction entails."[9] Arwen is full of these "dark drives" and as such her idealized female whiteness is constantly under threat.

Galadriel is also important here in terms of the way her idealized whiteness also hangs on an unhealthy life/death paradox. However, in the film Galadriel remains a figure of spirit and light and as such is free of the corporeal desire that haunts Arwen. Nonetheless, her coldness, her relative detachment from emotion and empathy, empties her of life, so that she is closer to the figure of the corpse, to the relatives of the living dead, than she is to the Virgin Mary. Saruman can also be read in this way: in fact, one can argue that he is as close to the figure of the white corpse as one gets in the film. His hollow face, bony, extended figures, and the long white shroud that is wrapped around his frame, mark him out as a spectre or zombie – in fact he closely resembles the "inverted" figures of the Black Riders/ringwraiths that we get to see when Frodo puts on the ring.

Galadriel and Saruman exist within a tradition of representing white people as the epitome of the walking dead. As Dyer writes in relation to *Night of the Living Dead* (Romero, 1969): "There is no difference between whites, living or dead; all whites bring death and, by implication, all whites are dead (in terms of human feeling) . . . Whites are dead, bring death and cannot stand that others live."[10] Death is often visualized in paintings, horror and folk stories as ghostly white. One only has to think of the ash-white vampire as the archetype of this, "ghastly white, disgustingly cadaverous, without the blood of life that would give colour".[11] Connected to this is the theme where illness or ill health is often represented through pale skin, as if white embodiment is actually a form of corporeal disappearance or wasting away.[12] In short, death seems to be much in evidence when it comes to white people, and even more so when it comes to what might be termed "thinking" hyper-white men: men who are overly cerebral, scientific, and who simultaneously underinvest in the(ir) sex drive, and who, as a consequence, fail to reproduce.

Saruman is again central here since, on one level, he embodies the racial myth that "scientific" white men are cerebral entities, all brain and no body, that can and do wondrous things with science and nature, through their experiments and research. However, on another level, Saruman is a fantastical version of the hyper-white mad scientist/professor: one who has let the logic and power of science go to his head, and this at the expense of "normal" heterosexual relationships and sexual relations. Saruman craves more of the power that idealized whiteness brings him: he has let the power that he has a "hyper-white" scientist turn him into a pathological figure of destruction.

Saruman will destroy the white species if he gets his way because, first, he will fail to seed properly. Instead of monogamous intimacy between two committed lovers, Saruman opts for a monstrous form of reproduction since he is the "creator" of the Uruk-hai. He is there to witness and parent their arrival in the film's bloody primal scene. Second, these (his) man-children are sent forth to literally eat white civilization to death. Saruman, then, is by proxy a flesh eater in classic zombie tradition. Nonetheless, the presence of the Uruk-hai also confirm what it means to be hyper-white: they allow Saruman to reproduce asexually and thus to become truly hyper-white – free of the "dark drives" of normal, human sexual contact. In essence, Saruman gets to fuck in the film but it is an absent, non-human form of intercourse which for him is "ideal".[13]

Through the figures of Arwen, Galadriel and Saruman the cultural paradox of what it means to be ideally white is clear. Achieve and reach for the higher state of whiteness – spirit, rationalism, logic, and purity – and you move a step closer to absence, negation, pathology and, ultimately, death. But this is also a cultural curse since white people who fail to reach for the heavens are always haunted by their "dark drives." Haunted by their dark drives, white people often feel compelled to reach for perfection but in so doing risk death – and so the horror story of being white goes on . . .

The whiteness of the *Rings*

The ring at the centre of the narrative trajectory of *Lord of the Rings: The Fellowship of the Ring* can be read as a metaphor of idealized whiteness. On the one hand, the ring is meant to have an unclouded purity about it and possession of it grants access to the eye that is all-seeing and all-powerful. When one puts on the ring it produces the invisibility that is itself the ideological and political marker of the white race – not to be seen as a race at all. The ring is wanted, desired by all who come close to it precisely because it is at the centre of things and has the power to grant one immortality. However, on the other hand, possession of the ring leads to madness and paranoia and the ring drains one of life and turns the wearer into a corpse, a blur in a shadowland where other deadly ghosts – mere skin and bone – roam. Frodo is nearly taken over by the ring and Boromir goes crazy with desire for it.

Lord of the Rings: The Fellowship of the Ring, then, allegorically "speaks" about whiteness in a contradictory way, precisely mirroring the life/death paradox at the core of this subjectivity. The film wants to throw the ring (idealized whiteness) into the fire of Mount Doom because it is death-inducing, and yet Frodo and Sam are the epitome of good white citizens, not only fearful of the ring but the bad bucks who have taken flight from their underground ghettos. In a sense, the film wants to have its racial cake and eat it: idealized whiteness is being rejected but whiteness per se is being re-centred, and the crude racial stereotypes used to fuel the fear of the Other mask the white trickery that sits in the belly of the film.

Finally, trickery or the alchemy of state-of-the-art digital effects is also central to the way *Lord of the Rings: The Fellowship of the Ring* situates the extraordinary power that whiteness has to shape the universe in its own image. The wonder of what can be done with digital technology is meant to be noticed: one is asked to gasp out loud at the most memorable of them, breaking the invisible wall that runs through much of mainstream fictional cinema.[14] These moments of technowonder are authored, the pioneering hands of Peter Jackson are symbolically witnessed, and revered. The film pays technophilic homage to this/his mastery, and in so doing situates itself within a wider discourse and history that connects science, technology and film innovation with white inventors. *Lord of the Rings: The Fellowship of the Ring* is part of a long line of spectacle-laden dramas that heralds the mastery of white auteurs to do incredible things with the moving image. Whiteness is this incredible; in cultural terms it remains a persistent representational and technological marker, shaping the way things are made and are seen.

Notes

With thanks to Tim Groves and Lee-Jane Bennion-Nixon for their supportive comments.

1   Alistair Bonnett, *White Identities: Historical and International Perspectives* (Harlow: Prentice, 2000).
2   Richard Dyer, *White* (London: Routledge, 1997), p. 27.
3   John Gabriel, *Whitewash, Racialized Politics and the Media* (London: Routledge, 1998), p. 13.
4   Marina Warner, *From the Beast to the Blonde* (London: Chatto and Windus, 1994).
5   Alistair Bonnett, "How the British Working Class Became White: The Symbolic

(Re)formation of Racialized Capitalism", *Journal of Historical Sociology*, 11, 3 (September 1998), pp. 316–40, p. 38.

6 Donald Bogle, *Toms, Coons, Mulattoes, Mammies and Bucks: An Interpretive History of Blacks in American Films* (New York: Viking Press, 1973), p. 10.

7 Dyer, *White*, p. 75.

8 Dyer, *White*, p. 28.

9 Dyer, *White*, pp. 28–9.

10 Dyer, *White*, p. 211.

11 Dyer, *White*, p. 210.

12 Judith Williamson, *Decoding Advertisements: Ideology and Meaning in Advertising* (London: Marion Boyars, 1978).

13 For an extended discussion of the pathological white scientist see Sean Redmond, "The Science Fiction of Whiteness", *Scope: An Online Journal of Film Studies*, 6 (October 2006).

14 Steve Neale, "'You've Got To Be Fucking Kidding!' Knowledge, Belief and Judgement in Science Fiction", in *Alien Zone: Cultural Theory and Contemporary Science Fiction Cinema*, Annette Kuhn (ed.) (London: Verso, 1990).

Chapter 6

Neo-abolitionists, colorblind epistemologies and black politics

The *Matrix* trilogy

Tani Dianca Sanchez

The *Matrix* movie trilogy, written and directed by Andy and Larry Wachowski, tells the futuristic story of Neo, who shockingly discovers that his and many of his fellow humans' lives have been lived in a computer-generated reality controlled by malevolent artificial intelligences. Throughout the series, Neo struggles alongside his love interest Trinity and a group of revolutionaries as they attempt to free the human race from virtual domination. *The Matrix* (1999), *The Matrix Reloaded* (2003) and *The Matrix Revolutions* (2003) have inspired websites and books offering intense discussions exploring questions of free will, reality, and predestination. The first film gained a cult-like following and the highly anticipated second film broke box office opening records for the year. When the third film came out six months later, however, many disappointed fans did not even bother going to theaters.[1] Audiences typically regarded the second film as action-driven, but incomprehensible and pointless. Many deemed the third mercenary and deceitful, with profit-driven directors offering pretentious gibberish designed to confuse and trick fans. Reviews in mainstream media as well as from academic analysts and online forum contributors rarely seemed to consider the increasingly radical disruptions of patriarchy and whiteness as the series progressed. These disruptions include the deaths of white females in stark contrast to surviving black women and the routine integration of authority within gender and race lines. Furthermore, in Zion, the only human stronghold and symbolically the utopian representation of a divinely sanctioned human order, Asians, Hispanics, and African Americans predominate rather than whites. In the last film, Neo, a savior coded as white, dies while a black female savior, an Asian man, and an East Indian child are the last faces seen onscreen, happily anticipating a brighter future. These disruptions are hardly typical of Hollywood, where, as Gwendolyn Audrey Foster notes, "one of the greatest lies of the cinema is that the world is largely made up of attractive white people who perform heroic acts and reproduce."[2] At least one possible explanation for these deviations lies in the trilogy's reliance on critical race theory *and* black philosophical thought, interpretive lenses not commonly used.

Race theory starts with the premise that race is intrinsic to cognition, experience, identity and politics in the United States. The "colorblind" nature of

American culture partly explain the unpopularity of race theory as an interpretive lens. This nature promotes ideologies attributing economic and social inequity to everything *except* white racism or a colonialist past. Further, a colorblind culture sees the continual emphasis nonwhites place on race as counterproductive, signaling an inability to face responsibilities, work hard, and adopt American cultural norms. These norms, of course, are associated with people identified as white and are part of a discourse labeled "whiteness." Implicit in whiteness, and accepted within colorblind culture, is the perception that whites almost single-handedly created America and that their economic success is due to their superior intellect, initiative, and morality. Because Western colonialists required a dehumanized labor force to subsidize economic ventures, a coexisting ideology of blacks as direct opposites of whites – indolent, disreputable, sexually excessive and aesthetically horrific – also developed.[3]

Black ideological thought, the worldviews of those of the African diaspora, is also a marginalized interpretative lens, almost surprising given that cultural theorist Cornel West has repeatedly stated in interviews that his writings (and in particular those that discuss "prophetic" black religious theology) influenced the *Matrix* trilogy.[4] Black ideology is rooted in both a history of brutal enslavement and in surviving aspects of African heritage. As a critical approach, black ideology promotes demystifying skills directed at the larger dominating culture and at human institutions in general. It becomes what West calls "prophetic" when it identifies "concrete social evils," conceives of how social change could take place, and then generates cultures of hope, faith, and love motivated to work for change.[5] With freedom and survival primary concerns, blackness is by necessity coalitional and action-oriented. Its authenticity, says West and others, is framed by race-consciousness, an orientation ingrained in a culture whose very humanity is under dispute precisely because of race.[6]

The failure to interpret the trilogy within frameworks of African American ideology or critical race theory speaks not just to colorblindness but also to a deep cultural disinterest in addressing racial issues. However, a *Matrix* reading that juxtaposes critical race theory *and* black epistemologies with whiteness and patriarchy yields logical, illuminating, and historically situated results. These results address discrepancies in interpretations, particularly for the last two films. They also supplement the brief racially oriented reviews and commentaries on the series and offer an extended, cohesive, race-centered analysis of the three films. The trilogy, in this light, is shown to use black ideology to challenge whiteness and to suggest possible routes into social change, human coalitions, and new understandings of what it means to be human.

What is the price of vision, of freedom?

The first *Matrix* film is centrally concerned with challenges to whiteness, "normalcy," the workings of hegemony and ideological domination. As in standard Hollywood form, the film begins with whites as dominant action figures – from the main protagonist Neo, played by Keanu Reeves, to Trinity, played by Carrie Ann Moss, to the enemy agents. Nevertheless, the movie very quickly questions seemingly unrelated core assumptions. During an arrest scene, Trinity, a freedom fighter, jumps above police officers and makes an impossible flying dive; in a bedroom, words type themselves on a computer screen; and later, an unseen person with the ability to see beyond understood realms directs Neo on a cell phone. In this first film, Neo, a white-collar corporate worker, begins to experience challenges to his, and by extension our, assumptions about the world and what is normal. Laws of nature, apparent reality, and other levels of existence continue to blur, as demonstrated in a scene where Neo is freed from the influence of a surveillance bug implanted in him during an interrogation sequence. Under the illusion that the implanting had been a dream, he exclaims, "That thing's real?!"

These breaks with reality apparently come after years of search for deep truths about a vaguely understood concept called the matrix. But Neo does not find his answers through the technology associated with Western breakthroughs, i.e. through computer searches for information. Instead, revelations come from Morpheus, an African American leader in an underground movement. Morpheus, played by Laurence Fishburne, tells Neo that he knows how Neo feels, that "something is wrong with the world" – wrong with its schools, churches, media, and everything around him. Morpheus further describes the human race as born in bondage and tells Neo he is a slave in a prison. Neo realizes the truth of Morpheus' words after he sees human bodies held captive in hives, fuel sources that power indifferent slave-holding machines. It is at this point, the usefulness of black ideology and black history surfaces. This ties to one of the most salient aspects of African American ideology in how it refutes the "naturalness" of racialized constructions by exposing the relationship between commonly accepted stereotypes and exploitation. Black ideology is patently color-conscious. In numerous pre-Civil War slave narratives and songs, blacks clearly understood that their lives fueled an economic system that enriched others while offering them little or nothing in return. Based on the severity of their experiences and in, many cases, on identification with the biblical Jewish exodus from slavery, many of these narratives invalidated Western constructions of skin color as markers of either morality or natural leadership. Particularly germane to this analysis is how black ideology and experience promoted widespread skepticism about Western discourses and epistemologies, instead prizing individual and collective self-realization with genuinely democratic processes. In slave narratives, the main characters lose their childish innocence and, through a number of terrifying experiences, become forcibly aware of colonialism, whiteness, and its horrifying effects.[7] Their testimonies correspond to Neo's move into the "real world" and his understanding of how humans, by virtue of mental constructs, support and keep alive the conditions for grotesque existences. Whereas in slave narratives, the condition of African Americans is gruesomely brutal, both physically and mentally, what is precarious in Neo's existence is the conceptual world he occupies, his idea of who he is and the rules of existence. The matrix-based discourse about his life, promoted in a variety of ideological state apparatuses such as the media, churches, schools and so forth, is revealed to be compromised and deceptive. As Morpheus says, "It is the world that has been put over your eyes to blind you from the truth." Morpheus' words reference Louis Althusser's theory that individuals live in ideologies, in distorted mental worlds that work to situate and name individuals as particular types of subjects. This misrecognition is part of a representation that disguises humans' "real conditions of existence," as Neo discovers and as black slaves knew. The very name "Morpheus," in Greek mythology, is that of a god sent to tell a dreaming sleeper of a death.[8] In *The Matrix*, Morpheus' message is both the beginning of an exodus from mental slavery and a series of death events for Neo, beginning with his perception of social reality.

Like African Americans, Neo faces the daunting task of trying to understand and exist outside, within, and around a system he now experientially knows is wrong. The true answers for his survival don't lie in the matrix culture in which he has been reared. Instead, his black sources of knowledge argue for hidden, unrecognized influences in the very discussion of freedom itself. In short, Morpheus' black face calls into question the perception of isolation and purity in modern Western philosophical traditions concerned with equity, a perception rarely challenged by whites but not uncommon among African Americans. Sociologist Paul Gilroy, for example, suggests modern critiques of freedom, slavery, and social oppression relate directly to global slave revolutions, that the insights of enslaved black intellectuals "flowed into social movements of an anti-colonial and decidedly anti-capitalist type."[9]

The trilogy does not deny white creativity or insights; the integration of races within Morpheus' ship, the Nebuchadnezzar, alludes to this. Nevertheless, its black leadership reflects the centrality of the issue for the enslaved and raises the possibility of black ideology as an historical, tangible catalyst for coalitional action. It also alludes to the biracial nature of American social change, as in the Civil War and in the modern civil rights revolution of the 1950s. The Civil War yielded emancipation and an expanded definition of citizenship that affected all races, as well as women. However, the people most affected, the oppressed people sharing and enacting black ideology and prophetic thought, arguably inspired its coalitional abolitionist societies, slave revolts, and protests. The modern black revolution similarly yielded new protections for women, the disabled, the poor, and all racial minorities; but again, its impetus came from black ideology, from black religious "prophetic" thought at the forefront of the movement, diffused throughout a culture. This suggests future social and political reform may also begin with nonwhite Othered faces, not with brave whites as inspirational saviors.

America's hegemonic colorblind world synchronizes with the deceptive matrix world. The motif of distorted reflections visually comments on Neo's and our actual states of being and the facades of misrepresentation. Inconsistencies symbolically surface in the slanted images of Neo in a motorcycle mirror, in Morpheus' glasses, in a mirror that engulfs Neo at the *Heart of the City* hotel, and in an image on a spoon. All of these warped reflections surface near Neo before he fully internalizes the truth. Neo's true self during his matrix existence is not actually a true self; it is instead a computer-generated image divorced from Neo as he really is – weak, with atrophied muscles and eyes that have never been used. Morpheus' explanation that Neo's appearance is no more than the "mental projection of your digital self" indicates that it is only apart from a matrix construction that Neo will determine who he really is and his true strengths. The racial parallels are obvious: white supremacy depends upon maintaining illusions and hiding not only the potency of female and nonwhite vision and leadership, but white male weaknesses and potential as well.

The Matrix seems to understand the dislocation its audiences will face when discovering the depths of socially constructed illusion and the vitality of radically challenging Othered epistemologies and ontologies. Youths who begin to understand that racial perceptions are a part of a knowledge system based on human exploitation are like Neo when he begins to discover the truth about the matrix. Like Neo, they can no longer trust given assumptions about truth or reality. To gain this knowledge, Neo's input and output signals (information received and sent) require disruption, much like anyone who questions rather than accepts racial platitudes about meritocracy and culture. Like Neo, only then can these youth begin a quest to determine their actual locations and identities.[10] At first, Neo finds it difficult to accept that his origins and life assumptions are false. He cries out, "No! I don't believe it. It's not possible," and wants out of the awareness. He tells those whose minds are not controlled by the matrix to stay away from him. Finally, Neo becomes ill, vomits and blacks out. Once Neo finally accepts the truth he realizes that he cannot go back to his former life. He instead chooses to join those committed to revolution and liberation. Twisted mirrors disappear as a motif, and he begins by the end of the first movie to discover doors.

The trilogy also parallels African American critical goals of revealing the relationship between cultural discourses and the acceptance of unspeakable existences, serving like the slave narratives, as Henry Louis Gates notes, "to indict both those who enslaved them and the metaphysical system drawn upon to justify their enslavement."[11] Authors of slave narratives aimed their communications directly at white audiences. In 1861, escaped slave Harriet Jacobs told her readers:

> You never know what it is to be a slave; to be entirely unprotected by law or custom; to have the laws reduce you to the condition of a chattel, entirely subject to the will of another. You never exhausted your ingenuity in avoiding the snares, and eluding the power of a hated tyrant.[12]

Today's increasing poverty, poor health care, and lives subjected to violence and social alienation function much like a matrix existence. We can read the term "matrix" itself as identical to "matrices of domination." Sociologist Patricia Hill Collins defines matrices of domination as historically specific, overarching social organizations where oppressions originate, develop, and are contained. They are extensive systems of control, she says, maintained by "elite white men" who dominate Western structures of knowledge.[13] Artificial intelligences known as agents are allegorical of these structures and are characterized by their complete indifference to human welfare. They represent both hegemony and the ideologies of racism, classism, genderism, and exploitation born in colonialism. As enforcers and guardians of hegemony, these artificial intelligences originated with mankind but gained independent life, becoming virtually indestructible. Although agents are deadly, the trilogy indicts the humans who choose to collude with them, humans fully aware of the agents' nature and purpose. Cypher, played by Joe Pantoliano, is a member of Morpheus' crew and a betraying Judas figure feigning commitment to human liberation. Negotiating with the agents for a return to delusional understanding, Cypher eats a steak in a matrix restaurant and observes, "I know this steak doesn't exist. I know that when I put it in my mouth, the matrix is telling my brain that it is juicy and delicious. After nine years, you know what I realize? Ignorance is bliss." His nine years of struggle represent the reality that genuine social change also requires a conceptual conversion, rather than mere appropriation or integration of ethnic cultural styles. The film contrasts Cypher's appreciation of an artificial meal with Neo's memory of matrix food. Neo points to a restaurant and remembers how he used to enjoy its noodles. He looks around and says, "I have these memories from my entire life but . . . none of them really happened." When Trinity tells him the matrix cannot provide answers about who he is, she suggests a need to jettison his past self and to incorporate different "intellectual food," other points of view, and a new self-construction. These contrasts between Neo and Cypher also highlight another black ideological thrust – that there are benefits for whites when they choose to work for change against a system giving them such heavily compromised privilege. Slave narratives consistently characterize slave masters as persons seduced into inhumane behavior and attitudes, becoming less than human. Like slave narratives, Lawrence Buell argues, the trilogy suggests it is impossible for whites "to rest in the delusion that slave territory exists in a hermetic elsewhere from which free people are immune."[14] Both blindness and collusion are ingredients needed to maintain fictions of white supremacy, but they are two-edged swords precluding change of the larger economic systems that victimize us all.

Refuting stereotypes: validating black women, validating Othered worldviews

Unlike Cypher, who could choose to understand or deny the exploitative effects and artificiality of the filmic matrix, many who live in multicultural communities have not had the option of ignoring Western matrices of domination. The most positive consequences of awareness are longstanding, well-developed traditions of oppositional, subjugated knowledges. These cultural and intellectual standpoints are alluded to in characterizations of Zion, beginning with the first native-born citizen introduced to audiences, brown-skinned Tank, played by Marcus Chong.[15] As "a genuine child of Zion," Tank is a freedom-fighter who bears no marks of the matrix on his body, no metal openings to hook into its delusional information system. Never plugged in, never attached, Tank (like his brother Dozer) has an identity based on different, expanded knowledges, experiences, and information. Neither Tank nor Dozer was ever subject to input and output programming signals; they are unlike Neo, who had to be removed from the matrix, its input and output signals disrupted, in order for him to discover his true position. These children of Zion, their lives rooted in a nonwhite human reality, do not require the same type of intellectual release although they share a common fight.

Further signs that the trilogy values subjugated communities and knowledges surface in the characterization of the Oracle, played by Gloria Foster and, later, Mary Alice, both African American women. Although the term "Oracle" references Greek priestesses who spoke for the gods, foretold the future, and offered advice, the black Oracle Neo meets says calmly, "not quite what you were expecting." In a major disruption of cultural stereotypes, she is obviously no standard Greek goddess or prophet – she is older and sturdy rather than thin and ethereal and hardly fits into Western depictions of feminine spiritual wisdom or beauty. The Oracle wears an apron and frequently inhabits the kitchen or a domestic setting such as a living room. Her cookie baking and constant care of non-black children clearly signify the enslaved black mammy and the post-Civil War domestic servant. Her contemporary language and demeanor also evoke the continuance of stereotypes suggested by the updating of Aunt Jemima images on pancake boxes a few years ago. But, unlike Jemima on the pancake boxes or the stereotypical mammy, the Oracle disrupts the lingering memory of black female as inferior and also challenges still-current understandings of black females measured by standards of white femininity. She is instead an "othermother." As sociologist Patricia Hill Collins notes, African American survival traditions required not just physical labor but a communal mothering, which produced women with moral authority born in experience, a critical aspect of black feminist thought. Often misunderstood, Collins says community mothering is a type of power, one recognized as strong, ethical and transformative. It is linked to concrete sustained social and political activism. The matrix Oracle has interests larger than the welfare of one white male or of any one group in particular. Her job is not mere caregiving but instruction to non-black children about the nature of reality and how it can be bent. Later identified as an artificial intelligence, the Oracle is also a type of intellect, but an endangered type of liberation ideology. She wants peace, and ultimately, in helping "white" Neo understand himself, she directs him not to privileged leadership, but to sacrifice.

Even more directly than the casting of a black leader (Morpheus), the casting of a black Oracle shows how "white" culture and wisdom may have very Othered and very female influences. The issue here is the disruption of another deeply held, but rarely overtly articulated, racist assumption – that Western culture developed in isolation, unique and pure. Ancient "interracial" borrowing is neither unknown nor is it discounted among many African Americans, but the very concept operates below the periphery in white cultures. Traditional black writers, such as Cheikh Anta Diop and George G.M. James, along with the contemporary white writer Martin Bernal, argue key ancient Greek philosophers are indebted to Egypt, a civilization that would have been considered black using colonial-based constructions of race. Equally important is a related belief that Greek oracles and priestesses imitated preexisting Egyptian models, and further, that the very first Greek priestesses were black women taken from Egypt.[16] Even to consider ancient Greek appropriations, much less to make a casting choice supporting the notion, radically undermines whiteness. This disruption relates to the earlier mentioned assumptions structuring modern knowledge as uniquely white. If basic Western intellectual discourses result from a bi-directional interaction between races and nations, then there is no actual legitimacy to an entire modern educational system promoting itself and rationality as primarily and organically white. Instead, philosophy and culture can be understood as a creolization, where the silence of origins and influences is just another function of Western hegemony.

The symbolic meaning of a black Oracle also has strong ties to Womanist/black feminist theories, which begin with dichotomous black and white feminine constructions. Western culture positioned white women as highly spiritual, sexually pure Virgin Marys.[17] This same culture depicted black women as direct opposites, as animals breeding without pain, neither human nor descendants of "Eve and her daughters."[18] This stereotypical black female could be dismissed as incapable of spirituality or "true womanhood." These representations, like other black stereotypes, obscured the profit motivations behind slavery, specifically the sale of black children, black female sexual exploitation, and inhumane labor for mothers and pregnant women. Connected to contemporary media portrayals, racist representations still tend to marginalize black women as either credible or moral, except in service to whites or as clones of a white female standard.

Many African American women did not and still do not accept these constructions of themselves. Prompted by psychological and physical survival, they instead developed critical orientations privileging female agency, creativity, assertiveness, and courageous articulation of truths from their own perspectives. Womanism or black feminism, like other black ideologies, provides an existentialist understanding of what it means to be female while surrounded by inescapable, inhumane conditions, and dehumanizing representations.[19] It is this Womanist orientation that provides the foundation for understanding Womanist Christianity. Theologian Stephanie Y. Mitchem characterizes a

Womanist theology as one that merges the sufferings of black females with those of Jesus and finds significant parallels. Black female suffering justifies social change and resistance, while her experiences become an interpretive resource for an entire community. When Christianity is understood from a Womanist perspective, sin becomes not only an act against the divine, but also an act of mental abuse against a larger human group and community. The terms *redemption* and *salvation* are broadened to include psychic liberations, while the black woman, as a Christ-like savior, embodies a family and community-oriented "ministerial vision . . . incapable of being destroyed by human evil."[20] In short, black women have a tradition of enacting and articulating truths that better an entire community. Their activism and right to speak is justified by the survival of dehumanizing experiences, and legitimized within an oppositional black ideological and theological system.

Understood within this tradition of analysis, action and survival, the trilogy's Oracle is not revolutionary and disruptive simply because she is a wise black woman or because she holds a lead role; she is revolutionary because she is a mainstream reference to underrepresented Womanist ideology and history. The Oracle is key to psychic liberation, guiding diverse characters according to her visions, realities, and her sincere desire to end the war. She is a radical transformation of Western denigration of black women and an amazing materialization of black women's own self-definitions. Her character reflects the life-sustaining insight, faith, and love for humanity that many scholars connect to black female culture. An early sign of her moral and spiritual positioning within the trilogy occurs when Neo and Morpheus enter her apartment building. They see a black man at the entryway, holding a staff, clothed in robes. As a black Moses figure, this unnamed character foreshadows the Oracle's role as savior and the notion of black and, in particular, black Womanist insights as central to emergence from damaging, enslaving constructions.[21] By the end of the third movie, the Oracle is revealed as the hidden catalyst for annihilation of evil. In *The Matrix Revolutions*, Agent Smith attempts to destroy her by absorbing her black essence and transforming it into a copy of himself. In this cloning process, she, like enslaved women during the colonial eras, is subjected to the loss of her body, insight, individuality, and her very existence. When cloning occurs, light blazes and computer imagery superimposes over the characters, suggesting a merging or meeting of two worlds. This imagery is an intertexual reference to Neo's resurrection and subsequent savior status in the first *Matrix* film. But, consistent with Womanist theologies, it also links the black woman as the Oracle to Christ. The final apocryphal battle scene between Neo and Smith similarly affirms her savior-like status. When Smith/ Neo disintegrates, the Oracle's body replaces his in the rain. She alone survives the ultimate showdown between good and evil. Although it appeared she had been destroyed, she was concealed, performing hidden critical intellectual work. This suggests that, despite attempts to appropriate and nullify nonwhite intellect and creativity, subjugated knowledges, particularly black female ones, are a potent force. They are the very essence of freedom, which, when adopted, understood, and strategically integrated, can subvert an entire system.

Niobe, played by African American actress Jada Pinkett-Smith, is a ship captain introduced in the second film. Not simply an inversion of power relations or a mere articulation of resistance, she, like the Oracle, proves she possesses the competency and ability to maneuver outside a dominant structure by developing and executing a critical alternate military strategy. Her plan eventually supersedes that of the white male commander previously in charge. In another scene, Niobe makes a contested decision to give Neo her ship for his sacrificial mission. In defending herself, Niobe references the words of the white male captain, invoking them to assert her own authority. This rhetorical move alludes to a double-voiced signifying as she takes the white male's words but turns them around to her own advantage. Even more remarkable is her identification of the spiritual force that inspires her actions. Unlike Morpheus and Trinity, she vocally articulates her doubts in a white male savior; she does not grant him credit as being central to her motivations. When choosing to give her ship to Neo, she instead acknowledges the black female savior/Oracle as her decisive inspiration. Niobe, freed from the matrix, resembles actual black women who define self and privilege their own agency. The name "Niobe" infers racial significance; in Greek mythology, Niobe was an Egyptian (black) queen who lost her children just like countless African American women.[22] In the Greek legend, a merciless god slaughtered her sons and daughters. In black American history, people who believed themselves to be racial gods sold away and molested black women's children. The Greek Niobe is known for her tears and mourning, corresponding to the deep suffering of many enslaved African American women whose children did not live out their natural lives.[23] This history of colonial era suffering is still retained in cultural memory; cultural theorist bell hooks characterizes these memories as an enduring "trauma of slavery holocaust."[24] Niobe's relationship with Morpheus also reflects a type of gender-independent, yet interactive relationship between oppressed black women and men. Facing a brutal system, they had a history of fighting and dying together in insurrections against American slavery and in agitations for civil rights.[25] It is Niobe, for example, who catches Morpheus in her car when he falls off a tractor-trailer, and it is she that later positions him to get back into a fight against an agent. Later, in *Revolutions*, Morpheus, who previously inspired and led an entire crew, often becomes virtually silent in Niobe's presence. In the final episode, he frequently takes a backseat to Niobe, whose piloting skills and risk-taking, at least temporarily, save Zion. Her role infers a female agency that does not ignore the male, but asserts as her given right independent action, an ideological position many African American women regard as a cultural resource and legacy.

Zion as racially transformed and multicultural

The city of Zion deposes yet another ingrained understanding of whiteness – that white people are central to human progress and the pursuit of divine utopias. The city alludes to the black ideological view that African Americans have a specific and useful insight,[26] and extends that concept to various Others. Heavily multicultural, Zion visually positions nonwhites and females at the center of its existence rather than at its periphery. Consistent with global reality, it is coalitional humanity that predominates – not groups of whites. This is also the population most besieged by matrix forces. Neo, the white male subject, does not lead Zion. Instead he, first learns from them, finds his place, and then fights in concert with an entire community mutually aware of the forces threatening them all. Zion's people are loving, intelligent, coordinated, and the only hope for the future. Their dance sequences are not reflections of stereotypical sexuality out of control; instead, they exude the essence of a creative, diverse humanity whose strength is a passionate, fiery hope for the future. They radiate an immediate vibrancy and enthusiastic life-force. Accordingly, Zion's cavern-like space pulsates with heavy drumbeats, metaphorically representing heartbeats that prefigure a new life. Dirty feet, transparent clothes, and strong, sexual emotions shout unpretentious, see-through humanity. Conversely, the techno music and props in matrix world clubs suggest enormous amounts of energy spent in maintaining contrived appearances and spaces. Matrix club dress continues the theme of artifice in the proliferation of tailored leather, stiff hairdos, and heavy makeup. While sexuality exists in the matrix clubs, its patrons wear dominatrix type clothing which positions sexuality as a perverse attraction associated with master/slave games. It is a clear contrast to Zion and another reference to slavery. In Zion, clearly identifiable humans make music, the symbolic framework for coordinated human action and movement. Citizens see the performers that stir them, suggesting hidden hegemonic forces are not in play. Music also plays in matrix clubs, but the rhythm that moves matrix dancers has an invisible or hidden source. The people who pull the strings and hit the beats are never seen. The communal meeting spaces of Zion are simultaneously a church/dance arena, one that integrates celebration, entertainment, spirituality and prayer. In Zion, religion flourishes and centers on human freedom. It is the black prophetic vision, tenaciously believing in futures as yet unseen. Religion as a belief in something beyond immediate survival, pleasure, and sensation never fully materializes in the matrix and is apparently not a goal. Illumination for Zion's flickering dance hall/church (metaphorically enlightenment) apparently comes from fires and torches, direct sources of energy. These coexist in harmony with other types of lighting, again evoking the notion of less contrived, or dehumanized sacred and secular approaches to life. Conversely, the matrix world has no integration of natural light sources, only artificial, technologically engineered illuminations for its dark interior places, suggesting a comparative imbalance between knowledge rooted in experience and abstracted, cold, florescent epistemologies.

The trilogy's Zion is in stark contrast not just to matrix clubs but also to common media representations normalizing nonwhite community as lawless and frightening. Two recent films, *Hotel Rwanda* (2004) and *Collateral* (2004), illustrate the concept of ghettos, and barrios as homes of the deviant. In *Hotel Rwanda*, immoral, brutal, and murderous black nationalist hordes rape and terrify a small group of blacks affiliated with whites. The film's black hero is humane, but his representation is telling. He refuses African dress, wears suits and ties, is a connoisseur of Western culture, has a pale wife with straight hair, and children who play European games. For all of the token discourse on how colonialism initiated the present ethnic rivalry, ultimately helpless, victimized blacks desperately seek white European saviors, horrified as the remnants of white colonialist forces leave their land. Almost every white pictured is empathetic and good, risking life and limb to help the blacks around them, affirming whiteness as preferable, fair and just. The black-ruled world is an oppositional nightmare.

Collateral's nonwhite underworld parallels *Rwanda*'s hellish black-ruled civilization. It takes viewers into a terrifying drug community prominently featuring Hispanics, a Korean, and a black on a hit list. All of these Othered characters have flaws that propelled them into their situations and none is innocent. The white assassin sent into this dark universe is perverse, but he is actually performing a service, eliminating undesirable criminals at the direction of a heartless Hispanic. The Latino club in *Collateral* is not a place of communal hope and pleasure; it is an operational headquarters where murders are negotiated. True to whiteness conventions, other races are moral deviations from an implied white ideal. Also true to whiteness conventions, the film infuses its surviving, preferable black characters with Anglo culture. Jamie Foxx does not especially like jazz and prefers Western classical music. Jada Pinkett-Smith appears in business dress and is the epitome of the corporate female; further, she is an active agent in society's attempts to control its dark Others, overdetermined as savage.

Zion also differs from the predominantly white futuristic cities in science fiction films such as *I Robot* (2004), *The Thirteenth Floor* (1999) and *Minority Report* (2002). In these thrillers, no multicultural group fights heroic life and death battles; the populations of these futures do not reflect contemporary global racial realities. The emphasis is on males working within a white systemic order. They correct problems within the system, but not the system itself. In *Dark City* (1998), a white male single-handedly returns humans to a pre-alien ideal, a "normalcy" lost when nonhuman strangers (read nonwhite Others) arrived to conduct reality-altering experiments. The doctor who colludes with them admits he has "betrayed his own kind." One of the most interesting contrasts to Zion is in *Gangland* (2004), a "B" movie aired on late-night satellite.[27] In this future, a plague originating in Africa threatens the globe.

White newscasters urge citizens to avoid contact with anyone infected. Meanwhile, as urban gangs take over, white blond female suburbanites and their white male heroes try to control the threat. Although the enemy gang that receives filmic attention is white, its vicious leader has skin color markedly darker than anyone else's. This dark-skinned, racially ambiguous character is named Lucifer. Evil in these films continues to express itself as a demonic, lawless Other threatening white societies.

The trilogy's twist on conventions becomes blatant and obvious within these contrasts. Rather than reinforcing ghetto or barrio stereotypes, Zion's conjoined humanity completely transforms them into sites of vibrant life with both religious and secular commitments to humanity. Going underground in the trilogy means human survival, however precarious, must move away from whiteness. Zion is not merely a backdrop to one white man's search for answers. Multicultural Zion *is* the answer.

The choice of Neo, a seemingly white hero (the actor, Keanu Reeves, is actually Asian and European American), as a pivotal personality does not necessarily negate a disruptive interpretation of the trilogy.[28] Realistically, Neo, perceived as white by most of mainstream America, and as symbolic of whiteness, indisputably has special privileges and powers.[29] Nevertheless, these powers and a star role do not translate into the expected narrative formations of privileged leadership and wisdom, but rather into privileged sacrifice and larger human freedom achieved by the ultimate denial of self – white death. As a symbolic white person, Neo's special power is in part authority; such authority can and must support dismantling of the system. This is suggested in the character of the Kid, a young white male who openly idolizes Neo as the one who "saved" him. It also comes through the many Zionist people of different nationalities who beg "white," male Neo to free loved ones still trapped in the matrix. These characters are testimony of the helplessness felt when interacting with people immersed in whiteness. Those afflicted with whiteness will not believe in nonwhite values unless an authoritative white endorses or appropriates a marginalized viewpoint. As West says, "it is unrealistic for creative people of color to think they can sidestep the White patronage system." He also identifies the existence of "white allies conscious of the tremendous need to rethink identity politics."[30] In alluding to interracial cooperation as necessary for transformation, Neo, Morpheus, the Oracle and others jointly function as interlocking role models working toward a transformed society.

Rejecting whiteness: understanding your idols

A break away from whiteness paradigms surfaces most clearly in *The Matrix Reloaded*, the second movie. *Reloaded* introduces the Merovingian, an artificial intelligence played by French actor Lambert Wilson. He relishes superficial extravagances and talks of contrivances, things done merely for the "sake of appearances." With his thick, exaggerated French accent, love of fine wine, and sampling of languages, the Merovingian embodies another concept of whiteness – that of Eurocentric notions of refinement and culture as the ultimate standard of human behavior. Western cultural capital is a traditional basis for Othering and assumes its social products are the results of advanced intellect in contrast to nonwhite culture, seen as based on primitive sexual and survival desires. As cultural theorist Stuart Hall comments: "Among whites, 'Culture' was opposed to nature. Amongst Blacks, it was assumed 'Culture' coincided with 'Nature'. Whereas whites developed 'Culture' to subdue and overcome Nature,' for blacks, 'Culture' and 'Nature' were interchangeable."[31] Reason (as a source of culture), says the Merovingian, separates "us from them." But, telling, the Merovingian compares speaking French to "wiping your ass with silk." Then, he admits, "beneath our poised appearance, the truth is we are completely out of control." He says this in the process of administering the technologically advanced equivalent of a date rape drug to a white female diner. The name "Merovingian" itself is that of an early French dynasty, a political precursor to European unity and the move of diverse people into a perception of themselves as white.

Various henchmen surround this symbol of culture, with the most visually compelling a set of twin albino assassins. A visual extreme of whiteness, they wear white suits and have unnaturally pale skin and bleached white hair. They are characterized by their ennui, monotone voices, and inability to engage in emotions; one, for example, observes languidly, "We are getting aggravated," when he is frustrated during a fight scene. They appear to be alive and perhaps even contemporary, *au courant* with their appropriated and dreadlocked hair, yet they are actually ghosts whose true state appears when they are attacked or attacking; they metamorphose, passing through tangible, real objects. Their ghostly features mirror the deathly qualities of the European intellectual legacy when it works to justify domination; the legacy of intangible ideas materialized in human bodies in the form of genocide, rape of enslaved women, and the exploitation of entire countries. When these gruesome allegorical albinos are finally destroyed at the end of the highway sequence, they dissolve into images of death, becoming translucent skeletons. It is the trilogy's indictment of the death and arrogance that has traditionally accompanied Western cultural capital.

Persephone, the Merovingian's wife, is also played by a European, the Italian actress Monica Bellucci. Her character similarly alludes to the lethal legacy of Western cultures and explores motivations of people with mixed allegiances to it. This white female has no intention of leaving her husband, nor does she particularly care about the rebels' cause. She will, however, help the Zion residents as an act of retaliation against her husband who has given her privilege but little fulfillment. When she leads Morpheus, Trinity, and Neo to henchmen watching TV in an inner room, she describes the henchmen as outdated programs kept alive to do her husband's dirty work. As she speaks, a vampire movie plays on a background TV. The metaphorical link is dead creatures (whites who constrict their existence into narrow, restricting lifeless conventions of whiteness), the murder of innocent beings (exploitation of third world peoples and resources) and survival by sipping the blood or life force of others (unacknowledged, insensitive cultural appropriations, or as bell hooks terms it, "eating the other").[32]

The Matrix Reloaded also makes commentary on nonwhite allegiances to whiteness ideology in Neo's fight against a second multicultural group of henchmen. These programs are intelligences working for the Frenchman and serve as reminders that, as bell hooks mentions, "the system of white-supremacist capitalist patriarchy is not maintained solely by white folks. It is also maintained by all the rest of us who internalize and enforce the values of this regime."[33] Asian, black, white and Hispanic programs fight for the Merovingian in a setting surrounded by icons of whiteness. Situated in a larger foyer, busts of European mythical gods are destroyed as the battle wages, each of their faces grotesque adaptations of the Merovingian's visage. European coats of arms are liberally sprinkled over the *mise en scène* while Renaissance era artwork adorns the walls, further suggesting links to whiteness, the start of Western colonialism and perceptions of whiteness as endowed with superior humanistic attributes. When the Merovingian leaves the room, these intelligences fight for him. As they struggle within a house shouting whiteness, they represent those who have learned to value themselves only as servants and imitators of whiteness. They show how domination and power is diffused throughout culture regardless of how one is racially classified. In this setting, Neo fights with the weapons available to him: tridents and swords linked to a European past. Although Neo wins this battle, he loses his larger objectives as the Frenchman tells him, "I will survive you," and moves to another location in what is apparently an enormous mansion. As Audre Lorde suggests, the effectiveness of using the tools and words of the West in attempts to contest white systems of domination may be doubtful.[34] However, this and other battles also reflect the multifaceted arenas of ideological and hegemonic struggles. The use of Westernized tools in fact may be necessary steps in the route for human liberation. The allegorical message in this fight scene suggests a direct confrontation with whiteness cannot be avoided in the contemporary journey to human freedom. The most radical challenge to whiteness appears in scenes with the Architect. Played by Canadian Helmut Bakaitis, his appearance signals the only time the movie makes a direct reference to race, the only time race is assigned to a character. As designer of the matrix, initially the Architect is aesthetically framed as a benevolent god. When Neo enters the Architect's sanctum, white light blazes, a familiar motif in life-after-death accounts and popular reports of encounters with deities. The Architect sits omnipotent, enthroned before computer screens showing various views of humanity. Cloaked in whiteness, he is an older white man with a white beard wearing an off-white business suit and shoes. But this god is actually contemptuous of people and indifferent to the destruction of most of the human race. He is not a benevolent God of humanity, but the god of the enslaving matrix world; his omnipotence is the horrifying specter of the panoptic prison.

The Architect is the metaphor of a worshiped idol, one who arrogantly and horrifically blends cultural concepts, religion, and logic to exploit others. The Architect frequently alludes to his superior mind and dismisses the black Oracle as "one less bound by the parameters of perfection." He speaks of a minority that could undermine the system, but his solution for humanity offers no liberation or freedom, only continuing cycles of slavery. He explains to Neo what the ultimate goal of a matrix white savior is – to save his own white life and, after slumming with the ethnics, to betray his diverse comrades, just as other versions of him have previously done. Neo's disillusionment and confusion in finally facing this white god figures in the overlapping, angry comments of past Neos confronting the Architect. Significantly, one angrily says, "You can't make me do anything, you old white prick!" These words, the only racial identifications made in the entire trilogy, indicate the past Neos recognize both hegemonic pressure as well as the possibility of choice when confronting whiteness paradigms and programming. The sixth Neo completely rejects this idol derived from culture and instead chooses love. He again suggests an alternative model for young whites who, after "eating the other," coolly walk away and are absorbed back into the system. The Architect's allegorical meaning can also easily be expanded to include any group of people who make their cultural, gender, or race constructions a force all must revere. The Oracle, as a signifier of Othered ideologies, contrasts his persona. As mother of the Matrix, she similarly is tied to systems and artificial intelligence, but she works in service of humanity. Continually, she offers choice, not domination. Her conversation is sprinkled with phrases such as, "Suit yourself," and "Make up your own damn mind." The trilogy suggests through the Oracle that philosophy can work for or against us. It can assist in obtaining knowledge or work to obscure it.

Merging gender and racial critiques

Critiques of the interlocking relationships between gender and race characterize the final movie, *The Matrix Revolutions*. It begins with white male characters dominating both scenes and dialogue. A strong, forceful white captain gives orders. Nonwhite males work in subordinate roles, and consistent with white patriarchal constructions, nurturing, loving white women are absent from the command arena; instead, they look after white males in the ship's medical bay. This initially seems to be a conventional patriarchal beginning. But it actually parallels the first movie because its normative beginnings are eventually reversed in subversive, and unexpected ways. Before the end of the film, Niobe, a black female, will be in charge of all the males first pictured, directing orders to everyone on the ship. Similarly, Neo, far from being the stereotypical white male tower of strength, starts the film trapped in a mysterious zone that appears to be an underground subway station. Neo is in a void, in a non-world, arriving there through forces he doesn't understand.

Neo's arrival follows a time of great disappointment and doubt. He has met the god of whiteness, found this idol inadequate, and then chosen an uncharted path. Neo's stay in the subway station can be read as a metaphor for the uncertainties and vagueness of maneuvering in intellectual territories outside whiteness, conceptual terrains that require non-Western moorings or newly created postmodern understandings. This unnamed netherworld is where beings make transitions, such as an East Indian family of intelligences who pass through it on their way to other destinations. Neo is initially confident his superior (read: white) powers will earn him a way out, but he learns he cannot leave. He is prevented from doing so by a Merovingian henchman. The netherworld subway is a living purgatory, a place where one realizes the enormity of the tasks of liberation and the price of ideological isolation and separation. It is also the confusion and vagueness felt after realizing hegemonic powers are overwhelming, committed to destruction, without mercy. His questions are our questions: How does one proceed forward in the struggle knowing the truth of the past but not the path to a truthful future? Is resistance a lost cause? Can one individual challenge a system alone or escape only through deals with its rulers? Neo runs in hopeless circles trying to escape this trap.

His release comes at the hands of a white woman, a black man, and an Asian man. These three, in turn, are operating under the visions of the black female Oracle. The rescue begins when Morpheus, Trinity, and Seraph, played by Collin Chou, the Asian protector of the Oracle, enter the world of the Frenchman and barter for Neo's life. The trio form a defensive tripod, back to back, each supporting the other against an evil white intelligence. This suggests unions not normally visualized in Hollywood cinema. The Frenchman, the embodiment of white cultural capital and pretensions, is compelled to choose between his own death and acquiescence to the trio's demands. It is the white female, Trinity, who decisively turns the tide in the standoff and initiates the Frenchman's capitulation. In Neo's rescue scene, Trinity alone meets Neo. She alludes to white female feminists who, with natural ties to white males, are a logical starting point for white male transitions into larger understanding.

Filmic critiques of white masculinity constructions proliferate throughout *Revolutions*, as Neo loses his sight and must be guided by Trinity. At the heart of Zion's battle against machines, Neo is removed from the screen for nearly thirty minutes, a clear commentary about the importance of collective utopian strategy. His constant self-questioning shows his primary task is to understand his role, not to direct and guide the Othered Zionists. He, as the symbol of whiteness's future, must in the end make a willing, deathly sacrifice. *Revolutions'* death throes of whiteness and masculinity are foreshadowed in Neo and Trinity's sexual scenes in *Reloaded*. Camera shots alternate between its rave-like dance and images of Neo and Trinity in a separate space making love. A mesh of primarily non-whites enthusiastically participate in a sensuous dance, and at one point, women touch each other provocatively. But Neo, the male hero, fails in the ultimate act of phallocentric masculinity and reproduction: ejaculation.

The physical appearances of African American characters Zee (Nona Gaye) and her sister-in-law, Cas (Gina Torres), address contrasts in black and white femininity as opposed to Womanist constructions. Both wear white, symbolic of purity and fleshly transcendence. Zee's displays of cleavage undeniably associate her with sexuality, but her quiet, almost demure persona suggest a spiritual purity traditionally associated with white women. Naturalized in both women and Niobe as well are tattoos and ethnic hairstyles, which include cornrows, Bantu knots, and flowing, frizzy curls. This places black female standards of beauty on a par with white ones, not as merely mimetic. Zee and Cas, unlike the other white women portrayed, are also traditional types of wives, loving and loyal women who wait for their men. Not surprisingly, children appear in their scenes together. Zee's version of traditional femininity is dramatized even more when, after she decides to join the war effort, the directors pair her with Charra, Rachel Blackman, a flat-chested white woman warrior who wears a butch haircut and masculine clothes. These inversions more than anything else call attention to the problems of routinely assigning psychological and physical characteristics to any single gender or racialized group. It also calls attention to variance, to the ways group members routinely *don't* fit stereotypes. What is also telling is the way the film portrays all of these women as contributors crucial to the struggle for human survival.

Another intersecting gender and racial critique is found in the trilogy's life and death choices. When viewed through phenotypic selection, the narrative shows the survival and reproduction of white people and white females are not privileged over that of nonwhites. This is a direct inversion of ideologies that reward white women for their affiliations and alliances to white men with survival. Challenges begin in *Revolutions'* sick bay sequences. Its doctor, Maggie, played by Essie Davis, cares for an ill white male, Bane, played by Ian Bliss. She appears nurturing; the doctor even enters the sick bay carrying an object resembling a serving tray. A ray of overhead light shines down on her and moments later, positioned before a computer, her face glows with light reflected from the screen, indicative of lighting choices aligning her to concepts of white women as Madonna-like and spiritually pure.[35] She is extraordinarily pale, with strawberry blonde hair and blue eyes. In control of her sick bay, she exercises power over the inert white male. Outside of the sick bay, the white male captain she works for seeks her advice. Maggie embodies film theorist Richard Dyer's notion of white women positioned between privilege and subordination. But, about halfway into the film, she understands too late that the white male she cares for has a hidden nature. Bane, an incarnation of evil intelligence, kills her. Her death occurs only after she attempts to administer a hypodermic that will force him to tell the truth about his past and events that have occurred. Close-ups highlight her expressions of fear, shock, and pain, a commentary on the feared results of hegemonic exposure and enlarged knowledge. For the white male, it is an anxious anxiety about possible loss, loss of prestige, phallocentric mystique, and white female connection.

Trinity is part of a group of white women with important roles. Another white woman functions, for example, as the leader of Zion's ruling Council and sits at the center of the decision-making table. Yet Trinity dies and the presence of white women in authoritative roles and positions does not signal a feminine version of white power structures. Trinity never enjoys a lasting union with Neo and her death contrasts with the joy of the black women (Niobe with Morpheus and Zee with Link) who celebrate with lovers as the war ends. Dyer alludes to the metaphorical significance of happy endings, of unions, in his descriptions of white women and what they signify. Dyer says white women are symbolic of home; reunion with her is allegorical reward for and the purpose of successful imperialism and colonial efforts. In killing the white male and his love interest, the trilogy suggests this is an imperialist understanding that, however romantic, should end in death. Whites survive in Zion, but it is clear their identities are no longer based on fictitious, exploitative hierarchies.

"Only human"

"Only human" is the contemptuous phase that an Agent throws at Neo during a fight sequence. The phrasing encourages a deeper analysis of what humanity really is — conceptualizations divorced from notions of earthly saviors or supermen. It also suggests an implied, indirect commentary on hierarchical racial divisions among peoples. The phrase supports an interpretation of character complexity along with a filmic storyline disinterested in pat answers.

In the trilogy, whiteness symbolically dies, but Morpheus' struggles and eventual silence and inactivity shows blackness is not given absolute moral stature. Whites do not dominate in Zion but they are significantly represented in its operations and life. Patriarchy, as seen in the East Indian family of intelligences, survives as does the continuance of a pocket of Western-based civilization, signified by the Merovingian and his club. The Frenchman's survival suggests white culture, as opposed to white supremacy with its henchmen of domination can figure into new existences. The Architect also lingers, but as a threat that has lost its former bite. This is signified in a clothing change — at the end of the film, he wears the same suit he wore in his god-like setting, but its color has changed from off-white to a pale, muted blue. His altered appearance and continuance suggests the threat of glorified systems of culture and race may still resurface and dominate with perhaps new racial or ethnic sources. The matrix world of abstract ideas and mental constructions also survives and, presumably, people choose to reside there. What changes is knowledge and choice. What also changes is the possibility of a neo-ideology outside of whiteness and beyond blackness, as represented by the East Indian child who creates a brand new intelligence, a program she says commemorates Neo and his abolitionist decision to sacrifice his life in support of humanity. The sunrise created by the East Indian intelligence respects sacrifice and proposes that privilege is not the most worthy or life-sustaining human goal.

The trilogy's phenotype selections signify the primary role of race in structuring American systems of domination. The interpretive gaps seen in cinematic commentary speaks to the effectiveness of color blindness as a cultural norm, as well as to the vast conceptual divides between white and nonwhite ideologies and experiences. These conceptual divides underscore not just filmic interpretive failure, but why the daily white supremacist assaults on nonwhite psyches are trivialized and go mostly unrecognized and misunderstood. With little mainstream cultural impetus for making whiteness and its narrative assumptions visible, the trilogy offers a unique starting point for Americans, encouraging whites in particular, to develop a "double-consciousness" that incorporates its *total* racial history. Like the Zionists who leave their city, travel to a virtual world to fight, and then return, contemporary viewers who internalize expanded knowledges can begin making culturally sophisticated choices. By redefining themselves as part of a multicultural global reality, they can decide to travel back and forth between constructed norms in a common fight for human liberation. The multifaceted nature of "only human" status with its allegorical doorways into ideology, history and larger systemic oppression is intrinsically linked to race and our contemporary culture.[36]

Notes

1 By the end of 1999, the first *Matrix* rated fifth top-rating film that year for total gross profits (see www.the-numbers.com/market/1999.php). The first film also won Oscars for editing, sound and visual effects, and sound. Given the high anticipation for its sequel, *The Matrix Reloaded* had the highest opening day gross for movies released that year and ranked #4 in total gross for 2003. Viewer dissatisfaction is indicated in that *The Matrix Revolutions*, released six months later in December, ranked #9 with an opening day gross that was almost half that of *Reloaded*. For a fairly representative mainstream assessment of the films and audience responses see the *Variety Magazine* movie reviews by Todd McCarthy ("The Matrix Revolutions," *Variety Magazine* (September 2003) and "The Matrix Reloaded" (May 2003)). These statistics are from *The Movie Times* at www.the-movie-times.com and from *The Internet Movie Database* at http://us.imdb.com.

2 Foster, Gwendolyn Audrey, *Performing Whiteness: Postmodern Re/Constructions in the Cinema* (Albany, NY: State University of New York Press, 2003), p. 138.

3 See Dyer, Richard, *White* (New York: Routledge, 1997), Bonilla-Silva, Eduardo, *Racism without Racists: Color-Blind Racism and the Persistence of Racial Inequality in the United States* (Lanham, MD: Rowman & Littlefield, 2003) and Thomas, Melvin, "Anything But Race: The Social Science Retreat from Racism," *African American Research Perspectives*, 79 (Winter 2000), p. 96. There is also a very good summary by

Charles W. Mills entitled "The Racial Policy" in *Racism and Philosophy* (eds Susan E. Babbitt and Sue Campbell, Ithaca, NY: Cornell University Press, 1999).

4 West specifically mentions *Race Matters* (New York: Vintage Books, 1994) and *Prophesy Deliverance!* (Louisville, KY: Westminster John Knox Press, 2002) in a number of print and online interviews. See Richard Corliss' "Unlocking the Matrix" and Belinda Luscombe's "The Five Burning Questions" in *Time Magazine*, 161, 19 (5 December 2003). The *New York Times* article "And the Oscar for Best Scholar . . . " by Michael Agger (18 May 2003), p. 15, is also very informative.

5 West, *Race Matters*, p. 39.

6 Two of the many other analyses of black thought can also be found in Sidney Wilfred Mintz and Richard Price's *The Birth of African-American Culture: An Anthropological Perspective* (Boston, MA: Beacon Press, 1992) and in Fred Lee Hord and J.S. Lee's *In I Am Because We Are: An Introduction to Black Philosophy*. Hord and Lee, eds (Amherst, MA: University of Massachusetts Press, 1995).

7 In developing this line of comparison, I used information from Henry Louis Gates and Hollis Robbins' anthology *In Search of Hannah Crafts: Critical Essays on the Bondwoman's Narrative* (New York: Perseus Books Group, 2004). In this work, literary experts list slave narrative qualities in order to determine the authenticity of an undocumented novel purporting to be authentic. The introduction section in Henry Louis Gates' *The Classic Slave Narratives* (New York: Penguin, 1987) was also useful. Specific texts I read included *Incidents in the Life of a Slave Girl* by Harriet A. Jacobs (1861), *The Narrative of the Life of Frederick Douglass, an American Slave, Written by Himself* (1845), and other classics.

8 Lies, Betty Bonham, *Earth's Daughters: Stories of Women in Classical Mythology* (Goldon, CO: Fulcrum Resources, 1999), p. 135. Electronic reproduction accessed 1 August 2005 from www.netlibrary.com.ezproxy.library.arizona.edu/Reader.

9 Gilroy, Paul, *The Black Atlantic: Modernity and Double Consciousness* (Cambridge, MA: Harvard University Press, 1992), p. 44.

10 Henry A. Giroux discusses movies as a source of white education in "The Discourse of Racial Identity: Towards a Pedagogy and Politics of Whiteness," *Harvard Educational Review*, 67, 2 (Summer 1997).

11 Gates, Henry Louis, *The Classic Slave Narratives* (New York: Penguin, 1987), p. ix.

12 Jacobs, Harriet A., *Incidents in the Life of a Slave Girl, Written by Herself* (Cambridge, MA: Harvard University Press, 1987), p. 55.

13 Collins, Patricia Hill, *Black Feminist Thought* (revised 10th anniversary edn, New York: Routledge, 2000), p. 251.

14 Buell, Lawrence, "Bondwoman Unbound: Hannah Crafts' Art and Nineteenth-Century US Literary Practice," *In Search of Hannah Crafts: Critical Essays on the Bondwoman's Narrative*, eds Henry Louis Gates, Jr. and Hollis Robbins (New York: Perseus Books Group, 2004), p. 27.

15 He is the brother of Rae Dawn Chong.

16 A brief summary of Herodotus' conclusions about black oracles and Greek religion is at http://academic.reed.edu/humanities/Hum110/Hdt/Hdt2.html. The complete text is in libraries and online at a number of sites, such as www.herodotus website.co.uk/Text/extext.htm. His writings, and other ancient sources, are used by those who further interracial arguments about Greek philosophy. See Martin Bernal's *Black Athena: The Afroasiatic Roots of Classical Civilization* (London: Free Association Books, 1987); Cheikh Anta Diop's *The African Origin of Civilization: Myth or Reality* (New York: Lawrence Hill Books, 1974); and George G.M. James' *Stolen Legacy: The Greeks were Not the Authors of Greek Philosophy, but the People of North Africa, Commonly Called the Egyptians* (reprinted by Africa World Press, 1992).

17 Dyer, Richard, *White*, p. 29.
18 Morgan, Jennifer L., "Some Could Suckle over Their Shoulder," in *Skin Deep, Spirit Strong: The Black Female Body in American Culture* (Ann Arbor, MI: University of Michigan Press, 2002), p. 56.
19 Patricia Hill Collins' *Black Feminist Thought* is an exploration of black feminism. The classic work *When and Where I Enter* (New York: Morrow, 1984) by Paula Giddings offers information about black women's activism.
20 Mitchem, Stephanie Y., *Introducing Womanist Theology* (Maryknoll, NY: Orbis Books, 2002), p. 116.
21 See Cornel West's comments in "The New Cultural Politics of Difference," in *Out There: Marginalization and Contemporary Cultures*, eds R. Ferguson, M. Gever, T. T. Minh-ha and C. West (New York: The New Museum of Contemporary Art, 1990), pp. 28–9, as well as *Black Feminist Thought* by Patricia Hill Collins.
22 Lies, *Earth's Daughters*, pp. 19–22.
23 Collins gives a black child mortality rate of two out of three children to the age of ten from 1850 to 1860 on p. 51. She also discusses communal types of motherhood and past and contemporary fears women had for survival, particularly female children, on pp. 178–99 in *Black Feminist Thought*. These communal concerns formed springboards for integrated types of political activism and social leadership that addresses racist and sexist cultures head on.
24 hooks, bell, *Black Looks: Race and Representation* (Boston, MA: South End Press, 1992), p. 187.
25 Giddings, *When and Where I Enter*, pp. 39–40.
26 This perspective is found in writings by W.E.B. Du Bois, David Walker and numerous others. Du Bois, for example, wrote in 1897, "We believe that the Negro people, as a race, have a contribution to make to civilization and humanity, which no other race can make." Du Bois, W.E. Burghardt, "The Conservation of the Races," in *Classical Black Nationalism: From the American Revolution to Marcus Garvey*, ed. Wilson Jeremiah Moses (New York: New York University Press, 1996), p. 83.
27 Dish TV, August 2005.
28 Many writers directly state Keanu Reeves is perceived as white by audiences or position him as such in their analysis – writers such as Gwendolyn Audrey Foster, Donald Bogle and, more pointedly, R.L. Rutsky. Richard Dyer has contended that "Stars are also embodiments of the social categories in which people are placed and through which they have to make sense of their lives, and indeed through what we make our lives, categories of class, gender, ethnicity, religion, sexual orientation and so on" (Dyer, Richard, *Heavenly Bodies: Film Stars and Society*. New York: St. Martin's Press, 1986, p. 18). I take the position that perceptions are more relevant signifiers of racial positioning than biology, particularly for persons who do not have or claim African American ancestry.
29 Rutsky, R.L., "Being Keanu," in J. Lewis, ed., *The End of Cinema as We Know It* (New York: New York University Press, 2001). Rutsky writes, "Despite the ethnicity of his name, Keanu is often perceived as a middle-class white boy, perhaps because of his early roles as an alienated teenager. Indeed, so strong is this perception that some have assumed that Keanu is simply an exotic-sounding stage name" (p. 191).
30 West, "The New Cultural Politics of Difference," p. 33.
31 Hall, Stuart, *Representation: Cultural Representations and Signifying Practices* (Thousand Oaks, CA: Sage, 1997), p. 44.
32 hooks, bell, *Black Looks*, Chapter 2, "Eating the Other."
33 hooks, bell, *Black Looks*, p. xii.

34 Lorde, Audre, "The Master's Tools Will Never Dismantle the Master's House," in *This Bridge Called My Back* (Watertown, MA: Persephone Press, 1981).

35 See Dyer's *White*, pp. 122, 126–42.

36 "Only human" is the term used by an enemy agent to contemptuously describe the freedom fighters.

Part III

Blood and bodies

Chapter 7

Vampires of color and the performance of multicultural whiteness

Dale Hudson

Billed as the "strangest" love story ever projected onto the silver screen, classical Hollywood's first vampire film, *Dracula* (1931), delivered handsome profits to its studio during the sparse years of the Great Depression by refiguring the Latin Lover as a vampire. Count Dracula is an unwelcome lover, who immigrates to London from central Europe but fails to assimilate to English mores and, consequently, is murdered. Drawing from pre-cinematic literary and dramatic conventions, vampire films resolve their narrative conflicts with the vampire's expulsion from the nation – often an expulsion via murder. As stories of nation and nation building, vampire films are stories of thwarted immigration and failed assimilation. Vampires, then, represent inassimilable immigrants; vampire films, sensationally encoded expressions of nativism. Although the United States began to imagine and represent itself as multicultural nation during the 1980s, whiteness continued to structure the power to be "just American" in much of the country and its film production. Even vampire films, a genre that takes considerable liberties with cinematic realism and cultural verisimilitude, are no exception. During the early decades of US multiculturalism, which replaced the "melting pot" model for assimilation, Hollywood updated its generic conventions by inserting "vampires of color" into conventional vampire-film narratives; the films, nonetheless, remained largely neoconservative and often reactionary.

This essay examines *Vamp* (USA 1986; dir. Richard Wenk), *Vampire's Kiss* (USA 1989; dir. Robert Bierman), and *Carmilla* (USA 1990; dir. Gabrielle Beaumont) – three films produced during a period largely defined by representations of diversity according to the promise of "America" as a nation open to all (legal) immigrants. Audiences are lured with more inclusive definitions of national identity and greater sensitivity to questions of immigration and cultural assimilation. Audiences are also lured by the suggestion of greater exoticism, adding a new frisson of xenophilia/xenophobia to the genre.[1] Divorced from the ethnic whiteness of eastern and central Europe, vampires are represented in these films as African and Asian Americans, model minorities and inassimilable immigrants alike, so that their expulsion from the nation signals social inequalities within US multiculturalism that sustain white privilege that are not so different from earlier moments in US immigration history. Audiences are free to adopt resisting or oppositional reading strategies, but cinematic representations and narrative conventions in these films are largely encoded to relay Hollywood's antiquated messages of what it is to be "American."

Due to their largely devalued cultural status, vampire films provide an under-acknowledged site for the analysis of cinematic representations of race and nation. Vampire films do not have the cultural status of other popular Hollywood genres, such as the Western. Over the past four decades, a large body of scholarship has argued that the Western gave cinematic expression to a complex nexus of US discourses at the intersection of race and nation.[2] Early films, such as John Ford's *Stagecoach* (1939) are critical of frontier democracy, that is, they qualify any emancipation from class-based oppressions associated with the east coast with "majority rules" conception of democracy; however, the films are largely uncritical of the genocide of Native Americans required for the "closing the frontier." Until the advent of McCarthyism, Hollywood Westerns unapologetically endorsed the Manifest Destiny and advocated US expansion into foreign lands. I would like to suggest that vampire films express another complex nexus of US discourses on race and nation that reflect changes in immigration laws and public perceptions of immigrants and immigration. Immigration function as an important means to sustain the global appeal of the "American Dream," while at the same time immigration functions within the national imaginary as a means of manipulating US voters, who often seem all to predisposed to envisioning waves of immigration, subsequent to their own, as a social "problem."[3] By situating vampire films within debates concerning immigration and assimilation, the fears and anxieties over miscegenation and passing that are expressed in the films come into focus symbolically as legacies of the forced immigration of slavery and indentured servitude.

The treatment of immigrant-vampires in classical Hollywood, for example, is suggestive of nativist hostility toward actual immigrants from eastern and southern Europe, who were occasionally lynched or gunned down by nativists, as legal formulations of "national quotas" were discussed, established, and later solidified under the Immigration Act of 1924.[4] Hungarian actor Béla Lugosi's portrayal of an eastern European immigrant-vampire in Universal's 1931 production of *Dracula* establishes an iconography for Hollywood's vampires, and the Lugosian vampire transitioned from the "strangest" of Hollywood's Latin Lovers into an ethnic buffoon, the "whitening" makeup signaling a clown more than a corpse, as whiteness expanded to include ethnicities that were then considered races. Appearing ethnically different yet racially same by today's definitions, the Lugosian immigrant-vampire was nonetheless an unmistakable "foreigner" in the 1930s.[5] Subsequent changes in US immigration law, and the demographics produced by these legal changes, suggest more diffuse displacement of nativist anxieties over the next several decades.[6]

It is critical to interrogate commercial genre films, seemingly innocuous forms of cultural production, since they often expose the unconscious workings of racism, chauvinism, sexism, homophobia, ethnocentrism, eurocentrism, religious (Christian) fundamentalism, and other forms of oppression based on social difference in the USA. Certain commercial genres, such as melodrama, have been examined for their power to narrate nation. The horror genre, however, has most often been discussed in terms of gender, sexuality, and class according to the universalizing strategies of early applications of structuralist, psychoanalytic, feminist, and marxist theories, as well as continental philosophy. With varying degrees of success, most of these paradigms have been employed to address race and racialization. Questions relating to the interplay of race and nation within the conventions of vampire films have not been sufficiently examined.[7] Involuntary bodily responses associated with the dominant affective modes of vampire films – melodrama and horror – suggest ways that US nationalism, as an unconscious partial repression of nativist impulses, is embodied by film audiences in response to entertainment media.

Vampires are represented as sexually predatory immigrants who infect and enslave the weak and the unwary. Vampires contaminate flesh and blood; they disrupt national and racial certainty. Vampires regenerate in "a new and ever-widening circle of semi-demons to batten on the helpless," to borrow a phrase from Bram Stoker's 1897 novel *Dracula*.[8] Moreover, vampires threaten to expose categories of social differentiation as illusions, categories that are powerful yet simultaneously fragile. Social differentiation requires constant reinforcement, not only through laws and institutional practices, but also through media representations, particularly when differentiation is deployed to legitimize social hierarchies. Ideological constructions of race and nation must be continually produced and reproduced, adjusted and readjusted, in order to sustain the illusion that they are natural, factual, divine, or biological – and even vampire films contribute to this discourse.

From its early articulation in pre-Civil War discourse to its elaboration in multiculturalist discourse, the gendered dimension governing US fantasies about, and anxieties over, miscegenation and passing seem adroitly suited for representation and reception in vampire films, particularly the horror and melodrama that they seek to evoke. Drawing largely from hypersexualized "vamps" in nineteenth-century literature by writers including Samuel Taylor Coleridge and Charles Baudelaire, as well as Count Dracula from Stoker's novel, the threat of the vampire is constructed in terms of contamination of current and future generations.[9] Vampires do not assimilate into the patriotism and loyalty demanded by national identity. They express complex and overdetermined desires and anxieties, threatening to destabilize the fantasy of national and racial purity. Vamps and vampires are imagined as sexually wanton, thereby potential threats to racial purity. Vampirism gives expression to fears over miscegenation and passing that are both historically and symbolically linked to the reciprocity between immigration and nationalism in the USA.

Vamp, *Vampire's Kiss*, and *Carmilla* represent white men as "the helpless," despite the sexual violence that white men initiate against women of color, whether human or vampire. I use the term "the helpless" from Stoker's novel, or, more precisely, from a diary entry written by his white male character Jonathan Harker, in an effort to expose the slippages in signification necessary to maintain white male privilege. The historical implications and legacies of the racial formations of African and Chinese Americans, as well as biracial Americans, are simultaneously evoked and disavowed in these three films through casting decisions, narrative strategies, and cinematic choices.[10] I argue that such representations of interracial violence suggest a displacement of (white male) fears of miscegenation and passing onto (human) fears of the supernatural. Despite on-screen representations of racial diversity in these films, the power of being "just human" is restricted to "white, thin, male, young, heterosexual, christian, and financially secure" characters.[11] Through analysis of *Vamp*, *Vampire's Kiss*, and *Carmilla*, I argue that, just as vampires are fantastic figures, vampire films may be considered as sites for social negotiations related to similarly fantastic constructions of race and nation.

Multicultural whiteness

Since the mid-1970s, Hollywood has employed homogenizing strategies to produce films suitable for "racially undifferentiated" audiences, typically generalized assumptions about a target market of suburban multiplex theaters. At the same time, Hollywood has also employed differentiating strategies to include representation of racial and ethnic diversity on screen, typically token minority characters as the multicultural setting within which stories featuring – often highlighting – white protagonists unfold.[12] At the intersection of these strategies emerges a reconception of whiteness that I am calling *multicultural whiteness*. Multicultural whiteness negotiates contradictions between an overstated racially blind inclusiveness of multiculturalism and an understated racial exclusiveness of whiteness. Multiculturalism responds in part to legislation such as the Immigration Act of 1965, which eliminated (racist) "national quotas," thereby permitting increased non-European immigration and changing the racial and ethnic demographics of the USA. In contrast to multiculturalism, whiteness ignores ways that nonwhites, whether born or naturalized as US citizens, are marked as "foreign" according to nativist assumptions.[13] As two primary discourses of contemporary US national identity, multiculturalism and whiteness produce overdetermined representations of race and ethnicity and evoke ambivalent readings of these representations among diverse audiences.

Whiteness studies within film studies provides insights into ways that constructions of whiteness produce and reproduce on screen the illusory stability that race is a biological or divine fact and that white privilege is part of the natural order of things. Richard Dyer suggests that the power of whiteness lies in its unacknowledged privilege of speaking for "the commonality of humanity."[14] "Raced people can't do that," he points out; "they can only speak for their race." Daniel Bernardi argues that whiteness "shifts and changes and is replete with contradictions" and that "passing as white, at least in the United States, has almost always had something to do with 'acting' or 'looking' – making – white."[15] Scholars, including Ruth Frankenberg and Gwendolyn Audrey Foster, have contributed to critical inquiry into whiteness.[16] Being white overlaps with being middle class and being heterosexual in the USA, so that these three vectors of social identity pass themselves as "invisible" as "just American." Films featuring white, middle-class, heterosexual protagonists continue to enjoy a privileged status in the popular imagination as being "just films"; they are seldom discussed as "white films," "middle-class films," or "straight films."

It is crucial to consider the social needs that are met in constructions of race and nation. In his analysis of racial domination as an integral component of US nation-building after the Civil War, specifically the establishment of a strong centralized state, Anthony Marx argues that intrawhite conflicts were resolved through the reestablishment of racial orders that emerged in relation to colonialism, slavery, and miscegenation.[17] David Roediger suggests that working-class European Americans self-identified as "white" to distinguish themselves from working-class African and Chinese Americans, equating "blackness with servility."[18] More broadly, Kenan Malik argues that the concept of race emerges "as a means of reconciling the conflict between ideology of equality and the reality of the persistence of inequality."[19] US multiculturalism serves as a powerful means of managing racial difference through representation and its reception, while ignoring racial oppression as an ongoing social reality. It serves as a means of abating racial conflicts by celebrating ahistorical and depoliticized conceptions of diversity, as well as outright ignoring the complexities of racial oppression that have been outlined in black feminism, borderlands theory, and ethnic studies.[20]

The performance of whiteness in recent Hollywood productions shifts in response to multiculturalism, so that it functions differently in Hollywood productions from the 1980s onward than it did at earlier moments. Within 1980s neoconservatism, whiteness and white privilege remain central to constructions of "America" in ways that are often less obvious.[21] Multiculturalism reconsiders racial identity, traditionally based on a selection and privileging of phenotypic characteristics, such as skin color and eye shape, and other cultural signifiers so that racial identity no longer functions entirely in opposition to whiteness. Whiteness no longer hides its racial constructivity behind the historical privileges of its purported invisibility, its absence of color, its passport to the national rights of citizenship. Whiteness begins to take on the qualities of color that have historically been deployed to legitimize racism and sexism. No longer confined to the production of classical Hollywood whiteness's invisibility/hypervisibility and its stabilization of the illusion of racially white identity, multicultural whiteness suggests greater emphasis on "Americanness." In so doing, it reproduces "American" national values – e.g. individualism, consumerism, patriotism, and ahistoricism – that sustain foundational myths of "America" as a "nation of immigrants," "land of opportunity," and "democracy."

Rather than defining whiteness simply in terms of a selection and privileging of physical ("white-looking") characteristics, as was largely the case in silent and classical Hollywood cinema, representations of multicultural whiteness are defined according to performative ("white-acting," "white-thinking," or "white-sounding") characteristics. Performing multicultural whiteness, then, is contingent on acquiring property (fixed residences), reproducing in (hetero-sexual) nuclear families, consuming material products, and assimilating into the socioeconomic order, yet the power of being "normal" largely remains quali-fied in representations of nonwhite, off-white, or partially white characters. Multicultural whiteness effectively manages racial and ethnic difference, rendering it into consumable styles of "ghetto chic" and "ethno-chic," while ignoring historical differences between forced and voluntary immigration, institutionalized racism – practices evident in property laws, public schooling, and racial profiling – and the investment of various immigrant groups to assimi-late into whiteness.[22] Multicultural whiteness is a form of passing, not racial passing, but *national passing*.

The confusion of nation and nation-states facilitates multicultural whiteness as a mode of national passing, as an expression of nationalism. As a social pro-cess, nationalism is itself overdetermined by its roots in ethnocentric ("common blood") and ascriptive (citizenship) discourses, by its outward (community of nations) and inward (multiethnic nations) expressions, and by its articulation in primordialist theories that insist nations evolve naturally, and by constructivist theories that insist that nations are imagined communities.[23] Postcolonial critiques of nationhood further complicate conceptions of nationalism with notions of difference and diversity and with definitions of identity as hybrid, complex, and fragmented.[24] Moreover, nationalism is remarkably "banal," to employ Michael Billig's analytical acumen: nationalism produces and repro-duces itself most substantially, not in heated moments of war and crisis, but in "unflagged" moments of everyday life.[25] The greatest lure of US nationalism is its purported openness to anyone, and Hollywood never tires of reproducing this "American Dream." Scott Robert Olson suggests that Hollywood and other US media "cater to as multicultural an audience as possible," one that "brings with its expectations for movies and television many different ethnic, religious, linguistic, and social backgrounds," so that "the media must pare down narratives to their essentials."[26] Thus, whiteness is poised perfectly to reflect the racial ambivalence of US multiculturalism, as well as its historical antecedents in US nation building. Multicultural whiteness is the performance of Americanness, an effort to universalize experience by divorcing history and power from representation.

"Historical amnesia toward immigration," argues Ali Behdad, is inseparable from the founding of the USA as a nation, which required forgetful represen-tations of violent conquests and exploitations of peoples, disavowals of the economic need for undocumented labor, and nativism as a crucial component of nationalism.[27] Nativism targets internal minorities, particularly visible ones, as well as immigrants. Miscegenation and passing disrupt the "collective racist fantasy" of a clearly defined binary of black and white based on "biology," such as the infamous "one drop rule" that was used to redefine mulattoes as black, so that they could be subjugated to segregation under the Jim Crow laws.[28] Racist conceits and failed searches for racial purity expose whiteness as a "copy lacking an original," in the words of Foster, who points out that "whiteness lack an original, yet it is performed and re-performed in myriad ways, so much that it seems 'natural' to most."[29] In comparable ways, "Americanness" lacks an original since indigenous nations signify a destabilizing pre-original; Americanness needs to be performed and re-performed, so as to pass itself as a legitimate and irrefutable identity. Americanness sustains white privilege without having to acknowledge it.

In vampire films, generic conventions complicate nations as "imagined communities," so that Hollywood's representation of multiculturalism exposes its underbelly in unimaginable community fears of "foreign contamination" expressed as fears of miscegenation and passing. The typical strategy of acknowledging multiculturalism in contemporary Hollywood vampire films by casting nonwhite actors in supporting roles, generally victims or villains, differs from the strategies in *Vamp*, *Vampire's Kiss*, and *Carmilla*. In these films, multiculturalism is represented in terms of interracial socialization motivated by sexual desire. The films offer more screen time to actors in racialized roles, yet they do so most apparently by enabling negative racial stereotypes.

As Katrina in *Vamp*, Grace Jones largely reads on-screen as a foreign vampire; as Rachel in *Vampire's Kiss*, Jennifer Beals reads as a biracial vampire; and as Carmilla, Meg Tilly reads as a white vampire passing as a white human. According to the films' narrative and cinematic strategies, the "helpless" victims of these female vampires of color are white men, who are tempted, threatened, or infected by female vampires of color. Through its efforts to distract attention from racial oppression, multiculturalism serves white men, enabling fantasies and evoking anxieties over miscegenation and passing. As a marketing strategy, female vampires of color appeal to a multicultural, multiplex and video generation, inviting the audience to participate in the privileges of white males. More significantly, these films represent white privilege through more than the demonization of women of color as vampires. Representations of human characters of color function within a narrative context that diverts attention from the ethically questionable acts (racial and gender oppression) of white male characters. People of color function largely to make the white male protagonists appear all the more heroic, all the more "American."

Vamp (1986)

Vamp opens with an initiation ceremony at a college fraternity in southern California. Figures, caped and hooded in white sheets, enter a room, where pledges are asked to place nooses around their necks, as a fraternity brother lip-synchs to a playback recording of an ominous voice that recalls the satanic–cult vampire films produced by Hammer Studios during the 1960s and 1970s. The generically self-conscious "gothic" *mise en scène* includes church-like windows but also a US flag, a fracture in the construction of this gothic space that calls attention to its artificial relocation to the contemporary USA. The main narrative, however, is set at the After Dark Club, a vampire strip club, located in a desolate inner city at a safe distance from the carefree world of the college fraternity. The set design for the vampire Katrina's crypt contrasts with that of the fraternity house: it is less generically self-conscious. The crypt is not marked with a US flag but designated as foreign (or contaminated by foreignness) by an ancient Egyptian bust and other pharonic motifs. Foreignness is constructed through the careful (or, perhaps, careless) conflation of the ancient and recent past. Katrina's Egyptian identity signals the ancient roots of African civilizations, by displacing blackness, as it is associated historically in the USA with the Middle Passage. Hardly affirming the activism of 1970s Afrocentrism and Black Power, if anything, Katrina's crypt satirizes African American self-empowerment. As a stripper exploited by her consorts to draw clientele into the club, Katrina signals the exploitation of African diasporic labor, an exploitation that is reproduced in the film's marketing campaign.

Grace Jones is given top billing and featured prominently in the film's trailers, yet her appearance is limited to a few short sequences – her elaborate strip tease, her sexualized victimization of A.J., a frat-boy wannabe; her murder of an Asian American woman; her satiation of Vic's addiction ("nasty habit") to her blood; her silent command that A.J. murder his friend Keith; and her death – and she had no lines of dialogue.[30] She is associated with hypersexuality and violence. Her agency is portrayed animalistic: she grunts and howls as she licks A.J.'s body, tasting his blood through the skin of his naked chest and neck. Her transformation into a vampire is rendered through close-ups of fangs extending from her mouth, her eyes, which roll back into her head, and long claws that grow out of her feet. Because *Vamp*'s protagonists are white, Jones stands out as the (muted or silenced) cultural other. Jones's star persona signifies exaggerated foreignness – whether Jamaican, British Caribbean, or African – an excess of animal, rather than human, instinct for mainstream US audiences.[31] Both Jones-as-celebrity and Jones-as-Katrina are situated, as Manthia Diawara observes more generally about black characters in Hollywood films, "primarily for the pleasure of white spectators (male and female)."[32] The film reproduces this structure of spectator pleasure by placing Jones in the role of a stripper whose performance entrances the white male protagonists.

Since Jones has no lines of dialogue, characterization of Katrina is developed solely through bodily gesture and facial expression, a standard practice of "Othering" in Hollywood that dates to the 1910s. Like an immigrant with no verbal command of the English language, she communicates through gestures and expressions. In the strip scene, Jones's black body is partly concealed beneath white body-makeup, including "white face," a red wig, and blue contact lenses, perhaps signifying the US national colors in a proprietary relationship over the black body. Foreignness is inscribed upon her body, which, in turn, is inscribed with the marks of commodification in the geometric African-like patterns of the body paint by artist Keith Haring. Associated with the vogue of graffiti art in the 1980s, Haring appropriates the visual vocabulary and painting style of subway graffiti, a form of social and artistic expression considered "vandalism" by the Metropolitan Transit Authority. As a white artist, Haring's appropriation of the vocabulary and style of subway graffiti empties it of its political content. No longer invested with its power to call attention to social inequalities that render certain citizens invisible, its function to mark their individual presence with "tags," subway graffiti becomes a commodified style.[33] On the body of Jones, Haring's painting may appear a voguish transgression but it serves as a reminder of white commodification of black cultural production, a means of simulating black pleasure without understanding black pain.[34] During the striptease scene, Jones's vocal performance of "Vamp," the film's theme song, plays on the film's soundtrack. Her stylized bodily movement and facial gestures suggest the discomfort of a captive or perhaps drugged victim. Her body, framed as animalistic sexuality, is literally caged in a spiral-accented metal bikini. The strip sequence is dominated by close-ups and medium close-ups that fragment Jones's body in performance, and low-angle shots that emphasize her seductive and dangerous power. Extending Laura Mulvey's thesis about "visual pleasure" in classical Hollywood narrative cinema, eye-line matches between medium shots of the white protagonists and this fragmentation of Jones's body structure spectator pleasure through encoding identification with the active white male protagonists.[35] The threat of black female sexuality and agency is simultaneously transformed into something pleasing and riddled with sadism. Jones's facial expressions and bodily movements suggest hesitation and uncertainty more than they do confidence and mastery as she performs on-stage. Although reaction shots of Katrina's audience are inserted into the performance sequence, none adopts her point of view. Katrina is always on-screen, always under someone else's gaze, even when she attacks her victims. Her dance is sexualized, culminating in a fellatio-like movement in which she buries her head in the crotch of a white, headless, anthropomorphic chair. After her strip tease, her body remains constrained: she wears a metal corset under her dressing gown, an instrument of female bondage that serves as a prop in her seduction of the frat-boy wannabe, playing into his sexual fantasies of professional strippers.

Vampirism in *Vamp* is given the ethical purpose of controlling the makeup of the US nation through selective "waste disposal," to cite the phrase used by Vic (Sandy Baron), one of Katrina's old, white, male managers. The vampires make victims of societal "dregs," who patronize the strip club, so that the strip club performs an "essential service" to US culture by eliminating itinerant men, who sustain the market for sexual voyeurism and prostitution, particularly ones attracted to (and repulsed by) Katrina's black sexuality. *Vamp*'s narrative, nonetheless, focuses on the interactions between the young, white characters: Keith (Chris Makepeace), A.J. (Robert Rusler), and Alison (Dedee Pfeiffer). The strip club is represented as an "unnatural" environment for all three. The club's ambiance is characterized by neon lights, chrome fixtures, miniature paper parasols as cocktail garnish, cockroaches crawling in a candy bowl, and Vic's pink tuxedo. The backrooms, accented with bare light bulbs and exposed pipes, resemble the exterior spaces of the deserted city streets and abandoned sewer system. These spaces reveal and conceal details of post-"white-flight," inner-city decay under highly stylized teal and pink lighting, particularly noticeable when it reflects on the surface of splashed water. Accepting employment under naïve pretenses, Alison renames herself "Amaretto" in partial disavowal of her circumstance, which she describes as a means to discover her "purpose in life," not a "permanent stop." In the film's comic resolution, following Katrina's death, A.J., resigned to his fate as vampire, tells Keith and Alison of his future plans. He will not revive the vampire strip club; instead, he will finish his formal education by attending "night school" and rejoin mainstream US culture by working the "graveyard shift." The comedy within A.J.'s word choices, their ability to convey silly in-jokes, suggests a means by which to acknowledge white privilege without really addressing its consequences. Although he initially prefers death to vampirism, finding the "living dead" to be too "boring" for him, he ultimately intends to recuperate the national privileges of young male whiteness. Nonwhite characters, by contrast, are cast out with the "dregs." Asian Americans appear at the periphery of the narrative and, as such, at the periphery of the film's conception of "America." African Americans and Latinos appear merely as part of the club's unsavory interior. They willingly patronize, or accept employment, at the strip club and, consequently, become Katrina's victims or slaves. *Vamp* does not frame their victimization as a loss in ways equivalent to the victimization (and recuperation) of A.J.

Basically reprising his role as Long Duk Dong in *Sixteen Candles* (USA 1984; dir. John Hughes), Gedde Watanabe portrays Duncan, a comic foil, who facilitates certain stereotypes of Asian Americans and complicates others.[36] He is a model minority whose financial resources are exploited by the white fratboy wannabes, but he expresses sexual desire for women of any color for which he is ultimately punished, transformed into a vampire and murdered by Keith. Unlike Keith and A.J., Duncan does not sufficiently perform masculinity: he hides in a diner toilet, posing as a plumber, leaving the others to fight vampires. Unlike the trendy 1980s fashions of Keith and A.J. – shirts with large geometric patterns under jackets with rolled-up sleeves – Duncan's costume is faux-WASP clothing, including white plaid golf trousers under a pink polo shirt. His mimicry of the "American establishment" seems misplaced in the modest southern Californian college, where Keith and A.J. aspire to an anti-establishment "cool" that is embodied by Alison's postmodern animal-print-on-primary-color jacket and tights. Like other stereotypical representations of Asian Americans, Duncan is simultaneously asexual and hypersexual. As a model minority, Duncan speaks flawless US-accented English, including slang expressions, in contrast to the accented English and pidgin expression of the only other speaking role cast with an Asian American. In a dragon-lady-like role, Leila Lee Olsen portrays the Asian American female vampire/waitress, Seko, who is similarly punished. Katrina rips Seko's heart from her body: Seko mistook A.J. as meeting the "profile" for suitable victims (itinerant, socially isolated) and gave him to Katrina as a "gift." Unlike the other, mostly white, vampires, she endangers the strip club business of "waste management." She has "screwed up," explains Vic; she's "sushi." Vic's expression plays upon ethnocentric notions of national foods: raw fish as a foreign cuisine that becomes "ethnic" in the USA, though without entirely losing its foreignness.[37] Asian American characters function as part of the setting, the "colorful" background – not unlike the pink and teal lighting of the interior (strip club), exterior (back alley), and subterranean (sewer) sets – against which to offset the white characters highlighting their "correct" performance of multicultural whiteness.

The film suggests that only white characters are capable of performing "Americanness" in the sense of frontier-like survival in a capitalist culture. *Vamp* is a narrative about consumption, about competing modes of consumption among social groups that must consume or be consumed. African and Asian Americans are consumed within a white-dominated system, and the ability to consume is redemptive. A.J. and Keith demonstrate their ability to adapt to new circumstances of social consumption early in the film, establishing themselves as heroes. Keith's practice of archery in their dormitory room later serves him well, as arrows provide an important means of stunning, if not killing, vampires. More significantly, A.J. is able to negotiate with the fraternity, deploying capitalism's logic of exchange value as a means to bypass the fraternity's hazing rituals. In exchange for the fraternity's provision of food, lodging, and social networking – the benefits of membership – he suggests the fraternity can most benefit by taking advantage of his labor. He and Keith can provide something of greater value to the fraternity than his willing subjection to the hazing rituals: the visual pleasure of a female stripper. Heterosexual sexual gratification carries greater exchange value than homosocial psychological humiliation.

The character of Duncan serves as more than a mere comic foil for the heroism of A.J. and Keith. Duncan serves as a reminder than even model minorities are still minorities within a system of white privilege. A.J. is distinguished from Duncan, a self-avowed "meal ticket" within the socioeconomic structure of the film's representation of the USA. Duncan's negotiation for a week's worth of A.J. and Keith's "pretend" buddydom in exchange for the loan of one of his cars does not demonstrate the economic acumen and enterprise of A.J.'s negotiation for a undergraduate career's worth of food, lodging, and, more importantly, social connections that extend beyond graduation in exchange for a stripper. Comparably, Keith is represented as more savvy than

Duncan in terms of attracting the attention of white women. Keith's archery skills not only defeat the vampires, they effectively win for him the amorous admiration of Alison. Keith carelessly forgets Alison and their grade-school kiss during a game of spin-the-bottle, but Duncan admits that he will carry Alison's image (dressed as Amaretto) with him for a lifetime. Moreover, Keith hesitates to enter the After Dark Club, sensing its potential dangers, whereas Duncan eagerly enters the strip club, singing "I'm in the mood for love, simply because they're naked." Duncan's unchecked sexual desire again contrasts with Keith's more "appropriate" performance of twenty-something sexuality. In every instance, the film constantly provides narrative reminders that model minorities cannot equal the white majority, even when they participate in equivalent consumerist practices. Even Katrina's parasitic manager Vic dies with a dignity (a quiet reflection on his seventy-five-year career and lamentation that he never saw "Vegas") that is not extended to Duncan. Duncan burns in a car explosion, his last audible word, "guys," a plaintive appeal for recognition and inclusion among the film's definition of "model" Americanness. Interracial socialization within a multicultural "America" is represented as riddled with inequalities and prohibitions. Duncan is only slightly more "American" than the overtly foreign vampire Katrina. In spite of its parodying of racial stereotypes in the name of comedy, *Vamp* would seem to suggest that white characters should not fraternize with nonwhite characters.

Vampire's Kiss (1989)

The implicit prohibition of interracial socialization is taken further in *Vampire's Kiss*. Set in the yuppie paradise of Manhattan during the late 1980s, when cell phones were rare but smoking was still permitted in public spaces, the film situates the potential dangers of miscegenation and passing at a distance from the intolerance of "middle America." The film's specific location is established in an opening-credit montage sequence of Manhattan at sunset, including images of landmarks such as the Empire State and Chrysler buildings, reestablished throughout the film with copious shots of streets and buildings, and reaffirmed with an end-credit shot of the financial district skyline. The film's young, white male protagonist, Peter Loew (Nicholas Cage), a successful yuppie literary agent, makes a secondary career of interracial dating until he believes himself to have been bitten by the biracial vampire Rachel and infected with vampirism. In order to make sense of the changes that he perceives in himself, Peter draws upon his knowledge of vampires from popular media. F.W. Murnau's *Nosferatu, eine Symphonie des Grauens/Nosferatu: A Symphony of Horror* (Germany 1922), for example, is presented in the film through extradiegetic inserts of its television broadcast into a scene of Rachel's seduction of Peter in a room that contains neither the television nor its off-screen sound. Crosscutting between Rachel's seduction of Peter and the Graf Orlok's televised seduction of Ellen places the white male yuppie in a feminized position. This feminization is confirmed in several shots of Rachel stretched atop Peter's body as she sucks blood from his neck, reversing the gendered hierarchy of positions in this stock bloodsucking-as-sex scene in vampire films. In the film, masculinity is largely equated with financial independence, reinforced visually through the ubiquitous exterior shots of Manhattan's heroic, architectural erections to capitalist enterprise. Unable to work, Peter's financial status declines. His charcoal-gray suits become dirty; his professionally ironed shirts, wrinkled; and his well-groomed hair, disheveled. Peter's brownstone apartment undergoes a similar transition from tidy to untidy with clothing and books tossed across the floor, furniture overturned or broken, and a blanket of feathers over the living room after he consumes a live pigeon. Cage's performance of Peter moves from affected pseudo-intellectual to raving lunatic. Peter is even forced to purchase the least expensive vampire fangs available on the market – the "cheapie" ones, in the words of the "Fang Vendor" (Stephen Chen) – perhaps a satire of the yuppie's equation of self-worth with over-inflated price tags since these fangs are undoubtedly mass produced in sweat shops. The "cheapie" fangs contrast with Peter's designer sunglasses, which he wears in the office, believing that his eyes have become abnormally sensitive to sunlight – another convention of vampire films.[38] Eventually, Peter wanders the streets of Manhattan, asking passers-by to thrust a makeshift wooden stake, which he himself has ripped from a crate abandoned on the street, through his heart. Within this ostensible parody of the yuppie, comedy is apparent, not only in Cage's performance of Peter as potentially sociopathic, but also in Peter's blatantly misogynistic and racist behavior, which is partially acknowledged as problematic through its ubiquity and exaggeration.

As a parody of vampire-film conventions and of the sadistically self-absorbed yuppie as an unacceptable performance of white masculinity, *Vampire's Kiss* further endows Peter with misogynist tendencies.[39] His sexual desire for women of color, in particular, represents a violent displacement of his fear of miscegenation, his fear of impregnating one of these women and potentially endangering his bachelor status.[40] Although his misogynistic relationships might be excused as symptomatic of his alleged vampirism, he insults his African American girlfriend Jackie (Kasi Lemmons) with racial slurs and murders a white woman (Jill Gatsby) at a disco. Moreover, he unremorsefully abuses his professional relationship with his Latina secretary Alva Restrepo (Maria Conchita Alonso). Over the course of his "infection," Peter is successively more brutal and humiliating in his acts of psychological and physical abuse of Alva, which generate material for jokes at the all-white-male boardroom table and which culminates in Peter's rape of Alva. In one scene, he explicitly informs Alva that she is "the lowest on the totem pole" since social position within the agency's hierarchies is based on date of hire. He orders her to search for a missing contract, a type of work that he would not order any other employee of the agency to perform, suggesting the types of work typically reserved for newly arrived immigrants, particularly undocumented ones ("the lowest on the totem pole") that sustain the agricultural industries in California and other states. Alonso's star status as a former Miss World, born in Cuba and raised in Venezuela, who "crossed over" to Hollywood success, may be read into the film, so that Alva becomes a tangible representation of migrations produced by US imperialism in the greater Caribbean region, as well as Spanish colonization which demanded a "whitening" of indigenous and enslaved populations through what would be considered miscegenation in the USA. The interactions between Peter and Alva suggest Manhattan's relationship to New York's "other" boroughs – Brooklyn, Queens, Staten Island, and the Bronx – with their large populations of people of color, both citizens and recent immigrants, as a source of cheap labor for corporate (white) Manhattan during the 1980s.[41] Peter himself feels tortured by Rachel who asks him to say that he loves her, something that he most likely did not say or feel for any of the women of color that he has dated.

That Peter is able to imagine Rachel's control over him would seem an ambiguous comment on the "jungle fever" of interracial dating. On one level, it supposes a racially blind environment; on another level it frames this environment as potentially exploitative to women of color and, in neoconservative terms, dangerous to white men. Fears of miscegenation – the "one drop rule" and the post-1910 elimination of mulatto as a racial category on the US census – may be read into Beals's role as Rachel who is implicated in bringing Peter's demise.[42] Yet fears of miscegenation are mediated and displaced via the pop-icon status that Beals achieved during the 1980s after her role as the talented and determined, yet underprivileged (in terms of racial and socioeconomic hierarchies), Alex Owens in *Flashdance* (USA 1983; dir. Adrian Lyne).[43] Rachel may be read as a predatory woman of color, as easily as she may be read as a celebration of biracial identity in a colorblind world. As a psychologically complex and, thus, "realistic" character, however, she is not fully developed.

The film actually implicates women of color in their own oppression. Terrified by Peter's unrelenting attacks and humiliation, Alva dreads going to work, telling her mother (Sol Echeverría) that she hates her boss. Alva's mother dismisses Alva's genuine fears and attempts to convince her that she (and, by implication, all women of color) does not have the financial luxury to choose to work for someone she does not hate. The film attempts to recuperate its ambiguous implication of women of color for their own oppression by having Alva's brother Emilio (Bob Lujan) give credence to Alva's complaints, avenging her rape by murdering Peter.[44] The shot of Peter's impaled corpse within his makeshift coffin (an overturned sofa) in his ransacked apartment is immediately followed by a shot of Rachel speaking directly towards the camera against a solid black background. The shot of Rachel is not situated within the film's narrative. It is extradiegetic, like the scenes of the televised film *Nosferatu*, and connotes power relations, actual or imagined. As such, it provides information for the viewing audience, not for the characters within the film. Her laugher is ambiguous, perhaps prompted by her destruction of a misogynistic

white man, and yet the extradiegetic shot primarily reduces Rachel to the spectacle of the cinematic vamp, whose agency is illusory under multiculturalism's
"victimized" (perhaps even masochistic) white male gaze. Although Peter's
"Continental bullshit accent," self-indulgences, and other questionable qualities work to demonize the character (or at least forestall audience identification
with him), the film's cinematography and editing work more forcefully to
demonize Rachel.[45]

Comparable to the camera movements and editing strategies that create
images of encirclement in Hollywood Westerns and represent Native Americans as intruders on what was their land by positioning spectators to identify
with the white "settlers," *Vampire's Kiss* positions audience identification with
Peter.[46] Before he has even met Rachel, the camera adopts the point of view of
a bat, hanging somewhere near a window in Peter's apartment. The private
space of Peter's apartment is represented as under the silent gaze and surveillance of Rachel, suggested by the use of high-angle shots, presumably from the
perspective of the bat at the window, intercut with standard eye-level shots of
the actors within the interior space. The shot that precedes the first shot in
which the bat is visible on-screen consists of a crane shot, the movement of
which mimics the bat's descent from the window as it prepares to bite Peter on
the neck. Elsewhere in the film, high-angle shots are employed to suggest
Peter's growing sense of self-estrangement, his paranoia about being controlled,
if not observed, by Rachel. Many of the interior scenes are established with
camera movements towards or through exterior windows, perhaps in homage
to the opening sequence in Alfred Hitchcock's *Psycho* (USA 1960), a film
whose ability to shock audiences resided in its representation of private (and
presumably safe) places, most notably the shower, as sites of terrifying murder.
While reestablishing shots in *Vampire's Kiss* showcase Manhattan, they also
suggest the vulnerability of private spaces, not only apartments and offices, but
the human body. Like the high-angle shots of Peter, these shots suggest the
encirclement strategy observed in Westerns. Here, the white man is menaced,
a potential victim of a "foreign" intruder. The constant framing and reframing
of audience identification with Peter (and, if not with Peter, then at least not
with Rachel) work to position Rachel as an intruder to the film's representation of the privileged yuppie lifestyle of a multicultural Manhattan.

The consequences of Peter's contamination by Rachel provide further
insights into the film's construction of white characters almost as victims of
multiculturalism. Although Peter abuses most of the women he encounters in
the film, he murders only one: an unnamed white woman in a disco. While it
could be argued that the racial designation of Peter's victim prevents the film
from reproducing early and classical Hollywood's overtly racist narratives,
within the context of the film's emphasis on racial and ethnic diversity as the
"dark" backdrop against which white tragedy is staged, the narrative detail of
the white woman's murder unwittingly reinforces the implicit danger of interracial socialization within the film. White women suffer when white men date

outside their race, the film appears to suggest. This suffering seems particularly the case when they date light-skinned black women. After gorging on the white woman's neck with his "cheapie" vampire fangs, Peter runs into the main room of the disco where he accosts Rachel, blaming her for his actions and attempting to convince the disco patrons that she is a "goddamned vampire." The disco patrons mock Peter's claims that he is a vampire and that Rachel made him one – one man even crosses two fingers to form the shape of a crucifix – nonetheless, the film's narrative, cinematography, and editing repeatedly contradict this reading of Peter by pointing to Rachel as the cause for much of sociopathic behavior. The camera repeatedly frames Peter as a victim of Rachel through high-angle shots of his movement through interior spaces, often motivated through editing as reproducing Rachel's point of view, suggesting that she observes him and, in so doing, renders him helpless.

In a scene in which Peter has completely disconnected with reality and given himself over to the hallucination (a symptom of clinical psychosis), the character wanders the streets of lower Manhattan in search of a willing assassin. He converses with the corner of a building, believing it to be a session with his therapist Dr Glaser (Elizabeth Ashley). After revealing to Dr Glaser that the cause of his "depression" is his need for genuine love, she presents him with his amorous fantasy woman: the white yuppie Sharon (Jessica Lundy). The hallucinated version of Dr Glaser facilitates Peter's psychosis: rape becomes "just a little id release," murder occurs "everyday in New York" – his actions are nothing that should stop his quest for romance. The hallucinated romance sustains itself for about ten minutes until Sharon pressures Peter in the ways that he has sensed pressure from any of the women he has dated. Perhaps craving the casual romance that only Rachel can provide, he violently rejects Sharon. Again, the film suggests that white women suffer, emotionally and physically, when white men date women of color.

Carmilla (1990)

Although *Vampire's Kiss* hints at the implications of passing through its casting of biracial and light-skinned women of color, the cable-television film *Carmilla* incorporates, perhaps unwittingly so, passing into its casting decisions, putting a biracial actor in the role of the female vampire. Meg Tilly's performance of the vampire Carmilla pivots on Tilly's star persona at the time as a racially white actor. Just as Tilly passes as white in the late 1980s, Carmilla passes as human in the film's representation of post-bellum Louisiana.[47] Passing is contingent on misrecognition, carrying associations with "community abandonment and self-annihilation," in Jane Gaines's analysis.[48] The historical structure of Hollywood complicates the question of passing, particularly in terms of the studio system's policies and practices of role stratification and segregation.[49] Under the Production Code, classical Hollywood tried to pass white actors as light-skinned black characters, such as Susan Kohner's portrayal of a biracial woman in Douglas Sirk's aptly named *Imitation of Life* (USA 1959), itself a (satiric) imitation of (real-life) biracial Fredi Washington's portrayal of the same character in an earlier adaptation (USA 1934; dir. John M. Stahl) of Fannie Hurst's novel. Even racially white actors in classical Hollywood required special makeup and special lighting to pass as white since they did not appear "white enough" on screen, erasing with "gluelike white face paint" and "special lighting" all traces of ethnicity in a practice Foster calls "whiteface."[50] Roland Barthes's peculiar fetishization of "the face of Garbo," its mask-like qualities, avoids recognition of the makeup's central function of stabilizing the illusion of whiteness, of a mythical white race, whose face could serve as an "archetype" for the human face. Even in close-up, Garbo's ethnic features dissolve under this thick substance, low-key lighting, and soft-focus.[51] Mulvey's reading of fetishistic scopophila as one option for the male protagonist (and audiences who identify with him) to turn the threat of castration into visual pleasure might be read in racial terms. Anxiety over racial purity requires the possible threat of passing on some level since race does not exist outside ideology.

Although the post-bellum South is an unlikely point of reference in representations of a multicultural USA, the implications of making such a reference in a vampire film produced during the late 1980s are illustrative of the mechanisms of multiculturalism. *Carmilla* adapts Joseph Sheridan Le Fanu's novella "Carmilla" (1871–2), displacing the setting of the narrative from nineteenth-century Styria, an Austrian province on the Hungarian border, to post-bellum Louisiana. With the possible exception of the vampire Carmilla Karnstein, who claims "Hungarian" ancestry, the characters in Le Fanu's story are transients or migrants within shifting nationalisms of nineteenth-century Europe. The half-English/half-Styrian character Laura (renamed Marie in the film) lives in Styria with her English father, whose "patriotic leanings" demand that the household be kept according to English customs. The horror and melodrama of the story emerges as the local character of Carmilla penetrates this imagined nation constructed through social hierarchies made evident in the analysis of two ancillary characters: a black woman, who arrives with Carmilla, and an itinerant hunchback, who recognizes Carmilla as a vampire. The two figures stand at roughly opposite extremes: the former representing a possibly corruptive influence on white (Western) Europeans, the latter representing a possibly redemptive influence on them. The hunchback does not appear in the film, but the black woman does: she is given a role equivalent to Laura's opinionated governess in Le Fanu's story. This change is ironic, given that Laura's governess describes a "hideous black woman, with a sort of coloured turban on her head, who was gazing all the time from the carriage window, nodding and grinning derisively towards the ladies, with gleaming eyes and large white eye-balls, and her teeth set as if in a fury."[52] This irony in the cinematic adaptation of a literary work, however, is lost within the legacies of Hollywood's negative racial stereotypes.

Carmilla opens like many "plantation fantasies" with a long shot of black servants working outside a white colonial-style house, surrounded by large oak trees, white fences, and dirt roads, followed by a medium close-up of a young white woman, who moves a light curtain to look out one of the windows from an upstairs bedroom. The servants appear happy to work for their white "master," as one of them calls him. The family servant, Miss Hodgett (Armelia McQueen), is costumed as a stock Mammy figure with a blue dress and large white apron. Like Mammies in classical Hollywood, Miss Hodgett sacrifices her own safety to protect her white employers and does not even seem to notice that she has no family of her own. Partly departing from this stereotype, Miss Hodgett reveals her faith in the voodoo necklaces she conceals under her uniform rather than in Christianity, thereby positioning the character as potentially disruptive insofar as she does not fully assimilate with the dominant Christian social (feudal) order of the Old South. Moreover, she expresses sexual desire by ogling the black male carriage driver to whom she gives one strand of her voodoo beads.

Nonetheless, the film continues the "mechanisms of cinematic racism," sublimated "under the stronger compulsions of romance, revenge, or sensation that belong to the allure of film narrative," that date to the earliest years of feature-length narrative films.[53] "The traditional slave stereotypes are eminently comforting," William Van Deburg points out; "the slavery film is one of Hollywood's most reliable vehicles for the mass sedation of race-based anxiety."[54] Marie's father, Leo (Roy Dotrice), fears that "outsiders" bring disease (and *dis-ease* in the sense of discomfort), and his definition of "outsider" takes on a racial dimension. Although Carmilla is welcomed to the household, Leo chides Miss Hodgett for allowing an orphaned African American boy to sleep outside the house. Leo's xenophobia and excessive protection of his daughter, who he will not allow to leave his property, is also rooted in personal misfortune. His wife abandoned him, running away with a "Yankee" after "the War." Carmilla is ultimately exposed as having abducted and integrated Leo's wife into a "family" of vampires. White men know best, the film suggests, as Leo and his daughter Marie (Ione Skye) join hands to drive a wooden stake through the repentant heart of his wife and her mother. Leo is even redeemed of his implicit racism. In response to the threat of the supernatural, he is able to overcome his early dismissal of Miss Hodgett's necklaces, which he thought attracted "only bad spirits," putting faith in their ability to protect him from harm.

Racial stereotypes for African Americans in the film facilitate Carmilla's ability to pass as a white Southerner, as well as Tilly's ability to pass as racially white. Still, Carmilla is marked as different. Close-ups are often shot under bright key lighting, masking Tilly's facial features and giving her an otherworldly aura, one that is underscored by a nondiegetic musical motif that is played when the character exerts her vampiric powers. By contrast, Skye is shot under diffuse, soft lighting, a difference in lighting that functions as an aspect of characterization that is most visible during the shot/countershot editing of their frequent intimate conversations. Until Tilly acknowledged that her father is

Chinese, mainstream audiences generally read her and her sister Jennifer as white, often "ethnic" in some nondescript way. As with Keanu Reeves, another "stealth" Asian American, who portrays the quintessential Englishman, Jonathan Harker, in *Bram Stoker's Dracula* (USA 1992; dir. Francis Ford Coppola), Tilly portrays the vampire Carmilla in ways that do not suggest she was cast according to associations with "yellow peril" discourses that demonize Asians and Asian Americans as a threat to white privilege. Yet Tilly's portrayal of Carmilla resonates with Hollywood's stereotype of Asian women as Dragon Ladies, not unlike the supporting character of Seko in *Vamp*.

Carmilla is sexualized by most of the older white male characters in the film, and she encourages this sexualization as a means to seduce Marie. The film also works to prohibit (or entice through its prohibition) interracial homosexuality. Gina Marchetti's observation that Hollywood uses "Asians, Asian Americans, and Pacific Islanders as signifiers of racial otherness to avoid the more imme-diate racial tensions between blacks and whites or the ambivalent mixture of guilt and enduring hatred toward Native American[s] and Hispanics" seems applicable here.[55] The latent yellow-peril and male-fantasies-of-lesbianism discourses serve, it would seem, to abate black/white tensions within the con-text of a 1990 television representation of the post-bellum US South. Carmilla appears as an "outsider," a woman of unknown, if not mysterious, origins. "Home," she confides to Marie, "that was another lifetime ago," suggesting that her past is one of immigration. Although Tilly-as-Carmilla's racialized identity is minimized within the black/white framework of racialization, she represents a threat to Leo which manifests itself in her seduction of his daughter Marie, her destruction of the nuclear family and its fixed residence, her threat to whiteness. At the same time, the threat to whiteness posed by Tilly-as-Carmilla requires a willingness on the part of television and film audiences to remain unaware of her biracial identity, so that she passes as white in the cultural imagination. *Carmilla* actually hinges on Tilly's ambiguous ethnicity to enable her character, the vampire Carmilla, to function as an embodiment of fears of miscegenation in the Old South.

Cast as extras in the role of the plantation's numerous unnamed servants, African American actors are shown, though rarely heard, in reestablishing shots between scenes. They enter into, and depart from, rooms, or otherwise do work. Black labor becomes part of the scenery for Old South nostalgia, visible yet unacknowledged within the film's historical mimesis. The vampire Carmilla actually reinscribes the brutal treatment of African and African American slaves and servants by their white "masters" through inciting a flock of bats to murder Miss Hodgett, the only character at this point in the narrative who suspects Carmilla of murdering the young orphan. Although Miss Hodgett's face remains unharmed, her back is grossly disfigured by the thou-sands of tiny bite marks, left as bloody and scarred flesh that suggests that sadistic punishment of slaves being flayed by slave owner and traders. Moreover, the bats have removed (perhaps eaten) Miss Hodgett's tongue. The disfigured black body is naturalized in a scene in which Inspector Amos (Roddy McDowall), holding a cup of tea in his hands above Miss Hodgett's corpse, debates with the Doctor the likelihood of the plague from the south as having caused her death, as another black female "Servant Girl" (Lisa Marie Russell) continues household labor in the background of the shot. Although the film's narrative does not explicitly suggest that Carmilla condones the implicit racism of Leo, it does suggest that Carmilla is able to conceal her foreignness all the more readily by not outwardly opposing the racial hierarchies. Her personal dislike of Miss Hodgett is camouflaged by assumptions on the part of the white protagonists that African Americans are inferior. By the same token, Tilly's star persona as racially white (or "ethnic") camouflages Hollywood's institutionalized racism. Read as an Asian American, Tilly would have disrupted the film's efforts at historical, if highly stereotyped, verisimilitude. Tilly's "ethnic" facial features suggest the nondescript foreignness inscribed upon the bodies and faces of non-WASPs, not unlike the "resistant ethnicity" and "pan-ethnic threat" posed to classical Hollywood by Pola Negri, best remembered for her portrayals of vamps and femmes fatales.[56] Indeed, Tilly's on-screen presence as Carmilla draws upon aspects of cinematic vamps since Theda Bara. As Carmilla is murdered, she becomes a spectral presence, rendered by use of a solarization effect that reverses some of image color tones as though the film were only partially developed, against fully developed images of Leo and Marie. The film ends with the ambiguous suggestion that Carmilla, though dead, lives through Marie, legitimizing Leo's xenophobic conception of a national family.

Conclusion

The production and reception of vampire films are part of the routinely familiar and everyday ways that US nationalism finds expression. My analyses of *Vamp*, *Vampire's Kiss*, and *Carmilla* suggest that to be heroic ("just American"), characters must act white. They must also participate in consumer culture, own property, and reproduce in nuclear families; they cannot be female vampires of color, who are associated with strip clubs, casual sex, itinerancy, and queer sexualities: they are anathema to the most conservative definitions of US nationalism. This statement is perhaps most emphatically made by the reduction of female vampires of color in these films to cinematic spectacle. Even human characters of color cannot sufficiently perform whiteness within the neoconservative multiculturalism of the late 1980s.

What is most telling about US nationalism is that even when vampires of color perform multicultural whiteness sufficiently to escape negative stereotypes, US audiences largely read them as ersatz imitations of white vampires. Consequently, vampires of color may be represented as citizens, yet they are de-privileged with associations of remaining transients and migrants, ruptures and weak points in the nation. Vampire films that feature predominantly African American casts, including *Blacula* (USA 1972; dir. William Crain),

Scream! (USA, 1973; dir. Bob Kelljan), *Ganja and Hess* (USA 1973; dir. Bill Gunn), *Def by Temptation* (USA 1990; dir. James Bond III), and *Vampire in Brooklyn* (USA 1995; dir. Wes Craven), have been largely dismissed for not reproducing faithfully the conventions of the (white) vampire film and the spectator pleasures it encodes. Critical analyses of the films' production and reception histories suggest that media critics and fans dismiss criticism of race and racial oppression in these films.[57] Although these films are acknowledged as "black films," rather than "just (white) films," race is seldom acknowledged in evaluations of the films' repetition and variation of vampire-film conventions. Media and fan responses to such films are hardly surprising. Audience expectations are largely framed within the acculturation to Hollywood production values, visual styles, and narrative strategies that produce "culturally trained citizens" – and Hollywood trains its audiences to value whiteness.[58] US audiences (and global audiences trained by Hollywood productions) read films in remarkably complex ways, largely unconscious of the unnatural movements of continuity editing and the unnatural constructions of race and nation.

In his analysis of whiteness, Dyer argues that, if blacks have more "life" than whites, then whites have more "death" than blacks.[59] Life is equated with the body, emotions, sensuality, and spirituality; death, with the mind, intellect, over-investment in the cerebral, everything that seeks "to crush life out of others and out of nature itself." Dyer uses the example of the predominantly white zombies in George Romero's *Night of the Living Dead* (USA 1969) and its sequels to remark that the living and dead white characters are nearly indistinguishable, that whiteness is like death. Unlike flesh-eating zombies, vampires would seem to embody aspects of both "life" and "death"; indeed, Stoker's famously labeled vampires as the "undead," suggesting a state of existence that operates in a different dimension than Romero's "living dead." Vampires are characterized by excessive sexual appetite, comparable to the sexually dangerous, often animalistic, negative stereotypes, such as the Black Buck, the Greaser, the Latin Lover, and the Dragon Lady. Unlike these early Hollywood stereotypes, vampires, especially if they are racially white, can suggest resistance to patriarchal structures, though not actual social revolution.[60] While white vampires may be invested with the power of resistance in terms of gendered, classed, and sexual hierarchies, the same does not seem to hold for vampires of color in terms of racialized hierarchies, even in films that directly address racism.

Vampire films that have fared better with media critics and fans represent a racially and ethnically diverse "America."[61] Conventionally, a vampire of color is "deterritorialized," to use Diawara's application of the term, thrown into a predominantly white world where he or she is invariably ridiculed, humiliated, or punished in an effort to maintain white privilege.[62] Although the *Blade* films (USA 1998; dir. Stephen Norrington; USA 2002; dir. Guillermo del Toro; USA 2004; dir. David S. Goyer) are critical of racism, culminating, at least for me, in the punishment of overt racist characters by Blade, the films are hardly a cause for celebrations of "breakthrough" roles. Wesley Snipes's character Blade becomes a "positive image" of a negative stereotype through a complex process of emptying race of its historical meaning: his black skin matches his black leather costume, a significant change from the Afrocentric attire of the character in the comic upon which the films are based. The films also divert attention from questions of miscegenation and orientalism with visually arresting *mise en scène* (lavish special effects, martial-arts choreography, extravagant costumes) and aurally enticing nondiegetic scores. Comparably, the casting of female African American singer-actor Aaliyah as the Egyptian vampire Akasha in *Queen of the Damned* (USA–Australia 2002; dir. Michael Rymer) "corrects" Hollywood's most famous depictions of ancient Egyptian (born, Ptolemy) royalty by the white actor Elizabeth Taylor in "brown face" in *Cleopatra* (USA–UK–Switzerland 1963; dir. Joseph L. Mankiewicz).[63] The "breakthrough" of this casting decision is undermined by the relatively minor role of Akasha, albeit inflated due to the press surrounding Aaliyah's death, which is consistent with role stratification. Akasha represents a threat to the film's narratives of heterosexual love between the white vampire Lestat (Stuart Townsend) and white human Jesse (Marguerite Moreau), as well as homosocial friendship/ sublimated homosexual love between the white vampire Marius (Vincent Perez) and white human David Talbot (Paul McGann). Akasha's racial identity is reduced to visual style rather than a narrative focus in the film, so that she is exploited as Grace Jones was nearly two decades earlier.[64]

The interplay of positive images and negative stereotypes of racial and ethnic minorities provides the setting for films in which, as Norman K. Denzin phrases it, "good and bad dark-skinned others could do battle with one another," positing an "acculturation to white goals (education and hard work) as the preferred path out of the ghetto."[65] In Hollywood, racial and ethnic minorities are often represented as embodiments of national legal and educational institutions, such as judges, lawyers, police officers, teachers, serving as what Sharon Willis calls "guest figures" who facilitate representations of an inclusive model of assimilation.[66] One of the first US-produced vampire films to revive the genre, *Fright Night* (USA 1985; dir. Tom Holland), includes one such character, Detective Lennox (Art Evans), the only speaking role in the film cast to a nonwhite actor. Such representations of the inclusion or assimilation of racial minorities into the national hierarchies of the "American dream," however, buttress and even normalize white privilege in a multicultural USA insofar as historical determinants of uneven and unequal access to sociopolitical resources are not addressed. Hollywood cinematic production and US audience reception, governed by multiculturalism, continue to represent and read nonwhite racial identity in ways that do not sufficiently challenge historically imbedded assumptions based on binaristic representations of negative stereotypes and positive images. In tandem with the ambivalence regarding race and nation within the production of cinematic representations of "America," mainstream media critics and fans tend to map characteristics of negative racial stereotypes onto the violence and social transgressions of vampires of color.

At the same time, the normative power of whiteness is not equally desirable, or desirable in the same way, to all actors and audiences. Diane Negra finds that "in an era in which 'white ethnicity emerges as a trope for empowerment', ethnic identity is valued for its own sake in opposition to a whiteness deemed sterile."[67] Though compelling, this argument seems to skirt the requisite of the white privilege required to pass as off-white. Robyn Wiegman reads the production of whiteness in all its contradictory performances from liberal whiteness to white supremacy as reproducing the fantasy of a continued threat of its own extinction.[68] Multicultural whiteness suggests one such seemingly benign contour of white power and privilege. It does not adequately challenge the power to be "just human" in classical Hollywood whiteness; it merely diverts attention from the ongoing processes of its powers and privileges. Multiculturalism in Hollywood vampire films does not represent the diversity of United States, its people, their different desires and fantasies; rather, multi-culturalism in Hollywood vampire films represents the structures of power within the United States, the persistence of whiteness as a normative definition of "Americanness." By the same token, Hollywood films do not represent the world; Hollywood films represent power structures of globalization. Hollywood diversity, then, is not real equality any more than vampires, races, and nations are real (biological) entities.

Notes

I am indebted to the generous comments and suggestions of Catherine Portuges, Anne Ciecko, Sarah Lawall, Sunaina Maira, and Daniel Bernardi on early drafts of this chapter, as well as to Sheetal Majithia for her sustained emotional and intellectual support. Special thanks also to Anita Mannur, Alix Paschkowiak, Géraldine Vatan, and Patricia R. Zimmermann.

1 Hollywood's blaxploitation cycle produced three vampire films – *Blacula* (1972; dir. William Crain), *Scream, Blacula, Scream* (1973; Bob Keljan), and *Ganja and Hess* (1973; dir. Bill Gunn) – which featured black vampires. Another film, *Old Dracula/ Vampira* (UK 1975; dir. Clive Donner), in which Dracula's wife turns "black" after drinking the blood of a black man, parodying fears of interracial romance, has also been read within the context of blaxploitation cinema. Vampires of color also appeared in earlier films produced outside the US, such as Jean Rollin's "surrealist" *Le Frisson des vampires/ Sex and the Vampire/ The Shiver of the Vampire* (France 1970) which features both an "African" and an "Asian" female vampire. In addition to films produced in predominantly white countries, vampires of color appeared in films from Japan and the Philippines that were exhibited in the USA during the 1970s. These foreign films, however, did not have access to mainstream theatrical distribution and exhibition.

2 Early examples of such scholarship include André Bazin's "Le Western, ou le cinéma américain par excellence" and "Évolution du Western" in *Qu'est-ce que le cinéma?* (Paris, France: Éditions du Cerf, 1955) and Jim Kitses's *Horizons West* (Bloomington, IN: Indiana University Press, 1968).

3 As I revise this chapter, I draw upon recent work in the area of racialization, nation-alism, and transnationalism, including Ali Behdad, *A Forgetful Nation: On*

Immigration and Cultural Identity in the United States (Durham, NC: Duke University Press, 2005), Inderpal Grewal, *Transnational America: Feminisms, Disaporas, Neoliberalisms* (Durham, NC: Duke University Press, 2005), and Eva Cherniavsky, *Incorporations: Race, Nation, and the Body Politics of Capital* (Minneapolis, MN: University of Minnesota Press, 2006). The appeal of anti-immigration films can be located partially within this manipulation of social fears. See Michael Dummett's *On Immigration and Refugees* (London: Routledge, 2001) for an extended discussion of the mobilization of anti-immigrant sentiments to forward suspicious political agendas that is suggestive of the appeal of vampire films during moments of political or economic crisis, whether actual or perceived.

4 Richard Alba and Victor Nee, *Remaking the American Mainstream: Assimilation and Contemporary Immigration* (Cambridge, MA: Harvard University Press, 2003), pp. 68–9. Roger Daniels refers to the Immigration Act of 1924 as the "triumph of nativism" in *Coming to America: A History of Immigration and Ethnicity in American Life*, second edition (New York: HarperCollins, 2002), p. 265.

5 For an analysis of ways that eastern Europeans assimilated into, and were assimilated by, Hollywood, see Catherine Portuges, "Accenting L.A.: Central Europeans in Diasporan Hollywood in the 1940s," in *Borders, Exiles, Diasporas*, edited by Elazer Barkan and Marie-Denise Skelton (Stanford, CA: Stanford University Press, 1998), pp. 46–57.

6 After the landmark Immigration Act of 1965, designed to redress the institutionalized racism against eastern and southern European immigrants, expressions of nativism found new racialized targets. Italian American actor Frank Langella revived Lugosi's role in Universal's 1979 remake of the *Dracula* film, pointing to the ever-present US ambivalence over its southern border.

7 Exceptions include Manthia Diawara and Phyllis Klotman, "Vampires, Sex and Addiction: *Ganja and Hess*," *Jump Cut* (April 1990), pp. 299–314; Stephen D. Arata, "The Occidental Tourist: *Dracula* and the Anxiety of Reverse Colonization," *Victorian Studies* 33.4 (Summer 1990), pp. 621–41; Judith Halberstam, *Skin Shows: Gothic Horror and the Technology of Monsters* (Durham, NC: Duke University Press, 1995); Harry M. Benshoff, "Blaxploitation Horror Films: Generic Reappropriation or Reinscription?," *Cinema Journal* 39.2 (2000), pp. 31–50; Kent A. Ono, "To Be a Vampire on *Buffy the Vampire Slayer*: Race and ('Other') Socially Marginalizing Positions on Horror TV," in *Fantasy Girls: Gender in the New Universe of Science Fiction and Fantasy Television*, edited by Elyce Rae Helford (Lanham, MD: Rowman & Littlefield, 2000), pp. 163–86; Leslie Tannenbaum, "Policing Eddie Murphy: The Unstable Black Body in Vampire in Brooklyn," in *The Fantastic Vampire: Studies in the Children of the Night*, edited by James Craig Holte (Westport, IN: Greenwood Press, 2002), pp. 69–75; and Teri Ann Doerksen, "Deadly Kisses: Vampirism, Colonialism, and the Gendering of Horror," in Holte, ed., *The Fantastic Vampire*, pp. 137–44.

8 Bram Stoker, *Dracula* [1897], authoritative text edited by Nina Auerbach and David J. Skal (New York: W.W. Norton & Company, 1997), pp. 53–4.

9 The word *vamp* enters the English language from the Ancient French *vampé* or *vanpé* and the Old French *avanpié* (later *avantpied*) as "that part of hose or stocking which covers the foot and ankle" (*OED*, 2nd edn, vol. 19 [1989], p. 421). Although etymologically distinct, *vamp* as an abbreviation of *vampire* was used as an intransitive verb in 1904 to mean "to behave seductively," "to act as a vamp," or "to be a vamp"; as a transitive verb, it came to mean "to act as a vamp towards" and "to attract and exploit (a man, occasionally a woman)" in 1918 (ibid.). The latter usage is related to the word's use as a noun for "a woman who intentionally attracts and exploits men" or "Jezebel," "frequently as a stock character in plays and film" in 1911 (ibid.). The word returns to modern French in 1918 as a "*mot anglo-*

américaine" meaning a "*femme fatale et irrésistible (d'abord, type du cinéma)*" (*Grand Robert*, 2nd edn [1985], p. 637).

Vamps and vampires appear in Samuel Taylor Coleridge's "Christabel" (1801), Charles Baudelaire's *Les Fleurs du Mal* (1868), Théophile Gautier's "La Morte amoureuse" (1836), J. Sheridan Le Fanu's "Carmilla" (1872), and Robert Louis Stevenson's "Olalla" (1885). As with literature, the first vampires in cinema were oversexualized women. As a counterpart to the "innocent girl" epitomized by Mary Pickford, the vamp dates back to Theda Bara's role in Frank Powell's 1914 *A Fool There Was*, though cinema had known of vampire women in films such as the Danish film *The Vampire Dancer* of 1911. See Antoine de Baecque, "De la vamp à l'actrice," *Cahiers du cinéma*, hors-série (Novembre 2000), pp. 30–1.

10 Female vampires of color appear in other films, including *Def by Temptation* (1990; dir. Bond) – and male vampires of color appear in subsequent films, such as *Vampire in Brooklyn* (1995; dir. Craven), *Blade* (1998; dir. Norrington), and *Blade II* (2002; dir. del Torro), as well as in the blaxploitation films mentioned above (see note 1) – but sexualized violence in these films is not represented as interracial. *Queen of the Damned* (2002; dir. Rymer) avoids the displacement of fears over miscegenation evident in *Vamp*, *Vampire's Kiss*, and *Carmilla* by situating sexualized violence between a female vampire of color and a male white vampire.

11 Richard Dyer makes the argument that whiteness has the power of being "just human" in *White* (London: Routledge, 1997), p. 2. Audre Lorde defines the US "mythical norm" as "white, thin, male, young, heterosexual, christian, and financially secure" in "Age, Race, Class, and Sex: Women Redefining Difference," in *Sister Outsider: Essays and Speeches* (Freedom, CA: Crossing Press, 1984), p. 116. For introductory readings in whiteness studies, see *White Privilege: Essential Readings on the Other Side of Racism*, edited by Paula S. Rothenberg (New York: Worth Publishers, 2002).

12 See, for example, Sharon Willis, *High Contrast: Race and Gender in Contemporary Hollywood Film* (Durham, NC: Duke University Press, 1997) and Norman K. Denzin, *Reading Race: Hollywood and the Cinema of Racial Violence* (London: Sage Publications, 2002).

13 This description of pre-1965 immigration quotas, which largely limited immigration to Europeans, is Joe R. Feagin's in "Old Poison in New Bottles: The Deep Roots of Modern Nativism," in *Immigrants Out! The New Nativism and the Anti-Immigrant Impulse in the United States*, edited by Juan F. Perea (New York: New York University Press, 1997), p. 28. Robert S. Chung's argument that people of color, specifically Asian Americans, are "discursively produced as foreign" and thus "carry a figurative border" with them appears in his "A Meditation on Borders" in the same collection, p. 249.

14 Dyer, *White*, p. 2.

15 Daniel Bernardi, "Introduction: Race and the Hollywood Style," in *Classic Whiteness, Classic Hollywood*, edited by Daniel Bernardi (Minneapolis, MN: University of Minnesota Press, 2001), pp. xx–xxi.

16 See Ruth Frankenberg, *White Women, Race Matters: The Social Construction of Whiteness* (Minneapolis, MN: University of Minnesota Press, 1993) and Gwendolyn Audrey Foster, *Performing Whiteness: Postmodern Re/Constructions* (Albany, NY: State University of New York Press, 2003).

17 Anthony W. Marx, *Making Race and Nation: A Comparison of the United States, South Africa, and Brazil* (Cambridge: Cambridge University Press, 1998), p. 25. According to Marx, northern whites conceded to the implicitly and explicitly racist practices of southern whites in order to maintain state unity. Northern interests in economic intervention in industry merged with Southern interests in maintaining and extending slavery into the West, so that regional antagonisms were reinforced in

the intrawhite conflicts that emerged. Due to the historical disenfranchisement of African Americans, even those emancipated from slavery, northern whites perceived African Americans as less threatening to postwar reunification than southern whites, who already had economic and political privileges, such as land ownership and enfranchisement. Marx argues that "it was not so much the mistreatment of blacks to which most Northerners objected, given prevalent racism, but rather that such mistreatment flaunted Southern disrespect for the Union's policies and authority" (p. 128). "The genius of federalism," Marx writes, "was that providing for the rights of states or regions to construct their own social order preserved a loose confederation of those states, avoiding conflict" (p. 120).

18 David R. Roediger, *The Wages of Whiteness: Race and the Making of the American Working Class* (1991; second edition, London: Verso, 1999), p. 174.

19 Kenan Malik, *The Meaning of Race: Race, History, and Culture in Western Society* (New York: New York University Press, 1996), p. 6.

20 See, for example, Lorde, "Age, Race, Class, and Sex," pp. 114–23; Jane Gaines, "White Privilege and Looking Relations: Race and Gender in Feminist Theory," *Screen* 29.4 (1988), pp. 12–27; bell hooks, *Black Looks: Race and Representation* (Boston, MA: South End Press, 1992); Gloria Anzaldúa, *Borderlands: The New Mestiza: La Frontera* (San Francisco, CA: Aunt Lute, 1987); Lisa Lowe, *Immigrant Acts: On Asian American Cultural Politics* (Durham, NC: Duke University Press, 1999); and Mike Davis, *Magical Urbanism: Latinos Reinvent the U.S. City* (London: Verso, 2000).

21 In *Racial Formations in the United States: From the 1960s to the 1980s* (London: Routledge, 1986), for example, Michael Omi and Howard Winant discuss "right-wing initiatives" in the 1980s in relation to the legacies of Civil Rights. "Since 1965," they argue, "it has been impossible to argue *for* segregation or *against* racial equality. Any 'legitimate' politics must claim to favor racial equality *in the abstract*, even if specific egalitarian measures are condemned" (p. 141).

22 For historical analyses, see Lisa Lowe, *Immigrant Acts*; Cheryl I. Harris, "Whiteness as Property," *Harvard Law Review* 106.8 (June 1993), pp. 1707–91; David R. Roediger, *The Wages of Whiteness* and *Colored White: Transcending the Racial Past* (Berkeley and Los Angeles, CA: University of California Press, 2002); and George Lipsitz, *The Possessive Investment in Whiteness: How White People Profit from Identity Politics* (Philadelphia, PA: Temple University Press, 1998).

23 For an example of primordialist explanations of nation, see Johann Gottfreid von Herder, "Germans and Slavs," in *Ideas for the History of Mankind*, volume 16 (1784–91), reprinted in *Nationalism: Its Meaning and History*, edited by Hans Kohn (New York: Van Nostrand, 1955), pp. 103–10. For an example of constructivist explanations of nation, see Ernest Renan, "What is a Nation?" (1882), translated by Martin Thom, reprinted in *Nation and Narration*, edited by Homi K. Bhabha (London: Routledge, 1990), pp. 8–22. Rogers Brubaker provides a comparative analysis between German, drawn from nineteenth-century romanticism, and French, drawn from eighteenth-century rationalism, models for nationalism in *Citizenship and Nationhood in France and Germany* (Cambridge, MA: Harvard University Press, 1992). He contrasts a tradition of ethnocultural differentialism that transcends the territorial boundaries of Germany in *jus sanguinis* with a tradition of political assimilation within the territorial boundaries of France in *jus soli* (pp. 7, 138–64).

24 See Stuart Hall, "New Ethnicities," reprinted in *The Post-colonial Studies Reader*, edited by Bill Ashcroft, Gareth Griffiths, and Helen Tiffin (London: Routledge, 1995); Homi K. Bhabha, *Location of Culture* (London: Routledge, 1994).

25 Michael Billig, *Banal Nationalism* (London: Sage, 1995).

26 Scott Robert Olson, *Hollywood Planet: Global Media and the Competitive Advantage of Narrative Transparency* (London: Lawrence Erlbaum, 1999), p. 85. The generic

conventions of vampire films tend to pivot on representations of racial, ethnic, and national stereotypes that date to the earliest years of cinema.

27 Behdad, *A Forgetful Nation*, pp. xii–xiii.

28 Marx, *Making Race and Nation*, p. 75.

29 Foster, *Performing Whiteness*, p. 2.

30 In "*Vamp*" (review), *Chicago Sun-Times* online (18 July 1986; accessed 30 October 2002), www.suntimes.com/ebert/ebert_reviews/1986/07/68895.html, Roger Ebert writes: "To judge by the ads, you'd think this was a vampire movie and Grace Jones was the star. But, once again, all she gets is a tantalizing supporting role while a bunch of college kids hog the main story. [. . .] Somewhere in the middle of all this, Jones gets lost. She has a couple of big scenes, and then they dump her. That's what always happens. Hollywood must know there are a lot of Grace Jones fans. That's why they advertise a movie as if she were the star. Now they should try making a movie where she is the star. Doesn't that seem to be the logical next step?"

31 Often described as "exotic," "androgynous," and "statuesque," Jones's career as a fashion model began in Paris, rather than the USA where her "look" did not conform to contemporary conceptions of female beauty. Signed as a singer, she came to be associated with Andy Warhol's New York "underground" scene. She was later cast as Zula in *Conan the Destroyer* (USA 1984; dir. Richard Fleischer) and as May Day in *A View to a Kill* (UK 1985; dir. John Glen). Both roles emphasize her star persona as a sexualized Amazon-like predator. In "*Vamp*" (review), *Science Fiction, Horror, and Fantasy Review Database* (2000; accessed 30 October 2002), www.fortunecity.com/lavender/fullmonty/706/horror/vamp.htm, Richard Scheib seems satisfied with these scenes in *Vamp* that "exploit the animal rawness of her musical performing persona without wimping the character out."

32 Manthia Diawara, "Black Spectatorship: Problems of Identification and Resistance," *Screen* 29.4 (Autumn 1988), pp. 70–1.

33 In *All-consuming Images: The Politics of Style in Contemporary Culture* (New York: Basic Books/HarperCollins, 1988), Stuart Ewen traces the expression "right on" from its relatively exclusive use in African American communities during the 1960s, including its use in a speech by Black Panther party leader Bobby Seale, to its reduction as a commodity in an advertising campaign for Bic ballpoint pens (biros) as "Write on!" (p. 251).

34 I adopt the notion of black pleasure without black pain from Gwendolyn Audrey Foster's reading of Mae West. Foster explains that "the problem is that West's celebrated transgressive identity depended on her return to whiteness and on her displaying herself against a backdrop of black mammies and black gay men" (Foster, *Performing Whiteness*, p. 34). Foster is reminded of bell hooks's reading of ways that Madonna imitates black pleasure without having to understand black pain. White women are free to enjoy the sexual pleasures associated with black women without the stigma of wantonness (p. 37).

35 Laura Mulvey, "Visual Pleasure and Narrative Cinema," *Screen* 16.3 (Autumn 1975), pp. 6–18.

36 Fans mock the character of Duncan. As A.J. and Keith battle three vampires in a diner, Duncan hides in the toilet, posing as a plumber. In "*Vamp*" (review), *Science Fiction, Horror, and Fantasy Review Database* (2000; accessed 30 October 2002), www.fortunecity.com/lavender/fullmonty/706/horror/vamp.htm, Richard Scheib describes Duncan as "a nerdish Oriental friend." In "*Vamp*" (review), *Bad Movie Night* (no date; accessed 04 November 2002), www.hit-n-run.com/cgi/read_review.cgi?review=49604_jd, Jeff DeLuzio conflates Watanabe with his character Duncan: "Gedde Watanabe, [. . .] as a wealthy wannabee [sic] out to buy friendship, struggles to convince us that the weak material he's forced to work with

is actually funny. I think we all knew guys like this character at some point in our lives. They become annoying on-camera, too."

37 See Anita Mannur, "Model Minorities Can Cook: Fusion Cuisine in Asian America," in *East Main Street: Asian American Popular Culture*, edited by Shilpa Davé, Leilani Nishime, and Tasha Oren (New York: New York University Press, 2005), pp. 72–94.

38 The character of Peter Loew is parodied in the *jiang-shi* film *Geung shut yee sang/ Jiang shi yi sheng/Doctor Vampire* (Hong Kong 1991; dir. Jamie Luk).

39 In "*Vampire's Kiss*" (review), *DVD Talk* online (1 August 2002; accessed 4 March 2003), www.dvdtalk.com/reviews/read.php?ID=4747, Earl Cressey writes: "Judging from the comments on the IMDb, it is also one of the more misunderstood films of the eighties, which I can understand, as the film is often ambiguous, complex, and subtle with many of the plot details." In "*Vampire's Kiss*" (review), *Needcoffee.com* (no date; accessed 8 November 2002, www.needcoffee.com/html/ dvd/vkiss.html), Dindrain questions the success of the film as a comedy, pointing out that, despite indications of parody in the misogynistic yuppie Peter, the comedy does not succeed because "intentions just aren't worth much when execution is lacking."

40 In the audio commentary to the DVD release of *Vampire's Kiss*, director Robert Bierman remembers the casting of women of color in the roles of Rachel and Jackie as last-minute replacements.

41 For a discussion of New York City and its Third-Worldlike socioeconomic structures, see Saskia Sassen, *The Global City: New York, London, Tokyo* (Princeton, NJ: Princeton University Press, 1991).

42 For an historical analysis of interracial sex in the context of film studies, see Lola Young, *Fear of the Dark: "Race", Gender and Sexuality in the Cinema* (London: Routledge, 1996), pp. 45–8.

43 The Beals-as-Alex fantasy of "passing," albeit with obvious exoticism and eroticism, by dancing her way out of the ghetto (or, at least, an equivalent to the ghetto) and "arriving in America" is undercut by the scandal over the film's oversight in acknowledging Beals's white double for the dance sequences. Beals's role as herself in *Caro diario/Dear Diary* (Italy–France 1994; dir. Nanni Moretti) draws attention to her star status as it is associated with *Flashdance*. A latinized version of the image of Alex appears in a recent Jennifer Lopez music video. Beals's biracial identity is also read into her role as the biracial Daphne Monet who "passes" as white in *Devil in a Blue Dress* (USA 1995; dir. Carl Franklin).

44 Emilio might be read as the film's hero, though his role is minor.

45 "Continental bullshit accent" is Pauline Kael's term for the accent that Cage models after the affected speech adopted by his father as a professor of comparative literature in "*Vampire's Kiss*" (review), *New Yorker* 65.17 (12 June 1989), p. 106.

46 This interpretation of the Hollywood Western is from Tom Engelhardt's "Ambush at Kamikaze Pass," *Radical America* (July–August 1972), pp. 480–98. In *Celluloid Indians: Native Americans and Film* (Lincoln, NE: University of Nebraska Press, 1999), Jacquelyn Kilpatrick argues that the most common motifs of the Western "owe their genesis to the ideas articulated by Frederick Jackson Turner in 1893" in his paper, "Frontier Thesis," delivered to the American Historical Association: "the Native American was presented as an obstacle to the civilizing of the continent, a stage in the evolution of human society that preceded agrarian development, which in turn would lead to full-fledged urban civilization" (p. 39).

47 The US South was also the setting for Universal's *Son of Dracula* (USA 1943; dir. Robert Siodmak) set in the Louisiana bayou.

48 Jane Gaines, "White Privilege and Looking Relations: Race and Gender in Feminist Theory," *Screen* 29.4 (1988), p. 19.

49 Role stratification and segregation are practices developed in Hollywood to relegate nonwhite actors to supporting roles, ostensibly based on assumptions that mainstream (white) audiences would not attend films featuring "minorities" in non-stereotyped roles. In *On Visual Media Racism: Asians in American Motion Pictures* (New York: Arno, 1978), Eugene Franklin Wong explains that, until the mid-1960s, role segregation worked to bypass the Motion Picture Production Code ("Hayes Code") prohibition of depicting miscegenation, often interpreted as the mere appearance of actors of different "races" on screen in a particular scene. This topic is further discussed in Carlos E. Cortés, "Them and Us: Immigration as Societal Barometer and Social Education in American Film," in *Hollywood as Mirror: Changing Views of Outsiders as Enemies in American Movies*, edited by Robert Brent Toplin (Westport, USA, and London, UK: Greenwood Press, 1993).

50 Foster, *Performing Whiteness* (Albany, NY: State University of New York Press, 2003), pp. 4, 47.

51 Roland Barthes, *Mythologies* (Paris, France: Éditions du Seuil, 1957).

52 Joseph Sheridan Le Fanu, "Carmilla," in *In a Glass Darkly* (London: R. Bentley and Son, 1872; reprint edn, Oxford: Oxford University Press, 1993), p. 257.

53 These quotations are made by James Snead in relation to D.W. Griffith's *The Birth of a Nation* (USA 1919), in his "Birth of a Nation" chapter in *White Screens, Black Images: Hollywood from the Dark Side*, edited by Colin MacCabe and Cornel West (London: Routledge, 1994), p. 38. Although Griffith's work was once admired, when it was still possible, desirable even, to divorce aesthetics from politics, Griffith is presently discussed in film studies textbooks alongside Leni Riefenstahl as "among the most interesting, unredeemable figures in film history." Robert Kolker, *Film, Form, and Culture* (1999), second edition (Boston, MA: McGraw Hill, 2002), p. 167. In the tradition of Hattie McDaniel's portrayal of the O'Hara family's Mammy in *Gone with the Wind* (USA 1939; dir. Victor Fleming), Miss Hodgett is not afraid to confront her master, motivated out of concern for the master's family, suspecting that Carmilla will bring harm to Marie.

54 William L. Van Deburg, "A Popular Culture Prophecy: Black American Slavery in Film," in Toplin, ed., *Hollywood as Mirror* (Westport, IN: Greenwood Press, 1993), pp. 34–5.

55 Gina Marchetti, *Romance and the "Yellow Peril": Race, Sex, and Discursive Strategies in Hollywood Fiction* (Berkeley and Los Angeles, CA: University of California Press, 1993), p. 6.

56 These descriptions of Pola Negri come from Diane Negra's *Off-white Hollywood: American Culture and Ethnic Female Stardom* (London: Routledge, 2001), pp. 55–6.

57 See, for example, Harry M. Benshoff, "Blaxploitation Horror Films: Generic Reappropriation or Reinscription?," *Cinema Journal* 39.2 (2000), pp. 31–50; and Leslie Tannenbaum, "Policing Eddie Murphy: The Unstable Black Body in Vampire in Brooklyn," chapter in Holte, ed., *The Fantastic Vampire* (Westport, IN: Greenwood Press, 2002), pp. 69–75.

58 Toby Miller, *The Well-tempered Self: Citizenship, Culture, and the Postmodern Subject* (Baltimore, MD: The Johns Hopkins University Press, 1993).

59 Richard Dyer, "White," *Screen* 29.4 (Autumn 1988), pp. 56, 59. In his analysis of Romero's *Night of the Living Dead*, Dyer writes that "it is significant that the hero is a black man, and not just because this makes him 'different,' but because it makes it possible to see that whites are the living dead" (p. 59). Hollywood vampire films of the late 1980s and early 1990s would seem to invert the political disillusionment of Romero's trilogy.

60 See Nina Auerbach's *Our Vampires, Ourselves* (Chicago, IL: University of Chicago, 1995) for an empowered feminist reading of vampires in anglophone literature and film.

61   These films generally feature white protagonists. *The Lost Boys* (USA 1987; dir. Joel Schumacher), for example, limits its representation on Chicano/as in southern California to an opening sequence montage, with an Echo and the Bunnymen cover version of the Door's "People Are Strange" on the soundtrack. More recently, *Vampires/John Carpenter's Vampires* (USA 1998; dir. John Carpenter) portrays vampires in ways that suggest illegal immigration over the US–Mexico border. Although portrayed by white actors, the vampires live in "nests" until they are murdered by vigilante vampire hunters.

62   Manthia Diawara, "Black Spectatorship: Problems of Identification and Resistance," *Screen* 29.4 (Autumn 1988), pp. 66–76.

63   The film is based on Anne Rice's novels *The Vampire Lestat* (USA 1986) and *The Queen of the Damned* (USA 1988). "A 4000-year-old Egyptian queen ought not to look like Elizabeth Taylor, even though the books describe her as being so," Rymer explains about his casting decision and departure from Rice's novel in an effort to represent Akasha with authenticity according to historical studies that suggest ancient Egyptians were black Africans. As quoted in Craig Reid, "Memories of Aaliyah: A Look at the Life and Tragic End of a Multi-talented Performer," *Femmes Fatales* 11.10–11 (September–October 2002), p. 13. According to Reid, the decision ignited a "flame war" between Rice fans and Aaliyah fans on the internet (p. 13). "On the one hand the Anne Rice fans are upset that Aaliyah is not white," explains Saralegui, "then, the Aaliyah fans start calling these fans racist."

64   The film's release was postponed twice: first, in August 2001, by Aaliyah's death in an airplane accident in the Bahamas, and second, in September 2001, by the terrorist attacks in the USA. In some places, the film was marketed as a vehicle for Aaliyah's acting career with heavy emphasis of hip-hop music in the theatrical trailers. "Aaliyah fans, as well as fans of charisma, sex, and violence, will be sorely disappointed," warns Jane Dark in "Creatures of Celluloid and Flicker" (review of *Crossroads* and *Queen of the Damned*), *The Village Voice*, 429 (5 March 2002), p. 122.

65   Denzin, *Reading Race*, p. 6. Denzin argues that, since "a majority of Americans know and understand the American racial order through mass media," the more than 500 "hood movies," produced between 1967 and 2000, that feature "the violent ethnic other in a variety of stereotypical situations, set the stage for the 1990s attacks on federal affirmative action, social welfare, and education programs" (pp. 3–5).

66   Sharon Willis, *High Contrast: Race and Gender in Contemporary Hollywood Film* (Durham, USA, and London, UK: Duke University Press, 1997), p. 5.

67   Diane Negra, *Off-white Hollywood: American Culture and Ethnic Female Stardom* (London: Routledge, 2001), p. 4.

68   Robyn Wiegman, "'My Name is Forrest, Forrest Gump': Whiteness Studies and the Paradox of Particularity," chapter in *Multiculturalism, Postcoloniality, and Transnational Media*, edited by Ella Shohat and Robert Stam (New Brunswick, NJ: Rutgers University Press, 2003), p. 228. She argues that an emphasis on the universalizing strategies of whiteness, such as Dyer's thesis, fails to recognize "the tension between particularity and universality that characterizes not simply the legal discourse of race (where early documents enfranchise the 'white person'), but the changing contours of white power and privilege in the past three centuries" (p. 228). About the seemingly "benign" cultural rhetoric of whiteness today, she argues that "until recently, seldom has whiteness been so widely represented as attuned to racial inequality and justice while so aggressively solidifying its advantage" (p. 230).

Chapter 8

The naked and the dead

The Jewish male body and masculinity in *Sunshine* and *Enemy at the Gates*

Peter Lehman and Susan Hunt

Undoubtedly one of the most disseminated images of the Jewish body since World War II has been that of mounds of naked corpses in concentration camps. Unlike images of the lynching of blacks in the American south which have only recently begun to permeate the entire nation, these images of dead Jews were seemingly authorized from the very beginning as images of taboo subjects which could and should be shown for a greater good: lest we forget. Yet as with the images of blacks circulated in, for example, the recent exhibition and book, *Without Sanctuary: Lynching Photography in America*, these images are more complex than the context of good intentions implies.[1] While on the one hand, they undoubtedly serve to remind us of the atrocities committed upon Jews and blacks in the past, on the other hand they may have additional unintended consequences. In this paper, we argue that images of Jewish masculinity in international cinema since WWII have been profoundly affected by documentary images of seemingly passive, weak starving, naked men on the verge of death or in fact dead: their naked bodies a testimony to a very public, failed masculinity. The conventional opposite of the body is the mind – a stalwart aspect of Jewish identity. In representation, however, the Jewish mind fares little better than the Jewish body, further complicating the imagination of a vibrant Jewish masculinity. To explore this issue we concentrate on *Sunshine* (2000) and *Enemy at the Gates* (2001) two seemingly dissimilar films that represent the Jewish male body as literally both naked and dead and the mind as metaphorically so.

Ever since the publication of John Berger's *Ways of Seeing* in 1972, his distinction between the naked and the nude has been widely accepted within the world of art, photography, and cinema.[2] Naked people are people without clothes whereas nude people have their bodies displayed to be looked at. As with many such categorical distinctions such as the one between art and pornography, the distinction may be too convenient. Much "art" contains elements of sexuality and eroticism similar to and at times identical with elements in pornography and if one simply accepts the basic distinction those elements of art may go undetected and unanalyzed. After Berger, nearly all scholars working on the representation of sexuality and eroticism have focused on the category of the nude. We argue that the category of the "naked" is in some manner sexual as is that of the nude and that in fact one single voyeuristic gaze underlies both, oscillating between the poles of the naked and the nude.

Heather Kravas, a dancer and choreographer, notes within the context of a discussion of what she calls dancing "naked": "We can't help but sexualize bodies. We put our own against others, or we rate them in terms of desirability."[3] We suspect Kravas uses the word "naked" because she refers to herself as dancing "without clothes." Yet, she quite rightly notes that even within that context and within a serious work of art, being naked does not somehow turn off the sexual component of the look. Both of her points are perceptive and crucial. All looks at bodies include a *sexual* component and an *evaluative* one and disturbing as it may be, that includes dead bodies, especially within the voyeuristic gaze of cinema, art, and photography.

Disturbing as it may be for many to acknowledge, the look at those dead and dying Jewish men includes a look at their penises. The constant circulation of these images for nearly sixty years makes it difficult, if not impossible, to imagine those pathetic bodies as vibrant, erotic spectacles that promise sexual fulfillment. In a sense, they have not only failed in the social, political, public arena but also in the private arena of the bedroom. Just as surely as with choreography, we sexualize those bodies and place them against more desirable ones. In fact, we seem to have done this so successfully that the notion of the sexually desirable Jewish male body has become something of an oxymoron, even for such Jewish male comics as Woody Allen, who jokes that he's the only man he knows who suffers from penis envy. Funny as the joke may be, he may have it wrong – far from being the only one, he may be speaking about Western Jewish masculinity in general.

In other words, a representation of a naked body is seldom just a naked body – it also contains an element of display and invokes a voyeuristic, even sexual, gaze. In this paper we argue that cinematic images of Jewish male bodies are always seemingly "naked" and never "nude," and that this has had profound implications on the representation of Jewish masculinity, sexuality, and intellectualism. The naked and the dead are not as far away from the nude and the dead as we think.

Sunshine closely examines three generations of Ashkenazi Jews in the same family during the twentieth century, with Ralph Fiennes playing the principal male character from each generation. The film contains what may be the quintessential image of the naked, dead Jewish male body. After Jews have been rounded up by Nazis in Hungary and taken to a camp, they are forced to watch the torture and death of one of their members (played by Fiennes). The crowd includes a teenage boy who is the son of the stripped and tortured man. During the first part of the humiliating torture, the naked man bound by his hands and feet to a horizontal pole, hangs with his penis visible, though not in the manner that films typically represent the penis as "impressive". Then the film moves to a level of insight almost too painful to watch as the tortured, naked body is hung vertically by the wrists, the victim still alive. In the freezing cold, a Nazi guard sprays the man with a hose, his body slowly icing as he freezes to death on public display.

Like the scene in *McCabe and Mrs Miller* (1971) where the body of a cowboy who has just been laughed at for having a small penis and then shot in a gunfight falls into a river with freezing chunks of ice, the death scene in *Sunshine* associates the public humiliation of male torture and death with the shriveling effect of cold water on the penis, phallic masculinity retracting even to the fearful point of disappearance. In a later segment with Fiennes playing the boy now as a man, a rhyming scene occurs when Communists break in on him while he showers. Once again his nakedness is a sign of his powerlessness and humiliation: this time the shower water falls on him in contrast to the water sprayed on his father.

Related images of Jewish men are common in cinema. Frontal male nudity abounds as an image of humiliated, vulnerable Jewish masculinity. Steven Spielberg lingers on images of pathetic-looking Jewish men in a concentration camp in *Schindler's List* (1993), their scrawny skin-and-bones bodies foregrounding their genitals even more. In Spielberg's *Munich* (2005), a Jewish man, Carl, is the victim of a female assassin's seduction. When his compatriot, Avner, discovers the dead body, Carl is lying on his back in bed with his penis fully visible. His body position contains several layers of humiliation. The beautiful assassin had earlier propositioned Avner who declined her with some hesitation. When Avner passes near Carl's room, he catches a whiff of the assassin's perfume and comments to himself that he saw her first, suggesting some jealousy of Carl's sexual exploit. Sex was more than deadly for Carl. Instead of using his penis for the intended masculine performance, he is killed by a woman who leaves him exposed. Furthermore, she leaves him in that humiliating position knowing that Avner will find him. In Agnieszka Holland's *Europa, Europa* (1990), we see the central character's penis in three scenes: first, when he frantically exits a bathtub and runs outside to hide in a barrel during a Nazi assault on his home, again when he attempts to hide his penis from a Nazi soldier who is playfully wrestling with him, attempting to see it, and yet again when he inspects his aching penis after an attempt to camouflage his circumcision. In all cases the boy is vulnerable: first from being discovered by Nazis while fleeing his home and then for being discovered as a circumcised Jew who is masquerading as a Nazi. The third time, his penis actually appears blackened and infected from his attempts to stretch existing skin over the head of his penis in order to appear uncircumcised.

In an episode of the HBO TV series *OZ*, a Jewish prisoner is murdered and his naked body is hung upside down, eerily recalling the events shown in *Sunshine*. As in that film, the spectacle of the penis is minimized, both by its being small and by the oblique camera angle, something which is all the more underscored by the extensive use of male nudity throughout the *OZ* series, including a later rhyming shot of the dead, naked body of the Aryan who killed the Jew. The Aryan's penis is larger than the Jew's, and filmed in a manner that more clearly displays it for the spectator. This is underscored and replicated in a bizarre manner on a website *The Men of OZ: Nude Scenes from HBO's TV Series "OZ"* which shows images of male nudity from the series organized around the actors. Fred Koehler, playing the Aryan who kills the Jew, is included, and a montage of images of him nude includes two frames from the shot in which he lies dead on his back, his penis prominently displayed as the camera moves up and away. Yet the Jew whom he killed is missing from the site, the dead Jewish penis and the actor who played the part not even memorable enough to be included, erased from the penile spectacle parade of the series, which, according to the site, "developed an enormous gay fan base." The reference to gay fandom makes explicit the site's assumption about the sexual component and eroticism of the display of the penis in *OZ*.

The Jewish penis is always shown in situations of humiliation, vulnerability, and death – never sexuality – never as potent; always as impotent. Even in films like *Sunshine* that grant sexual potency to Jewish males, that potency is always separated from the naked body. It is as if the mounds of dead bodies and naked living corpses of the concentration camps – whether in documentary photos and newsreels or in the cinema – have fixed the sight of the Jewish penis, thus profoundly effecting the notion of Jewish male sexuality. Indeed, this notion is actually represented in *Europa, Europa*. Near the end of the war, the Jewish boy masquerading as a Nazi surrenders to the Russians, revealing that he is Jewish and only in the German army to protect himself from persecution. A disbelieving Russian officer pushes his head toward a pile of photographs of concentration camp victims. One by one, the officer throws the pictures in front of the boy saying that if he was Jewish, he would look like the men in the pictures – emaciated and dead.

All the concentration camp images invoke a sexual look in several senses of the word: there is something inherently pornographic in the truest sense of that word in looking at these images. In an oft-identified pattern, the desire to look away in horror is countered by the desire to stare in fascination and of course sex and death have been strongly linked by many, including in the well-known works of Georges Bataille. Within this pattern the common distinction between naked and nude is worse than useless since it obscures what connects the nude erotically displayed body from the allegedly naked, merely unclothed body. They become horribly intermingled in these films leading to deep disturbances in the representation of the sexuality and masculinity of Jewish men.

We turn now to *Enemy at the Gates*, a film with no male nudity but one nevertheless plagued by the same problems. *Enemy at the Gates* is a mainstream film that narrativizes the dilemma of representing the Jewish male body as sexualized and potent in a particularly crude and revealing manner. A key stereotype of Jews centers on their intelligence and the value they place on education and the development of the mind. Jean-Jacques Annaud's *Enemy at the Gates* (2001) is part of a larger cinematic pattern in which intelligence is denigrated.

The narrative mechanism for this denigration is to have an intellectual male lose out in a competition for a beautiful woman to a male associated with the earth and his body. The intellectual male particularly fails in the arena of sexuality. In *Enemy at the Gates* this failure is specifically linked to a Jewish male, who flirts with the object of his desire – a beautiful Jewish woman – vis-à-vis their common love of ideas, books, education and Marxist ideology. The Jewish male attempts an appeal to the woman's intellect by noting how the two of them are different from another man who seeks the woman's affection – an uneducated, sharp-shooting, Gentile, shepherd. The woman's reply is to initiate sex with the shepherd. Her passion for the shepherd (and lack thereof for the intellectual) is so great that she seduces him for the first time while he sleeps on the floor in a cold cavern filled with filthy snoring men who could awaken at any moment. She is confident that the shepherd can perform well under these circumstances, and he does so to the point where he must stifle her orgasmic screams. The film cannot "imagine" that happening with the Jewish intellectual – neither granting him the competence of such a sexual performance nor granting the woman the desire for it with him.

The Jewish intellectual ultimately commits what amounts to suicide by taking a bullet in his "useless" brain, as he refers to it, to reveal the location of an enemy sniper for the shepherd. His decision to die coincides with his loss of the woman to the provincial shepherd *and* his disillusionment with Communist ideology, which he had previously embraced with gusto. His death denigrates the world of ideas and political activism, thus laying waste to the notion that a sexual relationship can develop from intellectual and/or ideological pursuits and passions. In addition, the woman's seduction of the uneducated, non-Jewish shepherd obliterates in an instant her cultural heritage and connection to men of her past – a connection the intellectual was certain he could exploit to his advantage.

Unlike *Enemy at the Gates*, *Sunshine* does not "deprive" the Jewish male characters of sex appeal or the ability to perform sexually. In fact, the opposite occurs: beautiful women in all three familial generations pursue and seduce the Jewish males, at risk to themselves in a variety of ways. The director, Szabo, however, posits other problems with Jewish masculinity, linking it to anger and brutality. The first generation male rapes his wife after she asks him for a divorce; the second feels guilt for having an affair with his brother's wife; and the third calls his lover a "cold bitch" when she refuses to leave her husband and children for him. Although the three generations of Jewish men have been represented as capable of torrid lovemaking, all of these men renounced their Jewish identity for the sake of assimilation. Indeed, all three generations of male characters are played by Ralph Fiennes, an actor who is not Jewish, or at least whose star image does not include public identification as Jewish. In addition, despite their identity alterations, all generations experience tragic falls from grace with the ruling class or party into which they assimilated. In the first two generations, neither the Jewish mind (an intellectual lawyer) nor the Jewish body (a world-class fencer) could save themselves from misery and premature death. Sander Gilman observes a related pattern about the representation of Jews in American mass culture in his book *Smart Jews* when he argues that the representation of intelligent Jews supports the notion that Jewish superior intelligence compensates for Jewish physical weakness, and consequently has been made a sign of flawed masculinity, always linked to dysfunction.[4] Similarly, we are arguing in *Sunshine* that as the Jewish male alignments with nation and state fail, so do their sexual relationships, indicating a dysfunctional, failed masculinity.

This difficulty at both the mind and body poles of Jewish masculinity is also narrativized in Werner Herzog's *Invincible* (2002), with the body issue specifically couched in terms of size. This film centers on an actual historical figure, Zishe Breitbart, a Jewish blacksmith from a rural town in Poland. Breitbart's intellect is limited, but he has a body-builder's physique – the polar opposite of the wasted Holocaust victim. Breitbart travels to Berlin in 1932 to perform in a cabaret. His employer, the brilliant Hanussen, intentionally designs the acts in the show to pit the intellect against the body, with himself as a clairvoyant representing the power of the mind. This mind–body opposition is doubled through Breitbart's close relationship with his younger brother who publicly displays his precocious intellect on several occasions. In that Hanussen is revealed to be Jewish, the film constructs a problematic dichotomy within the category of intellectual males. On the one hand, the younger brother is an innocent, physically fragile child, and on the other, Hanussen is powerful and sexually alluring, but sadistic and misogynistic.

Breitbart as the opposite of intellect becomes a Jewish folk hero when he publicly refuses to wear Aryan costumes in Hanussen's show; performing amazing feats of strength instead as the Jewish character, Samson. Whereas Breitbart becomes heroic, Hanussen's psychic powers are exposed as fraudulent and the Nazis execute him when his Jewish heritage is revealed. But the body pole of Jewish masculinity is also problematic. Breitbart is denied a conventional sexual potency when a woman he desires cares for him in return, but their sexual energy is displaced away from the body. Second, his impressive strength is rendered inconsequential when he returns to Poland and is incapable of articulating the Nazi threat he observed in Berlin; his public warnings ignored. In addition, when performing a feat of strength, Breitbart injures his own leg, it is later amputated, and he dies after a prolonged agony. The film ends with written text noting that Breitbart died two days before Hitler seized power. At one point, Hanussen says to Breitbart, "Jews should never be as strong as you." The rampant dissemination of Holocaust imagery from the immediate years following WWII to the present seems to substantiate that sensibility – the image of Breitbart's scantily clad behemoth body is replaced by the mounds of wasted corpses and living-dead bodies of the Holocaust.

With *Sunshine*'s third-generation male named Ivan, director Szabo – himself a Jew – constructs a utopian Jewish masculine subjectivity that had eluded

Ivan's intellectual grandfather, who had changed the family name from Sonnenschein to the less ethnic Sors to advance his law career, and athletic father, who converted to Christianity in order to fence for the Hungarian national team. Szabo has Ivan create an identity by happily reclaiming Judaism and the Sonnenschein family name. Through Ivan's euphoric self-discovery, Szabo extols the Jewish tradition of valuing the intellect, unlike *Enemy at the Gates* and *Invincible*, but does so, once again, at the expense of the sexual Jewish body.

The various Sonnenschein generations are linked by the motif of a lost booklet containing the recipe for a delicious and sensual herbal tonic concocted and marketed by Ivan's great-great-grandfather. After several unsuccessful searches, Ivan inadvertently locates the booklet, but absent-mindedly over-looks it to read a letter written by his great-grandfather. As Ivan reads the letter, the recipe book is thrown into a garbage truck. The tonic is associated with the body, but the letter is "of the mind", containing homilies such as, "You will be successful because you have knowledge. Study has always been our religious duty as Jews." Ivan's ultimate choice of "the word" over the sensuousness of the body, so to speak, is recapitulated when he relinquishes his mistress – the figure that allowed the representation of a potent Jewish male sexuality.

In yet another film about World War II-era Jews, *Nowhere in Africa* (2001), director Caroline Link endows her lead Jewish male character with sex appeal and performance potency and, unlike the Jewish characters in *Sunshine*, he succeeds in maintaining a relationship with the beautiful woman he desires. Yet, a sense of loss permeates the narrative and is once again tied to the valuing of the intellect at the expense of the sensual as in *Sunshine*. In Link's film, a German Jewish lawyer, Walter Redlich, presciently moves his wife, Jettel, and daughter, Regina, from 1938 Nazi Germany to live in exile in Africa. Walter gives up his career as a lawyer to work on another man's farm in Kenya. Jettel was initially resistant to the move, but, along with Regina, grew to love all things Kenyan, and is even attracted to another German expatriate who feels at home in his adopted country in a way that Walter never did. Jettel contemplates leaving Walter, but their relationship is salvaged when he decides to stay and work the land with her. His decision results in a passionate lovemaking scene between husband and wife in which the conventionally handsome Walter performs admirably, per conventional standards of filmic lovemaking.

Ultimately, to become a complete man, however, Walter feels he must return to Germany. This move is specifically linked to the intellect through the trope of Walter's jurist robe. At the film's start Walter gives the robe to his black Kenyan assistant saying, "You have to be smart to wear a robe. Here in Rongai [Kenya] you're smart. Not me." The robe is returned to Walter as he departs the country. Walter's masculinity depends on his intellectual work as a lawyer. The passionate sexuality that marked Walter's initial decision to stay in Africa resulted in a pregnancy, motivating Jettel's reluctant return to Germany. Walter's potency as a sexual being is displaced onto the child, and indeed the narrative ends with Regina's voiceover stating Jettel gave birth to a "big and strong" son. In addition, Walter's need for a masculinity defined by career and intellectualism is manifested at the expense of Jettel and Regina's deep-rooted connection to Africa. The Redlich family's departure for Germany is melodramatically linked to loss through Regina's tortured farewell to her Kenyan friend and through the imagery of the film's final scene: Jettel reaches from the train window to receive a banana from an African woman, and, in close-up, caresses her hand in the process. The film ends on a freeze frame of the woman running alongside the train as Jettel watches with an expression of longing and regret. The sensuousness of Africa, like the delectable elixir in *Sunshine*, is subordinated to the law and the word.

The choice of the intellect as a solution to the loss of Jewish identity and homeland creates a problem for representation. We contend that, in general, an erotics of intelligence is largely absent from cinematic representations, and films like *Enemy at the Gates* demonstrate this with a vengeance. How do you represent the abstract concept of intelligence, or perhaps more importantly, how do you eroticize or sensualize the intellect?

As we have argued in a prior essay, Sandra Goldbacher's film *The Governess* (1998) offers a potentially interesting answer to the above question, but with a Jewish woman, not a male.[5] The film's protagonist is a Jewish female who enthusiastically assists her employer with his scientific and photographic work before they become lovers. The Jewish woman's eventual erotic seduction of her employer is coupled with the work that they do together. In other words, her passion for him cannot be separated from the ideas they pursue and the work that they do together. This film, written and directed by a Jewish female filmmaker, is the polar opposite of *Enemy at the Gates* in which the Jewish woman not only rejects the cerebral male, but also abandons her job involving mental skill as a translator to pick up a gun and join her shepherd.

Like the distinction between the naked and the nude, the two are commonly thought of in opposition to each other: the intellect is abstract and the body is sensuous. However, much like we are suggesting that the naked and the nude really are two points on a continuum, so are the intellect and the sensuous body – the mind can be just as sexy as the body.

Notes

1   Hilton, Als, Jon Lewis, Leon F. Litwack and James Allen, *Without Sanctuary: Lynching Photography in America* (Santa Fe, NM: Twin Palms Publishers, 2000).

2   Berger, John, *Ways of Seeing* (New York: Penguin, 1972).

3   Quoted in Kourlas, Gia, "The Bare Essentials of Dance," *New York Times* (February 12, 2006), www.newyorktimes.com.

4   Gilman, Sander, *Smart Jews: The Construction of the Image of Jewish Superior Intelligence* (Lincoln, NE: University of Nebraska Press, 1996).

5   Lehman, Peter and Susan Hunt, "Passion and Passion for Learning in *The Governess*," *Jump Cut*, 44 (2001), www.ejumpcut.org/home.html, www.acropolis video.com/menofoz.

Chapter 9

Framing Jennifer Lopez

Mobilizing race from the wide shot to the close-up

Priscilla Peña Ovalle

The [beauty] pageant illustrates that women's natural "asset" continues to be primarily located in and through the body, whereas men's natural assets include talent, intellect, and entrepreneurial ambition.

Sarah Banet-Weiser, *The Most Beautiful Girl in the World*[1]

Just when I get them to focus on your assets, they're focusing on hers.
They're fantastic assets, don't you think?

Scripted exchange between Stanley Tucci and Ralph Fiennes, regarding a newspaper image of Marisa Ventura (Jennifer Lopez), in *Maid in Manhattan*

At the intersection of race and gender, the Latina body challenges the traditional binaries of racial representation, specifically the poles of whiteness and blackness. Recent scholarship has begun to theorize how Hollywood power structures reify whiteness by continuing to pose it as the central screen identity. Richard Dyer has illustrated how white subjects in film have historically been positioned as the default identity for protagonists. The illusion is that white bodies lack race: "At the level of racial representation . . . whites are not of a certain race, they're just the human race."[2] Layered film practices – from narrative to shot composition, but also including financial, aesthetic, technical, etc. – reinforce the status quo of this centralized position. This hierarchy of racial representation is arbitrarily organized according to the poles of whiteness (One) and blackness (the Other). Representations of gender (and heterosexuality) likewise work according to this dominant power structure. Filmmakers have actively constructed the representational difference of female bodies since Edward Muybridge.[3] As Linda Williams notes in her analysis of pornography, "Men's naked bodies appear natural in action: they act and do; women's must be explained and situated: they act and appear in mini-dramas that perpetually circle about the question of their femininity."[4] Through reiterated performance, the hierarchical systems of race and gender work to support and reify each other.[5]

Thus, whiteness may be endlessly nuanced through characterization while blackness/nonwhiteness *is* characterization. Whiteness remains a blank slate:

the white actor can simply be the character. Instead, the nonwhite (particularly black) body is so marked by cultural signifiers that the performance becomes complicated; the nonwhite performer's actions must be explained or understood as possible for someone of his/her race to perform. Hence, Hollywood has simplified complex categories of identity (race, gender, etc.) into polarized and formulaic narrative canvases for more convenient storytelling. Because two-dimensional representations of race continue to signify normalcy (whiteness) or difference (blackness), the white male remains the traditional lead protagonist while the nonwhite female is typically a supporting or, more commonly, a character actor.[6] Hollywood has thus continued a legacy of colonialism that supports what Charles Ramírez Berg identifies as a "preferred power relation."[7] These types coincide with long-held myths regarding the disposition and sexuality of Others – and the hegemonic values of our society possible through acclimation and assimilation.[8]

Jennifer Lopez's recent rise as a multimedia star is compelling given these traditional binaries and intersections of representation. Using Lopez's career, this essay shows how the screen Latina has remained tenuously between types throughout Hollywood's history, resulting in a malleable media and economic space ripe for Lopez to exploit at this specific multicultural moment in US history. In many ways, Lopez's on-screen Latina identity is composed within the tension of sameness (One) and difference (Other). Therefore, this essay explores the evolution of Lopez's appearance within the film frame by using the film language of the close-up and wide shot. I argue that the close-up encapsulates the cosmetic changes Lopez has made to access mainstream Hollywood film while the wide shot reiterates her difference by reinstating the popularity of her butt and the nonwhiteness it represents. By using these terms – particularly the way each composition has traditionally framed the female face and body – I will illustrate the continual and complex process of racialized representation that has depicted one of the most famous Latina stars in Hollywood.[9]

"Between and betwixt": the tempo(rary) of the dancing brown body

The screen depiction of Latinas has traditionally centered on the body, specifically the dancing body. Hollywood's best known Latina stars – Lupe Velez, Dolores Del Rio, Carmen Miranda, Rita Hayworth (Rita Cansino) and Rita Moreno – have each become famous by dancing onto the screen.[10] Jennifer Lopez is no exception. As Jane C. Desmond has shown, the belief in the "natural rhythm" of nonwhite bodies effectively positions race and nationality on/through the body to construct and perpetuate a division between "moving and thinking, mind and body."[11] Dance has traditionally limited the Latina film performer to the realm of the body, serving as both costume and characterization; in this way, Hollywood has economically connoted racialized sexuality through one action. This performance is true for the extra and star alike – from the "Cantina Dancer" (a Latina character frequently posed in the back of saloons as décor) of early cinema to Jennifer Lopez in *Shall We Dance* (2004).[12] As a result, the conventions of dance have come to "represent a highly codified and highly mediated representation of social distinctions" – collapsing passion and lust into the stereotype of the Latina.[13]

In this essay, I am interested in how the Latina body must change to simultaneously exhibit sameness and difference. Lopez is the first Latina whose celebrity has opened a Hollywood film at the box office since Rita Hayworth.[14] While Hayworth's mainstream success required an Anglicized revision of her name from the Spanish "Rita Cansino" in the 1930s, Lopez has remained "Jennifer Lopez."[15] Still, access to mainstream Hollywood film for both women has meant – to varying degrees – alterations in cosmetic appearance of the hair and face. While such physical negotiations are often considered necessary for both white and black actresses, Lopez conformed to idealized beauty standards yet retained an exoticized difference – a simultaneity that resulted in mainstream success in the late twentieth century. Yet, like Latina celebrities before her, dance has shaped the trajectory of Lopez's career.

If dance indicates a popularly recognized difference, the mainstream success Jennifer Lopez and Rita Hayworth achieved through it can be, at least partially, attributed to cultural citizenship. Here, I define this citizenship as a sense of belonging and investment in socioeconomic ascension – exemplified by an association with the work ethic and the American Dream. Velez, Del Rio, Miranda and Moreno were born, if not raised, abroad or outside of the continental USA; the perceived foreignness of their origins may explain how their personas, though successful, remained marginalized by mainstream roles.[16] Lopez and Hayworth were born in the continental United States – New York, to be specific. As such, Hayworth and Lopez ostensibly better support and sustain the nationalized narrative of the American Dream.

In Lopez's version of this Dream come true, her mother and father were born in Puerto Rico; both parents came to New York, making Jennifer – though technically already a US citizen – a first-generation mainlander and full cultural citizen of the United States. Both of Lopez's parents worked and expected their daughter to attend college; against their wishes, Lopez left college to pursue a career in dance. Despite early professional struggles, she eventually won a spot on the television program *In Living Color* as one of the Fly Girls. Gradually, Lopez earned television and film roles, capturing the public's attention when, after a national search, she was cast in the title role of *Selena* (1997). The breadth of the film's publicity and casting call as well as the tragic narrative of Selena's emerging crossover success proved an ideal springboard for Lopez's career.[17]

Because Jennifer's upbringing seems to straddle the working class and middle class, this biography is not exactly one of rags-to-riches. The fact that the Lopez family was able to purchase a home and expected Jennifer to attend college indicates intentions of upward mobility. Perhaps because of her fan base and persona, Lopez categorizes her own background rather vaguely; in one interview, Lopez identifies it as "lower to middle class, working class."[18] This vagueness is culturally crucial. First, it is in line with a general Americanness that imagines itself as middle class despite the economic truth. But secondly, in the case of Lopez's success, this back-story seemingly proves that with hard work anyone – even Latinos/as – can prosper in the United States. Despite Lopez's background, she corroborated the working-class status that was effectively collapsed into her persona by publicity to fulfill the bootstrap mythology and reinstate popular national narratives that largely cast Latinas as domestic, garment, farm or other low-wage workers (in the real and reel worlds).[19] Because of Lopez's fiscal accomplishments – particularly her triumph as the first Latina to earn over $1 million per picture – her persona ultimately bears the symbolic weight of a country invested in perpetuating itself as the land of opportunity.

Since the rise of her star in *Selena*, Lopez's body – particularly her derrière – has remained a site of public fascination.[20] Despite the public obsession with Lopez's physical assets, her career has continually maneuvered beyond the limitations that such attention might foster/forge. Instead, Lopez's image has capitalized on Hollywood's depictions of Latina-ness, which have historically straddled the prescribed codes of whiteness and nonwhiteness. In other words, as a Latina performer Lopez presents the most marketable components of both polarized representations to reap the greatest rewards during a period of multiculturalism and a shift in popular culture practices.

In the past century, the Latina has been cast into the media spotlight at specific and intermittently historical moments while the ebb and flow of whiteness has governed national identity within the United States. Whiteness has defined and rearticulated itself against blackness, using all Others as intermediaries in this process of defining cultural citizenship. As an intermediary, the Latina has flexed and bridged the boundaries of whiteness and blackness, despite – or perhaps because of – the double bind of a marginalized race and gender. It is precisely this "in between-ness" that makes brown female bodies desirable (and disposable) nation-builders.[21] In the colonization of the New World and American West, the Latina has served as a temporary woman, helping to populate conquered lands in the absence of Spanish or English female bodies. The impermanence of this flux echoes the malleable borders that have historically constructed and categorized whiteness according to national, political or colonial shifts.[22] As a colonized body, the Latina serves to reify these shifting ideals and thus explains the routine waves of attention that Latina (specifically) bodies foster in the United States. This temporal and racial oscillation between the supposed normalcy of whiteness and purported exoticism of blackness is the foundation of Lopez's ability to mobilize race. In other words, the codes of race in visual culture have been manipulated by, on and through the Latina body to effectively articulate difference and sameness in a nationalized body.[23]

As in the case of Del Rio and Miranda, Latinas previously depicted an inter-national Otherness; today, however, the national project of the United States is to articulate itself against an intra-national Other – nonwhite but assimilable persons operating within hegemonic US culture.[24] This project serves to reify the racial and structural status quo while offering the illusion of diversity and inclusion. Ideally, this intra-national Other works within (but never fully achieves) the dominant codes of whiteness, so as to be distinguished from so-called illegal or less assimilable immigrants. In this way, fetishized assets like the butt or actions like dance reiterate the necessary difference of the Other (even as it is being re-presented as diverse) while other bodily markers (hair, fashion, etc.) perpetuate the ideals to which beauty must strive. Lopez has utilized her in-between-ness to cultivate and manipulate a persona that simultaneously presents both as needed. By mobilizing race across various forms of media, Jennifer Lopez has cultivated celebrity by exploiting this transitional position to its fullest.

The prototypical Latina body – not too light or too dark by Hollywood standards – efficiently illustrates diversity and economizes representation: it diversifies both white and black venues. As a dancer, Lopez seemed conscious of this unique position.[25] A 1998 *Mirabella* interview finds Lopez musing on her early success in the Fly Girl world. Beyond her dance training, Lopez offered something different during a specific (multi)cultural moment:

> [Lopez] studied jazz and ballet, and aspired to dance on Broadway, but then, she says, "Hammer came out with 'U Can't Touch This,' and all the auditions started becoming hip-hop auditions. I was good at it, and they were like, 'Ooh, a light skinned girl who can do that. Great, let's hire her!'"[26]

Though classically trained, Lopez's skin seemed her most marketable feature in the competitive hip-hop dance world. While Lopez's complexion is arguably light, this statement suggests that Latinas with the right skin and hair remain privileged in the media – and assimilation – process. The lightening of skin and straightening of hair has long been a means of accessing the artificial hierarchy of whiteness, an attempt to assimilate through aesthetic and/or social identity. The history of African Americans in the United States illustrates the impact of Anglicized ideals on the perception of skin tone and hair texture as codes for the hierarchical arrangement of mainstream culture.

This ascent is not solely cultural or national, but also economical. The 1998 Coca-Cola commercial featuring Jennifer Lopez exemplifies the pervasive American Dream as hegemonic and economic access. The advertisement pres-ents Lopez's life as a then-and-now narrative: images of her glamorous Hollywood present are juxtaposed with sepia-hued footage of her re-enacted past. The commercial begins as an elegantly dressed Lopez runs into frame, rapidly exiting a mansion and forcefully climbing into a red Lamborghini. The car speeds away and the action sequence's intensity is heightened by the frenetic editing style and the sound effect of barking dogs. In voiceover, Lopez says: "Wow, things have really changed since my dad used to walk me to school." The past appears in faux home movie footage, showing a man and little girl standing before an urban stoop. The man's hands are full: one holds his daughter's hand while the other holds a Coke. The commercial cuts to the artificial present, with the getaway scene mid-action. Lopez then exits the Lamborghini and hugs the director of a film crew; the opening scene is revealed to be a (staged) film shoot.

Then Lopez states, "It wasn't easy to find an open door . . ." as the commercial cuts to the past and a young, brown-haired child actor playing Lopez extinguishes the candles of a birthday cake. With a Coke bottle prominently displayed in the foreground, Lopez continues that it wasn't easy ". . . to make my dreams come true." At the party, the girl/Lopez embraces an actress playing her mother. The real/present-day Lopez addresses the camera: "But here I am . . . working hard yesterday, working hard today." To illustrate the hard work of yesteryear, a pre-teen actress playing Lopez is shown completing a jazz dance turn. A wider shot reveals that she is dancing onstage and being evaluated by an anonymous gentleman. As he waves his hand in judgment, the expression of disappointment on the pre-teen's face indicates the judge's negative decision. But the success of Lopez's hard work "today" is clear when the commercial cuts to a chef serving the real Lopez food as she enjoys the Coca-Cola in her hand and laughs with others. Closing the commercial, Lopez reminds us that "what's important will never change" as she sits with her real (biological) mother. A separate shot shows her actual father with an obscured, yet unmistakable, Coke bottle in the foreground. After a glamorous sip from her Coke, Lopez directly addresses the audience in close-up to complete her thought: "Family, Friends" remain important to her. Lopez hugs her mother. A close-up then shows Lopez laughing and looking screen left; the reverse shot reveals that Lopez is addressing a little girl with dark and tight curls giggling at her. In the final shot, Lopez takes us in confidence, placing hand over heart as she says: "They'll always be here." And so will Coke, suggests the logo branding the top right of the screen.

The ad's insistent juxtaposition of Lopez's past and present marks it as an American Dream; this commercial narrative seems especially intended for Latinos/as, as the hard-work-and-family formula remains unique to national advertising aimed at marginalized communities, particularly the working class and/or nonwhite/immigrants.[27] The commercial is clearly negotiating a representational tension between the marginal past and mainstream present, a tension played out through ethnicity and cosmetic appearance. For example, a classic all-American birthday scene depicts Lopez's youth, but it is sonically marked as different by a musical bridge: the birthday-past is scored with the sounds of a folkloric guitar, beginning faintly then swelling as the young actress/mother embraces the child actress/Lopez. This musical moment cues the difference we are witnessing as Latino/a but seemingly subsides for the remainder of the commercial. Similarly, familial moments like the birthday hug signal Lopez's difference as a Latino/a in America: the overwhelmingly strong familial commitment keeps her family in heart and is the true secret of her success.

Further, Lopez's transition to success is marked in her clothing and hair. Lopez's costumes – both present and past – are primarily "Coca-Cola" red: a red gown in the present and a red leotard in the past. In this subtle way, Lopez is both branded and equated with the product itself. We can also see a transition in hair, from the first shot of Lopez as a wavy haired girl to the increasingly straightened and lightened hairstyle of the present. Such assimilation, the commercial suggests, is possible for every little Latina with a dream. The shot/reverse shot of Lopez looking at a girl with ethnically dark curls offers us this promise. Finally, the use of dance to link the past and present is of particular interest. Lopez's hard work of the past is depicted as dance auditions and rejection. The present-day Lopez, however, works in the similarly physical realm of an action film, as suggested by the commercial's recreation of a film shoot. Both present and past center on the body; the body is clothed in the color of the product, but all endorsements are composed in close-up.

The timing of Jennifer Lopez's presence and success might be considered temporal and transitional, a smoothing over of some of the historically constructed, racialized lines in mainstream media. Cornell West's assertion that we are experiencing a recent cultural shift towards the "African American-ization of American popular culture" sets the stage for Lopez's rise.[28] Beyond the skin tone that Lopez brought to hip-hop, the dance (and music) form's impact on Lopez's success is striking, as it signals the increasing importance of this music and dance form in mainstream representation. Despite the increased attention to black aesthetic practices like hip-hop or the current attention to diversity, a tension remains around the bodies that perform in line with blackness. The rise of a brown screen identity like Lopez from the world of hip-hop may be the result of black popular culture's emergence within the confines of hegemonic whiteness in the United States. Lopez's in-between-ness has helped soothe the anxiety of whiteness as representation has inched closer towards blackness.

The variety of visual media formats – including film, print, interactive, music videos and television appearances – offers multiple spaces through which Jennifer Lopez has mobilized her racial representation. Each medium encodes its message differently, creating multiple planes through which Lopez's image plays with bodily codes and narratives. Regardless of talent, the few types that women – particularly Latinas – can play in Hollywood film limit their careers. The Lopez interview in *Mirabella* illustrates Lopez's consciousness of her Hollywood identity – and the need to aim beyond her limited type.

> But all along, Lopez has been determined not to market herself as *just* a Latina actress. "My managers and agents and I realized that I'm not white,"

she says with a laugh, "so I've always wanted to show that I could play any kind of character. Not only a range of emotions, but also race-wise." [emphasis mine][29]

The importance of moving beyond Latina-type roles underscores the complexity of race and gender in Hollywood representation. In the case of Lopez, the compromises necessary for standardization have primarily occurred through hair and cosmetic style, echoing the conventions of lightness and whiteness in Hollywood film even as the films themselves reiterate her difference in ways beyond character name.[30]

Race, up-close

The close-up directs the audience's full attention to the subject of the frame's composition, reinforcing the cultivation of the Latina type by typically excluding her from its gaze. The close-up presents the audience with the most valuable or informative detail within a scene; the importance of a gesture, object or other visual cue is indicated by the way it is fully magnified within the frame. However, the shot's cultural value primarily resides in its use to capture the film star's face: within this frame, the star may use this space to emote, react, glow or simply be. Cinematography is organized around the proper exposure of the face and historically this face has been white. Dyer has identified the many ways that, technically but no less culturally, traditional cinematic lighting and framing techniques have reinstated whiteness by operating according to mechanical requirements standardized for white complexions – even when recording black bodies. On a symbolic level, the tradition of backlighting (creating a specific glow or halo around the star to signal importance) comes from a mythical representation of white virtuousness. This technique has most commonly been used with white female stars: brightness cues the framed subject's "idealized representation" by cultivating the illusion of a "glow."[31] The artificial glow effectively and economically collapses lightness, beauty and subject/narrative positioning in a single shot. While Dyer states that the moral and sexual superiority associated with such imagery is not as prevalent, "the language [and power] of this image remains powerful."[32] Thus, the fiery Latina type – relegated to character actor or supporting role – has typically been neglected by the full cultural weight of the close-up.

As visual real estate, the spatial value of the close-up is exemplified by the April 1997 cover of *Vanity Fair*. While the outer magazine cover features blondes Cameron Diaz and Claire Danes (with a red-haired Kate Winslet), the inside-cover highlights emerging actresses Jennifer Lopez, Charlize Theron and Fairuza Balk.[33] Captioned "Not Quite Ready For Their Close-Ups," these three actresses close out a ten-person spread, following other performers like Renee Zellweger, Minnie Driver, Alison Elliot and Jada Pinket (pre-Smith). Lopez's position in this Hollywood lineup indicates the newness of her celebrity but may also illustrate the unmet potential of her non-conformed image.[34] Like the front cover, the image of Lopez, Theron and Balk seems to privilege blondeness. Both brunettes, Lopez and Balk, are seated. Each flanks Theron's left and right sides. Theron stands front and center in the picture; the nude color of her dress, blonde hair and central placement in the light make her the image's focal point. While such composition may be a coincidence, Theron is given additional significance: on the same page is another inset, captioned image of Charlize sitting with her boyfriend. No additional images of Lopez or Balk appear on the page. Theron may not have her close-up, but she clearly deserved more screen/page time.

Much has changed since *Vanity Fair* first identified Lopez as an up and comer in the Hollywood Issue. In the early period of Lopez's career, she primarily appeared as a Latina actress in films like *Money Train* (1995), *Anaconda* (1997) and *Selena* (1997). In these films, Lopez's characters are identified by Spanish surnames such as Santiago (Grace), Flores (Terri) and Quintanilla (Selena) respectively. Over time, overtly Latina characters/names have disappeared from Lopez's films. In some cases, Lopez's Latina-ness was replaced by Italianness. The transition to Italian characters, besides providing some excuse for Lopez's ethnic body, signals a symbolic upward mobility: Italianness provided an intermediary station towards whiteness. This process mirrors the relational assimilation of new immigrants in the early 1900s, as noted by David Roediger's recent work on the whitening (incorporation into the collective definition of whiteness) of Italian, Jewish and Polish people in the United States.[35] The malleability of Lopez's visual representation, particularly her hair styling, has served to mobilize her climb in Hollywood film towards less ethnically defined roles. Though Hollywood was content to typecast Lopez as the love interest, her aspirations and consciousness caused her to instead select the B-film *Anaconda*. "'I was offered another movie at the same time. It was like, Am I going to be the woman between two men again, or am I gonna be a strong woman character who's a hero of an action movie, which is what I wanted to do.'"[36] We can conclude that such calculated decisions increasingly propelled Lopez into the mainstream roles that she desired. Similarly, she has decreasingly been (overtly) defined by ethnicity as her career matured; however, as we will see with the wide shot, marks of Lopez's difference have manifested themselves in other ways across her more recent performances.

One could argue that the Latin and Italian surnames have no impact on the narrative and that we should instead celebrate the appearance of a Latina character without overanalyzing these roles. Such an approach idealizes mainstream representation and overlooks the casting strategies of certain films. In *Money Train*, the Latina-ness of Lopez's character mediates the sexual and racial tensions between an unlikely pair of brothers, played by Wesley Snipes and Woody Harrelson. In one interview, Lopez remarks: "'They wanted a Latina. . . . They wanted somebody who could be with Wesley and with Woody.'" This comment prompted the *Buzz* magazine writer to (quite rightly) note,

"Apparently, in Hollywood, brown is some kind of mediating color between black and white."[37] In a film that challenges the racial taboos of biracial families, Lopez's in-between-ness served as a convenient bridge, a detail utilized by the film's publicity: one *Money Train* advertisement literally places the body of Lopez between and against close-ups of Snipes and Harrelson.

The process of becoming visually American in both Hollywood and the United States has played out through the politics of hair. While Americanness has primarily been determined by class, it has been normalized through beauty ideals. Access to the American Dream is a rite of passage requiring the marks of assimilation: a strong work ethic and/or acceptance of hegemonic beauty standards. Ayana D. Bird and Lori L. Tharps have noted that – as some members of the black community chose to resolve the process of assimilation – passing from one racial category to another was negotiated through "skin tone and hair texture."[38] The lightening of skin and straightening of hair became a currency to access the artificial hierarchy of whiteness, enabling a sort of cultural citizenship in the United States. Lopez's appearance has similarly required tailoring to conform to idealized notions of screen beauty, effectively moving her career beyond "just a Latina actress."[39] Since the beginning of Lopez's career, audiences have witnessed the transformation from her true hair in films like *Money Train* towards lightened and straightened hair in films like *Angel Eyes* (2001) or *Monster-in-Law* (2005).[40] Lopez's transformation has opened many doors, making her marketable beyond the ghetto of marginalized audiences. Curiously, as Lopez's hair moved from curly to straight, her star power in mainstream film increased.

Evidence of this transition to the mainstream exists in Lopez's leading men: each leading man in Lopez's films (and real life in the case of Sean Combs and Ben Affleck) has helped usher her racial mobility. Since *Anaconda*, Lopez's romantic leads have consistently been white (or white ethnic) males: George Clooney (*Out of Sight*), an animated Woody Allen (*Antz*), Matthew McConaughey (*The Wedding Planner*), Ralph Fiennes (*Maid in Manhattan*) and Richard Gere (*Shall We Dance*).[41] In this sense, *Anaconda* is the transitional film from Latina performer to mainstream star, theoretically pairing a curly haired Lopez with Eric Stoltz. This relationship is literally dormant over the course of the film; the narrative incapacitates Stoltz with a coma, effectively appointing Lopez heroine with Ice Cube as her sidekick. Yet, as Mary C. Beltrán has noted in her work on Lopez as a crossover star, it was Lopez's pairing with Clooney in *Out of Sight* that announced her status as a "rising global star property," particularly as she followed the film with her music career.[42]

The cultural desire for lightness has been routinely reified through cinematic practice of Lopez's image.[43] Cultural ideals become cultural norms when glorified and emulated through mass media's technical practice. Though Lopez has rarely gone completely blonde for a film role (with the near exception of *Angel Eyes* or *Monster-in-Law*), she routinely wears dramatic hair highlights. The coloring effect lightens and brightens Lopez's image, as the publicity stills for

Angel Eyes and *The Wedding Planner* illustrate. In *The Wedding Planner* publicity, Lopez's hair and complexion nearly match that of Matthew McConaughey while in *Angel Eyes*, Lopez's face becomes a blown-out ghost of whiteness.

Illustrating the equation of the American Dream with lightness is the hair coloring in *Maid in Manhattan*. Here, Lopez (Marisa Ventura) plays a maid employed at the elite Beresford hotel. Because the narrative centers on a domestic worker and because this role is occupied by Lopez, her hair remains true to the character type: Lopez is a dark-hued brunette in this film. In fact, hair coloring significantly and subtly connotes cultural capital in the film. Marisa's fellow maids each have dark hair: two of her friends are dark-haired black women while her confidante is a crass (Italian?) woman from Brooklyn with black hair. Beyond the maids, two female figures are significant in *Maid*: the housekeeping manager and a character residing at the hotel, nicknamed "The Goddess." The housekeeping manager is an auburn-haired white woman and the Goddess is a blonde socialite.[44] Significantly, both characters represent what Marisa – either directly or indirectly – aspires to be. Though Lopez is clearly the female lead, she remains subdued through hair coloring to remain consistent with her characterization. As a sort of compromise, Lopez's hair is never curly or even unruly; instead, it remains neatly slicked into a low ponytail or bun with the exception of a few key scenes, where hair is mobilized in performance. For example, Lopez's hair is used to show a transition at the beauty salon – from maid to princess – as called for by the narrative's love story.

The film negotiates an unlikely love story as a journey towards the American Dream, depicted here as a managerial position. Lopez's character is mistaken for a hotel patron and attracts a Republican New York Assemblyman named Chris Marshall (Ralph Fiennes). As a maid, Marisa is instructed by the Beresford managerial staff to strive towards invisibility and she is quite successful. When Marisa anonymously meets Fiennes' character while servicing his bathroom, the narrative asks us to believe that he does not recognize her upon their second meeting because her long brown bangs – for the only time in the film – obscured it the first time. It is not until Lopez illicitly tries on the Goddess's glowingly white Dolce & Gabbana suit that Chris (Fiennes) begins to woo her relentlessly.

The film's narrative, hinged on a case of mistaken identity facilitated by the white suit, creates a modernized passing narrative in a multicultural era. The brilliance of the suit – so white that several characters ponder how to keep it clean ("Scotch Guard") – works as a surrogate for whiteness (or whiteface?) in the film. Though this passing could simply be identified in terms of class, two moments suggest otherwise. First, Fiennes's character describes Lopez as "kind of Mediterranean," phrasing often used to soften Otherness by Europeanizing it.[45] Later, when Marisa Ventura's full name is revealed to Fiennes' character and his aide (Stanley Tucci), the aide's response is a quizzical "Ventura? Spanish?" Once Marisa's character is outed as an Other, she confirms her lineage by listing her childhood residence: "I grew up there [the projects]. I lived in a four block radius my whole life."

In the Lopez/Fiennes romance, each fills a lack for the other. Marisa legitimizes Chris' connection to nonwhite or poor people by offering her thoughts on public housing and poverty; in exchange, Chris fills the paternal gap left by Marisa's predictably unreliable ex-husband. This substitution of Fiennes for the missing father figure of Lopez's son signals a significant absence in Hollywood film: the Latino male. Unlike the Latina, Latinos rarely possess a vertical racial mobility; for example, leading Latino actors are rarely paired with white actresses. Their racial mobility (when possible) occurs laterally where their sexuality can be contained – as in the case of Anthony Quinn's ability to play other brown men such as Arabs, Greeks or (in a move towards white ethnicity) Italians. Perhaps this absence (or lack of mobility) explains why only two of Lopez's films since *Mi Familia* (1995) feature Latino love interests. Such a double standard suggests that Latinas – as near-white females – still serve as a "metaphor for the raising up of what were deemed primitive societies to a more civilized rung on the ladder of societies."[46] With a few highlights and a spotlight, we Latinas clean up real nice. However, such mobility is only possible so long as Lopez's difference is continually reinscribed upon the image – in cultural or media frames like publicity or films and music videos.

The asset shot

One year after *Vanity Fair* determined Lopez too new for a close-up, the magazine decided that she was ready for her wide shot: the infamous photo of a nearly naked Lopez (from the rear), wearing nothing more than lace-up satin bloomers and matching mules.[47] This image represents the general framing for media depictions of Lopez. In portraits like this one or through lingering shots of her butt on the film screen, Jennifer Lopez's difference is reiterated by the framing of her body. Her body performs – even when she does not – in the pages of magazine or tabloid articles, exposés, news clips and music video screens. If Jennifer Lopez were never to dance another step, exotic sexuality – like her ethnicity – would always already be inscribed on her body. The attention paid to Lopez's rear in every medium echoes past discourses around Saartje/Sarah Baartman, most commonly known as "The Hottentot Venus"; Saartje supposedly carried an excess of sexuality in her large derrière and was commissioned to simply exhibit herself as an example of difference in Europe.[48] As Beltrán states:

> [D]espite the generally positive discussion of Lopez's acting abilities in her publicity in late 1998, it was pretty hard to focus on her acting when most of what we saw of her was her backside. From this perspective, Lopez can be considered a modern-day Hottentot Venus with respect to this

publicity, kin to other nonwhite film actresses who have been similarly constructed before her.[49]

Like her predecessor Carmen Miranda, Lopez signifies excess. While the excess of Miranda was worn as a costume, Lopez's body is her excess.

A good example of this fascination with and overt fetishization of Lopez appears on the cover of the *Sunday Times* (London) "Style" section. Lopez fills the left side of the cover's frame, standing in profile with her face tilted downward and to the left. Her body is shown from the top of her head to her upper thighs. The cover's text settles on the right side of the frame, with the *Sunday Times* "Style" banner at the top. The magazine feature's title sits low right and reads: "Hot Bot: Why Jennifer Lopez is Hollywood's Biggest Star." The brightness/lightness of the lettering contrasts the dark background and dress that clings to Lopez's body. The words "Hot Bot," emboldened in a sans serif font, are level with the curve of Lopez's butt. The absence of text and image between the masthead and "Hot Bot" pulls the weight of the cover's composition, focusing the eye on Lopez's butt and the phrase "Hot Bot," a British English abbreviated allusion to the desirability of Lopez's bottom (buttocks). Because the article ran early in Lopez's career, her title as "Hollywood's biggest star" does not seem to be career-centric. Such a constant fixation on the butt orients discussion of Lopez's body in terms of excess and sexuality; its display is intended and linguistically affirmed as an example of difference – her bigness. While countless examples of such images reiterate that Lopez's difference is ample, her performance as a dancer has simultaneously functioned in line with and against these dominant cultural narratives.

While the suggestive movements of Latinas dancing on screen were built upon negative cultural beliefs about nonwhite women, these movements also challenge traditional inactive female roles and bodies in film. Lopez's paradoxical manipulation of bodily codes thereby offers us another way to read the wide shot: as a transgressive space. With the exception of Busby Berkeley, and particularly after Fred Astaire revolutionized the form, dance in film has primarily been exhibited through the wide shot. This framing illustrates a sense of authenticity in the movement, particularly how, where and when the body moves. Because the wide shot exposes the full body within a single frame's composition, attention is paid to the whole figure's movement. For the Latina, the wide shot further depicts her difference by the cues present – often little more than setting and costuming. As an in-between identity, however, representations of the Latina may transgress the ideals of both image and culture. The hybridity of the Latina's racial representation enabled her to perform dance styles that were not yet deemed appropriate for transfer between the lower to upper classes, as in the mainstreaming of hip-hop in the late 1980s and early 1990s. Dance has challenged the passivity of mainstream female representation by providing the screen Latina with a niche opportunity and narrative agency (however tenuous) typically reserved for men.

Yet the re-articulation of dance in film since the 1980s exposes another facet in the success of Lopez's dancing body: the slippage between dance and race in media representation, exemplified by the more recent phenomenon of 1980s dance films and MTV (Music Television). Though hip-hop emerged in New York during the 1970s, it did not permeate Hollywood until the 1980s. The slew of films which rode the first mainstream hip hop wave – including *Flashdance* (1983), *Beat Street* (1984), *Breakin'* (1984) and *Breakin' 2: Electric Boogaloo* (1984) – centered on the lives of inner-city youth. In this way, the terms "urban" or "youth" were/are used to describe (the process of commodifying) dance, music and fashion and have served as a code for race. With the exception of *Beat Street*, the dance films cited – easily the more popular urban dance films of the 1980s – featured female protagonists, specifically ambiguously raced women, none of whom were stars.[50]

The nonwhite female has become the most family-friendly means of depicting difference to a mainstream audience. For example, *Flashdance*'s lead character (Alex) is played by the biracial actress named Jennifer Beals.[51] The film is about a girl with a dream. But Alex is not just any girl – she is a welder by day and an erotic dancer by night. The working-classness of both jobs reinforces Alex's upwardly mobile dream of becoming a ballet dancer. Unfortunately for Beals, her emerging career was derailed by an inability to dance in the real world: Paramount studios misrepresented her talent by employing dance doubles throughout the film. The scandal that resulted from this (contractually silenced) revelation shows the significance of dance in the film career of a brown-skinned woman. While the dance film genre has faded with a few exceptions of late, its benefactor and successor MTV has continued to escalate the exposure and importance of hip-hop music and dance.

Lopez's dance ability, however, is bona fide, simultaneously authenticating her difference through one medium (her own music videos) to naturalize that difference in another (her film features). It should come as no surprise that Lopez would eventually "remake" *Flashdance* in the form of a music video for her song "I'm Glad." The videos for "I'm Glad" and "Get Right" provide interesting examples of the wide shot representation of Lopez's body. As promotional pieces for the records, Lopez's music videos always showcase her trendsetting abilities in fashion and style. The "I'm Glad" video, however, places Lopez in the "girl with a dream" narrative popularized by *Flashdance*, while she wears costumes inspired by (or actually from) the movie.[52] Beyond recreating the film, Lopez's dancing is the central component of the video; she commissioned David LaChapelle to specifically direct a dance video ("I'm Glad"), focusing on her solo performance.

Flashdance mirrors Lopez's own mythology – working-class girl works hard, lives dancing dream and makes millions – to fulfill what Angela McRobbie describes as a "narrative of desired social mobility."[53] But this mobility is not without compromise. While Beals's performance was criticized for its lack of dance, Lopez's bodily performance faced scrutiny for its excess. The combination of vigorous choreography and skimpy costuming reveal the "wiggle and jiggle" of Lopez's body in the video "I'm Glad."[54] The obvious athleticism of Lopez's body was overruled and the excess of her fleshy movement was edited:

> I really worked out and did the diet thing . . . and then after the video . . . there's always that one guy who's like, "We should retouch this." I was like, "You're going to leave everything the way it is. That's how it wiggles and jiggles in real life, that's how they're going to see it in the video." And I noticed − [the editors] sent [the video] to me and they had shaved off a little bit of my hips and − I was like, "That ain't me − those are not my hips. Just leave them the way they are. Do me a favor − don't touch my hips. Don't try to make me look skinnier. It's fine, it's fine the way it is." And that's what they did.[55]

Despite the training and physical intensity of the dance, Lopez's body did not represent the ideal performance of femininity. This desire to police Lopez's flesh illustrates the ingrained equation of unfirm flesh with a lack of physical and/or moral discipline.[56] In other words, Jennifer's body, like her Hollywood hair, seemingly required taming to conform to mainstream ideals. The attempt to slim Lopez is curious, however, when one compares the natural movement of her body with the thickness and jiggle currently in vogue for backup dancer bodies in (primarily) male-performed rap/hip-hop videos. As Lopez has moved from backup dancer to music video star, has her body become a *more* malleable commodity? In this case, however, Lopez's will to "keep it real" illustrates her significant creative control and representational agency. Lopez's authority over her music video image and ability to transform herself from close-up to wide shot are dependent upon the fact that she − body and all − remains a high-demand commodity. Lopez knows this fact and utilizes it.

For all the transgression and racial mobility, successful mainstream representations of Latinas still lean towards whiteness. For example, Lopez's 2004 video "Get Right" spans a spectrum of hair colors and character types. In the video, Lopez plays multiple characters, each congregating at a club where her song is spinning. We enter the narrative of the club through a female disc jockey (DJ) who is accompanied by her younger, brown-haired sister. As the DJ settles in her booth, places her sister under the counter and begins her musical set, we are introduced to several other Lopez characters: a cocktail waitress, go-go dancer and chola. Other characters − the diva and mousey girl − appear over the course of the video. Beyond showing the multiple sides of Lopez − in this way, the video serves as a microcosm of Latina-ness and Lopez-ness in Hollywood − the video also intercuts footage of Lopez, singing and dancing in a studio performance of the song.

Despite the many types of Lopez present in the video, the DJ is the most curious character. While all the other Lopez characters receive establishing close-ups, the DJ is only ever seen from behind, the outline of her afro providing a convenient distinction as she enters the crowded club. For the course of the five-minute song, the DJ remains anonymous to the audience, though we recognize the character as Lopez by her voice in the video's prologue. The DJ–Lopez face is not revealed until the final shot of the video. While the go-go dancer and studio dance sequences presumably appear in wide shots to best present the body and its movement, it is curious that the DJ remains in a wide shot until a final reveal in the very last frame of the video. It is possible that the DJ's difference of framing is a coincidence or that this delayed reveal marks it as somehow more important than the other representations, but it is equally possible that the frontal close-up of Lopez in an afro swung too closely towards blackness and was better left as a cameo from behind.

Conclusion

The rise of a Latina star like Lopez confirmed that – during a time of revoking affirmative action and other propositions against Latinos in the United States – minority members of the nation could prosper with a little hard work. Lopez symbolized the work ethic necessary to achieve the American Dream and was rewarded with a successful screen, music and fashion career. But despite the access it provides, the complications of in-between-ness are vast. Lopez's figure (as an actor and body) has presented contradictory messages throughout its career. In many ways, her emergence paralleled the ambivalence of her debut program.

As a Fly Girl for the 1990s variety show *In Living Color*, Lopez gained mainstream media representation – as did black sketch comedy. Like Lopez, the prime-time network program navigated through a complex and often contradictory agenda. For *In Living Color*, the show aimed to simultaneously present comedy sketches primarily organized around contemporary black issues while addressing a wider mainstream market/audience. This compromised position prompted Herman Gray to critique *In Living Color* as ambivalent in its "representations of blackness."[57] The commodification of culture has its casualties, but the brunt of this labor often falls on the doubly marked body of the nonwhite female. In this light, it is striking that the multicultural Fly Girls were used to transition *In Living Color* from commercial breaks to the program itself through dance. In effect, the Fly Girls were also represented in-between.

Jennifer Lopez's eventual negotiation of these polarized and racialized spheres, though problematic, offers a unique case study in the cultivation and necessity of a hybrid persona for contemporary nonwhite success. The "multicultural self" that Lopez embodies has worked particularly well after the US visual culture crisis between whiteness and blackness.[58] Ultimately, Jennifer Lopez cultivates a paradox of whiteness and nonwhiteness by mobilizing race for the sake of a mainstream career. Despite the access that dance has afforded Lopez and the Latinas before her, it has simultaneously marked their difference. The moving Latina body has clearly been visually and culturally coded as overtly sexual and in the process perpetuated and reified licentious myths about nonwhite women. Yet, Lopez actively wielded dance in exchange for an incredibly ambitious and successful career; she is now a performer, corporate entity and pioneer on many fiscal fronts.[59] The negotiations of her Hollywood success – minority representation in mainstream media, active female roles and autonomous (sexual) identity in exchange for a sexualized and narrowly defined characterization – mirror the complexities of nationality and sexuality that Latinas experience in everyday life (granted, with significantly less financial return).[60]

Despite this success, the threat of illegitimacy lingers beneath the surface. The 2005 Sony BMG (Lopez's music company) payola scandal thrust the legitimacy of Lopez's musical success into the spotlight; somehow, the scandal seemed less damaging to the credibility of Britney Spears or Beyonce Knowles, also represented by Sony BMG. Still, Lopez continues to push at the boundaries of mainstream culture from within, now that she is in it. The September 2005 issue of *Elle* features a glamorous and curly haired Lopez on the cover. Within, Lopez fills out the usual article/profile and fashion shoot. Of the six-page poses, four feature at least one article of clothing from Sweetface, Lopez's newly launched line in collaboration with the Hilfiger family: three outfits are fully Sweetface while the other two featured designers are Dior and Oscar de la Renta. The representation of Lopez's business and performance personas offers, at very least, a more complex depiction of the American Latina in 2005.

Fashion, cosmetics and hair coloring have long played a role in cultural and national transformations; breast and (more recently) butt implants now allow the body itself to be fully manipulated by everyone – white and nonwhite women inside and outside of Hollywood – to achieve a redefined/re-raced/re-packaged physical ideal. Such trends will only last, I contend, so long as the market will bear it. How, then, will the next Latina performer shake her assets into the national/media spotlight?[61]

Notes

1 Sarah Banet-Weiser, *The Most Beautiful Girl in the World: Beauty Pageants and National Identity* (Berkeley, CA: University of California Press, 1999), p. 65.
2 Richard Dyer, *White* (London: Routledge, 1997), p. 3.
3 Elizabeth Coffman, "Women in Motion: Loie Fuller and the 'Interpenetration' of Art and Science," *Camera Obscura*, 49, 17:1 (2002), p. 82. Also see Linda Williams, *Hard Core: Power, Pleasure and the Frenzy of the Visible* (Berkeley and Los Angeles, CA: University of California Press, 1989).
4 Williams, *Hard Core*, p. 43.
5 For the reiterative nature of performance, see Judith Butler, *Bodies That Matter: On the Discursive Limits of "Sex"* (New York: Routledge, 1993).
6 Examples of this permeate all areas of film, including the male authoritarian voiceover in movie trailers. Still, white female performers remain less prevalent than male performers in film.
7 Charles Ramírez Berg, *Latino Images in Film: Stereotypes, Subversion, and Resistance* (Austin, TX: University of Texas Press, 2002), p. 21.
8 While exceptions to this rule do exist – particularly as black audiences gain box

office power – Hollywood narratives are still determined according to longstanding expectations about types and taste.

9 I use these formal expressions to indicate a more general discussion of how the body is traditionally framed in mainstream film and how Lopez's career might be understood as navigating between the physical expectations of both. While I do analyze specific shots, my examination of Lopez's representation through the "close-up" and "wide shot" should be read metaphorically. For example, not all close-ups strictly focus on the face; I am certain that Lopez's derrière has commanded more than its share of these specific shots. For these reasons, this essay uses the terms "close-up" and "wide shot" more openly.

10 This list does not attempt to account for all of the Latinas who have been featured in Hollywood film. Rather, I compose a snapshot of Latina "leading women" in film – either in terms of mainstream popularity, box office records or other means of mainstream success in Hollywood. For this reason, actresses such as Rosie Perez, Salma Hayek and Penelope Cruz are not included as primary figures. Though I do not include Rosie in my overall analysis, it is striking that her career follows my central argument: she began as a dancer and served as a dancer/choreographer for *In Living Color*.

11 Jane C. Desmond, "Embodying Difference: Issues in Dance and Cultural Studies," in *Meaning in Motion: New Cultural Studies of Dance* (Durham, NC: Duke University Press, 1997), p. 33. Dancing "lump[s] together 'race,' 'national origin' and [a] supposed genetic propensity for rhythmic movement [to rest] on an implicit division between moving and thinking, mind and body." Also, "the ascription of sexuality (or dangerous, potentially overwhelming sexuality) to subordinate classes and 'races' or to groups of specific national origin (blacks, 'Latins,' and other such lumped together terms to denote non-Anglo-European ancestry) yields such descriptions [and depictions] as 'fiery,' 'hot,' 'sultry,' 'passionate'" (pp. 40–1).

12 Gary D. Keller, *A Biographical Handbook of Hispanics and United States Film* (Tempe, AZ: Bilingual Press/Editorial Bilingüe, 1997), p. 91. Caption appears under the heading "Dancing Señoritas."

13 Berg, *Latino Images in Film*, pp. 70–1.

14 Yxta Maya Murray, "Jennifer Lopez," *Buzz* (April 1997), p. 70. Murray notes, "But with the possible exception of Hayworth, none rose to high-roller, leading lady status."

15 Because Hayworth's father was Spanish and her mother Irish, Rita took her mother's maiden name as her screen name – reportedly re-Anglicizing the less refined "Haworth" into "Hayworth." Lopez's only change has been the temporary moniker/clothing line entitled "J.Lo."

16 Velez, Del Rio, Miranda and Moreno indeed experienced significant fame and fortune, but their personas remained fully Latina or Other, a difference that may have prevented a full mainstreaming of their careers in the vein of Hayworth and Lopez. Such Othering is complicated by Moreno's birth in Puerto Rico, a commonwealth of the United States.

17 For more on this, see Mary C. Beltrán, "The Hollywood Latina Body as Site of Social Struggle: Media Constructions of Stardom and Jennifer Lopez's 'Cross-over Butt,'" *The Quarterly Review of Film and Video*, 19.1 (January 2002).

18 "J.Lo" *Revealed with Jules Asner*, 1:00 (2002), talk show.

19 Angharad N. Valdivia, *A Latina in the Land of Hollywood* (Tucson, AZ: University of Arizona Press, 2000), p. 97. This collapse is also noted in Valdivia's work on Rosie Perez. Valdivia finds: "[Perez] is at once Latina because she is working class and working class because she is Latina. One codetermines the other in a classic case of piggybacking undervalued positions of dominant binary explanatory frameworks."

20 Frances Negrón-Muntaner's article does an excellent job of outlining the discourse

around Lopez's "assets" during *Selena*'s press junkets. Frances Negrón-Muntaner, *Boricua Pop: Puerto Ricans and the Latinization of American Culture* (New York: New York University Press, 2004).

21 By "brown female bodies" here, I mean Latinas – but a similar argument could certainly be made for other exoticized female bodies colonized by the United States, such as Pacific Islanders and some Asian communities.

22 Dyer, *White*, p. 57.

23 This mobilization of race comes from a term I call "mobile whiteness," a concept I explore in other work. Mobile whiteness synthesizes Richard Dyer's work on whiteness with that of Judith Butler's performativity. Intersecting these concepts, I imagine how the Latina body performs and maneuvers amidst and across the regulated and ordained poles of race and gender in popular culture (white/black/male/female). Here, whiteness is mobilized because it serves as the default form, its illusion of "normalcy" serving as the crux of its underlying representational power. By "mobilizing" whiteness, I destabilize the notion that whiteness is a fixed identity lacking a performance and limit of its own. Judith Butler, *Bodies That Matter: On the Discursive Limits of "Sex"* (New York: Routledge, 1993) and Richard Dyer, *White*.

24 A good example of this is the importation of Carmen Miranda during the Good Neighbor period. Miranda's presence signaled a symbolic cooperation between the United States and South America during WWII.

25 Lopez's complexion can certainly be problematized in this process: she is not exactly light complected, yet routinely elaborates her "brown-ness" with bronzer or her "lightness" with hair color.

26 *Mirabella* (July 1998), p. 84.

27 Arlene Davila, *Latinos Inc.: The Marketing and Making of a People* (Berkeley, CA: University of California Press, 2001), pp. 216–17.

28 Herman Gray citing Cornell West. Herman Gray, *Watching Race: Television and the Struggle for Blackness* (Minneapolis, MN: University of Minnesota Press, 1995), p. 148.

29 *Mirabella*, p. 82.

30 This de-ethnicizing can and does, of course, happen in wide shots. The incredibly light ad campaign for Glow by J.Lo perfume functions in both a wide and close-up. While the silhouette of her body is hidden behind a translucent sheet, her face becomes the focus of the advertisement, as it is revealed from behind the sheet (effectively re-framing it) and is easily the brightest element. The ability of Latinas to play other types of (specifically) nonwhite roles is also evident in classical Hollywood film, a subject I take up in my work on Lupe Velez and Dolores Del Rio.

31 Dyer, *White*, pp. 127, 132.

32 Dyer, *White*, p. 131.

33 *Vanity Fair* (April 1997), p. 88.

34 This conformity is supported by the fact that – as yet – Fairuza Balk has not achieved the same level of media representation as Lopez and Theron. Of the three, Theron's persona is the only full "blonde." Though Lopez's media exposure is arguably more vast than the other two, Theron is the only star of the trio to be recognized by the Academy of Motion Picture Arts and Sciences.

35 David R. Roediger, *Working Toward Whiteness: How America's Immigrants Became White: The Strange Journey from Ellis Island to the Suburbs* (New York: Basic Books, 2005).

36 *Entertainment Today* (c.1997), page unknown. Margaret Herrick Research Archive, Academy of Motion Picture Arts and Sciences.

37 *Buzz*, p. 72.

38 Ayana Byrd and Lori Tharps, *Hair Story: Untangling the Roots of Black Hair in America* (New York: St. Martin's Press, 2001), pp. 26, 27, 30.

39   *Mirabella*, p. 82. Emphasis mine.

40   *Jennifer Lopez: The Reel Me* (Sony Studios, 155 minutes, 2003), DVD. In the commentary for her video "I'm Glad," Lopez remarks that her hair is naturally curly like the style in this video.

41   Though Lopez and Harrelson exhibit romantic tension in *Money Train*, their relationship is tempered and mediated by her dance and eventual sex scene with Wesley Snipes.

42   Beltrán, "The Hollywood Latina Body," p. 76.

43   Diane Simon, *Hair: Public, Political,* Extremely *Personal* (New York: St. Martin's Press, 2000), p. 61.

44   Even the jewelry and department store clerks (in higher end service jobs) sport sandy/blonde hair.

45   Leland Saito's analysis of Atlantic Square shows how an architectural style can be "whitened" through a strategic use of adjectives. He shows how one shopping center can evolve from "Mexican" to "Spanish" to "Mediterranean" – without any modification to design. Leland Saito, *Race and Politics: Asian Americans, Latinos, and Whites in a Los Angeles Suburb* (Urbana, IL: University of Illinois Press, 1998), p. 47.

46   Jane C. Desmond, *Staging Tourism: Bodies on Display from Waikiki to Sea World* (Chicago, IL: University of Chicago Press, 1999), pp. 50 (citing Womacks), 110.

47   *Vanity Fair* (July 1998), page unknown.

48   Coco Fusco, *English Is Broken Here: Notes on Cultural Fusion in the Americas* (New York: New Press, 1995), p. 47.

49   Beltrán, "The Hollywood Latina Body," p. 83.

50   Jennifer Beals' race is never mentioned in the film and her family is never shown. Likewise, Kelly in *Breakin'* can be easily read a variety of ways, as one 1984 review noted.

51   Alex is a working-class erotic dancer striving for a "better life," indicated by her desire to become a ballerina. She does not have a visible family, simply a mysterious Russian "aunt," and her leading man is the ambiguously raced boss of the steel factory at which she works (Michael Nouri, of Lebanese descent).

52   The same red teddy worn by Jennifer Beals in the famous "water-bucket" dance number is worn by Lopez in the video *Jennifer Lopez: The Reel Me*, "I'm Glad" video commentary.

53   Angela McRobbie, "Dance Narratives and Fantasies of Achievement," in Jane Desmond, ed., *Meaning in Motion: New Cultural Studies of Dance* (Durham, NC: Duke University Press, 1997), p. 228.

54   *Jennifer Lopez: The Reel Me*, "I'm Glad" video commentary.

55   *Jennifer Lopez: The Reel Me*, "I'm Glad" video commentary.

56   Banet-Weiser, *The Most Beautiful Girl in the World*, p. 68.

57   Gray, *Watching Race*, p. 145.

58   I borrow the term "multicultural self" from Sarah Banet-Weiser's critique of beauty pageant's "nonthreatening" approaches to race. Banet-Weiser, *The Most Beautiful Girl in the World*, p. 105.

59   Not only is Lopez the highest-paid Latina in Hollywood (and the first to break $1 million per picture), but she was also the first performer to open at #1 in the box office and music charts with *The Wedding Planner* and the single "Love Don't Cost a Thing."

60   Dance challenges the passivity of female representation, granting the screen Latina with narrative agency (however tenuous) typically reserved for men in film, particularly in the musical genre.

61   This essay emerges from my dissertation entitled "Shake Your Assets: Dance and Latina Sexuality in Hollywood Film."

Part IV

Desire to desire

Chapter 10

Guess Who's Coming to Dinner with Eldridge Cleaver and the Supreme Court, or reforming popular racial memory with Hepburn and Tracy

Susan Courtney

Handcuffed, 1967/68

What does it mean that the first Hollywood film to unequivocally reject the miscegenation taboo was a Tracy and Hepburn film that would go on to become the most popular interracial text of its era, and arguably of the late twentieth century?[1] This question becomes all the more intriguing when we recognize that the film was in fact one of three tremendously influential interracial texts to appear within less than a year. Just months before the release of Hollywood's instantly celebrated and ridiculed verdict on the subject, the Supreme Court handed down its decision, *Loving v. Virginia*, that rendered laws prohibiting interracial marriage unconstitutional in June of 1967. And not long after the film's December release, Eldridge Cleaver, then Minister of Information for the Black Panther Party, published a collection of boldly personal and political essays that meditate extensively on fantasies of interracial sex that had marked his experiences as a young black man; that book, *Soul on Ice* (March 1968), quickly became a widely discussed and debated bestseller.[2] While *Guess*, *Loving*, and *Soul* thus form a trio of authors, agendas, and implied audiences that could hardly be more different from one another, together they cut across a wide swath of popular culture to suggest that dominant American legacies of miscegenation were being confronted more directly than ever before. This in turn makes all the more consequential the terms and conditions under which those legacies were publicly avowed and (still) repressed.[3]

While Cleaver exposed multiple forms of racial, sexual, and economic oppression regularly embedded in dominant fantasies and practices of interracial sex, the Court remained virtually silent on such histories in the *Loving* decision, and *Guess Who's Coming to Dinner* both couldn't see its way to openly admitting them, but also couldn't manage fully to avoid them. What is more, despite their varied thresholds of cultural knowledge and amnesia, these texts demonstrate a shared ability to divest conventional commitments to racial hierarchy secured through the miscegenation taboo only by reasserting rigid conventions of gender and sex. By reevaluating *Guess Who's Coming to Dinner* in this context I hope to clarify not only how that film so successfully masked the most critical histories of the phobia it allegedly renounced, but how classical cinematic forms of vision, space, and spectatorship were central to that project.

Each of the three texts in question could be said to revolve around one or more mixed couples that function as highly condensed figures within which a range of social conflicts converge. In a period marked by the felt limits as well as the successes of the civil rights movement, local and global crises over the Vietnam War, the resuscitation of the women's movement, and various counter cultures, divergent attempts to rethink such couples find in them the means to rearticulate shifting notions of race, gender, class, and generation. Indeed, they repeatedly demonstrate the difficulty of extricating each of these identities from the others. Whereas Cleaver's text critiques some of the powerful effects of that condensation, the more mainstream liberal texts compound it by insisting on the singularity of the racial questions these couples pose. This is apparent in the film when Spencer Tracy's character sums up the difficulties his daughter and her fiancé will face as the result of their "pigmentation problem." Reducing the dilemma to color, this formulation not only clouds the complex meanings of "race" at issue, but masks the film's use of this couple to simultaneously navigate contemporary anxieties about difference on multiple fronts.

Even a brief, introductory glance at *Guess* quickly reveals the much more complex constellation of differences tangled and untangled in and through its primary couple. Joey (Katharine Houghton), as Matt and Christina Drayton (Spencer Tracy and Katharine Hepburn) tellingly call their daughter, is "a very determined young woman" who wears pants, travels to Hawaii alone, suddenly brings home a black fiancé, frankly expresses her interest in sex with him, and demands that her parents immediately declare their approval of her imminent marriage. Yet she also continuously demonstrates that in the eyes and company of Dr John Prentice (Sidney Poitier), who alone insists on calling her Joanna, she is delighted to melt and mold her independent spirit into the supporting role of wife, second only in its devoted performance to the one Hepburn plays to Tracy's aging, but still firmly ruling, patriarch.[4] And while this gender drama of taming spunky Joey into the more docile Joanna is tended to through the more talked about "pigmentation" plot, the class conditions that underwrite any possibility of integrating the very white Drayton home are unmistakable: in the extravagance of their mansion overlooking the San Francisco Bay; in the black maids who keep it running and get the eponymous dinner on the table; and in John's working-class black parents who arrive as decidedly temporary guests, as if to assure that this proposed mixing need not seriously threaten the class structure upon which the Drayton household clearly stands. And finally, although viewers catching the film on cable decades later would be hard pressed to recall from the film itself *either* that the city in which it is so visibly located was widely known that year as host to the "Summer of Love" (and its public celebrations of sex, drugs, and rock and roll), *or* that loud calls for "black power" had been coming from just across the bay the Drayton home so spectacularly surveys, the dramatic day that marks the temporal sweep of the film's plot is nonetheless punctuated by vivid, albeit highly constrained, eruptions of those highly charged places and times.

Of the three texts under discussion it is *Soul on Ice* that most explicitly articulates such intertwined forms of identity and difference and the ties that can bind them through dominant fantasies of miscegenation. Cleaver insists that the social and psychic injuries that ensue from those fantasies, especially the "sickness between the white woman and the black man," "must be brought out into the open, dealt with and resolved," and that "all of us, the entire nation, will be better off if we bring it all out front."[5] As he analyzes this culturally produced "sickness," a larger model of identity and difference in US culture gradually emerges, organized simultaneously around two intersecting binary axes; male/female and black/white. For Cleaver, this results in four distinct positions – white man, white woman, black man, and black woman – each of which is defined in opposition to the others.[6] After describing the dominant scripts of these four mythic characters, a fictional character whose voice is rhymed with the author's reflects:

> All this is tied up together in a crazy way. . . . At one time it seems absolutely clear and at other times I don't believe in it. It reminds me of two sets of handcuffs that have all four of us tied up together, holding all black and white flesh in a certain mold.[7]

When we read these "two sets of handcuffs" as racial and sexual difference interlocked, the metaphor vividly articulates a structure wherein the position of any one of those raced and gendered subjects "tied up together" necessarily affects, or is affected by, the position of each of the others.

This essay seeks to analyze that tightly regulated movement as charted within and across *Loving v. Virginia*, *Soul on Ice*, and especially *Guess Who's Coming to Dinner*. Cleaver's double handcuffs – which his own conceptions of labor invite us to triple if we disentangle race from class, and which multiply and divide yet further when we factor in the calls for generational change implicit throughout his text – serve as a particularly apt metaphor with which to do so at a moment so marked by the multiple "movements" of the late sixties. What is more, it is precisely because of the simultaneously social and psychological consequences these texts still hold, "for all of us, the entire nation," that this essay queries the terms and conditions under which they variously confront the legacies of miscegenation handed down to them – from the courts, from Hollywood, and from experiences of everyday life. In short, this essay asks, what are the implications of Cleaver's metaphorical "handcuffs" for the textual production of popular American memory, and forgetting, in these unprecedented interracial texts of 1967 and 1968?

From miscegenation to marxism

Before turning to the more conservative terms of Hollywood and the Supreme Court, it is useful to further mine Cleaver's more radical reckoning of codes against miscegenation. For not only does his text speak of a black male experience that is invisible in the white texts, but it keenly moves between starkly personal reflection and equally stark analysis of the larger social structures the author's own preoccupations enact and resist.

Cleaver tellingly relates his intellectual history as having been marked by a pivotal shift from obsessions with miscegenation to a new obsession with the writings of Karl Marx and other "readings into the history of socialism."[8] He locates this shift just after a "nervous breakdown" in the wake of Emmett Till's murder, precipitated by the following event:

> One day I saw in a magazine a picture of the white woman with whom Emmett Till was said to have flirted. While looking at the picture, I felt that little tension in the center of my chest I experience when a woman appeals to me. I was disgusted and angry with myself. Here was a woman who had caused the death of a black, possibly because, when he looked at her, he also felt the same tensions of lust and desire in his chest. . . . It was all unacceptable to me. . . . In spite of everything and against my will and the hate I felt for the woman and all that she represented, she appealed to me. I flew into a rage at myself, at America, at white women, at the history that had placed those tensions of lust and desire in my chest.[9]

While the culpable "history" here named gets variously elaborated throughout Cleaver's book, it will prove central to his analysis that the announced cure to the breakdown set off by the white woman's picture is his discovery of Marx. Reading Marx, "although he kept me with a headache," "was like taking medicine" and "diverted me from my previous preoccupation: morbid broodings on the black man and the white woman."[10] This transformation narrative is complicated by the fact that such "morbid broodings" would not disappear: by his own account Cleaver would go on to rape white women after release from the prison term being served at the time of the breakdown and then, back in prison, he would write this essay that famously confesses, and less famously but emphatically renounces, his earlier performance of interracial rape as "an insurrectionary act."[11] Nonetheless, that Cleaver's narrative emphasizes this turn from "morbid broodings" over miscegenation to curative "headache[s]" over Marx, and that his writings suggest that turn to have marked something more like a junction between two conceptual paths he would continue to move between, strikes to the heart of his insistence throughout *Soul* that a series of social hierarchies – namely those of race, gender, sexuality, and class – intersect to form the peculiar handcuffs of social and psychic life in the USA.

Although Cleaver at times seems to conflate race and class, his understanding that race functions in part to sustain a class structure is occasionally made explicit by, and is always implicit in, his interlocked foursome. When the character who describes the double handcuffs tries to explain his sexual obsession with white women, he begins with a raced and sexed model of identity in which the meaning of "white" and "black" are free and enslaved, respectively:

> I know that the white man made the black woman the symbol of slavery and the white woman the symbol of freedom. Every time I embrace a black woman I'm embracing slavery, and when I put my arms around a white woman, well, I'm hugging freedom.[12]

This free/enslaved dichotomy is elaborated further as a mind/body dichotomy that in turn reflects and enforces a labor relation. All these meanings conjoin to script the handcuffed cast of four. "The white man wants to be the *brain* and . . . wants us to be the muscle, the *body*" [original emphasis]. He therefore "turned himself into the Omnipotent Administrator. . . . And he turned the black man into the Supermasculine Menial and kicked him out into the fields." This understanding of black defined as body and labor leads to its feminized version in "the myth of the strong black woman," "Aunt Jemima," which is in turn "the other side of the coin of the myth of the beautiful dumb blonde."[13]

Although seemingly at odds with this intersectional critique, also crucial to Cleaver's analysis are its rigidly sexed and gendered limits.[14] For example, at the outset of *Soul*'s penultimate chapter, "The Primeval Mitosis," Cleaver writes:

> The roots of heterosexuality are buried in that evolutionary choice made long ago in some misty past . . . by some unknown forerunner of Homo sapiens. Struggling up from some murky swamp, some stagnant mudhole, some peaceful meadow, that unknown ancestor of Man/Woman, by some weird mitosis of the essence, divided its Unitary Self in half.[15]

From this feverish mix of origin stories Cleaver theorizes a "dynamic magnetism of opposites – the Primeval Urge – which exerts an irresistible attraction between the male and female hemispheres, ever tending to fuse them back together into a unity in which the male and female realize their true nature."[16] This language of sexual "essence" and "biology" continues for several paragraphs, building to the startling suggestion that a heterosexual impulse is not only prior to, but "a driving force of the Class Struggle," and even "history" itself:

> Man's continual striving for a Unitary Sexual Image, which can only be achieved in a Unitary Society, becomes a basic driving force of the Class Struggle, which is, in turn, the dynamic of history. The quest for the Apocalyptic Fusion [of male and female] will find optimal conditions only in a Classless Society, the absence of classes being the *sine qua non* for the existence of a Unitary Society in which the Unitary Sexual Image can be achieved.[17]

While words like "Fusion" and "Unitary" might suggest a desire to overcome sexual binaries, no such overcoming is ever articulated. Instead, the language works to relentlessly shape, and sex, the book's movement towards race–class liberation, leaving little doubt as to which forms of difference Cleaver seeks to reconceive and which will forever determine us from the "misty," "murky" "mudhole" of primal "Man."

Sexual difference thus functions as a kind of absolute limit in this self-consciously revolutionary text – the one order of difference it thoroughly depends upon amidst its embrace of a series of radical transgressions and dismantlings. Cleaver announces as much when he writes:

> All men must have [a male "self-image"] or they start seeing themselves as women, women start seeing them as women, then women lose their own self-image, and soon nobody knows what they are themselves or what anyone else is – that is to say, the world starts looking precisely as it looks today.[18]

As we will see, it is precisely such deep commitments to the most conservative terms of sexual difference accompanying visions of racial progress that make this popular, "radical," black treatment of interracial sex from 1968 most akin to its more mainstream white counterparts.[19]

The memory of *Loving*

After Cleaver's fierce reckoning with dominant legacies of miscegenation, even with its rampant sexual essentialisms, the Supreme Court's could hardly seem tamer. And this is the product not simply of an admittedly jarring shift from Cleaver's baldly sexual and political language to the formal distance and legal obligations of juridical prose; it also reflects the different terms and conditions under which laws against interracial marriage could be denounced by dominant white culture. For while legal historian Adrienne D. Davis calls *Loving* a "legally radical decision," because it struck down laws that had worked to "promote and maintain the racial and gender caste order of slavery," I approach the landmark case from a different vantage point.[20] Without denying its progressive effects, or the radical implications Davis outlines, my reading of the decision itself in the larger context at issue here calls attention to the ways in which: 1) even as it boldly indicts the "White Supremacy" of antimiscegenation laws, *Loving* falls silent on the histories of institutional oppression they sanctioned; and 2) its final championing of marriage serves not only to affirm a normative sexual order, but arguably to restabilize orders of class and race implicitly at risk in the decision.

The first of *Loving*'s two numbered sections argues that the statutes prohibiting interracial marriage violate the Fourteenth Amendment. Invoking the Equal Protection Clause, the Court here concludes:

There is patently no legitimate overriding purpose independent of invidious racial discrimination. . . . The fact that Virginia prohibits only interracial marriages involving white persons demonstrates that the racial classifications must stand on their own justification, as measures designed to maintain White Supremacy.[21]

This final explanation echoes the Court's opening commentary in this section, where it rejected a prior Virginia ruling which had

concluded that the State's legitimate purposes were "to preserve the racial integrity of its citizens," and to prevent "the corruption of blood," "a mongrel breed of citizens," and "the obliteration of racial pride," *obviously an endorsement of the doctrine of White Supremacy.* [emphasis mine][22]

At the beginning and end of its main argument in *Loving*, then, the Court unflinchingly names "White Supremacy" as the cause and intended effect of the laws in question.

Because the rhetorical force of the decision so rests on this indictment, a consideration of its part in shaping the meaning and memory of interracial history begs the following questions: What explicit or implicit meanings of "White Supremacy" does *Loving* offer? And, in turn, how does it effectively interpret the miscegenation statutes for the legal record? Such questions quickly arise because, although the Court clearly argues that the statutes legitimate acts of "arbitrary and invidious discrimination" and white privilege, how exactly they do so – with what particular logics, mechanisms, or effects – is virtually impossible to discern from the decision. While the condemnation following the Virginia ruling cited above might be read to suggest that the statutes maintain white privilege by regulating whiteness as an exclusive social territory (e.g. "'preserv[ing] the racial integrity of . . . citizens'"), the Court never says this. What it does do, in the introduction, is invoke language that more explicitly reduces the terms at stake, as we've seen elsewhere, to color. This comes with a citation of the Virginia Court's assertion of a kind of divinely segmented global palette whose discrete, pure colors dare not be "mix[ed]":

Almighty God created the races white, black, yellow, malay and red, and he placed them on separate continents. And but for the interference with his arrangement there would be no cause for such marriages. The fact that he separated the races shows that he did not intend for the races to mix.[23]

Even though the High Court is here citing a segregationist vision it will flatly reject, this language of race as color nonetheless lingers in *Loving* without comment. And when the Court later cites from its own concurring opinion in another case, it affirms more directly the notion that racial discrimination is reducible to color bias: "Indeed, two members of this Court have already stated that they 'cannot conceive of a valid legislative purpose . . . which makes the color of a person's skin the test of whether his conduct is a criminal offense.'"[24] Coming near the climactic end of Section I, as the last sentence of the paragraph immediately preceding the one that will deem Virginia's laws to be "measures designed to maintain White Supremacy," this rejection of a legal test based solely on skin color textually resides as the nearest thing to an explanation of how, precisely, such measures operate or might be detected.[25]

While the Court had good reason to reject discrimination keyed to skin color, what becomes noticeable in our context is the accompanying absence of any clear articulation of the manifold forms of power historically secured beneath such surface rhetoric. The one muted trace of that history comes and goes quickly in *Loving*, when we read: "Penalties for miscegenation arose as an incident to slavery and have been common in Virginia since the colonial period."[26] While this unspecified relation to slavery is not explained, a footnote directs us to an "historical discussion" in a contemporary law review. Yet the inquiring reader who seeks out that bulky article will find nowhere in its detailed history of Virginia's criminal codes and punishments any discussion of their social or economic origins or effects.[27]

For readers suspecting that the Court's silence must at least partly be explainable by the terms with which the case was presented to it, the written arguments filed by *Loving*'s attorneys could not be more startling. For the appellant's brief to the Court, before offering arguments based on Equal Protection and Due Process, argues exactly what is most significantly absent from the Court's opinion; namely, that miscegenation laws were "originally passed primarily for economic and social reasons as means to foster and implement the institution of slavery" and continued to "perpetuate and foster illicit exploitative sex relationships [of the sort for which they were] explicitly designed."[28] And the brief gets very specific about how exactly the laws worked towards these ends. "Slaveowners wanted protection from the loss of their slave property through intermarriage with a free white," and laws that rendered "illegitimate [the children born of] Negro slaves and white masters" and determined the slave or free status of such children "according to the condition of the mother . . . led to intentional slave breeding by slave-owners." The brief also charges that these laws continue to function as "the State's official symbol of a caste system,"[29] citing in support one of the very texts the Court itself had cited in *Brown v. Board*, Gunnar Myrdal's *An American Dilemma*.[30] Yet *Loving* takes up none of Myrdal's claims, extensively reprinted for it in the brief, about relations between miscegenation taboos and social hierarchies. This omission is particularly noteworthy since Myrdal digs beneath precisely the superficial explanations referenced in *Loving*. As the brief cites him: "The great majority of non-liberal white Southerners utilize the dread of 'intermarriage' . . . to justify discriminations which have quite other and wider goals than the purity of the white race . . . what white people really want is to keep the Negroes in a lower status."[31]

As one reads pointed, elaborated claims like these leaping out from the pages of the appellant's brief, the Court's silence in *Loving* on anything like the mechanisms of sexual and economic exploitation embedded in the laws at issue only becomes louder and louder. Insofar as the Fourteenth Amendment arguments required the determination of "invidious" racial distinctions, the brief would seem to offer ample material. More to the point, that *Loving* refers to none of it suggests that even in 1967 the Court could boldly condemn antimiscegenation laws so long as the specific forms of power and oppression legitimated through them not be named.

Also relevant here is the way the Court supplements its treatment of racial institutions in Section I with a thorough embrace of the institution of marriage in Section II. There's a palpable sense of relief there at having maneuvered through the most difficult matters of slavery, segregation, and white supremacy, emerging with renewed certainty and simplicity to conclude the decision with a resounding call for among the most personal of liberties.

> The freedom to marry has long been recognized as one of the vital personal rights essential to the orderly pursuit of happiness by free men.
> Marriage is one of the "basic civil rights of man," fundamental to our very existence and survival.[32]

In addition to the obvious maleness of the named subjects of freedom, striking here is the language of essence and origin. The Court not only cites case precedent, but in its own words – and not wholly unlike its black nationalist counterpart – the declaration of marriage's "vital," "essential," "fundamental" function leaves little doubt as to the structuring role here granted the sexed, and sexing, institution.

Loving thus not only reminds us that the real problem with colorblindness is its muteness about institutionalized forms of inequality and exploitation, but also suggests once again that as the rigid borders and binary distinctions of one system of difference are increasingly challenged, the language of another is ready at hand to provide closure, order, and structuring hierarchy.

Thinking of the self as a man

After considering the terms with which its more expressly radical and conservative liberal contemporaries avowed and disavowed American legacies of interracial sex, those of *Guess Who's Coming to Dinner* come as even less of a surprise. Looking and sounding more like the Warren Court than Eldridge Cleaver, Spencer Tracy, as we have seen, sums up the young couple's dilemma as "a pigmentation problem," reducing the matter to a language of color that avoids histories of exploitation and privilege nonetheless evident in his hilltop mansion with seemingly all white interiors and all black servants.[33] In part, the history that seems to both surface and fade with the texts considered above reminds us that such avoidance is already significantly structured into the text by casting the couple in question as a black man and a white woman (not a black woman and a white man). For even as this pairing implicitly confronts white culture's most popular, violent fantasies of miscegenation, it also allows for the continued forgetting, in effect, of what happened on the plantation as well as of *What Happened in the Tunnel* (1903) — the first of a spate of early American short films to briefly (albeit comically) imagine an interracial kiss between a white man and a black woman before that interracial pair, and the history it might threaten to evoke, were more forcibly denied on the Hollywood screen.[34]

In addition, the precise way the plot poses the question — will the interracial couple's parents accept them? — sets the problem up as a conflict of husbands vs. wives, mothers vs. fathers, and its solution utterly depends upon the nostalgic casting of Tracy and Hepburn, the aging star couple who helped make the "battle of the sexes" a classic Hollywood subgenre.[35] Yet while the conventionality of such Hollywood rhetoric can make it difficult to immediately recognize the full reach of its impact in this case, the payoff of having traced similar rhetoric in the contemporary, non-filmic texts — I hope — is that we are now better positioned to consider *Guess*'s particularly cinematic contributions to the larger histories of memory and identity in question. I approach this below first by examining how the film's narrative structure enacts the wider cultural tendency to tolerate, at times even celebrate, the opening up of formerly restricted racial institutions only by refortifying sexual ones. Then, in the final section, I consider how this well remembered text elaborates this gesture in sometimes startlingly exact visual and spatial terms.

The centrality of sexual difference to this film is quickly demonstrated by the regularity with which contemporary reviewers understood it to be, at bottom, a Tracy and Hepburn movie. The nostalgia that saturates such accounts is compounded by the fact that *Guess* was the couple's first onscreen reunion in nine years and would also be their last. Fans knew before seeing the film that Tracy had died soon after shooting it, intensifying the already emotionally charged experience of watching him in a role in which he finally declares openly his passion for the woman long known as the primary but officially unrecognized woman in his life. So powerful was the performance, the reviews repeatedly insist, that even those who hated the film would love Tracy and Hepburn. Writing for *Life*, Richard Schickel judged *Guess* "false," "unbelievable," and "dishonest," but of the star couple he rejoiced: "They bicker fondly together in their patented manner, and for me, at least, their performances in this movie are beyond the bounds of criticism."[36] A reviewer at the *New Yorker* effectively describes the counterbalancing act detectable in many more reviews: "the movie insidiously charms us into ignoring its defects, and for this the credit must go to a superb cast."[37] While this praise is not exclusive to them, the reviewer makes it clear that Tracy and Hepburn are his shining favorites: "when, at [the film's] climax, he turns to her and tells her what an old man remembers having loved, it is, for us who are permitted to overhear him, an experience that transcends the theatrical."

The film itself provides ample cause to take such responses seriously. In addition to the particular charms of this particular star couple, central to the text are several sexually differentiated elements grafted to them. The father's rule, the mother's delicate handling of him, and the house designed around them (with his bay-view study, paintings presumably from her art gallery decorating interior walls, etc.) all provide a palpable sense of order and stability to a situation that nonetheless signifies the potential for significant social and personal upheaval. But clearly the most hallowed and central patriarchal structure of all is the father of the bride. For his "blessing" is the authoritative judgment around which the entire film revolves. Indeed, most everything in the film – the content and structure of the plot, familial happiness, the marriage itself, and the political statement it will make – hinges on the white father's decision. *Guess* thus explicitly registers, elaborates, and responds to its presumably racial "problem" by translating it and its solution into decidedly gendered terms. When John battles his own father (Roy E. Glenn, Sr.) near the end, championing his right to live as he chooses, his fierce speech climaxes with a line that not only reduces race to color, but finally sheers away both of those to suggest that sexual difference is now the only difference that should matter: "*Dad, Dad,*" John pleads, "you think of yourself as a colored man, I think of myself as a *man.*"[38]

Equally revealing is the fact that amidst the many deliberations of this marriage, there is little, if any, real discussion of race. Characters repeatedly remark on the match being unexpected, a "shock," and a few comments are made to the effect that others will make it difficult for the couple and any children they might have. Yet, while we see Matt debate with John about whether blacks have "a special sense of rhythm" and announce to Christina his astonishment that a black mailman could produce such a fine son (a doctor for the World Health Organization, a distinguished scholar, etc.), we hear none of the specific feelings or fears that make him initially object to his daughter's marrying a black man, even though he does so openly, almost immediately, and until the film's last scene. While it's not surprising that a proudly liberal Hollywood film would not make a "hero" like Drayton/Tracy speak the ugliest white phobias of miscegenation, such silences nonetheless signal the patriarchal plot's relative muteness on racial matters, despite its alleged preoccupation with them.

This reticence might be productively compared to the Court's apparent choice, albeit under very different circumstances, to not dig too deeply into the causes and practices underlying "White Supremacy" in *Loving*. For while that case obviously had considerably more authority and intent to change social institutions, the Hollywood film also made popular a message many still were not ready to hear. And yet in so doing it too inadvertently perpetuates the amnesiac effect the miscegenation taboo worked to secure in the first place, when it denied and secured social and economic territories staked out by "race" by displacing their defense onto a terrain feigned to be purely personal and sexual. And in *Guess* it would seem especially unthinkable to remember such structural histories, since the (beloved) Draytons' identity and position so clearly depend on forgetting them. (To John's parents Matt introduces his devoted maid, Tillie [Isabell Sanford], as "a member of this family for twenty-two years.") It thus goes without saying in this film, but is glaringly visible even before conventions of sex and gender can step in to work out the details, that any racial accommodations this family can make are only possible so long as they in no way disturb its class status. But keeping that condition as unspoken as it is intact, *Guess*'s patriarchal plot nonetheless secures the white man's authority over the white woman and her black lover by having the first finally declare that the *only* thing that matters is the love and regard of two individuals for each other.

That said, and despite the overpowering centripetal force whereby all textual paths lead back to Matt Drayton/Spencer Tracy in anticipation of his final judgment, *Guess* registers several potential forces that could, and in some other parts of the universe already do, seriously challenge the old white man's authority in ways the film itself does not.

The film's only references to contemporary black liberation struggles are channeled through Tillie and played for laughs in a not-so-modern minstrel style. Watching from the kitchen as John and Matt confer on the terrace, she muses: "civil rights is one thing, but this here is *some*thin' else!" Catching John unawares as he changes clothes in the guest room, she dresses him down as "one of those *smooth* talkin', *smart* ass niggers just out for all you can get, with your *black* power and all that other trouble makin' nonsense!" Railing on, she threatens: "You bring any trouble in here and you just like to find out what black power *really* means!" The sense here of the eruption of something otherwise contained is amplified by the camera's sudden tilt to a jarring canted angle, the only such deviation from standard framing conventions in the film. Linking the excessive performance here demanded of Isabell Sanford to a tradition of "faithful servants" dating back to *The Birth of a Nation* (1915), James Baldwin described Tillie as "prepared to protect her golden-haired mistress from the clutches of this black ape by any means necessary."[39] What his linguistic play signals is the textual reversal whereby the film denies and discredits black nationalism by applying its terms to a force here deemed purely sexual.

Less hysterical, but arguably even more contained, are the film's brief glimpses of youth culture. Never so explicitly named as "civil rights" or "black power," flower power might be said to silently flash upon the screen in the image of Joey's pale hand reaching into a medium shot of John's dark face – as he looks out across the city – to tuck a daisy behind his ear. Although the image of the clean-cut pair chatting on the terrace could hardly be more unlike stock imagery of hippies hanging out in the park and in the streets that summer, the daisy here commences a brief glimpse of a nonetheless modern romance, marked not only by the emphasized difference in skin tones, but also by Joey's tomboyish plunking down on a stool with knees apart as the two tease and confide in one another.[40] Yet, with a zoom-out we realize this image is being watched from inside the house by Christina, and then also by Matt, and soon what began as the image of a new kind of love is read by, and compared to, the image of Tracy and Hepburn. As we watch the older couple standing together, Christina describes how moved she is to see Joey so happy, and the film offers the promise that older form(ula)s of romance will eventually move the old man to accept the young couple.

More pronounced than these fleeting eruptions of civil rights and counter culture are the feelings of old age and conservatism they breed in a man like Matt Drayton. This is explicit when Matt, insisting that they get out of the house before the dinner party, takes Christina for a drive that ends up at Mel's Drive-In. Even here, where Matt is literally surrounded and confronted by youth culture, it appears exceedingly tame – neat, short-haired kids hang out in shiny cars and a carhop serves coffee and ice cream. Nonetheless, this is the setting in which the film elaborates the question of Matt's age; first through a scenario in which the cranky old man comes to like an unexpected new flavor of ice cream, and then through his confrontation with a young black driver whose car he blindly backs into. Matt's sense of generational assault is palpable as the other driver shouts: "Stupid old man! You ought to be put away in a home or something!"

What makes this didactic scene especially interesting is the way it tends to evident anxieties about the aging white patriarch with nostalgia for an earlier history of the classical (Hollywood) couple. Before Matt has to suffer new flavors and ageist name calling, the drive-in setting prompts Christina to reminisce about her own early marriage as she thinks about what lies ahead for her daughter. The gender politics are made plain when she remarks: "The work he's doing is so important. She'll be able to help him with it and share in it. It's the best break any wife can have." Less obvious is the way the scene revises the history it invokes. Watching Hepburn and Tracy alone, framed side by side, we are invited to read the scene as a celebration not just of Matt and Christina's good old days, but of Tracy and Hepburn's. Grinning sweetly, with a classically Hepburnesque delivery, Christina muses: "You know, for us it's all been great, but, you know what was the best time of all? It was in the beginning when everything was a struggle and you were working too hard and worried and sometimes frightened. And there were times when I felt, when I really *knew* that I was a help to you. That was the very best time of all, for me." In light of how set up we are to imagine ourselves to be reminiscing (with her) about this classical Hollywood couple as we once knew it, what is remarkable is how thoroughly this narrative rewrites it. For despite their capitulations to normativity, this team's early films were "battles" of the sexes precisely for their preoccupation with female independence – hence the dilemma of the first such film, *Woman of the Year* (1942), about the early stages of a relationship and a marriage in which a man feels eclipsed by said woman's fame and success. The sexual conservatism of the 1967 film thus arguably works not only to stabilize gender relations for its own senior and junior couples, offering the revised portrait ultimately as a model for Joey and John, but in doing so goes so far as to deny and rewrite the gender discord of the 1940s and the "classical" couple of the Tracy and Hepburn comedies. And these considerable efforts to revive and rewrite conventional terms of sexual difference work in turn to establish the safest possible context within which to confront the question of the white patriarch's decline.

Further evidence of this lies in the fact that the nostalgia conjured at the drive-in not only mitigates a crisis of age, but follows immediately after Tillie's mocking invocation of "The Reverend Martin Luther King," and is edited so as to bookend the scene of her threats to John and his "black power." Once again, although multiple challenges to Matt's authority are still clearly in the air, the nostalgic mode and wifely reassurances of the drive-in scene immediately soften the sharp verbal edges and visual angles of Tillie's defense of the white family's only daughter.

While conservative gender rhetoric thus works to manage looming racial and generational threats, it also clearly reinvigorates the dominant sexual order in the course of the film. For although we hear not even a fleeting utterance of "feminism" or "women's lib," there are signs of female forces beyond Matt Drayton's control. Joey asserts her own determination, and at least the hypothetical possibility of female political power (in the further diluted form of a second thought), when she tells her father of her decision to marry John: "you couldn't stop me . . . even if you were the Governor of Alabama, I mean if Mom were." And, in his climactic speech, after Matt first describes Joey as "a very determined young woman, much like her mother," within moments he reveals his intolerance even for her timid response to the news that John has secretly given the deciding vote about their marriage to her parents. When she turns to John and muses gently, "You didn't? What a funny thing to do," her father snaps: "Joey, this may be the last chance I ever have to tell you to do anything. So I'm telling you: shut up!" While this invocation of the end of paternal authority announces the fear that the young woman really *could* escape patriarchal control, the force with which the film has put Joey's entire future in Matt's hands, and defined her "best break" as becoming a dutiful wife (Joanna) to John, suggests again and again that this particular fear has been effectively put to rest.

The last (?) gasp of the Great White Spectator

While *Guess*'s heavily gendered narratives thus work overtime to replot multiple lines of difference and power, it is in the articulation of vision and space that these plots, and those of Cleaver and the Court, most dramatically collide. Specifically, the film's struggle to overcome racial prejudice provokes troubled meditations on a series of aging classical Hollywood forms, namely: the classical white male hero; regimes of vision and space organized around him; and the white spectator invited to see and be situated in analogously privileged ways.

That classical cinema was itself a key subject in *Guess* is indicated in part by the fact that reviewers regularly equated, as if interchangeable, its leading star couple, the classic screwball sex comedies they were known for, and the "magic" of Hollywood at its best:

> The magic (nothing less) which Tracy and Miss Hepburn had engendered in all of the previous screen outings, together works again.[41]

> Unfortunately . . . their [Tracy and Hepburn's] presence . . . reminds us of how really wonderful pictures like *Woman of the Year* and *Adam's Rib* were.[42]

> Spencer Tracy's final film and moreover a last teaming with Katharine Hepburn qualifies, all other considerations aside, as must-viewing for anyone who has ever cared about movies.[43]

At times the very same critics extended such commentary further, and less kindly, to read the film as an indicator of the exhaustion of virtually every register of Hollywood style. Champlin described it as a "comfortably old-fashioned picture, set in the comfortably old-fashioned upper-middle-class milieu of soundstage decor," but despite these comforts was left with "[t]he nagging uneasiness . . . that the problem has not really been confronted or solved, but only patronized." Arthur Knight ominously begins: "Revivals of old movies reveal a disconcerting fact. . . . The sets, the costumes, even the style of acting – all are dead giveaways, an idiosyncratic response to the way things are despite determined effort to create a vision of how they might have been."[44] And *Newsweek*, after declaring the young couple "a pair of pop-ups from some children's book on tolerance" and the film's treatment of the issue "an absolute antique," advances further: "In technique, too, the film might have been made a decade or two ago with its painted sunsets, sclerotic photography, glaucomic process shots and plastic flowers pummeled by floodlights."[45]

As these dismissive, occasionally vituperative, critiques accumulate alongside the nostalgic ones, a decidedly conflicted portrait of Hollywood cinema emerges. Excessive but exemplary in its movement between these extremes was *Newsweek*. Immediately following the diseased portrait of the film's visual style just cited, in that very same paragraph, it suddenly finds redemption in terms so lavish they must be read for full effect:

> No matter though, when Tracy and Hepburn are on screen doing their lovely stuff for the last time together; when she comes on like a fugitive from an old Red Cross poster, a slash of crimson fabric on her shoulder and

the old Supergirl gleam in her eye, when she screws up that screwy smile and shrugs that tomboy shrug and seems to be saying, "What the hell, life, you can do your worst but we'll still survive," and he stands there next to her looking grim and granite-good inside, with a face so full of valleys and crags that a space probe would find it unfit for landing.

When Tracy tries and fails to recall some newfangled flavor of ice cream he recently enjoyed, a teen-age temptress at a drive-in serves him fresh Oregon boysenberry sherbet. He tongue-tips it dubiously. "This isn't the stuff." Suddenly his face erupts with joy. "But I like it!" *That* is vitality and also good writing, scenarist William Rose's apt metaphor for the changes in life that the old folks must learn to accept [original emphasis]. And when Tracy gives his blessings to the lovers in a noble speech that was written as a melodrama's climax and may now serve as an artist's epitaph, when he says his say about youth and yearning and whether an old, white-haired man is necessarily a burned-out shell who can no longer remember the passion with which he has loved a woman, *then everything wrong with the film is right and we can see, through our tears, that the hero we worshipped was just what we always knew he was, an authentically heroic man.* [emphasis mine]

Coming just after the pan of *Guess*'s "pop-up" book tolerance and "glaucomic" visuals, this encomium is striking for the way it enacts, as well as states, the power of "Spence and the Supergirl" to put "right" the political and aesthetic flaws so harshly enumerated at the outset. Indeed, the power of the dynamic duo is so great that it grips the critic of tired Hollywood forms to interpret the didactic ice cream parable as "good writing"! Nonetheless, the criss-crossing rhetorics of aging and "vitality" that riddle both the scorn and the praise suggest that *several* classical Hollywood institutions – its style, its classical couple, its "granite-good" hero – are showing their age, albeit some more gracefully than others. (The publicity still beneath the text, of a sash-draped Hepburn combing the old man's hair, like a little boy's, visually reiterates the effect.)

The film itself further articulates the join between the aging classical style and the aging classical hero that the reviews tend to split apart. In so doing it also suggests that another subject being at once challenged, mourned, and nostalgically resurrected is that classical position from which the Hollywood spectator has been invited to see – not unlike Tracy's "authentically heroic man" who finally sees the light from his hilltop view overlooking the bay. And the film is startlingly literal in its enactment of such concerns. Not only do plot and cameras literally revolve around the aging patriarch gazing sternly about his house as he contemplates the situation, but the space in which this drama unfolds is crucial to that process. It's fitting, then, that the studio spared no expense to build what it touted as "one of the largest single sets in Hollywood history," designed "like a real house, all rooms connecting."[46] Save for a few strategic outings, the Draytons' remarkably situated modern mansion, and the placement and circulation of bodies within and around it for the better part of an afternoon and evening, serve as the literal and metaphorical space wherein the film works out the conditions under which this couple can come together and the interracial dinner party can finally take place.

James Baldwin first recognized how deeply *Guess*'s racial project depended on its representation of space:

> The setting . . . is the key. We are on the heights of San Francisco – at a time not too far removed from the moment when the city . . . reclaimed the land at Hunter's Point and urban-renewalized the niggers out of it. The difficult and terrified city, where the niggers are, lives far beneath these heights. The father is in a perfectly respectable, perhaps even admirable profession, and the mother runs an art gallery. The setting is a brilliant re-creation of a certain – and far from unattractive – level of American life. And the black doctor is saying, among other things, that his presence in this landscape (this hard-won Eden) will do nothing to threaten, or defile it – indeed, since in the event that he marries the girl, they are immediately going to the Far East, or some such place, he will not even be present. One can scarcely imagine striking a bargain more painless; and without even losing a daughter, who will, merely, in effect, be traveling, and broadening her education; keeping in touch via trans-Pacific telephone, and coming home to San Francisco from time to time, with her yet more various, toddling, and exotic acquisitions.[47]

To this I would add that the film goes out of its way not only to establish that the black man will not threaten to occupy or claim white space, but also that he will not threaten to challenge or disturb that position of mastery held out by it, that position from which the world below is looked at, contemplated, judged, and represented (Drayton runs a newspaper). In question are not only the authority and principles of a classical Hollywood hero like Matt Drayton, but the position of the white spectator who has long been invited to imagine himself, or herself, as the occupant of a similarly privileged place.

Before we analyze the enormous energy the film spends to establish, worry over, and preserve such places and the vistas they afford, another outside view helps to establish the larger cultural positions and relations at stake. For the same writer whose account of America's interlocked "handcuffs" of difference could be said to have its own implicit spatial analysis (the abstraction and remove of the "Omnipotent Administrator," the mired bodies of blacks, etc.) invoked related terms in a 1968 interview, there tying them explicitly to white spectatorship:

> The majority of white people are indifferent and complacent simply because their own lives have remained more or less intact and as remote from the lives of most blacks as the old French aristocracy was from "the great unwashed." It's disturbing to them to hear about Hough burning,

Watts burning, the black community in Newark burning. But they don't really understand why it's happening, and they don't really care, as long as *their* homes and *their* places of work – or the schools to which they send their children – aren't burning, too. So for most whites, what's happened up to now has been something like a spectator sport. There may be a lot more of them than there are of us, but they're not really involved.[48]

Immediately resonant here is the way Cleaver's description of a mainstream white political position is so explicitly tied to a simultaneously visual, spatial, and psychic one. So "remote" from black life and black rebellion, the relation of whites to the fires and what they represent is one of a spectator who is not disinterested, but whose position and interests are imagined to be wholly dislocated, and thereby distinct, from the scene of racial struggle.

The possibility of this state of affairs – the possibility for white Americans to imagine themselves removed from racial battles, even from "race" itself – surely depends upon a long history of segregation, hierarchy, and exclusion. At the same time, the history of moving image culture, and the spectatorial positions it solicits and affirms in particular, play a notable role in this process, rendering those physical, social spaces of white seclusion (the suburbs, "the hills," etc.) into widely disseminated, subjective experiences of whiteness ("remote," untouched, etc.).[49]

While Cleaver and, later, Baldwin openly expose and resist such literal and figurative architectures, Hollywood demonstrates mainstream culture's capacity to sustain them *even as* it calls for a liberal renunciation of white supremacy. Cleaver suggests how this is possible when he claims that "[a]ny liberality [the Omnipotent Administrator] might show . . . is itself a part of his lust for omnipotence. His liberality is, in fact, charity."[50] It is not, Cleaver implies, a renunciation of the privileged position, but a benevolent gesture bestowed from it. While such terms might be used, polemically, to describe the High Court's righteous but indistinct decree against white supremacy, they are excessively, graphically inscribed in Matt Drayton's final denunciation of those "bastard[s]" who would oppose the young couple's marriage. For, as we will see, this denunciation occurs precisely at the moment when his place at the critical, elevated center of the text has been utterly sealed through plot, editing, camera work, lighting, and the arrangement of bodies in his expansive white living room on the hill. To understand the full significance of these textual terms, a sketch of those they answer is first in order.

The most persistent visual trope in *Guess Who's Coming to Dinner* is the view of San Francisco Bay. Not only does the Draytons' home showcase a wide, panoramic sweep of that view, but it guides the camera, and even the script, from start to climax. The film opens with a quiet shot of the sky with an airplane coming slowly closer and louder as the names of the film's stars appear above it. The title slowly unfolds beneath the plane, each word projected separately to draw out the question. The anticipatory silence is dramatically filled in the second shot with a sudden swell of the hokey theme song ("You've got to give a little, take a little, let your poor heart ache a little . . .") and the revelation of the dramatic backdrop against which this narrative of compromise will transpire – a dazzling display of San Francisco and its bay spreading out beneath the plane. Although we don't yet see who is enjoying this view from on high with us, that ambiguity will turn out to be a thoroughly appropriate beginning to the film that ensues.

The film's first few scenes elaborate the visual terms put in question by the arrival of the interracial couple we soon meet. While the pair is marked as a spectacle in and of itself (the object of prying looks by the camera, a cab driver, and a nosy employee of Christina's), the possibility of John's assertion of a look of his own quickly arises. As they drive into the city from the airport, another dramatic display of the skyline is revealed (again punctuated by a sudden musical swell). And their first stop, at Christina's art gallery, quickly establishes Joey's family as being in the business of elite visual culture, only to pose the question: what will John's relation to that culture be? Although at first uncertain about some of the modern pieces on display, John proves a quick study. When the couple starts to leave the gallery, moments after Joey has explained a puzzling, blinking piece to be a "kinetic sculpture," he turns back with a knowing grin to switch it off, thus demonstrating his ability to manipulate, as well as appreciate, abstract art.

These preliminary setups are in effect just light warm-ups to the dramatic visual contest that ensues once John enters the Draytons' bay-view home. Although marked as a visual object right up to his approach to the front door (when, to Joey's amusement, he puts on her wide-brimmed straw hat to free his hands for suitcases and tipping), this status changes almost immediately upon entry. A brief stop in the foyer establishes the differences between the blacks who serve and are served here, as Joey introduces "Dr John Prentice" (in a suit and tie with briefcase) to "Miss Matilda Binks" (in a maid's uniform), and then asks "Tillie" to bring them lunch on the terrace. Having made that crucial distinction (in a film in which racial integration is possible so long as it remains disconnected from class equity), the film moves to introduce John first to the Draytons' home, then to Christina, and finally to Matt. And these scenes serve as much to introduce the visual and cinematic stakes at issue as the more obvious racial ones.

Even though Matt Drayton's gaze across the bay is finally insisted upon as the most controlling look in the film, the troubles that plague him with his daughter's interracial engagement are repeatedly represented as potential encroachments upon that entitled view. Before Joey has finished ordering lunch in the foyer, John's desirous eyes are drawn off screen to the living room, where he begins to look around. With neck and eyes craning forward, he quietly but deliberately strides about, peeking into corners and adjoining rooms to admire the extravagant expanse of well-appointed living space.[51] That Joanna, in a yellow-trimmed shift at John's right, is rhymed with one of the female figures, also standing and in yellow, in a painting that hangs to his left, makes literal the parallel between John's new relationship to the white woman and to this luxurious white space and its many visual attractions.

After allowing John, and the spectator, this initial orientation to the interior, Joey excitedly offers up the prime viewing spot just outside: "Come out and look from the terrace!" As the couple heads in that direction we can see that the living room John has surveyed is lined by a bank of picture windows, but at this point only partial glimpses of the bay appear. And just as they move through the open glass door to the terrace, John's look is swerved in the opposite direction. In midstride he suddenly stops, turns back to stare and squint in the direction of the foyer, and calls out a long, "Heeeey, who's that?" The camera answers with a point-of-view shot that traces his look back to its new object, a young black woman in a miniskirt. Further registering John's interest, a quick pan follows her as she steps out from behind a partly opaque glass partition, and a zoom-in draws closer for a head to toe inspection. While the racial politics of this look have been critiqued, its timing is also key.[52] For, in rerouting it, the film inclines John towards a sexual, "black," kind of looking at precisely the moment he's been invited to take in the prized, white-owned view.[53] And this deferral of his consumption of the view from the terrace is extraordinarily effective. After John stops Joey does too, resting her arms on either side of the door frame to confirm the pull of the distraction: "That's Dorothy, isn't she a knockout?" But even after she drags John outside in mock jealousy, we do not return to their original destination. When the camera cuts to follow them, still walking and giggling, their position and direction have changed entirely: they walk not towards the vista but with their backs to it, on the other end of the terrace, heading towards Matt's study.[54] Whether they have already gone to see the view, without us, or have forgotten about it entirely (along with the continuity editor) is unclear. Either way, many scenes ensue before we actually see John gaze out at the much-discussed view, and when he does so the territory will be much more extensively marked. It is not until Matt Drayton appears, indeed not until the belated moment in which he realizes John's relation to his daughter, that the visual turf in question is finally, fully revealed. When Christina arrives, at first stunned by what John here calls "a rather shocking pair," the trio moves to sit down on couches in front of the picture window. Although the view is still obstructed and out of focus, we can occasionally glimpse pieces of it behind them for the first time. But the equation between the news of this couple and the status of the view is undeniable when Matt arrives moments later. First, with Christina, the couple returns to the terrace to enjoy Tillie's sandwiches, and presumably the view originally offered with them. But again the camera manages to take us there without revealing it, instead framing the trio's conversation tightly with the house in the background. Because John proposes breaking the news to the soon-to-arrive father gently, when Matt appears the newcomer is introduced simply as a doctor Joey met in Hawaii. Thinking nothing of this, Matt quickly excuses himself to make a golf date. But halfway through the living room he does a slow double take, and we can see the larger meaning of John's presence start to dawn on him. In a cinematographic gesture that seems almost too remarkable to be unconscious, it is only in Tracy's performance of this recognition, turning himself 180° on his return to the terrace to re-inspect John and the situation (exactly undoing the course of the swerve that originally drew John's look back from the doorway), that the camera is finally set free of its former constraints: for only after turning entirely around with Matt, all in the movement of a single shot, does it move back out to the terrace to finally reveal the long-withheld view.

At the end of its dramatic rotation, this shot lands on a static setup of Matt and John standing side by side against the backdrop of the view between them. That they represent two competing positions of authority is further suggested by the placement of Chris and Joey, seated in the foreground in front of them (with their backs to us) as if to watch their respective men. After John initially explains his relation to Joanna, a shot-reverse-shot series capturing the men's exchange is anchored in Matt's point of view but is also marked by John's and the camera's considerable height above him. Matt then sits down, alone in a medium close-up in front of the view. The visual authority connoted by this reframing and the black-rimmed glasses that stand out from his white-haired head is simultaneously put into question by his half-loosened tie (interrupted in the double take) and the baffled looks that wash over his face.

With the visual-racial-patriarchal territory thus carefully marked, one final condition must be met before the black man is finally allowed to gaze directly at the view: he must relinquish all authority in the matter of his future with, or without, the white man's daughter. Annoyed and disturbed by the scene on the terrace, Matt retires to his study, where he calls his secretary to research John's background. After Christina joins him, John knocks and announces that although "Joanna doesn't know it, and I don't see any reason she should," he has decided that "unless you approve . . . there won't be any marriage." When Matt bristles at this as an "ultimatum," John reassures him it is not, and leaves as politely as he entered. Christina then makes it clear that she cannot disapprove, leaving the ball entirely in Matt's court.[55]

Only now does the film allow John a clear and direct look at the remarkable landscape: when the next scene begins we finally see him, in a close-up, gazing out across the bay in contemplation. But details from the ensuing scene, described above, reveal that John's long-awaited look from the terrace is nonetheless fleeting and forcefully contained by: the spectacle-rendering daisy Joey soon tucks behind his ear; her desirous look that pulls him in the opposite direction; and, eventually, the zoom-out from this romantic scene that exposes diegetic voyeurs to be watching the "problem" couple along with us. The "origin" of the zoom is first identified in Christina's look from the study, but the camera then further reveals Matt standing behind her and also watching the couple on the terrace. And it is at the moment of *that* knowing gaze from Matt's study, after John's has so fully surrendered, and as Christina speaks tearfully of her pride in her daughter's happiness, that the film has established the visual terms, as well as the romantic ones, under which Matt will eventually accept the marriage.

For all that, the film has in effect only just begun, and much anguish now ensues over the question of whether or not the "broken down old phony liberal" – as an old friend teasingly calls him – can sustain our faith in the justice of his vision. Only now, in fact, with these primary visual terms established, do the many forms of difference and authority in question get seriously discussed, or seriously erupt, in the hours between lunch and dinner: in Tillie's "civil rights" and "black power" outbursts from the kitchen and guest room; in the sexual confidences Joey shares with her mother in her childhood bedroom; in Matt's bafflement in the garden that a "colored mailman's son" could be so successful, etc. In short, having amassed the central cast on and around the terrace in the opening scenes to establish the critical terms and issues, the film then scatters it about the house's many spaces to address the couple's manifold implications.

That the film's climactic dinner party arrives on the scene of a visual crisis as well as a patriarchal one is detectable in one last dramatic view from the terrace taken in before the guests arrive. Having returned from their ice cream outing at sunset, Matt and Christina argue bitterly in the foyer as a vivid orange glow saturates the wall behind him. Despite her nostalgic invocation of a young couple's good old days, he now makes it clear that he has no intentions of relenting, and accuses her of "not behaving in [Joey's] best interest." For the spectator who has been invited to embrace the women's romantic terms, Matt's flaming anger now threatens a tragic ending. After he storms up the stairs, the theme song returns in a minor key with painfully slow, dissonant modulations. Christina strolls somberly, pensively, through the glowing living room, as if pulled towards the garish light streaming in from outside. The camera follows her attentively as she passes the empty dinner table and begins to remove her coat and scarf, at times pulling in close enough to reveal Hepburn's uncontrollable shake. The details are apt, because the scene contemplates the painful possibility that the pairing of Tracy and Hepburn might not be enough, that the man really is too "old" and too "phony" to come around. Christina clearly worries as much, her eyes filling and finally bursting in the scene's final shot. And this tormented performance is staged around the view that glows now as if on fire. We see it, with her, first through the windows, and finally as she gazes deliberately out from the edge of the terrace at the intensely dark, orange scene – by far the film's most extraordinary and excessive use of color. While previous scenes were shot with bright, shadowless lighting ("sclerotic photography"?), this is the sequence of "painted sunsets" and "glaucomic process shots." The subject and timing of such an afflicted visual style, therefore, precisely grafts the film's crisis of faith in the Hollywood hero to the evident crisis of the visual conventions typically attached to him.

The sense of impending tragedy persists as guests begin to arrive. Christina breaks down with the first, Monsignor Ryan (Cecil Kellaway), urging him to go upstairs and reason with her husband. Matt's loss of control is evident in his fumbling struggle to get dressed as he refuses to listen to his old friend's reason. Yet his real estate continues to function steadily without him. Upon her arrival Mrs Prentice (Beah Richards) immediately comments: "What a lovely home. . . . You have such a magnificent view." In a gesture that will initiate the choreography of negotiations soon to transpire, Christina invites her out to see it. When Matt just then joins the party, he barks at his wife: "The view? What in the hell are you talking about?! What view?!" Even granting his understandable preoccupation with the film's central "problem," the momentary amnesia of this utterance – in this house, in this film – has the distinct ring of negation (in the psychoanalytic sense), announcing by way of denial something that in fact matters very much.

A series of critical conversations follow. On the terrace the mothers discuss their husbands' stubborn disapproval; the fathers confer in Matt's study; and in the living room the Monsignor worries with John that his relationship, and his fiancée, will soon be destroyed. Later, also on the terrace, John's mother first voices her support to her son, prompting him to confide his newfound passion; she then confers with Matt. Again in the all-male space of the study, John and his father face off. And upstairs, oblivious to it all in a room still marked by her childhood, an ecstatic Joey giddily packs, blind even to her mother's visible dread. Compounded, these scenarios again suggest the importance of space and patriarchy to deciding the future of the interracial couple – as if the Drayton home just needs to be large enough, well designed enough, to accommodate all of these negotiations. And the trope of the view continues to play a central role. First in the conversation between the two mothers, then in the one between mother and son, and finally with Mrs Prentice and Mr Drayton, the most passionate and tormented exchanges are staged against the (artificial) backdrop of city lights shimmering over a dark bay.

With the first two of these, initial looks at the bay turn inward for face-to-face conversation. But the third appears mostly in a disjointed set of profiles, Mrs Prentice's in the foreground at left looking off screen towards the house at right, and Matt's behind her looking in the opposite direction towards the bay. As his eyes fix on the view, she gives a stunning speech, proposing with an unexpected directness that what is ultimately at stake is not the young lovers' races, but the fading perception and sexuality of their aging fathers:

> What happens to men when they grow old? Why do they forget everything? I believe these two young people *need* each other like they need the air to breathe in. Anybody can see that just by looking at them. But you and my husband, you might as well be blind men. You can only see that they have a problem. But do you really know what's happened to them? How *they* feel about each other? I believe that men grow old. And when sexual things no longer matter to them, they forget what true passion is. If

you ever felt what my son feels for your daughter, you've forgotten every-thing about it. My husband too. You knew once, but that was a long time ago. Now the two of you don't know. And the strange thing for your wife and me is that you don't even remember. If you did, how could you do what you're doing?

The power of this speech is registered in part by Matt's profound silence: he will require several more scenes of contemplative gazing to muster a response. And in keeping with the film's by now well established visual rhetoric, the staging here makes it evident that the sexual potency Mrs Prentice so poignantly puts into question is also bound up with the more symbolic forms of authority under discussion. For Matt's gaze at the view remains troubled throughout her speech, and is then featured in not one but three more short sequences just after it, each of which carefully focuses on him as he paces and stares at the landscape. The third of these culminates in a zoom-in to a close-up of his gaze again fixed on the view, at a distinct moment of recognition: he blinks, nods to himself, and mutters "I'll be a son-of-a-bitch" before turning to deliver his verdict inside.

Upon the film's release critics regularly read the climactic speech to follow as not simply the best thing about the film, but a memorial to Spencer Tracy himself and his command of his craft, even in the face of death. The *Hollywood Reporter* noted that it took five days to shoot because "the old trouper was so ill . . . he couldn't work more than two or three hours a day." But deeming "that last speech alone" worthy of "a posthumous nomination," it asserted: "Spence dying outacts most actors in the best of health."[56] The *New Yorker* cast the performance as a kind of self-conscious tribute: "the very words that he spoke were written for him deliberately as 'last' words"; and "being aware that it was the last picture he would ever make [Tracy] turned his role into a stun-ning compendium of the actor's art; it was as if he were saying over our heads to generations of actors not yet born, . . . 'Here is how to dominate a scene by walking away from it.'"[57] Such claims of immortality so tightly join "Tracy," his performance, and his role – the "vitality" of each invigorating the others – that it sometimes becomes impossible to pry them apart: "His final perfor-mance was just exactly what it should be: a sincere, concentrated, honest portrait of a sincere, concentrated, honest man who might as well have been Spencer Tracy."[58] Despite the suggestion that "Spencer Tracy" could be the model, or real ideal, behind such a "portrait," all signs point to its origins in a wider series of Hollywood traditions.

First and foremost among these is that "authentically heroic man," the one who finally emerged in the course of Tracy's speech as "the hero we wor-shipped . . . just [as] we always knew he was." This tradition of "authentic" masculine authority is described by another reviewer as "conviction," cham-pioned as "that basic and supreme gift" of the Hollywood actor:

> He was at all times what he said he was. . . . If he is not who he says he is,
> than [sic] he is an actor reading lines. Tracy was never, never that. His
> "great American eagle face," looking more than ever like something
> hewed in oak, had become part of that conviction. He did not start with it;
> it grew from within.[59]

The epithet comes from Joey, describing Matt (not Tracy) when he stares
fiercely but refuses to be read.[60] We see this expression repeatedly, especially in
the many shots of Matt alone looking out from the terrace before he renders his
decision. That the kind of man and look it refers to are bound up with a
substantial body of classical Hollywood values and forms is suggested when
another review not only deems Tracy the master of the film, but oddly imbues
him with the organizational principles of classical Hollywood narrative itself:
Guess is "the late great actor's picture and he dominates it with his vitality and
the *clarity and logic of his presentation.*"[61]

The devout tones with which such classical Hollywood aesthetics are thus
regularly celebrated ("worship," "transcend[ence]") turn decidedly biblical in a
short trade piece on the film's lighting design, entitled "FIAT LUX [Let There
Be Light]."[62] Invoking the first words of God himself, the divine illumination
of the phrase is here doubly apt. As intended, it referred to the technological
marvel whereby heavy arc lights were raised such that "all lighting [was]
suspended from . . . catwalks" and could be "alternately dimmed and intensified by remote control." And, fittingly, the scene that inspired such divine stage
craft was the old master's all-knowing speech, a speech staged to position him
not simply as the object of all lights and looks, but as the commanding subject
out from whom everything else would appear to radiate. Indeed, the film presents Matt's final words as more powerful than those of the priest invited to this
difficult party precisely for his gift, as Christina puts it, for expressing "beautiful
thoughts." Monsignor Ryan confesses to John's parents that the tools of his
trade, soothing words for "nearly every human condition," have failed him
here: "I'm completely stumped. There's simply nothing I can say." Mrs
Prentice concurs, silencing her husband, and at this very moment the film cuts
to Matt's flash of recognition that will lead him to finally speak his mind at
length.

The "personal statements," as Matt calls them, delivered to all assembled
guests and residents, and Tracy's knowing delivery, clearly seek to redeem the
"authentically heroic [Hollywood] man" earlier put into question. Matt's turnaround is rather sudden, but is brought on, he explains, by a deeply felt
response to Mrs Prentice's claim "that like her husband I'm a burnt-out old
shell of a man who cannot even remember what it's like to love a woman the
way her son loves my daughter." Having run through several others, he adds,
"this is the only statement presented to me all day with which I am prepared to
take issue." His objection leads him first to insist: "Old? Yes. Burnt out?

Certainly. But I can tell you, the memories are still there. Intact, indestructible." And those memories serve as the means by which he now recognizes that "[t]he only thing that matters is what they feel, and how much they feel, for each other. And if it's half of what we felt, that's everything." The lump in his throat verifies the authenticity of his claims, further confirmed by tears welling up in all the women's eyes. What is more, the power of this romantic sentiment renews the voice of liberal conviction. Of those who would still object, Matt further insists, "screw all those people!" Now it is only "some bastard" who would make a case against them, and "knowing what you two are, knowing what you two have, knowing what you two feel," the only thing worse than getting married "would be if you didn't get married." Having thus said his piece, he pauses, and barks once more: "Well Tillie, when the hell are we going to get some dinner?" The terms and conditions under which this interracial dinner party can finally be seated are thus made clear with a swell of sentiment for conventional marriage that handily tops the Supreme Court's. And this one is expressly delivered as a white patriarch's final words over all racial, sexual, and socioeconomic others.

Significantly, the only history Matt's long-anticipated speech invokes is his own asserted memory of an intensely potent masculinity, and the sequence cinematically commemorates the visual-spatial command long associated with such a figure. The speech begins with, and is anchored by, the image of the eagle-eyed sage holding forth: he stands at the center of a medium close-up, his sensible glasses framing the eyes cast out and downward in the direction of the diegetic spectators seated before him. Through reaction shots and shots that include the backs of his onlookers' heads in the foreground, all other eyes, like ours, are riveted upon him at the centerpoint where their looks converge. In each case, these looks reflect back to him the reach and force of his gaze and knowing presence.

This effect intensifies as the speech unfolds. Reconfiguring the original arrangement on the terrace, in the living room Matt now faces the view while Joey and John, seated, watch him quietly with their backs to it. When Matt recalls passionate memories of Christina, she at times looks on from his side, positioned as affirming witness and inspiring vision. The cinematographic climax occurs when Matt stands directly in front of John and Joey to declare his verdict in their favor. Looking sharply down at them, he announces that they'll "have no problem with me," but adds that they'll be "up against . . . a hundred million people right here in this country who'll be shocked, and offended, and appalled at the two of you." When the speech takes this social turn, the camera begins to turn as well, starting with a directly frontal full shot of Matt that then slowly pivots around him. The revolving camera soon cuts in for a close-up, still slowly encircling its subject, but now pivoting our look in an orbit entirely focused on his. And this insistence on the commanding centrality of Matt's judgment and determined gaze occurs exactly as his speech becomes most righteously liberal, urging the couple to "cling tight" against people's "prejudices, and their bigotry and their blind hatreds and stupid fears." When the camera's slow revolution finally halts, it lands on Matt in profile as he looks off screen to the right, in the direction of John and Joey and the view behind them, eyes cast outward with as much determination as his vocal delivery of the line that here implores them to "say 'screw all those people!'" With a few more reaction shots to register the pride, respect, and welling tears of the onscreen audience, the camera returns to the medium close-up with which the speech began for its conclusion. Only then does it break away for a long shot that captures all parties – smiling, rising, and moving towards the dinner table. Following them, the camera finally settles just outside the dining room, behind Matt at the head of the table. Now, after all the machinations described above, and with the affirmed couples and temporary guests seated appropriately and Tillie serving her way around the table, our look is positioned closest to his to acceptingly survey the new family snapshot so neatly laid out before it.

The formal terms in question thus emphatically mark the political, historical, psychological, and cinematic limits of the interracial acceptance the film is so proud of at the end. For, despite its evident crises of faith in the conventions in which it finally wants to believe, *Guess Who's Coming to Dinner* made popular for decades to come a set of forms whereby the legacy of white supremacy represented in the miscegenation taboo is selectively renounced from a position of white, patriarchal privilege that nonetheless further secures itself by retaining its noticeable remove from the territorial battles at issue. In other words, interracial desire is only speakable, and visible in 1967, when those who have the most to lose are still positioned as if telling and seeing the story, surveying and projecting the field in which it appears as if they have no part to play but that of liberal judge or benevolent father.

As a white writer at times absorbed in my own impassioned visions and at times pulled back to see all I have surveyed – and as one who grew up in the hills across the bay from the Draytons no less – I know firsthand how white people with good intentions can fail to see themselves in the racial picture. Just as I would hope that my own failures to fully divest from these and other forms of authority and privilege do not invalidate the work I have attempted, so I would not want to vitiate the value of the unprecedented embraces of interracial love considered here. Instead, my aim has been to learn from their all too familiar limits also on display.

Notes

1 *Guess Who's Coming to Dinner* was the second-highest grossing film of 1968, was nominated for (all of the) major Academy Awards of 1967, and received them for Best Actress and Best Original Screenplay (Cobbett S. Steinberg, *Film Facts* (New York: Facts on File, 1980), pp. 25, 241). Its oddly enduring status was confirmed in 1998 when the American Film Institute included it on its list of the hundred best American films of all time, albeit in next to last place. Very different interracial romance films from this period include the highly acclaimed *One Potato, Two Potato* (1964), *If He Hollers Let Him Go* (1968), and *The Landlord* (1970).

2 The book also made Cleaver famous. As one review later described that year: "Today Cleaver is nationally known. . . . His face shows up frequently on national television, his statements are widely reported in the press, he is important enough to have inspired the distaste and opposition of Governor Ronald Reagan, and Maxwell Geismar has called him 'one of the new distinctive literary voices.'" Jervis Anderson, "Race, Rage and Eldridge Cleaver," *Commentary* (December 1968), p. 63.

3 I consider the repression and eruption of interracial sex in popular American film up to this period, including the Production Code's express prohibition of "miscegenation" for nearly thirty years, in *Hollywood Fantasies of Miscegenation: Spectacular Narratives of Gender and Race, 1903–1967* (Princeton, NJ: Princeton University Press, 2005). The current essay has been extracted from that book's final chapter in condensed form.

4 Christina's boyish nickname, "Chris," on the other hand, is used only by her husband, though he and the film, as we'll see below, clearly have other means of taming her.

5 Eldridge Cleaver, *Soul on Ice* (New York: Dell, 1968), pp. 16, 17.

6 Leerom Medovoi claims Cleaver's "blind spot" to be his assumption that these identities are "social truths." "A Yippie-Panther Pipe Dream: Rethinking Sex, Race, and the Sexual Revolution," in *Swinging Single: Representing Sexuality in the 1960s*, ed. Hilary Radner and Moya Luckett (Minneapolis, MN: University of Minnesota Press, 1999), p. 145. Yet, despite Cleaver's escalating sexual essentialism (discussed below), his critical reflection upon the "myth" (pp. 162–3) and "social imagery" (pp. 183, 189) he discusses, and his evident desire for change, suggest that *at times* he understands these identities, or at least their racial components, to be mutable social constructs.

7 Cleaver, *Soul*, pp. 162–3.

8 Cleaver, *Soul*, pp. 16, 12.

9 Cleaver, *Soul*, p. 11.

10 Cleaver, *Soul*, p. 12.

11 Cleaver, *Soul*, p. 14. For a reading that at last takes seriously the renunciation as well as the "act," see Pamela Barnett, *Dangerous Desire: Sexual Freedom and Sexual Violence in American Literature Since the Sixties* (New York: Routledge, 2004), pp. 1–31. In addition to her manuscript, I am grateful for vital conversations, feedback, and research materials Barnett shared with me as I wrote this piece.

12 Cleaver, *Soul*, p. 160.

13 Cleaver, *Soul*, p. 162.

14 One of the first black feminists to do so, Michele Wallace articulated the masculinist terms of black nationalism in the *Village Voice*: "It took me three years to fully understand that . . . the countless speeches that all began 'the Black man . . . ' did not include me." "A Black Feminist's Search for Sisterhood" (1975). Reprinted in *Documentary History of the Modern Civil Rights Movement*, ed. Peter B. Levy (New York: Greenwood, 1992), pp. 199–200.

15 Cleaver, *Soul*, p. 177.

16 Cleaver, *Soul*, p. 177. Elsewhere in *Soul* this logic sanctions Cleaver's virulent homophobia, including his notorious textual assault of James Baldwin in "Notes on a Native Son" (pp. 97–111).

17 Cleaver, *Soul*, pp. 177–8.

18 Cleaver, *Soul*, p. 94.

19 Cleaver eventually moved away from his leftist politics to become an active Reagan Republican. "Covering a Controversial Figure: An Informal Survey," *Newswatch*

Project, San Francisco State University Journalism Department, 1998, www.news-watch.sfsu.edu/Critiques/1998/Cleaver.html.

20 Adrienne D. Davis, "*Loving* Against the Law: The History and Jurisprudence of Interracial Sex" (forthcoming).

21 *Loving v. Virginia*, 388 US 1, US Supreme Ct., 1967, p. 11.

22 *Loving*, p. 7.

23 *Loving*, p. 3.

24 *Loving*, p. 11.

25 Justice Stewart's brief concurring opinion also refers to the skin test (*Loving*, p. 13).

26 *Loving*, p. 6. According to Kenneth James Lay, "Twenty-nine states [had] statutes still on the books in 1951. In 1964, nineteen states still had anti-miscegenation laws." "Sexual Racism: A Legacy of Slavery," *National Black Law Journal*, 13.1–2 (1993), p. 175.

27 Walter Wadlington, "The *Loving* Case: Virginia's Anti-miscegenation Statute in Historical Perspective," *Virginia Law Review*, 52, 5 (1966) p. 1222.

28 Brief for Appellants, *Loving v. Virginia*, pp. 9, 26.

29 Brief for Appellants, *Loving v. Virginia*, pp. 16–17, 17, 28.

30 *Brown v. Board*, 347 US 483, US Supreme Ct., 1954, 495 n11. Brief for Appellants, p. 26.

31 Brief for Appellants, p. 27, citing Gunnar Myrdal, *An American Dilemma*, pp. 590–1.

32 *Loving*, p. 12.

33 See Ed Guerrero, *Framing Blackness: The African American Image in Film* (Philadelphia, PA: Temple University Press, 1993), p. 77, and Thomas E. Wartenberg, *Unlikely Couples: Movie Romance as Social Criticism* (Boulder, CO: Westview, 1999), p. 121. White spectators, Wartenberg writes, can "identify . . . as supporters of integration while believing that nothing is required of them to bring it about" (p. 125).

34 I discuss how *What Happened in the Tunnel* both announces and renounces its unseen sexual encounter between a white man and a black woman, and the relevance of that fleeting eruption to the history of American film, in *Hollywood Fantasies of Miscegenation*, pp. 6–9, 24–6. Among the multiple readings of *Tunnel* and related films referenced there, see especially: Jane Gaines, *Fire and Desire: Mixed-Race Movies in the Silent Era* (Chicago, IL: University of Chicago Press, 2001), p. 89; Jacqueline Stewart, *Migrating to the Movies: Cinema and Black Urban Modernity* (Berkeley and Los Angeles, CA: University of California Press, 2005), pp. 82–5; and Sharon Willis, *High Contrast: Race and Gender in Contemporary Hollywood Film* (Durham, NC: Duke University Press, 1997), p. 159. One could also compare *Guess*'s long-term popularity to the long-term trashing of *Mandingo* (1975), the first Hollywood film to depict the routine sexual abuse of black women by white men under slavery. On that film see Robin Wood, "*Mandingo*: The Vindication of an Abused Masterpiece" in his *Sexual Politics and Narrative Film: Hollywood and Beyond* (New York: Columbia University Press, 1998), p. 267.

35 Wartenberg recognizes this film's "patriarch[al] strategy for accommodating racial integration" wherein "[r]ather than compromise men's power over women, patriarchy will admit black men to the ranks of the privileged" (p. 120).

36 Richard Schickel, "Sorry Stage for Tracy's Last Bow," *Life* (15 December 1967), p. 16.

37 "Good Causes," *New Yorker* (16 December 1967), p. 108.

38 A vivid testament to the complex history attending such rhetoric is Ernest C. Withers's powerful photograph (taken just months after the film's release) of African American sanitation workers on strike in Memphis, carrying placards that

repeatedly declare: "I AM A MAN." Such an image reminds us of the deeply human and progressive contexts out of which such declarations can emerge. These contexts clearly inform John's remark as well. The photo is reprinted in Thelma Golden, ed., *Black Male: Representations of Masculinity in Contemporary American Art* (New York: Whitney Museum of American Art, 1994), p. 18.

39 James Baldwin, *The Devil Finds Work* (New York: Dial, 1976), p. 72.

40 The generational change in the air continues in the next scene when Dorothy, the young black maid, hooks up for a ride with a white delivery boy, and they groove in the driveway to the (not so) funky music emitting from his van. Although another tame image of youth culture, this one nonetheless again equates it with interracial (albeit intraclass) couples.

41 Charles Champlin, review of *Guess*, uncited newspaper, *Guess* clippings file, Margaret Herrick Library, Academy of Motion Picture Arts and Sciences, Beverly Hills, California ("Herrick").

42 Schickel, "Sorry Stage for Tracy's Last Bow," p. 16.

43 Champlin, review of *Guess*.

44 Arthur Knight, "The Now Look," *Saturday Review* (16 December 1967), p. 47.

45 "Spence and the Supergirl," *Newsweek* (25 December 1967), pp. 70+.

46 Production Notes, *Guess* file, Production Code Administration Collection ("PCA"), Herrick.

47 Baldwin, *The Devil Finds Work*, p. 70.

48 Robert Scheer, ed., *Eldridge Cleaver: Post-prison Writings and Speeches* (New York: Random House, 1969), pp. 175–6.

49 For extended consideration of the representation of whiteness in visual culture, see Richard Dyer, *White* (London: Routledge, 1997).

50 Cleaver, *Soul*, p. 180.

51 Production notes report that "[p]aintings, valued at more than $90,000, were rented from five leading Los Angeles art galleries to decorate the rooms." *Guess* file, PCA, Herrick.

52 Arguing that the film's visual representation refuses the colorblindness defended in the narrative, Wartenberg discusses the "determinedly desexualized representation of its central love affair" and cites John's eroticized look at Dorothy as the film's overt attempt "to emphasize that John's sexual interest is not limited to white women" (p. 127).

53 Poitier's looks at Joanna are never this overtly sexual. What is more, at the moment of this look he is (presumably) directed to "sound more black," something that happens in the film only when he speaks with other African Americans.

54 When John then goes into that study, his look and placement continue to gently toy with the absent white man's. He sits at Matt's desk – also with a view, but also withheld – admiring and fingering a photo of Joey and her mother. As if to again safeguard Matt's position a little longer with a black alternative, Joey teases that she better shut the door "in case Dorothy walks by."

55 Christina here makes explicit both Matt's liberal hypocrisy and the film's inability to articulate racism beyond the language of "color": "The way she is is just exactly the way we brought her up to be. We told her it was wrong to believe that the white people were somehow essentially superior to the black people, or the brown or the red or the yellow ones. People who thought that way were wrong. . . . That's what we said. And when we said it, we did not add, 'but don't ever fall in love with a colored man.'"

56 James Bacon, *Hollywood Reporter* (6 December 1967), *Guess* clippings file, Herrick.

57 *New Yorker* (16 December 1967), p. 108.

58 *Time* (15 December 1967), pp. 108+.

59 Bacon, *Hollywood Reporter*. A review in the *Motion Picture Herald* similarly posits the actor as the "deep" source of authentic emotion: "A lesser actor might have appeared to be giving a lecture; Tracy makes the words seem the spontaneous outflow of a man who feels deeply." *Guess* clippings file, Herrick.

60 When John, having just met Matt, says he cannot tell what he thinks, Joey concurs: "I don't know either. Nobody can tell when he puts on his American eagle face, except mom."

61 *Guess* review, *Daily News* (12 December 1967) (emphasis mine), as cited in an ad for the film in *Hollywood Reporter* (20 December 1967), *Guess* clippings file, Herrick. Sounding a good bit like Matt Drayton, director Stanley Kramer draws a related parallel when he defends his film against "the rebel intellectual" response of certain college students. Remarking on the aesthetics of "this new unsmiling generation," he writes that "the [current] student of cinema wants to be Godard – not Wyler nor Stevens nor Ford, – nor Kramer." But he rejects "the cover-all of [counter-Hollywood] technique. The 'nouveau vague,' the 'neo-realists' and the 'angry young men' have opened the gates to interrupted dialogue, mismatching, jump cuts, super-impositions, split screens. . . . Technique covers a multitude of sins." True to his film's faith in classical form, he concludes, "The seeds of the next revolution are planted during this one. I think there will be a massive return to utter simplicity. It remains the purest form – the most difficult to attain." Stanley Kramer, "Nine Times Across the Generation Gap," *Aah'ou* (April–May 1968), pp. 13, 12.

62 "Fiat Lux," *Hollywood Reporter* (18 April 1967), from *Guess* clippings file, Herrick, invoking Genesis 1:3.

Chapter 11

Master–slave sex acts

Mandingo and the race/sex paradox

Celine Parreñas Shimizu

Is pleasure possible within relations of domination? The question of how power works between those empowered and those enslaved persists as a moral and ethical dilemma within contemporary relations and representations. Representations of sexuality and race, in particular, raise particular challenges that the film *Mandingo* continues to bring to the fore today. Not quite blaxploitation and not quite plantation-genre film, Dino De Laurentis' *Mandingo* (1975) portrays the private sex act between masters and slaves as an intense paradoxical site of sexual pleasure and racial domination. Against a Hollywood history of representing rape and sexual assault of innocent white women by menacing black men such as in D.W. Griffith's *Birth of a Nation* (1915), *Mandingo* posits sex acts as the primary constitutive technology of racial domination in US slavery while raising the possibility of mutuality, recognition, and affection between masters and slaves. The film's polemic proposal evades more serious engagement when most frequently described as a "trashy southern gothic that uses interracial sex as its steamy selling point"[1] or as "a sadomasochistic Old South wonder"[2] that capitalized on sex for box office profit.[3] Prematurely, the film is dismissed as a pastorally racist project – a telling of slavery from the point of view of slave sexual contentment. In this article, I explore how paying attention to sexual relations and the explicit sex act acknowledges the paradox of pleasure and violence in racial subjection. Through a consideration of explicit sex acts between masters and slaves as both a form of disciplining subjugation and of liberatory self-formation for racial subjects, I will formulate better understanding of the relationship between sexual subjugation and racial subjectivity.

To understand racial relations within a very limited notion of absolute domination cannot accommodate *the confounding dynamics of power in relations within slavery* dramatized in *Mandingo*. Such analyses celebrate the film's masculinist militant politics,[4] and understand slavery as an institution of total domination that only revolution can adequately address.[5] Resulting from such criticism is the further dehumanization of slaves' and masters' subjectivities. Missing from such analyses are the occurrences of more nuanced and specific engagements at the level of emotions, the psyche and other human relations between masters and slaves as represented in the film. Both moralistic dismissal and uncritical celebration of the film avoid how sex and sexuality function in the cinematic oeuvre of racial representation. The film's hypersexual representations of plantation-era masters and slaves desiring each other exhibit a complex construction of racialized sexuality. Sexual practices, identities, and acts centrally constitute racial formation; therefore, sexuality complicates how we understand racial subjection. In *Mandingo*, what occurs when the racial order is challenged at the site of the sex act is a confrontation of the paradox of slavery, an antagonism between freedom and domination as defined by the Hegelian dialectic. That is, a Hegelian understanding of the dynamics of power between the lord and the bondsman shows how there is a dependency at work in how the other defines the self. The master cannot be the master without the slave and vice versa. Each requires the other in a mutual dependency in order to recognize oneself as not the other. To extend such analysis in *Mandingo* is to acknowledge how the moment of the sex act is not only a site of domination, but of self and subject formation as well.

To pay attention to the meanings of sexuality as such is to confront the general tendency to fear and flee from complications netted by the illicit sexuality that continues in racial discourses persistently embedded within representation today. Rather than flee from sex or ignore race, the racialized sex act is a scene where seemingly coherent racial identities fracture and transform, not only in the realms of the intimate but in the larger world. To study sex acts within the context of sustained daily brutality does not simply illuminate how enforced sexualized subjectivities for racialized others are perpetuated, but actually acknowledges the specter of violence haunting racial and sexual relations and self-formations, especially when desires transgress normative bounds.

Sexual practices and racial identities in slavery

Mandingo is set in the American South at the turbulent dawn of abolition, where an aging slave master prepares his only son to take over the family plantation, which breeds slaves instead of selling crops. The old master Maxwell instructs young Hammond to "purchase" a wife so as to sire an heir. For the purposes of breeding chattel, he must also buy a "Mandingo" buck, a male slave. In the film, a "Mandingo" represents the finest stock of slaves deemed most suitable for fighting and breeding. When Hammond realizes his new wife Blanche is not sexually pure, he purchases a virgin slave woman Ellen to be his "bed wench." In revenge, Blanche beats Ellen so she miscarries the master's child. Blanche also lures Mede, the Mandingo, into a sexual relationship that produces a mixed race child. As a consequence, the furious master orders the deaths of the child and Blanche, casts off Ellen, shoots Mede into a boiling cauldron, and then stabs him with a pitchfork. The violence leads to a slave rebellion culminating in old Master Maxwell's death and leaves Hammond more deeply bound to mastery, which is ultimately represented as dehumanizing to white men.

Mandingo interrogates the meaning of sexual pleasure within the enforcement of racial identities in slavery. The film shows how it is precisely sex that organizes racialized slaves and masters in a system of subordination through the routine discipline of bodies, the medical classification of superiority and inferiority, legal sexual defilement and forced consent, and the steely control of emotions and feelings in sexual transaction. The master ascertains power through his use and enjoyment of enslaved black men and women and constrained white women. Mastery in *Mandingo* includes the initiation of slave women into sexual life. The master enjoys many black women's bodies to fulfill his own sexual lust, while producing chattel for the security of his income. In these relations, he derives pleasure as he simultaneously applies his power. While his subjectivity is privileged over hers, she is also put in a position where she confronts this relation of power. I am most concerned with this question of her engagement with power. A slave woman either serves as the master's "bed wench" in demonstrating desire for him and providing him with sex, or she acts as his sow, breeding with bucks for the master's ultimate profit. Similarly, the "fighting slave" buck pleases the master, who gains virile pleasure through the slave's body as surrogate for his manhood in the exciting and heated public arena of boxing. The master also profits from mating the black male buck with wenches, regardless of incest, so as to populate his plantation. Furthermore, the master ignores his wife into a depraved position by limiting her ability to derive pleasure from her sexuality, on the basis that she is a proper white woman whose sexuality should only serve procreative purposes. Operating under the binary logic of Madonna–whore, his sexual performance with black women is very different than with his wife. Blanche is the only one with white, "human" blood qualified to sire racially legitimate heirs; she is therefore disallowed any sexuality for pleasure. Blanche, however, is a sexually experienced woman who, contrary to the master, initially finds neither sexual agency nor sexual pleasure within the system of slavery. I am most concerned with how each of these characters – the wench, the buck and the mistress – engages with power.

Sexual pleasure intertwines with violent punishment to maintain the racial order within the film. When Hammond's wife discovers his favored wench pregnant, she beats her frantically, kills the child, and calls her a "dirty fornicating animal." Mastery is ensured through the control of others who exist for the white patriarchal master in explicit bodily terms. To train for the fight, Mede is bathed in a boiling cauldron of water over a fierce fire so as "to toughen his hide." When beating slaves, the masters describe how "niggers" do not feel the same pain as white men. Through continual sexual and physical subjection of others, masters confirm their superiority. Masters continually work to instill fear so that slaves sacrifice their bodies to power.

At every crucial filmic instance, however, slaves resist the masters' violent construction of their bodies, psyches, and self-consciousness. The editing, shot compositions, performance, and character construction privilege the slaves' resistance to the masters' actions. Displayed in the public sphere of the auction block, they are priced and sold depending on the qualities of their bodies. Slave buyers fondle the chattels to emphasize their primacy as sexualized bodies. In the opening scene, the house-slave Mem leads a long procession of slaves for evaluation by the slave trader. Shots of the enraged rebel Cicero interrupt the ease of the transaction. He must spread his legs and bend over for the examination of the anus. Like a dog, he must fetch sticks thrown by the trader, but he defiantly throws it back upon his return. The slaves open their mouths for the intrusion of the slave trader's fingers as cigar smoke is blown into their mouths. Their steely looks and subsequent attempts to escape contradict the passivity of the scene. A German widow explores Mede's crotch on the auction block as he holds himself taut against the invasion. Here then, masters certainly discipline slave bodies by condoning their non-stop, daily violation by known and unknown hands. Slaves are seen as accustomed to such violence upon their bodies, which range from everyday unwelcome groping to sexual assault by virtual strangers. Sexual subjection disciplines the body so as to maintain and reproduce slavery in the everyday – *in ways that are also met with resistances that create ambiguity within the relations of power.*

While the master inflicts domination repeatedly in public and private, slaves do not always passively accept the continuous violence. Within a home life where her body is sanctioned for rape, a very young wench demonstrates that she understands her lot. Her master hands her over, gives her like a pillow to Hammond's cousin, who happily claims his entitlement to violate her. It would be incorrect to read her audibly silent response as passivity; she responds visually to the ritual sexual assault. The scene is shot to prioritize the violence of the experience. Her eyes widen to the agony of his spanking. No matter how accustomed she may be, the pain continues to be shocking to her. While she may seem to accept her slavery, her facial expressions and bodily convulsions show the forcible violence and demeaning subjugation contained within these acts. In forcing her to say she likes it, the master demands her complicity in order to secure his pleasure. Within this moment, she defends herself by making any semblance of her self and her experience unavailable to him. He shoves her to the bed, turns her over on her stomach, undoes his belt and whips her fiercely for her refusal. By assaulting her body, he forces her into a conscious acknowledgment of his mastery. She registers total contradiction through bodily, as opposed to verbal, speech. The shot shows the drama of the wench's rape: a close-up of her pain in the foreground, and looming behind her in fuller body shot, the white man with the power of his whip. Unseen by the master, the viewers see her facial expression of physical and psychic torment. The film aligns itself to her by focusing on her pain. She avoids expressing her pain to resist how the master appropriates it for erotic purposes as well as to affirm his power.

Within this particular system of domination, the slave experience of sexual acts seems to undermine what may be immovable roles of slavery and mastery as powerful and powerless. The representation of pain and coercion dispels the pastoral mythologies of naturalized hypersexual qualities or propensities, while also providing what Elaine Scarry calls the "insignia of the regime."[6] Within the film's symbolic representation, masters learn their superior position by taking up sexual entitlements just as slaves recognize their role within the system as forcibly prone to their masters. Sexuality is the site of domination in slavery within this representation. And within such experiences, the film represents slaves and masters forming selves that cannot be articulated outside of sexual subjection. The film makes the argument for sexuality as intrinsic to the institution of slavery. How do we understand the potential of these sexual relations to disrupt the roles of and the larger relations between masters and slaves?

Sex, race, and the master and slave dialectic

Mandingo presents certain sex acts as cracks within the slave system's house of terror. I now read the main sex scenes between two pairs of masters and slaves closely so as to show how they define sex – in both the infliction and subordination of racial slavery – as a substantial form of agency and protest in *Mandingo*. Within the film, the sexual subjection of slaves by masters is the mechanism that keeps slavery in operation, but paradoxically, at the same time, it provides the key to slavery's very dissolution. *Mandingo* aims to destabilize the claim that all master–slave sexual relations are always already scenarios of absolute domination that render slaves as property for the pleasure of the master. Through a sexual form of racial subjection, it actually posits a dialectical relationship between slavery and mastery.

A romanticized relationship transpires in the sexual interactions between the white master Hammond and his black "bed wench" Ellen. A tenderness constructed between master and wench seems to disrupt their locations in order to transform each of them into troubled new identities. The master's own uncharacteristic practice of having feelings for his bed wench Ellen, and her status as his "surrogate wife," disturb the permitted roles within the filmic world but also confront the audience by rewriting the terms of interracial pairing through sexual and "looking relations."

Organized as what E. Ann Kaplan calls new "looking relations" within slavery, the love scenes between Hammond and Ellen are constructed as desirable and progressive. Immediately after the whipping scene, the bewildered Hammond sits in bed while Ellen fearfully steals shy looks at him from the doorway of the bedroom next door. bell hooks asserts that "there is power in looking"[7] when describing it as a means for securing the master's dominant position within slavery, for "[t]he politics of slavery, of racialized power relations, were such that slaves were denied their right to gaze."[8] The master's gaze functions as a panopticon in the Foucauldian sense wherein the master's surveillance disciplines slaves by forcing them to "[turn] in on themselves" in a form of self-policing.[9] bell hooks points to how slaves did indeed look back at masters, albeit in secret so as to secure power in not looking. Slaves who choose not to look back strategize relations of self-protection by making unavailable their true feelings to the master and his gaze. Hammond commands Ellen to explain her acts of "looking back" so he may uncover what she really thinks. The question of his ability to know what his slave thinks even if she tells him is not posed here. Rather, what we see is an earnest presentation of a falling in love scene between a man and a woman, made particularly titillating by its context of master–slave sexual relations. Timidly, she expresses her surprise at his "care for what was being done to a wench by a white man." The conversation is framed as liminal, or a passing moment where master and slaves meet in a moment of recognition.

The film also eroticizes the mastery of the white mistress and the slavery of the black male slave. Mastery is contradictory for white women in slavery because they undergo injury in white patriarchy at the same time that they benefit from white supremacy. Blanche flees from her own childhood household where she must remain silent about incest. However, her only way out of the confines of family in that historical moment is marriage, which relies on her sexual purity. On their wedding night, Hammond discovers that she disqualifies from good white womanhood. Throughout the film, he punishes her by refusing her sexual pleasure. Her desperate whispers of "I craves you" worsen her predicament. He considers her strange and fearsome. The husband pathologizes her sexuality when he says, "You strange for a white lady." In a notable and ironic contrast, the black wench Ellen, who is stuck in a position where she must consent to sex, is constructed as the "proper" woman, while the master's wife is lascivious for desiring sex.

Within the sexual economy of slavery, white women do not possess any sexuality apart from reproduction. While sexuality is a site for her subjection, she defines her own mastery through her bodily subjection of slaves, including the Mandingo buck, Mede. Increasingly drunk as the movie progresses, the mistress ultimately commands Mede to please her sexually. She threatens him with death if he will not sexually fulfill her. In effect, she rapes him through the threat of falsifying a rape by him. She exerts the protection reserved for her racialized femininity as his endangerment. She tells him the master will listen to his wife and not a "nigger." While the mistress may at first be acting to insert herself within the homosexual relations between master and buck, the sex scene between her and the buck transforms to one of mutual desire. I must emphasize however, that he is bound to perform the sexual act; for if he flees, her word will condemn him to death as she rightly describes. He surrenders to the force of her threat, but, it seems within the representation of the sex act, also comes to fulfill his desire and his need for recognition from the other, in this case, the mistress.

In this way, the film constructs the mistress–Mandingo sex act as a different form of meeting than rape; it is meant to arouse the possibility of racial freedom through sex between a diminutive mistress (Susan George) and the bigger-bodied Mede, who is played by the recognizably famous boxer Ken Norton. The scene of their bodily contrast – big and small, black and white – and the particular emphasis on her pained face sets the stage for Blanche to expose the pain of her bodily subjection within slavery. Denied sex by the master and driven into a realm of asexuality, she imposes her need for recognition onto the slave Mede. She trespasses against the rules preventing her from desire. In the darkness of her room, she touches him very gently and very slowly strips his clothes in silence. Mede looks down on her as she strips him. As she strips herself, she supposedly strips off her mastery. An extreme close-up shot of her face reveals a very emotionally ripped expression as she rubs her cheeks against his chest. In an unspoken declaration of the need for a meeting of their person-hoods, she frames his face with her hands and they look at each other, directly in a way that is constructed as "new." Like the looking relations between Hammond and Ellen, this meeting is also framed as transformative of slave rela-tions. The characters' looks of intensity communicate the weight of the sexual act as a kind of threshold moment in the film, one with supposedly enough conscious and transgressive power to undo the racial order. If the Mandingo–mistress and master–wench sex acts presumably defy slave relations, is it simply a moment wherein two subjectivities meet in order to measure and mark their lack of freedom within slavery? Fulfilling self-invested sexual feelings for each other outside the white male master's grasp, the encounter between Blanche and Mede threatens slavery with new identities produced by corporal liaisons. Similarly, Hammond and Ellen present a seemingly rupturous new order in slavery through a relationship that is presented as a kind of transcendent love that must eventually fail. Do these scenes of sexual "love" between masters and slaves lead to freedom, or do they actually deepen the institution of slavery?

Hegel, sex, and race: mutual recognition

Different generations of thinkers on race – from W.E.B. Du Bois, to Frantz Fanon, Orlando Patterson, and Paul Gilroy – have appropriated Hegel's dialectic for understanding master–slave relations.[10] I bring together high (master, established, or canonical) and low (contemporary film, race, and sex) discourses to articulate how *Mandingo* enables a rethinking and rewriting of Hegel's dialectic in ways relevant to our understanding of race, sexuality, and representation today. Through a rewriting of the Hegelian master–slave dialec-tic, the film constructs a momentary breakdown of the slave system through the representation of outlaw sex acts meant to question slavery's absolute domi-nation. The sex acts seemingly trespass the most intimate laws of the racial order when the master affirms the humanity of the wench, and the rape is rewritten by desire and mutual recognition in the encounter between the black man and white woman. By the end of the film, for example, Mede even expresses surprise at the master's rage upon him when Blanche births a black baby.

The Hegelian notion of mutual recognition describes the process wherein the lord depends on slaves (and their work) for the acknowledgement of his (sic) mastery or self-certainty. The lord is the master who exists in and for himself, while the slave is dependent upon and works for another. The slave affirms the master and is in turn subjected into a position of servitude. He sacrifices his self-certainty in service of another. Through *Mandingo*, I propose a new appropriation of the Hegelian lord and bondsman relation, one that acknowledges the possibility of mutual recognition occurring during outlaw sex acts posing as social progress. Mutual recognition occurs in the self-conscious representation of sex as taboo within a system where recognition usually disciplines rather than transforms subjects.

In *Mandingo*, mutual recognition occurs when shared displacements are recognized through sexual meetings disallowed in slavery. In these sensuous moments, *Mandingo* frames slaves and masters as agents who have the potential to re-frame, but not radically turn over, subjected roles in slavery. The film argues that both masters and slaves reconfigure themselves against the brutalities of the system when a different form of recognition occurs between them through sex. Mutual recognition proposes that outlaw sex acts introduce liberatory potential born out of enslavement. This proposal questions the implications of sexuality, perhaps now read as a mechanism that not only forms subjects but liberates them from and within slavery – to a degree. Setting up masters and slaves in tender and/or ecstatic meetings across unequal power locations, the film uses sex to frame slaves' access to freedom and to certify their humanity. The slaves in *Mandingo* are the ones with the potential for redemption as revealed in the encounter of bodies, psyches, and self-consciousness during sexual engagement. This is the master–slave impasse upon which Hegel builds his idea of the dialectic.

Hegel formulates that the slave does have a self-consciousness but one that is checked by the master. Describing an original and ahistorical struggle between master and slave, the master secures his position of domination by "risking his life," while the slave "who has not risked his life may well be recognized as a person, but he has not attained the truth of this recognition as an independent self-consciousness."[11] In his original life-or-death struggle wherein two self-consciousnesses struggled with each other, the master wins and subsequently dominates the slave. In the master–slave dialectic, however, the slave's self-consciousness is still the one with potentiality for transformation; in other words, the one in the process of becoming. In other words, the master is already free – yet his freedom is contingent on the slave's bondage. Not free within the world of slavery, the slave holds the potential for revolt that can become a pursuit of freedom. In *Mandingo*, the sex act is constructed as the new life-or-death struggle between master and slave. The slaves "agree" to sex in fear of death. The slave performs labor in fear of the master's capacity to kill him.[12] Within the film, sex is the work the slave performs in fear of his and her own death.

This fear of death is precisely what enables the slave towards a new self-recognition, in an analogy of sex and work afforded by the film. Through this "fear, the being-for-self is present in the bondsman himself; in fashioning the thing, he becomes aware that being-for-self belongs to him, that he himself exists essentially and actually in his own right. . . ."[13] The slave realizes desires belonging to the self in ways that produce new identities that threaten the structures of slavery. Through the independence of the sex act, slaves come to recognize their own self-consciousness as apart from the master. The process of sexual work transforms them into recognition of their own self-certainty. They realize that the master usurps the work they perform in the bondage of terror and fear. In *Mandingo*, the slave consciousness is not fixed. Unlike the master who works to maintain his power at all costs, the slave can potentially transform, become, and progress out of his hold. Since the system disallows self-consciousness for slaves, the recognition of independent desires for the enslaved through sex could potentially bring an autonomous sense of self. In effect, feelings and emotions can emerge in the sex act that exceeds the project of domination or submission, specifically in the transformative act of recognizing one's bondage.

Within the film, the primary mechanism available to the slave for transformation out of the terror of slavery is sex as work. It must be said that engaging sex as work can also be a terrifying predicament. Yet, sex becomes a form of work that introduces the possibility of transformation. In *Mandingo*, the slave performs work in and through sexual service. Sexual service constitutes their thinghood in slavery. Sex is the work slave bodies produce for the master in *Mandingo*, replacing plantation and field "work" tying master to slave. Sex is the labor produced in bondage and is therefore that which "holds the bondsman in bondage; it is his chain from which he could not break free in the struggle, thus proving himself to be dependent, to possess his independence in thinghood."[14] If, as Alexandre Kojeve reflects, the slave transforms himself through the independence of "work," Mandingo's work of sexual service is the mechanism through which the slave can progress.

If sex is the work of the slave that benefits the master on the plantation, it is sex which "forms and shapes" self-consciousness. Kojeve describes the Hegelian process of becoming: "Through work the bondsman becomes conscious of what he truly is . . . Work . . . is desire held in check, fleetingness staved off; in other words, work forms and shapes the thing."[15] The potential process in which the slave can embark on a transformation out of slavery is through sex as subjugation and reclamation. Sex constitutes slave subjects who transform themselves by claiming entitlement (e.g. when Ellen negotiates freedom for her child) and pleasure (e.g. when Blanche and Mede experience orgasm). Sex also produces more workers – mixed race chattel – keeping more slaves in bondage while threatening the very order of slavery that prohibits interracial sex.

Master–slave sex acts: paradoxical freedoms

Attributing agency in the life of the enslaved is a contemporary historical and ethical dilemma. What does it mean that the very system that hails slaves into subjection enables the possibility of freedom? The hypersexual racial mythologies re-emerging in this formulation are precisely what make it so attractive and so arousing to viewers. Seduced into the romance of new looking and new corporeal relations, we follow the narrative of *Mandingo*'s sexual scenes, but are not meant to ask if such moments of mutual recognition can truly be viable possibilities between slave subjects.

I return to the two sex scenes so as to question the possibilities of freedom opened up by these particular master–slave sex acts. Hammond asks Ellen if she wants to perform sexual service for him, as if she had a choice! Her scripted response is as follows: "I like you, sir. I want to please you." Acting counter to the norms of sex practices in slavery, he kisses her on the mouth and encourages her to "look at [him]." This moment is constructed as a romantic meeting between two who are not meant to come together in love. The audience is meant to swoon. The film is sexy because the characters mutually recognize each other in ways not sanctioned by slavery but burgeoning in the contemporaneous era. The scene romanticizes and eroticizes the racial terror of master–slave sexual relations with representations of tenderness. This transgressive sexual scenario is attractive not only for imparting anew the Hegelian analytics of dependence and independence between master and slave but in its attempts to provide an explanation for contemporary interracial practices of sex and love. In the context of the 1970s, it asks historically relevant questions about the function of interracial sex within the lingering and unfinished entanglement between sex and slavery still present in society. Specifically, how do the legacies of such desires configure in the burgeoning occurrence of mixed marriages? How does the American racial past haunt intimate relations in the present? How do interracial babies function within rigid social orders?

In *Mandingo*, the two people who would normally struggle against each other's difference instead affirm each other's insufficiencies and dependencies within a system of dehumanizing brutality. In effect, the black man and white woman meet tenderly in an exceptional moment within violence. As independent self-consciousness, they mutually depend on the other to constitute themselves. His slavery supports her mastery. Her mastery depends on his slave's confirmation. *Mandingo* eroticizes this relationship of power so that the possibility of unlocking the master–slave dialectic transpires in the bed.

The sex scenes between the master and the wench eroticize racial difference as well. The light flickers from a fire and makes her dark skin glisten and his white skin brighten. Certainly, sexually overdetermined racial subjects who find liberatory promise in sex implies problematic racial mythologies. This is precisely the arousal sold in *Mandingo*. Sex between racial others sells in an era of racial disharmony. Or race sells in an era of sexual confusion. The master gently commands her to raise her head out of her deferential posture that signals her position within slavery. He permits her illegal gaze upon him. He tells her to "put your eyes on me . . . look at me straight into my eyes. She protests, "Niggers don't" look back. The master breaks with the gaze allowed in slavery when he says, "You can look at the white man in the eye if told to do it," then even more tenderly, "if asked." At this moment, race is forsaken so as to construct normative and romanticized gender roles: a powerful man is gentle to a powerless woman. She plays her gender role as demure, shy and waiting for instruction. With his hands gently directing her gaze, he commands a new form of looking relations to occur between them. The scene is deliberately racial in its titillation: a black woman acts as a proper (white) woman. In their meeting of gazes, she lets loose a tear that makes her vulnerable and normatively female. She is seemingly struck by the striking emotional power of looking outside the sanctions of the law. She is met with the master's own newfound and apparently bewildered gaze. Their looking relations are transformed from a panopticon situation; the white man does not punish her looking but allows his own looking to be challenged. He transforms his own looking beyond conferral of her object status.

Seemingly, the very notion of absolute mastery comes to be questioned by the master who gives up his power (albeit momentarily) to the slave through the power of physical touch and its emotional meaning. The black woman slave as sanctioned by the master comes to stand in for the white woman as his surrogate wife. Despite his father's discouragement and disapproval of "tenderness" towards Ellen, Hammond gives her presents "good enough for a white lady." He insists on transgressing the rules of his mastery. Indeed, he bestows the same presents upon his wife with much less expense of emotion. He pours emotional investment onto his relationship with his wench. He takes Ellen on his trips outside the plantation and leaves his wife Blanche to rot in the house without his attention. Ellen, unlike his wife, receives assurances of his devotion and commitment. Even if Blanche is pregnant, Hammond guarantees Ellen that "No one, black or white, gonna take your place." Ellen takes Blanche's place as his more legitimate partner in terms of an emotional marriage. As such, this relationship presumably defiles the system of domination in slavery, because the master no longer annihilates the slave to a certain death in life through her slavery but instead interrupts, or at least puts into question, her domination with affirmations of her value in life.

Is domination in slavery so total that any small pleasures, although readable as resistance, are not only insufficient but mistaken? Is sexual pleasure possible within relations of domination? In *Scenes of Subjection*, Saidiya Hartman emphasizes the problem of agency exemplified in assigning will to a subject who has no rights in the context of slavery. She argues that the "simulation of will disallows redress and resistance when slave subjugation is determinate negation."[16] But does not the lack of any will for the slaves reinscribe them into an unquestioned status of beasts of burden? Certainly, the crucial question is how to do the impossible measurement of agency without (1) obscuring the terror of slavery or (2) fulfilling Hartman's diagnosis of a "spurious attempt to incorporate the slave into the ethereal realm of the normative subject through consent and autonomy."[17] Consent, will, and choice are indeed questionable concepts in the context of slavery and racial domination. Yet sex acts in the film show both slaves and masters as subjects-in-struggle within circuits of power.

Furthermore, both looking and corporeal relations seemingly transform anew between the mistress and Mandingo. Against her tired and stained face, we see the Mandingo's large fragmented body. He is still, unresponsive, and frozen to the infliction of her touching. She strips off her robe and embraces him desperately in silence. After a long and painful pause, he surrenders, lifts her, and takes control of their sex by taking her to the bed for their carnal meeting. In a mutual act of vulnerability, he returns and affirms her self-exposure of displacement and alienation. The film constructs mutual participation in the sex act, in turning each other over and giving pleasure and kissing each other fully. In the previous sex scene Blanche performs with Hammond, she must pretend to fulfill the role of pure and high moral white lady. With Mede, there is supposedly no need to pretend. Blanche seeks the recognition that Hammond did not give her. She finds pleasure through the forbidden sex act that further secures her place as an impure mistress. In effect, through the filmic construction of their sex as love, they meet in an ecstasy that transports their psyches momentarily into a world outside their racial roles. Although liminal, they meet sexually in recognition of their mutual displacements within the alienating system of slavery. A liberation of self-consciousness is embodied through carnal sex so that their pleasures purportedly introduce possibilities for agency. Their resistance occurs in sex, paradoxically at the very site of their subjection as raped slave and ignored wife.

What supposedly occurs here is a mutual sacrifice of selves in which they recognize and meet in a sexual act that I describe, in Judith Butler's words, as not "purely consumptive" but "becomes characterized by the ambiguity of an exchange in which two self-consciousnesses affirm their respective autonomy (independence) and alienation (otherness)."[18] A meeting between the two reveals their independence from the master's grip. In a sense, they overthrow the master's control of their bodies when they experience the independence of pleasure for self. The power of this transgression is in the possibility of realizing a liberated self and one's self-consciousness.

The new relationship between transformed subjects cannot stay contained within secrecy. In subsequent scenes, the mistress Blanche and the Mandingo Mede avoid each other's gaze as suspect subjects in the master's presence. Looks of recognition based on a shared fear of discovery pass between them. Her sexual cravings for intimacy fulfilled, she no longer lays open her hunger for recognition onto the master. She no longer drinks alcohol nor looks like a haggard mess. In effect, her transgression immediately garners her power into a new self-certainty so much so that both masters (Hammond and his father) are intrigued by her new independence. The centrality of the master in controlling the relations of all selves in the system of slavery, is redirected in this case from mistress to slave, thus skipping mediation by the master. The slave affirms the mistress' selfhood with his own recognition and vice versa. They share a secret from their master and in effect, circumvent him, making him superfluous. Each sex act they repeat questions the master and slave's independence and dependence. The new relationship troubles the master's certainty in master–slave relations.

When the Mandingo's sexual acts exceed the master's laws at moments of recognition in sex, the independence of that action leads him to discover his own self-consciousness. The independence of his sex acts defies the master's claims on his self-certainty. The slave begins to exist for himself; his participation in sex acts normally outlawed in the system of slavery transforms him. The scenes of racial disruption through sexual tenderness help slaves see potential freedom through a seeing of the master as a similarly alienated other. This re-recognition is the transformative experience of pleasures garnered from forced sex. In *Mandingo*, this mutual recognition makes outlaw sex a racially liberating act. If ecstasy is the process of losing oneself, the self surrenders as a sacrifice to the possibility of re-recognition in and through sex. When the slave recognizes the bondage of his self-consciousness to the master as fallible, protest against slavery is made visible through sexual acts between masters and slaves.

Conclusion

However, we should be careful about buying the romance of freedom sold in *Mandingo*. In both transgressive situations of master–slave sex acts, Blanche and Hammond's imperfections lead to the betrayal and demise of mastery. Similarly, in the film's logic, Mandingo and Ellen must be punished for trespassing the boundaries of their enslavement and for engaging in the possibility of racial and sexual transgression. More precisely, sex both ensures slavery and undermines it in a complicated formulation of power. The potentiality for freedom presented in *Mandingo* is paradoxical; it presents sex as the way to freedom from slavery as it simultaneously enmeshes slaves further into servitude. By way of the master–wench and mistress–Mandingo relationships, the film disrupts the master's self-certainty and the slave's bondage so as to assert how sex opens up possibilities for de-stabilizing slavery as a total system of domination.

All the while, the sex scenes between masters and slaves occur within the slave system while appearing to be in the semblance of transgression. Hammond orders Ellen to new relations of recognition in sex. Ellen is surreptitiously seduced into a position of taking power from the master. Mede, who must have sex with Blanche, is in a similar position to Ellen. While the masters' dictates open up the possibility for freedom through new relations or freedom from the death in life that slavery entails, they also demonstrate how slaves are thoroughly enmeshed in servitude. Through sex, the master creates a paradox so as to get out of the master–slave impasse. Both masters Hammond and Blanche command the slaves to rewrite the power that inscribes them all into slavery and mastery. While the slave cannot initiate new relations in slavery, the masters are never supposed to give up their mastery. The slave, who must agree with the master, is placed deeper within the world of slavery for fulfilling the desires of the master. Whether slaves disagree or agree with the master, they face certain death within the Hegelian description of the encounter between others and the self. The paradox of mastery and slavery requires the notion that the site of the slave's complete powerlessness also comes to be the site where freedom is possible. Yet, freedom from slavery is fleeting as ever.

Notes

Thanks to Daniel Bernardi for the opportunity to revisit this work, to Deborah Gin for her production assistance and to Anitra Grisales for copyediting. I presented earlier versions of this work at the Real to Reel Conference in the University of North Carolina at Chapel Hill in 2001, the Modern Thought and Literature colloquium in 1999 and Humanities Center and Mellon Foundation-sponsored Race and Sex Workshop at Stanford University in 1999. An earlier version of this revised article was published in *Wide Angle* 21, 4 (October 1999), pp. 42–61.

1　Nelson George, *Blackface: Reflections on African Americans and the Movies* (New York: HarperCollins, 1994), p. 62.
2　Donald Bogle, *Toms, Coons, Mulattoes, Mammies and Bucks* (New York: Continuum, 1993), p. 243.
3　Ed Guerrero, ed., *Framing Blackness: The African American Image in Film* (Philadelphia, PA: Temple University Press, 1993), p. 31.
4　Guerrero, *Framing Blackness*, p. 35.
5　Robin Wood, *Sexual Politics and Narrative Film: Hollywood and Beyond* (New York: Columbia University Press, 1998), pp. 272–6.
6　Elaine Scarry, *The Body in Pain: The Making and Unmaking of the World* (Oxford: Oxford University Press, 1985), p. 56.
7　bell hooks, *Reel to Real: Race, Class and Sex at the Movies* (London: Routledge, 1996), p. 197.
8　hooks, *Reel to Real*, p. 198.
9　Michel Foucault, *Discipline and Punishment* (New York: Vintage Books, 1977), pp. 197–202.
10　See W.E.B. Du Bois, *The Souls of Black Folk* (Chicago, IL: A.C. McClurg & Co., 1903); Frantz Fanon, *Black Skins, White Masks* (New York: Grove Press, 1967); Orlando Patterson, *Slavery and Social Death: A Comparative Study* (Cambridge, MA: Harvard University Press, 1982); and Paul Gilroy, *The Black Atlantic: Modernity and Double Consciousness* (Cambridge, MA: Harvard University Press, 1993).
11　G.W.F. Hegel, *Phenomenology of Spirit*, trans. A.V. Miller (Oxford: Clarendon Press, 1977), p. 114, para. 187.
12　Hegel, *Phenomenology of Spirit*, p. 119, para. 196.
13　Hegel, *Phenomenology of Spirit*, p. 115, sec. 190.
14　Alexandre Kojeve, *An Introduction to the Reading of Hegel: Lectures on the Phenomenology of Spirit* (New York: Basic Books, 1969), p. 48.
15　Kojeve, *An Introduction to the Reading of Hegel*, p. 48.

16 Saidiya Hartman, *Scenes of Subjection: Terror, Slavery, and Self-making in Nineteenth-century America* (London: Oxford University Press, 1997), pp. 52–3.
17 Hartman, *Scenes of Subjection*, pp. 52–3.
18 Judith Butler, *Subjects of Desire: Hegelian Reflections in Twentieth Century France* (New York: Columbia University Press, 1987), p. 51.

Chapter 12

The tragedy of whiteness and neoliberalism in Brad Kaaya's O/Othello

Deborah Elizabeth Whaley

O, beware, my lord, of jealousy! It is the green-eyed monster, which doth mock. The meat it feeds on. Poor and content is rich, and rich enough; but riches fineless is as poor as winter. To him that ever he shall be poor. Good God the souls of all my tribe defend, from jealousy!

Iago to Othello, Act 3, Scene 3, lines 165–75

There is a level of evil which is human, and which defies explanation. There is a kernel of evil in all of us, which you cannot explain, and which will not be explained.

Tim Blake Nelson, director of O[1]

After viewing an early print of Brad Kaaya's screenplay come to life, the *Othello* remake *O* (2001), actor Lisa Binavides (who also has a small part in the film as an English teacher) proclaimed to its director Tim Blake Nelson: "Tim, it's extraordinary. It will never be released."[2] Unfortunately, she was almost right. Kaaya, who is a black American and graduate of the University of California at Davis, sold the film to a large motion picture conglomerate, i.e. Disney/Miramax Motion Pictures, despite that at the time he was a newcomer to film-making and a first-time screenwriter. The film benefited from the keen acting eye of its casting director, Avy Kaufman, who gathered a strong cast of established and new actors for a modest budget film of four million dollars. Meki Phifer signed on to play the role of O/Othello, Julia Stiles as Desi/Desdemona, Josh Hartnett as Hugo/Iago, Martin Sheen as Iago's father, Duke Goulding, John Heard as Desi's/Desdemona's father (Dean Brable/Brabintino), Elden Henson as Roger/Roderigo, Andrew Keegan as Michael/Cassio, and Rain Phoenix as Emily/Emelia. While the strong cast and their superior acting streamlined the film as an Oscar contender and as one of the best films of the year, its depiction of teenage violence, which involved death by firearms, caused concern among Disney/Miramax executives, thereby stalling the film's release.

A high school shooting in Littleton, Colorado, a few months before *O*'s scheduled release, simply referred to now as "Columbine," intimidated Disney/

Miramax from releasing the film. As supporters of the Gore–Lieberman presidential ticket, a platform that publicly denounced violence in Hollywood films in the spring of 1999 post-Columbine, Miramax executives – Harvey and Bob Weinstein – sat on the film with the intent to wait out the 2000 election. This, Miramax executives felt, would appease the trickledown pressure from Washington's neoliberals. As speculative rumors spread that the Columbine murderers used the films *The Basketball Diaries* and *The Matrix* as a template for their actions, the release of *O* became an extreme political risk. Director Tim Blake Nelson deemed Miramax's response to Columbine as selective and ill-conceived politics that misunderstood the work and reception of popular film.[3]

In an interview in the Canadian paper *The Vancouver Sun*, Blake Nelson commented that "Harvey [Weinstein of Miramax] felt that, given his political affiliation, he would be perceived as a hypocrite for releasing a movie that – however well intentioned – had such a bloody ending involving teenagers."[4] After another school shooting that year in San Diego, California, at Santana High School, Miramax refused to release *O*. Tim Blake-Nelson threatened to sue Disney/Miramax for delaying the film's release, but in its stead, Lions Gate, a Canadian motion picture company, bought the film from Miramax. In August of 2001, two years after the schedule release of the film, it opened in 15,000 theatres in the USA. This release number is slightly more than an art or independent film, but considerably low for it to compete with most major motion pictures. In April of 2002, Lions Gate released the film on video and a special edition, two-disc DVD set.

O's postmodern narrative, *mise-en-scène*, and tumultuous release provide textual examples to map ways of seeing – and not seeing – the advents of contemporary racism and social injustice in American society. *O*'s narrative generates from the dangers of jealousy taken to the extreme, where white students at a Southern prep school manufacture a scheme to annihilate the source of their insecurity – a black American star athlete named Odin James (nicknamed O by the white characters). For the white characters in the film, the stability of their gender, sexual, racial, and political self is dependent upon destroying or consuming O in order to affirm a previous liberal identity that the material presence of O, and their irrational jealousy of him, calls into question. The white characters in *O* appropriate popular forms of black culture and leisure; they listen to hip-hop music and employ black vernacular idioms. At the same time, they engage in a racialized drama that consumes blackness in a commodified form, even as they paradoxically try to destroy it in its embodied form. *O* works as a multivalent metaphor for disparate race and social relations in contemporary US society and brings to focus the ways that the neoliberal ruling force responds to and within those social relations. By defining the havoc of neoliberal ideology and providing a brief synthesis of Shakespeare's *Othello* in comparison to its postmodern filmic reinterpretation *O*, I pinpoint violent epistemological structures of solipsistic knowledge, which reveal ways of knowing and seeing race and difference as absent, as a commodity, or as pathological. The voice of Othello's main antagonist, the character Iago, appears throughout the essay in order to serve an experiential and literary purpose.[5] This insertion of voice illustrates a continuum and intertextual relationship between the two texts, that is, *O* and *Othello*, and it allows an opportunity to draw connections between these texts and the larger contexts of epistemological solipsism and neoliberalism in contemporary society.

"'Tis better as it is"

Much of contemporary neoliberalism in the USA is entrenched in a form of racially inflected historic amnesia and epistemological solipsism concerning the role and presence of historically marginalized groups in society. Contemporarily, neoliberalism works as a rationale of transnational government policies as reflected in discourses of globalized nations and as disseminated through macro-economic formations and institutions. As a form of ideology, neoliberalism represents a cognitive social reasoning that bolsters the legitimacy of a moderately liberal to conservative nation state that runs in direct opposition to material social justice for aggrieved populations. When it comes to a redistribution of wealth and cultural transformation, the inaction of neoliberalism echoes a telling line in Shakespeare's *Othello*, "'Tis better as it is" (Othello to Iago, 1.2.6). Concerning the prevalence of neoliberalism in the Americas, cultural theorist Pierre Bourdieu writes:

> Neo-liberal discourse is not just one discourse among many. Rather, it is a "strong discourse." It is so strong and so hard to combat only because it has on its side all of the forces of a world of relations of forces, a world that it contributes to making what it is. It does this most notably by orienting the economic choices of those who dominate economic relationships. It thus adds its own symbolic force to these relations of forces.[6]

As a false cloak of social and political change, neoliberalism masks itself with a shield of nebulous progressivism, in order to hide the calculated work of its reproduction of the status quo. Insofar as this position presents itself in the form of epistemological solipsism (i.e. a if I do not or choose not to see something it does not exist state of unconsciousness), its structures of knowledge are limited to seeing through an abject social-self that is unable to align itself with contemporary communities of struggle. An assumption of a monolithic, contemporary neoliberal movement is as blind and as hasty as neoliberalism's racial unconsciousness. Nevertheless, the advent of neoliberalism's epistemological solipsism is unmistakable. As cultural critic George Lipsitz argues:

> [Neoliberal] minded intellectuals who have never directly experienced the power of social movements in social relations can easily become isolated in their own consciousness and [intellectual] activity, unable to distinguish

between their own abstract ideas for social change and actual people and movements. Taking a position is not the same as waging a war of position. Changing your mind is not the same as changing society.[7]

This strand of neoliberalism wreaks havoc most intensely via ideological state apparatuses (i.e. state or culturally sanctioned institutions such as schools, organized religion, nuclear family structures, local and national government), and public sphere cultural politics, which view and deploy a misunderstanding of the lived implications of contemporary race prejudice to abstractions of past forms of racism and its assumed resolve.[8] Neoliberalism thus suffers from a subtle, but nonetheless violent way of seeing or not seeing race and difference, because of its contemporary shaping of the discourse on race prejudice and domestic policy. Cultural critic Adolph Reed Jr explains the political schema in the twenty-first century when he argues that contemporarily, there is a morphing of Republicans' "compassionate conservatism" with Democrats' "Republican Lite" form of government in the USA. Taken together, the two political entities have become a neoliberal monster where good (or bad) intentions keep aggrieved communities stagnate, while neoliberals can feel comfortable that they are making right or culturally progressive decisions by purporting change rhetorically without engaging in actions that lead to self and cultural transformation.[9] It is this form of racial amnesia and neoliberal politics that undoes a hoop star in Brad Kaaya's O.

"I am not what I am"

Shakespeare's Othello draws from a 1566 fictional piece by Giraldi Cinthio, Hecatmmithi, which bases itself on an actual sixteenth-century murder.[10] The play takes place in seventeenth-century Venice, and is about a highly respected black general of Moorish/African descent, whose jealous ensign Iago convinces him that Othello's Italian wife, Desdemona, is engaging in an extramarital affair with Cassio, who is Othello's second in command. Upon Iago's enthusiastic coaching and manipulative design, Othello strangles his wife to death in, as Iago says, "The bed she has hath contaminated" (Iago to Othello, 4.1.205). At the play's end, Othello learns of Iago's deceit and Desdemona's faithfulness and commits suicide as a form of remorse and sacrificial sentiment. Othello finds out at the end of the play what the audience learns throughout it by way of Iago's disturbing exegesis of his subconscious: Iago's lie of infidelity is retaliation for Othello electing Cassio as his lieutenant instead of him; he is resentful of the attention Othello receives by his constituents and his notoriety as a general; he is perplexed – in fact enraged – by the undying admiration and love "the Moor" (as Iago refers to Othello in private through the voice of mockery) receives from Desdemona. In addition, Cassio's higher socioeconomic class symbolizes to Iago his own lack of ability to transcend his more modest class background for promotion.

In a postmodern sense, Iago is a Freudian cliché; he embodies the psychological pathologies of emotional displacement and identity fragmentation.[11] As Iago says about himself, "I am not what I am" (1.1.64), meaning he is not what he presents to the world, that is, a rationale being, but rather, he is in actuality a broken and deeply wounded soul who desires the fruit and success of Othello and Cassio. His plot to destroy Othello – a man who, as Iago claims, is initially "without jealousies" – acts as a process to restore Iago's fractured identity. His jealousy of Desdemona's and Othello's relationship suggests he finds threatening the emerging social status and sexual autonomy of white women. Iago thus displaces his own insecurities onto Othello in order to cleanse himself of the feelings that he is incapable of fully understanding and accepting, and he elects the help of others to destroy the austerity of Othello, in order to claim a self-identity of austerity. The greatness and accomplishments of Othello, the power of Venice's aristocracy, and the growing sexual and gender autonomy of white women are all reminders to him of his inability to rely upon his identity as a white heterosexual male, and a mythical bildungsroman narrative to ensure his long-term career success. Despite his self-proclaimed and actual hard work and labor, Iago fears that he is being rendered invisible and is being eclipsed by all those around him who he subconsciously believes are inferior, i.e. black men and white women, and those who he fears will continue to keep him in a stagnant career position, i.e. a white male aristocracy.

"Were I the Moor, I would not be Iago"

In contradistinction to the original, Kaaya does not confine his rewriting to Shakespeare's Elizabethan inflections of language, a Venetian landscape, nor the historical moment of the seventeenth century. Instead, Kaaya's *Othello* artfully fissures itself from the original, by focusing on contemporary social relations in the USA through the lens of black male subjectivity. He trades Venice for a Southern prep school in North Carolina, the battlefield for a basketball court, and the Moor army general for a popular black athlete. The setting and circumstances change, but like Shakespeare's narrative components, Kaaya's story works as a metonymic symbol for the ways the characters struggle to operate within a postmodern society, and how they struggle with the presence of blackness.

O opens with Verdi's "Ava Maria" from *Otello* (an opera based on *Othello*) as the camera slowly focuses on a clearer shot of white doves that coo as they increase in number. The birds gather on a staircase and the Hugo/Iago character's voiceover immediately introduces the theme of jealousy, by proclaiming: "I know you are not supposed to be jealous of anything, but to take flight. Now, that's living." The camera jump cuts to a picture of a black hawk, which the spectator later learns represents O/Othello and blackness in the film. Verdi's opera fades into a fast-paced rap song "We Riddaz," by rapper Roscoe. The camera quickly focuses the spectator's eye on O and his speed and skill on the basketball court, as Othello would have likely displayed on the battlefield. Following a more typical narrative convention of basketball scenes in popular films, O makes the winning shot, all gather to the gym floor, everyone cheers, and they lift O above their shoulders in a simile of flight. The camera pans away from O to Hugo glaring at the celebration from the sidelines, and then reverses to a slow motion camera release to close in on Hugo's face. For the first time, the spectator sees the driving force in the film: Hugo's envy of the star black player.

From thereon, O's plot unfolds quickly. Hugo is jealous of O because he shares his Most Valuable Player (MVP) title with his teammate Michael instead of him. "I hate the Moor! And it is thought abroad that twixt my sheets. H'as done my office. I know not if it be true, but I, for mere suspicion in that kind, will do as if for surety" (Iago to Roderigo, 1.3.380). In addition, Hugo's father, who is also the basketball team's coach, publicly announces that he loves O like one of his own sons. This intensifies Hugo's jealousy, because Hugo and his father have a strained relationship. Hugo, like Shakespeare's Iago, is from a modest class background; he resides at the prep school and is a member of the school's basketball team because his father is coach. Hugo is intelligent and an exceptional scholar at the prep school; yet, his skill on the basketball court is lackluster. In order to keep up with other members on the team and to compete with O, he injects steroids laced (possibly) with psychotropic elements. To add insult to Hugo's self-believed injury, O dates a beautiful white woman – in this version Desi – just as Othello was married to one (Desdemona). In the eyes of the white characters, O flaunts the relationship, which causes a fury in Hugo, his girlfriend Emily, and the school's rich misfit Roger. While Hugo desperately desires to belong, O is aloof about it; he does not care to belong, despite that he is the only black person at the school. In Hugo's view, O has everything that Hugo has worked hard to achieve or fears losing: Coach Goulding's admiration, a star position on the team, popularity among others in the school, in short, the limelight.

If Shakespeare's Iago is a postmodern Freudian cliché, Kaaya's Hugo is a postmodern Freudian nightmare. Like Shakespeare's Iago, Hugo tells O that Desi is cheating on him with the character Michael (Cassio). "I will turn her virtue into pitch, and out of her own goodness make the net that shall enmesh them all" (Iago to Roderigo, 2.3.360). He uses Roger as a pawn for criminal acts and as a tool to spread the news of O's and Desi's love affair to her father, Dean Brable. "Call up her father. Rouse him, poison his delight. Proclaim him in the streets" (Iago to Roderigo, 1.1.65). He persuades Emily to steal an antique silk scarf for him that O has given to Desi, which belonged to O's great grandmother, who was a former slave. Hugo then suggests to O that Desi has given the scarf to her new white lover, and manufactures an opportunity for O to see Michael handling the scarf, thus sealing in O's mind Desi's infidelity. "I will in Cassio's lodging lose this napkin and let him find it. Trifles light as air are to the jealous confirmations strong as proofs of Holy Writ" (Iago, 3.3.320). Finally, Hugo masterminds a murderous plot that results in Michael, Roger, O, Desi, and Emily all dying by the end of the film. Has Hugo done all of this in the name of jealousy? "As I confess it is my nature's plague to spy into abuses and oft my jealousy" (Iago to Othello, 3.3.150).

In an interview, actor Josh Hartnett (Hugo/Iago) provides an interpretation of the violent and contradictory emotions that consume Hugo and overtakes his judgment:

> [Hugo is an] overly emotional and wounded individual. And a very smart and manipulative person at that. And a dangerous person. There's nothing wrong with being smart. There's nothing wrong with being jealous – it is a real emotion and you can use it for all sorts of things . . . But his fear of not being seen anymore is his downfall – he get's desperate. Race and drugs are clouding the real issue and the real issue is that this kid is screwed up really, really bad. He has feelings of guilt and envy, and he is experiencing loss concerning his relationship with his father.[12]

Hartnett's view, though leaning toward complexity, overlooks the role racial and class jealousy plays in Kaaya's interpretation of Shakespeare's text. In counter juxtaposition, cultural critic Cynthia Fusch argues in her review of the film that "in *O*, the resulting tragedy exposes the social tensions that shape the young adults' experiences – these tensions are also, of course, economic, racial, political and, above all, mediated."[13] This intersection convenes most disturbingly at the end of the film, when Hugo voices his justification for his treacherous deeds, which is a monologue of his self-alienation and distortion, and his insight into the social relations he is contributing to, but is in no way apologetic about. A non-diegetic music sequence of "Ava Maria" plays in a shrilling loud volume as the camera documents in slow motion the body bagging of those whom Hugo directly or indirectly murdered. There is a jump-cut between Hugo being handcuffed, to white doves fluttering in a cage. While Hugo willingly sits inside a police car, the camera jump cuts to the cage of doves. Yet, this time, the cage door swings open and one white dove escapes from the cage, thus representing the emotional freedom Hugo experiences now that Desi, O, Roger, and Michael are all dead. The camera jump cuts again to an image of the dead Odin, whose arms and body are stretched wide like a black hawk. The volume of "Ava Maria" softens to a low murmur and the camera jump cuts again to Hugo inside the police car glaring despondently out the back window. Hugo's voiceover ascends to begin the monologue of a deeply wounded, but newly confident soul:

> I know you are not supposed to be jealous of anything . . . but to take flight, to soar above everything and everyone . . . now, that's living. But

a hawk is no good around normal birds. It can't fit in. Even though all the other birds want to be hawks, they hate him for what they can't be – proud, powerful, determined, dark. Odin is hawk. He soars above us. He can fly. And one of these days, everyone is going to pay attention to me. Because I'm going to fly, too.

Before O's suicide, he demands Hugo confess as to why he has spun such a deadly web of distrust and evil, and Hugo responds in chill: "From now on, I say nothing." "Demand me nothing; what you know, you know" (Iago to Othello, 5.2.300). Hugo is a sociopath, but the emotions that drive his actions are certainly not limited to the mentally ill. Hugo's monologue and ineffectual response to O's demands reveal the suppressed sentiments of those who are resentful they must compete with people of color in a post civil rights society. O's success and good fortune in an arena of competitive sports and academe do not function in isolation as his own good deeds. To the contrary, O's peers view his success as taking away from or overshadowing their success. Hugo's plot therefore serves the multiple functions of (1) gaining O's trust so that his plan of deception will work and go largely unnoticed until the tragic end, (2) achieving notoriety via O's spiraling downward, and (3) reasserting power over the black subject, which Hugo feels has been lost given O's popularity and autonomy. "Make the Moor thank me, love me, and reward me for making him egregiously an Ass" (Iago to Roderigo, 2.1.310).

As blackness functions as pathology or as an article of trade in the subconscious mind of the white characters, they are unable to delineate between consuming and purporting a love for black culture in abstract terms, with realizing the actual humanity of black people beyond irrational fetish.[14] O's filmic narrative intimates that neoliberalism's bilateral blind spot constitutes viewing difference in the form of commodity, and therefore difference comes to signify and occupy the space of extrinsic value. An example of this is when Dean Brable and Coach Goulding accuse O of sexually forcing himself on Desi, who, recall, is Dean Brable's daughter. "I speak yet not of proof . . . for that I do suspect the lusty Moor" (Iago to Roderigo, 2.1.295). In response to the accusation, O responds, "Coach, you know I would never do anything like that. Besides, if you are so worried about me, why did you bust your ass to get me to come to this school?" Coach Goulding replies in a way that underscores the black body as extrinsic commodity, retorting, "Because you were worth it." The word "were" is key here, as the coach is at this moment marking O in terms of his utility, that is to say his worth, as an accessory commodity. Once the coach and the Dean realize they need O to win the state basketball championship – and only then – do their concerns about O's character take a back seat to filling an immediate need in the sport marketplace.[15]

Dell, who is the school's resident drug dealer, facilitates O's awareness concerning his use to the school, and he emphasizes the way O inadvertently plays a role in his own exploitation and commodification:

DELL: These white boys sure got you twisted all up.

O: What, you still here Nigger?

DELL: I know it is tough being "Mr. I am on my way to the NBA," I feel ya. But you got to think this thing through. See, what's gonna happen is they are going to parade you around in front of their friends, take you to parties, supply you with everything – money, coochie, white women, even their daughters. They are going to offer you a million dollars, and you gonna take it. And then, you are going to be their new, Million Dollar Nigger. But what happens if you bust out one of your knees or you fuck up some other way? I'll tell you what. They are going to take their money back. Now what do you call a Million Dollar Nigger, without a million dollars? Another Nigger.[16]

Dell's and O's dialogue suggest that O's primary function is to signify the white characters' and the school's liberal progressivism, and as a commodity he is exchangeable and replaceable. O thus represents the fetishism of the black male body as commodity in sports. Perhaps not surprising is that his use value quickly wanes as Hugo's self-fulfilling prophecy for him runs its course. "The Moor already changes with my poison" (Iago, 3.3.320). Indeed, by the film's end, O engages in illicit drug use, date rapes and murders his white girlfriend, allows jealousy and hearsay to destroy him, and, like Othello, kills himself at the end, solving the proverbial black (male) problem.[17]

"This may help to thicken other proofs that do demonstrate thinly"

The *mise-en-scène* in the film coupled with the dialogue underpins the racial divisions present. O's music score integrates opera and hip-hop to create continuity between Kaaya's O and Shakespeare's *Othello*; the two musical forms also double as a cultural marker of departure from the original text. The film manipulates popular iconography of the South (North Carolina) to trigger questions of racial harmony and change. One example of this is a confederate flag that hangs during a basketball game with the caption: THE NU SOUTH. Given the events in the film, the caption functions as an ironic question as to how far race relations have progressed in the twenty-first century South. In addition, in the first intimate scene between O and Desi, she wears a t-shirt with a confederate flag on it, which she disrobes before entering into a naked embrace with O. Desi's stripping away of the garment is symbolic to stripping away the sexual and racial boundaries enforced by the former segregated South, for which her t-shirt signifies. "All seals and symbols of redeemed sin. His soul is so enfettered to her love that she may make, unmake, do what she list, even as her appetite shall play the God with his weak function. How am I then a villain?" (Iago, 2.3.345). As they lay naked, Desi and O joke together to deflate (and therefore paradoxically intensify) the complicated history of slavery, miscegenation, and the white and black cultural politics that defy their sexual and romantic union:

O: You know I got them playa skills.

DESI: Oh, he's getting a little cocky.

O: Don't say little and cock when you are referring to me, especially when you know the deal . . . I pulled you cause I'm that type of Nigger. (*Desi turns away in embarrassment.*) Don't be like that. See I can say Nigger because I am one. You're not, so you can't. Don't be jealous.

DESI: And why can't I say it? My people invented the word.

O: You can't even think it.

DESI: You are the one who started it. You said I was so fine you'd let me dress you up and play Black Buck got loose in the Big House.

O: Don't go repeating that. If another Black person knew I said that, I could get my suffering-Negro-league-card revoked.

DESI: Then you better watch out, because it looks like I got some dirt on you, playa.

Kaaya's choice of dialogue serves several purposes. O's and Desi's verbal exchange plays with, and draws upon, colonialist fantasies of the big, black male phallus that looms in the popular imagination.[18] O's words signify an awareness of the historical construction and defaming of black male sexuality since the onslaught of the enslavement of Africans in the USA, where white mistresses assumingly sought after enslaved black men for their sexual gratification. Kaaya throws the viewer a cinematic curve, though, by indirectly suggesting that − conscious or not − the two *are* playing out a psychosexual drama dreamt up by white slavers and their mistresses in the Antebellum years. O's off the cuff "suffering-Negro-league-card" remark, and Desi's response to him via black vernacular, "I got some dirt on you, playa," provides a transition from the film's references to past constructions of white/black sexual unions during the Antebellum period, to contemporary views of white/black sexual unions as a more moderate threat.

Code switching is prevalent throughout the film concerning the use of language, and it is commonplace for the white characters to take on black personas before engaging in racialized behavior. The white characters' use of black vernacular language in the film calls into question neoliberal discourses of race, language, and the perceived, as well as imagined, areas of gray in this usage. For instance, Hugo and Michael casually use the terms "Big Ballers," "Playas" and "Niggas," but they also use this language against or to describe the main black character, thus asserting control over language and meaning to recoup their white supremacy. An example of this is when Hugo and Michael refer to each other as "Big Ballers," and seconds after Michael informs Hugo that "the ghetto has just popped out" of O and that "the Nigga is out of control." Racialized and vernacular language is a significant narrative technique used by Kaaya. He is able to show how the white characters simultane-ously appropriate black vernacular language structures and use them against black people without seeing any contradiction between this use and the power differential in that use.

Shakespeare literary critics critiqued *O* for such narrative liberties and symbolic inversions, citing the film's demolition and departure from the formal poetic structures of Shakespeare's language, and its dependency on presentist interpretations of class, race, sexuality, and gender.[19] Critics such as Harold Bloom opined that the creator of *O* and other recent renditions of the play fail to understand that *Othello*'s theme of race and miscegenation is secondary to its universal themes of jealousy and betrayal.[20] In tandem, James Welsh's article about the film, "Classic Demolition: Why Shakespeare is Not Exactly Our Contemporary, or Dude, Where's My Hanky?," argues that Kaaya's film is "an ill-advised treatment that turns Shakespeare's tragic plot into an absurd teen melodrama."[21] However, what many colorblind literary criticisms of the film fail to acknowledge is that *Othello* itself is a remake of a fictional piece, which bases itself on an actual historic event. This not only dismantles arguments of literary purity, but it also adds credibility to Kaaya's postmodern version doing what Shakespeare himself did, that is, embellishing an existing story to shed light on the current milieu. In this way, Kaaya's postmodern *O* carries the possibility to perform a kind of cultural work as a production of popular culture targeted at young adults that Shakespeare's *Othello*, as a popular response to modernity, is likely not to make as strongly in our current historical moment.

In the 123 film reviews of *O* in major newspaper publications and online film sites, the consistent response to the film was to applaud it for its transgres-sions, denigrate it for its departure from Shakespeare, or denounce it for reasons motivated by justice in representation. On the latter point, critics voiced concern that *O*'s/Othello's nemesis Hugo/Iago fooled the protagonist too easily, thereby reflecting and perpetuating the black stereotype of the fumbling, foolish black man.[22] "The Moor is free and open in nature. And will as tenderly be led by the nose, as Asses are" (Iago to Roderigo, 1.3.395). Indeed, *O*'s rape of his white girlfriend conjures up the racialized referent of the black male as sexual brute, and his descent into drug use defies the black respectability that his overwhelming success might otherwise infer.

In a pivotal moment that begins *O*'s spiraling downward and an emotional and power transferral to Hugo, he convinces *O* that using cocaine is the answer to anesthetizing his feelings and helping him cope with his personal problems, to which *O* gullibly concedes. Blake-Nelson frames the intimacy and intensity of this scene by directing the camera to move slowly into the space of the conversation through an open window, which places the spectator in the posi-tion of an eavesdropper to Hugo's and *O*'s conversation. As the camera moves closer into the room that the two men inhabit, a fracture composite of Hugo's reflection appears through a long lens shot of his dorm room mirror. The camera then quickly jump cuts to a mirror of cocaine that lies on the table dividing Hugo and O. Hugo separates the lines of cocaine from two to three, which works as a symbolic representation of the triangular web of deceit he has drawn for O, Desi, and Michael. While this moment foreshadows O's coming undone, it also simultaneously represents the beginning of Hugo's identity suture from a fragmented, wounded soul, to an individual whose identity will become complete once his jealousy-driven plot materializes. With an unrelenting facial expression of diabolical, manufactured compassion, Hugo whispers to O:

HUGO: I'm gonna take care of you man. This shit right here, is going to help you make it through.
O: I don't want to be doing this shit man.
HUGO: (*Sliding the mirror of cocaine to O*): Just makin' it through playa, just makin' it through (*O snorts two lines of cocaine and quickly swallows a shot of hard alcohol in concession*).

After this, Hugo falsely confides to O that Desi and Michael refer to him as "The Nigger" and he proclaims that, although he has not seen Michael and Desi together, he is most certain that they are having sex. "Her honour is an essence that's not seen . . . What if I had said I had seen [them] do you wrong? Or heard [them] say? They must blab. [He] lies with her, on her; what you will" (Iago to Othello, 4.1.15–40). In reaction to Hugo's lie, O begins to weep and the racial and masculine shield that had protected him, and that which incensed his white peers, breaks down. Hugo's lie transforms sexual dishonor to racial dishonor for the black male character, because not only has his manhood been questioned, but his naive sense of racial justice and equality that his interracial relationship signifies for him has been obliterated through Hugo's malicious gossip and innuendo.

While O's initial reaction to this news is to hold the character Michael accountable for the perceived affair thereby reclaiming his patriarchal dominance of the white female object, Hugo intervenes and insists that Desi and Michael must go down together, that O should murder Desi, and frame Michael for the crime. Through emotional, racial, and sexual displacement, Hugo manipulates the source of his jealousy, i.e. the black male character, to annihilate all other human factors that make him feel insecure, e.g. sexually autonomous white women and those who have class advantage. In so doing, he aims for the world order to restructure or return for him in a way that is congruent with his fantasies of blackness, his belief of subordinate white womanhood, and his irrational investment in a class bildungsroman that presents itself in the form of being a successful basketball player. "I have rubbed this . . . quat almost to the sense. Now, whether he kill Cassio, or Cassio kill him, or each do kill each other, every way makes my gain" (Iago to Roderigo, 5.1.10).

Compounding a perceived problem of racial representation is that the drug dealer in the film, Dell, is a black American, and the only other black character in the film besides O. Black women are absent from the film, although soft porn iconography of a black woman adorns one of the dorm walls of the character Hugo, thus indirectly commenting on black women's displacement from race, class, and sexual power hierarchies other than as objects of the white male gaze. Moreover, although Dell supplies Hugo with intravenous injections of steroids and powder cocaine, he ultimately comes to represent the pathology of black on black crime and the prejudicial ideology of blackness itself as always-already prone to illegal activity and illicit drug use. All of this – O's portrayal of race relations, heavy drug use, violence, and the willingness among the characters to do anything to belong – including murder – made it too dangerous in the view of critics on both sides of the political spectrum. The popular film critic Roger Ebert's review in the *Chicago Sun Times* speaks to the trappings of neoliberalism in Washington that threatened to kill the film, writing:

> To suggest that O was part of the solution and not part of the problem would have required a sophistication that our public officials either lack, or are afraid to reveal for fear of offending constituents. Hugo . . . and his allies are victims of that high school disease that encourages the unpopular to do anything in order to be accepted. Those who think this film will inspire events like Columbine should ask themselves how often audiences want to be like the despised villain.[23]

The film's question of representation notwithstanding, Brad Kaaya's O is a useful cinematic text for much of what it has received criticism for, and that is, its postmodern interpretation of the original play, its insistence to let the contradictions of the characters remain intact without resolve, and its controversial racial politics. Too many critics who denounced the film seemed to confuse representative justice with the desire for positive representation, thereby closing off a deeper discussion of human frailty and the intelligence, sophistication, and culpability of young adults. The film's refusal to portray the central black male figure as a victim and its ability to show the inner workings of the neoliberalist psyche without apologies provide insight to the complexity of social relations. Further, O sheds light on the pathology that racialized jealousy breeds in its characters. Kaaya's filmic remake thus manages to build upon Shakespeare's, and he keeps the narrative of career and race jealousy alive in ways that its critics and political censors too easily deny and dismiss in the name of literary purity and liberal politicking. Depictions of racism is not new to the silver screen, neither is jealousy, rape, and the use of drugs. Yet, Kaaya's writing takes the spectator into more risky territory, insofar as he refuses to create a text that leaves its spectator comfortable during its painful scenes of interracial date rape, white subterfuge, and emotional coercion, nor at its hyper-dramatized climax of murder and suicide. Instead of viewing Kaaya's O as a demolition of modernity's Shakespeare, one might rethink it as a postmodern improvement ripe for the twenty-first century.

"O, beware, my lord, of jealousy!"

Despite *O*'s tumultuous release, Kaaya was able to bring to the screen a film that explores racial jealousy and its relational partner, i.e. envy. Literary and Shakespeare critic Lily Campbell notes that, while jealousy can derive from love and comes about through "reason, pleasure, passion, property right, or honor," envy is an intensified emotion and a form of hatred that generally leads to an act of revenge. Envy, she writes, is a derivative of "grief and fear that comes from seeing another in possession of that which one would possess solely for one self, or from fear that another may possess it."[24] Campbell's discussion of jealousy and envy works well to place boundaries around terms not easily disentangled and defined, yet racially inflected jealousy, although symptomatic of the human condition, is not a rational emotion of reason. Rather, it is an irrational emotion and like envy, in the film *O*, it stems from racial insecurity. "I have told thee again, and again, and I retell thee again, and again. I hate the Moor. My cause is hearted; thine hath no less reason. Let us be conjunctive in our revenge against him" (Iago to Roderigo, 1.3.365).

O is elevated to the status of superstar, but he is not the only successful figure in the entire school. Kaaya's filmic question is indirectly suggested: why is it that the white characters fixate on the black subject's success, and why do they use him to displace and deny the human inadequacies from which they suffer? It appears race allows the white characters to have ultimate power over the black subject and race inequity allows Hugo to tap into dominant perceptions and fears of blackness that work to legitimate his devious behavior and to naturalize O's decline. "It is not honesty in me to speak. What I have seen and known. You shall observe him, and his own courses will denote him so that I may save speech" (Iago to Lodovico, 4.2.275). The white characters fear and/ or wish to consume O's blackness, but they also subconsciously fear the threat that blackness is not inferior to their whiteness. Their appropriation, consumption, and abolishment of blackness reify their whiteness and their actions uphold white supremacy.

In a material sense, epistemological solipsism and the current neoliberal ruling force has worked to repeal cultural citizenship (e.g. Propositions 187 and 22 in California), affirmative action in higher education (e.g. Proposition 209 and the brief filed by George Bush concerning the University of Michigan's admissions policy) and post 9/11 human rights (e.g. Patriot Act).[25] In a post civil rights society where members of the dominant culture have to compete with difference in the form of excellence, destroying measures that would increase opportunities for historically marginalized groups and denying their intellectual and cultural fortitude acts as a way to return power to a social order where the dominant culture rules supreme. Denying current forms of discrimination also allows structural inequities to remain frozen in time in the hegemonic, racialized psyche, which allows the absence of white success to come to mean the unfair advantages of historically marginalized groups. "Stamp and counterfeit advantages, though true advantage never presents itself" (Iago to Roderigo, 2.1.240). Put another way, because of the subconscious belief of black (read racial) inferiority in the racialized fragmented mind, black success equals unfair advantage that requires rectification, or, as the film *O* portrays, collective reversal and revenge.

Given recent public policy over the past three decades, cultural critic Cameron McCarthy seems correct in the assertion that "traditional distinctions between conservatives and liberals, Democrats and Republicans, the Left versus the Right, have collapsed."[26] What is left is a neoliberal and neoconservative agenda that often doubles as each other in convenient, and at the most destructive and dangerous of, times. This was especially evident in the move on liberals' part to censor the film and/or stall its release. To illuminate the connection between career jealousy and the neoliberal condition, I return to Bourdieu's explanation of the prevalence of organizational toxicity that buttresses competition in individuals and workers to the detriment of forming political collectives and working toward social justice. In the influential essay "The Essence of Neo-liberalism," Bourdieu's keen observations on neoliberalism, modern capitalism, and organizational toxicity are worth quoting at length:

> Competition is extended to individuals . . . through the individualisation of the wage relationship [in the workplace]: establishment of individual performance objectives, individual performance evaluations, permanent evaluation, individual salary increases or granting of bonuses as a function of competence and of individual merit . . . This pressure toward "self-control" extends workers' over-involvement in work and work under emergency or high-stress conditions. And [this] converges to weaken or abolish collective standards or solidarities. In this way, a Darwinian world . . . finds support through everyone clinging to their job and organisation under conditions of insecurity, suffering, and stress. [Neoliberalism] would not succeed so completely without the complicity of all of the precarious arrangements that produce insecurity and . . . employees rendered docile by these social processes that make their situations precarious, as well as by the permanent threat of unemployment.[27]

Kaaya's *Othello* illustrates the violence of middle and upper middle class sensibilities of Darwinian survivalism instigated by capitalism that Bourdieu refers to in his essay. For Shakespeare's Iago, Cassio, and Othello, the macro-economic and relational forces of modernity and the bureaucratic ranks of the military shore up their competitive and violent drama. For Kaaya's Hugo, Michael, and Odin, excellence in sports and the white female object is the sign of autonomous and successful masculinity that they struggle to master, possess, and control. In both versions, Iago's/Hugo's irrational competitiveness with the central black subject suspends ethics.

In explaining the cultural work and relevance of *O* in the context of high school and the lives of young adults, director Tim Blake Nelson offers the following in view of Columbine:

> I think the point of this film is pretty obvious in its very concept. And that is, we've been able to take a Shakespearean tragedy and set it, credibly, in an American high school. *Othello* in high school is something that when you put the two words together and say them rather quickly it sounds silly. But we're at a point in America, right now, in which it is not silly; it is serious. And it's believable.[28]

A Southern prep school can thus stand in for Venice, the university can stand in for the Southern prep school, and corporate America can stand in for the university, because all of these metonymic relationships function in a similar way under a racist, sexist, and capitalist society. "Make all the money though canst. If sanctimony and a frail vow betwixt an erring barbarian and a super subtle Venetian be not too hard for wits and all the tribe of hell therefore make money. A pox of drowning thyself!" (Iago to Roderigo, 1.3.335–60). The Iago complex is not merely a figment of Shakespeare's theatrical imagination then, nor is he only the literary manipulations of Giraldi Cinthio's biographical fiction of domestic murder. As Shakespeare historian Tina Packer and the specialist in CEO management styles John Whitney remind in their comparison of the textual plot of *Othello* to the environmental context of cut-throat corporate America: "*Warning*: Some Iagos are so patient and crafty that they can work their mischief for years without being exposed."[29]

Conclusion

In 1971, the black writers John Dover Wilson and Alice Walker published an edited edition of *Othello* for Cambridge University Press.[30] Their preface, introduction, explanatory notes, and analysis of scenes read race into the text at a time when such analysis was speculative and secondary to the thematic focus of universalism. In Dover's introduction, he indicates that those who do not see an intersection of race, jealousy, class, gender, and sexuality in Shakespeare's *Othello* have not read it closely with a discerning eye. He also includes that understanding the character Othello as a "Negro" – or via black subject formation and its abortion – is essential to a full understanding of the play. Since Walker's and Dover's edition and before, writers and literary critics have been fascinated with Shakespeare's lead protagonist, the noble Moor, and his creation of an antagonist who is unbelievably believable as evil incarnate: the ensign. In the tradition of this edition that came out of the racial consciousness of the 1970s, I have meant to revisit their intentions. I have also hoped to go further in order to think through the possibilities in understanding the *Othello* narrative as envisaged through the eyes of a contemporary black American male screenwriter.

Kaaya's rewriting of *Othello* depicts that in the age of neoliberalism, rational beings relinquish agency and humanity to compete with each other, and race and other forms of difference exacerbate this competition. It also shows the pathology and power of racialized jealousy as it morphs into prejudicial envy. Under these conditions and because of epistemological solipsism compounded by twenty-first century racism, commodifying and consuming race too often replaces progress toward social justice for historically marginalized groups. *O* challenges us to understand the violent way epistemological solipsism is symptomatic of the neoliberal condition, and the violence that results from needing to belong and succeed by any means. Like the original *Othello*, there are no heroes in *O* and the culpability and motive of the contradictory characters in their deeds eschews easy answers to the vexing problems the film presents to its audience. The cultural work of the film thus lies in its latent possibilities. Kaaya shows us that as social actors under the guise of neoliberalism and modern capitalism, even young adults are not outside of the ideology that informs this disparate structure in *O*, and his cautionary postmodern *Othello* may help them to begin to see and perhaps, encourage them to work at rejecting it.

Notes

1 Quoted from Daniel Derkson interview with Blake Nelson, "To Adapt, or Not Adapt." Retrieved July 31 2003, from the Writing Studio website: http://home. mweb.co.za/al/aladar/page139.html. Derkson was an editor for Kaaya's screenplay.

2 Kevin Simpson, "Shelved After Columbine, Film to Debut," *Denver Post* (April 30 2001), A01.

3 Lawrence Grossberg, for example, reminds us that popular culture studies and practices have the potential for political registration, but that the political effects are not assured ahead of time, because they depend on context and cultural practice being analyzed, among other things. See *Dancing in Spite of Myself: Essays on Popular Culture* (Durham, NC: Duke University Press, 1997), p. 209.

4 Jamie Portman and Katherine Monk, "The Hollywood Film Only a Canadian Firm Would Touch: Disney Dropped Othello 'Remake' Because of School Violence," *Vancouver Sun* (August 28 2001), A1.

5 I cite Iago's dialogue by act, scene, and line from Robert Southwick, ed., *Othello*, Longman Literature Shakespeare Series (Harlow: Longman, 1994). I use Iago's voice to help point out similarities between Shakespeare's text and Kaaya's filmic text, and as a literary device to underscore Iago's/Hugo's emotionally driven actions that have racialized implications. While many critique the play and recent renditions as privileging Iago's irrationality and behavior at the expense of other complex characters in the play, I agree with the Royal Shakespeare's troupe director of *Othello*, Michael Attenborough, when he insists that such critiques miss the point. In an interview, Attenborough informs:

> Shakespeare's play is not about Othello's jealousy, it's about Iago's jealousy, of everyone. Iago is paranoid, he has a ruined marriage, he's frustrated in his

career, all his motivations glue together in jealousy, and he passes that on like a disease to Othello.

See Attenborough's interview with James Inverne, "Dark Side of the Bard: You Can Wait Years for an Update of *Othello*, Then Two Turn Up at the Same Time," *Sunday Telegraph*, London edition (December 9 2001), p. 6.

6 Pierre Bourdieu, "The Essence of Neo-liberalism," *Le Monde Diplomatique* (December 1998). Retrieved September 5 2003 from Mondediplo.com. Available at *Le Monde Diplomatique* online journal website: http://mondediplo.com/1998/12/08bourdieu.

7 George Lipsitz, *American Studies in a Moment of Danger* (Minneapolis: University of Minnesota Press, 2001) p. 81.

8 On post-1960s neoliberalism see Stephen Steinberg, "The Liberal Retreat From Race in the Post Civil Rights Era," Wahneema Lubiano ed., *The House That Race Built* (New York: Vintage, 1998), pp. 13–47; Melvin Thomas, "Anything But Race: The Social Science Retreat From Racism," *Perspectives* 6 (1) (Winter, 2000), pp. 79–96.

9 Adolph Reed Jr., "The 2004 Election in Perspective: The Myth of the Cultural Divide and the Triumph of Neoliberal Ideology," *American Quarterly* 57 (1) (March 2005), p. 11.

10 For background on the origins of the play see Don Nardo, "William Shakespeare and the Moor of Venice," *Readings on Othello* (San Diego, CA: Greenhaven Press, 2000) and Alvin B. Kernan, "Othello, An Introduction," in Harold Bloom ed., *William Shakespeare: The Tragedies* (New York: Chelsea House Publishers, 1985), pp. 79–88.

11 I draw from Freud's theory of wish displacement where one projects their desires, insecurities, and anxieties onto an Other, in order to deny the existence of their own desires, insecurities, and anxieties. Psychoanalytic analyses of *Othello* are common, John Bernard's "Theatricality and Textuality: The Example of *Othello*," *New Literary History* 26 (4) (Autumn 1995), pp. 931–41 being a useful example. In response to Freudian readings of *Othello* in particular, critic Harold Bloom opines: "Freudian readings of Shakespeare . . . give us neither Shakespeare nor Freud, but a Shakespearean reading of Freud is capable of giving us both. Iago is subtler than Freud." See the "Introduction" to his anthology *Iago* (New York: Chelsea House Publishers, 1992), p. 2. To the contrary, I argue that, while psychoanalysis is not the only way one might read this character, as a theoretical tool psychoanalysis provides the most convincing lens to understand Iago and his irrational quest to destroy Othello.

12 See Josh Hartnett's interview on the special edition DVD, "*O*" (dir. Tim Blake Nelson, Lions Gate Films, 2002).

13 Cynthia Fusch, "Transgressions." Retrieved October 10, 2003 from Rotten Tomatoes Website. Also available at *Popmatters* website: www.popmatters.com/film/reviews/o/o.html.

14 Writer Jill Nelson, for example, argues that the dominant culture's assumption that black people are pathological is so pervasive that contemporary black writers continue to create counter-narratives in fiction and non-fiction to combat this racialized ideology of blackness. See Jill Nelson, "Hiding in Plain Sight," *The Nation* 258 (16) (April 25 1994), p. 3.

15 While this chapter does not detour into recent events concerning black athletes Kobe Bryant, Patrick Dennehy, and Maurice Clarett, I note these figures as an allegorical epilogue and evolving text-to-context future parallelism. Kobe Bryant is a popular black athlete who was on trial for and accused of raping a young white woman in 2003. He faced disfavor in the public's eye and temporary loss of finan-

cial endorsements because of the accusation. Patrick Dennehy is a deceased athlete who played basketball for Baylor University. To sway suspicion away from the sports community and the basketball conglomerate at Baylor concerning Denney's 2003 murder, the team's white coach later admitted to lying concerning insinuations Denney was involved in drug use to help facilitate the case's closure. Maurice Clarett is a football player who was engaged in an ethics dispute at Ohio State University because of exaggerating insurance claims and allegedly accepting unauthorized gifts. On these cases see Jim Vertuno, "Tapes Reveal Ex-Baylor Coach Told Players to Lie About Dennehy," *Associated Press News Wire* (August 17 2003); Stephen Ohlemacher and Bruce Hooley, "Clarett's Tale: From Hero to Outsider; Off-field Troubles Derail OSU Back," *Plain Dealer/Sports Final* (September 14 2003); Earl Ofari Hutchinson, "Symptoms of Simpsonitis?; Media Circus Covering Kobe Bryant's Case is Reminiscent of O.J.'s Trial of the Century," *Daily News of Los Angeles* (October 26 2003), pp. VI, 860.

16 This scene appears in the special edition DVD, but was not included in the theatrical release.

17 It was common in early psychological and sociological texts in the 1960s to study the black community, most especially the black male, as "a problem" to solve, instead of delving into larger systemic forms of racism and oppression as the problem of a global community. Contemporary race theory reminds us that prejudice is not the problem of the target, but, rather, it is the problem of the perpetrator and society as a whole. The late James Baldwin described this phenomenon and its motivations eloquently when he wrote "a vast amount of energy that goes into what we call the Negro problem is produced by the white man's desire not to be judged by those who are not white." See James Baldwin, "The Fire Next Time," in *The Price of the Ticket: Collected Non-fiction, 1948–1985* (New York: St. Martin's Press, 1985), p. 333.

18 On the sexual stereotypes and colonialist fantasies of the black male phallus see Herman Gray, "Black Masculinity and Visual Culture," *Callaloo* (18) 2 (1995), pp. 401–5; Kobena Mercer and Isaac Julien, "True Confessions: A Discourse on Images of Black Male Sexuality," eds, Rowena Chapman and Jonathan Rutherford, *Male Order: Unwrapping Masculinity* (London: Lawrence and Wishart Publishers, 1988).

19 Analyses of *Othello* that unearth themes of gender, race, sex, class, and sexuality in current times include Robert Matz, "Slander, Renaissance Discourses of Sodomy, and Othello," *ELH* 66 (2) (1999), pp. 261–76, and as mentioned earlier in reference to psychoanalysis, John Bernard's "Theatricality and Textuality: The Example of Othello," *New Literary History* 26 (4) (March 1995), p. 931. The latter points to the relevance of popular theatre as a site to work through and display dominant ideologies. In our current historical moment, Kaaya's *O* serves this purpose for a demographic that is likely not as familiar with Shakespeare's text.

20 I refer here to remarks Harold Bloom made in response to Masterpiece Theatre's British version of *Othello* and Kaaya's *O* on the *National Public Radio Show* (March 2 2002). See also Harold Bloom ed., *William Shakespeare: The Tragedies* (New York: Chelsea House Publishers, 1985); Jeanne Hoffa, "'O' No, Another Shakespeare Remake," *Daily Forty Niner* (September 4 2001).

21 James Welsh, "Classic Demolition: Why Shakespeare is Not Exactly Our Contemporary, or Dude, Where's My Hankie?" *Literature and Film Quarterly* 30 (3), p. 223.

22 Film criticisms that questioned the gullibility of the postmodern Othello character in O include Cynthia Fusch, "Transgressions," Popmatters website, www.popmatters.com/film/reviews/o/o.html; and Amy Taubin, "Character Flaws," *Village Voice* (September 4 2004), p. 115.

23 Roger Ebert, "Green-eyed Monster: Jealousy Undoes a Hoops star in an Updated *Othello,*" *Chicago Sun Times* (August 31 2001), p. 29.

24 Lily B. Campbell, "Many Faceted Jealousy Leads to Tragedy," *Readings on Othello* (San Diego, CA: Greenhaven Press, 2000), p. 122.

25 Proposition 209 aimed to end affirmative action at the University of California. Proposition 187 attempted to limit the rights and benefits of undocumented workers that do not have legal citizenship. Proposition 22 intended to make same-sex marriage illegal. Although these are all California initiatives, similar pending or passed legislation exists in other US states, for example the Michigan brief filed by George W. Bush. The Patriot Act (HR Bill 3162) was introduced after the 9/11 terrorist attacks on the USA. The language of the document proclaims to "deter and punish terrorist acts in the United States and around the world," and "to enhance law enforcement investigatory tools" via increased access to the areas of citizen life that had been previously deemed as protected and private under the law.

26 Cameron McCarthy, "Living with Anxiety: Race and the Renarration of Public Life," Joe L. Kincheloe [*et al.*], *White Reign: Deploying Whiteness in America* (New York: St. Martins Griffin, 1998), p. 333.

27 Bourdieu, "The Essence of Neo-liberalism."

28 See Tim Blake Nelson's interview on the special edition DVD, "*O.*"

29 John Whitney and Tina Packer, "The Trusted Lieutenant," *Power Plays: Shakespeare's Lessons in Leadership and Management* (New York: Simon and Schuster, 2000), pp. 83–7.

30 John Dover Wilson and Alice Walker eds, *Othello* (New York: Cambridge University Press, 1971), pp. xi–xiii.

Chapter 13

Romeo Must Die[1]

Interracial romance in action

Gina Marchetti

Perhaps Aaliyah kissing or having a nipple in Li's mouth would have disturbed a number of black penises. Perhaps these would be the same brothers we see sporting a fetish for Asian women in current hip-hop videos. Perhaps Aaliyah and Jet embracing would have disturbed Asians, blacks, and whites.

Latasha Natasha Diggs, "The Black Asianphile"[2]

. . . insofar as Asians and Africans share a subordinate position to the master class, yellow is a shade of black, and black, a shade of yellow.

Gary Okihiro, *Margins and Mainstreams*[3]

Blending action, music, and romance, *Romeo Must Die* should fit neatly into the Hollywood commercial mold. However, as Latasha Natasha Diggs points out, the pairing of Chinese action star Jet Li with African American chanteuse Aaliyah disrupted the way "visual pleasure" normally operates along the axis of race and sex in American cinema. The genesis of the project, however, does not seem to be atypical of current Hollywood feature filmmaking. Polish-born director Andrzej Bartkowiak worked as a cinematographer in Hollywood before his directorial debut with *Romeo Must Die* in 2000. Specializing in action, his credits as a cinematographer include *Twins* (1988), *Speed* (1994), and *Lethal Weapon IV* (1998).[4] Since he worked with Chinese martial arts star Jet Li in *Lethal Weapon IV*, it is not surprising that Bartkowiak would choose Li to star in *Romeo Must Die*. The same year as *Lethal Weapon IV* made its appearance, the Disney action cartoon *Mulan* (1998) paired a Chinese woman (voiced by Asian American Ming-Na Wen) with a red dragon, Mushu, whose voice was performed by African American comedian Eddie Murphy.[5] Again, in 1998, the pairing of Hong Kong star Jackie Chan with African American comedian Chris Tucker in *Rush Hour* proved to be enormously successful at the box office. In fact, Bartkowiak was following a Hollywood trend when he conceived of a film featuring an Asian/African American pairing, which could comically foreground cross-cultural misunderstandings and appeal to a multiracial, multi-ethnic, global audience for action.[6] What is surprising is the fact that the "buddy" formula made popular by the meeting of "the fastest hands in the

East" and the "biggest mouth in the West" in *Rush Hour* gives way to an inchoate romance between Han Sing (Jet Li) and Trish O'Day (Aaliyah, who tragically died in a plane crash after making the film).[7]

Although action and romance occasionally mix in action plots (particularly in the action-adventure genre) and "Romeo and Juliet" stories are a staple of Hollywood fiction, the pairing of a Chinese man and an African American woman in a mainstream commercial film challenges many deeply held prejudices about Asian masculinity, African American femininity, and the racial politics of romance in Hollywood. Within America's racial hierarchy, fascination mixes with suspicion, and fantasies of racial conflict as well as multicultural harmony fuel *Romeo Must Die*. Although computer graphics, rap music, and martial artistry may eclipse the relationship between Han Sing and Trish, the appearance of lovers who find themselves on either side of a criminal as well as racial divide merits serious attention in order to better understand the way in which representations of race and sexuality continue to evolve in Hollywood.

Genre politics: blaxploitation, kung fu, and transnational action

Although rare, African American/Asian romances do appear in American cinema. Mira Nair's *Mississippi Masala* (1991), for example, revolves around a romance between an African-born South Asian, Mina (Sarita Choudhury), and African American Demetrius (Denzel Washington). Another feature Timothy A. Chey's *Fakin' Da Funk* (1997) includes an Asian/African American romance between Julian Lee (Dante Basco), an Asian raised by African American parents, and a young upper-middle-class black woman who has difficulty coming to terms with her racially Asian and culturally black boyfriend. Chi Moui Lo's *Catfish in Black Bean Sauce* (1999) romantically pairs Dwayne (Asian American Chi Moui Lo) with African American Nina (Sanaa Lathan) in a feature about the reunion of Vietnamese refugees, raised by an African American family, with their birthmother.[8] However, the focus in all three of these films is on romance; whereas, *Romeo Must Die* highlights martial arts and music through the casting of its two stars, Jet Li and Aaliyah.

In many respects, casting defines this film and its anticipated market quite clearly. Jet Li brings in Asian martial arts aficionados, and Aaliyah draws in rhythm and blues fans. DMX, who plays club owner Silk, brings stellar rap credentials to the project.[9] Anthony Anderson, who plays Maurice, has been an African American television comedy fixture since the mid-1990s. Russell Wong, playing Kai, brings a certain global cult following into this mix with his ties to syndicated television in *Vanishing Son* (1994) and his occasional film appearances in Hong Kong (where his brother Michael is a very popular star).[10] Francoise Yip, another biracial North American performer, also brings in a certain Hong Kong cachet in her cameo as the unnamed motorcyclist Jet Li/ Han Sing has difficulty hitting because she's a "girl." Although her role is minor, she does bring a recognizable face from another martial arts film in which Canada stood in for the United States, the Jackie Chan vehicle *Rumble in the Bronx* (1995).

Even in the casting of minor and supporting roles, *Romeo Must Die* presents a package that promises a certain quality to music and martial arts fans. In addition, the film features notable actors from both sides of the Pacific – Isaiah Washington as Mac (*Get on the Bus, Bulworth, Clockers, Crooklyn*), British-born Delroy Lindo as Trish's father, Isaak O'Day (*The Cider House Rules, Clockers, Crooklyn, Malcolm X, Get Shorty*), and Henry O as Han's father, Chu Sing (who had supporting roles in *Snow Falling on Cedars, Red Corner,* and *The Last Emperor*). Behind the camera, Joel Silver, the producer, was still on a roll from *The Matrix* (1999) the year before, and Corey Yuen (himself a star performer) was brought in from Hong Kong to work on the fight choreography.

The combination of African American comedy, drama, and musical talent (Aaliyah, DMX, Anthony Anderson, Isaiah Washington, and Delroy Lindo) with Hong Kong/transnational Chinese star power (Jet Li, Russell Wong) revives the links between late 1960s and 1970s blaxploitation and kung fu films.[11] Although the trend reached its apogee with films like Jim Kelly's *Black Belt Jones* (1974) and Tamara Dobson's *Cleopatra Jones* (1973), the possibility of moving beyond the African American and global Chinese market into the more profitable American multiplex mainstream continues to be attractive. Taking a page from Quentin Tarantino's "book," Andrzej Bartkowiak develops a conversation with these genres from the 1970s, drawing from the past to update the definition of "cool" at the millennium. While African American fascination with Asian martial arts films has a history dating back several decades and white audiences (particularly young, male, working-class viewers) enjoy martial arts action as part of Bruce Lee's transnational legacy, the importance of African American culture in Asia and among Asian Americans should also be taken into account. Eric Koyanagi's *Hundred Percent* (1998) features a black-identified Asian American character, and Renee Tajima-Pena's *My America . . . Or Honk if you Love Buddha* (1997) includes a segment on the "Seoul Brothers," two Korean American rap singing brothers. Enamored of hip-hop style, Japanese youth use blackface as a form of subcultural expression, and African American music plays on MTV across Asia.

The first scene announces this updating of black/Asian cool by citing a common generic past. A montage of Chinese characters, credit titles, neon signs, cars, guns, rap music and the streets of the Bay Area melts into a disco scene featuring open sexuality, black music, and dance. Russell Wong as Kai arrives strikingly dressed in a red shirt, black leather jacket, and sunglasses (worn at night as a definition of "cool" since the earliest days of blues music). Kai faces off against three African American assailants who each conjure up a different era in black popular culture – one has dreadlocks (Reggae/Rasta), one an Afro "natural" (Black Power), and one a pomade ("Superfly"). All of blaxploitaton is summed up in a single kung fu bar fight.

The entire film revolves around the meeting of African American and Chinese popular culture. Aaliyah carries with her the legacy of Pam Grier and Tamara Dobson, while Jet Li stands in for Bruce Lee, Wang Yu, David Chiang, and Ti Lung. Aaliyah also represents a tradition of R and B, rap, and house music's sampling of kung fu culture in its lyrics from Carl Douglas' "Kung Fu Fighting," which Jackie Chan revived to help market *Rumble in the Bronx* in North America, to the hits of the Wu Tang Clan. *Berry Gordy's The Last Dragon* (1985) also brought black music, kung fu, and blaxploitation together. However, kung fu, blaxploitation, and hip hop do not coexist without discord. Following the cross-racial violence in South Central Los Angeles in the wake of the acquittal of the police who beat Rodney King captured on video in 1992, Ice Cube's "Black Korea," from his 1991 rap album *Death Certificate*, proved to be prophetic in articulating tensions between the Asian and African American communities. Although common ground exists, popular culture also provides a platform for conflict.

Although *Rumble in the Bronx* features a comic romance and kiss between an African American woman and a Chinese man, the interracial kiss seems to have separated the genres of blaxploitation and kung fu for decades. In *Romeo Must Die*, the plot throws Trish and Han together and the orchestration of the spectacle calls for physical contact; however, generic conventions pull Trish and Han apart. Neither blaxploitation nor kung fu promises romance, even tragic romance, and *Romeo Must Die* does little to defy the conventions at the heart of each genre where revenge, male bonding, and individual heroism supersede heterosexual love, romance, and marriage.

The plot (rather than the visual spectacle) of *Romeo Must Die* does, however, bring the couple, and, symbolically, African Americans and Asians, the closest to fulfilling the romantic promise of the film's title. In fact, the structure of the film provides a symmetrical organization that places Trish and Han in comparable positions within the narrative. Isaak O'Day and Chu Sing head the feuding African American and Chinese crime families. Mac and Kai serve as their presumably loyal lieutenants. Prodigal sons, Po Sing (Jon Kit Lee) and Colin (D.B. Woodside), who die in the gang war, try to prove their worth under the shadow of their powerful fathers. The patriarchs O'Day and Sing both have dealings with young, white, white-collar criminal, Vincent Roth (Edoardo Bellerini), who promises legitimacy and hefty profits in a real estate deal involving the NFL and the building of a waterfront stadium. Mac and Kai do the dirty work of killing off members of their own communities in order to pave the way for O'Day's/Sing's dream of being a black/Asian "Donald Trump."

After Po's death, O'Day fears he will be the target of Chu Sing's wrath, so he places protection around his daughter Trish in the person of Maurice, who serves primarily as comic relief. Hearing of his brother's death, Han escapes from a Hong Kong prison and makes his way to the Bay Area for revenge. Trish, the potential object of vengeance, and Han, the avenger, meet coincidentally and form a bond. An important part of the plot, then, revolves around the O'Day clan protecting Trish from Han, the representative of the Sing family, and the couple, as in Shakespeare's *Romeo and Juliet*, serves as the focal point of the drama.

As the events unravel, it seems that Po and Colin had an agreement to move in on their fathers' deal. Mac and Kai also planned to turn against their mentors. Not only are they responsible for killing their allies in order to get the real estate deeds that they need for Roth, they are also guilty of killing their bosses' sons. However, the symmetry ends when Mac wounds O'Day, who seems not to have known about the murders, while Chu Sing is revealed to be the mastermind behind the mass slayings of the other Chinese gangster families.

The two patriarchs also seem to come to different conclusions about their children's romance. Whereas Chu Sing refers to Trish as a distraction, Isaak O'Day seems to become fond of the "little guy" with a firm handshake as he lies wounded after Mac's attack. Since Han helped to destroy O'Day's enemy and save his daughter from danger, his softened attitude toward Han does not come as a surprise. Although far from an enthusiastic endorsement of the relationship, it would seem to pave the way for something more than the brief embrace and walk away from the camera with their arms behind each other's backs at the film's end.[12]

While the conventions of blaxploitation and kung fu would not require a kiss, the other narrative conventions structuring the film – namely, the musical and the Shakespearean screen drama – demand it. While gangster machinations and revenge shape the primary structure for the plot, the romance in the making between Han and Trish does receive a fair amount of narrative attention beyond the promise of the title. In fact, following Shakespeare's *Romeo and Juliet*, the film provides a "masked ball" in the form of Han, disguised as a hip hop fan, dancing with Trish at Silk's casino, a "balcony" scene in which Trish looks out her window fondly on Han as he escapes from her apartment after fighting with O'Day's gang, a romantic interlude in Trish's bedroom when Han enters from the balcony and must hide from his paramour's father behind the bedroom door, and, of course, plenty of fights, comic interludes, coincidences, and reversals similar to elements in Shakespeare's play. However, in exchange for a "happy ending" in which neither principal dies, the film denies the couple a kiss.

Where for art thou, Romeo? Why no kiss?

At first, the racial politics of the film industry seems to explain the lack of a kiss. The taboo against interracial sexuality runs deep, and, particularly when stars are involved, can be strictly enforced. As Diggs notes in "The Black Asianphile," the embrace may disturb whites, blacks, and Asians. However, since romances involving Asian women with white (and, occasionally, black men), and, to a lesser degree, Asian men with white women have been part of

Hollywood cinema since the silent era, it appears that something beyond generic conventions and Hollywood taboos may be operating against Trish and Han's kiss.

As in *China Girl* (1987) and many other Hollywood screen romances, the "Romeo and Juliet" story has been used to look at interracial romance – entertaining fantasies of miscegenation with the promise that death will put an end to the illicit liaison.[13] Generally, these romances point to problems within both racial groups. Typically, the nonwhite community is depicted as cruel to its women, "uncivilized," and "barbaric," while the white community appears as prejudiced, closed, and racist. The film may call for interracial understanding, but, as in Shakespeare's play, the illicit union exacts its price – usually death. As in many Hollywood "Romeo and Juliet" interracial romances, *Romeo Must Die* provides many reasons for the couple to be alienated from their families/ethnic communities.

No suitable romantic partners appear from within the community for either Trish or Han. For example, Trish's African American suitors are either comic like Maurice or dangerous like Mac. Han has even fewer alternatives in the narrative, since his only physical exchange with an Asian woman occurs during a fight. Trish and Han survive the threats from their respective communities, but they take no step to consummate their romance.

Star power may, in fact, tear Trish and Han apart, since either Aaliyah or Jet Li may have felt the kiss would hurt a tenuous Hollywood film career. Since neither was an established American screen star (the film marks Aaliyah's first feature film appearance), but both had fan bases outside of Hollywood, perhaps neither wanted to take a chance on alienating fans who might object to the romance. Within the film, Maurice and Mac both deride Trish for her interest in an Asian man; they find the hint of romance unbelievable. Again, as Diggs notes, this may involve a certain possessive sexism within the African American community, since she insinuates a relationship between a black man and Asian woman would not be treated the same way. Moreover, Sing cannot take his son's interest in Trish seriously and dismisses it as a distraction. Thus, the larger communities within the film that parallel the film's audience of African Americans and global Asians find the romance difficult to believe or take seriously. The film does little to counter these characters' responses, and, instead, allows the romance to remain undeveloped.

Although the title could be read so that Po, Han's lusty brother (who does, indeed, die), becomes the "Romeo," this does not clarify the matter. Rather, the perplexing question remains as to why Jet Li was cast as "Romeo," but denied a kiss with "Juliet." Does this say more about Jet Li's fears of returning to Hong Kong or transnational Chinese productions after an on-screen kiss with an African American woman? Could Li, for example, have returned to China to be Zhang Yimou's titular *Hero* (2002) if he had kissed a black woman in a Hollywood film? Or, does it say more about Aaliyah's protection of her image as an African American star? Does the romantic joining of Asia and

Africa (a dream of unity against white racism envisioned by W.E.B. Du Bois in *Dark Princess*, 1928) provide too potent an image of rebellion against the white establishment for the mainstream audience?[14] A closer look at how the film presents Han and Trish's relationship within the narrative as well as in moments of spectacle involving fighting and dance may shed some light on the ways in which *Romeo Must Die* draws Han/Jet Li and Trish/Aaliyah together only to erect an impregnable wall between them.

What's in a name? What's in a story? White visions of black/Asian relations

While unusual for Hollywood, the type of unfulfilled romance of opposites that characterizes Han and Trish's relationship has been a key part of Jet Li's career in Hong Kong and an important component of his star persona. In fact, Jet Li began his screen career as a monk in *Shaolin Temple* (1979), so being sexually unobtainable has been part of his star image from the start. As Wong Fei-Hung in the *Once Upon a Time in China* series (1991–7), Li finds himself in a very chaste relationship with his longtime paramour Auntie Yee (Rosamund Kwan).[15] As a Western educated "modern" woman, Auntie Yee provides a foil for the traditional Wong and also helps him deal with the dramatic changes taking place in China at the end of the Qing Dynasty. As an allegory for the momentous changes racking global China at the turn of a new millennium, the relationship between Wong and Yee also speaks to changing political, cultural, and social relations played out against sexual mores and gender roles still salient within the Chinese world. Miscommunication, crossed cultural signals, radically different value systems, and mixed loyalties typify the Wong/Yee relationship, and the same attributes characterize the relationship between Han and Trish as well. The mutual attraction between the characters propels the plot, but the historical, social, and cultural forces that the characters represent pull them apart.

However, *Romeo Must Die* does not take place in the world of late-Qing China in which the heirs of the Chinese knight-errant tradition remain shy in the presence of women and reluctant to engage in any indecorous displays of heterosexuality.[16] Rather, the opening scene of *Romeo Must Die* features a lesbian dance sequence in which two Asian women kiss on the lips before one exposes the other's breast and begins to suck her nipple. Po, Han's brother, lustily watches the display and passionately kisses his girlfriend. Thus, the film opens with an erotic spectacle in an African American disco-casino in which the blatant display of sexuality on the dance floor is meant to be a provocation. Po does, indeed, get "lynched" for his hubris, and he hangs from an electric pole in the next scene – alluding to the horrific tradition of public hangings for black men accused of public displays of lust for white women in the Jim Crow South. The sexual spectacle leads to punishment, but not before Po uses the salacious display to provoke and to showcase the power of his rebelliousness. While the errant brother openly flaunts his power through his sexuality, Han remains reserved, and the opening kisses do not find their parallel in a socially accepted heterosexual kiss between the principals at the film's "happy ending."

This is far from the world of Wong Fei-Hung, and *Romeo Must Die* is less a story about China's continuing conversation with the forces of globalization and modernity and more a Hollywood story of gangsters, ghettoes, and the woes of the American immigrant.[17] Directed by an emigré from Poland, the film presents a fantasy of ethnic/racial community divided by the temptations of white money and upward mobility. Both Chu and Isaak dream of leaving Chinatown and the black ghetto behind in order to transform their impoverished, racially stigmatized, ghetto real estate into the coveted cash cow of a major sports arena. Their blood and fictive crime families both crumble from the strain of reaching for the American dream.

Within this context, Han and Trish survive as remnants of the impossibility of an Asian/African connection in the corrupt corporate world represented by Roth. Although Trish owns and runs a prosperous boutique, the action fantasy maintains that access to American riches remains outside the reach of most nonwhite outsiders. As the "legitimate" individuals in their corrupt families, Han, the former policeman, and Trish, the businesswoman, seem to have quite a bit in common. Han, the refugee, and Trish, the daughter of a gangster, manage to build a life away from their families. For Han, Trish represents what he has lost in prison; i.e. a legitimate life away from the stigma of his Chinese (PRC) roots.

Going abroad to encounter African America brings him face to face with his own dilemma of loyalty to an ethnic family and a maligned racial community versus the American myth of the "self-made man" free from traditional obligations and archaic blood ties. From this perspective, like Wong Fei-Hung, Han provides a way of coming to grips with the fact of Chinese abroad – a fantasy that has meaning for both those within global China and those who routinely encounter the Chinese in diaspora. In many respects, Jet Li's star biography parallels his character's history. Born in the People's Republic, after establishing themselves in Hong Kong, Jet Li and Han end up in the United States. Jet Li, like Han, and like many others within the Chinese diaspora, leaves an Asia in which he may have a bleak or uncertain future in order to make his way in America. However, he does not enter the American mainstream or even the world of European immigrants; rather, he enters a multicultural mix in which he is positioned between the white and black communities and coolly received within the established world of Chinatown. On screen, Jet Li, paired with Aaliyah, finds himself on the margins as well. Not quite what he was in the mainland or Hong Kong, but not completely a part of either Asian America or African America. His star image only accommodates itself to the Hollywood screen with difficulty.

Like *Rush Hour*, much of the interaction between the Asian and African American stars revolves around the negotiation of cultural (and subcultural) "capital"[18] – knowledge of the rules of language, deportment, music, film, and popular culture. Han learns to be "American," specifically, a minority in

America, through his encounters with black culture, and this knowledge ensures his survival. Han is seduced by America, and America, for him, is not the corporate world of Roth, but the counter-cultural world of Trish – and her connection to a particular style of clothing, music, dance, and argot. She brings him into the world of the "yellow Negro" – and affirms that imprisoned Chinese former policemen can still be "hip" and know about hip-hop. White America remains closed, but black America promises a warmer welcome to the nonwhite immigrant – but only to a point. Racial antagonism between the two communities still forms a taken-for-granted part of the plot. As in many of the films about African American and Asian relations, *Romeo Must Die* does not play this up as drama, but as farce, in which both minority communities, ignorant of each other's cultures, become embroiled in a comedy of miscommunication and cross-cultural blunders that plays well to an audience (presumably primarily white) that may see itself as superior to both. When this comedy happens between two attractive stars with their own followings, the self-deprecating aspect of the humor can be mitigated by the power of celebrity.

Trish and Han meet in the "melting pot" of American multiculturalism. Getting into a cab to elude her bodyguard Maurice, Trish runs into Han, who has just stolen a taxi from a South Asian/Muslim driver named "Ahkbar" (Manoj Sood). Ahkbar, on break, had refused to take Han, saying, "Can't you understand English? Off duty." When Trish insists on a ride, Han, imitating Ahkbar, tries "off duty" as well. Trish responds by throwing a fifty-dollar bill onto the front seat. Although Trish quickly realizes she is not in a cab with the licensed driver, Ahkbar, she continues her banter with Han, whom she calls "Ahkbar." The exchange plays on stereotypical notions of Asian men. Clearly, Han cannot drive, and, when he says he learned to drive in Hong Kong, Trish immediately asks if he knows kung fu and can break a board over his head. He answers in the affirmative, "Of course, state law." Han asks if she is afraid of him. When she replies that she knows far more dangerous men, Han is smitten by the promise of a "dangerous" interracial encounter, and he watches her appreciatively when she exits the taxi.

Their mutual understanding as a couple begins with a common misunderstanding of their respective cultures – from assumptions about Chinese kung fu to the "dangerous" eroticism of black women. Han and Trish also fail to recognize their respective positions within the plot, since they only realize that their brothers knew each other much later in the film. Trish does not give her name, and "Ahkbar" remains Han's only moniker at this point in the film. The Muslim name mediates and serves as a signifier of their tacit agreement to misunderstand each other. Within the American "melting pot," unbridgeable gulfs remain within the multicultural mix, and any romance or union among minority groups remains unquestioningly unattainable. A white norm and racial hierarchy maintain absolute divisions and argue against common interests outside white America. Although racial difference throws them together, white definitions of America keep them from mutual understanding.

In the moments of spectacle that erupt throughout the rest of the film,

Trish/Aaliyah acts as the catalyst for Han/Li to misconstrue American culture, primarily African American culture, for his own ends. The scenes play as comedy. Han mangles modes of behavior, mishandles situations, and misreads cultural cues, but manages to keep Trish's interest. For example, Trish's exchange with Han in the taxi sets up the first fight scene with Han that Trish witnesses. As he demonstrates in the taxi, Han has a certain familiarity with Western stereotypes of Chinese men, and he is adept at using these stereotypical notions for his own ends. Like Bruce Lee in *The Chinese Connection* (1972), Brandon Lee in *Rapid Fire* (1992), and scores of other Chinese martial arts stars, Jet Li takes on the persona of a working class Chinese as a disguise to evade non-Chinese. In this case, Han becomes Trish's "delivery boy" when Maurice and the O'Day gang turn up at her apartment. When the disguise fails to work because Maurice cannot smell the food, a comic battle ensues. Like Trish, Maurice articulates his skewed version of Chinese culture by calling Han "dim sum," adopting a *Karate Kid* (1984) version of the kung fu crane stance, and getting kicked in the groin as a result. While Han can use his belt as a flexible weapon, O'Day's thug simply drops his drawers when he tries to imitate him. Although Han may not break a board over his head, he does disarm his opponents and win an appreciative glance from Trish when he leaves. While the "delivery boy" serves as a mask, the "kung fu master" becomes the "authentic" embodiment of Chinese masculinity.[19]

From this perspective, Han operates as a racist fantasy of keeping black masculinity (i.e. sexual and athletic prowess) in check.[20] Throughout the film, Han wins Trish's respect and admiration by besting her father's African American minions. For example, O'Day's gang has a rematch with Han in the park. Trish has taken some kids to the park, and her father's gang has followed to play football. Taking advantage of Han's ignorance of American football, O'Day's men set him up for the fall, and the hefty Maurice tackles him first as the others pile on top. Han quickly learns to break the rules as he kicks and punches his way to win goals. His opponents fall in agony on the grass, and Han, triumphant, goes over to enjoy an ice cream with Trish.

Jackie Chan also used kung fu to gain the upper hand in a "soccer" game in *Dragon Lord* (a.k.a. *Young Master in Love*, 1982), and Stephen Chow used a soccer/kung fu combination as the premise for *Shaolin Soccer* (2001). However, the use of American football here resonates beyond the comic intersection of martial arts and Western styles of football in the action film. Rather, in this case, football serves not only as a comic reconfiguring of American culture to serve the needs of a Chinese immigrant, but also as the source of corruption in the film. The promise of the NFL stadium destroys the black and Chinese communities. Isaak dreams of bringing African Americans off the field and into the owners' box, but he ends up destroying icons of the black community – from the disco to the corner barbershop – on the way.

Another icon dear to American sports and symbolic of African American hopes for access to the American Dream – the basketball – also resonates with this scene. When Han enters his dead brother's apartment, he finds a deflated basketball.[21] In a flashback, the basketball serves as the brothers' lifeline as they swim from the People's Republic to Hong Kong. Although Yao Ming had not yet entered the NBA, the symbol of the American Dream for blacks becomes the conduit for the realization of the mainlanders' dream of success outside the People's Republic in *Romeo Must Die*. The basketball takes Po and Han to Hong Kong, and, eventually, leads them both across the Pacific to the "gold mountain" of California.[22] The deflated basketball provides an apt symbol for the Sing family's broken dreams. Han, an escapee from a Hong Kong prison, Po, hung in the street, and Chu, a suicide, represent the emptiness of the promise of escape, freedom, and fortune. In contrast, Roth and Isaak play golf – a game that signifies wealth and mainstream acceptance rather than a way out of China, Chinatown, or the African American ghetto. In fact, Isaak goes beyond escape to become a destructive force within his ethnic community. Golf, symbolically (Tiger Woods aside), takes him away from his ethnic roots.

In this respect, Han provides no alternative. He also represents a force of destruction within his own ethnic community. After the massacre at one of the Chinese-owned businesses associated with his family, Han and Trish engage in a chase with the murderers on motorcycles. Startled to find his motorcycle-riding opponent Chinese and female, Han cannot "fight a girl," and, instead, manipulates Trish's body to defeat the other woman. In this scene, the body of the black woman becomes the emblem of Han's division from the Chinese world and the medium of its destruction. A hug ends the scene. Han clings to Trish, who must save him from the corruption of his own clan. Similarly, Trish holds on to Han to rescue her from Mac and the mutiny within her father's African American gang.

While this fight may draw Trish effortlessly into the world of Chinese kung fu, the expectation is that Han will need to blend into the multicultural mix of America, and this may require more effort. When Trish and Han need to infiltrate Silk's casino, Trish must create a "disguise" for Han to make him "cool" enough to get past the club's bouncer. Trish turns Han's baseball cap around, pulls a lock of his hair over the sweatband, and says, "Now you're giving me something to work with – hip-hop." Han takes out a stick of gum, says he knows hip-hop, and pulls down his pants below his hips. Imitating black style, Han makes his way into the club, but still cannot seem to blend in. However, comic awkwardness gives way to flirtation. Trish encourages him to dance, and he begins to get the hang of things before O'Day's men step in to put a stop to the budding romance.

Han's final duel with Maurice again plays for comedy. After insisting that Trish could never be interested in Han romantically, the jealous Maurice, the O'Day gang, and Han fight. Stalking Han with a gun, Maurice, imitating the gang members from *The Warriors* (1979), calls, "Dim sum, come out and play." Using a fire hose to blast guns from their hands and whip them (in choreography similar to *Once Upon a Time in China*), Han finally gets the upper hand and dangles Maurice out a window by his tie before both drop on a car, and Han falls on top of Maurice. Han calls him "moron," and Maurice, defeated, replies, "It's Maurice, bitch." If Han's invective questions his African American opponent's intelligence, then Maurice counters by putting Han's masculinity into doubt. In fact, throughout the entire film, the cross-cultural banter does not move beyond racial stereotypes widely circulated within mainstream Anglo-American culture. Asians and African Americans remain sealed within their own cubicles of misunderstanding constructed by racist ideology.

At the film's climax, Trish and Han each exact revenge on their brothers' murderers. During a fight between Han and Mac, Trish arrives on the scene to blast Mac off the roof with a gun. Han, in turn, crushes Kai's vertebrae, after learning he had killed Po. However, as the police come in to clear up the mess, Trish and Han share little passion beyond a chaste embrace. Although their respective ethnic communities have been revealed to be corrupt and destroyed, the way has not been paved for a new world of interracial harmony and multi-cultural understanding. Rather, the "happy ending" remains somber, and the Hollywood fantasy of reconciliation and renewal remains muted.

Taking action in America

To return to Diggs, it seems Hollywood feels that its global audience cannot accept a kiss between an Asian man and an African American woman. However, that audience can tolerate racial invective, ethnic corruption, moral decay, and images of self-loathing and self-destruction. Trish and Han do not unite against mainstream white American, but, rather, against the African American and Chinese communities. They remain far from W.E.B. Du Bois' vision of the unity of African and Asian peoples against the forces of racism and colonialism.[23] While hip-hop and kung fu promise "cool" for the young audience for action around the world and across racial lines, *Romeo Must Die* kills off any hope for subversive pleasure by not sealing the film with a kiss.

Both Hong Kong and Hollywood maintain a distance from the African American community on which both rely for talent and consumer revenue. While Hong Kong and Hollywood draw on the energy of maligned and marginalized genres like kung fu and blaxploitation, they strike a balance between the raw anger of these genres and the more general appeal of the transnational action film. Furthermore, Hong Kong filmmakers have not let their forays in Hollywood overwhelm their careers in Asia. Directors and stars who have dipped their hands into the American melting pot – from Wayne Wang, Peter Chan, Tsui Hark, and John Woo to Chow Yun-Fat, Jackie Chan, and Jet Li – have all remained "flexible," and they continue to work on projects on both sides of the Pacific. Unlike the first "kung fu craze" that reached its apogee with Bruce Lee's *Enter the Dragon* (1972), the current influx of ethnic Chinese stars into the Hollywood action film occurs under very different circumstances.[24] However, while mainstream Hollywood may be more open to the possible profitability of Asian and African American stars and the complexion of Hollywood directors may also be gradually changing, the industry remains quite conservative – fantasies of dissent titillate, as they always have, but stay safely boxed in by a racial and sexual status quo that proves resistant to radical change.

Notes

1 I am grateful to Frances Gateward for kindly commenting on an earlier draft of this essay. I would also like to thank Daniel Bernardi for encouraging me to write on this topic.

2 Latasha Natasha Diggs, "The Black Asianphile," *Everything but the Burden: What White People Are Taking from Black Culture*, ed. Greg Tate (New York: Harlem Moon, Broadway Books, 2003), p. 200.

3 Gary Okihiro, *Margins and Mainstreams: Asians in American History and Culture* (Seattle, WA: University of Washington Press, 1994).

4 Information on credits taken from the Internet Movie Database, http://imdb.com.

5 See the discussion of *Mulan* in Sheng-Mei Ma, *The Deathly Embrace: Orientalism and Asian American Identity* (Minneapolis, MN: University of Minnesota Press, 2000).

6 See Gina Marchetti, "Jackie Chan and the Black Connection," *Keyframes: Popular Cinema and Cultural Studies*, eds Matthew Tinkcom and Amy Villarejo (London: Routledge, 2001), pp. 137–58.

7 For more on interracial "buddies," see Yvonne Tasker, *Spectacular Bodies: Gender, Genre and the Action Cinema* (New York: Routledge, 1993).

8 For further insight into both these films, see Frances Gateward, "Adopting Identities: *Catfish in Black Bean Sauce* and *Faking the Funk*," *Black-Asian Encounters* (conference, Boston University, Boston, MA, 12–14 April 2002).

9 For discussions of hip-hop and kung fu films, see Frances Gateward, "Wong Fei Hong in Da House: Hong Kong Martial Arts Films and Hip Hop Culture," paper presented at *Year 2000 and Beyond: History, Technology and Future of Transnational Chinese Film and TV – The Second International Conference on Chinese Cinema* (Hong Kong Baptist University, 20 April 2000); Cynthia Fuchs, "Slicin' Shit Like a Samurai: Hiphop, Martial Arts, and Marketing Styles," paper presented at the Society for Cinema Studies Conference (Chicago, IL, 10 March 2000); Grace Wang, "What's Asia Got to Do With It? Asian Sampling in Hip-Hop Culture," paper presented at the Association for Asian American Studies Conference (Tucson, AZ, May 2000).

10 See Gina Marchetti, "Race, Class, Gender, and Television Action: *Vanishing Son* and *Martial Law*, *Film International* 2 (2003), pp. 33–43.

11 For more on this relationship, see David Desser, "The Kung Fu Craze: Hong Kong Cinema's First American Reception," *The Cinema of Hong Kong: History, Arts, Identity*, Poshek Fu and David Desser, eds (New York: Cambridge University Press, 2000), pp. 19–43; also see Verina Glaessner, *Kung Fu: Cinema of Vengeance* (London: Lorrimer, 1974); for an exploration of African/Asian American relations and the kung fu film, see Vijay Prashad, "Bruce Lee and the Anti-Imperialism of Kung Fu: A Polycultural Adventure," *positions: east asia cultures critique* 11 (1) (Spring 2003), pp. 51–90; Vijay Prashad, *Everybody Was Kung Fu Fighting: Afro-Asian Connections and the Myth of Cultural Purity* (Boston, MA: Beacon, 2001); for an illuminating account of the African American encounter with the Asian martial arts, see Bill Brown, "Global Bodies/Postnationalities: Charles Johnson's Consumer Culture," *Representations* 58 (Spring 1997), pp. 24–48.

12 It should be noted, too, that other emigré Hong Kong actors have found themselves in similar passionless screen relationships with white women. The Chow Yun-Fat/Mira Sorvino vehicle *The Replacement Killers* (1998) is just one example.

13 See Gina Marchetti, *Romance and the "Yellow Peril": Race, Sex, and Discursive*

Strategies in Hollywood Fiction (Berkeley: University of California Press, 1993). Also, Gina Marchetti, "America's Asia: Hollywood's Construction, Deconstruction, and Reconstruction of the 'Orient,'" *Out of the Shadows: Asians in American Cinema*, ed. Roger Garcia (Milan: Edizioni Olivares, 2001), pp. 37–57. (Produced in conjunction with the 54th Locarno International Film Festival.)

14 Quite a bit has been written on the politics of African/Asian relations worldwide, specifically the politics of the African American and Asian American communities. See Gary Okihiro, *Margins and Mainstreams*; Frank H. Wu, *Yellow: Race in America beyond Black and White* (New York: Basic, 2002); Snow Philip, *The Star Raft: China's Encounter with Africa* (Ithaca, NY: Cornell University Press, 1988).

15 For analyses of this series, see Yang Ming-Yu, "China: Once Upon a Time/Hong Kong 1997 – A Critical Study of Contemporary Hong Kong Martial Arts Film," PhD dissertation (University of Maryland, College Park, 1995); Hector Rodriguez, "Hong Kong Popular Culture as an Interpretive Arena: The Huang Feihong Film Series," *Screen* 38:1 (Spring 1997), pp. 1–24; Tony Williams, "Under 'Western Eyes': The Personal Odyssey of Huang Fei-Hong in *Once Upon a Time in China*," *Cinema Journal* 40:1 (Fall 2000), pp. 3–24.

16 For an explication of the links between traditional Chinese culture and contemporary visions of masculinity in the action film, see Kam Louie, *Theorising Chinese Masculinity: Society and Gender in China* (London: Cambridge University Press, 2002).

17 For more on the ideology of the action film, see Gina Marchetti, "Action-Adventure as Ideology," *Cultural Politics in Contemporary America*, eds Ian Angus and Sut Jhally (New York: Routledge, Chapman and Hall, Inc., 1989), pp. 182–97.

18 For a definition of this term, see Sarah Thornton, *Club Cultures: Music, Media and Subcultural Capital* (Hanover, NH: Wesleyan University Press, 1996).

19 For more on Asian masculinity and American cinema, see Eugene Franklin Wong, *On Visual Media Racism: Asians in the American Motion Pictures* (New York: Arno Press, 1978); also, see Jachinson Chan, *Chinese American Masculinities: From Fu Manchu to Bruce Lee* (New York: Routledge, 2001); David L. Eng, *Racial Castration: Managing Masculinity in Asian America* (Durham, NC: Duke University Press, 2001); specifically on the transnational action hero and the martial arts film, see Yvonne Tasker, "Fists of Fury: Discourses of Race and Masculinity in the Martial Arts Cinema," *Race and the Subject of Masculinities*, eds Harry Stecopoulos and Michael Uebel (Durham, NC: Duke University Press, 1997), pp. 315–36.

20 For a broader discussion of Chinese/African American masculinity in Hollywood, see Gayle Wald, "Same Difference: Reading Racial Masculinity in Recent Hong Kong/Hollywood Hybrids," Society for Cinema Studies Conference (Chicago, IL, 10 March 2000).

21 For an insightful analysis of *Romeo Must Die* that begins with an analysis of this scene, see James Kim, "The Legend of the White-and-Yellow Black Man: Global Containment and Triangulated Racial Desire in *Romeo Must Die*," *Camera Obscura* 55 (2004), pp. 151–79.

22 It is interesting that *Romeo Must Die* is shot in the new "gold mountain" of British Columbia where Canadian laws favor immigrants with cash reserves. After 1989, Hong Kong emigration to Canada, Australia, New Zealand, as well as England, the United States, and elsewhere escalated, and the number of Asian Canadians appearing as extras in the film bears witness to the growing communities of Chinese in that country.

23 In addition to the novel *The Dark Princess*, see W.E.B. Du Bois, *The Souls of Black Folk*, eds Henry Louis Gates, Jr. and Terri Hume Oliver (New York: Norton, 1999).

24 See Aihwa Ong, *Flexible Citizenship: The Cultural Logics of Transnationality* (Durham, NC: Duke University Press, 1999).

Part V

Provocateurs

Chapter 14

The dark side of whiteness

Sweetback and John Dollard's idea of "the gains of the lower-class negroes"

Thomas Cripps

This essay is about an unintended impact that a legendary, even notorious, movie, Melvin Van Peebles's *Sweet Sweetback's Baadasssss Song* (1971), is said to have had on the cultural life of urban African American youth. This outcome derived not so much from the movie itself, but rather from the vast culture-producing machinery of America that turned its attention to defining and playing to a black urban culture inspired by the box office success of *Sweetback*. Its hero could either take the role of "bad nigger" who actively resisted the rigid, race-based "Jim Crow" social order, and expect to die young or, as a survival strategy, play to type as a carefree, lazy, sexually driven, often violent lowdown black man. *Sweetback*, as we shall see, chose to flee rather than suffer either fate. The result was ambiguous, as Van Peebles left the moviegoer with a last-frame promise of a vengeful sequel that never came. In the ensuing years, the rules changed a bit, opening closed doors, giving blacks unheard access to power and wealth formerly open to only, as an old black friend put it, "damn few white folks and no niggers."

My point here is that *Sweetback*, set as he was in dreary, defeated south central Los Angeles, was entitled to his choices, indeed as though he were in Mississippi in 1936. But afterward, in the age of the so-called blaxploitation movie and commercially driven hip-hop and rap music, there emerged a one-dimensional portrayal of African American culture that insisted on a sort of retreat to the ghetto, a surrender to the status quo, indeed a conservatism on the part of men − *Sweetback* is mainly about men − who had little to conserve. In such a setting, options that deferred gratification in favor of, say, education left a black kid open to the charge of traitor to his "roots."

Such a perplexed man was Carmelo Anthony, a high-school sports hero, who recently made news in Baltimore, not in his role as a star player for the Denver Nuggets of the National Basketball Association, but in a locally produced videotape, *Stop Snitching* (Sci-Bercellar, 2004), that purports to be a documentary about streetlife in the city, but has also been read as a threat to intimidate witnesses to killings (Baltimore averages one murder per day). Anthony is heard to say "I'd put some money on his motherfucking brains [place a price on his head?]." Not a rapist or murderer, nor even a mock-thuggish rapper,

Anthony was only a kid who happens to play the game of basketball better than anyone on the planet – ironically a white game, invented in a New England YMCA to fill a gym in the down-days of winter, a deliberate game that, without eventual black style and overawing skills, might have remained a fill-in sport between football and baseball seasons.

What was going on in this little melodrama of the streets? Anthony, it seemed to me, was caught between his two tribes – the mesmerotic world of white celebrity and his black tribe with its distinctive coded names, trappings, and argot, that he linked to his roots – a choice offered to few young black men. His was the rare opportunity to choose the romance of life in his old posse – if only as a carpetbagger and sojourner – and to show off his new life of unimagined gifts wealth and idolatry. As the gritty story of the film played out in the local press, the legislature in Annapolis proposed tougher laws against threatening witnesses, whereupon Anthony first denied the intent of the film then, prodded by his keepers, offered to atone for it by promising to campaign against drug use. "I just want to help," he is quoted. "The power of his image," said Congressman Elijah Cummings, "would have a positive impact."[1] But what next? He had achieved what historians have come to call "black agency" – the ability to vie for a piece of the "wages of whiteness." Yet could he have *both* – his new world of plush hotels, fawning women, and admiring white fans, as well as his posse from his old 'hood?

Anthony's "Hobson's choice" resonates in newspaper coverage of yet another black success story that demanded a hard choice between one's "roots" and a strange, welcoming new world. As compelling as Anthony's story, is that of Roland G. Fryer, Jr., a professor of economics at Harvard and currently a member of its distinguished Society of Fellows, because he is not only an exemplar of the black man with a choice but also a researcher into the nature of black success in entering white circles of achievement and power. Far from rejecting black culture, Fryer remains marinated in it – as he drives to a lecture "gig" (as he says), the rapper, 50 Cent, is on the radio. That is, success in a white arena means, to him, he "got game" in *two* worlds. Moreover, his options arose out of life itself: one part of his family drifted into a life of crime, cooking "crack" in the kitchen, doing time for violent acts, and dying young and abruptly, while Fryer picked his path through black Bethune-Cookman College, major universities, and thence to Harvard.

The crux of his research is a macrocosm of his own life, resulting, perhaps, in a "unified theory of black America" grounded in cultural choices controversially centered in the question of, as he says, "where blacks went wrong." Not so much blaming the victim, he merely argues for a new model black strategy based upon deliberately cultivated systems of reward for achievement. Sensing that black critics might see him as "acting white," he ran a study, "An Economic Analysis of 'Acting White,'" in which he measured the impact of hazing by low-achievers aimed at potential high-achievers.[2] To suggest that Fryer is onto something rests on a faith that American society is capable of responding favorably to black strategy and that the prospects for a change are optimal. So, soberly, we might profitably contrast his ideas with the despairing witness made by John Dollard during a sojourn in the South in the throes of the Great Depression. When scholarly inquiry into the near-foreign terrain of the American South had only just begun, Dollard, a young professor of psychology at Yale and eventually director of its respected Institute of Human Relations, spent five months in Indianola, in the Mississippi Delta, a Yankee "alone" and fearful that the locals might think him "a labor organizer or some-thing." The result was *Class and Caste in a Southern Town* (1937), an inquiry influenced by Lloyd Warner and other scholars of "the Chicago school," who viewed social class as hardened in time and place, indeed, as he wrote, "poised and timeless in the frieze of class of structure."[3]

A reader in more recent times might be startled by one perversely titled chapter – "Gains of the Lower-Class Negroes" – and its resonance in recent portrayals of African Americans in movies, beginning with Van Peebles's angry, picaresque black man on the bottom rung, *Sweetback*. Dollard wrote that the black man on the bottom in Mississippi enjoyed a white tolerance for his seeming genetically driven petty thievery, hyper-sexuality, and invincible lazi-ness a sort of balm for the pains of racial segregation.

Sweetback, at first glance, rebelled against this narrow range of black choices. But his profoundly influential movie only stammered a last-reel promise of his return that left his fans with only a hoped-for second coming. Van Peebles bears little of the onus for this, except in the sense that his admirers (or copyists) in scores of movies ground out legions of often violent, erotic, crime-ridden epigones dubbed, by *Variety*, blaxploitation movies. What Van Peebles might wish to accept credit for is that such movies served both as stark reportage of a city life that had been untouched by the Civil Rights Movement and a sort of collective saga of the black struggle against intractable oppression. Still later, the music industry would reprise the imagery in hundreds of hip-hop and rap videotapes cablecast on BET and other outlets – minus the politics.

But Hollywood was not Mississippi. Struggle happens. Things *do* change. And so must old obsolescent strategies. Here I am thinking back to the "gains" meagerly granted to Dollard's "low-class Negro" of Indianola. In 1936 allow-ing black men to loaf, steal (most stereotypically, chickens), and to prey on women (as a sole assertion of manhood) acted as a sort of wage that bought silence which, if refused, might end a black life in a lynching. That is, however hateful and demeaning, it was a strategy of "the man lowest down." But late-twentieth-century racial arrangements were different at least in degree and, for many, even substantively so.

Also in 1936, this lowest-down black man not only played his role but turned his envy on a privileged class: not white men who invented *caste* and invested it with such damnable meanings, but on black strivers, an elite *class* within their caste – a "talented tenth," W.E.B. DuBois called them; a "black bourgeoisie," in E. Franklin Frazier's wry coinage – whose "cultural script" emulated the larger white society in a dark parallel world. This thin elite of the churched, the affiliated, the employed – the women who did white people's chores and the men who held steady jobs as unskilled laborers in lumberyards, or prestigious jobs such as Pullman porters, waiters or, more rarely, preachers and teachers – clung to "respectability," their lives of quiet striving in home or church or fraternal orders often passing unnoticed in the daily press, while the black "riffraff" often offended them with its violence and criminality. In effect, they enjoyed a shadow-show of what white men enjoyed: a life conferred upon them as a reward for striving, though never the full "gift of whiteness" awarded by European skin.[4]

This meager share, bargained from a position of weakness, *also* came as a sop for accommodating to oppression. They perforce accepted a genteel "making do" as a way of life – a *bricolage* in Claude Lévi-Strauss's usage. An old, now deceased friend told me such tales of his father, a lumberyard sweeper, and his mother, a seamstress, who, together with their two sons, lived in an "alley house" in black Baltimore, yet set a table with silver napkin rings and ate pigeon (which they called "squab") on Sundays after church (where his father was choirmaster). An African Methodist Episcopal bishop lived across their alley.

Advice on how to cling to this shaky ladder of status was rife: black mothers taught their children a bourgeois ("white," its critics said) decorum; Booker T. Washington urged his own Tuskegee community (and the black nation at large) to shop in midweek when the town squares might be free of men who insulted decent women and gave the race a bad name; the black press offered exemplars on its "society" pages; and when the National Association for the Advancement of Colored People (NAACP) protested the movies' slurred speech, raucous laughter, and gambling, they tutored moviemakers in the ways of the "talented tenth." Two rival philosophers of black life, Washington and DuBois, opposed the white handouts of "gains," preferring instead "self-help," the former urging "working with the hands," the latter offering the "talented tenth" as a model.[5]

Dollard easily saw that this ladder of black striving was short and shaky for a reason – that "patterns" of inferior education were calculated to hobble black aspiration and thus compel a settling for small "gains." To strive higher – to act "uppity" – was to overreach one's "place" and risk worse. To illustrate, in an incident thirty years before Dollard's arrival in Indianola: the town's black post-mistress, Minnie Cox, and her husband, a sometime railroad mail clerk, together acquired property in Indianola, later opened the Delta Penny Savings Bank, and displayed other entrepreneurial skills, a black pattern of success which, in its "uppitiness," enraged a gubernatorial candidate who then taunted her white patrons for their "tolerating a negro wench as a postmaster," ulti-mately forcing her to resign. That is, black "gains" in a white game, rather than lowdown black criminality, set off white retaliation.[6]

The "gains" of Dollard's "lower-class Negro," poorer and ridden with indignities, came with a white paternalism that expected in return only an unctuous etiquette – "uncle tomming." As Dollard heard with "haunting insistency, 'The Negroes have all the best of it down here.'" Yet the gifts of loafing in the slow cadence of "colored people's time," sexual liberties, and petty thievery – "the weapons of the weak," as the anthropologist, James C. Scott, called them – were accompanied by, indeed caused, a simmering rage and displaced aggression that festered under local white law and custom, to be vented safely only on *colored* people. This perverse "gift of blackness" had its uses for the white South: such a social order shaped by a rigid racial etiquette not only lubricated the daily round but also served to validate the worst stereotypes of its racial ideology. A fair trade? Hardly. As the young DuBois in 1898 studied black life in Farmville, Virginia he *also* observed the "lazy, shiftless, [and] dissolute," but as marginal men idled by an industrialism that had no place for them.[7]

The point here is that for better or worse, black life possessed a complexity that black popular culture after *Sweetback* tended to discount, preferring the romance of streetfighters dashing themselves against white barricades as against a black bourgeois tale of working, like yeast, from within. But beginning with *Sweetback*, popular culture mostly celebrated, first in movies, then music, a post-civil rights, urban streetscape version of the Dollard's "gains of the lower-class Negroes," often in which a life of petty crime and loose women, salted with a few swipes at "the man," sufficed as a new black politics. Few critics reckoned Dollard's "gains" for what they were: an obligatory tactic to survive in the old South, nor saw that in a more recent racial political economy they had become fools' gold. That is to say, in Roland Fryer's calculus, if one is to assail the surviving walls of the American racial system, streetcraft must be augmented by new skills for a new game. He means not to lecture the man on the bottom rung, but only to study Hollywood's (and Tin Pan Alley's [if that is still a useful term]) misguiding of the alienated, disaffiliated, and almost calculatedly idled poor by exalting as culture-heroes figures from a distant past that no longer exists.

Like most cultures anchored in tradition, the white South portrayed itself as changelessly rooted in a benign, romantic narrative. Yet, far more than a regional myth, it slowly drifted northward like a ground-mist. At first, most white Americans knew the legends of the Old South mainly through the written word – the sentiments in Walter Hines Page's *Two Little Confederates* or John Esten Cooke's memoir, *The Wearing of the Gray*, or Joel Chandler Harris's *Uncle Remus* stories, or much later, in the year of Dollard's sojourn, Margaret Mitchell's fable of the New South, *Gone with the Wind* (1936). But in the years following the fiftieth anniversary of the Civil War (1910–1915), movies also weighed in the balance – indeed, dozens of them ranging from Edwin S. Porter's *Uncle Tom's Cabin* (1903) through D.W. Griffith's *His Trust* and *His Trust Fulfilled* (1911) to King Vidor's movie of Stark Young's novel, *So Red the Rose* (1936), but particularly the beau ideal, Griffith's rabidly Southern epic,

The Birth of a Nation (1915). In time, the Civil War grew into a white intersectional lovefeast, as though a triumph of Northern arms must be followed by a peacetime victory of Southern culture.

The movies' Southern bias derived from a confluence of forces: the need to please audiences, a fear of losing the "Southern box office," and the producers' own censor who kept a wary eye on "controversy." Together, these forces erected a broad national code of movie morals (and politics) – a menu of "do's and don'ts" that replaced a gaggle of state and local censor boards and reduced blacks to narrow "gains" of steady but merely incidental work as hoofers, singers, and servants save for occasional mavericks such as *Hallelujah* (1929), *Imitation of Life* (1933), and *The Green Pastures* (1936).[8]

Only with the onset of World War II with its propaganda as "the people's war" and its catchwords of "brotherhood, tolerance, equality" did a promised new racial order – a "Double V" (the term was the *Pittsburgh Courier*'s) over both foreign fascism and domestic racism – result in movie efforts to integrate African America into a national war effort. And at war's end, a booming documentary film movement and the studios' own run of "message movies" carried wartime integrationist sentiments into peacetime.[9]

The resulting trend opened a door into which Sidney Poitier stepped, fresh from bits of work in a "race movie," *Sepia Cinderella*; an army training film for chaplains, *From Whence Cometh My Help*; and a role in a black *Lysistrata*. Thereafter, almost single-handedly he extended the message movie era for a quarter of a century, and withal broadened its range. His movies sketched a formula for a generation, an endless pitching of the goal of admitting a worthy Negro to a lilywhite club. For Poitier and his millions of fans the films were, as Henry Luce described in the documentary fables in his *The March of Time* series, "lies told in the service of truth" – the growing truth that doors had, in fact, begun to open to blacks (the *Monthly Labor Bulletin*, May–June 1965, p. 502, reported a black "sizeable middle class").[10]

For much of its history the NAACP had urged Hollywood to accentuate the "positive image" and eliminate the "negative." Thus the movie moguls and their icon of black progress, Sidney Poitier, were thrown together with the NAACP in portraying the black struggle as a goal to be won through learning and preparation, a pattern that, despite its gradual successes, minimized, even excluded, the "brother on the block." The public rhetoric of the NAACP, then, implicitly accepted narrowly simplistic "positive roles" as the gold standard of racial politics, thereby freezing black performance in the mode of the "message movie" era and its extension, the age of Poitier. As Julian Bond, a central figure in both the Movement and the NAACP, appraised black movie politics *vis á vis Sweetback*'s genre: "Some of us want only the best depiction, that is the upright, the triumphant, law-abiding hero," rather than "films that didn't conform to what we thought our image ought to be." That is, they preferred a successful formula – Poitier's lone black image frozen in time, thereby closing off lower down life and its edgier roles.[11]

By then, the civil rights movement had spent its fervor and lost its leader, Martin Luther King, Malcolm X, and the two most public white allies of black activists, the Kennedys. In the midst of such public despair, "The Great Society" programs and civil rights acts of Lyndon Johnson's government seemed of little moment. Black hopes faded; familiar street tactics faltered; optimistic civil disobedience soured into civil disorder; cities emptied, their citizens fleeing to suburban cocoons. Worse, youthful opponents of the war in Vietnam filled the streets *and* the Movement's accustomed place on television, "the chosen instrument of the civil rights movement," as one newsman recalled the era.[12]

In the ruins of the movement, Dollard's "lower-class Negro" enjoyed a revival of fortune in a new role, not merely a village rakehell but the newly militant "bad nigger" who stared down the cops – "the occupying army," as the Black Panthers put it. Black East Palo Alto, California even seceded from America and became "Nairobi."[13]

At the same time the new urban demography provided a seedbed in which a new black cinema – Van Peebles's and *Sweetback*'s – thrived, its audience high on the rough politics of the street. The white "downtowns" of American cities, abandoned by their bourgeoisie, left behind derelict "picture palaces" – "rundown rialtos," said *Variety* – then neighborhood theatres, went dark, all victims of new multiscreen "complexes" in suburban malls. The palaces soon reopened to city kids in search of new cultural icons (Poitier and King both wore gray suits). Disinhibited by the absence of ushers (or adult moviegoers) their market achieved a *new* gain of blackness – a shared solidarity as disinherited moviegoers who talked back and vented tribal rage upon the action on the screen. Thus the "brother on the block" – the urban cousin of Dollard's Indianola "lower class" – was ready for his close-up. *Variety* broke the story in a trickle: in 1962, studios began "special previews" wherever black grosses were newly "important" (May 16, 1962, p. 70); by 1969 the paper ran a page-one banner, "Negro Teenagers Rampage" (January 1, 1969, p. 1); and soon the "Breen Office" censors gave in and allowed a laundered version of the portmanteau word, *motherfucker*, "our word," as a black colleague once portrayed it. Thus the tune Van Peebles wrote in *Sweetback* was waiting to be strummed.

Neither Van Peebles nor *Sweetback* created this new audience; but they rode with it, fed it fresh political nutrients, and recast it from an audience into a community. From the earliest days of silent film, the progressive critic, Mary Heaton Vorse, felt this in "picture show audiences" who responded to movies with ethnic (and noisy) voices as though, she wrote, in a "Tuscan hill town." Albert F. McLean, Jr, thought oldtime vaudeville houses also stirred a sense of "a community of city-dwellers" with shared "norms of taste and behavior." And the essayist, Harold Cruse, saw something akin to it in a 1926 projectionists' strike in Harlem's Lafayette Theatre – an action driven, he wrote, "by the impact of the developing American cultural apparatus on . . . the social development of the black community." Much later, also in black audiences,

Annette Powell Williams caught similar nuances of ethnicity, collectivity, and *gains*.[14]

Then, as though in agreement, two youth cultures, black and white, began to merge in the form of "rock 'n' roll," a music culture deeply indebted to African American sources but, more than any popular form since jazz in the 1920s, a vibrant "crossover." Driving this interracial movement were two genres of movies, apart from each other but sharing a common source in black musical performance, a sort of pop-cultural version of bebop, cool, and "modern" jazz. On the one hand was Louis Jordan and his white mimic, Louis Prima, both advocates of frenetic, sometimes comic, jazz style briefly known as "nut jazz." Jordan's "race movies," made for African American audiences, such as *Caledonia*; *Beware*; *Tall, Tan, and Terrific*; and *Reet, Petite, and Gone*, were energetic, rollicking films that turned on plots in which a social goal – in one, saving a Negro college from closure – was attained by means of the music. Crossovers followed in the manner of such "white" youth movies as Roger Corman's urgently transgressive AIP release, *Rock All Night* (1957); Fred Sears' *Rock Around the Clock* (1956); and Hal Kanter's and Elvis Presley's *Loving You* (1957), the latter of which marked the entry of the major studios into the swelling market. This hard-driving idiom, soon known as "rhythm and blues," became the sacral music of the urban young, black and white, who shared a common enmity against adult authority and a sense of outlaw "gain" in their ability to bully it.[15]

I felt some of this as a lingering resentment in years of cabdriving under the thumb of the police or being stiffed by fares richer than I was. So I knew the import of a story told me by Richard Brooks, director of *Rock Around the Clock* (1954), in which he blared Bill Haley's "Rock Around the Clock" on the set of *Blackboard Jungle* in order to heighten the sense of impending rebellion that the cast was meant to feel; it worked; yet when I saw the film in a throng of screaming youngsters I blanched: I had just signed my first teaching contract and these kids were howling for the heads of *teachers*! Later in the fabled Royal Theatre on black Baltimore's "Avenue," I saw James Brown and the Famous Flames also arouse a crowded house, sending rent-a-cops to the footlights to protect the wailing star from his fans. In the same era, while jammed into a throng of black and white protesters of a Ku Klux Klan rally in a public park, we spooked the police into marching upon us in a phalanx of jabbing nightsticks as though they were the Tsar's Cossacks against the Decembrists. We were the nascent audience for the *Sweetback* who had only just begun to slouch through Van Peebles's psyche waiting to be born.

Together, auteur and icon, like Rabbi Loew and his Golem in sixteenth-century Prague, entered the ghetto to smite the enemies of the race – to "take names and kick ass," as Van Peebles phrased it. Of equal parts urban mood and Van Peebles's outlaw shtik, steeped in a broth of lowdown black male street culture, *Sweetback* was to be a political animal who might challenge the Poitiers' heroic black "firsts" that mattered little to the man "deep down in the jungle."

If only he could fuse inchoate rage into the communal force that he, in fact, would dedicate his movie to – "the black community."[16]

In any event, in 1970, as Van Peebles drove – no, drifted – through the Mojave, mulling the nugget that became *Sweet Sweetback's Baadasssss Song*, he wandered back through memory to 1949 and one of Hollywood's first message movies on race in America. It was *Home of the Brave* – he had forgotten the title, but its simplistic solution to racism still nettled twenty years later – a white doctor in a white coat, ministering to, as though a medical missionary, an "Uncle Tommy" Negro soldier. Contrarily, he wanted a "big film," "a victorious film" that would free African Americans to "walk out standing tall." In a rush, he sketched a theme on a brown paper bag, then a scrawled back-story under the main titles – a fore-image of his hero, a black towel boy in a brothel, cozened into the crib of a black prostitute where his virginal performance throws her into wails of ecstasy (it is she who dubs him *Sweetback*). His hero must be a black man deep down in the Los Angeles basin, trapped and living off the same "gains" as Dollard's "lower-class Negroes" of 1936: a bit of petty crime, the empty romps of a sexual athlete, dressed in cool "threads" – and caught in a high wind between the fading mores of the Old South and those of a cold ghetto in Los Angeles. No "New Negro" here, no Poitier "coming to dinner," only a cool, vengeful hero who might just alter the rules of the game.[17]

Yet Van Peebles (and *Sweetback*) faced a dilemma. To "take names and kick ass" is merely getting even, not revolution. In his sketched back-story under the main titles he has *Sweetback* enjoy his "gains" as a performer in a brothel playing to leering, repressed white voyeurs – casual sex, an easy life, clothes, status – all under the paternal gaze of white cops. He rebels *only* when the cops violate the code by beating a prisoner, and even then is more a man on the run who will return for retribution – not "revolution."

He is Lenin in Zürich rather than Lenin in the Winter Palace, a fugitive rather than a revolutionary. Yet he can no longer enjoy the "gains" of a down-home black man loafing against a pole in the courthouse square, paring his nails, awaiting his main chance, perhaps a pliant young black woman or a hand of Three Card Monte or settling an old score in a jukejoint fight. He would have been a heller in Indianola – rogue, feckless rebel, refusing to play "white man's nigger," and surely dead at an early age – remembered along with other black legends such as Staggerlee, Leadbelly, and even the young Louis Armstrong. Perhaps, the black bourgeoisie behind its well-worn lace curtains might have taken heart from him and passed his legend to the young. But this is Los Angeles, not Indianola; the old movies, with their stock Uncle Toms, Stepin Fetchits, Bojangleses – and Sidney – will not serve. Who then, what new legend?

Already, Van Peebles had crafted a public self, an urbane variant of Dollard's subjects and their "gains," a "ghetto-gamin-prodigy," as he put it, wrapped in a trickster identity he called "Br'er Soul." Slim and fortyish, he readily looked the part of the "brother on the block" – trim "bomber" jacket, jeans, lowcut boots, a cigar stub – auteur and dude were as one. Enough so that taxicabs passed him by. Cool; impulsively abrupt in addressing powerful whites; with an edgy, jiving wit peppered with black rhetoric – "man," "groovy," "dig," "fuck" – a studied "rep" for "being mean" and living off "obliging ladies;" he was possessed by an unremitting drive to be "the first one to attack the citadel itself [Hollywood]." Yet, like all rebels, he remained a romantic with a history that included drifting to Mexico to "paint," living among "winos," feeling kinship with the "grass roots," and likening a stint as a San Francisco cablecar gripman to "the gondoliers of Venice." Yet, like an unspoken oath, he bore a resentment of the black bourgeoisie, so that part of his legend remained quietly blurred – his honors diploma from Ohio Wesleyan, his graduate studies in astronomy in the Netherlands, and such.[18]

Meanwhile, as he drifted toward *Sweetback*, black America stood ready for him; the civil rights strife in the 1960s burned out although not before its televised legend had created a rapt national audience. Meanwhile, the movies gingerly felt for their path to the future: Van Peebles himself had crept around the guards of the citadel and managed to make a black comedy at Columbia that began as a sight gag and ended as a dead serious insurrection; Sidney Poitier stepped up and with his friend, Robert Alan Aurthur, and made *The Lost Man* (1969), a black version of Carol Reed's movie of the Irish troubles, *Odd Man Out* (1947), in which the hero dies fighting against an oppressor; the football player, Jim Brown, had already made a half dozen action movies as a sort of muscular Poitier; and films like Shirley Clarke's *The Cool World* (1964), with its gritty, black-and-white portrayal of Harlem, had broken the barrier between documentary and commercial films. In Baltimore's revered Royal Theatre, a centerpiece "on the avenue" of black West Baltimore it played under a catchy title, *Cool World in Harlem*, drawing the crowd that anticipated not only Van Peebles but the coming "blaxploitation" era.[19]

So time and the man had arrived on the cusp of an eventual genre of black film with black heroes in familiar modes of behavior and dress, in a ghetto, and in dramatic conflict with the status quo. Such a black cinema, then, might become, as Peggy Harper has written of tribal art, "not mere entertainment" but "a significant part of the cohesion of its peoples." Not that Van Peebles would be pleased with the new genre. "Yes," he would say, *Sweetback* was a first, "but it really doesn't belong with the others," by which he meant the oldline studios' rush to be second in the race for black tickets with a lengthy cycle of movies laden with pimps, prostitutes, grifters, junk-dealers, and their enforcers.[20]

In any event, in 1971 *Sweet Sweetback's Baadasssss Song* went into release and at once became a half-told legend wrapped in the persona of its maker. The tales that clung to the making of every movie reminded the prospective moviegoer that it had been shot on the run, ahead of the cops, and outside of union rules, a genuine "guerrilla cinema" in the making, and one that would, "liberate third world people." As its tag line said "You bled my momma – you bled my poppa – but you won't bleed me." "Rated X by an all-white jury," said its wry dig at the Hollywood system. As promised, the main titles also hammered at the theme; the stars were "The Black Community" and "Br'er Soul."[21]

Yet the politics of both *Sweetback* and his auteur, with all their powers of African American rhetoric, had an unintended dual political outcome. On the one hand, *Sweetback* gave heart to the urban black disaffiliated, but on the other created an iconic figure, the "street blood 'gone bad,'" the black urban thug, Dollard's "lower-class Negro" moved to the big city, whose style, voice, and idiom acted as more of a *juju* in his own ghetto rather than against the caste enemy – white "downtown." With each new Hollywood film no more than "the same only different," *Sweetback* stood up, cleared his throat, and, it seemed, presented a radicalized black cinema. No more Poitier, he seemed to say, with his gray suit, white shirt, and sensible tie, tilting at windmills.

The tactic of such a self-conscious movie is similar to making the pilot for a hoped for long running television series in the manner of, say, Steven Bochto's *L.A. Law* or *Hill Street Blues*. The ensemble – the community – matters, indeed is the core of its being; the hero is Everyman, not a lone wolf. And so the role of the hero also holds the fate of community. Like Bochto's bumbling Columbo who prevails despite his shuffling manner, smelly cigar stub, and shabby raincoat, the collectively flawed stationhouse cadre in his *Hill Street Blues*, and the equally human law partners in *L.A. Law* – they are *Menschen* – humankind, ever "making do" with their plight. So *Sweetback* rises from low-class Negro with his "small time" – that is Van Peebles's term – "gains" to become a *Mensch*, a man of, but not greater than, the community.

As in the first scribblings, *Sweetback* is a towel boy in a bordello, shoveling in a poorboy's meal, then the cool star in the house's sex shows (attended by all-but-slavering white men) – shows protected, like black "gains" in Indianola, with the winking forbearance of white cops (the boss eying them, steers the show away from a white woman in the audience who rises to join in). All is smooth in the darkened squalor until the cops need a momentary fall guy – *Sweetback* – a fake suspect to run in as a sign of their working a case. Along the way to jail, they stop to pick up (and rough up) a street activist to whom *Sweetback* is handcuffed – "sorry, man," says one of the cops apologetically, as they go at their work, whereupon *Sweetback* intervenes, saves the kid from a licking and stirs a black crowd to torching their cruiser.

Here, in a departure from the theme asserted by the movie's populist ad-campaign, *Sweetback* goes underground and loses touch with the black community that turns inward, rebuffing him at every turn. Why does a "dead man" need money, they ask. Intensely colored, jangling, fleeting shots of *Sweetback* reveal empty omens – a red-washed sign says "Jesus Saves," but a preacher in modish buba and dashiki, who says the black community is dying of "an overdose of black misery," can offer only "a black 'Ave Maria.'" "Buy yourself a last supper; you're a dead man," says a gambler. A lone woman helps get his cuffs off, but only as a payoff for using his sexual artistry. He flees in the dry concrete bed of the Los Angeles river, southward past the oilfields with their birdlike pumps, pecking. Along the way he loses touch with African Americans entirely. Far into the desert he takes up with white bikers with whom he puts on a sex show, then, aided by Mexican migrants and living off moisture sucked from lizards, he eludes the police.

Gradually, it becomes clear: "the black community" that he has given billing are mainly extras on a location shoot. Even when a black biker in the desert hopes for the future, *Earth, Wind, and Fire* on the soundtrack are singing only "Come on feet, do your thing." So we have seen only a teaser of the revolution to come. "WATCH OUT," the final frame promises in boldface, "a baadasssss nigger is comin' back to collect some dues. . . ." So *Sweetback*, like Zapata's horse, the spirit of a Mexican populism, becomes a legend.

Where does that leave "the black community?" Waiting for its Godot who never comes? Its ship that does not come in? Its yellow brick road that dead-ends? The answer is not given in Mario Van Peebles's *Baadasssss* (2003), a Columbia Tristar and Sony DVD that finds the cruiser-burning scene "revolutionary" and his father an "in-your-face black power director." How to account for this disconnection? Van Peebles remained active in a vast field of various media. Perhaps the sheer burden of life as a polymath denied him the focus needed to return to the promised *Sweetback*. Or he knew that sequels rarely match the attainment of their parents. Or perhaps Hollywood took its revenge as it had done upon Orson Welles, another rebel who harbored a vision of a *personal* movie that was meant to define the future of film art.

Sweetback did creditably well among a range of critics. True, the *New York Times* man, Roger Greenspun, when it opened in midtown *and* at Loew's Victoria in Harlem (April 24, 1971), wrote that this "man on the lam, whatever he stands for, comes to look like nothing much," a point taken by the *Times'* Vincent Canby a month later (May 9) – "too simple," he wrote, "a slight pale escape drama." But speaking from a populist angle, the critic, Charles Peavy, heard "delighted exclamations" at *Sweetback*, the "badass cat," reckoned the movie, "answers a psychic need of black audiences," but agreed with black critics who knew that "nobody ever f***ked their way to freedom." Among black critics, Lerone Bennett, in glossy *Ebony*, predictably found him an illusionary loner lacking both theoretical base and organization, and thus the political rigor needed to take up "revolutionary questions." Worse, he saw *Sweetback* as if in Indianola in 1936 – a "sexy, violent, emotional . . . drinking, wenching lot, and a little thievish." Yet doctrinaire cultural nationalists in the Black Panther Party agreed with their founder, Huey Newton, that it was "the first truly black revolutionary film."[22]

Since there was no second coming, the endgame was left to a new generation. Van Peebles had led the assault on the citadel, and marked the path. It was left to others to raise the promised revolution, reject the old "gains of the lower-class Negroes" and press on to the *real* gains to be won. What emerged, sadly, was an often politically garbled black movie and music culture – this in an era that held greater promise than at any previous time since post–Civil War Reconstruction.

At the time, I agreed with Newton to a point, but as years passed, the absence of a *Sweetback Returns* rendered moot the prospects for an alternative politics of the urban poor. In popular culture, an unyielding ghetto game began to play out, even as Fryer's academic forebears sought new strategies linked to learning skills and competencies to alter how black kids played the game – strategies that challenged both the style of the game and its rules. This happened once, on the eve of *Sweetback*, when black neighborhoods in America's cities burned. Jesse Jackson, with the Head Start program already in place, charged black youth not to "burn, baby, burn" but to "learn, baby, learn;" in *Wattstax* (1973), an optimistic hymn to ghetto hopes drawn from a seven-hour daytime concert trimmed into a feature film calling for a "Watts Tax" – funds to rebuild the south central ghetto burned in the risings of the 1960s.

For a time, the first generation of blaxploitation movies that followed in the 1970s – Van Peebles's ideological spawn – took up the theme by fabricating urban heroes who at first lived the ghetto game and its lowdown "gains" of sex, indolence, and crime, then, as though the "before" image in a self-improvement ad, turned ghetto-style heroes against the enemies of the race. In this way, the code of the streets, coupled with a sort of conversion experience, acted to plead for future generations. Such movies would run to hundreds, often exalting the streetscape of the pimp or the dopedealer, each at first centering on some seeker after no more than a city version of old "the gains of the lower-class Negro," until maddened by some vile white miscreant who becomes a straw man to be vanquished by *The Mack*, *Shaft*, or *Superfly*. Formulaic? Sure. But as the historian, Mark Reid, points out "black popular audiences were starving for black heroes" (often merely martyrs in white movies). Besides, those shot on location, as *The Mack* was in the Black Panthers' Oakland, were made blacker when "that energy spilled over into the film," as the actor, Carol Speed, remembered. Black critics, as assembled by Ed Guerrero, in his *Framing Blackness*, vigorously debated their merits: Junius Griffin of west coast NAACP thought them nothing short of "cultural geno-cide;" the singer Curtis Mayfield stood up for them as reflectors of "conditions that exist;" as for the filmmakers, Gordon Parks, Jr, focused on a black "wish to be entertained," while *Superfly*, himself, Ron O'Neal dismissed attackers of the films as "handkerchief-head Negroes moralizing on the poor black man."[23] But by their sheer numbers, whatever the accuracy of their reportage, their melo-dramatic, visual imagery of the street let slip an elusive point: if in Indianola in 1936, the "gains of the lower-class Negro" were the *only* options, black movie-makers in the 1970s held sway enough that they might have taken Van Peebles where he said he wished to go. He showed by example that LA was not Indianola, that the "citadel" had been stormed, and that options had opened.

Van Peebles himself stood aloof, partly because some heroes were *cops*, newly cool black cops, but still *cops*, thus "counterrevolutionary." Yet the blax-ploitation film appeared as though with his imprimatur. His stamp was in their gritty streets, the cool duds, life set in a timeless, unrelieved squalor, redeemed in a last-reel assault on the heavies – almost always white people who broke their own rules – "the mob," dirty cops, oily politicos, priggish teachers (as though ending racism required only a few personnel changes). In fact, easy victory was a conservative flaw in some black film. Like Warner Bros' social dramas of the late Depression a lone crusader routs the heavies – a weak warden, a cop on the take – instead of the systemic flaws at the root of black despair. Yet, in the hands of a New York sensibility, as in Ossie Davis's film of Chester Himes's *Cotton Comes to Harlem* (1970, actually scooping *Sweetback*) this "black city cinema," as Paula Massood called it, offered a rounder portrait of the ghetto, "a complete world," as Davis himself said.[24] Far from failing their audiences, many served as morality plays in which blackness stood with uncommon grit against the grain of American racial culture.

Even when some were bloody awful, taken together they revealed a sleeping market and knocked on its door. They drew Jimmy Cliff's reggae movie, *The Harder They Fall* (1973) into the country; freed Michael Schultz to do his rousing *Carwash* (1976), and made it safe for the majors do classier and riskier material in the ensuing years: Charles Fuller's play that became *A Soldier's Story* (1981), Alice Walker's *The Color Purple* (1985), Toni Morrison's *Beloved* (1998), among many; daunting historical epics such as the mutiny of the *Amistad* and the saga of the all-black 54th Massachusetts volunteers; and daring independent pictures like Bill Gunn's *Ganja and Hess* (1973), Julie Dash's *Daughters of the Dust* (1991), and Haile Gerima's dreamlike *Sankofa* (1993). To dismiss blax-ploitation movies is to miss this freshened wind that freed movies from the narrow "gains" offered in prior decades.

This is not to say the day of jubilee had come for urban popular culture. There followed the most corrosive assault on black culture since the age of Dan Emmett's traveling minstrels, an era marked by the co-opting of African American street music, notably hip-hop and rap. I refer here not so much to music but to its dominance by a cabal of music oligopolies that peddled it as a mean, sensual thug-culture offered as the sole source of black authenticity and thus cultivated a permanent core of ghetto listeners. Its daily pitching of material excess – *bling bling* in the argot – and exotically modified motor cars, the scene garnished with thinly clad, slithery women, is offered as though a free lunch. This narrowly focused, workless setting insulted African American history by selling its youth market on a retreat to the "gains of the lower-class Negro," the slack lives and petty crime with which white men in Indianola stifled "their Negroes."

This is not a rap against a black musical idiom but rather, what has become of it. It had not always been this way. A quarter of a century ago (or more) I met the filmmaker, Warrington Hudlin, in a conference in the old Huntington Hartford building in Columbus Circle. We had met in passing, once at Yale when he was a student and I was shooting a film there for which he agreed to be a "talking head," and once when he asked about an aunt of his whose image

I had used in a book. It seemed we, at a long table, were being asked about the future of black film. Hudlin, between sessions, excitedly described the street-corner groups of black youngsters breakdancing, showing their stuff, and chanting what became "rap." They were everywhere in midtown doing their thing, for money or not. Boomboxes had only just happened and they carried the beat. I mentioned I had seen can-bangers for the first time in the subway stations – young men seated on cartons, rhythmically banging on the bottoms of huge pretzel cans, more in the idiom of tribal drummers rather than Philly Jo Jones. Wondering whether the breakers and bangers ever worked Lincoln Center, the shrine of Euro-music, on a break I walked to 64th and Broadway and there they were all vying for the rapt attention and admiration of an urban audience. It was like being in on the creation of something – minus, as an old movie title had it, the *Money, Women, and Guns.*

Flowing from this energy of the street came a musical politics, albeit briefly. The group, Public Enemy, in 1989 released its "Fight the Power" with its call to urban arms in Chuck D's angry lyric of the romantic guerrilla: "Our freedom of speech is freedom or death," they chant. "We got to fight the powers that be/Lemme hear you say/Fight the power." Then a chorus: "It's a start, a work of art/To revolutionize make a change nothin's strange." As Laura K. Worrell wrote on Salon.Com, the group and their rap "will hold a place in pop music's canon," not only because of its theme "at a crucial period in America's struggle" that was "confrontational in the way great rock has always been" and that touched "every kid in America" with its "uncompromising cultural critique." She credited the group's outrageously creative producer, Hank Shocklee, coupled with "the booming, preacherlike rhythm of rapper Chuck D's rich baritone" that gave it the mood of "a Black Panther revival meeting." A point taken by Spike Lee who used it as a thematic thread in his signature film *Do the Right Thing* (1989).[25]

But then, cut to the present as a clash of cultures simmered. The issue was sharply framed first by aggrieved black artists themselves, specifically in the book, *Fight the Power: Rap, Race and Reality* (New York: Delacorte Press, 1997), by Chuck D and Yusuf Jah, in which they argue that "the 1990s have been filled with Black men being systematically ripped down and overexposed in the media like we're the worst criminals on earth."[26] Theirs was the opening word in a debate as to whether or not to let pass unanswered the electronic, commercial portrayal of black youth as an idle, sex-charged thuggery – the metaphorical return to the cheap "gains" of Indianola 1936. Much later, in 2004, the square sector of black circles, most famously led by the comedian and survivor of the streets of South Philadelphia, Bill Cosby, Ph.D., and opposed, among others, by Professor Eric Dyson who sees Cosby as blaming the poor for their plight. Standing as a scholar, not so much between the camps, but researching the context, is Roland Fryer, who, on the one hand, studies ways to free the black young from the thrall of goalless behavior (which he blames not on music videos but poor strategy) and to replace it with the tools of black achievement, while on the other, he remains steeped in the same contemporary black music culture that Cosby excoriates as a self-damning barrier to black scholarship, discipline, and aspiration – the paths the music portrays as "acting white," "playing the game," or "selling out."

This was Cosby's point in his Constitution Hall speech that commemorated the 50th anniversary of the benchmark Brown vs. Topeka Board decision, which had been a long step toward an open society but, as he told his powerful, well-placed hearers, one that placed the onus for future failure on African American families. His ragging, barbed talk raised hackles not for what it said, but how and before whom. Kweisi Mfume, then the leader of the NAACP, had often quipped that "if you want to conceal something from a black person, hide it in a book" – but mostly *within* black circles.[27]

Most emblematic of the middle range of critics was the stance of Rev. Al Sharpton who has led a charmed life on the frontier between black hip and black square. Evasively, he feared "the artists" might "be the only ones to bear the brunt of what is going on," yet, in a comment on the rapper Li'l Kim, and her conviction for lying to a jury over a 2001 shootout between rival rappers, he asked for a dialogue "on the whole climate of violence in hip-hop" as a step toward dealing with "the broader problems in the industry and *broader solutions* [italics added]."[28]

Such voices resonated even in mainline comicstrips that took up Cosby's side of the debate. Aaron McGruder's *The Boondocks* pointedly took up the case: his two boys, both black-essentialist in racial politics, recently spoke of a "beef" between 50 Cent and The Game. "We gotta do something," says the younger; "Yes," says the older, "we can go to college so we don't end up like 50 Cent and The Game." Ray Billingsley's *Curtis* took a side in a parent–child skirmish over the issue – in which his father prevails. One day it began with, "Curtis, turn that rap junk down," referring to a rapper's "newest release since his *release*." In another, his father lectures Curtis: "The constant images of young black men as thugs, and young black women as promiscuous: it's more than a bit unsettling!"[29]

The beef here, *my* beef, I suppose, is an unintended outcome, like the epigones of *Sweetback* that Van Peebles thought counterrevolutionary. The range of such pre-political tastes has been, at bottom, a rebellion against the next rung up on the ladder, or, as the sociologist, Robert Merton, wrote, to seek an "alternate ladder of success." Perhaps the urge begins with the wish to assert a sort of anti-social tribal loyalty as a first break from one's square parents: for example, to wear penny loafers rather than office-style wingtips, or wear ballerina shoes (that did something sexy for your ankles) to school rather than only to ballet class, or, as in the case of the dozens of placid suburban high schools who named their teams "Rebels" and "Pirates,"[30] to take up the tribal argot of corner-culture, which, for black youth, meant mouthing endless variations on, as a black colleague once dubbed it, "our word" – *motherfucker*. The oldest black gangs had always led double lives, first as rebels against the square life, then as scufflers on the alternative ladder of success, the same one European immigrants found. As a Chicago Blackstone Ranger put it to an informant: "A black kid, see, he ain't got nothing choice to look up to. . . . You ask most black kids what they want to be and, like, they'll go and tell you: a pimp. . . . Because a pimp, man, that's the only impressive man they ever see out in the street. They see a man with a Cadillac car, who has expensive-looking threads . . . and they think to themselves, 'shit, that's the way of livin' right.'" Or, they settle for lower rung as Dan Rose found in Telemachus, a back alley mechanic and rough mentor to Philadelphia kids who lounged about, ragging, "signifying," and talking "play talk" ["the dozens?"] – the verbal exercises that helped young men to achieve a "cool."[31]

Often, when streetgang tribalism required codes of manner, dress, "colors," and tests of fealty to the group, life became lethal: "bloods" wearing a "wrong" color might end in a killing for the smallest affront; Pachucos in Los Angeles wearing the totemic "zoot suit" might end in Sleepy Lagoon; even shielded by white skin, folkloric hippies ("white Negroes," in Norman Mailer's term) might fall victim to a shootout with the National Guard. When rappers and hip-hoppers attain notoriety it is not only by their professional work in the recording studio but also as public persons acting out, often violently, even criminally, the old ways of the street, *but* with the certain knowledge that their costly lawyers will get them off. Thus, as Gilberto Freyre once said of his native Brazil, "money whitens;" or put in terms of "whiteness theory," rappers may act out old transgressive ways with impunity not open to "the brother on the block;" *beefing* on the bleak streets of East Baltimore leads to, rather than a new *Benz*, a life-damning criminal record. As Li'l Kim's attorney was quoted upon her conviction recently, "She thought she was above the law."[32]

Thus, the worlds of show business and professional sports have turned the privilege of "whiteness" on its ear. Rich black musicians and athletes had clawed their way out of the ghetto to live a posh life while purveying their former ghetto style as still eminently to be desired both to sojourn in – to go slumming in – and to teach their fans how to squander their lives in, thereby selling a mindlessly conservative hedonism as a ghetto politics. In so doing, not entirely consciously, whether in music or sport, they lived on the "wages of whiteness," only posing as allies of a black underclass, earning mock "street creds" by profitably styling, then dressing in, the costume of the alienated, adorned with "bling bling," flaunting self-absorbed excesses of drugs, alcohol, or sex, and building police blotter records that testified their fellowship with the ghetto. Taken together, these survivals of old ways authenticated the musicians and athletes while indulging them in the fantasy that they had not deserted the old "'hood." Never mind the unintended outcome that, as Cosby, Chuck D and Yusuf Jah argued, idealized a prototype of thuggery marked by its low slung, baggy pants, fingerpopping gestures, its lingo of the streets with its spewed out scatologies and its anti-womanist rhetoric of "hoes and bitches" – all so evocative of life in the ghetto as to serve as a prison wall that denied black kids access to any job or classroom "uptown." That is, the athletes and musicians "half create the environment [they were] half created by."[33]

Sometimes, they crossed over to a new audience in the square world, leaving the old 'hood to its lowdown fate. The crossover singer, Beyoncé, for example, appeared on the Academy Awards – the "Oscar" show – wearing no less than four gowns, each presumably, as they say, "original." The sometime rapper, P. Diddy, starred on Broadway as Walter Younger, the Poitier wannabe struggling to reach the suburbs in Lorraine Hansberry's prizewinning drama, *A Raisin in the Sun*, and was a presenter at the Oscars, turned out in an all-velvet frock-coated tuxedo from his own Sean John line. An older rapper, Ice Cube, has played in Hollywood movies, as have Ludakris, Snoop Dogg, and Ja Rule. All without surrendering the rough-edged style of the street.

This is where Carmelo Anthony found himself, caught in a high wind between the two cultures that defined him, each a badge of a kind of success. In the one, his youthful success in basketball allowed him to enter and be idolized by a privileged white world denied most African American males, while in the other, he clung to the raffish world of his old posse, whose "privileged" state extended only to the old "gains of the lower-class Negro." True, both are privileged. But only Anthony, by virtue of his passport *out* through basketball, presumed to make an infomercial advertising the harsh rules of the ghetto game – "stop snitching" – or *else*. In the end, he played the conservative role rather than "fight the power," as Public Enemy sang a quarter of a century ago. Thereby, he validated Cosby's charge and rendered Fryer's research all the more urgent.

To leave it to the athletes and musicians who play among the stars, returning to the ghetto only as though for spring break at Virginia Beach, is to narrow the choices of yet another generation and doom it to the low horizons of Dollard's Indianola in 1936. Not to act forthrightly is to lose all choice, as Finley Peter Dunne, a Chicago newspaperman in the midst of the *first* Republican hegemony in 1900, wrote of it in the Irish brogue of his mouthpiece, the bartender, "Mr Dooley." "'What's goin' to happen to th' naygur [Negro],'" asks a drinker. "'Well,' said Mr Dooley, 'he'll ayther have to go to th' north an' be a subjick race, or stay in th' south an' be an objick lesson. T'is a har-rd time he'll have anyhow.'"[34] We can do better.

I wrote this last, hopeful line in early April 2005. Then, on April 6, *The City Paper*, Baltimore's "alternative" press, ran a piece by Bret McCabe, a regular on the paper. Almost audibly sighing in despair over "the latest political theater" in hip-hop circles, a reconciliation of feuding rappers 50 Cent and The Game, which he saw as mainly a marketing dodge by a "culturally conservative" industry "cynical enough to reward getting shot as a career move and promote black on black violence, while white American businessmen make bank on the art and bodies of dead black men." I close instead with the rhetorical question often asked by a popular comic strip – "The pain, when will it end?"[35]

Notes

1 *Sun* (Baltimore), beginning December 4, 9, 28, 2004, and January 20, 25, 31, 2005 on the backlash in the Maryland legislature which struggled to change "witness intimidation" from a misdemeanor to a crime and on January 31, 2005, on Anthony's disavowing the tape and his offer to "help" in a campaign against drugs and violence, a gesture complicated, said David Nitkin in the *Sun*, February 1, 2005, by Anthony's other world, the NBA season. See also Associated Press story, www.baltimoresun.com, February 2, 2005; and *Baltimore* magazine, February 2005, 21 for a story on Anthony's commercial appeal.

2 I know Fryer's work from Stephen J. Dubner, "Toward a Unified Theory of Black America," *New York Times Magazine* (March 20, 2005), pp. 54–9. Fryer prefers group incentives because it avoids stigmatizing individual achievers. He saw both worlds: school years with his father in Texas, summers in Florida with his crack-dealing mother and where he only just missed a bust because he lingered at a dog track. In seeking a changed cultural strategy he even asks if naming kids "DeShawn and Imani" might alter the odds negatively.

3 *Caste and Class in a Southern Town* was published for the Institute for Human Relations by Yale University Press, and in England by Oxford University Press, in 1937. Recently Dollard's work has been reassessed in the light of current concepts and research – a task he disavowed being "up on" when his book was reprinted in 1957 – by, among others, William R. Ferris, in his "John Dollard: Caste and Class Revisited," *Southern Cultures*, 10, 2 (Summer 2004), pp. 7–18. Dollard's own work was immediately augmented by Hortense Powdermaker, *After Freedom: A Cultural Study in the Deep South* (New York: Viking Press, 1939); Allison Davis, Burleigh B. Gardner, and Mary R. Gardner, *Deep South: A Social Anthropological Study of Caste and Class* (Chicago, IL: University of Chicago Press, 1946); and by the 1936 decision of the Carnegie Corporation to support Gunnar Myrdal's monumental study of race in America that became *An American Dilemma: The Negro Problem and Modern Democracy* (New York: Harper & Brothers, 1944).

4 Dollard, *Caste and Class in a Southern Town*, particularly Chapter XVII, "Gains of the Lower-Class Negroes;" DuBois's "The Negroes of Farmville, Virginia: A Social Study," *Bulletin of the Department of Labor*, 14 (January 1898), pp. 1–44, cited in David Levering Lewis, *W. E. B. DuBois: Biography of a Race, 1868–1919* (New York: Henry Holt and Company, 1993), p. 196. See David Gordon Nielson, *Black Ethos: Northern Urban Negro Life and Thought, 1890–1930* (Westport, CT: Greenwood Press, 1977), pp. 52–7. Lois W. Banner, *Intertwined Lives: Margaret Mead, Ruth Benedict, and Their Circle* (New York: Alfred A. Knopf, 2003), p. 101, is the source for the term "cultural script;" "riffraff" and "respectables" are borrowed from James Weldon Johnson's *The Autobiography of an Ex-Colored Man* (New York: Hill & Wang, 1960; repr. of 1912 edn), pp. 55–6; see too E. Franklin Frazier, *Black Bourgeoisie: The Rise of a New Middle Class* (New York: Free Press, 1957, 2nd edn, 1962), a scholarly but wry look at class in black circles; on NAACP, see Cripps, "The NAACP's Hollywood Bureau: A Cautionary Tale," forthcoming.

   See King Vidor's film of Stark Young's novel, *So Red the Rose* (1935), as a sign of this unspoken white expectation. A rebellious slave (Clarence Muse) stands on the back of a wagon, railing against life as it is, but promising "Yankee men in blue coats" were on the march to free them: "no more breakin' new ground," he says, "no more choppin' cotton," listing the burdens of slavery, only then to evoke a promised future when "we don't work no mo', just sittin' in the sun."

5 Recollections of Professor Walter Fisher, Morgan State University (deceased); and the memories of dozens of Morgan colleagues who remembered the admonitions of youthful years to mute one's manner, utter appropriate "yes ma'ams," and do

homework on time, indeed do *everything* on time. On the role of the black press as bourgeois tutor, see Frazier's *Black Bourgeoisie*, Chapter VIII. On protests of movie-made African Americans, see, among many, Ann Tanneyhill, Urban League, to Guichard Parris, November 21, 1946, NUL Records, Library of Congress, on Uncle Remus in Walt Disney's *Song of the South*, cited in Thomas Cripps, *Making Movies Black: The Hollywood Message Movie. . . .* (New York: Oxford University Press, 1993), p. 193, in which she complains of that "which we have all learned to abhor . . . loud, long, sustained and vulgar" laughter; and on *Cabin in the Sky* and *Stormy Weather* in the midst of World War II, pp. 81–5.

6   Thomas Cripps, "Booker T. Washington and the Lily White Republicans: The Party, the Negro, and the South in the Progressive Era" (College Park, MD: Ph.D dissertation, 1967), see chapter on Indianola; Louis R. Harlan, *Booker T. Washington: The Wizard of Tuskegee, 1901–1915* (New York: Oxford University Press, 1983), p. 12; *Nation*, 75, 1960 (January 22, 1903) (www.nationarchive.com/ Summaries/v76i1960_10.htm).

7   In 1958, in the midst of a Ku Klux Klan rising against whites "consorting" with Lumbee Indians – by far the majority of students in Pembroke State College (NC), where I lived and taught – the (covertly land-rich) black woman who kept house for us explained in elaborate detail the intricacies of life. Dollard, *Class and Caste*, pp. 390–3. DuBois, in Lewis, *W. E. B. DuBois*, p. 196. Recent historians have found in other groups transgressive behaviors and styles as ways of asserting identities that challenge the hegemony of one's "betters" – a servant's sassiness, stylish dresses, or bungled assignments, say. Crossing lines thus served the needs of "subalterns" (as the literature has come to call them) much as in the lives of the riffraff. See, for example, Gunja Sengupta, "Elites, Subalterns, and American Identities: A Case Study of African-American Benevolence," *American Historical Review* (October 2004), pp. 1104–40, in which black servants live in hierarchies of their own; and David W. Stowe, "The Politics of Café Society," *Journal of American History*, 84, 4 (March 1998), pp. 1384–1406, in which the point is taken that lefties, black or white, dropped into Barney Josephson's *Café Society* in Greenwich Village for a drink and a show where a doorman presided in appropriately worn-out gloves, the matchbook motto touted "the wrong place for the right people," and a racially mixed cast played to a racially mixed audience – all of it meant to satirize effete *actual* "café society." Stowe cites the anthropologist, James C. Scott, *Domination and the Arts of Resistance: Hidden Transcripts* (New Haven, CT: Yale University Press, 1990) in noting "transcripts" of the "weapons of the weak," that included trangressions – flippancy, pilfering, malingering.

8   The literature grows unabated, starting in the 1970s with Donald Bogle, *Toms, Coons, Mulattoes, Mammies, & Bucks* (New York: Viking Press, 1973); Daniel J. Leab, *From Sambo to Superspade: The Black Experience in Motion Pictures* (Boston, MA: Houghton Mifflin, 1975); Thomas Cripps, *Slow Fade to Black: The Negro in American Film, 1900–1942* (New York: Oxford University Press, 1977); and Cripps, *Making Movies Black* (New York: Oxford University Press, 1993), for treatments of this era. On the presumed impact of race on the box office, see Cripps, "The Myth of the Southern Box Office: A Factor in Racial Stereotyping in American Movies, 1920–40," in Lewis Gould and James Curtis, eds, *The Black Experience in America: Selected Essays* (Austin, TX: University of Texas Press, 1970), pp. 116–44.

9   For a useful survey, see Cripps, *Making Movies Black*, pp. 1–249; for an argument that there is less here than meets the eye, see Clayton R. Koppes and Gregory D. Black, *Hollywood Goes to War: How Politics, Profits, & Propaganda Shaped World War II Movies* (New York: Free Press, 1987), Chapters IV and VI, particularly pp. 84–90 and pp. 178–84.

10 There is a rich literature on Poitier, capped by Aram Goudsuzian, *Sidney Poitier: Man, Actor, Icon* (Chapel Hill, NC: University of North Carolina Press, 2004).

11 Bond quoted in Hal Hinson, "Birth of a Genre: The Black Hero Who Talks Back," *New York Times* (August 11, 2002), A26. On NAACP and Hollywood, see Cripps, *Making Movies Black*, especially Chapters II and III.

12 The television newsman, William B. Monroe, quoted in Paul L. Fisher and Ralph L. Lowenstein, eds, *Race and the News Media* (New York: Frederick A. Praeger, 1968), p. 83.

13 My family of five lived both in the critical center of Baltimore at the time of urban risings and for a year in Palo Alto where we delivered books and food to "Nairobi." No telling, but flames, the National Guard patrolling the streets in Jeeps, the kids thrilling to it either as theatre or as the dawn of a new day must have moved or influenced Van Peebles, wherever he was.

14 Mary Heaton Vorse, "Picture Show Audiences," *Outlook* (June 24, 1911), pp. 441–7; Albert F. McLean, Jr., *American Vaudeville as Ritual* (Lexington, KY: University of Kentucky Press, 1965), p. 131; Harold Cruse, *The Crisis of the Negro Intellectual* (New York: Morrow, 1967), p. 81, cited in Stowe, "The Politics of Café Society," p. 1384; and Annette Powell Williams, "Dynamics of a Black Audience," in Thomas Kochman, ed., *Rappin' and Stylin' Out: Communication in Urban Black America* (Urbana, IL: University of Illinois Press, 1972).

15 A history of this expressive subculture is Shane White and Graham White, *Stylin': African American Expressive Culture from its Beginnings to the Zoot Suit* (Ithaca, NY: Cornell University Press, 1998). See also, R.T. Sale, *The Blackstone Rangers: A Reporter's Account. . . .* (New York: Random House, 1971); and Dan Rose, *Black American Street Life: South Philadelphia, 1969–1971* (Philadelphia, PA: University of Pennsylvania Press, 1971). The other side of the coin of racial arrangements is to be found in the constraints on white behavior – the "inner taboos" that hobble white gratification, which, in turn, stirs white envy of black habits and provides "another good reason for being a nigger!" – a white regret, Dollard reckoned, that extended to Harlem cabarets. See his *Caste and Class in a Southern Town*, pp. 393, 400.

16 Rabbi Judah Loew, after much prayer, raised up a clay Golem, a champion of the downtrodden Jews of Prague. See a child's version of the tale in Barbara Rogasky, *The Golem* (New York: Holiday House, 1996).

17 Melvin Van Peebles, *Sweet Sweetback's Baadasssss Song* (New York: Lancer Books, 1970), pp. 8–9. I borrow a phrase here from Roger D. Abrahams, *Deep Down in the Jungle. . . .: Folklore from the Streets of Philadelphia* (Hatboro, PA: Folklore Associated, 1964). For Van Peebles in a nostalgic mood – "memory without pain" – see Melvin and Mario Van Peebles, *No Identity Crisis: A Father and Son's Own Story of Working Together* (New York: Simon and Schuster, 1990), *passim*; and *Unstoppable* [a filmed conversation hosted by Warrington Hudlin, featuring Ossie Davis, Gordon Parks, and Van Peebles] (Black Starz, 2004).

18 Van Peebles, *Sweet Sweetback's Baadasssss Song*, p. 47; by "crafted" I mean a press agent's sort of legend; see also Cripps, "*Sweet Sweetback's Baadasssss Song* and the Changing Politics of the Genre Film," in Peter Lehman, ed., *Close Viewings: An Anthology of New Film Criticism* (Tallahassee, FL: Florida State University Press, 1990), pp. 243–8 and notes.

19 Van Peebles, *Sweet Sweetback's Baadasssss Song*, pp. 24–5. Van Peebles had already embarked on a cinematic career: two short pieces, *Three Pickup Men for Herrick* (1957) and *Sunlight* (1957); a French film *Cinq Cent Balles* (1968) made possible, according to the legend, by writing novels in French, thereby earning a union card that enabled him to make a wryly done French feature, *The Story of a Three Day Pass*

(1968); and *Watermelon Man* (1970), a wry Hollywood racial comedy that twitted Columbia studio, particularly its writer whose script had been quietly bent to Van Peebles's will.

20 Harper, "Dance in a Changing Society," *African Arts/Arts Afrique* (Autumn 1967), pp. 10ff, quoted in Cripps, "*Sweet Sweetback's Baadasssss Song*," p. 239; Van Peebles quoted in Hinson, "Birth of a Genre."

21 On the advertising tag lines, see a poster reproduction in Cripps, "*Sweet Sweetback's Baadasssss Song*," p. 244, that anticipates the line in the film that reminds the audience it is experiencing "a hymn from the mouth of reality," p. 249. See also Charles D. Peavy, "Black Consciousness and the Contemporary Cinema," in Ray B. Browne, ed., *Popular Culture and the Expanding Consciousness* (New York: Wiley, 1973), pp. 189–200.

22 Peavy, "Black Consciousness," pp. 194–8, cites Lerone Bennett's "The Emancipation Orgasm: Sweetback in Wonderland," *Ebony* (September 1971), pp. 106ff and Don L. Lee, "The Bittersweet of Sweetback/or Shake Yo' Moneymaker," *Black World* (November 1971), pp. 43–8 as critics, but is himself hopeful. Not only did he sense "that the black masses who attended the film's screening" found its "immediacy . . . overwhelming," but predicted, "doubtlessly," sequels. The Museum of Modern Art clipping file reflects still more of this "yes and no" sentiment. This ambivalence is at the core of an interesting unpublished (to my knowledge) paper by Christina Violeta Jones, "Changing Male Images in *Nothing but a Man* and *Sweet Sweetback's Baadasssss Song*."

23 Mark A. Reid, *Redefining Black Film* (Berkeley: University of California Press, 1993), pp. 77–8; Gerald Martinez, Diana Martinez and Andres Chavez, *What It Is . . . What It Was: The Black Film Explosion of the '70s in Words and Pictures* (New York: Hyperion Miramax, 1998), p. 168, a Carol Speed memoir. Ed Guerrero, *Framing Blackness: The African American Image in Film* (Philadelphia, PA: Temple University Press, 1993), pp. 100–3, neatly captures the range of the black debate over blaxploitation and its presumed impact on black life.

24 A Van Peebles memoir in Martinez, *et al.*, *What It Is*, p. 38; Paula J. Massood, *Black City Cinema: African American Urban Experiences in Film* (Philadephia, PA: Temple University Press, 2003), p. 87. Yet Reid, *Redefining Black Film*, p. 77, notes Van Peebles's debt to loners like that in Clint Eastwood's *Hang 'Em High*.

   The density of black urban life neglected by filmmakers of the day is palpable if, for example, one stands at the corner of 135th and Malcolm X [*née* Lenox], the black-managed Jock's bar, center of many a political bargain, a long block west – indeed the *first* black block in Harlem (1907); historic Harlem Hospital across Malcolm X, the Schomburg Center for the Study of African American History and Culture is on the corner; across to the south are the James Weldon Johnson Apartments; a block to the west are the sites of Small's Paradise, the Lafayette Theatre, and the Harlem YMCA (site of generations of poetry readings); southward past Sylvia's restaurant is fabled 125th Street, home to Daddy Grace's House of Prayer for All People, Michaux's black nationalist bookstore, and the Apollo Theatre. Dunbar Apartments, Adam Clayton Powell's Abyssinian Baptist Church are but a block north. What a location shoot!

25 www.stlyrics.comlyrics/aligindahouse/fightthepower, Ali G Indahouse lyrics; Laura K. Worrell, on *Fight the Power* in Salon.com/emt/masterpiece/2002/06/03/ fight_the_power/; on Chuck D see Public Enemy official website, www.public enemy.com; on a recently recorded "cover" see www.billboard.com on "Korn, Xzibit Fight The 'Power' On 'XXX.'"

   "Googling" reaps a broad reportage, including the critic, Stanley Crouch, on a conscious "thug culture." The earliest works on the impending "revolution" include Frank Kofsky (who dedicated his book, evocatively, to John Coltrane and Malcolm X), *Black Nationalism and the Revolution in Music* (New York: Pathfinder Press, 1970); Brian Cross, *It's not about Salary. . . . Rap, Race and Resistance in Los Angeles* (London: Verso, 1993), a book of interviews that links hip-hop and Chicano cultures and features a discography and a chronicle of "police abuse in LA;" a solid piece of "early" scholar-journalism masquerading as a fan letter, Nelson George, Sally Banes, Susan Flinker and Patty Romanowski, *Fresh: Hip Hop Don't Stop* (New York: Random House, 1985), particularly for its groundbreaking "sources;" Adam Sexton, ed., *Rap on Rap: Straight-Up Talk on Hip-Hop Culture* (New York: Delta, 1995), an anthology of both hip and square criticism; Chuck D., with Yusuf Jah, *Fight the Power: Rap, Race, and Reality* (New York: Delacorte Press, 1997), an essay by a practitioner with a link to Spike Lee; George Lipsitz, *Dangerous Crossroads: Popular Music, Postmodernism and the Politics of Place* (London: Verso, 1994), in an international setting, notably Chapters 2 and 3; Adam Krims, *Rap Music and the Poetics of Identity* (Cambridge: Cambridge University Press, 2000), a first critical piece set in the context of anthropological and cultural criticism, one of a series on "new perspectives;" Cheryl L. Keyes, *Rap Music and Street Consciousness* (Urbana, IL: University of Illinois Press, 2002), one in the scholarly series, "Music in American Life," with no less than thirty pages of discography and bibliography; on up to the recent essay on "Gangsta Rap," Eithne Quinn, *Nuthin' but a "G" Thang: The Culture and Commerce of Gangsta Rap* (New York: Columbia University Press, 2005), angled on African and Caribbean roots of urban music and its transgressive values. Most recently see Jeff Chang, *Can't Stop Won't Stop: A History of the Hip-Hop Generation* (New York: St. Martin's Press, 2005), in which *Mother Jones* (March/April 2005), p. 86, sees in the 1970s "an enormous amount of creative energy was now ready to be released from the bottom of American society."

26 Chuck D with Yusuf Jah, *Fight the Power*, p. 1.

27 Cosby's speech reported in *WorldnetDaily* website, May 20, 2004, which also recorded Theodore Shaw's (NAACP Legal Defense Fund) and others' attempted rebuttals; and CNN.com, November 12, 2004. As a panelist on Mfume's TV show, *Look at It This Way*, I was astonished when he said it to a studio (and broadcast) audience.

28 Lola Ogunnaike, "Sometimes 'Guilty' is a Good Thing, Rap Insiders Say," *New York Times* (March 18, 2005), and *Beat King* website (March 30, 2005), on her case.

29 *Sun* (Baltimore) (March 14, 2005), 23, 3.

30 Sometimes kids see the irony in protesting too much their wished for outlaw or "street creds," as in the case of the basketball team of Baltimore's nationally ranked inner-city high school named for the black poet, Paul Laurence Dunbar – whose athletes are named not "Outlaws" but "Poets."

31 R.T. Sale, *The Blackstone Rangers: A Reporter's Account of Time Spent with Blackstone Rangers in Chicago's South Side* (New York: Random House, 1971), p. 91; Dan Rose, *Black American Street Life: South Philadelphia, 1969–1971* (Philadelphia, PA: University of Pennsylvania Press, 1987), pp. 146 and 169.

32 Anonymously quoted on *Beatking*'s website (March 30, 2005). On excesses of dress and crossover gigs, particularly P. Diddy and Beyonce, see *Sun* (Baltimore) (March 6, 2005).

33 Paine cited in Cripps, *Making Movies Black*, p. viii.

34 Finley Peter Dunne, *Mr. Dooley on Ivrything and Ivrybody*, selected and with an introduction by Robert Hutchinson (New York: Dover Publications, Inc., 1963), p. 140, taken from *Mr. Dooley's Philosophy* (New York: R.H. Russell, 1900).

35 Bret McCabe, "The Reign of Beef," *The City Paper* (April 6, 2005), pp. 29–30.

Chapter 15

Black like him

Steven Spielberg's *The Color Purple*

Lester D. Friedman

A note on blacks and Jews in America

As a film directed by a Jewish man based on a book written by a black woman, *The Color Purple* (1985) remains a part of both the sprawling history of the American cinema and the complicated relationship between blacks and Jews in the United States. The arduous fight for black civil rights during the 1950s and 1960s highlighted the obvious commonalities between these minority groups, molded their conceptions of themselves and each other, and fostered an effective alliance for social change.[1] Marginalized as outsiders and stigmatized as pariahs – blacks because of their color and Jews because of their religion – these groups recognized a mutual, diasporic heritage permeated with discrimination and persecution at the hands of fearful often hostile, white and Christian societies.[2] Homegrown organizations, such as the Ku Klux Klan and the Aryan Nation, made no distinctions between blacks and Jews when spewing their hatred and perpetrating their violence. It is not surprising, therefore, that black leaders often referred to passages from the Old Testament to draw parallels between their own struggles in America and the plight of Jewish slaves in Egypt. Citing their long history as the victims of oppression, many Jews provided money, manpower, and political support to assist the black campaign for equality, linking arms with them in marches, protests, and lawsuits against racism. For most Americans, the two most pervasive and vivid historical examples of intolerance, brutality and genocide are the institution of slavery and the advent of the Holocaust, a fact which further entwines blacks and Jews in the public's consciousness and in their own minds as well.[3]

Ultimately, however, the center did not hold. As the heated campaign for civil rights died down and was replaced by ongoing economic and cultural conflicts, some in the black community began to see Jews as part of the oppressive white majority rather than as brothers and sisters working alongside them for equality. Incidents of distrust, anger, and even outright violence testified to an escalating antagonism between blacks and Jews, signaling the collapse of the coalition they had forged together. For an increasing number of blacks, Jews were no longer freedom fighters but instead landlords, corner-store owners, bankers, and lawyers – often the most conspicuous examples of the white-dominated economic and legal systems that discriminated against them. While acknowledging that Jews came to these shores to escape persecution, black leaders nonetheless noted that no Jews had been kidnapped, manacled, and sold into slavery. Many blacks saw the rise of Jews to the highest levels of business, education, and government as certifying that mainstream Americans viewed differences in religion far more benevolently than they did differences in race.[4] Jews, for their part, expressed surprise and a sense of betrayal at the growing hostility directed towards them, since they still envisioned themselves as part of the country's minority culture.[5] Despite their current social and economic advances, Jews knew that their history was replete with bitter lessons about the illusion of assimilation and the impermanence of acceptance. They hoped that America would be different, but cautious Jews didn't need a weatherman to tell them how quickly the political and social winds could shift and how rapidly tolerance can turn into tyranny. Today, tensions between these groups remain palpable if less visible, a constantly simmering flame ready to flare up at perceived insults or outright provocations from one side or the other.

The American cinema was not immune from these changes in black/Jewish relations. Increasingly, black leaders and scholars assailed Hollywood for its long history of racist stereotypes, and some explicitly conflated these depictions with the industry's Jews. The Committee to Eliminate Media Offensive to African People, for example, declared that Hollywood's Jews "with rare exceptions . . . have depicted Black men as criminals, pimps, drug addicts, clowns and fools [and] Black women as fat, loud, bossy mammies who dominate their husbands and families [or] as whores."[6] The Nation of Islam's leader, Louis Farrakhan, told a Michigan State University audience that Jews have "sucked the blood of the Black community" and specifically cited the Jewish influence in mainstream filmmaking: "You wrote us in as clowns and buffoons. I never did that to you, but you Jews did that to Black people."[7] Professor Leonard Jeffries, chairman of the African–American Studies Department of the City University of New York, vilified Jewish Hollywood at the 1991 Empire State Black Arts and Cultural Festival, contending that there was a conscious "conspiracy planned and plotted and programmed out of Hollywood, with people named Greenberg and Weisberg for the destruction of Black People."[8] Admittedly, such comments represent examples of heated rhetoric, but they were rarely challenged by others within the black community. Given the intensifying debates swirling about commercial filmmaking, the most successful Jewish director in Hollywood, the man who adapted Alice Walker's book for the screen, unwittingly became part of the ongoing controversies between blacks and Jews; "Not Jolson in blackface but Steven Spielberg, the adoptive father of two Black children, has become the lightning rod for today's Black Nationalist attacks on Jewish Hollywood."[9]

The Color Purple: Steven Spielberg and Alice Walker

Though he had previously converted an immensely popular novel into a blockbuster film (Peter Benchley's *Jaws*) and would subsequently make films based on the works of critically acclaimed writers (J.G. Ballard's *Empire of the Sun*, Thomas Keneally's *Schindler's List* and Philip K. Dick's *Minority Report*), Spielberg's relationship with novelist Alice Walker represents a creative collaboration with a literary figure never duplicated at any other point in his career. Both participants, as well as those who closely observed their interactions, attest to the affection, warmth, and mutual respect that grew between the black feminist writer and the white Jewish filmmaker. Initially, Walker knew little of Spielberg's works and, before they met, had only seen *The Sugarland Express*. On his part, Spielberg understood that his first visit with Walker in her San Francisco home was an audition, since she controlled the film rights to her book: "Basically, I was going to be interviewed, as I hadn't been since 11 years before when I was up for jobs, starting out as a director."[10] That the world's most successful director would willingly submit himself to this rudimentary process documents Spielberg's passion to bringing Walker's novel to the screen, as does his willingness to draw no salary beyond the Director's Guild minimum $40,000 – most of that ultimately spent on overages not covered by the film's budget.

Unfamiliar with his work, Walker immediately sensed that "for all his worldly success," Spielberg "remained a minority person. . . . She recognized that his sensitivity enabled him to share the feelings of characters of another race and another gender."[11] She was also "worldly" enough to retain a large amount of influence over the filmmaking. In what must be one of the more unusual pre-production agreements, Walker's contract stipulated that at least "half the crew members would be women or blacks or Third World people."[12] She also brought Whoopi Goldberg, a relatively unknown young comedian who had never made a movie, to Spielberg's attention; ultimately, she was cast in the film's lead role of Celie. Walker further suggested Tina Turner to play Shug, a part the singer eventually turned down as being too close to her own experiences with spousal abuse. The novelist even tried her hand at writing a screenplay for the film (reprinted in her book *The Same River Twice*) which both she and the director ultimately agreed not to use as the script for the movie. Nonetheless, Alice Walker was on the set for about half the shooting schedule, adding lines of dialogue when requested, helping the actors get the proper Southern speech patterns, working with Menno Meyjes on the screenplay and with Quincy Jones on the musical selections, and showing photographs of her grandparents' home to the film's production designer, J. Michael Riva.

Most importantly, Spielberg understood Walker as an interpreter, a guide, who helped him cross over from his culture to her own experiences: "Alice could take my hand and take me into a world that, at first, I didn't know anything about."[13] Walker and Spielberg talked for hours about the movie – and about their lives as well. "She has a kind of beneficence about her, a light," he recalls in a 1988 interview, "She's very kind."[14] Walker was on the set during the particularly painful scene where Mister separates Celie and Nettie. Spielberg did the master in one shoot, feeling that such a sense of continuity would make the actors feel the horror of the moment. He also wanted to affect Walker: "I turned to Alice and she was a wreck. Really crying. And that was good for me because I wanted to impress her."[15] Once Walker gave her approval for Spielberg to adapt her work, the fact that he was white was never raised as a problem: "the issue was not the color of my skin, but whether I'd make a good movie out of the book."[16] On the set itself, says Spielberg, Walker would provide specific help if asked to do so by the director, but primarily "Alice was a spiritual presence throughout the movie."[17]

In her recounting of this time over a decade later, Walker reveals the various physical and psychological traumas that afflicted her during the making of *The Color Purple*, including her mother's incapacitation from a major stroke and her own painful bout with Lyme disease. Suffering from what she characterizes as "the hidden trauma I endured during its creation," she recounts feeling "exactly as if I were being attacked from the inside at the same time I was being attacked from the outside."[18] As the filming progressed, she:

> sat under a tree and offered speech lessons and tarot readings, painfully conscious of my fuzzy thinking and blotchy skin, my soul-deep exhaustion and almost ever-present nausea. I was unequal to the task of pointing out to Steven every "error" I saw about to be made, as my critics later assumed I should have, or even of praising the exquisite things he constantly thought up, which moved me to tears each evening as we watched "dailies."

Even though she was on the set as much as possible, the novelist felt, as Spielberg noted, "more like a spirit than a person." The director never knew the extent of Walker's physical and emotional pain, but she firmly believes that "Steven intuited that I was extremely fragile as our film was being made, walking some days as if in a dream."[19]

Spielberg's film follows the general outline of Walker's novel. The narrative, set in rural Georgia, begins in 1909 and follows the life of Celie (Whoopi Goldberg), a poor black woman suffering under the crippling yoke of sexism and racism. After being raped by her father (Leonard Jackson) and giving birth to Adam (Peto Kinsaka) and Olivia (Lelo Masamba), Celie's children are handed over to the Reverend Samuel (Carl Anderson), and she is forced into a marriage with the brutal Albert Johnson, known to her only as Mister (Danny Glover). Even worse, she is separated from the person she loves most in the world, her sister Nettie (Akosua Busia). Mister, who loves the flamboyant singer Shug Avery (Margaret Avery), treats Celie like a domestic servant, beating her mercilessly and making her rear his unruly son, Harpo (Willard Pugh), who eventually marries the domineering Sophia (Oprah Winfrey). When Shug comes to Celie's and Mister's home to recuperate from an illness, the two women form a strong emotional and sexual bond. Sophia is sent to jail for hitting the mayor's wife, a sentence that breaks her physically and emotionally, Shug leaves and then returns with a new husband (Bennet Guillory), and Celie finds that Mister has been hiding Nettie's letters from Africa. Tearing them open, she discovers that her sister has joined Reverend Samuel's missionary work and that Celie's children are thriving in their new home. Finally, Celie summons up the courage to confront Mister and leave him. She returns home after her father's death – learning the man was actually her stepfather – and establishes a successful clothing store. The film ends with Celie's tearful reunion with Adam, Olivia and, of course, Nettie.

Walker's first reaction after seeing the finished product in a nearly empty theater was overwhelmingly negative. "Everything seemed wrong, especially the opening musical score, which sounded like it belonged in *Oklahoma*."[20] She "noticed only the flaws."[21] In particular, the novelist articulated concerns about the following points, most of which are echoed by the film's critics: (1) the de-emphasis of Shug's bisexuality; (2) the lack of fullness in Harpo's character and his frequent falls through various roofs; (3) the "bluntness" of Celie's erroneous statement about being raped and impregnated by the man she supposes is her father; (4) the falseness of Shug pretending not to understand why Celie can't speak up when left alone with Mister; (5) the absurdity of Mister not knowing where the butter is kept or how to start a fire; (6) the lack of forgiveness for Mister; (7) the avoidance of an erotic, sensuous relationship between Shug and Celie; (8) the characters being overly well dressed; (9) the distortion, at times, of the folk speech; (10) the sentimentality of the carved heart in the tree and the imposition of *Oliver Twist* into the story; and (11) the misinformation present in the African scenes about the location of the village, the sanctification ceremony, and the placement of the rubber plantation.

After that disastrous first screening, and as part of a far larger audience, Walker warmed to the film as an adaptation not a transcription, seeing "its virtues rather than its flaws."[22] Even with some significant reservations, she feels generally positive about the movie and consistently maintains her admiration and affection for Spielberg: "When I think of Steven Spielberg's 'version' of my book, my first thought is of Steven himself. His love and enthusiasm for my characters. His ability to find himself in them."[23] The song "Sister," written by Quincy Jones, Rod Temperton, and Lionel Ritchie remains, for Walker, particularly powerful, "a signal of affirmation that women could hum to each other coast to coast, an immeasurable gift to the bonding of women."[24] The scenes she particularly admires include the emotional parting between Celie and Nettie, the kissing scene with Celie and Shug, the section where Shug and

Celie find the hidden letters (especially when she smells the dried flower petal), Shug's first song in the juke joint, and the moving ending (though she reaffirms her wish that "Mister had been up on the porch, too.")[25] Years later, on the DVD interview, Walker sums up her feelings by declaring, "I love it as a gift given to our people. A kind of medicine."

In an insightful and sympathetic summation of her personal connection to Spielberg, Walker hits upon a crucial element which directly and viscerally links the director with a wide range of viewers: "In more modern times, people say you think with your brain. Only there are a few of us who still actually think with our hearts, and after talking to Steven, I had a lot of confidence that he was one."[26] That Spielberg "thinks with his heart" does not deny his brain, nor for that matter his technical skills; it does, however, reveal one significant reason for his unparalleled success: the ability to transform his deepest emotions and pervasive obsessions into powerful visual images that strike broadly responsive chords in audiences. The ability to connect emotionally with audiences remains a primary reason for Spielberg's popularity, but it also accounts for the wariness expressed by some critics as the director himself notes:

> Everybody loves the movie for the first few months, and then when it starts breaking records, some'll say, "Well, wait a second. I'm being tricked. There's some kind of evil seduction afoot. I don't trust that Spielberg. I know, I enjoyed it. I saw it four times, but that little bastard manipulated me!"[27]

Walker also recognizes that, at the time the film was made, Spielberg was trying to move beyond his self-imposed limitations as a filmmaker. "Perhaps Harpo is Steven," she speculates, "falling down the stairs of his life at the time, breaking his bones against his parrot's cage, needing to rattle his own."[28]

Both Spielberg and Walker instinctively knew that making *The Color Purple* represented a turning point in their lives. Looking back with some historical perspective, the novelist observes that "oddly, the experience of making a film of my work, as bewildering and strange as any labyrinth, and as unpredictable as any river, was an initiation into the next, more mature, phase of my life."[29] Similarly, Spielberg recognizes the inherent hazards in adapting this particular book to the screen. "I've been playing in the sandbox for years," he said on the eve of the film's release, "something in me would say go for the easy challenge and not the hard task. So I went for the fast-paced, energetic entertainments."[30] Becoming a father during the making of the movie – his son Max was born just as he was shooting Celie's childbirth sequence on June 12 – Spielberg must have realized that his new role as an adult would ultimately be mirrored in his art, just as his childhood had played such a major role in his previous work. "It's as if I've been swimming in water up to my waist all my life . . . but now I'm going into the deep section of the pool."[31] Spielberg was clearly aware of the dangers involved in venturing beyond the shallow water: "the biggest risk, for me, is doing a movie about *people* for the first time in my career – and failing. . . . It's the risk of being judged – and accused of not having the sensibility to do character studies."[32] Looking back over his career, one can characterize *The Color Purple* as his first conscious attempt to create a mature film, the project that launched him into the rougher, more challenging currents of *Empire of the Sun, Amistad, A.I., Minority Report* and *Schindler's List*.

The Color Purple: the controversies

Of the many controversies that swirled around *The Color Purple*, two dominate much of the discourse that surrounded it: the charge that the film is fundamentally racist due predominately to the way it constructs black men; and the charge that Spielberg's alterations distort Walker's literary vision. Walker's feminist work, which won both the National Book Award and the Pulitzer Prize for Fiction in 1983, sparked heated disputes because of its frank presentation of incest, spousal abuse, female sexuality, and lesbianism within black society. The movie ignited a larger firestorm by bringing these incendiary issues to a far wider audience than the book ever could hope to reach. Outside the black community, critics initially castigated Spielberg for candy coating Walker's graphic narrative: typical of the hostile responses were David Ansen (*Newsweek*) who had "the disorienting sensation that I was watching the first Disney movie about incest," John Powers (*L.A. Weekly*) who wrote that "Spielberg's suburban background shows all over the place," and Rita Kempley (*The Washington Post*) who called the director's version of rural Georgia "a pastoral paradise that makes Dorothy Gale's Kansas farm look like a slum."[33] But these objections were tame compared to those arising from inside the black community and typified by Donald Bogle's accusation that the film ignores "the broader context in which any of the characters must live: the larger dominant white culture that envelops – and certainly enslaves them all."[34] As such, Spielberg's "sensibility informs almost every frame, turning an intimate tale into a large scale, overblown Disneyesque Victorian melodrama, full of 'big' moments and simplified characters."[35] The controversies spilled from the page into the streets, starting with boycotts from the Coalition Against Black Exploitation and the Hollywood branch of the NAACP, as well as protest meetings in black churches across the country.

Controversy I: The Color Purple maligns black men

This movie "depicts all blacks in an extremely negative light," claimed Kwazi Geiggar of the Coalition Against Black Exploitation. "It degrades the black man, it degrades black children, it degrades the black family."[36] Three pieces from within the black community – one from the popular press by talk-show host and columnist Tony Brown, the second by Gerald Early in the scholarly literature, and the last a sophisticated critique and audience analysis by Jacqueline Bobo in her book *Black Women as Cultural Readers* – represent the general charges leveled against Walker, Spielberg, and the movie.[37] Brown begins by bemoaning the "growing inability of black men and women to love one another."[38] Historically, he argues, the brutality of slavery forced humiliated black men to deflect their hostility from whites towards those with even less power than themselves, "women being the most vulnerable."[39] Brown credits Walker for brilliantly capturing this "self-hatred." He refuses to see the movie – making the analogy that "a Jew does not have to go into a gas chamber to understand Hitler's motives" – which does not stop him from criticizing it and contending that "lesbian affairs will never replace the passion and beauty of a free black man and a free black woman."[40] He asserts that because so few films are produced with black themes, *The Color Purple* will become a definitive statement about black men and broadly attacks the white-dominated publishing industry for only publishing "books by black women or homosexual men with degrading themes or passive attitudes – and then makes them into movies of 'the black experience.'"[41] In retrospect, *The Color Purple* never became the definitive statement about black men in America, and Brown's hyperbolic critique appears far more connected to his own political agenda than to the movie he chooses not to see.

Walker admitted that the accusation she found hardest to tolerate was that she hated black men: not only does she admire many contemporary and historical black male figures stretching from Langston Hughes to Bob Marley to Nelson Mandela – including those within her own family – but she asserts that she "felt close to, and always affirmed by, the black male spirit within myself. This spirit's indomitable quality is fierceness of emotion, tenderness of heart, and a love of freedom."[42] Even more importantly, the writer has "always considered men of color brave and daring beyond compare; it is from them I have learned much of what I know of gracefulness, of how to love and how to fight."[43] But she has also been irrevocably saddened by seeing and experiencing "that which destroys beauty in anyone: oppression of those over whom one has power."[44] Anita Jones, writing in the same journal as Tony Brown (January 4, 1986), responds directly to his article, contending that:

> *The Color Purple* is not a story against black men: it is a story about black women. The fact that the men in the story are not all good guys needs no justification, for it is not the obligation of any work of fiction to present every possible angle or every possible situation. Walker chose a particular feminist theme and dealt with it, which resulted in many black men protesting and licking their egos.[45]

Even with such spirited defenses, Walker, and by extension Spielberg, never fully escapes the allegation that *The Color Purple* viciously slandered black men, spotlighting the violent deeds of a few to the detriment of the many. As such, argued many critics, both the book and the film reinforce the worst white stereotypes about black families.

Gerald Early's blistering rebuke makes Tony Brown's objections seem calm and circumspect, as he savages both Walker's book and Spielberg's film from a variety of aesthetic, sociological, historical, ideological, and racial perspectives. He dismisses the literary work "because it fails the ideology it purports to serve . . . only *appears* to be subversive and . . . is far from being a radically feminist novel;" similarly, the film is "so undeniably bad that one wonders how Steven Spielberg ever acquired any sort of reputation as a competent artist." Early sarcastically surmises that Spielberg "was really directing a parody or a comedy and was not succeeding." The blatant artistic failure of *The Color Purple* seems inevitable to Early, who characterizes the director's works as very expensive B movies that "combine hokum and splendor. . . . Spielberg's films essentially have the same moral and artistic visions as a professional wrestling match: the experience of an exaggerated morality in an excessive spectacle that is, I think, not an experience of art, but an experience of the negation of art."[46] Early goes on to list the film's historical flaws, reaffirming the "bourgeois pretensions and moral integrity" of the "chronically insecure American audience," alleging that it alienates blacks from their own history, and censuring black viewers who enjoyed the movie and (like Quincy Jones) participated in its creation.[47]

Castigating the film as "narcotic art" that "moves an audience without disturbing it," Early utterly rejects any notion that it contains radical impulses. Instead, *The Color Purple* is "the ideal American protest art, freeing Americans from any criticism of their social or political order by denying that the film presents a problem open to any implication of a social or political solution." Lumping Walker and Spielberg into culpable representatives of a stridently bourgeois orthodoxy (which certainly must have surprised Walker if not Spielberg), Early contends that *The Color Purple* simply recycles the Victorian cliché that "the individual still has the power to change and that power supersedes all others." Walker's book "lacks any real intellectual or theological rigor or coherence, and the fusing of social protest and utopia is really nothing more than confounding and blundering;" as such, the novel – and by extension the film – endorses a "dim witted" pantheism that resembles a "cross between the New Age movement and Dale Carnegie." Early concludes his one-dimensional critique by charging that the success of the book and the movie graphically illustrates American society's unwillingness to face the pervasive evil within its midst. Both works confirm the desperate and perilous middle-class illusion that "there are no devils in the end, no evil that cannot be repented and, indeed, no final rendering up of things because there will be no sin."[48]

In many ways, Jacqueline Bobo's discussion of *The Color Purple* is the most fascinating of these three documents, in that she offers both a critical feminist reading of the film and an enlightening dialogue with representative black female cultural consumers who responded far less negatively to the film than did black males, mainstream reviewers, or radical commentators. Unlike Early, Bobo believes that Walker's novel incorporates both "subversive form and content" and situates it "within the continuum of black female creativity and activism." In particular, she argues that the writer "continues the task of revising images of black women by taking the familiar and negatively constructed sexual images and imbuing them with power." The fact that Celie, Shug, Sofia and Squeak (Rae Dawn Chong) fashion a mutually beneficial, fundamentally supportive, and ultimately liberating female community as a counterbalance to the male brutality that surrounds them endows the book with a power that allows these women to move beyond "being dependent on men for emotional and economic support." Thus, her analysis makes a stark distinction between Walker's words and Spielberg's images.[49]

For Bobo, Spielberg's most unforgivable transgression is to dilute these robust literary figures, replacing them with tired clichés and negative stereotypes, recycled caricatures from the mainstream media: Sofia becomes "the overbearing matriarchal figure . . . the castrating Amazon," Shug "the licentious cabaret singer . . . a victim of her insatiable sexual appetite who . . . longs for her preacher father's approval and regrets her life," and Celie simply "a victim of racism, sexism and patriarchal privilege . . . An Orphan Annie." Although Spielberg, in his DVD interview, contends that the movie is "Celie's story, a woman's story. Not Mister's," Bobo maintains that he turned Walker's novel into "a chronicle of an abusive black man's journey toward self-understanding." Resorting to these conventional formulations of character and plot, Spielberg harkens back to Hollywood's shameful history and his film becomes, in effect, a "revision to past racist works." Although she admits that only "Spielberg could have obtained the financing to mount the kind of production that he did," Bobo bemoans the fact that no black woman has been "allowed to develop the track record" of white male directors like Spielberg and thus none could command the industry confidence and monetary clout to make *The Color Purple*.[50]

Given her pejorative reading of the film, Bobo is astounded by the mostly favorable responses it garners from black female viewers. How to account for these accolades for a film that "did not aid the cause of black women?" She first attempts to explain this puzzling phenomenon by adopting the basic premise of Marxist philosopher Louis Althusser, contending that the positive reactions were "another instance of certain audiences having been manipulated by the mechanisms of mainstream media into accepting its repressive ideology without question." Somehow, these women "read against the grain of the film and reconstructed more satisfactory meanings" than should have been expected in a movie that "portrayed black people disparagingly." Bobo situates these "oppositional readings" within a history of black women's resistance: "it is a challenge to the mandate, given dominant media coverage, that black people should not have positive responses to the film." In essence, then, the black women who "clung tightly to their positive feelings about *The Color Purple*" resisted the authoritative, sanctioned readings of the dominant media, not to mention of Bobo herself. Finally, she offers the possibility that "the pervasive absence of black people in the mainstream media" motivates black audience members "to enjoy" rather than to "critically evaluate" works, thereby failing to "distinguish a harmful image from just the pleasure of seeing black women in roles other than comics or domestic workers."[51]

So, which is it? Has Spielberg "manipulated" these black women into responding positively to a movie which belittles them, or is their enjoyment a radical act of "oppositional" reading? To my mind, the former implies being controlled and duped; a compliant viewer falls under the sway of powerful visual images and consequently cannot dispute (or perhaps even distinguish) the negative ideas carried within them. Contention is not part of this process, nor is disputation or resistance. The latter response, however, explicitly incorporates a rejection of dominant readings and a conscious estrangement from both the black community and the white mainstream press. In this sense, then, the two ways of readings appear mutually exclusive, one grounded in acquiescent passivity and the other in rebellious opposition. Bobo's third option – that these viewers derive pleasure merely from seeing a variety of black women on the screen – suggests that black women are so starved of representational images that they willingly and uncritically accept negative stereotypes and harmful clichés because these are the only things available to them. Again, this assumption sits far from a vigorous, consciously oppositional interpretation with implications for a radical reading of the text. In essence, then, Bobo insists that anyone who responds positively to *The Color Purple* must have been overpowered, deluded, or lacking in critical judgment. In an ironic manner, her willingness to ignore her own data both condescendingly minimizes and ultimately essentializes the responses of black audience members.

Bobo, of course, ignores the most obvious possibility. Though her subjects consistently find "moments in the film that resonated with elements in their lives," she never considers that – even with all the sins he commits against Walker's vision – Spielberg actually manages to make her book into an emotionally moving film, one that "resonated" with a broad range of black women.[52] Given their responses, one could easily conclude that these women fully recognized many of the negative issues raised by the film's critics, including Bobo herself, but that they found "Celie's urgency to fulfill her own destiny and to discover the things that belong to her self" so touching that it counterbalanced their reservations and allowed them to negotiate a space within which they could enjoy the movie.[53] Such basic motivations never occur to Bobo. Given her negative response to the film, she could not understand why her subjects did not feel the same way. McBride gets closer to the truth when he observes that the director's "full-throated romantic mode of visual storytelling is not fashionable by the postmodernist standards of contemporary films criticism," a fact which often accounts for the gap between the "mass audience's often tearful enjoyment of a film such as *The Color Purple* and the distaste of critics who view any evocation of strong emotion as a form of directorial manipulation."[54]

While one might ascribe ulterior motives behind her defense of the film, Whoopi Goldberg defends *The Color Purple* by arguing that "There is not a 'mammy' or a 'nigger' in this film. I resent the fact that people think we actors would be involved in something that shows stereotyped behavior. Do people think that neither I am capable of judging what's exploitative, nor Danny Glover nor Oprah Winfrey?"[55] Apparently critics such as Brown, Early, Bobo, and a host more believe that neither the actors in the film, the people who enjoyed watching it, the woman who wrote the book upon which it was based, nor the man who directed it are capable of making such judgments. That said, I don't want to leave this portion of the conversation about *The Color Purple* controversies without stating that I fully agree with some of the criticisms leveled at this film, particularly those stated by Bobo at her most incisive. Though she consistently undervalues the emotional appeal of the film – as do many other critics who attack Spielberg throughout his career for being simply a manipulator of feelings – as well as its more positive feminist aspects, her comments offer perceptive insights about a variety of important issues that need further exploration and discussion, particularly how the director toned down Shug's brassy sexuality and eliminated Mister from the joyous reconciliation scene at the film's conclusion.

Controversy 2: Spielberg distorts Walker's book – Shug's domestication

In responding to challenges about his film's historical authenticity, Spielberg often cites Walker as his factual authority, thereby deflecting some of the slings and arrows back against those who originally launched them. When accused, for example, of transforming rural Georgia into an idealized pastoral and sprucing up the lives of blacks living there in the early years of the twentieth century, the director responds that his sets accurately recreated photographs supplied by the novelist and that some southern blacks, including Walker's grandparents, had not resided in miserable poverty during this period. He argues that the writer's ancestors were financially successful, even considered wealthy, by the standards of the day. Given this fact, Spielberg wryly notes that his detractors "had a kind of *Uncle Tom's Cabin* view . . . their own inclination for racial stereotyping, which is what some of the same people said we were guilty of."[56] Walker did originally point out to the film's set and costume designers that "these particular black landowners did not dress in rags and could afford wallpaper," but she ultimately feels that everyone in the film was "too well dressed."[57] Similarly, although Spielberg incorporates the basic design of her grandparents' house into his design for Mister's home, his addition of columns, which Walker "lobbied against," turns that edifice into "the big house." Spielberg's attempt to hide behind Walker strikes me, at best, as ingenious.[58] Although he based many of his creations on Walker's artifacts and remembrances, he clearly embellished them beyond her expectations and recollections. It was, after all, his film, not hers.

More substantial than these charges about set design issues and historical authenticity, Spielberg's detractors indict him for drastically attenuating Walker's sexually liberated stance, particularly by eliminating the overt lesbian scenes she so lovingly describes between Celie and Shug. Given his acute discomfort about depicting any type of sexuality on the screen, Spielberg's decision to eliminate the more physically explicit scenes from the novel, such as when Shug convinces Celie to hold a mirror between her legs and examine herself, or when the women passionately kiss and hungrily caress each other, seems unsurprising. Walker claims that it took her gentle insistence "in talks with Menno, Steven, and Quincy, simply to include 'the kiss,' chaste as it was."[59] Instead of overt sexual scenes, Spielberg takes a more "poetic route" by substituting Shug's insisting that Celie take her hands away from her mouth and, for the first time in the film, smile openly. Shug's attentions enable Celie to accept herself as a woman, much as does her sexual awakening in the novel, and the women seal this scene of personal emancipation with a kiss that clearly indicates a sexual relationship, though with a discreet 1950s obliqueness rather than a 1980s frankness.

"I don't think a full-out love scene would say it any better," Spielberg contends on the DVD interview. In her interview on the DVD edition, Kathleen Kennedy, one of the film's producers and the person who first brought Walker's book to Spielberg's attention, says she believes that "the whole notion of anything that alludes to a same-sex relationship would have been considered borderline taboo at the time that we were making the movie." While Walker was initially "annoyed that there was not more cuddling and kissing and making love," she looks back on the DVD interview and concludes that this scene "was very very well done because it captures the sweetness of their relationship." One does not need to be cynical to see that it also allowed Spielberg to keep the film's PG-13 rating, thus providing access to a wider audience than would have been possible with a more restrictive "R" in its advertisements. Ultimately, then, Spielberg made an artistic, a psychological, and a marketing decision in depicting the physical connection between Shug and Celie far more obliquely than Walker did in her book. Spielberg conceptualizes the powerful bond between Celie and Shug as "a love relationship of great need. No one had ever loved Celie other than God and her sister. And here Celie is being introduced to the human race by a person full of love."[60] Yet his downplaying of the physical acts between Celie and Shug elicits criticism from both those who claim he showed too much and those who assert he did not go far enough.

Along with constraining the love scenes between Celie and Shug, Spielberg makes two significant alterations to the spirit of Walker's novel that overtly demonstrate his persistent psychological drives and tie *The Color Purple* securely to his other works: the inclusion of Shug's father (John Patton, Jr.), and the refusal to reconcile Mister with Celie. Shug's intense desire to be loved and accepted by her minister father does, as many critics contend, domesticate the sexy jazz singer; her desperate need to gain his approval reinforces the practice and power of patriarchal privilege which the book, and sometimes the movie, seeks to expose and undermine. In the novel, Walker emphasizes Shug's "completely unapologetic self-acceptance as an outlaw, renegade, rebel and pagan; her zest in loving both women and men, younger and older."[61] In the movie, distinctly opposite to this rebellious exuberance, "Shug is seen as someone who regrets the life she has lived and who assents to others' perception of her as a loose woman. Her constant quest for absolution from her preacher father takes away her central source of power in the novel – that she does what she wants and has the economic means to do so."[62] This "disempowerment" becomes evident early in the movie.

During the sequence entitled "Shug's bath," a time when the singer must recover from physical illness and spiritual depravation, she reveals the emotional frailness lurking just beneath her bravado. It opens with jazz music from a victrola filling the room as Celie obsequiously attends Shug, adding hot water and bubble oil as the singer belittles her. We view Shug from behind the metal tub, her hands holding a bottle of whiskey and a cigarette, her voice heard before we see her face: "What you staring at?" she barks at Celie. "Never seen a naked woman before?" Almost immediately, the singer turns the talk toward children, interrogating Celie about where hers might be. "You got kids?" asks Celie, tentatively responding. "Yeah," says Shug, "They with my ma and pa. Never knowed a child to come out right unless there's a man around. Children gots to have a pa. Your pa love you? My pa loves me. My pa still loves me. 'Cept he don't know it. He don't know it." Shug entwines both childhood and motherhood with the yearning for a masculine presence and recognizes the lack of such a figure in her life; slowly, she sinks back into the water, convulsed in tears of pain and sobs of regret. Celie, mesmerized but sensing Shug's need for warmth and human contact, begins gently to brush her hair. Lingering in her past for a moment longer, Shug melts into the rhythms of the brushstrokes and begins to hum snatches of a melody which will eventually become "Miss Celie's Blues."

This poignant moment of contact between Celie and Shug – two women whose children have been taken away from them, two women whose fathers have either abandoned or raped them (as we believe at this point), two women who have suffered irreparable emotional trauma inflicted by their fathers – sets the tone for the rest of the movie; it indelibly defines Shug's character. From this point on, even when we see her provocatively gyrating in her shimmering red dress and belting out lusty lyrics in Harpo's juke joint, we always understand that a fundamental sadness pervades Shug's life, a grief that no music can fully drown out and a thirst that no whiskey can ever quench. On the other hand, this moment also plants the seeds for Celie's eventual liberation. For the first time since Mister so brutally separated her from Nettie, Celie feels something for someone else. She has seen pictures of Shug before, since Mister keeps one prominently displayed in their bedroom. But as she stares into this woman's face, a moment of quiet reverence steals over her, a calm that blossoms into love despite the obviously awkward situation. Eventually, Shug's appreciation of Celie's kindness and warmth will evolve into a deeply reciprocal love. Only by seeing herself through Shug's eyes will Celie ultimately recognize herself as a person of worth and substance and, as a result, attain the inner strength needed to escape the physical and psychological oppression represented by Mister.

As the film progresses, Shug becomes more and more traditional in both her dress and actions. Recovering from her illness – clothed conservatively in a light purple outfit, her hair pulled back and tucked neatly under a large hat with a prominent bow, and carrying a pink parasol – she attempts to visit her father in his empty church. "What life like for her?" wonders Celie as she shyly follows Shug down the country road, "And why she sometime gets so sad? So sad just like me?" Greeting her father tentatively, Shug tells him that she has been sick, that she is better now, and that she is staying down the road with Albert and Celie. He keeps sweeping the church, never looking at her or even acknowledging her presence. Finally, he sits down, his broad back to his daughter. "This place brings back memories," she tells him, revealing how she watched him in church, "the best preacher in the world." She continues to inch tentatively forward, the camera sometimes capturing them in a tense two-shot and other times alternating between her face and his back. As she offers him some snatches from the gospel songs she once sang in his choir, her father slowly gets up and heads toward the back door of the building. "It's alright," says Shug, retreating in the opposite direction, "I know you can't say nothing to me anymore 'cause things so different. Just thought I would stop and say hello." They leave through separate exits, shutting doors and closing themselves off from each other.

After her marriage, Shug and her new husband Grady pay a surprise visit to Celie and Mister, both of whom are disappointed and somewhat bewildered by her new status as a wife. No longer does she resemble the raucous singer who shimmied in sparkling red sequins and outlandish headdresses, packed Harpo's juke joint, and caused men to nearly faint with lust and mutter how they would "drink her bathwater." Instead, she looks like a conservative, middle-class lady, her mid-calf blue dress and straightened hair evidence of a newly acquired sense of respectability and modest comportment. She even smokes cigarettes through a fancy holder, though her desperation for fatherly acceptance remains unfiltered. Unexpectantly, he drives his horse and buggy past Mister's house, his outmoded vehicle and dark suit in stark contrast to Grady's snazzy yellow convertible and vivid clothes. Shug breaks into a smile, then trots hopefully out to the road to greet him. "I's married now," she yells out, holding up her hand and pointing to the ring on her finger. Silence. "I said I's married now," she calls after him, as he whips his horse and drives past her without a word or a glance in her direction. The smile fades from her face. Dejected, she lowers her hand, stares forlornly at the gold band encircling her finger, and softly begins to hum "Sister," as she approaches the mailbox and retrieves the letter that will lead to Celie's liberation.

Shug's reconciliation with her father comes, not surprisingly, through music. But, it follows an important scene taken almost verbatim from Walker's novel, though with less pantheistic emphasis and without her character's bitterness about "Man corrupting everything."[63] Celie and Shug casually stroll amidst a frame filled with exuberant purple flowers. "More than anything," Shug tells Celie, who trails after her holding an umbrella to shade herself from the sun, "God loves admiration. . . . I think it pisses God off if you walk by the color purple in a field somewhere and you don't notice it." Celie responds hesitantly, "Are you saying it just want to be loved like it say in the Bible?" "Yeah," responds Shug, "everything want to be loved. Us sing and dance and holler just trying to be loved. . . . Oh, Miss Celie, I feels like singin!" Interestingly, Spielberg keeps his distance from the characters in this crucial scene. We see them only from the waist up in the mid ground of the frame, the fore and backgrounds filled with flowers. Instead of concentrating on their faces as they utter these words, he lingers on their surroundings, creating a moment in which the words seem more like voiceovers than dialogue. Here, as elsewhere, the director focuses on the visual and emotional import of the language as mediated through the images, on the visceral connection between sights and sounds, image and language.

The reconciliation scene between Shug and her father begins with ostracism: Mister sits rocking alone on the front porch, banished for his litany of sins. He never utters a word in the film again. He has lost his voice. As so often happens in this film, we hear characters before we see them; the sound of Shug singing "Sister" wafts over the forlorn and isolated figure of Mister before Spielberg brings us to the crowded site of her musical performance. This time, however, both the joint and Shug have noticeably changed. No longer is she solely the focus of heated masculine gazes. In fact, the scene begins with well-dressed men and (conspicuously absent earlier) women swaying to her voice, as Harpo lowers the drawbridge between his place and the mainland. Dressed conservatively in a long, pale yellow dress with matching earrings and holding a bouquet of purple flowers in one hand and a blue handkerchief in the other, Shug continues to croon as Spielberg crosscuts between the juke joint and her father's Sunday church service. "All of us been prodigal children at one time or another" booms the preacher from his pulpit, "And I tell you children it's possible for the Lord to drive you home. To drive you home to truth. And he can fix things for you if you trust him." But his flock is already distracted. Hearing the sweet sounds of Shug's music, they fidget on the hard wooden benches, craning their necks backwards toward the music flowing from Harpo's.

Sensing their dwindling attention, the preacher turns to the choir standing behind him who, dressed in white robes with collars nearly replicating the color of Shug's dress, rise to his call and harmoniously answer "Yesssss." Cut back to Shug who hears the faint music emanating from her father's church, as his congregation just heard hers. She pauses for a moment, the past calling out to her, the prodigal child of her father's sermon. The jazz music slides to a halt, and the choir's blended voices fill Harpo's now silent building. Cut back to the church. "If I were you I would say 'Yes,'" belts out the lead singer, a young black woman who holds the place no doubt once occupied by Shug. Cut back to Shug. "Speak Lord," she sings, as we hear the choir singer echo the same phrase from across the river. "Speak to me," she continues. Quick cut to Mister, a smile playing across his lips. Again, her words are echoed by the church choir: "I was so lost until He spoke to me." Now the people pour out of Harpo's, cross the drawbridge, and head toward the church with Shug leading them onward. "Oh speak, Lord, / Speak to me" belts out Shug, as she guides the crowd through the dark woods and toward the plain white church. Spielberg continues to crosscut between the choir, who slowly become aware of another voice, and Shug; they occupy different frames but now seem to be singing together. Finally, her father recognizes the voice from outside, struck dumb by hearing it enter his sanctuary. "Oh you can't sleep at night," sings both Shug and the choir leader. Finally, Shug throws open the doors to the church she had so sadly closed earlier in the film; "Maybe / God is / Trying to tell you something" she sings out as she and her father finally face each other across a divide of hurt and pain.

As the patrons of the juke joint stream into the church, clapping and singing joyously along with Shug, she looks directly into her father's eyes and continues to implore him through her lyrics: "Maybe God is trying to tell you something" she repeats again and again, "Save me." The preacher gingerly removes his glasses to see his daughter more clearly, the woman standing before him, not the girl who defied him. "I praise your name," sings Shug, the choir responding, "God's trying to tell you something." Slowly the preacher slips from behind the pulpit. As father and child stare at each other in a shot/counter shot structure, Shug at last falls silent. As earlier, we see his back, but this time his daughter stands fully present in the same frame, momentarily caught in his gaze and her need. She rushes forward to hug him, tears streaming down her cheeks. "See Daddy," she whispers into his ear, "sinners have soul too." The preacher slowly raises his arms, still a bit uncertain about how to respond to the woman clinging tightly to him; then, he returns her embrace, Shug's face breaking into a broad smile of happiness and relief. The church erupts into even louder song, the patrons of the juke joint freely mixing with those in the congregation. Only Celie, in a close-up, remains silent. Though a small smile forms on the edge of her mouth, she remains apart from the celebration, perhaps remembering the cruelties of her own father, her pain at the hands of Mister, and her still absent children and sister.

The scene I have just transcribed into words provides a good example of why some viewers feel emotionally moved by Spielberg's films while, at the same time, others harshly reject his overt sentimentality and conservatism. Remember, first, that the inclusion of the preacher as a character is wholly Spielberg's invention; he is not found in the Walker novel. Then, depicting a daughter singing a gospel song about God the Father, while at the same time imploring her biological father to forgive her, surely provides ammunition for those who label him a reactionary filmmaker, one conspicuously merging religious obedience and patriarchal submission into a single moment. Yet the archetypal union of a child with a parent, here depicted as a spectacle both witnessed and shared by the surrounding community which is simultaneously joined together as well, possesses an almost irresistible visual power heightened even further by the mixture of black musical traditions that permeate the scene. The action resembles a Vincente Minnelli musical number more than it does any other part of the film's narrative, but it simultaneously demonstrates Spielberg's sustained thematic obsessions, proficiency at finding unique ways to express them, and mastery of engaging audiences in them.

Controversy 3: Spielberg distorts Walker's book – Mister's ostracism

As the music continues on the soundtrack in the reconciliation scene between Shug and the preacher, Spielberg cuts back to a close-up of Mister's hand as he opens the mailbox and reads the return address on the letter it contains: US Naturalization and Immigration Service / Washington D.C. / Important Official Mail. To the sounds of the gospel hymn he turns, digs up his hidden strong box, retrieves his money, journeys to the office from whence the letter came, and pays the funds necessary to bring Celie's children and sister back to America. This is Mister's act of contrition, his attempt to earn Celie's forgiveness and, perhaps, even his own redemption. But it will prove to no avail. In the final scene, all the film's major characters gather together on the porch or in the front yard of Celie's house: Squeak and Shug, Harpo and Sofia. Across a field of purple flowers, Celie spots a group of black men and woman standing beside their overloaded car. Their brightly colored scarves, pink and purple, billow upward in the breeze. Slowly, and then more rapidly, she realizes who it is: "Nettieeeeeee!" she screams dragging out the last vowel and running through the field toward her long-lost sister and, as she is soon to discover, her children as well.

Mister, who makes this touching reunion possible, is never allowed back into the family fold dominated by women. Following Shug's glance into the field, we catch a glimpse of him, standing beside his horse, as Celie's joyful reunion continues. He watches the events, breathes a sigh, drops his head slightly downward, and smiles to himself. Spielberg situates Mister in long shot beyond the field of purple flowers, not in it. The film's last image shows Celie and Nettie replaying their childhood clapping game as the lengthening shadows of the setting sun grow deeper behind them. Mister, silently leading his horse, slips by them in the foreground, never glancing at them and receiving no hint of recognition in return. In *The Same River Twice* (and repeated again in her DVD interview), Walker regrets "that Mister was not 'forgiven' by Steven as he was by me" and proclaims that "the ending was moving. But I wanted Mister up on the porch too!"[64] Indeed, at the end of Walker's novel, Celie and Mister sit together "seeing and talking and smoking our pipes."[65] In his DVD interview, Spielberg claims that he saw Mister not as "a villain but as a victim. A victim of his father. A victim of his era." He contends that the film contains a moment of silent forgiveness as Mister stands in the darkened street outside Celie's pants shop, but this moment barely, if at all, registers a glimmer of forgiveness.

In a very real sense, then, Spielberg's film is both more conservative and less compassionate than Walker's novel. The director's inclusion of a strong patriarchal presence in Shug's life undercuts her rebellion and, at times, tames her outlandish spirit. Bobo correctly concludes that "instead of a woman who lives her life according to the dictates of her values system . . . the film version of Shug is obsessed with winning her father's approval." As such, the film "casts a moral judgment on Shug" and in the reconciliation scene her song is one "of repentance." Spielberg's refusal to incorporate a contrite Mister into the final family reunion speaks of his deep anger, perhaps touching upon his own psychological relationship with his often absent father. Here Bobo misses the point entirely when she claims that:

> the black female characters . . . are displaced as the center of the story. The film is a chronicle of an abusive black man's journey toward self understanding. . . . The film grants the male protagonist salvation because he has arranged for a happy ending for the woman he misused throughout the film.

Quite the opposite, Celie's journey from abuse to independence remains Spielberg's clear and consistent focus, and as I have argued, no hint of "salvation" filters into his portrayal of Mister, who is less accepted than in Walker's book.[66]

The Color Purple: conclusion

I have purposely conjoined Spielberg's version of *The Color Purple* with the book upon which it is based and the woman who wrote it because, at no other point in his career, did this director ever approach a literary work with such reverence or collaborate so closely with an author he respected as he did with Alice Walker. Yet despite these facts, Spielberg still infuses the work with his overriding personal concerns. Along with a number of other critics from both inside the black community and beyond its borders, Bobo ultimately castigates the filmmaker for creating a production "in line with Steven Spielberg's experiences, cultural background, and social and political worldview. . . . He tapped into his consciousness and experiences and produced a work that was in keeping with his philosophy and knowledge of Hollywood films about black people."[67] But what kind of artist would Steven Spielberg be if he didn't make a Steven Spielberg film? Bobo condemns Spielberg for incorporating his persistent thematic preoccupations into his interpretation of Walker's text; I would contend that such acts are inevitable for creative directors who base films on novels. Unlike Bobo, I believe that Spielberg's characters in *The Color Purple* often transcend racial stereotypes, but her statements offer a congruent articulation of my fundamental approach to the director's work.

To expand on this just a bit further, the best film adaptations seek the spirit rather than the letter of their original source. Transferring that spirit to the screen often demands violating the letter of the work. This is one reason for the standard critical assumption that the better the novel the worse the film. Director Lewis Milestone aptly observes: "If you want to produce a rose, you will not take the flower and put it into the earth. This would not result in another rose. Instead, you will take the seed and stick it into the soil. From it will grow a rose. It's the same with film adaptation."[68] Take, for example, a classic example of this process. If one judges Akira Kurosawa's *Throne of Blood* (1957) by how well it reproduces the external events in Shakespeare's *Macbeth*, one might well deem it a rather poor attempt. But once we examine the themes and moods of Shakespeare's drama, and then analyze how Kurosawa uses cinematic devices to recreate those ideas and feelings visually, we can easily see that, far from being a weak adaptation, *Throne of Blood* remains extremely faithful to the spirit and meaning of *Macbeth*. Thus, the best directors become not illustrators of the written text, but artists who draw inspiration from original sources, as Shakespeare himself drew from Holinshed's Chronicles. All adaptations offer subjective responses to their primary sources. In this sense, artists can never fully duplicate the black experience in the early twentieth-century south but simply mediate it through their own eyes. That said, if one wants Walker's vision of that time, then one should read the novel. If one wants Steven Spielberg's interpretation of Walker, then one should see the film.

Few would contend, myself included, that *The Color Purple* stands as one of Spielberg's best films; but, in light of his future career, it was necessary for him to attempt such a challenging project in order to move forward as an artist. Ultimately, the ambitious movie fails because the director does not seem to trust himself or, at times, allow his images to carry the narrative. The frames are too loaded, the music too intrusive, the action too overblown, the comedy too broad, and the film simply too long. Yet one cannot deny the substantial power of some scenes, particularly the ripping apart of Celie and Nettie, the sadness of Sofia's first homecoming and her ultimate resurrection, the frightening brutality of Mister, and the joyful reunion of Celie with her family. It would also be important to acknowledge the marvelous performances Spielberg elicits from two first-time actors: Whoopi Goldberg and Oprah Winfrey. The reception to *The Color Purple* left Spielberg with some deep scars. The film received eleven Academy Award nominations, though Spielberg was not selected to compete in the "Best Director" category. It won no Oscars while an intrinsically more racist film, *Out of Africa*, captured the statuette for Best Picture. Spielberg, however, did obtain some consolation by winning the Director's Guild of America Award. Most importantly, however, the film's reception and controversies neither deterred Spielberg from making another predominately black film, nor prevented him from tackling more complex and demanding subjects.

Notes

Segments of this essay were published as part of my discussion of *The Color Purple* in *Citizen Spielberg* (Urbana and Chicago, IL: University of Illinois Press, 2006).

 1 Milly Heyd, *Mutual Reflections: Jews and Blacks in American Art* (New Brunswick, NJ: Rutgers University Press, 1999).
 2 Nicholas Mirzoeff, *Diaspora and Visual Culture: Representing Africans and Jews* (London: Routledge, 2000); Jeffrey Melnick, *Black–Jewish Relations on Trial: Leo Frank and Jim Conley in the New South* (Jackson, MI: University Press of Mississippi, 2000); Robert Philipson, *The Identity Question: Blacks and Jews in Europe and America* (Jackson, MI: University Press of Mississippi, 2000).
 3 Laurence Mordekhai Thomas, *Vessels of Evil: American Slavery and the Holocaust* (Philadelphia, PA: Temple University Press, 1993).
 4 Cornel West, *Race Matters* (New York: Vintage Books, 1994).
 5 Michael Lerner and Cornel West, *Jews and Blacks: A Dialogue on Race, Religion, and Culture in America* (New York: Plume, 1996).
 6 Harold Brackman, "The Attack on Jewish Hollywood: A Chapter in the History of Modern American Anti-Semitism," *Modern Judaism* 20, 1 (Winter 2000), p. 8.
 7 *Syracuse Herald Journal* (February 21, 1990).
 8 Brackman, "The Attack on Jewish Hollywood," p. 8.
 9 Brackman, "The Attack on Jewish Hollywood," p. 7.
10 Lester D. Friedman and Brent Notbohm, eds, *Steven Spielberg: Interviews* (Jackson, MI: University of Mississippi Press, 2000), p. 123.
11 Joseph McBride, *Steven Spielberg: A Biography* (New York: Simon and Schuster, 1997), p. 368.
12 McBride, *Steven Spielberg*, p. 369.
13 Steven Spielberg interview, *The Color Purple: Special Edition* (dir. Steven Spielberg, 1985. DVD. Warner, 2003).
14 Steven Spielberg, "Dialogue on Film," *American Film* (June 1988), p. 14.
15 Spielberg, "Dialogue on Film," p. 14.
16 Friedman and Notbohm, *Steven Spielberg*, p. 124.
17 Friedman and Notbohm, *Steven Spielberg*, p. 123.
18 Alice Walker, *The Color Purple* (New York: Harcourt Brace Jovanovich, 1983), pp. 23, 27.
19 Walker, *The Color Purple*, p. 30.

20 Walker, *The Color Purple*, p. 21.
21 Walker, *The Color Purple*, p. 161.
22 Walker, *The Color Purple*, p. 21.
23 Walker, *The Color Purple*, p. 30.
24 Walker, *The Color Purple*, p. 31.
25 Walker, *The Color Purple*, p. 161.
26 Walker, *The Color Purple*, p. 176.
27 Spielberg, "Dialogue on Film," p. 16.
28 Walker, *The Color Purple*, p. 35.
29 Walker, *The Color Purple*, p. 32.
30 Friedman and Notbohm, *Steven Spielberg*, p. 121.
31 Friedman and Notbohm, *Steven Spielberg*, p. 121.
32 Friedman and Notbohm, *Steven Spielberg*, p. 120.
33 McBride, *Steven Spielberg*, pp. 365; 373.
34 Donald Bogle, *Toms, Coons, Mulattoes, Mammies, and Bucks: An Interpretive History of Blacks in American Films* (New York: Continuum, 1986), p. 292.
35 Bogle, *Toms, Coons, Mulattoes, Mammies, and Bucks*, p. 293.
36 McBride, *Steven Spielberg*, p. 274.
37 Tony Brown, "Blacks Need to Love One Another," *Carolina Peacemaker* (January 4, 1986); *Antioch Review* 44, 3 (1986); Jacqueline Bobo, *Black Women as Cultural Readers* (New York: Columbia University Press, 1993).
38 Walker, *The Color Purple*, p. 223.
39 Walker, *The Color Purple*, p. 223.
40 Brackman, "The Attack on Jewish Hollywood," p. 8; Walker, *The Color Purple*, p. 224.
41 Walker, *The Color Purple*, p. 225.
42 Walker, *The Color Purple*, p. 23.
43 Walker, *The Color Purple*, p. 42.
44 Walker, *The Color Purple*, p. 42.
45 Anita Jones (January 4, 1986), p. 226.
46 Gerald Early, "*The Color Purple* as Everybody's Protest Art," *The Films of Steven Spielberg: Critical Essays*, ed. Charles L.P. Silet (Lanham, MD: The Scarecrow Press, 2002), pp. 94–102.
47 Early, "*The Color Purple* as Everybody's Protest Art," pp. 96, 98.
48 Early, "*The Color Purple* as Everybody's Protest Art," pp. 101–6.
49 Bobo, *Black Women as Cultural Readers*, pp. 64–8.
50 Bobo, *Black Women as Cultural Readers*, pp. 68–87.
51 Bobo, *Black Women as Cultural Readers*, pp. 87–93; 128.
52 Bobo, *Black Women as Cultural Readers*, p. 102.
53 Friedman and Notbohm, *Steven Spielberg*, p. 122.
54 McBride, *Steven Spielberg*, p. 736.
55 Friedman and Notbohm, *Steven Spielberg*, p. 124.
56 Spielberg, "Dialogue on Film," p. 14.
57 Walker, *The Color Purple*, p. 161.
58 Walker, *The Color Purple*, p. 161.
59 McBride, *Steven Spielberg*, pp. 375–6.
60 Friedman and Notbohm, *Steven Spielberg*, p. 124.
61 Walker, *The Color Purple*, p. 35.
62 Bobo, *Black Women as Cultural Readers*, p. 68.
63 Walker, *The Color Purple*, p. 168.
64 Alice Walker, *The Same River Twice: Honoring the Difficult* (New York: Washington Square Press, 1996), pp. 41; 161.

65 Walker, *The Same River Twice*, p. 230.
66 Bobo, *Black Women as Cultural Readers*, pp. 69–72.
67 Bobo, *Black Women as Cultural Readers*, p. 76.
68 Lester Friedman, "The Blasted Tree: Mary Shelley and James Whale," *The English Novel and the Movies*, eds Michael Klein and Gillian Parker (New York: Frederick Ungar Publishing, Company, 1981), p. 60.

Chapter 16

Crossover diva

Whoopi Goldberg and persona politics

Bambi L. Haggins

> I've never seen anyone like her. . . . One part Elaine May, one part Groucho, one part Ruth Draper, one part Richard Pryor and five parts never before seen.
>
> Mike Nichols[1]

Since her landmark one-woman show in 1985, Whoopi Goldberg has been somewhat of an entertainment anomaly: a black comic diva. On stage and screen, Goldberg has gained a degree of critical and financial success attained by few African American comics – and industrial clout accorded to even fewer women. With the notable exception of Jackie "Moms" Mabley and Pearl Bailey, whose careers, like Goldberg's, straddle stage and screen, Whoopi has acquired what few black female comic entertainers of either the pre- or post-Civil Rights era have been able to gain: access to white main stages and the entertainment mainstream. All of these women, with varying degrees of success, knew how to play to their audiences. Although one might also assert that Goldberg's divadom began with Mike Nichols' directed Broadway debut, thus making the emergence of Whoopi her moment of crossover, the comic actor, like her predecessors, has navigated crossover waters by mobilizing multiple personae, dependent upon both intended audience and the limitations of the given medium. Unlike Mabley and Bailey, the many facets of Whoopi often seem at war with each other – particularly in relationship to her comedic work.

In exploring Goldberg's comic personae in relationship to those who came before and those who followed her, one begins to discern how race, along with sexuality and gender, are played with and against by female black comic actors and how the constructions of their personae are inextricably tied to tropes of black femininity – for better *and* for worse. In her introduction to *Not Just Race, Not Just Gender*, Valerie Smith mobilizes Kimberle Crenshaw's concept of *intersectionality* "as a mode of cultural or textual analysis, what it means to read at the intersections of constructions of race, gender, class and sexuality."[2] This concept seems particularly apt for the discussion of the multiple ideological and sociocultural impulses that inform the personae that are Whoopi Goldberg. It is in this intersection that we all exist – our identities and our articulation of them, fluid and never fixed, always already being impacted by our past and present as well as histories of race, class, gender and nation. Undoubtedly, the complex process of identity formation for black women in the United States is in conversation with Goldberg's evolving comic personae. As one might expect when dealing with an individual who consistently endeavors to defy both convention and expectation, it is not always a friendly conversation. On one hand, the evolution of her persona and her sometimes contentious relationship with her audiences (black and white) calls to mind Dick Gregory's reflections on the nature of being a black comic:

> I've got to go up there as an individual first, a Negro second. I've got to be a colored funny man, not a funny colored man. . . . I've got to make jokes about myself before I make jokes about them and their society – that way they can't hate me. Comedy is a friendly relation.[3]

This "relation" is further problematized for Whoopi by gendered notions of "how to be funny" and those tied to the function of racial and cultural specificity in stand-up comedy, in the theater and on the big and small screens in the post-Civil Rights era. On the other hand, even as the choice of her stage name – "Whoopi," of cushion fame, and "Goldberg," either a homage to borscht belt comics or the name suggested by her mother (depending upon which bio one consults – and there are many differing accounts) signified the former Caryn Johnson compulsion to challenge and defy pre-determined conceptions of who and what she would be like, the comic actor was consistently engaged in the practice of crossover.[4] In fact, one might argue that Whoopi began *crossed-over*. Thus, Goldberg's outspokenness, her unabashed disdain for being "niched" and her idiosyncratic sense of humor and appropriateness have sometimes had the effect of setting her apart from the black community – for which, like it or not, she will always be seen as representative.

The phrase "crossover diva" is used in the title of this study to try to capture the conflicted and conflictual position that Goldberg occupies in American comedy. A slew of adjectives come to mind when one thinks of a diva: gifted, unique, uncompromising and, of course, prima donna.[5] I choose to mobilize the word as a signifier for a unique black female comic presence, who occupies a space in the entertainment world that, as much as possible, she defines. Thus, the choice to focus upon persona rather than a star, which necessarily forces one to foreground the comic actor's body of work rather than his/her personal life, is further complicated because the diva, one might argue, is always "on." In order to understand the significance of Goldberg's personae, one must see it how their trajectory was directed by and, in turn, directs, other black women's comic personae. Goldberg's choices of comic personae, as annunciated in her stand-up/stage performance and in film comedies, reflect and refract articulations of African American womanhood in myriad forms: constructed as alternately quotation and opposition to the hypersexualized *and* desexualized, to the stereotypical and the anomalous, within "integrated" milieu and homogeneous media texts. Again, the notion of intersectionality comes into play, not only in the construction of the persona, but also in the ways she is perceived at the intersections of race, class, gender at particular sociohistorical and sociocultural moments.

Given the few niches afforded women in mainstream comedy, one might assume that the voice of a comic who is a black and a woman might be marginalized. Surprisingly, in reality, Whoopi Goldberg has been afforded a dually – albeit mitigated – privileged space from which to speak for – if not always to – the African American community. Sadly, for audiences whose knowledge of Goldberg is limited to questionable comedic fare like *Bogus* and *Homer and Eddie*, the onstage prowess of the actor seems more like an antiquated legend than a popular cultural reality. One just might question Pryor's iconic status in American comedy if one had only viewed his Gene Wilder buddy films and not the pinnacle of the comedy performance film, *Live on the Sunset Strip*. Those who came to know Whoopi in the late 1990s and the first decade of the new millennium, have a woefully limited picture of her comedic discourse. While this study focuses upon the cinematic constructions of Whoopi, one must recognize the (minimally) bifurcated nature of her comic persona – existing as if the split between the onscreen and onstage personae, between the audacious sociocultural critic and the amiable trickster, is the function of sort of a willed schizophrenia. Like Richard Pryor, the cinematic construction of her comic personae often provide only the vestiges of the scathing sociopolitical critique and expansive notions of the American condition. Yet, in order to discern the nature of that bifurcation and to understand the multiple functions of Goldberg's personae, it is necessary to return (albeit briefly) to the moment of Whoopi – her emergent comic voice and the times in which it came to prominence.

The moment of Whoopi

Onstage, Goldberg was able to move fluidly from satire to pathos, from stand-up comedy to the brink of tragedy, whether in her self-titled Broadway debut where the series of monologues in the show attested not only to Goldberg's range as an actor (playing diverse characters from a black male junkie to teen-aged white surfer chick), which revealed her affinity for those on the margins of society or her scathing monologues addressing the complexity of race relations and media representations after the Rodney King beating (*Chez Whoopi*, 1991) and LA uprising (*Comic Relief V*, 1992).[6] In retrospect, one can see pieces of later iterations of Whoopi's stand-up and cinematic personae in each character's monologues as well as the sociocultural themes that will inform her work for the next two decades, and it was the comic prowess of this onstage Whoopi that initially established her divadom. However, when attempting, albeit elliptically, to illustrate Goldberg's onstage comic voice, one must go back to the character that she has revisited twice since his initial off-Broadway inception in *The Spook Show*: Fontaine.

Fontaine, who opens her one-woman show, comes closest to the voice of Whoopi – then and now – irreverent, outrageous and, arguably, outraged. Fontaine's entrance immediately lets the audience know that this is not going to be a night of traditional theater. He is heard – singing, "Around the World, in 80 Motherfucking Days" – before he is seen. On the second time through the chorus, the audience sees Goldberg as Fontaine, scarf tied around her head, dark glasses and a slow, hipster strut. Fontaine continues to sing as he moves towards the center of the stage. Like all the characters, Fontaine speaks directly to the audience; unlike the others, he expects them to answer back. Breaking the fourth wall (the virtual barrier between the audience and the world presented onstage), Goldberg disrupts the audience's notions about the breadth of Fontaine's cultural fluency, and perhaps, more important, as she speaks through Fontaine, Goldberg immediately establishes with the audience: he is in a position of authority. Goldberg, speaking in a low growl reminiscent of a blaxploitation movie hustler, endows Fontaine with toughness and just a touch of menace – the kind that might induce the clutching of pocketbooks if the upscale Broadway patrons were to pass him on the street. Fontaine, aware of this possible perception further toys with the audience: "Lot of people real uptight around me – I don't understand it. I think I'm real friendly. (*Pauses, staring over his dark glasses out at the audience.*) Don't you?"

In Fontaine, Goldberg found a comic alter ego that, if not autobiographically informed, was certainly inflected by her lived experience. As a former addict, one might argue that Goldberg's understanding that the addict is more than the addiction, certainly is part of what allows Fontaine, a junkie-thief with PhD in literature, to be the most fully realized character in the show. Moreover, Fontaine's irreverently incisive critique and his candid self-assessment provided the truest indication of Goldberg's actual comic voice to date. Interestingly, endowing Fontaine's monologue with the greatest degree of discursive power provided a masculine voice for Goldberg's persona. Thus, in this instance, gender is displaced by race, which informs not only Fontaine's world-view but also the authority with which he speaks – even if he is speaking from the margins.

When Goldberg revived Fontaine in August of 1988, in her second HBO special, *Fontaine: Why Am I Straight?*, her reputation for being outspoken in terms of her political beliefs was well established. While the construction of the junkie philosopher in its earlier iteration had been informed less by a political agenda than a common sense form of humanism, the clean and sober Fontaine of 1988 ripped into multiple status quo with a vengeance, critiquing the futility of the "Just Say No" campaign, the administration and the public's deafening silence on the AIDS epidemic and its victims. As Mel Watkins notes, "In that special, Goldberg proved that she could be as blasphemous as [Eddie] Murphy but her humor spotlighted social and political satire as well as straight out parody."[7] Watkins' comparison to Murphy, while apt on some levels, draws attention to the gendered dimensions of stand-up comedy, in which, the audaciousness of the male's content is viewed differently than that of a female's – with greater license being granted to the former in terms of being as "nasty as you want to be." Furthermore, while the audaciousness of Murphy's humor, particularly in *Raw* (1987), was rooted in masculinist discourse on sexual politics, popular culture and celebrity, Goldberg, who was always overtly political, at this point in her career did not use extended discussions of sexuality as a comic staple.[8] In fact, one might argue that Goldberg's initial decision to disseminate her scathing critique through the masculine filter of Fontaine speaks to these gendered assumptions and the era's de facto prohibition of frank discussion of social practice, namely, sexual agency. Through Fontaine, Goldberg engaged in a contentious dialogue with the cultural politics of the Reagan era and, like her ex junkie/philosopher alter ego, the comic actor confounded and was confounded by the times of which she, often incredulously, spoke.

Goldberg's rise to national prominence in the mid 1980s coincided with an increasingly difficult period for black America. When the gift of Reaganomics was the ever-expanding gap between rich and poor, poverty among blacks was at an all-time high and the crack epidemic, accompanied by the expansion of violence (gang and drug related), wreaked havoc in urban black America. In the same era when Martin Luther King Jr's birthday was being established as a national holiday and Jesse Jackson's run for presidency seemed to act as testaments to how far we had come in the struggle for civil rights, the incarceration of black men rose to then record numbers. The 1980s marked a period in which African American women writers (from Toni Morrison and Alice Walker to Terry MacMillan), whose work gave voice to a multiplicity of black women's experiences, at the same time that media images spun new tales of black female archetypes to join the mammy and the Jezebel, namely, those of the welfare queen and, the black female "Buppie" (black urban professional) or the "black lady." Taken in tandem, these emergent tropes of black femininity, like their predecessors, served as yet another means by which black women could be blamed for their own oppression and could be used to offer justification for the cutting of social welfare spending or the limitations sought in relationship to affirmative action. As Wahneema Lubiano notes, "Whether not achieving and passing on bad culture as welfare mothers, or by virtue of having achieved middle-class success . . . Black women are responsible for the disadvantaged status of African Americans."[9] By the mid 1980s, the administration's domestic policy had a devastating impact on the underclass – namely, the homeless and the working poor – especially in urban America: from the loss of revenue sharing to cities and reduced funding for public service jobs and job training, to the elimination of the anti-poverty Community Development Block Grant program and the reduction of funds for public transit. One of

Goldberg's first public political acts responded to this glaring need in the "greed is good" days in the land of plenty. Goldberg, along with Billy Crystal and Robin Williams, became the public face of Comic Relief, a non-profit organization created by writer-producer Bob Zmuda in 1986, which used the increased popularity of stand-up to raise funds and awareness to fight homelessness in the 1980s. For Goldberg, the telethon stand-up show provided a venue to espouse her strongly held political beliefs with like-minded comic actors. Goldberg became associated with this crusade against homelessness, a cause that cut across boundaries of race, gender and region and, in so doing, became a high-profile equal-opportunity activist.[10] By the early 1990s, emboldened by the significant industrial currency from her Academy Award winning role in *Ghost*, Goldberg became even more insistent upon bringing her particular political agenda to the public's attention – regardless of the venue. No longer using characters as vehicles for her discourse, Goldberg's voice, unfiltered, expounded upon glaring social and political ills.

On stages for over two decades – in stand-up (HBO specials), in hosting duties (the Academy Awards and multiple iterations of Comic Relief) or as celebrity cultural critic (on the talk and new show circuit from *Hardball* with Chris Matthews to *The View*) – Goldberg has cultivated her self-professed "equal opportunity offender" status. While the broad swath of Goldberg's critique establishes her affinity with multiple communities; it also makes clear her unwillingness to being limited by the political agenda of any one of them. While one might argue that Goldberg's construction of her comic personae onstage (literally and figuratively) was tailor made for her very personalized politics, the intentionality of the comic in the creation of his/her persona is only half of the story; the way in which the personae are seen to mobilize, represent and speak to varied ideological and cultural impulses in the American popular culture of his/her day is the other half. Clearly, Goldberg's forthright comedic persona posits her in unique and problematic space within the entertainment industry: a sort of A-list star with an asterisk next to her name. The power of that asterisk signifies both her highly politicized public persona and reveals a negative spin to the early praise given her by the director of her Broadway debut, Mike Nichols – "I have never seen anyone like her." In the film industry, which never seems to know exactly what to do with her, her uniqueness is not necessarily a good thing. This fact becomes progressively and more painfully apparent when examining the body of her comic film work.

> I've never been offered a lot of scripts because nobody is sure what to do with me.[11] – Whoopi Goldberg

Onscreen, Whoopi plays with and against these iterations of black womanhood – sometimes subverting and sometimes reinscribing problematic constructions. While Goldberg's personae offer unique voices for comedic sociopolitical discourse, I would argue that the lineage of their divadom can be traced back to the humor of black women, who – onstage and around the kitchen table – offered their reflections on their American condition. Goldberg is not the only comic presence to play with expectations and to use humor to forward both critique and complacency. Indeed, Jackie "Moms" Mabley and Pearl Bailey are two such black female comic figures who, while not having achieved either the industrial success or the widespread notoriety of Goldberg, managed to cross over to the mainstream promised land with their divadom intact. If, indeed as Valerie Smith states, "by reading intersectionally," one might ascertain "the ways racism, misogyny, homophobia, and class discrimination have functioned historically and in the present to subordinate all black people and women," one might also be able to address the manner in which industrial and cultural practices play out in the movement of mediated images (like comic personae) and the ways in which the images themselves are in conversation with multiple forms of limitation and/or subjugation generated by those aforementioned practices.[12] While the rewards for crossover – in terms of exposure, industrial cachet and fiscal remuneration – are not insignificant, neither is the price of the ticket, determined by American taste culture as well as the times. Bailey, Goldberg and Mabley thrived in an era not particularly hospitable to black women in a male-dominated genre – but the terms of success, like the times themselves, offered unique struggles and unexpected opportunities.

At first glance, race and humor might be seen as the only qualities that join together Pearl Bailey, Moms Mabley and Whoopi Goldberg. Bailey's Pearlie Mae persona blended lackadaisically saucy sexuality with "down home" acceptance (and, even celebration) of the sociopolitical status quo. Bailey used humor "to communicate her view of the world as a joyous, harmonious place that had no great problems or tensions."[13] Mabley adopted the wise, folksy and risqué "Moms" persona to speak to social and political issues not seen to be within the purview of female comedians during her five decades in show business. Like the multiple and multifaceted personae of Goldberg, Bailey and Mabley each possessed a distinctive style that captivated audiences across boundaries of class and color, each used humor tied to her respective era to illuminate her worldview and each was able, within the limits of her chosen medium and persona, to articulate an idiosyncratic, sociopolitically, socioculturally informed brand of comedic discourse. While one might place Goldberg to the left of the political spectrum, Bailey on the right and Mabley somewhere in the (liberal-leaning) middle, both their bodies of work and the working of their bodies (how they were visually constructed) speak to historical constructions of black womanhood. Undoubtedly, both Bailey and Mabley could easily merit studies of their own; however, for the purposes of this study, their comic kinship with Goldberg will be examined in relationship to their articulations of sexual and political agency and integrationist Americanism, respectively, as well as, of course, their shared diva status and the audience and industrial understanding of that construct.

Remembrances of divas past, Part I: Moms Mabley

By the time Dick Gregory did his famous stint at the Playboy Club in Chicago in 1961, Jackie "Moms" Mabley, using the granny persona as a means to cut her biting sociocultural critiques (and to lighten the "blue" of some of her more salacious material), proved to be primed for crossover success – only 40 years after she started working on the Theater Owner Booking Association circuit. "Her matronly, off-beat appearance and down home ruminations about politics and the Civil Rights movement, and her fondness for younger men, were perfectly suited to the club's racy image."[14] (In the years that followed this appearance, Moms' crossover success, which had been a long time in coming, was impressive: after her auspicious debut album, "Moms Mabley at the UN," she made over 20 recordings on the Chess label and remains the highest charting comedienne on Billboard.[15] As Elsie A. Williams notes:

> With the integrated audiences of the sixties and seventies, the comedian continued to perform, basically, the same kind of folk humor that she had developed on the earlier "chitlin' circuit," where the boundary of segregation made the question of boundary practically irrelevant.[16]

Like those of Goldberg, her black comic diva daughter, Mabley's choices, in terms of the construction of her persona and the content of comedy, played with audience expectations and won popular claim even as they were inherently constrained not only by the times but by the ideological impulses that inflect the choices themselves.

Interestingly, as with Goldberg's, there was subversiveness built into Mabley's choices – both of name and of the purposefully desexualized (in Goldberg's case, androgynous) construction of gender. Whereas there was a certain arbitrary (and, arguably, anarchic) component to Goldberg's choice of moniker, Loretta Mary Aiken became Jackie Mabley in response to the actions of two men her life: a brother, who expressed his embarrassment about his sister's life on the boards and her first boyfriend whom she said took so much from her that the least she could do was take his name; the "Moms" nickname was given to her because of the maternal streak that she endeared to her fellow performers on the TOBA circuit. Moms' choice to literally *take* Jack Mabley's name signaled the feminist underpinnings of her persona – as did her choice to construct her appearance. Goldberg's consistent choice of baggy unisex clothing corresponds to Moms' attire, which was, arguably, suggestive of a mammy of sorts (frumpy, oversized housedresses, mismatched colorful clothing, floppy hats, socks with slippers) in that neither had made a fashion choice intended to construct their bodies as objects of desire – rather, they had purposefully covered their bodies in ways that made their female sexuality unobtrusive. The physicality of their personae seemed intended to directly contrast with the content of their comedy; the early onstage Goldberg persona used the dark-skinned, dreadlocked androgyny of her body as a sort of *tabula rasa* upon which she could detail the characters she embodied. Mabley, on the other hand, modeling "Moms" physically after her own grandmother, constructed a purposefully desexualized persona with touches of both masochism and pathos. Nonetheless, the disparity between the libidinous nature of monologues (often on the merits of young men and the deficiencies of the old) and her rubbery faced mugging, gravel-voiced delivery and desexualized appearance did not diminish the liberatory potential of her comedic discourse which forwarded the "public discussion of the female's sexual needs and . . . the inadequacy of the [usually old] male to fulfill such needs, both off-limits as subjects in comedy routines by women until very recently."[17]

In her commentaries on civil rights, however, Mabley's adherence to the revolutionary directives of the movement were unequivocal, as were her observations about both racial violence and the struggles of black activists, which were encased in vaudevillian-styled joke series and provided pointed critique within the guise of old-fashioned entertainment:

> Colored fellow down home died. Pulled up to the gate. St Peter look at him, say, "What do you want?" "Hey man, you know me. Hey, Jack, you know me. I'm old Sam Jones. Old Sam Jones, man, you know me. Used to be with the NAACP, you know, CORE and all that stuff, man, marches, remember me? Oh, man, you know me." He just broke down there, "You know me." He looked in his book. "Sam Jones," he say, "no, no you ain't here, no Sam Jones." He said, "Oh, man, yes, I am; look there. You know me. I'm the cat that married that white girl on the capitol steps of Jackson, Mississippi." He said, "How long ago has that been?" He said, "About five minutes ago."[18]

While the (light) blueness of her humor and the barely disguised sociopolitical commentary may seem mild by contemporary standards, Moms Mabley was an innovative force in American comedy. Moms' persona still operated within a stone's throw of the mammy, thus supplying some degree of comfort to audiences to whom the minstrel archetypes still appealed, but the content of her comedy was inflected by a mitigated sense of rebellion. Her construction of a comic persona that subverted long held social predispositions as the desexualized, alternately cantankerous and kindly sort of revisionist mammy, who uses comedic strategies associated masculine forms of the black humor (like "signifying") to position her, not simply within the black comic traditions of the past, in which the critique of mainstream America had to be coded and hidden, but also, in the spirit of the Civil Rights era, with a new form of direct comedic sociopolitical discourse, in which the voices of marginalized people – including black women – could be heard.

Cinematic convergences: de-wexed, de-raced – Moms, Whoopi and agency

Jackie Mabley made her big screen debut in the small role of Marcella in the 1933 version of *The Emperor Jones* starring Paul Robeson; her big-screen time has been quite minimal, and she made only six films in her career of almost six decades. Only in her first and last film, however, was Mabley actually asked to actually play a role, as Marcella, which was uncredited, and, the title role in Stan Lathan's *Amazing Grace* (1974), more memorable as a final showcase for the mugging and preaching aspects of Mabley's persona[19] and the appearance of black stars from the cinematic and vaudeville past like Slappy White, Butterfly McQueen and Stepin Fetchit, than as an uneven social comedy about inner-city politics (with the system eventually "working" because Mabley's Grace *reminds* the parties in question how the system should work). Perhaps more significant is Mabley's positioning of both herself and the film made during the blaxploitation age:

> I'm not a Black moviemaker. I'm everybody's moviemaker all nations and all colors. I don't want to make any of my brothers and sisters angry so I can't say what I want to say about a lot of those Black films. But Moms don't make that kind of movie. Ours is a family movie.[20]

By the time Mabley made it back to the big screen, both her comic sensibility and her notion of blackness seemed slightly out of step with the post Civil Rights era. Grace, unlike her previous cinematic constructions of the randy granny/mammy, was full of hopefulness and certainty that the sociopolitical ills of the black community could be solved by working within the existing institutional structures – absent was any edge or cynicism embedded in either the film's narrative or in the nuances in Mabley's performance. Furthermore, the ethos of colorblind family entertainment puts Moms squarely in the integrationist camp – particularly given the contrasts she makes between her film and, not only to the films associated with Black Power informed agency (*Foxy Brown* or *Truck Turner*, both 1974), but also those that worked with a post Civil Rights culturally specific comedic framework like *Uptown Saturday Night* (also 1974). While it is not surprising that Civil Rights era sentiments informed Moms' comedic social discourse, the language of her differentiation between her film and the 1970s black cinematic fare, in this instance, seems oddly deferential. As though aware that this colorblind assertion was somehow controversial at a decidedly not colorblind time in the nation's history, Moms Mabley, comic diva, seemed reticent to speak her mind. In its previous stage and small iterations, the Moms persona, desexualized with her race, simultaneously centered and elided because of the randy granny/revisionist mammy construction, was able to speak to and of aspects of the African American experience – without causing undue discomfort to mainstream audiences. On the cusp of the post Soul Era, the cultural, political and economic realities of life in the African American community problematized the notion of "overcoming someday" – when the integrationist rhetoric did not assuage fears and hostilities in Boston in 1976 anymore than it had in Little Rock over two decades before.[21] Thus, one might assume that the notion of colorblind comedy coming from a desexualized black woman, one that seemed dated in the 1970s, would have undoubtedly passed out of cinematic favor – one would be wrong.

In Goldberg's comic roles, the films featured a de-sexed and de-raced Whoopi.[22] Even in her Academy Award winning supporting role as Oda Mae Brown in *Ghost* (1990), Goldberg, as the spiritualist conduit for the recently deceased Sam and his grieving lover, Molly (played by Patrick Swayze and Demi Moore), besides providing comic relief in what would have otherwise been a supernatural weepie, gives her body in service to the tragic white couple. Interesting opportunities to play with both race and sexuality are squandered: play with this visual of Goldberg, in a big bad bouffant hairdo (rather than her usual dreadlocks), kissing Moore, in her eponymous pixie cut, could have been a means to question the nature of love (à la *Prelude to a Kiss*), taking the easier route, the hug and kisses shared between Molly and Sam via Oda Mae begin with Whoopi leaning in to Demi only to cut to Swayze touching Moore. While direct references to race were minimal ("white men trying to kill me"), given the narrative's less than adventurous spirit, the lion's share of the humor and Oda Mae's construction harkened back to all too familiar cinematic constructions of black folks and ghosts. The way in which Oda Mae's body is used in service to white happiness shows more than a passing similarity to the function of the mammy as does the almost absurd de-sexualized physical appearance of the character, a fact that neither the warmth nor the humor of Goldberg's performance can negate. Goldberg's comic persona was repeatedly positioned within narratives that cut any possible socio-political edginess with integrationist sentiments in colorblind comedic morality plays. Nowhere was this more apparent than the 1992 vehicle penned for Bette Midler, *Sister Act*.

Like that of Moms' Grace, Goldberg's Deloris Van Cartier's construction was informed by a colorblind comic sensibility that seemed out of sync with both post-King-beating America and Goldberg's own stand-up comic discourse. *Sister Act* is fundamentally a fish-out-of-water comedy in a nun's costume. First shown as the bespangled Diana Ross wannabe in a budget version of the Supremes, playing to a single unenthusiastic patron in a Reno casino, Goldberg is made to look intentionally absurd – and of questionable musical talent. The ill-fated romance between Deloris and Vince LaRocca (Harvey Keitel), which ends when the former sees the latter directing a hit, is the plot device than hurls Goldberg's fish out of water. However, race is purposefully avoided: no mention is made of the fact that her mobster boyfriend is white.[23] At times, the colorblind ethos strains credulity – in the frantic casino chase climax of the film, no one thinks to cite the race of the only black nun in the convent as an identifying detail.

Given that the film was not written for Goldberg, when "race as subtext" appears in the narrative, it goes uninterrogated. For example, one can easily read the other inhabitants of the convent immediate fascination with Sister Mary Clarence as a racialized moment – although their fetishizing of the activities of her fictional "progressive" order acts as the unwitting signifier for the "hipness" factor of black culture. When put in charge of the order's abysmal choir, Deloris/Sister Mary Clarence makes them into "chorus girls" with choreography and song styling influenced as much by gospel production numbers (their sanctified version of "Salve Regina") as by those found on the Reno strip (their retooling of the Motown Classic into "My God") – although the influence of the former is never recognized. Furthermore, as Janet Maslin notes, race continues to inflect the audience's reading of the film:

> [Deloris/Sister Mary Clarence is] scorned by Mother Superior (Maggie Smith), who disdains loud clothes and vulgar manners. Scenes that might have played as mere snobbery with Ms. Midler have the hint of racism, which might have been dispelled if the film had only addressed it head on.[24]

The elision of race is further codified with the progressive de-sexualizing of Deloris. A nun's habit serves even better than a frumpy housedress in terms of establishing the character as fundamentally asexual. Despite protestations to the contrary (throwaway lines like "and they don't even have sex"), the adjustment to convent life was not rooted in a sexual being's forced celibacy but rather in one who loves the night life being forced to be good and go to bed early. The transformation is complete once Deloris has the priorities of Sister Mary Clarence – willingly endangering herself (and, unintentionally, the rest of the convent) in order to perform the "big show" for the Pope, no less. Once rendered asexual and color-less, Goldberg's persona in Deloris/Mary Clarence is comfortably contained – and that made for good box office. At $232 million worldwide, *Sister Act* is the highest-grossing film in which Goldberg has starred and was, arguably, her last film to win popular, if not critical acclaim.

Given the success of this film (and Goldberg's willingness to conform her comic persona to mainstream cinematic imperatives), one would think that she would have no difficulty in continuing to be one of the few black female comic actors able to open a film. That has not always been the case – and the reasons why are by no means transparent. On one hand, the disparity between the comic film roles and her outspoken comedic sociopolitical discourse, although apparent, might not necessarily account for a decline in her cinematic popularity. On the other, her undeniable comic prowess and the purposeful construction of her comic personae may be at times, in contentious conversation with the times. Unlike Mabley, who read such moments warily and trod gingerly in positioning herself and her responses to those who positioned her, as the lines between Goldberg's person and persona began to blur extratextually, Goldberg's outspoken nature gave greater license (and fodder) for criticism and scrutiny.

Remembrances of divas past, Part II: Pearl Bailey

The kinship between the personae of Pearlie Mae and Whoopi may seem a bit more tenuous than the ties between those of Goldberg and Mabley. While Pearl and Whoopi occupy opposite ends of the political and comedic spectrum, the comic personae of Goldberg are clearly inflected by her unabashed liberalism (which, only on occasion, actually informs her cinematic construction) just as Bailey's Pearlie Mae, while not directly addressing her unapologetic conservative political beliefs, invested heavily in the creation of idyllic constructions of Americanism, where the discussion of race was simply deemed unnecessary. Their personae were honed in their early stage performance – for Goldberg, in small theaters before heading to Broadway and for Bailey, in Chitlin' Circuit theaters and, quite early in her career, white, as well as black, nightclubs before becoming the unequivocal star of a Broadway show.

In their debuts on the great white way, as originators of roles, Whoopi, in her retooled *Spook Show* debut and Pearl as the first Aunt Hagar in *St Louis Blues*, Goldberg and Bailey, each caused a sensation on Broadway. While the former tapped into the wellspring of her multiple personae, the latter, despite the high critical praise, only sampled a narrow swath of hers. Interestingly, each was involved in "non-traditional" casting coups when they took over roles in Broadway musicals from white actor predecessors. In each case, the "fact" of race was downplayed. When Goldberg followed in Nathan Lane's role of Pseudolus in the revival of Stephen Sondheim's *A Funny Thing Happened To Me On The Way To The Forum*, much more was made of the fact that a woman was taking over the role than the fact that a black actor was playing the role of a "smart slave." Playing the role with equal parts broad vaudevillian style (utilized by both Lane and, the original Pseudolus, Zero Mostel) and sly androgynous trickster, Goldberg fit with the bawdiness of the show's humorous tone. When Bailey followed Carol Channing in the role of Dolly in a black-cast version of Jerry Herman's *Hello Dolly*, seen as a risky venture in 1967, the character was remade into an ideal vehicle for the Pearlie Mae persona. The ad-lib-prone Bailey enhanced the original with a swagger and sassiness that Channing's effusive Levi (and Streisand's Fanny Briced-Levi) lacked. However, although the Pearlie Mae persona made its way into her stage roles (although not, for the most part, into her screen roles), the nightclub was its perfect habitat.

The nightclub Bailey used her act to establish her persona, Pearlie Mae, a woman who has been done wrong (and has done wrong, too) comes through, not only in the double-entendre-filled songs, but also in the asides and ad-libs that play with audience sensibility. More naughty than genuinely blue, Bailey's act, when brought to the small screen, retained many of the mildly provocative elements that had won her mainstream popularity. By the late 1940s, Bailey, already a nightclub veteran and having won raves for her supporting role in "St Louis Woman," was performing on television variety programs like *Cavalcade of Stars: Starring Jackie Gleason*. Her mannerisms are the same in January of 1949 as they would be in January of 1970 onstage in the premiere of her own television variety show – she is sassy. Clad in a very feminine black strapless dress with jeweled bodice, tight waist and full skirt, Bailey is definitely not desexualized nor is her song selection: "Good Enough For Me." Alternately talking and *singing* her way through the number, Pearl Mae crosses musical theatrics with down home earthiness in her performance:

> When I settle down and get married
> I want all of my in-laws to be
> Simple country folk like the Vanderbilts, The Whitneys, The Morgans,
> That's not a bad selection there.
> They're good enough for me.

Watching Bailey perform on her ABC variety show almost two decades later, the schtick is very much the same – although the content has been made even more family friendly. Her interactions with the audience, with asides and free floating "darlings," create a sense of small club intimacy in a large auditorium. Moreover, by her series premiere in 1970, both her clothing and her act had become more modest: with higher necklines replacing strapless fare, pants replacing full skirts; and rampant double entendre replaced by Pearl's pearls of wisdom. One only need to see the opening number of her series' premiere to see the convergence of personae (Pearl as Dolly as Pearlie Mae) particularly when Bailey makes the kind of entrance one expects from a diva: with a chorus singing her praises. Reminiscent of Dolly's descent into the show's production number, "Hello Dolly," Bailey stands at the back of the house in gold lamé gown, diamond jewelry and a chinchilla coat as an integrated group of chorus boys, dressed as ushers in red jackets with gold braid, sing, "Here comes joy, here comes love, here comes Pearlie Mae." An usher hands her roses as she saunters down the center aisle. Singing the chorus from another diva musical, "Applause," Bailey adlibs freely between the lines of lyrics. The presence is diva but comforting kind of diva – making her audience at home in *her* theater. "Pearl never pushed her humor to the point where it might disturb an audience. [Whereas] Moms or Redd [Foxx] . . . seemed bent in driving up the wall with their incisive barbs, Bailey . . . was always a soothing figure."[25] Her guests were her musical contemporaries, past and present: Andy Williams, Bing Crosby and Louis Armstrong. With the exception of a touching duet with Armstrong (clearly in his waning years), which was filled with reminiscences about "the old days" on the club circuit, Bailey's divadom was dimmed by deference to her "star" friends. Bailey literally gushed about the A-list talent she had proffered for her series' premiere to such an extent that it almost seemed sycophantic. While this audience was clearly enthralled by the onstage Pearlie Mae, the viewing public did not appear to be; the show lasted only one season. While one might argue that this was due to the waning popularity of the variety show, there were regressive aspects of the Pearlie Mae persona that some found troubling. Whereas her moments of self-aggrandizement were normal diva fare, her moments of deference as well as her chronic lamentations about fatigue from performing has more than just a trace of minstrelsy – acting as yet another spin on the revisionist mammy, in this case, one whose "people" are working her too hard. The co-existence of the diva and the mammy in the Pearlie Mae persona, in actuality, corresponds with the extra-textual construction of Bailey in American popular consciousness: comforting to and comforted by the sociopolitical status quo, Bailey manages to occupy her own color-coded yet colorblind space in terms of her persona and social and industrial position, respectively. When one begins to examine how Bailey's espoused ideologies and her personal politics were received on the broader stage of popular opinion, one sees surprising correlations between the star's mediated construction and that of Goldberg, the comic diva on the other end of the political spectrum.

Extratextual convergences: Pearl, Whoopi and (inter)racializing ways

As with many performers, like Goldberg and Mabley, whose strong onstage personae define the popular conception of both the performer and her relationship to the era, the later iterations of Pearlie Mae, in the late 1960s and early 1970s, became a de facto poster girl for a conservative form of integration: like the version utilized on network television during the same time period, it meant there was only one persona of color. For those in the African American community who begrudged Bailey the "mammying" in her act, "her penchant for hamming it up with Republican presidents" was even more disturbing. "Sure, [Bailey's] an ardent Republican, but many blacks wondered why she flaunted it with Nixon and Reagan – presidents many blacks and whites considered downright hostile to black advancement."[26] Not only was Bailey a welcomed visitor in the Nixon White House, she was appointed Special Ambassador to the United Nations by Ford in 1975 and was awarded the Presidential Medal of Honor by Reagan in 1988. Her friendships (particularly with First Lady Betty Ford, with whom she did a song and dance in Kraft's *All Star Salute to Pearl Bailey*) established her affinity with Republican administrations in much the same way that Goldberg's presence on the campaign trail and in the 1992 Inaugural Celebration did with the Clinton White House. In both instances, the comic divas maintained their allegiance to their presidents, regardless of the changes in the political climate – Bailey through Nixon's resignation and Goldberg through Clinton's impeachment.[27] While one can find other female comics – black and white – for whom the identity politics of their personae impact the way audiences do or do not embrace them, for Bailey and Goldberg, two particular personal policies, the rejection of the prevailing racial label and the commitment to interracial relationships, considered controversial back in each of their day, from either end of the political spectrum, play extremely different roles in how both the comic divas were seen inside and outside of black community.

On the short lived CBS Cable interview series, *Signature*, in 1982, Bailey articulated a color-less identity politics: "[Those who feel] 'I am mistreated because I am this color' then I feel sorry for them. . . . I am looking for this Blackness because I don't use the word . . . I think that's a fad to go along with 'I need my identity, baby.'"[28] Like many of the remarks made by Bailey about race in the past, the content of her commentary and its rejection of blackness as a designation are not as significant as her unapologetic and unwavering tone. "Black" was the term, associated with Civil Rights struggle and racial pride, that was used to signify both solidarity and empowerment in the days before "African American" became the (ostensibly) preferred expression. Thus, Bailey's rejection of the term seemed fairly consistent with her individualistic ideologies. Her "dismissal", not only of the word, but of both the recuperation and agency embedded the naming process as part of the "identity fad," denigrates myriad efforts within the black community to have some sense of history and cultural pride. Interestingly, Bailey's vocal aversion to "black" is matched in intensity by Goldberg's aversion to "African American." The chapter entitled "Race" in Goldberg's *Book* begins:

> Call me an asshole, call me a blowhard, but don't call me African American. Please. It divides us as a nation and as a people, and it kinda pisses me off. It diminishes everything I've accomplished and everything every other black person has accomplished on American soil. . . . Every time you put something in front of the word *American*, it strips it out of its meaning. The Bill of Rights is my Bill of Rights, same as anyone else's. It's my flag. It's my Constitution. It doesn't talk about *some* people. It talks about *all* people – black, white, orange, brown. You. Me.[29]

Goldberg's association of hyphenate American terms with the denigration of national identity presents an interesting thesis. Written in 1997, long before the post 9/11 "patriotic" elisions of race, Goldberg's chapter presents a separation of national and racial identity that speaks to the complex construction of clearly delineated racial and national identities. One could argue that the naming process is intensely personal, informed and inflected by lived experience as well as multiple ideologies – clearly this is the case for both Goldberg and Bailey. What is far more significant, for the purposes of this study, is both the way they defiantly frame and privilege their assertion of identity – not in terms of highly personalized statements, which, given their persona, one might expect, but rather, as clearly annunciated ideological directives. In other words, both Bailey and Goldberg were telling it, not necessarily like it is, but as they feel it should be.

As celebrities involved in interracial relationships, one might expect that both Goldberg and Bailey have received their share of criticism from black and white communities and one would be correct. What is far more interesting is the disjuncture between the level of ferociousness of the criticism and the time period in which Bailey and Goldberg's life experiences actually occurred. Married to Big Band drummer Louis Bellson, in 1952 – six years before Mildred Jeter and Richard Loving, a black woman and a white man, would marry in Washington DC; seven years before the Lovings were convicted of violating anti-miscegenation laws in the state of Virginia, where they had hoped to make their home; and eleven years before the Warren Court held that the Virginia statutes banning interracial marriage violated the equal protection and due process clauses of the Fourteenth Amendment – Bailey's career appeared to be unhindered by her status as part of a "mixed" couple. If she experienced any animosity, she chose not to share it in public venues. Rather, Bailey talked of the acceptance that she and her husband had received and positioned it as the norm, thus refuting notions of intolerance: "Lou and I got to sleep in Lincoln's bed – a mixed couple. Oh, dear."[30] Like much of Bailey's discourse on race, she framed her interracial marriage, and public reactions to it, as an issue only if someone, misguided by the "identity fad," wanted to make it an issue. While the extra-textual construction of her life as part of an interracial couple may have challenged the race relations status quo simply by its existence, *no* status quo was ever the target of her Pearlie Mae persona, which might explain why, in a decidedly less tolerant time, she fared so much better (industrially and personally) than did Whoopi Goldberg.

During the 1980s and 1990s, Goldberg's relationships with white actors, Timothy Dalton, Frank Langella, and Ted Danson, often fueled controversy and served to delegitimize her position within the African American community.[31] Nowhere is this more apparent than in the furore over the public aspects of her relationship with Ted Danson and their romantic comedy, *Made in America* (1993). While, in numerous interviews, Goldberg tried to turn the focus back to *Made in America*, her first romantic comedy, the subtext often dealt with her relationship with Danson as well:

> You know, when I said [to studio executives in the past], "Gee, I'd like to, you know, act with Dustin Hoffman," they'd go, "Well, you can only do a comedy. You can't do a love story because nobody's ready for an interracial love story" . . . I think there's been enough interracial couples around. With a war in Bosnia, am I really going to worry about it?[32]

Like most of her comedies, *Made in America* was not written with Goldberg (or any black actor) in mind. At Goldberg's behest, the revisions in the script attempted to embrace both her race and comic style as well as the resurgence of Afrocentric sensibility emerging in the early 1990s. *Made in America* follows Goldberg's Sarah Matthews, the owner of an Afrocentric bookstore called The African Queen and widowed mother of Nia Long's Zora, from her discovery that the sperm donor in her 18-year-old daughter's conception was not the ideal specimen of black manhood that she requested but, rather, the local, very white, faux cowboy car dealer, Hal Jackson (Ted Danson). As is the case with most romantic comedies, creating verisimilitude is not necessarily a guiding factor in the story. *Made in America*, while by no means a perfect romantic comedy, garnered more attention – particularly after the film's release – because of the flood of press coverage given to the high profile of Goldberg and Danson as a couple. The extra-textual constructions of Goldberg and Danson and of Sarah and Hal onscreen were in a fascinating dialogue with the times, the early 1990s, when interracial marriage appeared to be on the rise and a genre, romantic comedy, continued to fundamentally ignore these couples. As Donald Bogle notes, this interracial romantic comedy takes "precautions not to scare away patrons with too explicit an interracial couple."[33] *New York Times* critic Janet Maslin saw the chemistry of the couple as the film's greatest asset with the pairing of Danson and Goldberg as providing "a funny, disarming and believable screen romance, the first . . . in Goldberg's career."[34] Nevertheless, I would argue that the narrative seems to work against allowing the couple to slip into what I like to call the "sparkable period," when the romance of the romantic comedy becomes apparent. There seemed to be an ongoing deferment of this period: "The audience is led to believe that Goldberg has had Danson's child through artificial insemination, certainly not physical contact. Just when it appears that Goldberg and Danson will actually have a love scene, their romantic interlude turns into an unconsummated comic romp."[35]

While the reviews in the mainstream press might have hinted at the extra-textual realities of the coupling, the critique in the black press was clearly not solely about the film. In Yusef Salaam's review for *The New York Amsterdam News*, his analysis is rooted less in the film's quality than in its ideological agenda: "*Made in America* is a continuation of Hollywood's offer of racial assimilation to Black women. . . . The plot, like all of the white men–Black woman romantic tales, has no Black men in Sarah's life."[36] Whereas Salaam bemoans the presence of Goldberg, "a beautiful woman . . . one of the few Black women stars who has rejected fake hair weaves and wigs in favor of her natural kinky hair"[37] acting as love interest in an assimilationist text, Abiola Sinclair offers a different spin on "black looks":

[Goldberg] is Black enough [in terms of] Afrocentrism and commerce, mind you. It's not that Whoopi Goldberg is Black but how Black! If she were a Denise Nicholas or Mariah Carey, who is, as to be expected, marrying a wealthy white man; if she had her hair straight, by nature or nurture, if she looked like Halle Berry, the visual contrast would not have such an effect.[38]

Her allusion to the role played by color politics inside and outside of the black community reveals a certain quandary for black women in the industry – and in the black community. According to Sinclair's logic, one might assume that it would be just as acceptable for Denise Nicholas, a light-skinned black woman considered beautiful in Eurocentric terms, to act as the love interest of Carroll O'Connor on the television series *In the Heat of the Night* as it would be on the big screen. I would contend that the answer is yes and no. While Halle Barry has gone on to star in roles with varyingly problematic interracial relationships, like her Academy Award winning role in *Monster's Ball*, the realm of romantic comedy – the date movie and, arguably, the most easily digestible genre for American audiences – remains the domain of same-race coupling. In Goldberg's case, the process of judging just "how black is she?" has double meaning – as her extra-textual existence bleeds into the reception of the filmic texts and its iterations of her personae. In 1993, Goldberg was in a no–win situation – seen as too black, in relationship to her constructions as a romantic lead, and not black enough, because of her relationship with a white man, which was considered more than tabloid worthy. The tenuousness of her position was only exacerbated by the events at the Friar's Club Roast of Goldberg in October the same year.[39]

Using material, written mostly by Goldberg, Ted Danson, in blackface, gave a profane, racial epithet ("Nigger" and "Whitey") filled tribute to Goldberg, spending a great deal of the bit discussing "whoopie with Whoopi." Neither Danson nor Goldberg anticipated the fervor of the outcry against their minstrel-parodying antics. The black press took Goldberg to task, not only for the incident but also for the aspects of her persona/person that had been previously considered "suspect."

> Goldberg, who is Black but has taken on a Jewish name and white boyfriends, apparently to bolster her career, finds nothing disturbing about racial jokes being made, the casual usage of the pejorative "nigger" or a white man appearing in blackface at a function in her honor. . . . Goldberg should not allow her seeming assimilation into white culture [to] give her amnesia as to how blackface, a longtime staple at minstrel shows, is a gross caricature of Negro people.[40]

Not surprisingly, Goldberg's defense came in the form of offense. Citing the no-holds-barred history of the down and dirty Friar's Club Roasts, Goldberg questioned, not the content of the comedy, but the sensibilities of the audience:

If people on the dais and in the audience were not aware of what the day was supposed to consist of, they should have checked to see what the tenor of these roasts are, and then made a decision as to whether or not they wanted to participate.[41]

The impact of Goldberg's personal politics on the public perception of her celebrity – and, by extension, her film work – reveal how blurred the boundaries between the person and the personae had become for Whoopi. Goldberg's public personae (outspoken, unabashedly liberal and resistant to being "niched") often seemed in struggle with roles that seemed only to utilize narrow swaths of "Whoopi," contained in fairly conventional narrative framework. It seems both telling and ironic that when a role appeared (Sarah Matthews in *Made in America*) which did afford a certain degree of convergence between the personal and personae, the reception of the text was tied inextricably to the extra-textual controversies. Moreover, the events at the Friars Club and the subsequent outcry obscured the popular and critical opinion regarding Goldberg playing a role that challenged the ways that she had previously been constructed in film comedy: with all of its flaws, there was clearly liberatory potential in the construction of Sarah Matthews – for Goldberg and, arguably, for the romantic comedy representation of black women. Yet, one wonders whether, even without the Friars Club debacle, Goldberg's reception as a character like Matthews would have been more than tepid at best.

The extra-textual construction of Bailey did not have a negative impact on her stage and screen presence, since, arguably, her iterations of Pearlie Mae, regardless of venue or medium, never posed a significant challenge to her audiences. Goldberg, on the other hand, seems simultaneously trapped and empowered by her personae, her personal politics and the public perception of them both. Both Bailey and Goldberg, in true diva style, clearly announced their personal ideologies in relationship to their interracializing ways – and faced the implications of doing so. In the end, Bailey's ways, had minimal impact on either audience affinity with Pearlie Mae or her growing industrial cachet in the 1950s and beyond, while, for Goldberg, they facilitated a color-coding of the popular conceptions of her personae more thoroughly than at any other point in her career during the burgeoning multicultural moment of the early 1990s.

In *Black Looks*, bell hooks outlined directives for radical empowerment of black women:

> When black women relate to our bodies, our sexuality, in ways that place erotic recognition, desire, pleasure and fulfillment at the center of our efforts to create radical black subjectivity, we can make new and different representations of ourselves. To do so, we must be willing to transgress traditional boundaries [and] no longer shy away from the critical project of openly interrogating and exploring representations of black female sexuality as they appear everywhere especially in popular culture.[42]

I would argue that, at that same historical moment and the years that followed, Whoopi Goldberg has endeavored to present and represent a radical black subjectivity – with varying degrees of success. Undoubtedly, the extratextual construction of Whoopi Goldberg's personae has resulted in a certain mitigation of its significance to the development of black comedy – particularly in relationship to women in black comedy. In the age of the narrowcast and the niche, Goldberg's crossover capability continues separate her from other black comic sisters. Nonetheless, as Adele Givens states, "Without Whoopi, there would be no 'Queens of Comedy' . . . I'm just grateful that she was there before me, because without her there would be no me."[43] Moreover, there are other black female comics for whom crossover is both a goal and a possibility – one of whom, as will be discussed in more detail later in this chapter, is Wanda Sykes.

New millennial divadom

In the first decade of the new millennium, Goldberg has garnered high praise and intense criticism – which actually describes the previous decade as well. In 2001, Goldberg joined the ranks of Richard Pryor, Carl Reiner and Jonathan Winters when she was awarded the Kennedy Center's Mark Twain Prize for American Humor. The honor was bittersweet; presented with it a little over a month after the events of 9/11, the native New Yorker expressed the national sentiment with great candor and sensitivity:

> The events that hit our nation hit us all hard . . . I didn't know where what I did fit into the fabric of the nation anymore. Tonight, all the people who came here to this show remind us that along with the tragedy, we must exist. We must be a part of life.[44]

In the years that followed 9/11, Goldberg's activism went into full throttle – nowhere more significantly than in Democratic Party politics. Goldberg found herself at the center of controversy and criticism after her now infamous monologue at the Kerry/Edwards fundraiser in New York in the summer of 2004. It is not surprising that Goldberg's statement at the campaign fundraiser, which played with the double entendre and President Bush's name, in many ways, could be seen as vintage Whoopi – irreverent, funny, pointed and, for some, of questionable taste. When she appeared on *Hardball with Chris Matthews* in January of 2005, Goldberg stressed that, because the text of her talk had not been made public, people were commenting upon what "people would think I would say." Although on the program to promote a new project, when asked about her controversial use of double entendre, Goldberg recounted, "I said that I loved bush and that someone was giving bush a bad name . . . I think it's time for bush to be in its rightful place, and I don't mean the White House."

When Matthews questioned Goldberg as to whether she thought the joke appropriate, she replied simply, "For a comedian, yes."[45]

As a result of the way her words were mobilized in the opposing party's camp, Goldberg, from whom the Democratic campaign and party pundits distanced themselves, gained (temporary) quasi-pariah status in the party and lost her endorsement contract with the Florida-based Slim Fast company. As had been true in the past, Goldberg remained steadfast in her claims that it was her right to freedom of expression, not the content of her comedy, that was at issue here. Slim Fast's punitive measures did not chasten Goldberg's activism nor her tongue. By November of 2004, Goldberg was able to reflect upon not only the actions of the company that fired her, but also the party that abandoned her, "Slim Fast knew who I was when they hired me and made its move without having the facts. Everyone else made the decision to back away – including Kerry and Edwards. It's indicative of what's wrong with our party."[46] It is striking that, once again, in the face of public controversy, Goldberg chose to take the offensive and make her position clear – no matter whom it might serve to anger or berate. Always, outspoken, Goldberg has continued her divadom in the new millennium, although, one might argue that her choices of roles and venues mark both departure and return for Whoopi.

Cinematic Whoopi: portraits of restraint

Goldberg's choices of roles in films like *Kingdom Come* (2001) and *Good Fences* (Showtime 2003) can be seen as significant departures in terms of character and in terms of the industrial construction of the films. Interestingly, one could make the argument that the black-cast dysfunctional family comedy and the Showtime black melodramedy are the first in Goldberg's career that are actually niched – targeted for black audiences. Both Raynelle, the not-grieving widow and matriarch of the Slocumb clan, and Mabel Spader, a wife and mother of two who slides uncomfortably into suburban assimilation, are almost the antithesis of the hyperverbal comedic roles often associated with Goldberg's big-screen personae. Deliberately seeking to play comic roles that differ from those in the past, with the subdued Raynelle in *Kingdom Come*, Goldberg challenges audiences' – particularly black audiences' – previous assumptions about the comic Whoopi. As Stephen Holden notes,

> Her devoutly religious widow, Raynelle, has harbored so much pent up anger at him that she calmly insists that the engraving on his headstone read "mean and surly." Ms. Goldberg, giving one of her more restrained performance, projects an appropriate mixture of long suffering wisdom and curdled sanctimony with her Mona Lisa smile.[47]

The same can be said of Mabel Spader, the female protagonist of the Showtime film, who slides into isolation and alcoholism as she is taken from her comfortable working-class neighborhood to the toney suburb of Greenwich, Connecticut, in the 1970s. Mabel is pulled into the upper middle class by her black attorney husband, Tom (Danny Glover), who is determined "to end the colored man's losing streak" by any means necessary. The progressive disintegration of the family drives Mabel to the couch and the bottle (watching daytime television with scotch in hand). Again, the performance is restrained and contained, as Mabel loses her sense of self and her connection to a community of color, Goldberg plays the pathos with a light touch.[48] Goldberg's choices to play these repressed characters in a supporting role in the broad comedy of *Kingdom Come* and the co-starring role in the melodramedy morality play of *Good Fences* speaks to a desire to redefine herself on film – and, perhaps, with the very community that she is seen to represent in American popular cultural consciousness.

Not ready for (network) primetime sisters: Whoopi and Wanda

Upon returning to television in her NBC sitcom, *Whoopi* (2003), Goldberg was adamant that the sitcom set in Manhattan actually be filmed in New York rather than Los Angeles, thus providing a literal and figurative return for the comic diva.[49] However, in some significant ways, Goldberg was not the only black comic diva making her way to prime time as part of television's class of 2003. While Goldberg's choice of recent film roles played against her personae, the character of Mavis Rae, the one-hit wonder songstress turned hotelier, seemed to be the distillation of the most extreme aspects of Goldberg's comic persona: the hard-drinking, self-righteous, opinionated, outspoken, chain-smoking, intolerant of intolerance, unapologetically liberal (and anti-Bush) Mavis Rae is Whoopi to the tenth power. Not insignificantly, there was another hard-drinking, outspoken, opinionated black woman in the televisual class of 2003, Wanda Sykes in *Wanda at Large* on Fox. Although dissimilar in terms of the set-ups for the sitcom protagonists (Goldberg's Mavis is a Manhattan hotelier and former one-hit-wonder girl group star and Sykes' Wanda Hawkins is a Washington DC stand-up turned political pundit), the series' sociocultural milieux and the infusion of the comics' personae into the central characters reveal a striking kinship between the two televisual texts. Both series present milieux that act as a microcosm of their city setting. Whoopi's hotel is like a model UN, with Nasim (Omid Dhjalili) as the Iranian handyman/bellman; Jadwiga (Gordana Rashovich) as the Eastern European maid; Courtney Rae (Wren T. Brown) as Mavis' Republican, unemployed, former Enron executive brother; and Rita (Elizabeth Regen) as a white girl-friend, who provides a caricature of what it looks like to "try to be black." In *Wanda*, the milieu is defined in black, white and bi-racial terms: with Bradley Grimes (Phil Morris) as Wanda's black conservative colleague, foil (and possible love interest); Keith (Dale Godboldo) as her black dreadlocked cameraman/

buddy; Jenny Hawkins (Tammy Lauren) as Wanda's widowed white sister-in-law; Mark McKinney as Max, the high-strung station manager; and Barris and Holly Hawkins (Robert Bailey Jr and Jurnee Smollett) as Wanda's bi-racial nephew and niece. Each series is purposefully bawdy – the sexual innuendo is a dialogue staple – and each plays with notions of political correctness and is defiant in regards to imposed values systems. Each provides a sister-friendly iteration of a black woman protagonist on series helmed by impressive creative teams: Sykes, along with another alumnus of *The Chris Rock Show*, Lance Crouther, Les Firestein and Bruce Helford for *Wanda at Large*, and, for *Whoopi*, Goldberg along with Marcy Carsey, Caryn Mandabach and Larry Wilmore, sitcom heavyweights responsible for *The Cosby Show*, *Roseanne*, and *The Bernie Mac Show*. While one might think that these qualities would assure success, unfortunately for the comics, that was not the case. The final salient feature between the shows is that neither survived past its first season.

One might argue, not incorrectly, these series represent fairly traditional sitcom fare. Furthermore, it could also be said that, in socio political terms, *Whoopi* and *Wanda at Large*, provide comic fare that are pedantic and pedestrian, respectively. Despite these narrative flaws, I would suggest that both series, inculcated with the comic voices of their black female comic stars, is industrially significant – arguably, more so for Sykes than for Goldberg. *Wanda at Large*, which was given a deathly Friday night at 8 pm time slot, was the first network sitcom venture for Sykes, whose humor may well be better suited for cable. Her guest appearances on HBO's *Curb Your Enthusiasm*, while sporadic, have received rave reviews and have positioned her within a highly successful piece of "quality television" programming.[50]Nevertheless, Sykes' presence on HBO and in her current Comedy Central quasi-reality series, *Wanda Does It*, which showcases its slightly egocentric star declaring her ability (and willingness) to do just about any job, reveals an important aspect of Sykes' comic personae – her crossover capability. Whereas, from the very beginning of her career, Whoopi was engaged in crossover, Sykes's early association with *The Chris Rock Show* (as a writer on the Emmy Award creative staff and as cast member) positioned her within a black comedy elite, thus, providing a degree of both cultural cachet and legitimacy with African American audiences – something for which Goldberg has had to struggle. Sykes' comic persona, with its candid conversational and contentious sociocultural critique, has the edginess of Goldberg's early work but the ease of delivery is strangely reminiscent of Moms Mabley's when she took on the role of storyteller as truth-teller. Capturing the nuances and inflections of black vernacular speech, Sykes' voice, often brassy and a bit curt, speaks across cultural boundaries without seeming to make an effort to do so. Sykes emits a comfortable sexuality and self-assurance that shows no sign of either self-deprecation or self-denigration – neither too grateful to be in front of an audience nor too haughty to play to the crowd. Like the comic with whom she is most closely associated, Chris Rock, and her comic diva predecessor, Goldberg, Sykes has crafted a distinct comic persona which, on stage, has the potential to reach and appeal to multiple audiences without contorting either her voice or diluting the content of the comedy. However, as can be seen in Goldberg's comic filmography, even the most distinctive persona can be the square peg shoved into round hole of mainstream American comedy; Sykes' performances in supporting roles in upcoming mainstream comedies, *Monster-in-Law* with Jennifer Lopez and Jane Fonda and *In The Pink* with Tim Allen, Cher and Bette Midler, will provide a better indication of how she will survive the comedic middle passage. Nonetheless, one can safely assert that Sykes is a crossover comic diva-in-training.

Conclusion: Whoopi returns

When one looks at the comic personae of Goldberg, now a veteran of crossover divadom, in the latter half of the millennium's first decade, it appears to be in both an introspective and retrospective period. It seems somehow appropriate to have endeavored to reassess and reread Goldberg's comic personae, her body of work and its reflection and refraction of blackness and womanhood in the same year that Goldberg returns to the text that marked the moment of Whoopi. Goldberg's return to the Lyceum Theater in November of 2004 marked the twentieth anniversary of her landmark one-woman show. In *Whoopi Live*, Goldberg revisited the characters that she had embodied in the retooled *Spook Show* in 1984. Along with the Surfer Girl, the Crippled Girl, the Little Girl with the Long Luxurious Blonde Hair, Goldberg added Lurleen, "a menopausal Texas matron, who provides a personal hygiene products and reflections on a suicide attempt."[51] The longest monologue of the new *Whoopi Live* belonged, as it did before, to Fontaine, Goldberg's male junkie alter ego. In this iteration of Fontaine, the ex junkie is a junkie again. Speaking through Fontaine, Goldberg immediately launches into an attack on the Bush administration, which acts as his justification for his relapse: "We had a president who lied about getting some and we impeached him. We got a president who lied about all kinds of shit. And people are dying. And we put him back. And I thought 'I need more drugs.'"

In his review, Charles Isherwood noted that Fontaine's friendly discourse with the audience "evolves into a preachy lecture, and long before its conclusion, the pretense that we are being treated to the character's opinions rather than the performer's becomes transparent."[52] While admittedly saddened by the change in the Fontaine/Goldberg persona, which had previously acted as such an ideal vehicle for her comedic sociopolitical discourse, I was not surprised by Isherwood's conclusion. Given that the boundaries between Goldberg's personae and person have been in varying levels of collapse for over a decade, how could Fontaine/Goldberg escape unscathed? In his earlier iterations, Fontaine had afforded Goldberg an anonymous voice through which to speak, unencumbered by gendered or personalized presuppositions about his/her political agenda. Like *The New York Times* critic, most in the audience at the Lyceum, or who watch the special HBO presentation of the performance, will not be able to see Fontaine – rather, it will be Whoopi doing Fontaine. While this may seem like a semantic difference, it underscores the quandary in which Goldberg has been placed; it seems that, in achieving the status of "Whoopi," a single name recognizable to supporters and detractors alike, the conflation of the personae and the person is complete. The actor who stated two decades earlier, "I can play anything," is now always playing herself playing a role.

What may seem like an existential dilemma is actually rooted in Goldberg's status as crossover comic diva in the industry and in her communities. When I began this study I believed that by tracing the convergences and divergences between Goldberg's personae and those who came before (Mabley and Bailey) and those who came after (Sykes), I would be able to discern how and why Goldberg had achieved the status of crossover black comic diva while, at the same time, being socioculturally and industrially disempowered. The analytical path was far from linear and the shifts in her personae were not simply causal. The individualistic, idiosyncratic and overtly political nature of her comic personae, for which she was known (and, in some circles, revered), combined with the sociopolitical predispositions – about interracial relationships, political activism, purposeful androgyny, personalized gender and racial identities – frame aspects of the personal as culturally, politically and racially suspect. In so doing, Goldberg is put into an even more problematic version of the representational bind faced by many black women in the entertainment industry. The view of her blackness, from inside and outside of the African American community, from inside and outside of the entertainment industry, colored the lens through which her personae and her work were viewed, judged and classified – which is exactly what Goldberg had consistently fought to avoid. In the end, Goldberg is a black comic crossover diva, but she also remains an anomaly – celebrated by both the entertainment industry and the black community and, yet, fully embraced by neither.

Notes

1 Enid Nemy, "Whoopi's Ready, But Is Broadway?" *New York Times* (October 21 1984), sec. 2, E1.
2 Valerie Smith, *Not Just Race, Not Just Gender: Black Feminist Readings* (New York: Routledge, 1998), p. xiv.
3 Philip Berger, *The Last Laugh: The World of Stand Up Comics* (New York: Cooper Square Press, 2000), p. 121.
4 As a black woman, who is also "Bambi from Southern California," I understand, on an empathetic level, the pleasure of defying expectations generated by one's name.
5 The term "diva" is thrown around a lot these days – usually in association with events starring a few pop stars *du jour* and a couple of one-of-a-kind performers whose body of work has given them venerated status or when referring to someone's unreasonable self-importance or selfish demands.

6 The extended version of this chapter, which appears in *Laughing Mad: The Black Comic Persona in Post Soul America*, provides detailed analyses of Goldberg's onstage persona.

7 Mel Watkins, *On the Real Side: A History of African American Comedy from Slavery to Chris Rock* (New York: Lawrence Hill Books, 1999), p. 565.

8 The candid discussion of sexuality became more prevalent in her humor later in her career. In fact her use of a particular colloquialism for a sexual organ, as will be discussed later in the chapter, caused unanticipated controversy.

9 Wahneema, Lubiano, quoted in Patricia Hill Collins, *Black Feminist Thought: Knowledge, Consciousness and the Politics of Empowerment*, 2nd edn (New York: Routledge, 2000), p. 81.

10 This is not to say that this was the only cause which Goldberg has been involved – it is just her most high-profile activism, aside from Democratic Presidential campaigns.

11 Kam Williams, "Whoopi Goldberg: The Kingdom Come Interview," *Washington Informer* (April 18 2001), p. 21.

12 Smith, *Not Just Race, Not Just Gender*, p. xxiii.

13 Dorothy Gilliam, "The Puzzle of Pearl Bailey on her Philosophy of Life," *Washington Post* (October 17 1989), Style, p. C2.

14 Watkins, *On the Real Side*, p. 514.

15 In 1969, she even scored a Top 40 hit with her heartfelt version of "Abraham, Martin and John."

16 Elsie A. Williams, *The Humor of Jackie "Moms" Mabley: An African American Comedy Tradition* (New York/London: Garland Publishing, 1995), p. 89.

17 Williams, *The Humor of Jackie "Moms" Mabley*, p. 89.

18 Trudier Harris, "Moms Mabley: A Study in Humor, Role Playing, and the Violation of Taboo." *Southern Review*, 24 (1988), p. 772.

19 Mabley died within a year of the film's release in 1975.

20 "Amazing Grace opens . . . 'My Picture Different:' Moms Mabley," *Tri-State Defender* (August 10 1974), p. 10.

21 This is in reference to the violence surrounding the desegregation of the Little Rock schools, as a result of *Brown v. Board of Education* in 1955, and the similarly intense social upheaval caused by school busing for purposes of integration in Boston schools in 1976.

22 One might assert that, in her dramatic roles, Goldberg has played her share of revisionist mammies: the Jamaican housekeeper who heals the wounds left by the loss of her son, transforming the coming-of-age experience of her young white charge in *Clara's Heart* (1988); the stoic maid whose decision to respect the bus boycott transforms her white employer's understanding of the civil rights struggle in *The Long Walk Home* (1990); the musically adept babysitter, who transforms the lives of her white family by fulfilling their professional and emotional needs in the first of Goldberg's interracial romances, *Corinna, Corinna* (1994), and even as a free-spirited, lesbian singer who is transformed by her (unrequited) affection for her uptight white former real-estate broker, for whom Goldberg's character becomes caretaker as she is dying from AIDS in *Boys on the Side*.

23 The only line that makes even passing reference to race is when Deloris questions the origins of her new name, Sister Mary Clarence, inquiring whether "Clarence" refers to Clarence Williams III, who played Linc, the black member of television's *Mod Squad*.

24 Janet Maslin, "Goldberg on the Run Disguised as A Nun," *New York Times* (May 29 1992), p. C10.

25 Gilliam, "The Puzzle of Pearl Bailey," p. C2.

26 Gilliam, "The Puzzle of Pearl Bailey," p. C2.

27 It is interesting to note that Bailey's advocacy was never seen as a liability while Goldberg's became significantly less prized by the campaign she had so ardently supported.

28 CBS Cable, *Signature: "Pearl Bailey, Pt. 2"* (August 1982).

29 Whoopi Goldberg, *Book* (New York: Avon Books, 1997), p. 123.

30 CBS Cable, *Signature*.

31 Goldberg's interracial relationships have become comic fodder for black comedy so much so that in Spike Lee's *Bamboozled*, the character of Junebug (played by veteran comic Paul Mooney) jokes that the Hollywood blockbuster that he would make would be a sci-fi film called *The Last White Man on Earth* and "Whoopi Goldberg and Diana Ross will be fighting over him." While jokes about the personal lives of celebrities have become progressively more common in American comedy, in Goldberg's case this extratextual reality is often mobilized to critique her onscreen choices and the reading of her comic personae.

32 Jacqueline Genovese, "Whoopi Goldberg Again Reaching the Top: Up from Drugs and Welfare, Black Actress now Highest Paid Woman in Hollywood," *WE MBL* (June 13 1993), p. 10.

33 Donald Bogle, *Toms, Coons, Mulattoes, Mammies, & Bucks: An Interpretive History of Blacks in American Films* (New York: Continuum, 1973/1994), p. 332.

34 Janet Maslin, "A Man, A Woman and A Sperm Bank Yield a 90s Romance," *New York Times* (May 28 1993), p. C5.

35 Bogle, *Toms*, p. 333.

36 Yusef Salaam, "Whoopi Goldberg's Made in America, Another Hollywood Hoax," *New York Amsterdam News* (June 5 1993), p. 25.

37 Salaam, "Whoopi Goldberg's Made in America," p. 25.

38 Abiola Sinclair, "Whoopi and Ted's Excellent Adventure," *New York Amsterdam News* (June 12 1993), p. 32. Sinclair also notes, in response to Salaam's argument, that, "Not once in any film produced by a Black male has a Black woman worn her hair in a natural or in braids. Black women who were in braids are laughed at via Martin . . . when he [the Black film producer] dreams, apparently he dreams of women with long straight hair who can pass the paper bag test."

39 Founded in 1904, the Friars Club is a fraternal organization whose members have included scores of the biggest names in show business of the past century, from Irving Berlin and George M. Cohan to Frank Sinatra and George Burns, to Jerry Seinfeld and, of course, Whoopi Goldberg. Besides being involved in philanthropic activities, they are best known to the general public for the legions of comic/comic actors in their membership (like Billy Crystal, Drew Carey and Bill Murray) as well as for their uninhibited and notoriously harsh "roasts" of their celebrity members.

40 "Whoopi Goldberg: No Slapstick Comedy," *New Pittsburg Courier* (October 28 1993), p. A5.

41 "Whoopi Goldberg Defends Actor Ted Danson's blackface," *Los Angeles Sentinel* (October 14 1993), p. A1.

42 bell hooks, *Black Looks: Race and Representation* (Boston, MA: South End Press, 1992), p. 76.

43 Jawn Murray, "Talking Whoopi," *BVBuzz* (March 21 2005), http://bv.channel. aol.com/entmain/bvbuzz /20050321 (accessed March 21 2005).

44 Marc Warren, "Whoopi Goldberg Receives the Kennedy Center's Mark Twain Prize for American Humor," *Afro American Red Star* (October 21 2001), p. B4.

45 MSNBC, "Hardball with Chris Matthews" (January 14 2005).

46 Jeffrey Resner, "10 Questions for Whoopi Goldberg," *Time* (November 22 2004), p. 8.

47 Stephen Holden, "'Kingdom Come,' Off to the Cemetery with Laughter, Tears and Belches," *New York Times* (November 11 2001), p. Arts11.

48 Interestingly, her female counterpart and antagonist is Ruth Crisp, played by Mo'Nique as a derivative of Nikki Parker, her television sitcom character, which in itself is a derivative of her stand-up persona. Crisp wins the lottery, moves in next door and brings half of the hood with her, which inspires fear and dread in Tom. Mabel's budding friendship with Ruth, at the film's end, brings her back to (black) life and acts as a call for solidarity among black women.

49 Goldberg's first foray into the sitcom world was the short-lived CBS sitcom, *Baghdad Café* (1990), with Maureen Stapleton. She had also acted as producer (and center square) on *The New Hollywood Squares* (1998–2002).

50 The same is true of her feature segments on HBO's *Inside The NFL*, which may have acted as the inspiration for the offset, stunt-driven sequences of the Fox sitcom.

51 Charles Isherwood, "One Woman, Uh-Huh, But So Many Guises," *New York Times* (November 18 2004), p. E1.

52 Isherwood, "One Woman," p. E1.

Chapter 17

Surviving *In Living Color* with some *White Chicks*

Whiteness in the Wayans' (black) minds

Beretta E. Smith-Shomade

I know many souls that toss and whirl and pass, but none there are that intrigue me more than the Souls of White Folk. Of them I am singularly clairvoyant . . . I view them from unusual points of vantage. Not as a foreigner do I come, for I am native, not foreign, bone of their thought and flesh of their language . . . Nor yet is my knowledge that which servants have of masters, or mass of class, or capitalist of artisan. Rather I see these souls undressed and from the back side . . . my tired eyes and I see them ever stripped – ugly, human.

W.E.B. Du Bois, *Darkwater*, p. 29

Sometimes I really feel more sorrier for the white woman than I feel for ourselves because she been caught up in this thing, caught up feeling very special.

Fannie Lou Hamer, NAACP Legal Defense Fund Institute
speech in New York, May 1971

During the 2004 NBA playoffs, the trailer for the film *White Chicks* aired. Flashes of *Some Like It Hot* (Wilder 1959), *Soul Man* (Miner 1986), *Coming to America* (Landis 1988), *The Crying Game* (Jordan 1992), and *Big Momma's House* (Gosnell 2000) immediately crossed my mind. And as I thought more of these films, I realized that all of them pose one central conundrum: they focus on one category of identity, either race or gender, to create humor or pathos. None of the aforementioned films attempt to engage multiple identities – to simultaneously transgress race and gender.

In *The Associate* (Petrie 1996), Whoopi Goldberg's character Laurel Ayres comes close to crossing this identity divide. Recognizing the depth of sexist and racist behavior on Wall Street (as evidenced by her treatment as a financial analyst), Ayres starts her own firm but advertises it as headed by a white male. And toward the conclusion of the story, she actually assumes a white male personage to continue the masquerade. But it is only for a moment, as she quickly transforms to her "real" black woman self.[1] With so little precedence for it, the promise of *White Chicks* loomed large in my mind as a vehicle for illustrating gendered whiteness in the black mind – or at least in the minds of the Wayans brothers.

I rushed to the theater on opening weekend. Upon seeing the film, I thought: "Wow, the Wayans really don't do long form very well." While I can smilingly recall multiple skits from the Emmy-nominated *In Living Color*, from Homey the Clown to brother Oswald in jail to Oprah's show, their films, on the other hand, are easily forgettable (*Blankman* anyone?). My initial premise of gaining critical understanding of gendered whiteness from a black perspective seemed thwarted after viewing the film. The evidence of dynamic identity crossing failed to surface readily from the narrative and performances of the two main protagonists Kevin and Marcus Copeland (Sean and Marlon Wayans).

White Chicks did, however, force me to think about the articulation of whiteness generated by black folks in a larger frame. It allowed me to consider other projects created by this now successful Hollywood-insider familial group, the Wayans clan, to glean valuable critiques of whiteness across film and television. By examining several works created and controlled by the Wayans family, *In Living Color* (Fox 1990–4),[2] *Scary Movie* (2000), and *White Chicks* (2004), this essay attempts to paint a fuller picture of contemporary African-American "outsider-inside" knowledge of whiteness, gendered whiteness, and rationales for why these particular areas need more concerted and sustained scholarly exploration.

The whites of their eyes

In 2006, the preponderance of U.S. research on race representation centers (still) on the African-American figure and interpretations of what that figure means.[3] Historically, the bulk of these writings and foci have come through Caucasian lenses.[4] Early media culture found many ways to describe and disseminate ideas of blackness and gender. Minstrelsy, not to mention early cinema, provided a space where both men and women blacked up to perform blackness.[5] In vaudeville, men often performed as women. Whether through Sapphire and Jezebel on the radio version of *Amos 'n Andy* or the disembodied Mammy Two-Shoes on *Tom & Jerry*, feigning black and black women's culture specifically proved to be popular and profitable. As the preceding examples demonstrate, actual black people were more often than not physically absent. In fact, the segregationist economies, laws, and culture of the Jim Crow era required their absence.

Even with the late-twentieth-century scholarly focus on whiteness, analyses return frequently to a structured antithesis of blackness. Or conversely, the study of whiteness is patterned after the discourses of blackness. As Gwendolyn Audrey Foster argues:

> Whiteface is about space ownership and identity claims. It is therefore possible that whites become their own other in whiteface and that whites carry their own burden of representation, which is the burden of representing that which does not really exist, that which has come to be known

as *whiteness*. Perhaps it could also be argued that whites share with blacks a split, or double, identity.[6]

From this perspective, it seems that whether one describes blackness or whiteness, a Caucasian interpretation emerges as central and dominant.

In a 1992 essay, bell hooks argues that Caucasian lack of consciousness about evaluations of themselves comes from their ability to render those outside of themselves invisible. Using James Baldwin's *Native Son* as a reference, she says: "Baldwin links issues of recognition to the practice of imperialist racial domination . . . Absence of recognition is a strategy that facilitates making a group 'the Other.'"[7] Discussions of gendered white representations receive even less line space in scholarly and popular discourses. More important to my argument here, the idea that black folks have, for good or for evil, a fairly sophisticated, longstanding, and extensive view of whiteness – and gendered whiteness in particular – appears only limitedly in mainstream and academic discussions about race and representation. I illustrate this assertion below.

According to Mia Bay, black slaves associated whiteness with power and authority: "the hostility that some of them expressed toward all white people as a consequence, are the strongest elements of a coherent racial ideology that can be found in black folk thought."[8] African-American intellectuals and writers have a long history of theorizing white subjectivity. For example in 1920, W.E.B. Du Bois writes about whiteness as the "strut of the Southerner, the arrogance of the Englishman amuck, the whoop of the hoodlum who vicariously leads your mob."[9] Late 1940s' and early 1950s' "white life" literature gave black writers an opportunity to express their knowledge of whiteness – at least in fictional terms – by creating white scenarios and characters for their novels.[10]

In the latter part of the twentieth century, several North Carolina teachers found that in an exercise conducted with middle school students: "black children generally had a clear sense of how they were seen by white people and how white people saw themselves, [while] white children often could not see themselves as racially defined beings."[11] In this study, for example, Sheldon, an African-American eighth grader, writes of his white persona: "White Me: (1) corny, (2) smart, (3) nice, (4) playful, (5) weak, (6) Country, (7) Too confident, (8) Too tense, (9) My name 'Billy Bob,' (10) Get better jobs, (11) Be a vegetarian, (12) Listen to Garth Brooks."[12]

At the 77th Annual Oscar Awards in 2005, host Chris Rock gives comedic insights into how representation is quite literally taken up by black audiences. In a man-on-the-street sequence, Rock interviews 15 movie patrons at the Magic Johnson Theater in Los Angeles about their knowledge of "Best Picture" nominated films including *Million Dollar Baby*, *The Aviator*, *Finding Neverland*, and *Sideways*. Of the 14 black patrons interviewed, none has seen any of these films, while white actor Albert Brooks responds that he had seen all of them. But when Rock asks him and the other interviewees if they have seen *White Chicks*, they all reply enthusiastically in the affirmative. All of these examples are offered to make clear that discerning whiteness (and blackness) is not a new phenomenon in black popular culture. Moreover, perspectives on whiteness in black culture are not necessarily tied to white definitions or frameworks generally accepted and presented as normative. Black spectators interrogate whiteness consistently, even if light-heartedly.

This same outsider–inside knowledge applies to discursive insights held by African-Americans on gendered whiteness. Notions of the "outsider within" are explicated in many texts, (often using different terms but voicing the same idea), but tied most in this essay to Patricia Hill Collins's idea of "social locations or border spaces occupied by groups of unequal power."[13] These spaces find African-Americans structured betwixt and between visibility and invisibility – spaces where African-Americans have access but no authority. Hill Collins maintains: "Under conditions of social injustice, the outsider-within location describes a particular knowledge/power relationship, one of gaining knowledge about or of a dominant group without gaining the full power accorded to members of that group."[14]

Through systemic inequality and sexism, white women have been historically more accessible to and more a daily part of African-American life (initially as mistresses of the house and later as school teachers, nurses, social workers, and owners of homes with black servants) than white men. Caucasian men, on the other hand, have served as omniscient or certainly prescient forces that oversee the flows of living in the USA (agriculture, politics, economy, and the military). Consequently, black insights into gendered whiteness (especially about white women) are as cultivated as the ones about whiteness itself (largely masculinized).

Returning to Bay's work on nineteenth-century African-American thought, humanity reigns as a grounding principal to fight racism – across gender and class lines. Yet in her autobiography, former slave Harriet Jacobs writes about a new mistress as indicative of many Southern white women:

> She had not strength to superintend her household affairs; but her nerves were so strong, that she could sit in her easy chair and see a woman whipped, till the blood trickled from every stroke of the lash. She was a member of the church; but partaking of the Lord's supper did not seem to put her in a Christian frame of mind.[15]

Audre Lorde maintains that too often "white women ignore their built-in privilege of whiteness and define *woman* in terms of their own experience alone . . ."[16] bell hooks argues, as a contemporary example, that singer-actress Madonna's *Truth or Dare* (1991) does not "display . . . feminist power, [she offers] the same old phallic nonsense with white pussy at the center."[17] And Nikki Giovanni wonders aloud:

"Should I mention," the poet continued, "that we get tired of your impatience? That snappy white-girl way you have of saying something to us? That . . . well . . . debutante way you have of thinking what you have said is significant and important and must be responded to right away?"[18]

Indeed, a critical, cultured familiarity with the manifestations of gendered whiteness exists in the everyday and artistic venues of African-American thought. This wisdom finds acknowledgement, if not sustained development, in the works of the Wayans family.

The Wayans

The Wayans family consists of a ten-member sibling clan hailing from Harlem, New York. Sibling elder Keenen Ivory Wayans, born in 1958, introduced the family into the entertainment industry with his initial striving to act and do stand-up comedy, but more significantly by his creative co-writing skills of *Hollywood Shuffle* (Townsend 1987). Keenen, Damon, Kim, Shawn, and Marlon are the five Wayans who actively participate in the entertainment industry. They have pursued everything from stand-up to acting. They have also worked in film and television as producers, writers, and directors. As comedians, the Wayans family excels at lampooning what they know best – various manifestations of blackness. Simultaneously, however, they offer insights on black interpretations of whiteness.

With comedy as their foundation, the Wayans have made a significant impact on Hollywood. Individually and collectively, they've been nominated for and won Emmy Awards, NAACP Image Awards, and People's Choice Awards. As a family, they received BET's Inaugural Comedy Icon Award in 2004 for "outstanding career body of work and overall contributions to the comedy genre."[19] Oprah Winfrey hosted them on her program the week before *White Chicks* premiered, Tuesday, June 16, 2004, and praised the family for both their ability to negotiate Hollywood successfully and for creating an extremely funny film. Keenen, the film's co-writer and director, suggested that with the film they wanted to tap into every area that could be uncovered about notions of white women. This exploration of whiteness, however, was preceded by the family's comedic interrogations of blackness.

In Living Color

While neither *Scary Movie* nor *White Chicks* target a black market specifically, the Wayans initial forays into the entertainment industry did just that. *In Living Color* aired on Fox in the network's formative years when it was trying to carve out a space for itself by targeting an underserved African-American audience. Fox executives wanted it to be the "rebel" network.[20] After Keenen Wayans' highly successful film *I'm Gonna Get You Sucka* (1988), a parody of exploitative films featuring blacks, Fox gave him free rein to produce a hip and multicultural skit-driven variety program. The goal was to target the 18–34-year-old black market while also luring in hip, white 18–34-year-olds.

Though various assessments of blackness dominate its narratives, *In Living Color* offers black thoughts on whiteness in many of its skits. One of the early examples of this is in its parody of the beloved *Star Trek* series. Aired during its first season (April 21, 1990), the skit "The Wrath of Khan" features Nation of Islam leader Louis Farrakhan as portrayed by Damon Wayans. Farrakhan boards the starship of the USS Enterprise to open the eyes of its enslaved 'colored' crew members. In an exchange with Captain Kirk (played by Jim Carrey) who calls his ideas "poppycock," Farrakhan replies, "It is that same lie that kept Elvis the king; that made that poor Latoya Jackson think she could sing. It is that same lie that's got white boys rappin' and the Fat Boys actin'." And in his best James T. Kirk (William Shatner) imitation (both in voice and body movement), Carrey exclaims, "Hey Mister, you can't come in here and talk to me like that." The statement acknowledges not only the centrality of Kirk as captain of the ship but also his position as a white male directly in charge of a multicultural crew.

Norma Schulman argues that stand-up comedy (from whence all the comics on the program emerge) offers a place for African-Americans to talk back to the oppressive and exploitative discourses that circulate around blackness. She writes that in many routines:

> specific differences between blacks and whites are highlighted, only to be made ridiculous: white people "have stuff"; black people "have Jesus." "White boys" can't dance; black men can't keep their hands off attractive black women. White mothers tell their children to stay close to them in shopping malls; black mothers shriek, "You sit your ass down!" so loudly that strangers stop in their tracks. White people, when they trip over something, just try to regain their footing; black people, as Buddy Lewis of Def Comedy Jam sees them, "have to make an athletic event out of it."[21]

Herman Gray believes that whiteness becomes the object of ridicule, satire, and commentary in the narratives of *In Living Color*. He observes: "This satire is often staged through a kind of racial role reversal, where . . . white foolishness simply replaces black foolishness . . . it is the show's willingness to construct and parody whiteness explicitly from the angle of blacks that makes its disturbances all the more unsettling."[22]

For example in the recurring skit "The Brothers Brothers: Tom and Tom," Damon and Keenen mock the 1960s comedic/singing duo the Smothers Brothers. The difference between the two groups of brothers is simply, the logic of the skit tells us, the blackness of the Brothers' skins. Their p.o.v. comes from a perceived quintessential whiteness associated with the Smothers Brothers. In their attempt to join the Dixie Hills Country Club, for example, Tom and

Tom commend the work of Jesse Helms (having no idea who Jesse Jackson is), understand the need for aspirin to be white (so they will work for you), and joke that a black man in a three-piece suit can only be a defendant. Turning racist behavior on its head, Tom and Tom (as self-perceived white men) refuse to confine their critiques to perceptions of whites and ne'er do well black folks. African-Americans deemed "acting" white such as Bryant Gumble, Byron Allen, O.J. Simpson, and Clarence Thomas get called out as well.

Two white comedians, Kelly Coffield and Jim Carrey (as Fire Marshall Bill, Vera DeMilo, and other characters), serve as the requisite white cast members on *In Living Color*. The two participate in making the ways of whiteness visible through comedy. Whether through the aforementioned characterizations, within jibes at Sally Struthers' girth set against black African hunger, or the ridiculousness of Lassie's communicative ability, the wages of whiteness barrel through a black telescopic lens. *In Living Color* attempts to be an equal opportunity offender where understandings of both blackness and whiteness make for irreverent humor and profitable television.[23] This same impulse helps transition the Wayans from the small screen to the big one.

Scary Movie

According to July 2000 box office reports, *Scary Movie* grossed more than $42 million in its opening weekend. Released by Dimension Films, the film parodies many of the highly successful teen films of the late 1990s – teen representations particularly associated with whiteness (and directed toward white teen audiences), in order to critique that whiteness. In it, the Wayans humorously visualize the tropes of whiteness that permeate black discourses. Scenarios exist as binaries, specifically white against black, although not stringently. The film offers stupidity laced with poignant satire.

In the "Movie Mongrel" scene, for example, the trailer to the feature film mocks *Titanic* by having a black man (Keenen Ivory Wayans) stand on the bow of a ship shouting happily: "Whoo, I'm the king of the world!" That is, until he feels the lash of the overseer's whip on his back. This 30-second promotion for the fictionalized *Amistad II* conveys several critical conceptions about whiteness and mainstream representation that many African-Americans harbor: (1) the ridiculousness of historical fiction set during slavery with narratives operating as if blacks didn't exist while foregrounding white characters; (2) films that structure characters' lives without commenting on the cultural specificity of those lives (in other words, making whiteness normative); and (3) themes deemed important or consequential to the present that bear no obvious significance to daily living experiences. Comedian Steve Harvey captures this last assessment best in *The Original Kings of Comedy* (Lee 2000). Referring to the accolades heaped upon *Titanic* he quips: "White people always running to jump on some bullshit . . . movie had a been about black people, it wouldn't been no movie."

In another example from this same scene, the one black female character, Brenda Meeks (Regina Hall), is stabbed to death by the white movie patrons for disrupting their visual pleasure. They accompany the killing with epitaphs in remembrance of presumed black disruption of films such as *Thelma and Louise*, *The Fugitive*, *Schindler's List*, all Jackie Chan movies, and *Big Momma's House*. From the very old to the young, from priests to just average-looking white people, *Shakespeare in Love* (the film they were screening) is avenged by the slaughter of this young, black woman against the backdrop of Gwyneth Paltrow's Viola. While offered as humor, the scene revisits the all-too-naturalized occurrences of black women's death to the deafening sound of silence. While the Wayans's comedy usually tilts toward the obvious absurdity of a situation, this scenario points to the tragedy of continued debasement and disavowal of black women's existence and their perceived expendability and irrelevance.

Their commentary on white women is equally compelling. For example on multiple occasions, they invoke black assessments of white women's behavior: (1) as lascivious, (2) as privileged, and (3) as idiotic. Beyond the narratives of 1990s teen horror, these representations exist in horror films from previous decades (*Carrie*, *Halloween*), within comedies (*Grease*, *Sex and the City*, *Desperate Housewives*), and in drama(dies) (*Legally Blonde*, *Beverly Hills 90210*, *Ally McBeal*). Thus, the ideas that the Wayans employ come from many proliferating film and television examples.

Scary Movie positions the Wayans as cultural commentators – ones able to move within the system undetected, or at least allowed. The narrative allows for white audience pleasure based on familiarity and comfort of the generic form as well as a feeling of youthful inside the jokiness. Black audiences are availed to this same pleasure in the text but also get to enjoy the covert, implicit insights made manifest within the subtext of black narrative critiques of whiteness. For example in *Scary Movie 2* (2001) when "scary shit" starts to happen, a call for splitting up is made. While Brenda (Regina Hall) questions this common practice of white folks (especially in visual culture), the dissolution still occurs. To this prospect the only black characters look directly into the camera as she whimpers, "We gonna die y'awll" – as they begin walking toward their representationally predicted deaths. Unlike either *In Living Color* or *White Chicks*, *Scary Movie* privileges white stories with blacks as periphery. This allows for the Wayans's outsider-inside knowledge to become quite piercing.

White Chicks

Columbia Pictures clearly marketed *White Chicks* to a hip, young, 12–24-year-old audience. Trailers before the screening of this film included: *The Grudge*, with a grown-up Sarah Michelle Gellar from *Buffy, the Vampire Slayer*, *Mr 3000* (Bernie Mac), *Taxi* (with Queen Latifah and Jimmy Fallon), and *Anacondas* (hosting a multiracial, 18–34-year-old cast). *White Chicks* received a PG-13 rating. Grossing nearly $20 million on its first weekend, the film has garnered $112 million, domestically.

The Wayans positioned this film as "classic comedy . . . not for a race, not for a gender . . ." They constructed it as essentially a film about gender roles and expectations – pitching it as "*Some Like It Hot* meets *Big Momma's House* on a diet with *Mrs. Doubtfire*'s make-up."[24] According to their interviews on the film's DVD, they thought about how a black man would act in a certain situation, how a woman (presumably black like them) would act, and finally, how a white woman would act. Journalists Desa Philadelphia and Sora Song asked the brothers how they made sure that they knew and understood white women:

KEENEN: We hung out with them.

SHAWN: We watched *Sex and the City*, and we went to some clubs and hung out with those types of girls.

MARLON: We went to dinner with some white girls, and all the sisters in LA were sitting there going "They sellin' out too? First O.J., then Bryant Gumble, now the Wayans?"

These seemingly superficial responses belie, however, a running commentary that pervades African-American discourses about whiteness and in particular, gendered whiteness. The fact that these perceptions of whiteness are ongoing and available to the Wayans is clear in their body of work that precedes *White Chicks*.

Explicit ideas of whiteness and blackness abound in this film. For example, musical lyrics include a remake of Grand Master Flash's "White Lines" (their version referencing cocaine) changed to "White Girls" by Mighty Casey for the film. Keenen explains: "we wanted to explore race, class, gender with neither getting a leg up." Adds actor Terry Crews who plays Latrell Spencer: "with comedy it's gotta be the truth. If it's not the truth, it's not funny."

The humor of this film comes at the expense of both conceptions of whiteness and blackness and with an assumption of a static gendered being. Whether it's the assumption and performance of white women's bodies by the Copeland agents, the presumed insider access (and acting up) when no one else is around (for example, the "girls" ability to sing "nigga" in a song), or the embodied moves of blackness personified in the impromptu dance competition, the Wayans observe adroitly and move beyond stereotype to inform mainstream audiences about themselves. In other words, the Wayans position themselves as informants – making the conversations about whiteness within black life available for white (and black) consumption. So I turn to the "truth" of the funny undergirding the Wayans' ideas about whiteness in these media texts.

Whiteness revisited

In her book on whiteness, Ruth Frankenberg insists that "[a] far-reaching danger of whiteness coded as 'no culture' is that it leaves in place whiteness as defining a set of normative cultural practices against which all are measured and into which all are expected to fit."[25] Addressing this fallacy, several threads within the Wayans' media projects work to debunk notions of whiteness as normative, without culture, including ideas about white privilege, class disparities, and cultural appropriation. For example, the line, "Dear Mr Hotel Manager: I'm a white woman in America," appears at the very beginning of the agents' masquerade as Brittany and Tiffany Wilson in *White Chicks* and contextualizes the BF (bitch fit) Tiffany promises. The dialogue illustrates an unreflected and unfounded depth of privilege and normativity that seems to exist in white consciousness as shown through behavior. These expressions of white entitlement resound also in blacks' overt interpretation of the ways of whiteness.

The actions presented by the Wayans, the performances of the black men as white women, position these women as not only shallow and stupid but also as uncultured. Their wealth-based actions undermine decorum and civility – thrusting the same charges that are leveled at African-Americans based primarily on their physical presence, back at them. In a similar vein, much of *Scary Movie*'s humor comes from the confluence of white privilege and perceived idiocy. For example, the setting for the killings both at home and in school foregrounds suburban communities, well-funded schools, and minimal integration (almost limited to "colored" sports participants).

In Living Color speaks to white privilege quite poignantly in the skit, "Ted Turner's Very Colorized Classics – *Casablanca*." While referencing the then cable owner's colorizing of films in the MGM collection he acquired, the skit has Turner (Jim Carrey) change the actual lead character from Humphrey Bogart to Billy Dee Williams with Stevie Wonder playing Sam. While funny, a black perception of whiteness comes from Turner's positioning. Sitting in a luxurious leather chair watching films from a home projector, he says: "Now the colorization of these films may not agree with some people's artistic [spit] sensibilities. But, they're mine and I can do anything I want with them." Possession is the key. African-Americans understand that Caucasian ownership allows for visioning the world in any form imaginable. Thus, the Wayans' examination of ownership and wealth speaks to another way in which African-Americans come to know whiteness. Rationales calling for black representational control, access, and numerical balance find their underlying logic in the ways black folks have come to understand the economics of white and black representation. The narratives also address black interpretations of class and how class plays itself out in blacks' imaginings of whiteness.

Mia Bay's research finds that former slaves expressed acute awareness of white class status and their economic privilege. Specifically she suggests that while not much distinction was placed on white folks across class lines, all whites were by law to be respected and feared. Furthermore, some mentioning of "white trash" emerged in many of the interviews.[26] According to Dina Smith, the historic definition of white trash:

> often anchored the term to a racialized economic and occupational class status – the white trash sharecropper, the white trash migrant worker, the white trash miner, the white trash mill worker, all of whom are stuck in place. At once white and trash, a metonym for blackness, the term historically designated a *border position* between white privilege and black disenfranchisement.[27]

And while the larger white community harbors one definition of white trash (with that definition evolving into commodity according to Smith), African-Americans maintain another.

For example, *In Living Color*'s "Elvis Sighting" skit features Bill Bixby (Carrey) as a reporter who interviews a hunter tracking the elusive (dead) Elvis. The hunter, white, mountainous, scraggy, and spitting snuff, talks about "the King" as a knowledgeable, breathing quantity – a prize. The monstrous Elvis, even with three tranquilizers in him, emerges but refuses to stay down. He attacks the hunters and Bixby. The moral of this story – good ole' boys don't die, especially white icons. Eurocentric imaginings like these impact people of color in direct and often problematic and dangerous ways.

Wayans' comedy also addresses the many occurrences of white appropriation of black culture. Appropriation has been discussed across many aspects of Cultural Studies, most consistently with respect to music (jazz, r&b, and hip-hop). Yet attempting to acquire, to emulate, to put on black cultural norms and style is not confined to music and has cut across fashion, literature, and performance. The Wayans acknowledge these instances in multiple ways in almost all of their works. For example, *Scary Movie* spoofs black director Charles Stone III's Budweiser "Whassup" commercials. In the film, Shorty (Marlon Wayans) sits smoking weed and watching TV when the killer calls. One of his (white) "boyz" enters and says, "whassup." All the other friends (white boys) jump on board with the gregarious greeting, "whassuuuuuuuup," invoking a certain black coolness (or black authenticity – "true"). They usurp or at least sponge off Shorty's black vernacular to position themselves as trendy and de facto black – or as Eric King Watts and Mark Orbe argue, as "universal."[28] In this instance, the Wayans present an example of how appropriation is expressed without explaining it.

In Living Color, however, brings a different type of review to this phenomenon of appropriation – critique. For example in its spoof of *The Tonight Show with Johnny Carson*, Joan Embry (Coffield) from the San Diego Anthropological Institute appears on the talk program with a "show and tell" normally reserved for animals. Instead, she piggybacks in Calvin (Tommy Davidson), a homeboy sapien, indecipherable, evolving, and endangered. When the Carson-wannabe host (Carrey) elicits anger from Calvin by saying the word "boy," anthropologist Joan calms him by saying "Yo, yo, yo Calvin man, cool out. The man's just buggin." At the end of the interview, Calvin shows that he can actually talk. He grabs the microphone and raps about his humanity – a notion that elicits both audience and host applause – not for its ideology but for Calvin's ability to entertain. This example gives insight into blacks' awareness of the differences between white and black laughter.

While seemingly best positioned to show a reorientation of gendered whiteness, *White Chicks* failed adequately to invoke African-American intra-community dialogues about white women. In these "familial" discourses, the Other becomes those traditionally positioned in the space of privilege: Caucasians and in terms of beauty and status, white women. Despite its lack, black notions of gendered whiteness are still available within the film's narrative.

Gendered whiteness

"It may be summer time in the Hamptons but it is snowing up in here."
Latrell Spencer, *White Chicks*

One of the most cultivated ideological areas of contention between whites and blacks is white women – black men's perceived desire of them, black women's perceived envy. *White Chicks'* character Latrell Spencer provides the most insightful (and funny) commentary on white women in the black male mind. Spencer occupies the space of big black ballplayer who keeps visions of only white sugarplums dancing in his head. The comedic timing and dialogue of the character encourages laugh way-out-loud humor. His very physical presence provides an expected antithesis to all of the whiteness (white girls, old white money, and white accoutrements) that surrounds him in the film. For example in the beach scene, Spencer emerges all shiny and buff with a quasi-Barry White "I'm Gonna Love You Just a Little More" bass beat as his soundtrack. As he eclipses the sun by standing over his intended paramour Tiffany (Marlon), he purrs, "Easy white chocolate, I wouldn't want you to melt." In his many commentaries about (and presumably to) white women, we learn a great deal about the Wayans' notions of whiteness and gender in black men's minds.

Similar to Spike Lee's *She's Gotta Have It* (1986) (where the story is supposed to be about an independent black woman and her life), we learn who white women are through the thoughts of men in *White Chicks*. In the film, the faux white girls spend much of their time discussing (with the "really" white girls), relationships and gender discrepancies, shopping, and the negotiation of their new bodies. The incorporation of piano, lack of bass, and sublime melody, make an included song by Vanessa Carlton especially white sounding. Spencer not only knows Carlton's "A Thousand Miles" but loves it and becomes quite animated in expressing the lyrics – showing his sensitivity and knowledge of what appeals to white girls. When the valet tries to help open the door for Tiffany (Marlon), Spencer jumps in front saying, "Oh no my brother, you have to get your own," linking their date to the literal winning of a most valued prize.

In *Scary Movie*, the politics of representing white women are less obvious. Yet, the parodic elements of what occurs in the narrative also foreground many of the circulating ideas about white women's behavior, thought processes, and ways of being for black folks. The Wayans illustrate some of this thinking in the opening scene when the killer calls, and Drew Decker (Carmen Electra) moves toward her death, engaging the killer, tripping, and being generally idiotic. In these instances, the white girl always serves as both paramour and stupid (expected) victim. Even the character Buffy Gilmore (Shannon Elizabeth) gives credence to thinking about gendered whiteness, as Gwendolyn Audrey Foster argues: "Bad-white women are almost always good under-neath . . ."[29] That is, in this case, until their white ways get them killed. Bad behavior and gentle music, privilege and performance, all coalesce to paint a certain racialized and gendered picture of white girls for black folks.

Why does this matter?

Actress Whoopi Goldberg suggests, "You can sort of define periods of time by who was hosting the Oscars."[30] Using Chris Rock's Oscar hosting in 2005 as a barometer, what can be said about race and representation in the beginning of the twenty-first century? Is the mocking and acknowledgement of whiteness a sign of economic and social progressiveness? Is it an acknowledgement that everyone is racialized? Tellingly, even in the 2005 Awards show when black and Latino performers, category announcers, or actors are featured, the televi-sion audience can imagine the omniscient director's voice saying to his cameramen, "find the blacks, find the Latinos" in the auditorium, to visually accompany their race mates' presence on screen. Why? Because this is what is shown. Noticeably, all other audience members flashed during these same types of sequences generally have some connection to the topic at hand – beyond their perceived racialized tie.

Employing the writings of French philosopher Jean-Paul Sartre, the ways of looking and being looked upon continue to be situated around whiteness without acknowledgement of the Others' existence as human. Humanizing these Others, who are perceived as objects, would force a "congealed sliding of the whole universe, to a decentralization of the world which undermines the centralization which I [white male] am simultaneously effecting."[31] In our current visual parlance, Sartre's assertion is tantamount to a *Matrix*-like shifting of dimensions with Neo, the reluctant hero who escapes false consciousness, effectively making this happen. Understanding this Hollywood framework,

Wayans' productions attempt to reorient popular narratives to make assessments of whiteness visible.

Does *In Living Color*, *Scary Movie*, or *White Chicks* move us beyond the stereotypical meanderings of Caucasians and gendered whiteness? In many regards, the answer to this question is "no." However, with their many extremely successful mainstream media offerings, the Wayans expose the fact that, at a minimum, surface versions of race have always occupied a space in people of color's minds, especially about white folks. Cross-dressing/masking/whiteface – all different terms for occupying spaces not normally inhabited by those constructed as Other – make room for critiquing whiteness. Yet in an article reviewing *The Human Stain*, David Pilgrim remarks: "When whites put on blackface, the result is comedy . . . when characters of African ancestry say they are white, the result is tragedy."[32]

Foster suggests that definitions of good and bad whiteness may be changing in these postmodern times. She muses that:

> The ability to be a good *consumer* is now more important, it seems, than being a good, chivalrous, young, white male or sport. As long as one has plenty of money, one can be a single mom, a gangsta thug, or an abusive superstar athlete and still be a hero in the white world. Class now has more to do with cash than with birth relations. Yet with the changes in Western culture, there is a deep nostalgia for a white class that had been based on royal birth and marriage.[33]

Programs like *I Want to Be a Hilton* validate her claim. But while class has become increasingly more significant, the foundations of racism and sexism remain firmly intact and functioning.

For all the discussion of whiteness that has claimed scholarly space since the early 1990s, only limited work focuses on how people of color conceptualize and represent whiteness. In comparing *White Chicks* to *Scary Movie*, most reviewers focus on the slapstick humor of crossing one of the lines, either race or gender (and sometimes even class). For example, David Rooney says in Variety.com: "Most of the best jokes are at the expense of unhip white folks or vacuous, rich ho-bags, driven by reverse racial stereotyping . . ."[34]

Yet, understanding this racialized critique of whiteness is critical to the Wayans' body of work. They write broad and slapstick humor – wanting people to not just chuckle but have a deep down belly laugh. Whatever the narrative pretexts, humor is the goal. However, as noted by Gary Taylor:

> A white suburban teenager, listening to Tupac Shakur tell him "both black and white, is smoking crack tonight," may be doing nothing more than the safest version of slumming. The murder of black rappers like Tupac and the Notorious BIG enhances the thrill of the spectacle without ever endangering white consciousness or prejudices about black men.[35]

In other words, the Wayans provide a crucial, if flawed, intervention into "we are the world," twenty-first century mantras that maintain their nineteenth-century ways of being. If scholars and audiences want to move beyond the bamboozle of black silence, they must call for, listen to, and incorporate the ruminations of black folks on whiteness – beyond commercial imperatives – in order to make the low down dirty shame of Hollywood's shuffle a part of media history instead of its present.

Notes

The author thanks Deborah Elizabeth Whaley, Dana E. Mastro, and Daniel Bernardi for their fastidious and insightful reviews of this essay.

1 For insightful critiques of this film and Goldberg in general, see Mark A. Reid's *Black Lenses, Black Voices* (Lanham, MD: Rowman & Littlefield, 2005) and Bambi L. Haggins' contribution to this collection.
2 Technically, the Wayans were part of *In Living Color* only through the middle of the 1992–3 season. They left after disputes with Fox over repeats.
3 Though many scholars write about other aspects of race and representation beyond the black–white binary, two things ultimately bring the discussion back to African Americans: (1) Racial representation, as taken up in many disparate fields beyond the humanities/arts (such as communication, psychology, sociology, etc.), finds the black–white binary holding sway. (2) Frequently, implicit understandings of whiteness and race ground themselves in blackness. See Toni Morrison, *Playing in the Dark: Whiteness in the Literary Imagination* (New York: Vintage, 1993).
4 The term Caucasian here is used purposely. Its historic connection to science and veracity plays itself out in modern-day discourses about race – despite academics' attempts to undo it through language.
5 Many good works exist on minstrelsy. See Michael Rogin, *Blackface, White Noise: Jewish Immigrant in the Hollywood Melting Pot* (Berkeley, CA: University of California Press, 1996) and Eric Lott, *Love and Theft: Blackface Minstrelsy and the American Working Class* (New York: Oxford University Press, 1993).
6 Gwendolyn Audrey Foster, *Performing Whiteness: Postmodern Re/Construction in the Cinema* (Albany, NY: SUNY Press, 2003), p. 51.
7 bell hooks, "Representing Whiteness in the Black Imagination," *Cultural Studies*, eds Lawrence Grossberg, Cary Nelson, and Paula Treichler (New York: Routledge, 1992), p. 339.
8 Mia Bay, *The White Image in the Black Mind: African-American Ideas about White People, 1830–1925* (New York: Oxford University Press, 2000), p. 161.
9 William Edward Burghardt Du Bois, *Darkwater* (New York: Harcourt, Brace and Howe, 1920), p. 32.
10 See novels such as Ann Petry's *Country Place* (Chatham, NJ: Chatham Bookseller, 1971; first published 1947), Frank Yerby's *Foxes of Harrow* (New York: Dial Press, 1946), and Willard Motley's *Knock on Any Door* (New York: D. Appleton-Century Company, Inc, 1947) as examples of this literature.
11 Maurice Berger, *White Lies: Race and the Myths of Whiteness* (New York: Farrar, Straus, Giroux, 1999), p. 208.
12 Berger, *White Lies*, p. 209.
13 Patricia Hill Collins, *Fighting Words: Black Women and the Search for Justice* (Minneapolis, MN: University of Minnesota Press, 1998), p. 5.

14 Hill Collins, *Fighting Words*, p. 6.

15 Harriet Jacobs, *Incidents in the Life of a Slave Girl* (1861) as found in *The Norton Anthology of African American Literature*, eds Henry Louis Gates, Jr. and Nellie Y. McKay (New York: W.W. Norton & Company, 1997), p. 214.

16 Audre Lorde, "Age, Race, Class, and Sex: Women Redefining Difference," *Sister Outsider* (Freedom, CA: Crossing Press, 1984), p. 117.

17 bell hooks, "Madonna: Plantation Mistress or Soul Sister?" *Black Looks: Race and Representation* (Boston, MA: South End Press, 1992), pp. 163–4.

18 Nikki Giovanni, "Annual Conventions of Everyday Subjects," *Racism 101* (New York: William Morrow, 1994), p. 203.

19 As found on Variety.com.

20 Keenen Ivory Wayans recalls the mood of Fox in the early 1990s in Kristal Brent Zook's *Color by Fox: The Fox Network and the Revolution in Black Television* (New York: Oxford University Press, 1999), p. 5.

21 Norma Schulman, "The House That Black Built: Television Stand-up Comedy as Minor Discourse," *Journal of Popular Film and Television* (Fall, 1994): online.

22 Herman Gray, *Watching Race: Television and the Struggle for "Blackness"* (Minneapolis, MN: University of Minnesota Press, 1995), p. 141.

23 Certainly, *In Living Color*'s homophobia, as seen through their "Men on Film" and other skits, provides another central indication of their preoccupations. However, their ranting generally centers black homosexuality and black community discourses surrounding it, rather than ideas about whiteness and sexuality.

24 Marlon Wayans, *White Chicks*, DVD featurette, 2004.

25 Ruth Frankenberg, *White Women, Race Matters: The Social Construction of Whiteness* (Minneapolis, MN: University of Minnesota Press, 1993), p. 204.

26 Bay, *The White Image*, p. 156.

27 Dina Smith, "Cultural Studies' Misfit: White Trash Studies," *Mississippi Quarterly* 57.3 (Summer 2004), p. 370.

28 Eric King Watts and Mark P. Orbe, "The Spectacular Consumption of 'True' African-American Culture: 'Whassup' with the Budweiser Guys?" *Critical Studies in Media Communication* 19.1 (March 2002).

29 Foster, *Performing Whiteness*, p. 117.

30 Oscars 2005.

31 Jean-Paul Sartre, *Being and Nothingness* (Paris: Gallimard, 1943), p. 192.

32 Quote by David Pilgrim in John Leland, "The Perils of Improvising a Racial Self," *The New York Times*, 10 November 2003, E1.

33 Foster, *Performing Whiteness*, p. 125.

34 David Rooney, Review of *White Chicks*, Variety.com, 22 June 2004.

35 Gary Taylor, *Buying Whiteness: Race, Culture and Identity: From Columbus to Hip Hop* (New York: Palgrave Macmillan, 2005), p. 350.

Glossary of terms

Absent/present paradox In cultural terms, one of the powers of whiteness is that it remains "absent" or "invisible" as a racial category. However, to be "present" in culture it needs to be seen or brought into representation. This is the absent/present paradox of whiteness.

Alterity The state or condition of being different from or other than the norm; otherness.

American Dream The belief that the USA represents the possibility of financial success and democracy for all of its citizens.

Americanness A pervasive image of the American citizen as, typically, white and middle class. Alternative representations of the American citizen do exist, but often reinstate the primary image.

Auteur A theory that certain filmmakers possess both an individual style and artistic control over the production of their films. For example, proponents of the auteur theory often argue that Steven Spielberg is an auteur because his films possess persistent visual and thematic characteristics and because he retains a great deal of control over pre-production and production processes (including "final cut"). For further study, see James Dudley Andrew, *The Major Film Theories: An Introduction* (New York: Oxford University Press, 1976).

B-film A term used to indicate a studio's less prestigious films. B-films usually do not feature major stars or well-known filmmakers and are usually produced for less money to ensure a greater profit for less investment.

Bad buck A derogatory racial stereotype that positions black men as criminal, dangerous, and threatening (particularly to white people).

Bildungsroman A novel or work of fiction that follows the spiritual, moral, psychological or social growth of the main character. The story usually starts at childhood and ends with maturity.

Binary opposition Refers to power-saturated opposites, such as good/evil, gay/straight, black/white, that structure a great number of films in terms of moral value, ideology and identity.

Black ideology Traditional black ideology prioritizes community well-being and coalitional politics as a means of achieving social liberation. As a critical approach, black ideology promotes the practice of demystifying dominant culture (whiteness) and its various institutions (e.g. the media). Black ideology also references aspects of African heritage, a complex history that includes slavery, and is concerned with self-definitions and creative expression.

Blackness   A term used to identify the cultural and "racial" markers of "blacks" or African Americans. Like whiteness, blackness has been institutionalized to support the status quo; unlike whiteness, blackness has alternately come to encompass traditions of resistance and community liberation. See also **Brownness**, **Redness**, **Whiteness** and **Yellowness**.

Blaxploitation   A cycle of low-budget films from roughly 1971 to 1976 that featured black actors and themes but were financed, produced and directed by white-controlled production companies. The films were aggressively marketed to African Americans who, though comprising only 15 percent of the US population, accounted for nearly 30 percent of ticket sales during the late 1960s through the mid-1970s. Blaxploitation films are widely considered to have played a key role in restoring financial solvency to several foundering studios during the early 1970s. The term "blaxploitation" gestures to the exploitation of black moviegoers, black performers and the overall exchange value of "blackness" in the popular culture by primarily (though not exclusively) white interests. Though popular among many black audiences and profitable for many white production companies, these films were also a political lightning rod, drawing sharp criticism from organizations such as the NAACP, Jesse Jackson's PUSH Coalition, the Congress on Racial Equality, and the Coalition Against Blaxploitation. The two films most frequently credited with starting the blaxploitation phenomenon are Melvin Van Peebles's *Sweet Sweetback's Baadasssss Song* (Cinemation, 1971) and Gordon Parks Sr's *Shaft* (MGM, 1971).

Bootstrap   A popular reference to a person who advances him- or herself or accomplishes something without the aid of others; an abbreviation of the phrase, "to pull yourself up by the bootstraps." In the mid-twentieth century, "Operation Bootstrap" was the name given to an institutionalized shift in the economy of Puerto Rico, from an agricultural to industrial base.

Box office   A popular term that refers to the financial success of a film. The term is derived from the theater's "booth" (or box office), which was the place where tickets to movies were and in many cases still are sold.

Brownness   A term used to identify the cultural and "racial" markers of Latinos. See also **Blackness**, **Redness**, **Whiteness** and **Yellowness**.

Caucasian   A problematic term that is often used to classify people that share certain characteristics, including light skin and straight hair, and that can trace their origins to Europe. Although in everyday parlance it is often considered synonymous with white, as in "white people," most anthropologists discount the value of this term because its use stems from faulty scientific attempts to classify humans into biological races (e.g. Caucasoid, Mongoloid, Negroid, etc.). For further study, see Stephen Jay Gould, *The Mismeasure of Man* (New York: W.W. Norton & Company, 1996).

Character actor   An actor routinely cast as an eccentric, unusual or unheroic character. In terms of race, this eccentricity may simply be the performer's nonwhiteness, which, by contrast, often supports the lead performer's whiteness.

Chattel   A term used to describe the non-human status of slaves as property. In many ways slaves were considered to be like cattle.

Close-up   A cinematic composition that frames the detail of a subject on film. The close-up indicates that additional attention should be paid to the object in close-up, whether it is a key clue in the narrative or a star performer's face.

Commodification   Process of transforming an object, service or concept into a commodity; that is, something to be consumed.

Composition   The arrangement of visual elements within a film frame. See also **Mise-en-scène**.

Conglomeration   A conglomerate is a large corporation consisting of a number of smaller corporations that function independently from one another yet still serve the interests of the whole. In the context of the film industry, a conglomeration refers to the industrial reorganization that occurred in the 1960s and early 1970s. During this period a number of Hollywood studios were acquired by corporations and companies that were not primarily entertainment-related (e.g. Gulf & Western's acquisition of Paramount Pictures in 1966).

Coyote   In indigenous American folklore, the coyote is an archetypal fool or trickster known for upsetting social agreements, pursuing unreachable desires, or creating parts of the cosmos. Coyote's sexual or greedy activities usually meet a disastrous and somewhat humorous end. In many traditions, the Coyote never dies, giving him the name Old Man Coyote. In the Spanish Empire, coyote was one of several racially mixed categories used to divide peoples into *castas* or castes as a result of European, indigenous, African and Asian mixing or miscegenation. Specifically *el coyote* represented the "thieving" offspring of an Indian and Mestizo who fell below the ranks of "pure" Spaniards yet above many "full-blooded" Indians and Africans.

Coyotl   In modern Nahuatl speaking communities of Mexico, formally known as Aztec, "coyotl" is a term that describes the exploitative aspects of whiteness. More specifically, it refers to a white gentleman who, through trickery and other tactics, accomplishes success through the exploitation of others. Race, class, ecological and sexual exploitations are included within this definition, which can also describe anyone who adopts greed and oppressive ways to assimilate into whiteness.

Crossover   An entertainer whose popularity and financial success spans two or more media markets and/or a performer of color (or from another marginalized group) who parlays in-group acclaim into success in the entertainment mainstream. For example, Chris Rock is a crossover star in that he began his career in the black comedy niches (*Russell Simmons' Def Comedy Jam, Eddie Murphy's Uptown Comedy Express*) and has gone on to achieve popular and financial success in stand up, television and cinema.

Cultural capital   A term that refers to the notion that power and status are maintained and justified through the acquisition of attributes associated with high culture, such as titles, genealogies, culturally specific manners, higher education, and so forth. These symbolic resources have genuine value since society regulates their dispersion and they are generally not available to a mass public. In this way, cultural capital functions as a system of domination. Different cultures have different manifestations of cultural capital.

Cultural citizenship   A sense of belonging and investment in socioeconomic ascension, exemplified by association with a strong work ethic and democracy. See also **American Dream**.

Cultural geography   A term used to designate the spatial expression and impact of cultural products, values and practices on human geography.

Diegesis   The fictional world of the story. For example, Middle Earth forms the diegesis of the *Lord of the Rings* trilogy (2001; 2002; 2003).

Difference   A marked exoticism and otherness often linked in the USA to African Americans, Asian Americans, Jews, Latinos and Native Americans. See also **Other**.

Discourse   An integrated approach to a specific topic (conversation), such as race or gender; it encompasses representations in television, film, art, literature, politics, laws, etc. Framed by ideologies, discourses work to shape a society's understanding about life and people but, in a circular fashion, the specific understandings (or ideologies) of a society also shape the discourses. People born into discourse systems may believe that their concepts, words and arts are universal because they consistently appear throughout the worlds they inhabit and because they are accepted uncritically by a majority of people. Alternate discourses covering the same subject and the same representations can exist in the same society but these may be suppressed and discounted by dominant groups that position their representations and ideologies as the norm. For further study, see Michel Foucault, *The Foucault Reader* (New York: Pantheon, 1984).

Diva   Refers to a gifted, unique and uncompromising singer or performer; a prima donna. In the contemporary vernacular, the word has also been used to describe someone with unreasonable self-importance or selfish demands – a particularly fierce drag queen, for example – as well as female stars and singers with bodies of work that have given them venerated status.

Dragon Lady   A negative stereotype of an Asian or Asian American woman as a sexual predator.

Ethnicity   Related to the sociopolitical definition of **Race**, the term generally refers to social groups that share national, religious, cultural and/or linguistic traditions and affiliations.

Ethnography   A method of analysis that seeks to describe the range of human behaviors, cultural practices and social relations that occur within a group or community. Common in social science and anthropological disciplines, ethnographic writing draws conclusions based primarily on sustained observation, interviews and qualitative analysis.

Eurocentrism   A strategy to interpret the world in terms of European values and experiences, thereby placing them at the center of authority and power. For further study, see Ella Shohat, *Unthinking Eurocentrism* (New York: Routledge, 1984).

Exploitation film   Mode of filmmaking, from production to exhibition, that eschews prevailing standards of aesthetics, narrative form and subject matter. Exploitation films have existed since at least the 1930s and frequently target subcultural or marginal audiences (e.g. **Blaxploitation** films). Sometimes dismissed as "schlock," "kitsch" or just "trash," exploitation films frequently and explicitly address a range of topics that commercial cinema avoids (e.g. teenage, pre-marital or extra-marital sex; drugs; forms of physical or psychological difference, etc.). To this end, early exploitation film is often understood to have challenged mainstream movies' control over representation. By the 1960s and 1970s, amidst sweeping changes in both the ratings system and the studio system, exploitation films became less overtly oppositional.

Flexible citizenship   Ability of people to bend their national/racial/ethnic identities to accommodate movement within the contemporary postmodern global economy. Based on research on middle-class professionals within the Chinese diaspora by Aihwa Ong in *Flexible Citizenship: The Cultural Logics of Transnationality* (Durham, NC: Duke University Press, 1999).

Gaze   In film studies, a term used to identify the more powerful subject within a film narrative as indicated by the point-of-view shot. For example, classic Hollywood film often privileges the male in film by giving them point-of-view shots that reveal a female character from his perspective. For further study, see Robert Stam, *Film Theory: An Introduction* (Oxford: Blackwell, 2000).

Gender   Traditionally gender has been used primarily to refer to the categories of "masculine" and "feminine," but in recent years the word has come to refer to sex-based forms of identity. In this usage, gender is a social construct. This usage is supported by the practice of many anthropologists who reserve "sex" for reference to biological categories while using "gender" to refer to social or cultural categories. For further study, see Judith Butler, *Gender Trouble* (New York: Routledge, 1999).

Hegelian dialectic   A theory developed by the German philosopher, George Wilhelm Friedrich Hegel, that, in its application to questions of race, has led scholars to reveal the dependency at work in how the Other (the slave) defines the self (the master). For further reading, see George Wilhelm Friedrich Hegel, *Phenomenology of Spirit* (New York: Oxford University Press, 1979).

Hegemony   Control and domination of one group by another. However, this occurs not only through laws and policing forces, or physical force, but through social discourses and ideologies that convince both the dominated and the dominating that the social order of control is legitimate and should exist as it does. For a more detailed definition, see Tom Bottomore, *Dictionary of Marxist Thought* (Oxford: Blackwell, 1991).

Idealized whiteness   The highest, purest, most appealing version of whiteness and therefore the type of racial identity that one should aspire to be. See also **Whiteness**.

Ideological state apparatuses (ISAs)   Identified by a prominent Marxist theorist, Louis Althusser, to describe how specific institutions perpetuate ideology. These institutions, or ISAs, include religion, law, politics, trade unions, media and the family. ISAs are different from repressive state apparatuses (RSA) such as the army and police in that they produce consent through ideology rather than the use of physical force and violence. For further study, see Louis Althusser, "Ideology and Ideological State Apparatuses," in *Lenin and Philosophy and Other Essays* (London: New Left Books, 1989).

Ideology   A notoriously slippery term to define, ideology can be understood simply to designate a set of beliefs, or a "common sense," about the world. At its most effective, ideology remains more or less invisible to us and is perpetuated through language and culture. In addition, ideology represents its view of the world as "natural" in order to occlude its origins in and promotion of the cultural, economic and political interests of dominant groups (often at the expense of non-dominant groups). For a more detailed definition, see Tom Bottomore, *Dictionary of Marxist Thought* (Oxford: Blackwell, 1991).

In-between-ness   A term that identifies the simultaneous display of whiteness and blackness in visual representation. If whiteness and blackness are the traditional poles of visual culture, in-between-ness oscillates betwixt these categories.

Intercut   To cut between two or more scenes to create a new scene.

International Other   An Other that is positioned by Hollywood as originating from another country. Often, this Otherness is marked by an accent, costuming or other characterization that connotes foreignness. See also **Other**.

Interpolate   A term most commonly used in Marxist cultural criticism to describe the process by which an individual is "hailed," or called to take up a position, by a representative (a person, an institution, an image) of the dominant ideology. By acknowledging that representative's authority to speak for and/or to you, the individual becomes interpolated, tacitly consenting to the dominant ideology and the social relations to which it gives rise. For further study, see Louis Althusser, "Ideology and Ideological State Apparatuses," in *Lenin and Philosophy and Other Essays* (London: New Left Books, 1989).

Intersectionality An analytical paradigm often adopted in cultural, ethnic and women studies that operates upon the assumption that forms of oppression within a given society – homophobia, racism, sexism, etc. – do not act independently of one another. Instead, various modes of oppression intersect based upon various markers of difference. Women of color, for example, are often oppressed simultaneously by racism and sexism (as well as class, sexual preference, etc.). By extension, intersectionality can be applied not only to the analysis of multiple annunciations of identity (class, race, gender, etc.), but also their interrelation with industrial and cultural practices (e.g. the media).

Intertextual The interrelatedness of two or more visual or written texts, making the meaning of all texts partly shaped by other texts. It can refer to an author's use of a prior text, directly or indirectly, as well as a reader's use of one text to interpret another. In this way, all texts (films, television programs, etc.) are intertextual. For further reading, see Julia Kristeva, *Desire in Language: A Semiotic Approach to Literature and Art* (New York: Columbia University Press, 1980).

Intra-national Other An Other that is positioned by Hollywood as a second or third generation immigrant within the US. This Otherness is rarely affiliated with whiteness. Most commonly, the intra-national Other is typically represented as an assimilable nonwhite person, for example Latino/as, born within the USA. See also **Other**.

Latinaness A limited characterization (or type) that denotes a female of Latin American or Latina origin in Hollywood film. This type often involves specifically ethnic markers like accent, skin color, hair type, exuberant sexuality or the ability to dance.

Latin Lover A stereotype for a "foreign" man, generally Latino, as a sexual predator. To achieve his sexual conquests, which are generally focused on white women, the Latin Lover uses seduction rather than rape. He often appears effeminate in comparison to white men.

Lead The person playing the primary role in a film narrative; generally the protagonist or main character.

Love interest A character – often a supporting actress – whose main function is to provide a romantic narrative for the protagonist (lead) in a film.

Marxist ideology A view of the world based upon the writings of the German philosopher Karl Marx, emphasizing class conflict and revolution. See also **Ideology**.

Masculinity A cultural notion of being a man.

Melting pot A metaphor for homogenization through assimilation that is often contrasted with multiculturalism. The phrase is generally attributed to Israel Zangwill's adaptation of William Shakespeare's *Romeo and Juliet* in 1908, which he titled *The Melting Pot* and set in New York City.

Minstrelsy Refers to a form of entertainment that was popular in the USA in the nineteenth and early twentieth centuries. It originated in the 1830s with white performer Thomas D. Rice, known as "Jim Crow," who placed burnt cork on his face and performed songs and dances in a stereotyped imitation of African Americans. Blackfaced white minstrel troupes were particularly popular in the USA and England. Minstrel troupes composed of African Americans were formed after the Civil War and were, in general, the only theatrical medium in which black performers of the period could support themselves. While minstrel shows effectively disappeared by the early twentieth century, the effects of their racist import continue to persist in performance media and expectations within popular culture. For further reading, see Eric Loss, *Love and Theft: Blackface Minstrelsy and the American Working Class* (New York: Oxford University Press, 1993).

Miscegenation The so-called mixing of the races in terms of cohabitation, marriage or sexual intercourse. For over a century it was used by racists to promote the fear of race mixing that they argued would dilute the purity of the white race.

Mise-en-scène Literally "setting in the scene," a French term used to describe not only the objects, people and set design in the film frame at any given time but also the relationship between all of these to one another and to the camera. Mise-en-scène, together with editing and camera work, is a central aspect of a film's visual style.

Model minority "Positive" stereotype for minority groups that was originally applied to Asian Americans. Used to describe those who "outperform" other minority groups ("problem minorities") in terms of economic success, education and income.

Montage A type of film editing in which a series of short shots is formed into a sequence to create symbolic meaning and/or condense narrative (for example, to suggest that passage of time). For further reading on film theory, see James Dudley Andrew, *The Major Film Theories: An Introduction* (New York: Oxford University Press, 1976).

Mulatto Term used as a racial category on the US census until the early twentieth century to describe a person of mixed European and African ancestry.

Multiculturalism Paradoxical US national discourse that facilitates representation of different racialized and minoritized groups, glorifying each group's heritage without calling attention to inequalities between these groups in terms of access to material and legal resources.

Narrativize   The process of placing information (images, characters, plot devices, etc.) within a structured story.

Narratology   The study of stories and how they are told. It encompasses dramatic structure (the most common being beginning–middle–end), characters and how they are developed (characterization), genres, story-telling conventions (like the happy ending in many Hollywood films), plot devices, and settings.

Nativism   Policies or sentiments that convey prejudice against immigrants, children of immigrants, or other minoritized groups.

Negrophobia   Irrational fear of African Americans that finds its way into a great many media representations.

Neoliberalism   A post Civil Rights discourse and political position that advocates for social justice by working from within democratic and capitalist institutions and principles. Neoliberals believe that social justice can come about through a free market economy. This ideology often obscures the social, material, and grassroots work necessary for long-term change in social relations and confuses change and advancement in market forces with material (or actual) social change.

Neo-Marxism   A twentieth-century school of thought that, though based in Marxism and thus critiques of class-based forms of power and exploitation, rejected economic determinism, or power determined by one's relation to the economic mode of production (e.g. capitalism). Neo-Marxism focuses instead on relational causes that included, among other factors, economics, ideology, psychology and culture. For further reading, see Tom Bottomore, *Dictionary of Marxist Thought* (Oxford: Blackwell, 1991).

New Black Cinema   A period of black film roughly beginning with Spike Lee's *She's Gotta Have It* (1986) and continuing through the "second generation" of film school trained filmmakers such as Lee, Reginald and Warrington Hudlin, John Singleton, and Robert Townsend.

New Hollywood   A catchall term used to describe the prevailing industrial standards of production, distribution, marketing and exhibition in Hollywood from the mid-1970s forward, during which time Hollywood re-established its global hegemony after a period of steep decline in the 1960s and early 1970s. In the area of production, New Hollywood generally seeks a balance between big-budget, high-concept, effects-heavy, star-driven "blockbusters" that favor plot and style over character and substance on the one hand, and more modest, character- or genre-driven films that can be marketed to niche audiences. In the area of distribution, New Hollywood generally prefers to "frontload" films by scheduling national releases, that allow a film to recoup as much of its costs as fast as possible. New Hollywood embraces a wide range of marketing practices; one of the most important of these is the synergy it seeks with other markets and media outlets. Along with the consolidation of the media in the USA, this has given rise to a broad-based, multimedia entertainment culture, in which motion pictures are frequently seen as platforms to promote a soundtrack, music videos, video games, toy sales, product tie-ins, DVD sales, and so forth. With respect to exhibition, the New Hollywood ushered in the era of the multiplex and the reorganization of the release calendar, holding blockbusters and films with strong youth appeal for summer and holiday breaks while relegating films with narrower markets to the fall and spring periods.

Oedipal Complex   From Greek mythology of King Oedipus who killed his father and had sex with his mother. In Freudian psychology and psycho-analytic film contexts, the Oedipal Complex describes the developmental power struggle that children sexualize in relation to both parents. While the mother is the primal object of sexual desire, the father may use castra-tion to fend off children from sexually claiming the mother. The Oedipal Complex defines incest taboos and the tension that arises when people test the limits of those taboos.

One drop rule   Rule enforced until the mid-1920s that considered a person with "one drop of nonwhite blood" as nonwhite. See also **Miscegenation**.

Other   Like **Difference**, a term used critically to draw attention to the representation and positioning of people of color and other groups as different and thus not normal (white).

Overdetermined   The idea that a single effect has multiple causes. In contemporary criticism, the term is associated with Freud, who first used it to argue that elements in dreams came from several sources that might include recent experiences, repressed memories, fears, and wishes. Later, Marxist theorist Louis Althusser used Freud's term in an ideological way to explain how a single political act might be the result of many and some-times contradictory influences. For further reading, see Sigmund Freud, *The Interpretation of Dreams* (New York: Avon, 1980), as well as Louis Althusser, "Contradiction and Overdetermination," in *For Marx* (New York: Verso, 1985).

Panoptic   In the panoptic multiple subjects are surveyed from a centralized position. Michel Foucault associated "panopticisms" with modern soci-eties that discipline and control their masses through scientific, political and judicial surveillance, determining official standards for sanity, sexuality, deviance and so forth. With apparent objectivity, institutional forces can then incarcerate threats to social equilibrium and, at the same time, create understandings about the very nature of normalcy. For further reading, see Michel Foucault, *Discipline and Punish: The Birth of the Prison* (New York: Random House, 1975).

Passing   Posing or appearing as another race. The term most commonly refers to black bodies posing or appearing as white and draws attention to the artificial racial hierarchy that assigns white bodies more social, legal, cultural or symbolic weight than black bodies.

Payola The (recording industry) practice of illegally paying radio stations or other broadcasters to play music or promote artists in exchange for payment without identifying sponsorship.

Persona Refers to an assumed role or personality adopted by an individual. The persona(e), constructed to facilitate the performance of multiple identities, enables the individual to elicit specific emotional, ideological and intellectual responses from his/her audience – whether it happens to be in a comedy club, or on the floor of the Senate.

Phallic masculinity A cultural notion of manhood centered upon the phallus – a symbol of the penis – as strong and powerful.

Plantation genre Early Hollywood representations of master–slave relationships as pastoral and idyllic. For further reading, see Ed Guerrero, *Framing Blackness: the African American Image in Film* (Philadelphia, PA: Temple University Press, 1993).

Political economy Names the interconnectedness between economic structures (e.g. labor, capital, markets) and political institutions and processes (e.g. policy decisions, laws, etc.). Because these are often mutually reinforcing, such that the government and market shape, strengthen and benefit one another, "political economies" often express a range of ideological values in material terms. For a more detailed definition, see Tom Bottomore, *Dictionary of Marxist Thought* (Oxford: Blackwell, 1991).

Race Socially constructed category of differentiation, or meaning, among humans that attempts to pass itself as biological or divine fact. See also **Racial formation**.

Racial formation Term developed by Michael Omi and Howard Winant to describe that racial categories are shaped, defined and revised by social and historical forces. The concept further asserts that "race" is produced by, experienced in and negotiated through cultural practices and representations. See Michael Omi and Howard Winant, *Racial Formations in the United States: From the 1960s to the 1990s* (New York: Routledge, 1994).

Racial mobility The process of manipulating the codes of race in visual culture to maximize the types of film roles one can play. See also **Passing** and **Crossover**.

Real/representation dialectic Refers to the relationship between reality and representation of reality in which racial, sexual and gender identity is a product of both. In other words, real/representation dialectic posits that race, sex and gender are constructs and as such the production of these identity constructs is the process of representation. For further study, see Teresa De Lauretis, *Technologies of Gender* (Bloomington, IN: Indiana University Press, 1987), pp. 1–30.

Realism Practice of approximate fidelity in cinema (or other art forms) to reality without idealization. Realism in film is always a construct, a representational strategy, and in this way it is also ideological.

Redness A term used to identify the cultural and "racial" markers of Native Americans. See also **Blackness, Brownness, Whiteness** and **Yellowness**.

Reification Process by which an idea, value or ideology assumes a material form or is mapped onto an already existing landscape, geography or built environment.

Resisting gaze Term for a film-screening strategy that actively creates pleasure by reading against dominant and preferred meanings. See also **Gaze**.

Sameness (one) A seemingly unmarked yet privileged representation of normalcy often linked with whiteness.

Subaltern Most frequently associated with post-colonial theory, a term that describes a subordinated person or group with little or no agency, often of the non-Western world. Race, social standing, even history are projected onto the subaltern by colonial and other dominating powers.

Subcultural capital Knowledge of the rules of language, deportment, music or film associated with a particular subculture. Based on Pierre Bourdieu's concept of "cultural capital." For further study, see Sarah Thornton, *Club Cultures: Music, Media and Subcultural Capital* (Hanover, NH: Wesleyan University Press, 1996).

Supporting actor/actress A performer playing a secondary, non-lead role in a film.

Symbolic exchange Term used to describe the process by which individuals and/or groups produce and organize meaning through the exchange of non-material items such as symbols, values, knowledge and cultural capital.

Taboo Something a culture strongly prohibits doing, looking at, or talking about (e.g. incest).

Technophilia Love of technology. In film, this might manifest as extended special effect sequences where one is asked to express awe and wonder at what is visualized.

Tejano A person of Mexican descent living in Texas. In the 1820s and 1830s, Tejano referred to the native Mexicans who lived in Texas.

To-be-looked-at Displaying the body in a manner that invites an assessing look. See **Gaze** and **Resisting gaze**. For further study, see Laura Mulvey, *Visual and Other Pleasures* (New York: Palgrave Macmillan, 1989).

Type A simplified characterization used in film to efficiently convey specific information about a character within a narrative.

Verisimilitude Qualities that suggest truth in representation.

Visual pleasure Refers to the operation of looking relations in Hollywood film that constructs viewing pleasure around active male viewers and female objects of the gaze. Elaborated on by Laura Mulvey, "Visual Pleasure and Narrative Cinema," *Screen* 16.3 (1975), pp. 6–18. See also **Gaze, To-be-looked-at** and **Resisting gaze**.

Whiteface A play on the term "blackface," the use of make-up and stereotypical tropes by white performers to mimic black people, whiteface is used to identify how a nonwhite performer is marked as white through cosmetic or fashion. See also **Blackface**.

Whiteness   A term used to identify the cultural and "racial" markers of people that pass as white. In critical race theory and whiteness studies, the racial category "white" has been institutionalized as the dominant racial identity. In Hollywood film, for example, white characters are seemingly unmarked by race; therefore, whiteness superficially represents the human race and acts as the status quo against which difference is constructed. See also **Blackness, Brownness, Redness** and **Yellowness**. For further study, see the bibliography at the end of this book.

Wide shot   Also known as a "long shot," the wide shot is a composition that frames a full body or landscape to establish or contextualize the subject on film.

Xenophilia   Irrational attraction to strangers or foreigners.

Xenophobia   Irrational fear or hatred of strangers or foreigners.

Yellowness   A term used to identify the cultural and "racial" markers of Asians and Asian Americans. See also **Blackness, Brownness, Redness** and **Whiteness**.

Select bibliography

Compiled by Young Eun Chae

Whiteness studies

Alcoff, Linda Martin. "What Should White People Do?" *Hypatia* 13 (3), summer 1998: 6–26.

Allen, Theodore. *The Invention of the White Race: Volume One: Racial Oppression and Social Control.* London: Verso, 1994.

Anderson, Margaret L. "Whitewashing Race: A Critical Review Essay on 'Whiteness,'" in Ashley W. Doane and Eduardo Bonilla-Silva, eds. *Whiteout: The Continuing Significance of Racism.* New York: Routledge, 2003.

Appiah, Kwame Anthony, and Henry Louis Gates, Jr. *Identities.* Chicago, IL: University of Chicago Press, 1995.

Appiah, Kwame Anthony, and Amy Gutmann. *Color Conscious: The Political Morality of Race.* Princeton, NJ: Princeton University Press, 1996.

Arnesen, Eric. "Whiteness and the Historians' Imagination." *International Labor and Working Class History* 60, Fall 2001: 3–32.

Babb, Valerie. *Whiteness Visible: The Meaning of Whiteness in American Literature and Culture.* New York: New York University Press, 1998.

Berger, Maurice. *White Lies: Race and the Myths of Whiteness.* New York: Farrar, Strauss Giroux, 1999.

Bernardi, Daniel, ed. *The Birth of Whiteness: Race and the Emergence of US Cinema.* New Brunswick, NJ: Rutgers University Press, 1996.

——, ed. *Classic Hollywood, Classic Whiteness.* Minneapolis, MN: University of Minnesota Press, 2001.

——. "Cyborgs in Cyberspace: White Pride, Pedophilic Pornography, and Donna Haraway's Manifesto," in James Freidman, ed. *Reality Squared: Television Discourse on the Real.* New Brunswick, NJ: Rutgers University Press, 2002.

——. "Interracial Joysticks: Pornography's Web of Racist Attractions," in Peter Lehman, ed. *Pornography: Film and Culture.* New Brunswick, NJ: Rutgers University Press, 2006.

Bernasconi, Robert. "Who Invented the Concept of Race? Kant's Role in the Enlightenment Construction of Race," in Robert Bernasconi, ed. *Race.* Oxford: Blackwell, 2001: 11–36.

Bhabha, Homi K. "The White Stuff." *Artforum* 36 (9), May 1998: 21–4.

Bonilla-Silva, Eduardo. "Rethinking Racism: Toward a Structural Interpretation." *American Sociological Review* 62, 1997: 465–80.

——. *White Supremacy and Racism in the Post-Civil Rights Era.* Boulder, CO: Lynne Reinner Publishers, 1997.

Brodkin, Karen S. *How Jews Became White Folks and What that Says about Race in America.* New Brunswick, NJ: Rutgers University Press, 1998.

Bush, Melanie E.L. *Breaking the Code of Good Intentions: Everyday Forms of Whiteness.* Lanham, MD: Rowman and Littlefield Publishers, 2004.

Courtney, Susan. *Hollywood Fantasies of Miscegenation: Spectacular Narratives of Gender and Race, 1903–1967.* Princeton, NJ: Princeton University Press, 2005.

Crenshaw, Carrie. "'Resisting Whiteness': The Problems and Projects of a New Research Agenda." *Theory, Culture and Society* 13 (2), 1996: 145–55.

——. "Color-Blind Dreams and Racial Nightmares: Reconfiguring Racism in the Post-Civil Rights Era," in Toni Morrison and Claudia Brodsky Lacour, eds. *Birth of a Nation'hood: Gaze, Script, and Spectacle in the O. J. Simpson Case.* New York: Pantheon Books, 1997.

Daniels, Jessie. *White Lies: Race, Class, Gender, and Sexuality in White Supremacist Discourse.* New York: Routledge, 1997.

Delgado, Richard and Jean Stefancic. *Critical White Studies: Looking Behind the Mirror.* Philadelphia, PA: Temple University Press, 1997.

Dixon, Deborah, and John Grimes. "Capitalism, Masculinity, and Whiteness in the Dialectical Landscape: The Case of Tarzan and the Tycoon." *GeoJournal* 59 (4), 2004: 265–75.

Doane, Ashley W. "White Identity and Race Relations in the 1990s," in Gregg Lee Carter, ed. *Perspectives on Current Social Problems.* Boston, MA: Allyn and Bacon, 1997.

Doane, Ashley, and Eduardo Bonilla-Silva, eds. *Whiteout: The Continuing Significance of Racism.* New York: Routledge, 2003.

Dominguez, Virginia. *White By Definition: Social Classification in Creole Louisiana.* New Brunswick, NJ: Rutgers University Press, 1994.

Duster, Troy. "The 'Morphing' Properties of Whiteness," in Birgit Brander Rasmussen, Eric Klinenberg, Irene J. Nexica, and Matt Wray, eds. *The Making and Unmaking of Whiteness.* Durham, NC: Duke University Press, 2001.

Dyer, Richard. *White.* New York: Routledge, 1997.

——. "The Matter of Whiteness," in Paula S. Rothenberg, ed. *White Privilege: Essential Readings on the Other Side of Racism.* New York: Worth Publishers, 2002: 9–14.

Fanon, Frantz. *Black Skin/White Masks.* New York: Grove Press, 1967.

Farley, R. "Blacks, Hispanics, and White Ethnic Groups: Are Blacks Uniquely Disadvantaged?" *American Economic Review* 80, 1990: 237–41.

Feagin, Joe R., and Hernan Vera. *White Racism: The Basics.* New York: Routledge, 1995.

Fields, Barbara. "Whiteness, Racism, and Identity." *International Labor and Working Class History* 60, Fall 2001: 48–56.

Fine, Michelle, Lois Weis, Linda C. Powell and L. Mun Wong, eds. *Off White: Readings On Race, Power, and Society.* New York: Routledge, 1997.

Fishkin, Shelley Fisher. "Interrogating 'Whiteness,' Complicating 'Blackness': Remapping American Culture." *American Quarterly* 47, 1995: 428–66.

Foster, Gwendolyn Audrey. *Performing Whiteness: Postmodern Re/Constructions in the Cinema.* Albany, NY: State University of New York Press, 2003.

Frankenberg, Ruth, ed. *White Women, Race Matters: The Social Construction of Whiteness.* Minneapolis, MN: University of Minnesota Press, 1993.

——. *Local Whiteness, Localizing Whiteness*. Durham, NC: Duke University Press, 1996.

——. *Displacing Whiteness: Essays in Social and Cultural Criticism*. Durham, NC: Duke University Press, 1997.

Friedman, Lester D. *Citizen Spielberg*. Chicago, IL: University of Illinois Press, 2006.

Frye, Marilyn. "On Being White: Thinking Toward a Feminist Understanding of Race and Race Supremacy," in *The Politics of Reality: Essays in Feminist Theory*. Trumansburg, NY: Crossing Press, 1983: 110–27.

Gabriel, John. *Whitewash: Racialized Politics and the Media*. New York: Routledge, 1998.

Ganley, Toby. "What's All This Talk about Whiteness?" *Dialogue* 1 (2), 2003: 12–30.

Gates, E. Nathaniel, ed. *Cultural and Literary Critiques of the Concepts of "Race."* New York: Garland Publishing, 1997.

Gates, Jr., Henry Louis, Anthony Appiah, and Michael Vasquez. *The White Issue: A Special Issue of Transition*. Durham, NC: Duke University Press, 1998.

Gaule, Sally. "Poor White, White Poor: Meanings in the Differences of Whiteness." *History of Photography* 25, Winter 2001: 334–47.

Gilman, Sander L. "Black Bodies, White Bodies: Toward an Iconography of Female Sexuality in Late Nineteenth Century Art, Medicine and Literature," in Henry Louis Gates, Jr., ed. *Race, Writing and Difference*. Chicago, IL: University of Chicago Press, 1985.

Giroux, Henry. "Rewriting the Discourse of Racial Identity: Towards a Pedagogy and Politics of Whiteness." *Harvard Educational Review* 67 (2), 1997: 285–320.

——. "White Squall: Resistance and the Pedagogy of Whiteness." *Cultural Studies* 11 (3), 1997: 376–89.

Goldberg, David Theo, and Philomena Essed, eds. *Race Critical Theories: Text and Context*. Malden, MA: Blackwell, 2002.

Guglielmo, Jennifer, and Salvatore Salerno, eds. *Are Italians White? How Race is Made in America*. New York; London: Routledge, 2003.

Guglielmo, Thomas A. *White on Arrival: Italians, Race, Color, and Power in Chicago, 1890–1945*. Oxford: Oxford University Press, 2003.

Guterl, Matthew Pratt. "A Note on the Word White." *American Quarterly* 56 (2), June 2004: 439–47.

Hale, Grace Elizabeth. *Making Whiteness: The Culture of Segregation in the South, 1890–1940*. New York: Pantheon Books, 1998.

Haney López, Ian F. *White by Law: The Legal Construction of Race*. New York: New York University Press, 1996.

Harris, Cheryl. "Whiteness as Property." *Harvard Law Review* 106 (8), June 1993: 1707–91.

Hartigan, John Jr. "Establishing the Fact of Whiteness." *American Anthropologist* 99 (3), September 1997: 495–505.

Hartman, A. "The Rise and Fall of Whiteness Studies." *Race and Class* 46 (2), 2004: 22–38.

Hatt, Michael. "Ghost Dancing in the Salon: The Red Indian as a Sign of White Identity." *Diognes* 45 (1), Spring 1997: 93–110.

Helms, Janet E. *A Race Is a Nice Thing to Have: A Guide to Being a White Person or Understanding the White Persons in Your Life*. Topeka, KS: Content Communication, 1992.

Hill, Mike. *Whiteness: A Critical Reader*. New York: New York University Press, 1997.

Hoelscher, Steven. "Making Place, Making Race: Performances of Whiteness in the Jim Crow South." *Annals of the Association of American Geographers* 93 (3), 2003: 657–86.

hooks, bell. *Black Looks: Race and Representation*. Boston, MA: South End Press, 1992.

——. "Representing Whiteness in the Black Imagination," in Lawrence Grossberg, Cary Nelson, and Paula A. Treichler, eds. *Cultural Studies*. New York: Routledge, 1992.

Horsman, Reginald. *Race and Manifest Destiny: The Origins of American Racial Anglo-Saxonism*. Cambridge, MA: Harvard University Press, 1986.

Hyde, Cheryl. "The Meanings of Whiteness." *Qualitative Sociology* 18 (1), 1995: 87–95.

Ignatiev, Noel. *How the Irish Became White*. New York: Routledge, 1996.

Ignatiev, Noel, and John Garvey. *Race Traitor*. Cambridge: Race Traitor, 1996.

Jacobson, Matthew Frye. *Whiteness of a Different Color: European Immigrants and the Alchemy of Race*. Cambridge, MA: Harvard University Press, 1998.

Jackson, Ronald L., II. "White Space, White Privilege: Mapping Discursive Inquiry into the Self." *Quarterly Journal of Speech* 85 (1), February 1999: 38–54.

Jordan, Winthrop D. *White Over Black: American Attitudes Toward the Negro, 1550–1812*. Chapel Hill, NC: University of North Carolina Press, 1968.

——. *The White Man's Burden: Historical Origins of Racism in the United States*. New York: Oxford University Press, 1974.

Kaplan, Sidney. *American Studies in Black and White: Selected Essays, 1949–1989*. Amherst, MA: University of Massachusetts Press, 1991.

Kincheloe, Joe L., Shirley R. Steinberg, Nelson M. Rodriguez, and Ronald E. Chennault, eds. *White Reign: Deploying Whiteness in America*. New York: Palgrave Macmillan, 2000.

Knadler, Stephen P. "Untragic Mulatto: Charles Chesnutt and the Discourse of Whiteness." *American Literary History* 8 (3), 1996: 426–48.

——. *The Fugitive Race: Minority Writers Resisting Whiteness*. Jackson, MS: University Press of Mississippi, 2002.

——. "Traumatized Racial Performativity: Passing in Nineteenth-Century African American Testimonies." *Cultural Critique* 55, 2004: 63–100.

Kolchin, Peter. "Whiteness Studies: The New History of Race in America." *The Journal of American History* 89 (1), 2002: 154–73.

Lazarre, Jane. "Color Blind: The Whiteness of Whiteness," in Gary Colombo, Robert Cullen, and Bonnie Lisle, eds. *Rereading America: Cultural Contexts for Critical Thing and Writing* (5th edn). New York: St. Martin's Press, 2001.

Liera-Schwichtenberg, R. "Passing or Whiteness on the Edge of Town." *Critical Studies in Media Communication* 17 (3), 2000: 371–4.

Lipsitz, George. *The Possessive Investment in Whiteness: How White People Profit from Identity Politics*. Philadelphia, PA: Temple University Press, 1998.

Lott, Eric. *Love and Theft: Blackface Minstrelsy and the American Working Class*. New York: Oxford University Press, 1993.

——. "White Like Me: Racial Cross-Dressing and the Construction of American Whiteness," in Amy Kaplan and Donald E. Pease, eds. *Culture of United States Imperialism*. Durham, NC: Duke University Press, 1993: 474–95.

——. "Whiteness: A Glossary." *The Village Voice*, 18 May 1993: 38–9.

Lott, Tommy L. *The Invention of Race*. London: Blackwell, 1999.

Mahoney, Martha R. "Segregation, Whiteness, and Transformation." *University of Pennsylvania Law Review* 143, 1995: 1659–84.

Marx, Anthony. *Making Race and Nation*. Cambridge: Cambridge University Press, 1998.

McIntosh, Peggy. "White Privilege: Unpacking the Invisible Knapsack," in Bart Schneider, ed. *Race: An Anthology in the First Person*. New York: Crown, 1997.

McMillen, Liz. "Lifting the Veil from Whiteness: Growing Body of Scholarship Challenges a Racial Norm." *Chronicle of Higher Education*, September 8, 1995: A23.

Michaels, Walter Benn. "The Souls of White Folk," in Elaine Scarry, ed. *Literature and the Body: Essays on Populations and Persons*. Baltimore, MD: Johns Hopkins University Press, 1988.

Morrison, Toni. *Playing in the Dark: Whiteness and the Literary Imagination*. Cambridge, MA: Harvard University Press, 1992.

Mullen, Harryette. "Optic White: Blackness and the Production of Whiteness." *Diacritics* 24 (2–3), 1994: 71–89.

Nakayama, Thomas K., and Robert L. Krizek. "Whiteness: A Strategic Rhetoric." *The Quarterly Journal of Speech* 81 (3), 1995: 291–309.

Newitz, Annalee. *White Trash: Race and Class in America*. London: Routledge, 1996.

Nguyen, Viet Thanh. *Race and Resistance: Literature and Politics in Asian America*. Oxford: Oxford University Press, 2002.

Oliver, Melvin L., and Thomas M. Shapiro. *Black Wealth/White Wealth: A New Perspective on Racial Inequality*. New York: Routledge, 1995.

Pfeil, Fred. *White Guys: Studies in Postmodern Domination and Difference*. London: Verso, 1995.

Puar, Jasbir K. "Resituating Discourses of Whiteness and Asianness in Northern England." *Socialist Review* 24, 1995: 21–53.

Rafter, Nicole Hahn. *White Trash: The Eugenic Family Studies, 1877–1919*. Boston, MA: Northeastern University Press, 1988.

Rasmussen, Birgit Brander, Eric Klinenberg, Irene J. Nexica, and Matt Wray, eds. *The Making and Unmaking of Whiteness*. Durham, NC: Duke University Press, 2001.

Roediger, David, ed. *Towards the Abolition of Whiteness: Essays on Race, Class and Working Class History*. New York: Verso, 1994.

Roediger, David R. *The Wages of Whiteness: Race and the Making of the American Working Class*. London: Verso, 1991.

——. *Black on White: Black Writers on What It Means to be White*. New York: Schocken Books, 1998.

——. *Colored White: Transcending the Racial Past*. Berkeley, CA: University of California Press, 2002.

——. *Working Toward Whiteness: How America's Immigrants Became White: The Strange Journey from Ellis Island to the Suburbs*. New York: Basic Books, 2005.

Rogin, Michael P. *Blackface, White Noise: Jewish Immigrants in the Hollywood Melting Pot*. Berkeley, CA: University of California Press, 1996.

Rothenberg, Paula, ed. *White Privilege: Essential Readings on the Other Side of Racism*. New York: Worth Publishers, 2002: 9–14.

Sacks, Karen B. "How Did Jews Become White Folks?," in Steven Gregory and Roger Sanjek, eds. *Race*. New Brunswick, NJ: Rutgers University Press, 1994.

Sanchez, George J. "Reading Reginald Denny: The Politics of Whiteness in the Late Twentieth Century." *American Quarterly* 47 (3), September 1995: 388–94.

Saxton, Alexander. *Rise and Fall of the White Republic: Class Politics and Mass Culture in Nineteenth Century America*. New York: Verso, 1991.

Shome, Raka. "Outing Whiteness." *Critical Studies in Media Communication* 17 (3), 2000: 366–71.

Slotkin, Richard. *Gunfighter Nation: The Myth of the Frontier in Twentieth-Century America*. New York: Harper Perennial, 1993.

Smith, Shawn Michelle. "'Baby's Picture Is Always Treasured': Eugenics and the Reproduction of Whiteness in the Family Photograph Album." *Yale Journal of Criticism* 11 (1), Spring 1998: 197–220.

Stowe, David W. "Uncolored People: The Rise of Whiteness Studies." *Lingua Franca* 6 (6), September/October, 1996: 68–77.

Swain, Carol. *The New White Nationalism in America: Its Challenge to Integration*. Cambridge: Cambridge University Press, 2002.

Tardon, Raphael. "Richard Wright Tells Us: The White Problem in the United States." *Action* (October 24, 1946). Reprinted in Kenneth Kinnamon and Michel Fabre, *Conversations with Richard Wright*. Jackson, MS: University Press of Mississippi, 1946.

Taylor, Mark C. "Malcolm's Conk and Danto's Colors; or, Four Logical Petitions Concerning Race, Beauty, and Aesthetics," in Peg Zeglin Brand, ed. *Beauty Matters*. Bloomington, IN: Indiana University Press, 2000.

Tuch, Steven S., and Jack K. Martin, eds. *Racial Attitudes in the 1990s: Continuity and Change*. Westport, CT: Praeger, 1997.

Walter, Bronwen. *Outsiders Inside: Whiteness, Place and Irish Women*. London: Routledge, 2001.

Ware, Vron. *Beyond the Pale: White Women, Racism and History*. New York: Verso, 1992.

Warren, John. "Whiteness and Cultural Theory: Perspectives on Research and Education." *The Urban Review* 31 (2), June 1999: 185–204.

Warren, Jonathan W., and Winddance Twine. "White Americans, the New Minority? Non-Blacks and the Ever-Expanding Boundaries of Whiteness." *Journal of Black Studies* 28 (2), November 1997: 200–18.

Waters, Mary. "Optical Ethnicity for Whites Only?," in Gary Colombo, Robert Cullen, and Bonnie Lisle, eds. *Rereading America: Cultural Contexts for Critical Thing and Writing* (5th edn). New York: St. Martin's Press, 2001.

Wiegman, Robyn. "Whiteness Studies and the Paradox of Particularity." *Boundary 2* 26 (3), 1999: 115–50.

Wildman, Stephanie M. "Reflections on Whiteness: The Case of Latinos(as)," in Richard Delgado and Jean Stefancic, eds. *Critical White Studies: Looking Behind the Mirror*. Philadelphia, PA: Temple University Press, 1997.

Winant, Howard. "Behind Blue Eyes: Whiteness and Contemporary US Racial Politics," in Michelle Fine, Lois Weis, Linda C. Powell, and L. Mun Wong, eds. *Off White: Readings on Race, Power, and Society*. New York: Routledge, 1997.

Wray, Matt, and Annalee Newitz, eds. *White Trash: Race and Class in America*. New York: Routledge, 1997.

Yancy, George. *What White Looks Like: African-American Philosophers on the Whiteness Question*. New York: Routledge, 2004.

Young, Robert. *White Mythologies: Writing History and the West*. New York: Routledge, 1990.

——. "The Jewish Nose: Are Jews White? Or the History of the Nose Job," In Sander Gilman, ed. *The Jew's Body*. New York and London: Routledge, 1991: 169–93.

Race and contemporary Hollywood cinema

Abraham, Linus K. "The Black Woman as Marker of Hypersexuality in Western Mythology: A Contemporary Manifestation in the Film *The Scarlet Letter.*" *Journal of Communication Inquiry* 26, 2002: 193–214.

Adams, Rachel. "'Fat Man Walking': Masculinity and Racial Geographies in James Mangold's *Copland.*" *Camera Obscura* 14 (42), September 1999: 5–29.

Aleiss, Angela. "Race in Contemporary American Cinema: Part IV – Native Americans: The Surprising Silents." *Cineaste* 27 (3), 1995: 34–5.

Baker, Laura. "Screening Race: Responses to Theater Violence at *Boyz N the Hood* and *New Jack City.*" *The Velvet Light Trap* 44, Fall 1999: 4–19.

Bartley, William. "Mookie as 'Wavering Hero': *Do the Right Thing* and the American Historical Romance." *Literature/Film Quarterly* 34 (1), 2006: 9–18.

Beltrán, Mary C. "The New Hollywood Racelessness: Only the Fast, Furious, (and Multiracial) Will Survive." *Cinema Journal* 44 (2), Winter 2005: 50–67.

Benshoff, Harry M. "Blaxploitation Horror Films: Generic Reappropriation or Reinscription?" *Cinema Journal* 39, 2000: 31–50.

Berg, Charles Ramírez. "Stereotyping in Films in General and of the Hispanic in Particular." *Howard Journal of Communications* 2 (3), Summer 1990: 286–300.

Bernardi, Daniel. *Star Trek and History: Race-ing Toward a White Future.* New Brunswick, NJ: Rutgers University Press, 1998.

Berrettini, Mark. "Can 'We All' Get Along? Social Difference, the Future, and *Strange Days.*" *Camera Obscura* 50 (17:2), August 2002: 155–89.

Brinson, Susan L. "The Myth of White Superiority in *Mississippi Burning.*" *Southern Communication Journal* 60, 1995: 211–21.

Calafell, Bernadette Marie, and Fernando P. Delgado. "Reading Latina/o Images: Interrogating Americanos." *Critical Studies in Media Communication* 21 (1), 2004: 1–24.

Cameron, Kenneth M. *Africa on Film: Beyond Black and White.* New York: Continuum, 1994.

Chan, Kenneth. "The Construction of Black Male Identity in Black Action Films of the Nineties." *Cinema Journal* 37 (2), Winter 1998: 35–48.

Charles Jr., Richard Alfred. *Contemporary Hollywood's Negative Hispanic Image: An Interpretive Filmography, 1956–1993.* Westport, CT: Greenwood, 1994.

Colombe, Audrey. "White Hollywood's New Black Boogeyman." *Jump Cut* 45, Fall 2002. Available from: www.ejumpcut.org/archive/jc45.2002/colombe/blackmen txt.html

Cunningham, John. "A Second Look." *Cineaste* 22 (2), 1996: 40–1.

Dates, Jannette L., and Thomas A. Mascaro. "African Americans in Film and Television: Twentieth-Century Lessons for a New Millennium." *The Journal of Popular Film and Television* 33 (2), Summer 2005: 50–4.

Denzin, Norman K. *Reading Race: Hollywood and the Cinema of Racial Violence.* London: Sage, 2002.

Dessommes, Nancy Bishop. "Hollywood in Hoods: The Portrayal of the Ku Klux Klan in Popular Film." *Journal of Popular Culture* 32 (4), 1999: 13.

Diawara, Manthia, ed. *Black American Cinema.* New York: Routledge, 1993.

——. "Noir by Noirs: Toward a New Realism in Black Cinema," in Joan Copjec, ed. *Shades of Noir.* London: Verso, 1993: 261–78.

Donalson, Melvin Burke. *Black Directors in Hollywood*. Austin, TX: University of Texas Press, 2003.

Dunkerley, James. "All That Trouble Down There: Hollywood and Central America," in John King, Ana M. Lopez, and Manuel Alvarado, eds. *Mediating Two Worlds*. London: British Film Institute Publishing, 1993.

Ezekiel, Raphael S. *The Racist Mind: Portraits of American Neo-Nazis and Klansmen*. New York: Viking Press, 1995.

Fienup-Riordan, Ann. *Freeze Frame: Alaska Eskimos in the Movies*. Seattle, WA: University of Washington Press, 1995.

Flory, Dan. "Black on White: *Film Noir* and the Epistemology of Race in Recent African American Cinema." *Journal of Social Philosophy* 31, 2000: 82–116.

Fregoso, Rosa Linda. "Hanging out with the Homegirls? Allison Anders's *Mi Vida Loca*." (Race in Contemporary American Cinema: Part 4.) *Cineaste* 21 (3), 1995: 36–7.

——. "Homegirls, *Cholas*, and *Pachucas* in Cinema: Taking Over the Public Sphere." *California History* 74, 1995: 316–27.

Gabbard, Krin. *Black Magic: White Hollywood and African American Culture*. New Brunswick, NJ: Rutgers University Press, 2004.

Georgakas, Dan, and Miriam Rosen, eds. "The Arab Image in American Film and Television." *Cineaste* 17 (1), 1989: 1–24.

Gillian, Jennifer L. "'No One Knows You're Black': *Six Degrees of Separation* and the Buddy Formula." *Cinema Journal* 40 (3), Spring 2001: 47–68.

Gubar, Susan. "Racial Camp in *The Producers* and *Bamboozled*." *Film Quarterly* 60 (2), December 2006: 26–37.

Guerrero, Edward. *Framing Blackness: The African American Image in Film*. Philadelphia, PA: Temple University Press, 1993.

——. "Review of *Devil in a Blue Dress*." *Cineaste* 22 (1), 1996: 38, 40–1.

——. "A Circus of Dreams and Lies: The Black Film Wave at Milddle Age," in Jon Lewis, ed. *The New American Cinema*. Durham, NC: Duke University Press, 1998: 328–52.

——. "Black Violence as Cinema: From Cheap Thrills to Historical Agonies," in J. David Slocum, ed. *Violence and American Cinema*. New York: Routledge, 2001: 211–25.

Gutiérrez, Gabriel. "Deconstructing Disney: Chicano/a Children and Critical Race Theory." *Aztlán* 25 (1), 2000: 7–46.

Hall, Alice. "Film Reviews and the Public's Perception of Stereotypes: Movie Critics' Discourse about *The Siege*." *Communication Quarterly* 49 (4), 2001: 399–423.

Harris, Keith M. "Visual Culture and the Black Masculine." *Wide Angle* 21 (4), October 1999: 2–5.

Hicks, Heather J. "Hoodoo Economics: White Men's Work and Black Men's Magic in Contemporary American Film." *Camera Obscura* 18 (53), 2003: 27–56.

Hilger, Michael. *From Savage to Nobleman: Images of Native Americans in Film*. Metuchen, NJ: Scarecrow, 1995.

Holland, Sharon P. "Death in Black and White: A Reading of Marc Forster's *Monster's Ball*." *Signs* 31 (3), Spring 2006: 785–814.

Hunt, Leon. "Kung Fu from Bruce Lee to Jet Li." *Framework* 40, 1999.

Kakoudaki, Despina. "Spectacles of History: Race Relations, Melodrama, and the Science Fiction/Disaster Film." *Camera Obscura* 17 (50), 2002: 109–54.

Kim, James. "Global Containment and Triangulated Racial Desire in *Romeo Must Die*." *Camera Obscura* 19 (1), 2004: 150–79.

Knee, Adam. "The Weight of Race: Stardom and Transformations of Racialized Masculinity in Recent American Film." *Quarterly Review of Film and Video* 19, 2002: 87–100.

Kuo Wei Tchen, John. "White Patriarchy," in Russell Leong, ed. *Moving the Image: Independent Asian Pacific American Media Arts*. Los Angeles, CA: UCLA Asian American Studies Center, 1991.

Kusz, Kyle W. "'I Want to Be the Minority': The Politics of Youthful White Masculinities in Sport and Popular Culture in 1990s America." *Journal of Sport and Social Issues* 25 (4), November 2001: 390–416.

Lehman, Peter, and Susan Hunt. "Severed Heads and Severed Genitals: Violence in *Dead Presidents*." *Framework* 43 (1), 2002: 161–73.

Lentz, Kirsten Marthe. "Quality versus Relevance: Feminism, Race, and the Politics of Sign in 1970s Television." *Camera Obscura* 15 (43), June 2000: 45–93.

Lhamon, W.T. Jr. *Raising Cain: Blackface Performance from Jim Crow to Hip Hop*. Cambridge, MA: Harvard University Press, 1998.

Lipsitz, George. "Genre Anxiety and Racial Representation in 1970s Cinema," in *Refiguring American Film Genres: History and Theory*. Berkeley, CA: University of California Press, 1998.

——. "Learning from Los Angeles: Another One Rides the Bus." *American Quarterly* 56 (3), September 2004: 511–29.

List, Christine. *Chicano Images: Refiguring Ethnicity in Mainstream Film*. New York: Garland, 1996.

Lopez, Ana M. "Are All Latinas from Manhattan? Hollywood, Ethnography, and Cultural Colonialism," in Lester D. Friedman, ed. *Unspeakable Images: Ethnicity and the American Cinema*. Chicago, IL: University of Illinois Press, 1991.

Lott, Eric. "The Whiteness of Film Noir." *American Literary History* 9, 1997: 542–66.

Luhr, William. "The Scarred Woman Behind the Gun: Gender, Race, and History in Recent Westerns." *Bilingual Review/La Revista Bilingue* 20 (1), 1995: 37–44.

Madison, Kelly J. "Legitimation Crisis and Containment: The 'Anti-Racist-White-Hero' Film." *Critical Studies in Mass Communication* 16 (4), 1999: 399–416.

Man, Glenn. "Marginality and Centrality: The Myth of Asia in 1970s Hollywood." *East-West Film Journal* 8 (1), 1994: 52–67.

Margolies, Harriet. "Stereotypical Strategies: Black Film Aesthetics, Spectator Positioning, and Self-Directed Stereotypes in *Hollywood Shuffle* and *I'm Gonna Git You Sucker*." *Cinema Journal* 38 (3), Spring 1999.

Marubbio, M.E. "Celebrating with *The Last of the Mohicans*: The Columbus Quincentary and Neocolonialism in Hollywood Film." *Journal of American and Comparative Cultures* 25 (1–2), 2002: 139–54.

Mask, Mia. "*Monster's Ball*." *Film Quarterly* 58 (1), Fall 2004: 44–55.

Massood, Paula J. *Black City Cinema: African American Urban Experiences in Film*. Temple, PA: Temple University Press, 2003.

Modleski, Tania. "In Hollywood, Racist Stereotypes Can Still Earn Oscar Nominations." *Chronicle of Higher Education* 46 (28), 2000: B9.

Natter, Wolfgang. "'We Just Gotta Eliminate 'Em': On Whiteness and Film in Tim Cresswell and Deborah Dixon eds, *Matewan*, *Avalon*, and *Bulworth*." *Engaging Film: Geographies of Mobility and Identity*. Boston, MA: Rowman and Littlefield, 2002.

Neale, Steve. "Vanishing Americans: Racial and Ethnic Issues in the Interpretation and Context of Post-War 'Pro-Indian' Westerns," in Edward Buscombe and Roberta Pearson, eds. *Back in the Saddle Again: New Essays on the Western*. London: British Film Institute, 1998.

Negra, Diane. *Off-White Hollywood: American Culture and Ethnic Female Stardom*. New York: Routledge, 2001.

——. "Ethnic Food Fetishism, Whiteness and Nostalgia in Recent Film and Television." *The Velvet Light Trap* 50, Fall 2002: 62–76.

Negron-Muntaner, Frances. "Jennifer's Butt." *Aztlán* 22, 1997: 181–94.

Nero, Charles I. "Diva Traffic and Male Bonding in Film: Teaching Opera, Learning Gender, Race, and Nation." *Camera Obscura* 56 (19: 2), August 2004: 47–73.

Nickel, Joyce. "Disabling African American Men: Liberalism and Race Message Films." *Cinema Journal* 44 (1), Fall 2004: 25–48.

Nieland, Justus. "Race-ing Noir and Replacing History: The Mulatta and Memory in *One False Move* and *Devil in a Blue Dress*." *The Velvet Light Trap* 43, Spring 1999: 63–77.

Nishime, LeiLani. "The Mulatto Cyborg: Imagining a Multiracial Future." *Cinema Journal* 44 (2), Winter 2005: 34–49.

Noakes, John. "Racializing Subversion: The FBI and the Depiction of Race in Early Cold War Movies." *Ethnic and Racial Studies* 26 (4), 2003: 728–49.

Norgrove, Aaron. "But Is It Music? The Crisis of Identity in *The Piano*." *Race and Class* 40 (1), 1998: 47–56.

O'Hehir, Andrew. "*Windtalkers*." *Sight and Sound* 12 (9), 2002: 79–80.

Owens, Louis. *Mixblood Messages: Literature, Film, Family, Place*. Norman, OK: University of Oklahoma Press, 1998.

Patton, Cindy. "White Racism/Black Signs: Censorship and Images of Race Relations." *Journal of Communication* 45, 1995: 65–77.

Quart, Leonard. "The Triumph of Assimilation: Ethnicity, Race and the Jewish Moguls." *Cineaste* 18 (4), 1991: 8–11.

Reckley, Ralph, ed. *Images of the Black Male in Literature and Film: Essays in Criticism*. Baltimore, MD: Middle Atlantic Writers Association Press, 1994.

Reid, Mark. *Redefining Black Film*. Berkeley, CA: University of California Press, 1993.

Renov, Michael. "Warring Images: Stereotype and American Representations of the Japanese, 1941–91," in Abe Mark Nornes and Fukushima Yukio, eds. *The Japan/ America Film Wars: World War II Propaganda and Its Cultural Contexts*. Philadelphia, PA: Harwood Academic Publishers, 1994.

Rhines, Jesse Algeron. "Race in Contemporary American Cinema: Part IV – The Political Economy of Black Film." *Cineaste* 21 (3), 1995: 38–9.

——. *Black Film, White Money*. New Brunswick, NJ: Rutgers University Press, 1996.

Robinson, Cedric J. "Blaxploitation and the Misrepresentation of Liberation." *Race and Class* 40 (1), 1998: 1–12.

Rockler, Naomi R. "Race, Whiteness, 'Lightness,' and Relevance: African American and European American Interpretations of *Jump Start* and *The Boondocks*." *Critical Studies in Media Communication* 19 (4), 2002: 398–418.

Rollins, Peter C., and John O'Connor, eds. *Hollywood's Indian: The Portrayal of the Native American in Film*. Lexington, KY: University Press of Kentucky, 1997.

Shaviro, Steven. "Supa Dupa Fly: Black Women as Cyborgs in Hiphop Videos." *Quarterly Review of Film and Video* 22 (2), April–June 2005: 169–79.

Shaw, Deborah. "'You are Alright, But . . .': Individual and Collective Representations of Mexicans, Latinos, Anglo-Americans and Africans in Steven Soderbergh's *Traffic*." *Quarterly Review of Film and Video* 22 (3), July–September 2005: 211–23.

Shim, Doobo. "From Yellow Peril through Model Minority to Renewed Yellow Peril." *Journal of Communication Inquiry* 22, 1998: 385–409.

Shohat, Ella, and Robert Stam. *Unthinking Eurocentrism: Multiculturalism and the Media.* New York: Routledge, 1994.

Shome, Raka. "Race and Popular Cinema: The Rhetorical Strategies of Whiteness in *City of Joy*." *Communication Quarterly* 44 (4), 1996: 502–18.

Slane, Andrea. "Pressure Points: Political Psychology, Screen Adaptation, and Management of Racism in the Case-History Genre." *Camera Obscura* 45 (15:3), December 2000: 71–113.

Smith, Susan. *The Musical: Race, Gender, and Performance.* London: Wallflower Press, 2005.

Smith, Valerie. "Reading the Intersection of Race and Gender in Narrative of Passing." *Diacritics* 24 (2–3), Summer–Fall 1994: 143–57.

Stoddard, Jeremy D., and Alan S. Marcus. "The Burden of Historical Representation: Race, Freedom, and 'Educational' Hollywood Film." *Film and History* 36 (1), 2006: 26–35.

Suner, Asuman. "Postmodern Double-Cross: The Crisis of the Western, White, Male Subject in *M. Butterfly*." *Cinema Journal* 37 (2), Winter 1998: 49–64.

Taylor, Clyde R. *The Mask of Art: Breaking the Aesthetic Contract – Film and Literature.* Bloomington, IN: Indiana University Press, 1998.

Thi, Thanh Nga. "The Long March from Wong to Woo: Asians in Hollywood." *Cineaste* 21 (4), 1995: 38–40.

Thompson, Cliff. "The Brothers from Another Race: Black Characters in the Films of John Sayles." *Cineaste* 22 (3), 1996: 32–3.

Thompson, David. "The Last Frontier." *Sight and Sound* 14 (2), 2004: 12–15.

Thornley, Davina. "White, Brown or 'Coffee'? Revisioning Race in Tamahori's *Once Were Warriors*." *Film Critique* 25 (3), 2001: 22–36.

Wang, Jennifer Hyland. "'A Struggle of Contending Stories': Race, Gender and Political Memory in *Forrest Gump*." *Cinema Journal* 39 (3), Spring 2000: 92–115.

Watkins, S. Craig. *Representing: Hip Hop Culture and the Production of Black Cinema.* Chicago, IL: University of Chicago Press, 1998.

Williams, Linda. *Playing the Race Card: Melodramas of Black and White from Uncle Tom to O. J. Simpson.* Princeton, NJ: Princeton University Press, 2001.

Willis, Sharon. *High Contrast: Race and Gender in Contemporary Hollywood Film.* Durham, NC: Duke University Press, 1997.

Winokur, Mark. "Marginal Marginalia: The African-American Voice in the Nouvelle Gangster Film." *The Velvet Light Trap* 35, 1995: 19–32.

Young, Lola. *Fear of the Dark: Race, Gender and Sexuality in the Cinema.* New York: Routledge, 1996.

Index

A Funny Thing Happened To Me On The Way To The Forum 327
A.I. 298
Aaliyah 253–6, 258–60, 262
abuse, spousal 301
addict 318
adolescent: market 29–30, 32; sexuality 35, 37–9; white 32
Affleck, Ben 174
African American: and Asians *see* Asian/African American; family 58, 60; femininity 54–5, 60, 254, 261, 315, 319, 321; and Jewish *see* Jewish/African American pairing; masculinity, 51–2, 54–63, 81, 262, 298–9, 319; music 254–7, 261, 307–9, *see also* hip-hop; popular culture 255, 260; sexuality 51, 80–1, 333–4; stereotypes *see* stereotypes; unification 54, 59, 60
Afrocentrism 51, 54, 60, 134, 332
AIDS 57–8
Alamo, the 18–25
Alamo, The: John Wayne's 4, 20, 22; John Lee Hancock's 22–5
albino 115
Alice, Mary 108
aliens 77
All Star Salute to Pearl Bailey 329
Allen, Woody 174
Alonso, Maria Conchita 139–40
Amazing Grace 324
American Dream 17, 132, 169–70, 174–5, 262–3
American International Pictures 28, 31–3, 46–7
American Peace Society prize 14
American Releasing Corporation *see* American International Pictures
American Revolution 21
Americanness 131–3, 137–8
Amistad 298
Anaconda 173–4

Anderson, Anthony 254–5
Angel Eyes 174–5
anti-immigrantion 77
anti-Semitism 82; *see also* Jewish
Apache tribe 78
Arizona 14
Arkoff, Samuel 30–1, 33
Aryan Nation 292
asexual *see* de-sexualization
Asian/African American discord 256, 261; pairing 253–4; romance 254–61; unity against racism 259–64
Asian American 127, 134, 136–7, 145–6; popular culture 255
Asian: feminization of 81; masculinity 81, 254, 262, 264; stereotypes *see* stereotypes
assimilation 33, 127–9, 132, 147; of Jews 293; physical 169, 171, 173–4, 179–81
Associate, The 344
Aunt Jemima 108
Austin, Stephen F. 11
Avalon, Frankie 28, 39, 42, 45
Avery, Margaret 296

B movie 113
Baartman, Sara 176
backlighting 172
Bailey, Pearl 315, 321, 327–34
Bailey, Robert Jr. 338
Bakaitis, Helmut 116
Bartkowiak, Andrzej 253–5
Battle of San Jacinto 12, 24
Baudelaire, Charles 129
Beach Blanket Bingo 28, 45
Beach Boys, The 44–5
Beach Party 28
beach: culture *see* surfing; as private space 29–30, 40; as public space 30, 40, 43–4; as white space 28, 43
Beals, Jennifer 133

Beaumont, Gabrielle 127
Bellson, Louis 331
Belluci, Monica 115
Bernie Mac Show, The 338
Berry, Halle 333
Bierman, Robert 127
Big Momma's House 344
Bikini Beach 28, 45
Birth of a Nation 71
Birth of Texas, The see *Martyrs of the Alamo*
Black Belt Jones 255
black ideology 103–10, 112
blackface 255, 333
blackness 42–3, 47, 51, 61, 63, 91, 168,
    180, 340; as the Other 165
Blacula 146
Blade 147
Blankman 345
blaxploitation 46–8, 62, 254–7, 324
body: African American female 54; as
    colony 168; Jewish 157–64; as racial
    intermediary 173; racialized 145,
    165–9, 177; white female 71, 94–5
Bogus 317
Book 330
bourgeois 33; idealism 300
Bowie, Jim 18
Boyz N the Hood 51–2, 58, 61
Bram Stoker's Dracula see *Dracula*
Brennan, Walter 5
Brothers, The 63
Brown, Wren T. 337
brownface 148
Bulworth, 255
Bush, George W. 335, 337
Busia, Akosua 295

Cage, Nicholas 138–9
capitalism 137–9
Carey, Mariah 332
Carmilla 127, 142–6
Carrol Naish, J. 20
Casablanca 15
castration 72, 74, 80–1
Catfish in Black Bean Sauce 254
Catholicism, anti 12
Chan, Jackie 253, 255–6
Chan, Peter 264
chattel 219–21, 226
Chen, Stephen 138
Chey, Timothy A. 254
Chi Moui Lo 254
Chiang, David 256
China Girl 258
Chinese Connection, The 262
Chou, Collin 118
Chow, Stephen 262
Chris Rock Show, The 338

Citizen Kane 15
citizenship 167–8
civic creed see *civil religion*
civil religion 3–6, 9–11, 18–21, 25
Civil Rights 40–1; comedy during
    322–3
class 53
Cleopatra 148
Cleopatra Jones 255
climax 15
Clockers 255
Clooney, George 174
Coalition Against Black Exploitation 298
Coca Cola 169–71
Coleridge, Samuel Taylor 129
Collateral 113
colonialism 9, 11, 20, 69, 104, 168; see also
    imperialism
Color Purple, The 292–312
colorblind: comedy 324–5; ideology 103,
    105
Combs, Sean 174
Comic Relief 320
Coming to America 344
coming-of-age story 58
community 73
Coppola, Francis Ford 145
Cosby Show, The 338
cosmetic alteration 166–7; see also
    whiteness, idealized
counter culture 55
coyote 69–72, 73–4
coyotl 82–8
Craven, Wes 147
creolization 108
Crockett, Davy 18, 20, 22
Crooklyn 255
crossover 316, 321
Crow, Jim see Jim Crow
Crying Game, The 344
Crystal, Billy 320
Curb Your Enthusiasm 338

Dale, Dick and the Del-tones 42, 45
Dalton, Timothy 331
dance, as racialized movement 177–8
Danson, Ted 331
Dark City 113
Dark Princess 259
darkness 96–9; as sexuality 72
Darth Vader 70–1
Davis, Essie 119
Davy Crockett, King of the Wild Frontier
    (Walt Disney) 4
Def by Temptation 147
Del Rio, Dolores 166
del Toro, Guillermo 147
democracy 9, 10, 70

Democratic Party 335
de-sexualization 136, 325–6
Devil in a Blue Dress 63
Dhjalili, Omid 337
diva 316
DMX 254–5
Dobson, Tamara 255–6
Dollard, John 268–86
domestication 303–05
Douglas, Carl 256
Down in the Delta 63
Dracula 127–9
Dracula, Bram Stoker's 145
dragon lady 137, 145
Dragon Lord (a.k.a *Young Master in Love*)
  262
Dru, Joanne 17
drug use 47; *see also* counter culture
Drums Along the Mohawk 19
Du Bois, W.E.B. 259, 264

Eastwood, Clint 24
Echeverria, Emilio 22
Echeverria, Sol 140
Edwards, John 335
Egypt 108, 134, 148
Elitism 69, 72, 87
emancipation 105
Emerson, Ralph Waldo 11
Emperor Jones, The 324
Empire of the Sun 294, 298
empire *see* imperialism
Enemy at the Gates 160–1, 163–4
Enter the Dragon 264
epistomology 103–4, 106, 113
ethnocentrism 129
Eurocentrism 9, 83, 115
Europa, Europa 159
Eve's Bayou 63
exotic other *see* Other
exploitation cinema 32; *see also*
  blaxpoitation

Fakin' da Funk 254
fatherhood, as masculinity 59–60
feminism 85–6; African American
  109–12, 298–303
Fetchit, Stepin 83
fetishization 80; *see also* Other
Fishburne, Laurence 104
Fisher, Carrie 76
Flashdance 140
Fonda, Henry 19
Fontaine: Why Am I Straight? 318
Ford, Betty 329
Ford, Gerald R. 329
Ford, Harrison 85
Ford, John 24, 72

Fort Apache 24
Foster, Gloria 108
Foxy Brown 324
framing, as racial representation 172,
  176–7
Friars Club Roast 333–4
Friday 63
Fright Night 148
From Hell 63
Funicello, Annette 28, 42, 45

Gangland 113
Ganja and Hess 147
Gatsby, Jill 139
Gaye, Nona 119
gaze 135, 141; male 55
gender 319, 339–40
Gere, Richard 174
ghetto 46–7, 260
Ghost 320
Glover, Danny 295, 303, 337
Godboldo, Dale 337
Gold Rush 78
Goldberg, Whoopi 294–5, 303, 312,
  315–41, 344
Goldman, Ronald 62
Good Fences 337
Gordy, Berry 256
Goyer, David S. 147
Greek: civilization 108–9; oracle 108–9
Gregory, Dick 316
Grier, Pam 256
Griffith, D.W. 4, 18–19, 71
Guess Who's Coming to Dinner 76,
  187–217

hair: as a racial signifier 54; *see also* body
Hamlet 15
Hancock, John Lee 4–5, 22–5
Hardball with Chris Matthews 335
Haring, Keith 135
Hark, Tsui 264
Hartnett, Josh 233
Hawks, Howard 3–7, 24
Hayworth, Rita (Rita Cansino) 166–7
Hello Dolly 327
Hepburn, Katharine 187, 208
Herman, Jerry 327
heterosexuality 59
hip-hop 52, 54, 55, 61, 256
Hispanic *see* Latinos/as
Hitchcock, Alfred 141
Hitler, Adolf 9
Hoffman, Dustin 331
Holland, Tom 148
Hollywood musical 53
holocaust 162, 292
homelessness 319–20

Homer and Eddie 317
homoeroticism 73–4
homogeneity 38–40, 130
homophobia 74
homosexuality: male 52; violent 57;
    see also lesbianism
Hotel Rwanda 113
Hottentot Venus *see* Baartman, Sara
House of Mirth, The 15
House Party 55–7, 59–61
Houston, Sam 12, 24
How to Stuff a Wild Bikini 28
Hudlin, Reginald and Warrington 52, 55
Hughes, John 136
humanism 70
Hundred Percent 255
hybridity, racial 34, 37

I Robot 113
Ice Cube, 256
immigration 127–30, 132–4, 139–40,
    260–2; illegal 12
imperialism 3, 5–9, 25–7; anti- 72; *see also*
    colonialism
In Living Color 167, 180, 350, 353, 345
In the Heat of the Night 333
In The Pink 339
Indian genocide 78
indigenous: sexuality 69; stereotypes 69,
    77, 78
inner city *see* ghetto
integration 28, 37, 43
interracial relations 331–2; sexuality *see*
    miscegenation
intersectionality 315, 317
Invincible 159

Jackson, Leonard 295
Jackson, Peter 100
Jar Jar Binks 83
Jaws 294
Jeter, Mildred 331
Jewish: bodies *see* body masculinity
    157–64; stereotype 96
Jewish/African American pairing 292–4
Jim Crow 259, 133
Jones, Grace 133
Jones, James Earl 72
Jones, Quincy 294
Julius Caesar 15

Kaaya, Brad 233–49
Kahanamoku, Duke 34
Karate Kid 262
Kerry, John 335
King Ranch 5
King, Rodney 62, 256
Kingdom Come 336

Kinsaka, Peter 295
Koyanagi, Eric 255
Ku Klux Klan 72, 292
kung fu: in African American culture
    254–6; films 253; in music 256

Lane, Nathan 327
Langella, Frank 331
Last Command, The 4, 20
Last Dragon, The 256
Last Emperor, The 255
Lathan, Stan 324
Latin lover 127–8, 147
Latinos/as 76–7; as racial intermediary
    168, 173
Lauren, Tammy 338
Lee, Brandon 262
Lee, Bruce 255
Lee, Spike 51–2, 55, 57
Lemmons, Kasi 139
lesbianism 299; African American 304;
    see also homosexuality
Lethal Weapon IV 255
Li, Jet 258–60
lighting: as whiteness 91, 93–4
Lincoln, Abraham 14
Live on the Sunset Strip 317
Livermore, Abiel Abbott 14
Lloyd, Frank 4
Long, Nia 332
Lopez, Jennifer 165–181
Lord of the Rings: The Fellowship of the Ring
    91–100
Los Angeles 34, 59
Louisiana Purchase, The 11
Loving, Richard 331
lower class: Negroes 269–86; *see also*
    working class
Lucas, George 69, 75
Lugosi, Bela 128
Lujan, Bob 140
lynching 259
Lyne, Adrian 140

Mabley, Jackie 315, 321–7, 338
McCabe and Mrs Miller 159
McCarthyism 128
McConaughey, Matthew 174–5
McGann, Paul 148
McKinney, Mark 338
MacMillan, Terry 319
Madame Butterfly 87
Made in America 331
Maid in Manhattan 174–5
mainstream: culture 29, 31; film 30–33;
    ideology 301
Makepeace, Keith 136
Malcom X 255

Man Who Shot Liberty Valance, The 24
Mandigo 218–31
Manhattan 138–42
Manifest Destiny 3, 5–9, 18–21, 25
Mankiewicz, Joseph L. 63
Maori 83–4
martial arts *see* kung fu
Martyrs of the Alamo 4–5, 20
Masamba, Lelo 295
masculinity 80, 136, 139
matrices of domination 107–8
Matrix, The 102–21, 255
melting pot 127
mestizo 12–13, 76
Mexican-American War 7, 18–20
Mexicans: racism against 13; stereotypes
    see stereotypes; in Texas 6, 12, 19; war
    see Mexican-American War
MGM 52
Mi Familia see *My Family*
middle-class 33, 38; as Americanness 168,
    174
Midler, Bette 325–6
Minority Report 113, 294, 298
Miranda, Carmen 166, 169, 177
miscegenation 13, 37, 43, 76, 80, 85, 97,
    129–33, 138–40, 187, 189–97, 258;
    anti-miscegenation laws 192–5, 331
mise-en-scène 116, 134
misogyny 85–6, 139
Mississippi Masala 254
Miwok 77; sequoia forests 78
Molla, Jordi 23
Money Train 173–4
Monroe Doctrine 9
Monster's Ball 333
Monster-in-Law 174, 339
Moore, Demi 325
Moreau, Marguerite 148
Moreno, Rita 166–7
Morris, Phil 337
Morrison, Temueura 83
Morrison, Toni 319
Moss, Carrie Ann 104
Motown 52
MTV 255
Mulan 253
mulattos 77
multiculturalism 70, 112–14, 127–48,
    260–1
Munich 159
Murnau, F.W. 138
Murphy, Eddie 253
Muscle Beach Party 28, 34–40, 42–4
Mussolini 9
*My America . . . Or Honk if you Love
    Buddha* 255
My Family 176

NAACP 298
Nair, Mira 254
Nation of Islam, The 293
National Organization for Women 86
nationalism 128–33, 143, 146–8
Native Americans 5, 7, 12, 14, 20–2,
    75–6
nativism 127–30, 132–3
Negrophobia 96
neoliberalism 233–49
New Black Cinema 51, 61, 63
New Mexico 14
New York Times 332
Nicholas, Denise 332–3
Nichols, Mike 315
Nicholson, James 30
Night of the Living Dead 147
Night of the Living Dead 98
Nixon, Richard 329
noble savage *see* Other
non-western 33
non-white *see* Other
Norrington, Stephen 147
Nosferatu 140
Nosferatu: A Symphony of Horror 138

O 233–48
O'Henry 255
O'Connor, Carroll 333
O'Sullivan, John L. 11
Odyssey, The 10
Oedipal complex 11–13, 80–1
Olsen, Leila Lee 145
Once Upon a Time in China 259, 263
one drop rule 133, 140
Orientalism 81–2
ostracism 309
Othello 233–48
Other 91, 95, 100, 140–7; exotic 34, 40;
    fetishizing of 34, 135, 177, *see also*
    Baartman, Sara; primitive 34, 37, 40, 79
Owens, Alex 140

Pantoliano, Joe 107
patriarchy 52, 54, 74, 86–7, 120
Pearlie Mae 321, 327–40
Peckinpah, Sam 24
Perez, Vincent 148
personae 315–17, 320–1, 327, 334–40
Pfeiffer, Dedee 136
phallic masculinity 52, 73, 79–81, 119,
    159
Phifer, Meki 233
pieta 78
Polk, James 13
pop culture 31
Prelude to a Kiss 325
primitivism *see* Other

Promised Land 3, 9–10
prostitution 47
Pryor, Richard 317
Psycho 141
Pueblo Indians 78
Pugh, Willard 296

Quaid, Denis 22
Queen of the Damned 148
quest–story 4

racelessness 29, 32, 43; *see also* whiteness
racial hierarchy 76, 95–6, 120
racial mixing 76–78, 80; *see also*
    miscegenation
racial mobility 174, 176
racism: institutionalized 47; in Manifest
    Destiny 7, 12
Ralph Fiennes 165, 174–5
rap *see* hip-hop
rape 55, 78–9
Rapid Fire 262
Rasovich, Gordana 337
Reagan era 319
Reaganomics 319
Red Corner 3
Red River 5–11, 17–19, 22, 24
Reeves, Keanu 104; as white 114, 145
Regen, Elizabeth 337
Rio Grande 13
riots 61, 256
Robeson, Paul 324
Romeo and Juliet plot 254, 258
Romeo Must Die 253–65
Roseanne 338
Rumble in the Bronx 256
Rush Hour 253–4, 260
Rusler, Robert 136
Rymer, Michael 148

Saartje *see* Sara Baartman
St. Louis Blues 327
St. Louis Woman 328
Same River Twice, The 294
Santa Anna, Antonio Lopez de 12, 18, 20,
    22
Scary Movie 345
Schindler's List 159, 294, 298
School Daze 52–4, 58–9, 61
Scream, Blacula Scream! 147
Searchers, The 7, 24
Seguin, Juan 23
Selena 167–8, 173
Seoul Brothers 255
Set it Off 63
sexuality 52, 319, 323; in adolescents 8,
    10–13; racialized 37–8, 40–3, 130–45;
    white 29, 39

Shakespeare 15, 234–48
Shall We Dance 167, 174
Shaolin Soccer 262
Shaolin Temple 259
She's Gotta Have It 51
Silver, Joel 255
Simpson, Nicole Brown 62
Simpson, O.J. 62
Sing, Chu 255
Singleton, John 51
Sir Gawain and the Green Knight 10
Sister Act 325–7
Sixteen Candles 136
skin tone 169, 174; as class signifier
    53
slavery 54, 104–5, 109–12, 292; sexual
    abuse 220–3, 229
Slim Fast 335
Smith, Jada Pinkett 111, 113
Smith, Maggie 326
Smits, Jimmy 77
Smoke Signals 75
Smolett, Jurnee 338
Snipes, Wesley 147
Some Like It Hot 344
Sondheim, Stephen 327
Soul food 63
Soul Man 344
South Central 59
space: white 43–4
Spaniards12
Spielberg, Steven 292–312
Spook Show, The 318, 327
Stagecoach 128
Star Wars 15, 69–81, 84–8
Steinem, Gloria 85
stereotypes: African American 55–6, 58,
    97, 144, 300–3, 319, 352; African
    American female 108–10; Asian 81,
    261–2, 264; Latino/a 14, 22, 127–47,
    165–81; reversal of 112–18; white
    345–58
Sterling, Hayden 20
Stiles, Julia 233
Stoker, Bram 129
Stoltz, Eric 174
Strange Days 63
suburbia 40, 44–6
Sugarland Express, The 294
Summer of Sam 63
Sunshine 157–64
supreme court 187, 192, 210, 212
surf subculture *see* surfing
surfing 33–4, 47; culture 33–4, 37; music
    35, 44–5
Swayze, Patrick 325
Sweetback 270, 279
Sykes, Wanda 335

Tajima-Pena, Renee 255
Tales from the Hood 63
tanning 38; *see also* cosmetic alteration
Tarantino, Quentin 255
Taylor, Elizabeth 148
Taylor, Zachary 13
technology: as racial inferiority 78; as
    white masculinity 74–5
technophilia 75–6
teens *see* adolescents
Tejanos 12, 23
Texan War *see* Mexican-American War
Texas 5–7, 11, 13–14, 21–3
Texians 12, 19
Theatre Owner Booking Association
    322
Thirteenth Floor, The 113
three-act quest 3, 10, 15–25
Tiomkin, Dimitri 5
Torquemada 9
Torres, Gina 119
Townsend, Stuart 148
Tracy, Spencer 187–208
Tragedy 15
Transcontinental Treaty 11
Travis, Colonel 20
Treaty of Guadalupe Hidalgo 13
Truck Turner 324
Tucker, Chris 255
Turman, Glynn 76
Turner, Tina 294
Twins 253

Unforgiven 24
unification 53–4
Uptown Saturday Night 324
upward mobility 260
urban youth *see* adolescents
urbanization 96
utopian world 53, 56

Valley Forge 21
values, white 29, 33, 35, 47
Vamp 127, 133–8
Vampire in Brooklyn 147
Vampire's Kiss 127, 138–42
vampires, female 133, 137, 142
vampirism 129, 135–6, 138–9
Vanishing Son 254
Vanity Fair 172–3, 176
Velez, Lupe 166–7
verisimilitude 127
violence, in westerns 8–9, 24

Wachowski, Andy and Larry 103
Waiting to Exhale 63

Walker, Alice 293–312, 319
Wanda at Large 337–8
Wanda Does It 338
Wang, Wayne 264
Warriors, The 263
Washington, Isaiah 255
Watanabe, Gedde 136
Wayans, family 344–58
Wayne, John 4, 5, 7, 20–22
Wedding Planner, The 174–5
Welles, Orson 15
Wen, Ming-Na 253
Wenk, Richard 127
Western culture 107–8
westerns 3, 7–8, 22–5
White Chicks 344–58
white masculinity 70, 73
white supremacy 78–9
white, femininity 84–8, 237, 241
white/black dualism 70, 94
whiteface 134, 143, 345, 357
whiteness 61–3, 69–72, 103, 130: from
    African American perspective 344–58;
    as class 285; as death 92, 94–5, 98–9;
    exploitative 82–4; idealized 70, 72, 77,
    91–100, 172–4; multicultural 130–3,
    145–7; as non-race 165; politics 74–5,
    92; sexuality 69, 71; as space 28, 91; as
    social norm 51
Whoopi 337
Whoopi Live 339
wide shot 177
Wild Bunch, The 24
Williams, Billie Dee 86
Williams, Robin 320
Wilson, Lambert 115
Winfrey, Oprah 296, 303, 312, 345
womanist ideology 110
Wonder, Stevie 42
Wong, Russell 254
Woo, John 264
working class 69, 72–5, 83, 88, 96, 167–8;
    see also lower class
Wu Tang Clan 256

xenophilia 127
xenophobia 127, 144

Yip, Francoise 254
youth market *see* adolescent
Yu, Wang 256
Yuen, Corey 255
Yun-Fat, Chow 264–5

Zion 112–15
Zmuda, Bob 320